PRACTICE OF
MUNICIPAL ADMINISTRATION

THE CENTURY
POLITICAL SCIENCE SERIES
EDITED BY FREDERIC A. OGG, *University of Wisconsin*

VOLUMES PUBLISHED

Frederic A. Ogg and P. Orman Ray, INTRODUCTION TO AMERICAN GOVERNMENT (3d ed.); Walter F. Dodd, STATE GOVERNMENT IN THE UNITED STATES (2d ed.); John M. Mathews, AMERICAN FOREIGN RELATIONS: CONDUCT AND POLICIES; Herbert Adams Gibbons, INTRODUCTION TO WORLD POLITICS; Pitman B. Potter, INTRODUCTION TO THE STUDY OF INTERNATIONAL ORGANIZATION (3d ed.); Graham H. Stuart, LATIN AMERICA AND THE UNITED STATES (2d ed.); Charles G. Fenwick, INTERNATIONAL LAW; Raymond G. Gettell, HISTORY OF POLITICAL THOUGHT, and HISTORY OF AMERICAN POLITICAL THOUGHT; Thomas H. Reed, MUNICIPAL GOVERNMENT IN THE UNITED STATES; Lent D. Upson, THE PRACTICE OF MUNICIPAL ADMINISTRATION; Edward M. Sait, AMERICAN PARTIES AND ELECTIONS.

VOLUMES IN PREPARATION

Andrew C. McLaughlin, CONSTITUTIONAL HISTORY OF THE UNITED STATES; Edward S. Corwin, CONSTITUTIONAL LAW OF THE UNITED STATES; Francis W. Coker, RECENT AND CONTEMPORARY POLITICAL THEORY; William Y. Elliott, PRINCIPLES OF POLITICAL SCIENCE; William S. Carpenter, COMPARATIVE GOVERNMENT; Joseph P. Chamberlain, THE THEORY AND PRACTICE OF LEGISLATION; John A. Fairlie and C. M. Kneier, COUNTY GOVERNMENT AND ADMINISTRATION; Thomas H. REED, MUNICIPAL GOVERNMENT IN EUROPE; Charles Seymour, EUROPEAN DIPLOMACY SINCE 1914; Edwin M. Borchard, HISTORY OF AMERICAN DIPLOMACY; J. R. Hayden, COLONIAL GOVERNMENT AND ADMINISTRATION; Stanley K. Hornbeck, AMERICAN INTERESTS AND POLICIES IN THE FAR EAST; Harold S. Quigley, JAPANESE GOVERNMENT AND POLITICS; Frank M. Russell, THEORIES OF INTERNATIONAL RELATIONS; Edward M. Sait, OUTLINES OF POLITICS.

OTHER VOLUMES TO BE ARRANGED

March, 1929

PRACTICE OF MUNICIPAL ADMINISTRATION

BY
LENT D. UPSON
DETROIT BUREAU OF GOVERNMENTAL RESEARCH

THE CENTURY CO.
NEW YORK   LONDON

Copyright, 1926, by
The Century Co.
229

Printed in U. S. A.

To

THE PRESENT AND PAST TRUSTEES OF THE
DETROIT BUREAU OF GOVERNMENTAL
RESEARCH, WHOSE INTEREST IN
PUBLIC AFFAIRS MADE ITS
WRITING POSSIBLE.

FOREWORD

Increase in the number, importance, and cost of municipal activities has made desirable the adoption of the most effective methods for their administration. Only through the use of advanced practices by cities can public work of high character be secured at a cost that taxpayers will tolerate. This book attempts to review present-day municipal procedure and to suggest such improvements as experience has proved feasible. The discussion is intended not for the professional administrator,—the administrative manuals for several municipal services are more suitable,—but for the lay citizen, in or out of public office, who wishes some acquaintance with the problems that perplex the professional.

In writing on this subject, it is disconcerting to be obliged to state continually that the methods discussed are not commonly accepted by cities, or are not concurred in by many authorities. Such qualifications leave one with the uncomfortable feeling that public administration is a long way from an exact science, the processes and results of which are subject to experimental verification. Perhaps government will never be an exact and distinct science, but, rather, only the application of many sciences to the problems of community action. If so, the practitioner of politics must wait for accounting, engineering, medicine, sociology, and economics to develop precise processes that are usable in government. But whether as a distinct science or a combination of sciences, it is hoped that a summary of the most effective practices may be helpful to those concerned with them.

Aside from this brief statement of purpose, this preface is utilized to make general and specific acknowledgment to the many persons who have contributed to the preparation of this book. I make no pretense that the volume has been written wholly from my own experience in government. Woodrow Wilson has said that "No man knows enough to write a whole book," and this is particularly true of a book on municipal administration, covering as it does the many and diversified activities carried on by a modern large city. I am indebted to several colleagues for collaboration in the writing of a number of chapters and to such extent am editor rather than author—to Mr. Harrington Place, on *Engineering, Pavements, Sewerage,* and *Civil Service;* Mr. Place and Mr. Ernest B. Schulz, of the Department of Political Science, University of Michigan, on *Wastes;* Mr. Arch Mandel, Secretary of the Dayton Community Chest, on *Police;* Mr. Solon E. Rose, Secretary of the Detroit Traffic Committee, on *Traffic* and *Education;* Mr. George V. Branch, Commissioner of Markets of Detroit, on *Markets;* and Mr. R. Lee Humbert, of the staff of the Detroit Bureau of Governmental Research, for assistance on *Lighting, Safety, Planning, Fire, Traffic,* and *Water.*

I have also drawn freely from the numerous reports prepared by bureaus of governmental research and similar agencies, and particularly from those of the Detroit Bureau of Governmental Research, including the *Government of Cincinnati and Hamilton County,* and from the several admirable administrative manuals that have been published. In borrowing the ideas of others, I hope I have correctly reported their opinions and clearly demarked them from the added opinions of my own. I trust, too, that due acknowledgment has always been made. If not, the neglect is not willful, and I hope that these errors, with any others, will be brought to my attention for correction.

In writing concerning practical methods that vary from city to city, there is danger of unduly emphasizing the procedure with which one is most familiar. For that reason, I have had practically every chapter read by one or more persons familiar with the subject discussed, and the original text has been much modified by their criticisms and additions. I wish specifically to acknowledge help from the following persons: on *Elections,* Mr. C. A. Crosser, Director, Des Moines Bureau of Municipal Research; Mr. Oakley A. Distin, Chief Supervisor of the Detroit Election Commission; Prof. Joseph P. Harris, Department of Political Science, University of Wisconsin; Mr. William P. Lovett, Secretary, Detroit Citizens' League; and Mr. Frank L. Olson, Assistant Director, Pittsburgh Bureau of Municipal Research; on *Civil Service,* Mr. Harry W. Marsh, Secretary, National Civil Service Reform League, and Mr. William C. Beyer, Director, Philadelphia Bureau of Municipal Research; on *Revenues,* Mr. Ernest B. Schulz, Department of Political Science, University of Michigan; and Mr. K. J. McCarren, Engineer, Detroit Board of Assessors; on *Budget,* Mr. Arthur E. Buck, National Institute of Public Administration; on

FOREWORD ix

Treasury, Mr. David Ponnusky, Chief Clerk, and Mr. Eugene P. Deimel, Accountant, Treasurer's Office, City of Detroit; on *Accounting,* Mr. Henry Steffens, Jr., formerly Controller, City of Detroit; Mr. L. A. James, Governmental Accountant, Cornell & Company, Chicago; and Mr. Edward C. Coughlin, Chief Accountant, Controller's Office, Detroit; on *Law,* Mr. Robert M. Goodrich, Secretary, Taxpayers' League of St. Louis County (Duluth) Minn.; Mr. Clarence E. Wilcox, formerly Corporation Counsel, City of Detroit; and Prof. Thomas H. Reed, Professor of Political Science, University of Michigan; on *City Planning,* Mr. T. Glenn Phillips, Consultant, Detroit City Plan Commission; Mr. P. B. Augur, City Planner, Detroit; on *Engineering* and *Pavements,* Mr. Ezra Shoecraft, of Hoad, Decker, Shoecraft and Drury, Consulting Civil Engineers, Ann Arbor, Michigan; on *Sewers,* Mr. Clarence B. Hubbell, of Hubbell, Hartgering, and Roth, Consulting Engineers, Detroit; on *Water,* Mr. George H. Fenkell, Superintendent and General Manager, and Mr. William F. Wallace, Filter Superintendent and Chief Chemist, Department of Water Supply, Detroit; on *Lighting,* Mr. Frank R. Mistersky, General Superintendent of Public Lighting, Detroit; and Mr. C. W. Atkins, Director, St. Louis Bureau of Municipal Research; on *Safety,* Mr. Frank Burton, Commissioner of Buildings and Safety Engineering, Detroit; Mr. W. J. Canada, Electrical Field Secretary, National Fire Protection Association; and Mr. George Althorn, Jr., Industrial Engineer, San Francisco Bureau of Municipal Research; on *Health,* Dr. Henry F. Vaughan, Commissioner of Health, Detroit; Mrs. Blanche Bartlett, Detroit Tuberculosis Society; Dr. Carl E. McCombs, National Institute of Public Administration, New York City; and Dr. John Sundwald, Director of Student Physical Welfare, University of Michigan; on *Education,* Dr. Charles L. Spain, Deputy Superintendent of Education, Detroit; Dr. William H. Allen, Director, Institute for Public Service, New York City; and Prof. Arthur B. Moehlman, Professor of Education, University of Michigan; on *Recreation,* Mr. C. E. Brewer, Commissioner of Recreation, Detroit; on *Charities,* Mr. William J. Norton, Secretary, Detroit Community Fund; on *Fire,* Mr. C. A. Crosser, Director, Des Moines Bureau of Municipal Research; Mr. C. Hayward Murphy, member Detroit Board of Fire Commissioners; and Mr. Paxton Mendelssohn, of Detroit; on *Correction,* Mr. Fred M. Butzel, former Commissioner, Detroit House of Correction; on *Courts,* Hon. Pliny W. Marsh, former judge; and Dr. Arnold L. Jacoby,

Psychiatrist, Detroit Recorder's Court; and, on *Control of Utilities,* Dr. Delos F. Wilcox, Grand Rapids, Michigan; and Professor H. E. Riggs, Department of Civil Engineering, University of Michigan.

In addition, every writer on municipal administration places himself in the debt of Professor W. B. Munro, whose excellent pioneer texts have done so much to stimulate an interest in applied political science.

Especial thanks are due to present and former staff members of the Detroit Bureau of Governmental Research—Messrs. C. E. Rightor, A. H. Place, Solon E. Rose, John S. Rae, Glendon J. Mowitt, R. Lee Humbert, J. M. Leonard, and Mr. Arch Mandel, and to Prof. Thomas H. Reed of the University of Michigan, who have assisted in the collection and preparation of material and who have read all or part of the manuscript, not once, but several times, criticising with a frankness born of old friendship.

Professor Frederic A. Ogg, Editor of the *Century Political Science Series,* has contributed many helpful suggestions and has been very patient with interruptions and delays.

LENT D. UPSON.

Detroit, Mich.

CONTENTS

CHAPTER		PAGE
I	Administrative Organization	3
II	Elections	16
III	Civil Service	30
IV	Budget	53
V	Revenues	76
VI	Debt	105
VII	Treasury	126
VIII	Accounting	135
IX	Purchasing	153
X	Motor Transportation	167
XI	Law	177
XII	Planning	186
XIII	Safety	204
XIV	Fire	224
XV	Health	243
XVI	Education	266
XVII	Recreation	294
XVIII	Charities	309
XIX	Police	320
XX	Traffic	341
XXI	Courts	360
XXII	Correction	379
XXIII	Markets	399
XXIV	Engineering	416
XXV	Pavements	428
XXVI	Wastes	447
XXVII	Sewerage	469
XXVIII	Water	485
XXIX	Lighting	506
XXX	Control of Utilities	523
XXXI	Municipality Ownership	552
	Index	571

PRACTICE OF
MUNICIPAL ADMINISTRATION

PRACTICE OF MUNICIPAL ADMINISTRATION

CHAPTER I [1]

ADMINISTRATIVE ORGANIZATION

The intelligent direction of urban affairs that is called the science, or, if preferred, the art, of municipal administration has grown out of the compelling needs of the modern city. Had the municipalities of today only the modest tasks and the simple organization of those of a hundred years ago, there would be little demand for the improvement of their methods of administration. There would be no political (and usually abortive) promises of a "business administration," nor halting and somewhat disorganized research into the business processes of government, because government would not be the great and important business that it is. But the modern city is as different from the city of our grandfathers as scientific and social conditions are different from the science and society of a few generations ago. Cities have assumed new obligations. They facilitate industry and commerce, aid the sick and poor, protect the well, safeguard life and property, and provide uncounted conveniences for the householder. Such expansion of service has created a dependence of the public upon government, and has so increased its cost that it has become essential that governmental activities be well and economically performed. If they are not, the comfort, property, and even life, of citizens are jeopardized, and financial burdens are created which are exceedingly difficult to bear. *(Cities are increasing services and costs)*

The causes of this rapid and important growth in municipal services are interwoven with the economic and social changes of recent times. Perhaps the greatest single force has been the unparalleled production of material wealth resulting from scientific discoveries and their exploitation. Consider simply the changes wrought by the fabrication of steel, the harnessing of electric energy, and the development of the internal combustion engine. These inventions have made possible modern office buildings, automatic machinery, electric lights, automobiles, and trucks—innovations that have profoundly affected urban life and government. *(The fundamental causes of these increases)*

[1] Leonard D. White, *Introduction to the Study of Public Administration* (Macmillan, 1926).

4 PRACTICE OF MUNICIPAL ADMINISTRATION

CHAP. I

The immediate causes:
Congestion of population

The immediate causes are even more evident.[1] Modern industry requires a relatively dense population from which to secure its workers, creating in turn satellite industries—rapid transportation, banking, wholesale and retail distribution—each aggravating congestion of population. Incident to congestion are the changes that arise from surrendering rural life—expensive parks and playgrounds supersede the free open spaces of the country; costly fire and police protection stand in place of the volunteer fire brigade and the town marshal; pavements are built to carry heavier and more vehicular traffic; streets are widened and extended; viaducts and tunnels are built; and the educational system is developed to meet the changing requirements of business and industry.

Higher standards of living

Higher standards of living create an insistent demand for public activities not known or considered a decade or two ago. One by one, services usually performed or left unperformed by the individual in the smaller community, are taken over by the government in a growing municipality, to the general relief and satisfaction of the householder. The city not only supplies water, but with a view to greater convenience and comfort, pipes it into various parts of the home; streets are widened and parkways planted for pleasure drives and boulevards; educational facilities are expanded to include high schools, and even municipal universities; ashes and rubbish are carted away; drainage and sewerage are extended; street lighting is amplified; traffic is regulated; police and fire protection are increased; monumental public buildings are constructed—all being improvements not considered necessary in other times and other places.

Changing social concepts

A changing concept of social justice impels the community to ameliorate conditions resulting from social and economic causes or individual deficiencies. The public is no longer willing to leave the complete care of the sick and poor to the ministrations of private and ecclesiastical charity; city prisons cease to be institutions for exemplary punishment and for making profit from labor of inmates, and tardily become instruments of correction; the insane, the destitute, and the incapacitated requiring institutional treat-

[1] The results of the causes as seen in the growth of city activities in Detroit will be found in "The Growth of a City," *Public Business*, No. 70 (June 1, 1922); and Lent D. Upson, "Increasing Activities and Increasing Costs," *Nat. Mun. Rev.*, XI, 317-320 (October, 1922). Prof. William Anderson has a better arrangement of the same matter in *American City Government* (Holt, 1925), 404-405. See also Thomas H. Reed, *Municipal Government in the United States* (Century, 1926), Chap. III; and "Fifty Years of It." *Toledo City Journal*, XI, 285-297 (June 12, 1926).

ment are given larger opportunities for cure and are provided with less frugal and rigorous living conditions; vice—gambling, obscenity, prostitution, and vicious sports—is vigorously repressed, and commercial recreation regulated.

Modern scientific progress, also, has played no small part in the increase of municipal activities and costs. For example, in medicine the discovery of the germ basis of contagious disease has made possible its effective control. Following this, the public has realized that disease prevention is more important than efforts at cure. Consequently, public health activities have been expanded with great rapidity. The citizen of the new city pays for and enjoys the benefits of quarantine enforcement, food inspection, visiting nurses, tuberculosis treatment, medical examination of school children, purification of water supply, disposal of sewage and other wastes, and kindred efforts for the reduction of morbidity and mortality.

Confronted with this situation, citizens and officials seek some means of insuring an administration of municipal affairs which will guarantee that public acts will be adequate to public needs, and will be performed economically. Happily, there is a wholesome discarding of the idea that proper city administration is predicated alone upon the type of organization through which administration is secured, upon the character of the administrators themselves, or upon citizen interest. Unprejudiced experience indicates that satisfactory administration has its origin in all of these elements—in greater centralization and responsibility of authority; in a body of trained administrators, utilizing modern, scientific methods, and directly responsible to the representatives of the public for results produced; and in a more intelligent, though not necessarily increased, participation in government by the people.

The first step to the attainment of these requirements must be the complete divorcement in the public mind of policy determination from the actual administration of policies. The essential feature of democracy is the right of the public to determine what shall be done by government—to choose representatives who determine policies. To attempt in a similar way to decide the technical processes by which those policies shall be carried out is a perversion of republican principles, of which there are all too many evidences in the costly and incompetent government of American cities. Successful government must be a science, in the sense that its operations must be systematized through knowledge gained by exact observations, and being so, the public is not equipped to determine its technique. Policy determination requires a wide and intelligent interest on the part of citizens in the selection of their representatives, and in passing judgment upon accomplishments. However, if the administrative processes of government have grown so large, so complex, and so specialized that the average citizen cannot understand them, and so cannot be interested in them, then only two courses are open. Either government must remain a bungled effort and colossal failure in the hands of incompetents, or its technical processes must be removed from public meddling and made a responsibility of trained administrators whose work will be measured by well-defined standards and whose conduct will be subject to specific controls.

Centralization of responsibility

The increasing importance of public responsibility for the determination of policies, but not for technique of administration, is shown in a number of ways. Many states by means of home rule sections of their constitutions now permit their cities a considerable measure of local autonomy, placing the responsibility for local questions squarely upon the citizens and officials of these communities. Simultaneously, cities have sought to find some order in a chaos of elected officers, segregating those that should be elected from those that should be appointed. City councils have been reduced in membership, elected on non-partizan ballots, and the duties of these bodies clearly demarked from those having to do with administration. The number of elective administrative positions has been materially reduced, in favor of direct appointment or selection through a formal merit system. The strong-mayor and city-manager plans of government have in part superseded the disorganized and irresponsible types of organization common to American cities at the beginning of the century.

Defects in present centralized governments

Changing the organization of government so as to emphasize the distinction between policies and administration has not necessarily produced effective government. Small non-partizan city councils are not always fully representative, responsive, and non-political; but they are more so than their political, ward-elected predecessors. Perhaps some method of election will eventually become popular that will in a measure remedy these defects. Nor do city managers always deal with administration, and not at all with policies. Too often the city manager plan, as now operated, subordinates the policy-determining council to the administrative manager, confusing the two functions in the public mind, to the

ADMINISTRATIVE ORGANIZATION

detriment of the latter.[1] Always does the "strong-mayor" deal with both policies and administration, and more often than not the best of administrations are destroyed by the public because of disapproval of policies. The good public administrator is seldom a good public representative. As has been said of Mayor Mitchell in New York: "He thought that city government was taxation and administration, never realizing that it was people—and so into the mayor's office came a young humanitarian with no sense of humanity. . . . He would not kiss dirty babies; he would imperil his career to fight conditions which had kept them dirty."[2] It is a reasonable prediction that, eventually, modifications must be made in both the strong-mayor and city-manager types of government to insure executive leadership independent of administrative activities. In the city-manager plan this modification may take the form of emphasizing the position of mayor, increasing his authority over that exercised by the other members of the council, and requiring that he assume leadership in the formulation of policies, rather than being merely one of several coequal legislators to endorse policies advanced by the manager.

In the strong-mayor plan, an administrative organization yet to be tried is that of permanent appointment of one or preferably more professional administrators, subordinate to the mayor. It is believed that such a scheme would delegate to the mayor and the council all proposing and authorizing of policies, freeing the administrators for purely administrative duties, and shielding them from the public clamor of approbation or condemnation that attends any connection with policies.

In the newer types of municipal organization, the chief administrator—mayor or manager—is responsible for the conduct of all, or nearly all, departmental activities, each department embracing correlated services. Such correlation, however, has been largely a matter of custom as modified by the personalities involved and by the gradual accretion of new services. In many instances no orderly division of functions prevails. In commission and city-manager cites, five, or sometimes six or seven departments, have been instituted to embrace all activities, the num-

Departmental organization

---

[1] For an opposite view see Ellen D. Ellis, "The City Manager as a Leader of Policy," *Nat. Mun. Rev.*, XV, 201-204 (April, 1926). This article is, in part, an answer to J. W. Routh, "Thoughts on the Manager Plan," *ibid.*, XII, 176 (April, 1923); and I. G. Gibbon, "Municipal Government in the United States: Some Impressions," *ibid.*, XIV, 78-81 (February, 1925).

[2] Emanie N. Sachs, "Being Human," *Century Magazine*, III, 385-398 (February, 1926).

ber being increased in larger communities as activities become sufficiently important to warrant independence. This haphazard determination of organization too frequently results in an overlapping of services, or in services being rendered by departments not particularly interested in them.

Centralization into a few departments has advantages and aids in securing both inter- and intra-departmental coöperation. However, a department head, under these circumstances, is frequently responsible for work which he is not qualified to supervise. In such cases the department head stands between the chief executive and the actual administrator and prevents the direct contact that makes for sound administration. If the department head thus becomes simply a mouthpiece of his subordinates, he is really a supernumerary and might better be eliminated by decentralization. The logical arrangement is the correlation of kindred activities into a sufficient number of departments, each of such size only that the department head may be expected to be entirely familiar with its detailed operation. Such a system of departmental organization for a large city should follow somewhat the following outline of municipal functions, in which activities have been arranged in such natural divisions that they will be conducive to the greatest efficiency of operation within themselves and to the greatest ease of supervision and inspection on the part of the legislature and administrative authorities:

Municipal Functions [1]

A. Direct services to the public
 1. In the field of cultural development
    1. To provide instruction
    2. To provide library service
    3. To provide art service
    4. To provide recreation
    5. To provide parks and boulevards
 2. In the field of social and physical control
    6. To care for the indigent
    7. To prevent and repress disease
    8. To prevent and repress anti-social conduct

[1] This outline may be usefully expanded by listing under each function the specific objectives desired to be obtained, and further by enumerating the activities pursued to attain each such objective. For example, under the function of waste collection are the specific objectives of street cleaning, garbage collection, ash collection, and rubbish collection. Under street cleaning are the activities of handbrooming, machine brooming, flushing, etc. These activities are composed of work units which furnish the basis for cost comparisons and efficiency studies.

ADMINISTRATIVE ORGANIZATION

     9. To prevent and suppress fire
    10. To correct offenders
    11. To plan city development
    12. To regulate structures
    13. To regulate traffic
  3. In the field of public utilities
    14. To provide water
    15. To provide or regulate heat, light and power
    16. To provide highways
    17. To provide or regulate public transportation
    18. To collect and dispose of wastes
    19. To collect and dispose of sewage
    20. To regulate food supplies by providing markets
B. Indirect or overhead functions
    1. To conduct elections
    2. To provide legal advice and action
    3. To control personnel
    4. To assess property for taxation
    5. To plan, control, and audit finances
    6. To collect, safeguard, and disburse public money
    7. To transport employees and materials (if centralized)
    8. To purchase materials (if centralized)
    9. To supervise public property (if centralized)

The most important question in connection with establishing a theoretically correct city organization relates to inter- and intra-departmental activities, *i.e.*, activities conducted by one department for another, or by divisions within a department, which facilitate city activities but do not directly affect the public. Legal advice is an example of such inter-departmental activity, and in this instance, by precedent and experience, all legal matters are usually centralized in a department of law. Purchasing is still on the border line between centralization in a single department and dispersion through the numerous departments that have buying to do, although in recent years there has been a marked tendency towards centralization. There still remain a number of inter-departmental services which it appears logical and desirable to consolidate. Thus, the maintenance and repair of motor vehicles is still largely undertaken by departments using motor vehicles; the maintenance of public buildings is largely performed by the departments immediately concerned; as are activities having to do with the architectural design and construction of public buildings, and the control of public property. In moderately large cities these activities will ultimately be centralized in single departments, and will not be administered by individual departments whose primary purposes are of entirely different nature. The character of administration will be improved accordingly.

Many cities make use of bi-partizan or non-partizan boards for the administration of departments.[1] Probably this arrangement originated as a means of eliminating politics from certain branches of the city government, notably those having to do with public health, education, and the operation of utilities. Such commissions have demonstrated a large degree of usefulness in this aspect. The members, whether appointed or elected, usually serve without pay, and give an unselfish interest to their duties. There are, however, objections to this form of administrative organization. Not infrequently, departments so administered become almost separate corporations within, but not of, the city. They often operate without consideration for other departments and with the maximum degree of independence of the legislative authority, particularly if they have revenues of their own. In addition, these boards, because of their semi-independent positions, offer the chief executive—mayor or manager—means of disclaiming responsibility for the conduct of their branch of the city government. Also, such boards usually are unduly protected from criticism of their administration, even by the mayor, particularly when their membership consists of persons well established in the community. As a result their personal aggrandisement through extravagance must go unchecked. Further, the professional administrator serving under such a board feels that he is under obligation to the board and not to the chief administrator or mayor. In order to secure the removal of an incompetent official it may be necessary to bring about the removal of the entire board and the selection of a new board holding different opinions.

[1] "With the growing complexity of government problems it has been necessary for Congress to delegate to the executive side many secondary legislative functions in the making of regulations, and many secondary judicial functions in the enforcement of them. That is the socalled administrative law. And there has been the crudest mixing of these semi-legislative and semi-judicial functions with purely executive functions. These semi-judicial and semi-legislative duties are frequently entrusted to single officers, while purely administrative functions are often carried on by boards. All of this is exactly the reverse of the basic principles of sound administration. Boards and commissions are soundly adapted to the deliberate processes necessary to semi-judicial and semi-legislative and advisory functions, but they are absolutely hopeless where decisive administrative action is necessary. And likewise most of such functions should not be entrusted to a single mind. There is not a single successful business organization in the country that confuses such functions the way we do in government." From an address by Herbert Hoover, Secretary of Commerce, before the Thirteenth Annual Meeting of the Chamber of Commerce of the United States, May 21, 1925.

ADMINISTRATIVE ORGANIZATION

It is now generally accepted that in any department the best type of administration will be secured by a single head appointed directly by the mayor or manager. Certain exceptions may be made for the time being in respect to the administration of schools and public utilities, but even here the desirability of a citizen board intervening between the department head and the mayor is open to some question. The use of boards or commissions is of more importance as an expedient to prevent abuses than as an aid to efficient administration, and in a city not bed-ridden with politics, they probably do more harm than good.

CHAP. I

The essential qualities of a professional administrator differ little from those necessary for success in any field of endeavor. The administrator must bring to his task personal acceptability, energy, tact, courage, and honesty. These qualities are fundamental. Additional characteristics should be determined by the nature of the task and of the people served. Men like their own kind and the way of the administrator will be hard who has personal habits and manners substantially different from those of his associates.[1]

Characteristics of the administrator

It is impossible for a chief administrator to have training that will give him a detailed knowledge of how each public service is conducted. He should, however, know the ideals of every service and be able to test the approach made to them in practice. While the administrator cannot know how to do everything necessary in conducting a city, he should at least know what should be done, and be able to judge results. Routine application of adequate performance tests is of far greater importance than the intrusion of personal ideas into the detail of activities. How can administrators such as these be selected? Certainly not by the methods now generally employed by city councils and mayors in the employment of city managers and department heads. What legislative body in need of a city manager has ever, before undertaking its search, set down in black and white the qualities that a successful candidate must possess—the physical and mental characteristics, personal habits, training, and experience? There would be better city managers and better managed cities had this been done. How many department heads have been chosen because of eminent fitness for the tasks imposed upon them? Or even in accordance with any qualifications definitely established in advance of selection—omitting political ones? Yet if effective municipal administration

Selection of administrators

---

[1] See several chapters in William H. Allen, *Universal Training for Citizenship and Public Service* (Macmillan, 1917).

is to depend in part upon competent administrators, means must be devised for selecting them out of the unnumbered individuals who, in whatever other respects they may have failed, retain full confidence that they can run a government. Up to the present, little can be said for formal civil service as an instrument to be used in this selection. Yet one must not confuse the civil service of other days with that developed in recent times. In competent hands, modern civil service is indicating new possibilities of really differentiating between competency and incompetency in the selection of personnel.

But, given proper organization and able administrators, there remains the need of proper methods; this must be met before effective administration can result. Unfortunately it is in this field that local government has lagged most woefully. The progress of governmental administration into a science implies the same careful examination of methods as is found in private industry; the same trial and error processes of improvement; and the same development of standards by which results may be measured. Fortunately certain city activities, such as public utilities, health, and engineering, have fields of private experience and experiment from which to draw. If administered by technically trained men, this experience will be used to public advantage. On the other hand, such departments as police, fire, recreation, parks, courts, prisons, and city planning are practically unique to government and cannot profit from private endeavor.

Concede that public officials have the same initiative and intelligence as employees of similar responsibility in private business. Even so, what time, and what funds, have they to make experiments in the more effective and economical conduct of departments? If experiments were made, and they revealed desirable changes, what imperious pressure will not be brought to maintain existing conditions, in the interest of the incompetent, in jobs, in contracts, and in political preferment? And what machinery is available to give to other communities the results of such local research? What communities recognize that government is a science in which research will produce as profitable results as in private industry?

The desirability of such experiments in public administration has prompted public-minded citizens to support the making of experiments on a modest scale, in some larger cities, and the bringing of the available experience of other communities to the attention

ADMINISTRATIVE ORGANIZATION

of local officials.[1] But such activities are not concerned with pure research in the best sense of the word. Such citizen activity is engaged principally in determining the facts of local government and securing the adoption of the best known methods in a few communities. To be sure, such activities have resulted in some very notable work that has saved the taxpayers many millions of dollars and permanently elevated standards of service. The whole budget movement in America, which began in 1907 with an experiment in the health department of New York City made by the New York Bureau of Municipal Research in coöperation with public authorities, and which has culminated in the adoption of a national budget system, was the outgrowth of private research in government. Similarly, the as yet incomplete adaptation of private accounting methods to public business has been brought about largely through the experiments made possible by private philanthropy.[2] But compare the vast importance of government and the meager amount of pure research in its problems with the state of research in other fields. In science and engineering there are available the results of work done in ten thousand industries; in agriculture, the experiments of half a hundred university experiment stations; in education, the results of experiments in a few private schools of outstanding character, in institutions for the training of teachers, and in many city educational systems; in health there are the results of private medical research, as well as the results to be obtained from the numerous medical foundations.

With little improvement in methods, government is expanding its services in inevitable response to natural causes, building structure upon superstructure, expanding details, and increasing costs. In the meantime little or nothing is being done on many problems of municipal administration—governmental organization, metropolitan area, the incidence of taxation, the contracting of debt, the levy of special assessments, refuse collection and disposal, control of crime, correction of offenders, limits of free education, city planning, traffic regulation, transportation, budget making, accounting, methods of selecting personnel, pensions, standards for appraising results, etc., etc.

[1] Since the establishment of the first bureau of municipal research in New York City in 1906 similar agencies have been created in Philadelphia, Chicago, Detroit, Cleveland, St. Louis, San Francisco, Kansas City, and a score of smaller communities.

[2] Mr. Herman Metz, former comptroller of New York City, financed the first studies of public accounting.

14 PRACTICE OF MUNICIPAL ADMINISTRATION

CHAP. I

Operating audits and public interest

Sound organization, competent personnel, and scientific methods are essential to effective city government, but in addition there must be an intelligent compulsion by the public that is served. If the public is to keep its hands off of the technical processes of government, such compulsion can only come by measuring the results that these technical processes produce, and condemning or rewarding public servants accordingly. What standards of measurements can be used? In government there are no cash profits to be distributed to share holders, the amount of which will roughly gage the efficiency of production. The dividends of government appear as reasonable taxes, a low death and sickness rate, education, pure water, good pavements, clean streets, frequent garbage and rubbish removal, adequate fire protection, crime suppression, generous park and recreation facilities, regulated traffic, ample transportation, etc. Citizens cannot casually examine these services and say that they possess the quality, quantity, and cost that are most desirable from the public viewpoint. This means that certain definite standards must be established by which public services may be judged intelligently,—measurements against which the services of a particular city over a period of years can be evaluated and compared with similar results taken from comparable neighboring communities. Such tests have not as yet been devised, but efforts are being made in that direction. The business of government cannot be placed on the high plane that is commonly ascribed to the business of private industry until the process is perfected.[1] Nor will the existence of such standards be sufficient unless they are applied. This requires the incentive and authority to audit operations with the same care that at present we audit financial transactions. We are much interested in examining expenditures to insure that administrators are honest. The application of an operating audit will determine whether administrators are efficient—a quality of equal or greater importance. Usable public reports follow as a logical consequence.[2]

---

[1] Professor W. B. Munro discusses twenty-five criteria of good government in *The Government of American Cities* (4th ed., Macmillan, 1926), Chap. XXIII. For certain tests applied in one foreign city, see Charles A. Beard, *Municipal Government of Tokio* (Macmillan, 1923). For a more detailed use of tests see Lent D. Upson, ed. *The Governments of Cincinnati and Hamilton County* (1924).

[2] "In our time it's waste and incompetence not graft or bad arithmetic that menaces public service. For that reason ordinary auditing gives almost no protection against unnecessary or bungling expenditure. For example, Governor Smith (New York) recently reported that a state agricultural school has been spending $8700 to graduate a boy into actual farming, and

It has been predicted that in the coming age psychology, sociology, and politics will do for human relations what other sciences have done for material things. If this is to be so, there must be done for government what private initiative has done for industry, and what the philanthropies of the Rockefellers, Carnegies, Sages, and many others have done for medicine, education, and charity. This great institution we call government, which touches us so intimately, and upon which we are so anxious to thrust burdens, must be analyzed with disregard for prejudice and precedents, and organization and methods must be created that will do many new things effectively, but with a minimum of spiritual and material friction upon all whom government concerns.

that it would have been cheaper to ship over railroads at state expense all freight carried by the barge canal than carrying it by the canal at canal rates actually cost! These expenditures, now officially called worse than wasted, were all carefully audited. Additions were O.K. Amounts on vouchers for payments were just like those on bills. Payroll items were O.K. Dotted lines were appropriately signed on. Everything was attended to properly but the public's right to benefit in proportion to outlay." W. H. Allen, *Public Service*, No. 463 (April 6, 1926).

CHAPTER II

ELECTIONS [1]

Interest of the administrator in elections

Theoretically, administrators should be concerned only with the methods of selecting and appointing subordinate officials and employees, in which field are found the directly appointed officials exempt from civil service, and the larger group chosen under the merit system. Practically, officials responsible for carrying out policies cannot ignore the machinery for selecting personnel by election. In some instances, the administrator may be responsible for the operation of elections; all elective officials with whom he has contacts will be chosen by this machinery; and it will be used to determine public policies vitally affecting the success of the administration.

Development of the electoral machinery

Early voting was usually oral, the will of the elector being recorded by the election official. Sometimes there was an actual count of hands, or of beans and corn dropped into a box by the voters.[2] Later came the printed ballot furnished by the several political parties, and properly marked in the interests of the party concerned. The introduction of the printed official ballot—the "Australian ballot"—was fought vigorously by the politicians.

Incidental abuses

With the very gradual development of the electoral system, it would be expected that grievous abuses would characterize its growth. Sometimes election returns were and are deliberately forged regardless of the ballots actually cast; ballot boxes "stuffed" with fraudulent ballots after the polls closed; votes purchased at a fixed price in cash or by pre-and-post election favors; ballots

---

[1] The best reference on the subject of elections is the election laws of the state with which the student is concerned, and which can usually be secured from the secretary of state. An outline of a model election system will be found in "A Model Election System," Supplement, *Nat. Mun. Rev.*, X, 603-616 (December, 1921). This pamphlet was prepared by the Committee on Electoral Reform of the National Municipal League, the membership of which included a number of persons familiar with election procedure in the United States. For a brief discussion of some election problems, see C. A. Crosser, "Some Election Facts and Tendencies," *American Review*, IV, 204-213 (March-April, 1926).

[2] Older citizens of Detroit still tell of an election on the question of purchasing a park which was decided by the voters lining up at a given time on one or the other side of a rope stretched across a main street.

not completely voted marked while being counted, or excessively marked so as to be void; non-residents "colonized" in boarding houses so as to be on hand to vote on election day, and frequently voted in a number of different precincts as "repeaters"; decent citizens so intimidated as to remain away from the polls in certain sections; and sometimes ballot boxes removed and fradulent ones substituted. As one corrupt but jovial election official remarked when a group of "reformers" were casting their ballots in his district: "Let the boys have their fun; we ain't going to count that box."

Perhaps with a view to honesty and efficiency, but more probably because it is impractical to divorce from one another the numerous elections held in cities, school districts, townships, and counties of the state, and because local, state, and national officials must be voted upon by all of these units of government, the control of elections has been made a state function. The state enacts the statutes (usually in great detail) under which elections are conducted by local authorities, and retains general statutory, but seldom administrative, control over election operations. Ordinarily, local legislative bodies and local administrators have nothing to do with the formulation of election laws, although they may be wholly or partially responsible for their proper administration.

While the general control of elections rests with the state, and is exercised by a state election commission, the secretary of state, or similar authority, no uniform practice prevails with respect to the delegation of this authority for the purpose of operating local election machinery. In some instances, as in Ohio, the board of elections of each county is appointed by the governor upon the nomination of the two major political parties, there being two representatives for each. In other cases, as in Michigan, the election boards are exofficio bodies consisting of important local officials, there being separate boards for cities and counties. In still other instances, responsibility rests with a single individual, either elected by the public or appointed by the governor, mayor, or council. Bi-partizan boards are frequent as an ostensible but somewhat unreal safeguard against fraud. Experience indicates that the best practice with respect to the selection of local election authorities is the appointment of a single commissioner in each locality by the governor of the state.[1] This practice has at least

[1] The Committee on Electoral Reform of the National Municipal League says: "He should be appointed by the governing body of the municipality." See "A Model Election System," *op. cit.*, 608.

18   PRACTICE OF MUNICIPAL ADMINISTRATION

CHAP. II

Duties of local election authorities

Size of election districts

a tendency to minimize the political control that is the curse of American election procedure. Honest and economical elections will not be had until the political parties are pried loose from their almost complete domination of the electoral machinery.

The duties of the local election authorities are threefold—legislative, administrative, and inspectorial. Circumstances not covered by state law must be met by rules of the local election authorities; the routine procedure of conducting elections, counting ballots, certifying returns, and issuing certificates of election must be attended to; and the conduct of the numerous subordinate agents must be supervised. If the local election authority be a board, the legislative and inspectorial duties are carried on by the board members, the administrative responsibility resting with subordinates. Among such administrative duties are those of supplying, and lighting and heating places of election, providing ballots and other necessary supplies, procuring police protection, seeing that all ballots and properly tabulated election returns are sent to headquarters, and finally consolidating the returns for certification to the proper authorities.

For the convenience of voting, a city is divided into election districts or precincts, in each of which is located a place of election. The size of these election districts is determined either by state law or by the judgment of the state or local election authorities. The number of voters in a district should never be more than can be handled easily by the facilities provided, nor so small as to make the cost of elections unduly high.[1] A fair majority of registered electors turn out once in each four-year period when the president is to be elected. If the number of electors allotted each district for this election be fixed at say 500, it means that during the three intervening years from 50 to 150 persons will vote, making the cost of casting each vote excessively high. Mr. C. A. Crosser, who has given considerable study to the subject, believes that the best practice is to make the districts rather large for a heavy vote, the number of voters being

[1] The size of voting precincts prescribed by law differs in the several states. In Ohio a voting district cannot contain more than 500 voters, with a minimum of 200. The New York law prescribes 450 voters as a minimum when paper ballots are used. Missouri and Illinois allow 500 voters, and Minnesota, 400 voters, as a maximum. Washington allows 300 voters, Michigan, 600, and California, 200, as a maximum. Pennsylvania allows a range of between 250 and 1,000 voters. Massachusetts sets a maximum of 2,000 voters, and the largest districts are found in New England. See C. A. Crosser, "Registration by Precincts," *Toledo City Journal*, VIII, 447 (September 15, 1923).

ELECTIONS 19

automatically reduced at subsequent light elections.[1] In other words, if the voters are willing to stand in line a little while when they go to vote once in four years, the taxpayers can be saved considerable money. Apparently this occasional overcrowding does not reduce interest in elections. Scrutiny of 1924 election returns shows that the voting turnout in Boston, Detroit, Minneapolis, and New York, which have a large number of voters for each precinct, was as large as in other cities with smaller precincts.[2]

The voting places are usually in public or semi-public buildings, such as schoolhouses, libraries, churches, and fire and police stations, supplemented largely by private stores and garages rented for the occasion. A few cities use small movable booths, in place of rented quarters, a practice that is satisfactory but relatively expensive. On election day the booths are placed on vacant lots or street curbs, and at other times are stored wherever convenient. During the storage period between elections, the booths can be cleaned, painted, and maintained in a condition commensurate with the dignity that should surround elections. Utilization of publicly owned property, where possible, as places of election, reduces costs and provides most suitable facilities for election purposes. However, the presence of voters in schools, and in fire and police stations, handicaps the proper activities of these units unless special provision has been made for election purposes.[3] Probably the

CHAP. II

The place of election

---

[1] In Cleveland in 1924, 776 districts were used to cast the presidential vote of 197,082. In the presidential primaries in 1924, only 35,000 votes were cast in about the same number of districts. The variation among cities in the size of voting precinct, and the number of election officials, as given by Mr. C. A. Crosser, is as follows:

Cities	Average No. Voters per Precinct	No. Voting Districts	Total 1924 Vote or Vote for President	No. Officials per Booth
Detroit	711	458	325,678	3-7
St. Louis	417	624	260,190	6
Cleveland	254	776	197,082	6
Minneapolis	519	308	160,607	7
Kansas City	370	413	152,860	6
Cincinnati	244	638	155,880	6
San Francisco	181	882	159,649	6
Rochester	488	227	110,705	4
Denver	457	211	90,750	5-10
Newark	397	226	90,712	4
Seattle	323	294	94,437	3-4
Oakland	245	337	82,516	6
Columbus	229	406	92,272	6
Portland, Ore.	211	467	98,375	10
Toledo	200	423	84,335	6

[2] Ibid.
[3] Rigid wooden or iron booths are used in Toledo, Columbus, Cleveland, Detroit, and Cincinnati; collapsible booths of canvas or wood are used in San

CHAP. II

Selection of election officials

most desirable procedure involves the liberal use of public buildings and rented quarters, with movable booths when other desirable facilities cannot be obtained.

Routine operations of the election machinery within the voting place are conducted by district officials. These officials are the foundation of the election system, and upon their character and capacity depends the honesty and accuracy of elections, so essential to successful popular government. The selection of these district officials is properly a duty of the local election authorities, although in some instances they are elected. This latter practice is an absurdity, the results of which can be equaled only by the universal appointment of political henchmen to these positions. Even with appointed district officials, either by law or custom, the selection is really made by the party organizations, and these positions are looked upon as petty political patronage to be distributed among a large number of individuals who have rendered some real or fancied service to the political parties. While the compensation and honors are small, the number of workers who can be so rewarded is large. For example, New York has 17,800; Philadelphia, 7,000; and Cleveland, 4,500 booth officials.[1]

In a few cities, however, the election authorities have made a genuine and commendable effort to select district election officials of a high character.[2] Men and women of integrity, without regard to party recommendation, and particularly that group of citizens who are freed from labor on legal holidays, as bank clerks, are urged to present their names for consideration. From this group, the election authorities designate a proper number of local officers, continuing them in service over long periods of time, and promoting the most competent to the positions of chairmen. It has been suggested that the civil service authorities must eventually be called upon to furnish eligible lists of persons qualified to serve as judges and clerks of elections, and who would be willing to perform this temporary work on the few days in the year that it is required. There is no doubt that such a method of selection would produce booth officials of a distinctly improved mental and moral caliber as compared with those selected under generally prevailing

Francisco, Oakland, Boston, and Milwaukee; small portable booths or stalls that are set up in police and fire stations and rented storerooms are used almost exclusively in Pittsburgh, Portland, Los Angeles, Jersey City, Omaha, St. Louis, Chicago, Newark, Denver, New York City, and Richmond, Va. See C. A. Crosser, "Housing the Voter," *op. cit.*, VIII, 371 (July 28, 1923).

[1] C. A. Crosser, *op. cit.*
[2] Notably Detroit, Omaha, and St. Louis.

conditions. The results should be more correctly counted returns, and better handling of reports and records. A record of officials appointed in each district is maintained in the central office, as is a record of available candidates who can be enlisted to fill vacancies. These records provide information with respect to the character and general availability of officials and candidates, and the manner in which the duties of the officials have been discharged.

The number of election officials in a polling place is from three to a dozen, depending upon the possible number of voters to be cared for, and the number of separate ballots to be voted at the election. This group of booth officials is often supervised by a chairman of the voting precinct, who is designated to his position by the local election authority or elected by the local board. In such instances it may be the duty of this chairman to make all decisions in accordance with his interpretation of the election laws and regulations, with opportunity for his colleagues and watchers to record a protest. More often the chairman has only equal authority with the other members. In larger cities complete detailed instructions are made available to each precinct official, governing challenged, non-registered, and transferred voters, spoiled ballots, etc., and any question out of ordinary can be referred to the central authorities. The precinct officials must accord facilities for voting within legal hours, determine that applicants are proper voters in the district, count the ballots cast, and make a proper return of both ballots and election property to the local election authority.

These official representatives of the election authorities are supplemented by rather ineffectual challengers or watchers appointed by the political parties, and more effectual ones appointed by responsible civic organizations, in accordance with the legislation governing this subject. These challengers are permitted to be present at the voting, and usually at the count of the votes. They may challenge the vote of any person, requiring that such voter must "swear in" his vote, the oath being to the effect that he is a legal voter. Record is made of such challenged votes, to permit of prosecution of the voter should later investigation indicate perjury.

The purpose of preliminary registration, required in all large communities, whether it be annual, biennial, quadrennial, or permanent, is to insure in advance that voters meet all legal qualifications, and thus prevent fraudulent voting. In cities, all voters are required to register in person, either at a stated time in the voting district, or at a definite period before elections at some central point. Such registration lists must be checked to insure their integrity, particularly in districts where fraudulent registration may be anticipated. This checking is usually done by regular election officials, or by the police, although occasionally registered letters are used. The revised lists are open to inspection by political parties, civic organizations, and citizens for further investigation. As a control of the routine method of checking registrations, and to prevent fraud, some authorities recommend the creation of a permanent official agency to audit the work of the police or other persons responsible for checking,[1] but in actual practice such agencies have been of little worth. The registration lists may be published some weeks prior to the election and posted in each district in order that the public itself may serve as a check upon fraud and error, although the principal use of such published lists is by the party machines to canvass and get out the voters favorable to them. In addition, the challengers or watchers, already discussed, should serve as an effective check on fraudulent voting, although unhappily, challengers are sometimes refused admission to the voting place by election officials, or, when appointed by the political parties, often connive in the neglect of their legitimate duties. Under the permanent registration laws of Boston, Baltimore, and Milwaukee the police make a yearly house-to-house canvass and prepare a check list of all voters or adult residents. With the aid of this list, the election commissions may examine the file of eligible voters, make transfers, and drop those names not appearing on the list.

The registration itself usually involves the setting down of the name, residence, place of birth, age, when and where naturalized (if foreign born), record of last registration, length of residence in the state, city, and election district, sometimes followed by the voter's signature.[2] The signature is not always taken, but is a principal safeguard against impersonation and false voting, particularly if the voter is required to sign when voting and the signature is compared with the registration signature.[3]

In addition to preventing fraudulent practices, registration of

[1] "A Model Election System," *op. cit.*, 607.
[2] *Ibid.*, 608.
[3] A detailed study of registration is being made by Professor Joseph P. Harris, to be published shortly under the title *Registration for Voting in the United States.* For a brief statement see Helen M. Rocca, *Registration Laws* (National League of Women Voters, 1925).

ELECTIONS

the annual and biennial type is supposed to serve as a frequent reminder to citizens of their electoral duties and bring out a heavy vote. Many authorities on election matters believe that the large additional expense involved by annual registration is not offset by possible elimination of fraudulent practices,[1] and that an annual police check of permanent or quadrennial registration lists, coupled with the automatic removal of persons failing to vote in two successive years, and of names appearing in the death lists, would serve to prevent fraud just as effectively. Furthermore, it is held that annual registration does not bring out an additional vote, but on the contrary the annoyance of such frequent enrolment keeps some away from the polls.

Central registration of a permanent or semi-permanent character is rapidly coming into use.[2] Under the most desirable plans of permanent registration, only newly qualified voters, those having failed to vote for a specified time, or those moved to a new address are required to register, and these may register at the office of the election commission at any time, or sometimes in their respective election districts at certain intervals. A list of eligible voters is made up each year after checking a police or other official listing. The semi-permanent plan of registration provides for periodic registration in the districts, say once in four years, new registrations and changes in residence being recorded at the election headquarters, at any time, except for a few days immediately prior to an election. On the whole, these plans are probably best for the voters as the time of registration is made to fit their convenience, and there is an obvious saving in cost over maintaining registration places and registration officials in the districts for several days each year.[3]

The printing of election ballots, the arrangement of the names of candidates and questions upon the ballots, and the means of distributing ballots are determined by the general election law.

[1] The Kansas City Public Service Institute reports that the annual cost of permanent registration in Topeka is 8.4 cents per registered voter; Milwaukee, 12.1; Portland, Ore., 12.6; Denver, 19.7; and Omaha, 26.0. These figures compare with an annual registration cost in Kansas City, Mo., of 84.2 cents.

[2] Permanent registration is used in Boston and other Massachusetts cities, Milwaukee, Omaha, Portland, Ore., Denver, Minneapolis, St. Paul, Duluth, Louisville, Indianapolis, Newark, and Jersey City. A series of articles discussing registration in some of these cities appears in the *Nat. Mun. Rev.* for 1925 and 1926.

[3] For the arguments against permanent registration see Frank H. Riter, "Permanent Registration for Elections Unsuitable for Large Cities," *Nat. Mun. Rev.*, XIV, 532-535 (September, 1925).

24 PRACTICE OF MUNICIPAL ADMINISTRATION

CHAP. II

Ballots

The ballots provided for the election of persons to office may enumerate the names of such persons under the heading of their party, or preferably list the names under the head of the office that they are seeking, the name of their party being printed after each name. This plan is called the "Massachusetts Ballot," or sometimes the "Birdless Ballot," and makes it impossible for the ignorant or uninformed voter to register his adherence to some party emblem at the top of the ballot. It is customary to arrange for rotating names in printing ballots, when there is more than one candidate for an office.

As a control, during the printing, watchers are ordinarily stationed at the printing establishment day and night to see that no ballots are taken away, and that no surplus is printed over and above the quantity specified in the contract. After being printed, boxed, and sealed, with a certificate showing the number in each package, the police or election authorities take possession of the ballots, and see that the proper package is delivered to each voting precinct on election morning, the officer making the delivery getting a receipt showing the number of ballots so delivered. Ballots are frequently of the coupon character, *i.e.*, in one corner of the ballot is a coupon numbered with a serial number. Each ballot is usually initialed by an election official, below this detachable coupon. When an elector enters the polling place, his name is located on the registration book, and if he is found to be registered properly, he is handed a ballot or set of ballots, properly initialed, and his name and address, together with the numbers of such ballots, are entered on record on poll books.

Voided ballots

A ballot is voted by marking crosses or numbers in the properly designated spaces. The procedure by which a ballot, or portion of a ballot, is voided is determined by state law. Ballots are most frequently voided by voting for more candidates than there are offices to be filled, by voting with other designation than that required, by using a pencil other than that provided by the election authorities, by placing any identifying mark on the ballot, etc. A voter has the privilege of an additional ballot or ballots in case the original has been unintentionally voided.

After the ballot or ballots have been voted, the official at the ballot box, before depositing same, should call the numbers of the ballot stubs, to be sure they correspond with the numbers issued, as shown by the poll book. If correct, the detachable corners are then removed and the ballots placed in the box.

The official at the box should also see that only regularly initialed ballots are cast.

After the count is concluded the ballots are usually tied in packages, and returned to the ballot box, which is locked and sealed before the officials adjourn. A record is also made of ballots cast, ballots voided, and ballots unused, the total of which must equal the number of ballots delivered to the precinct. The returns of the election count, with the tally sheets and ballots, are made to the central authorities, who are responsible for transmitting the results to the proper city, county, and state officials. The precinct board delivers the ballot boxes to the police officer stationed at that particular booth or to other authorized persons. The ballots are usually kept inviolate for a number of months, and the tally sheets are frequently retained for a number of years. The payment of a small deposit as a guarantee of good faith by any defeated candidate should make a recount possible. This is most essential. The difficulties in the way of securing a recount in some states are a constant incentive to fraud.

To avoid delay, the counting of the ballots is done usually in the districts except when a method of election is used such as the Hare system of proportional representation, under which central counting is compulsory. The chairman of each board of local officials directs the count of the ballots, which should be observed by the authorized watchers. The votes for the various candidates are usually taken off by a crew of three officials, one person calling the vote, and two others tallying simultaneously. This gives a control which prevents slipping in more votes for a candidate than should be credited, and the challengers, who should remain during the count, act as a further check against irregularities. The law sometimes requires that all ballots voted must be marked with pencils of blue or other colored lead furnished by the election authorities, and that none of the booth officials shall have such a pencil in his possession during the canvass. As nearly all ballots are marked with the official regulation pencil, and a black "X" on a ballot otherwise voted in a distinctive color would be immediately noticeable, this rule has been a material check on the old political practice of either voting unfinished ballots, or placing extra "X's" on ballots to void them. Sometimes complicated methods are designed to check fraud in the tally. These methods normally will be ignored by the booth officials, who by common consent will adopt the least laborious plan of counting.

CHAP. II

Voting machines

Mechanical voting by means of voting machines is used in many communities as a means of eliminating both fraud in balloting and the long and tedious counting that follows the closing of the polls.[1] There are several varieties of voting machines, but all of them operate in substantially the same manner. The names of the various candidates are displayed, either vertically or horizontally, under the name of the office to be filled, or under the name of the political party if so required by law. A choice is indicated by operating an indicator of which there is one for each candidate, and such movement automatically locks the mechanism against indicating additional choices for the same office, unless there be two or more candidates to be voted for. The voter can change his choice only after readjusting the mechanism to its original position. The vote cast for each candidate is automatically registered on a concealed counter when the voter manipulates a lever, which sometimes pushes back the curtains surrounding the booth and rings a bell. This procedure also locks the machine, preventing further operation until the lever has been moved by the next voter. All machines make provision for counting the total numbers of votes, and some of them provide for an enumeration of the male and female voters, for indicating protested votes, and spaces for writing in additional candidates if the voters so desire.

Advantages

The chief advantage of the machines are secrecy of the ballot, absence of void and doubtful ballots, elimination of fraud, and speed of operation and tally. The returns are, of course, known instantly after the polls close. A reduction in the cost of elections is claimed from the fact that the number of districts can be reduced; fewer election officials are needed in the districts retained; the officers obtained work shorter hours; the expense of supplies and the cost of ballots is lessened; and the expense of litigation attending contests is practically eliminated.[2]

Objections

On the other hand, some legitimate objections to the machines

---

[1] A thorough discussion of mechanical voting from which this description is summarized, will be found in T. David Zukerman, *The Voting Machine, Report on the History, Use and Advantage of Mechanical Means for Casting and Counting Ballots* (Political Research Bureau of the Republican County Committee of New York, January, 1925).

[2] As evidence on the point of possible reduction in the number of districts, the experience of Seattle and Rochester may be cited. Both of these cities utilize voting machines exclusively, yet with a vote approximately the same as in Toledo, Columbus, and Portland, Ore., which require between 400 and 500 polling places, the cities first mentioned have about 200 precincts. In 1924, the election cost in Rochester was $98,000; the expense in Toledo and in Columbus was in excess of $150,000. See footnote, p. 19.

have been raised. It is argued that there is a lack of assurance to the voter that the vote will be counted in accordance with his desires, since he does not see an actual paper ballot; that there are difficulties in using the machine intelligently; and that there is an inclination to cast a straight ballot. It is also alleged that there are occasional breakdowns and necessity for repairs. Probably the principal objections are the large initial cost of installation, and the dislike of the political parties for an innovation that makes fraud so difficult.[1]

Many states have provided that electors who are necessarily absent from their legal residence on election day may vote by mail, although little use is made of the privilege.[2] The right to cast a vote by mail is sometimes made dependent upon the reason for the absence, a provision that invites litigation in event that votes so cast have an important bearing upon the election. There is also danger that sufficient ballots may be secured through this device to permit the operation of "chain balloting" in certain precincts. Absent voting has not been tried out sufficiently to afford a thorough test of its methods or effectiveness, but it has not been entirely abandoned by any jurisdiction that has undertaken it.[3] In practice, a person expecting to be absent on election day secures a ballot by application to the central election authority, which in turn tabulates such votes as may be received before or on election day.

However, the question of absent voting suggests the entire question of balloting by mail.[4] The casting of votes by mail, in

[1] Mr. Zuckerman, in summing up his conclusions with respect to voting machines, says, "They are not perfect. In a district where the entire body of officials connive at dishonesty, they are not an absolute guarantee of an honest election. Neither can they prevent certain types of fraud, certainly not the kind that arises from illegal registration; but they can reduce bribery to a dubious speculation, and eliminate entirely fraudulent changes made in ballots, and errors in counting. They cannot develop intelligence and thought in the careless voter; they cannot insure worthy candidates nor lure the absent elector to the polls; they cannot even make certain that there will not be indirect influences determining the result. They can, however, undoubtedly eradicate the evils and wastes of paper ballots and insure a more honest and efficient election. And while more far-reaching reforms may be sought and attained in later years, there is an immediate problem which should be met now. It can best be met by the use of voting machines."

[2] Only four states are without absentee voting laws, although three other states grant the privilege only to the military. For an enumeration of states see James K. Pollock, Jr., "Absent Voting," *Nat. Mun. Rev.*, XV, 282-292 (May, 1926).

[3] "Absent Voting," *Bulletins for the Massachusetts Constitutional Convention.*

[4] Mr. Russell Thompson has compiled information on the subject of voting by mail which is distributed by the More Democracy Press, 104 W. Monroe

28   PRACTICE OF MUNICIPAL ADMINISTRATION

CHAP. II

lieu of the present rather cumbersome method, has been advocated now and again by writers in both England and America. It is urged that complete voting by mail would eliminate the largest element of expense in the holding of elections, would secure an expression of opinion from the numerous persons who now do not take the trouble to go to the polls, and would remove the element of fraud which arises largely through faulty counting by district election officials. It is suggested that the ballots could be sent by registered letter to all voters on the registry list, and that the voter's ballot could be placed in the post at the convenience of the person voting, the same to be counted if it carried the postmark of the day of the election. On the other hand, it is argued that the present secrecy of the ballot would be lost, influence could be brought to bear upon the marking of the ballot, which is not now possible, that fraud might be perpetrated in the forging of ballots, and that an unusual, and perhaps impossible, burden would be placed upon the postoffice authorities. Sundry schemes have been devised to meet these arguments, but their details are too extensive for repetition. Recently the problem has been discussed more seriously by election authorities, and it is anticipated that with the growing cost of elections this method of balloting will receive sufficient attention to bring it within the realm of possibility.

Compulsory voting

Compulsory voting is of little interest to the administrator, except as it may be occasionally advanced by well-meaning citizens as a panacea for part or all of the ills that afflict municipal government. A successful democracy is believed to depend upon an intelligent expression of opinion from all of its members. When on an average about one-half of the qualified voters go to the polls, it is but natural that some form of compulsory voting should be suggested as a remedy.[1] The forms of compulsion proposed are several—that the negligent voter should be disfranchised for a limited period, extra obligations in the way of jury duty imposed, or poll taxes and small fines levied. At the present time, com-

St., Chicago, Ill. A bill has been considered by the Wisconsin legislature that would permit the experiment to be made in certain Milwaukee districts.

[1] See C. E. Merriam, "Compulsory Voting in Czechoslovakia," *Nat. Mun. Rev.*, XIV, 65-68 (February, 1925); and Thomas H. Reed, "Compulsory Voting in Belgium," *op. cit.*, XIV, 335 (June, 1925). Reference also may be made to W. T. Donaldson, *Compulsory Voting and Absent Voting*; and J. D. Barnett, *Compulsory Voting in Oregon*, in the *Amer. Polit. Sci. Rev.*, XV, 265; and "Compulsory Voting," *Bulletins for Massachusetts Constitutional Convention*. Suggestions on how non-voting may be reduced are contained in C. E. Merriam and H. F. Gosnell, *Non-Voting* (Univ. of Chicago Press, 1924), Chaps. IX-X.

pulsory voting does not exist anywhere in the United States, and as a practical proposition, it would be difficult to enforce any law requiring voting in communities where more than one-half of the citizens are at times offenders. In this connection, Professor C. E. Merriam suggested, however, that with forty-eight states and many cities in a position to experiment with the plan, some useful facts could be secured by actual trial.[1]

[1] *Op. cit.* The Chicago study of 5300 voters summarized the reasons of non-voting as follows: physical difficulties, 25.4 percent; legal and administrative difficulties, 12.6 percent; disbelief in voting, 17.7 percent; and inertia, 44.3 percent. It has been suggested that the amount of non-voting as well as election costs would be reduced by permitting citizens to vote as they pay taxes, over a period of several weeks. Many excuses for non-voting would be eliminated and the conduct of elections could be handled by a comparatively small staff.

CHAPTER III

CIVIL SERVICE [1]

The public as employer

The most important group of public servants consists of those numerous employees who are appointed rather than elected to office, and whose duty it is to conduct the many activities undertaken by local governments. From modest beginnings, this number of persons has increased with the expansion of public activities, until it is estimated that for every ten workers gainfully employed in the United States one person is now on the payroll of some governmental unit.[2] Obviously, the effectiveness of government depends in a large measure upon the honesty and efficiency of these men and women. These characteristics of honesty and efficiency are determined partly by the methods used in the selection, promotion, dismissal, and retirement of public employees.

Early theories of public employment

Public employment was once commonly considered to be the property of the political party in power, with the result that after every electoral turnover, whether in nation, state, county, city, or village, there was an almost complete change in the personnel in public positions. Employment depended upon the fortunes of the party leaders, so employees worked industriously for party success.[3]

Genesis of the merit system

Early in the nineteenth century the absurdities of such a system of

---

[1] A brief study of some phases of the merit system is *The Personal Problem in the Public Service, Report of the Conference Committee of the National Assembly of Civil Service Commissions*, the National Municipal League, the Governmental Research Conference, the *National Civil Service Reform League*, and the *Bureau of Personnel Administration* published in *Public Personnel Studies*, IV, 1-44 (January, 1926). Arthur W. Procter, *Principles of Public Personnel Administration* (Appleton, 1921) is an outstanding but more extended treatise. Present-day tendencies in the practice of the merit system will be found in *The Character and Functioning of Municipal Civil Service Commissions in the United States* (Committee on Civil Service of the Governmental Research Conference, 1922); *Report of the Committee on Civil Service of the National Municipal League* (1922); *Public Personnel Studies* (monthly); *Proceedings of the National Assembly of Civil Service Commissions* (annual); and the numerous publications of the National Civil Service Reform League.

[2] In 1925, a total of 2,800,000 persons were on the public payroll; 900,000 were supported by pensions; and 500,000 were in public institutions, *Report of the National Industrial Conference Board*, 1925. Other estimates range from 2,300,000 to 3,250,000. See *Report of the Committee on Civil Service of the National Municipal League*, 1, note.

[3] Edward C. Marsh, *Civil Service* (National Civil Service Reform League, 1922), 4.

public employment began to be recognized in England.¹ In the United States the necessity for the merit system in the selection of public employees was established by the multiplication of positions that followed the Civil War. In a nation governed for many years by one party it now became necessary to remove Republicans in order to make way for new and better ones, just as Democrats had been previously removed. Several efforts were made to end this situation by measures of civil service reform, and in 1883 Congress passed legislation (the Pendleton Act) providing for open, competitive examinations for testing the fitness of applicants for public service, now classified or to be classified subsequently; and since this date a steadily increasing number of positions have been classified under the terms of the law.²

The merit system for the selection, promotion, and dismissal of employees is one of the few governmental reforms which have started in the national government and slowly filtered down into the smaller administrative units. Since the inauguration of civil service reform in the Federal domain, ten or a dozen states have adopted the system, in whole or in part; and more than 330 cities with a population of more than 32,000,000 are now under some form of civil service control, including all but one city of the sixty-eight cities of more than 100,000 population.³ Of the hundred largest cities in the country, no less than seventy-two have adopted the merit system, in whole or in part, and this number includes the twenty cities of largest population. In Massachusetts and New Jersey all cities are under the direct jurisdiction of the state civil

Extension to cities

---

[1] In 1822 at the instance of Sir Robert Peel the metropolitan police law for London provided that only those who had been trained by actual service in each subordinate rank should be qualified for the position of inspector or superintendent. In 1854 the merit system was for the first time put into actual practice on a large scale by the adoption of a plan of open competition for places in the Indian service, and a year later a system of competitive examination was introduced in the English home service. The final step was taken in the last quarter of the nineteenth century, when official patronage was abolished and open competition substituted in practically all branches of the government. See E. C. Marsh, *op. cit.*; and Robert Moses, *Civil Service in Great Britain* (Longmans, 1914).

[2] The movement reached its crisis in 1881, when President James A. Garfield was assassinated by a disgruntled office seeker. See the pamphlets, Edward C. Marsh, *op. cit.*; and Imogen B. Oakley, *A Sketch of the History of Civil Service Reform in England, India, and the United States* (General Federation of Women's Clubs). For later developments in the National Government, see William D. Foulke, *Fighting the Spoilsmen* (Putnam, 1919); and for a study of national personnel administration, Lewis Mayers, *The Federal Service* (Appleton, 1922).

[3] *Report of the Committee on Civil Service of the National Municipal League* (1922).

32 PRACTICE OF MUNICIPAL ADMINISTRATION

CHAP. III

The civil service authority

service commission, and in New York and Ohio the state civil service commissions have supervisory jurisdiction over municipal commissions.

The administration of the merit system ordinarily rests with a civil service commission, consisting of from one to five members, and appointed by the chief executive or the legislative body of the jurisdiction concerned. Sometimes it is required that the commission represent the two major political parties in the community; or that the members be active in no political party. Often this latter requirement, intended to secure non-partisanship, has only forced the appointment of persons sufficiently inconspicuous in party activities to warrant being given non-political classification.[1]

The incongruity of selecting by other than the merit system a commission to administer such a system is frequently pointed out. Seldom are persons selected who are qualified by training for the work of employment administration, or who have any large knowledge of employment conditions. On the contrary, many appointees are petty politicians or individuals with a leaning toward machine politics. As a correction for this situation, it has been urged recently that the principle of administering the merit system by a commission be discarded, and that there be appointed by merit a personnel director, occupying the same position and having the same responsibilities in public matters as has an employment officer in private industry.[2] The secretary of a civil service commission should have substantially this position; but unfortunately the members of commissions frequently trespass beyond their proper field of activities.

Duties of the civil service authorities

The duties of a civil service commission are three-fold—legislative, judicial, and administrative.[3] The principal legislative duties are the formulation of rules and regulations having the force of law, and which supplement the principles laid down by the merit law itself, and sometimes the classification of positions and recommendations to the legislative body of a standardized wage for the

---

[1] *The Character and Functioning of Municipal Civil Service Commissions in the United States*, 23 et seq. For a discussion of the several types of commissions, see *Personnel Problem in the Public Service*, 12-18.

[2] Recommended by the three recent reports on civil service conditions and program—*The Report of the Conference Committee* (1926), *The Report of the Committee of the Governmental Research Conference* (1923), and *Report of the National Municipal League* (1922).

[3] Procter, *op. cit.*, 31 et seq., in which the enumerated duties are discussed in detail.

positions within each class. The duties of a judicial character relate to hearing appeals from the ratings given on examinations, and sometimes appeals from suspension and dismissal, including any charges of incompetency, insubordination, or misconduct. The administrative functions are numerous, and include the following:[1] (1) establishing and maintaining contact with sources of labor supply; (2) testing the qualifications of applicants for employment; (3) testing the relative fitness of employees for promotion; (4) classifying positions according to duties and establishing lines of promotion; (5) examining the fairness and adequacy of the compensation of employees and recommending proper rates of pay to the legislative body; (6) passing upon cases of discipline and dismissal; (7) preparing, installing and supervising service records and efficiency ratings; and (8) certifying payrolls to insure that only properly appointed persons are being employed.

In addition to these fundamental duties, however, it is desirable that a civil service commission be concerned with the more modern tendencies in employment as suggested by these further activities: (1) promoting and organizing the instruction of new employees; (2) promoting the establishment of standard policies in respect to working conditions, health, and safety; (3) promoting the establishment of standard practices in regard to hours of employment, vacations, holidays, and sick leave; (4) promoting and encouraging recreational and social activities among employees; (5) establishing methods of transfer rather than discharge of employees who are unsuited for their positions; and (6) carrying on research for the purpose of improving the administration of employment policies.[2]

Only in the exercise of its legislative and judicial duties does a civil service commission ordinarily act as a body, the administrative details being left to a secretary. This secretary usually has certain technical assistants, including examiners who prepare, conduct, rate examinations and persons who make investigations into the character and previous experience of candidates for public employment. In preparing and rating examinations, the examiner

---

[1] As enumerated in *The Character and Functioning of Municipal Civil Service Commissions in the United States*, 30.
[2] *Ibid.*, 33. For further details, see *Personnel Problems in Public Service*, 27, 28. Lewis Mayers, *The Federal Service* (Appleton, 1921), 529 *et seq.*, argues that the personnel activities other than recruiting and selection should be delegated to a separate authority.

34 PRACTICE OF MUNICIPAL ADMINISTRATION

CHAP. III

Recruiting

Classes of service

is frequently assisted by competent persons from the city offices, and by others who may be particularly conversant with the subject under consideration.[1]

The work of the civil service authorities begins with securing competent persons who will present themselves for examination. Ordinarily, the law requires that notice of examinations be advertised in one or more newspapers for a suitable period prior to the actual examination. Such restricted publicity is not sufficient to insure competent applicants since people are not in the habit of reading legal advertisements. For certain positions, suitable workers can be secured only by personal solicitation on the part of the commission among individuals who might be induced to take the examination. In other instances, notices must be published in trade journals that will reach high grade employees, bulletins sent to institutions, which prepare persons for employment, and news items inserted in the local press. A civil service commission that limits its publicity activities to mere legal advertisement is by no means measuring up to modern employment standards.[2]

The announcement of an examination should contain among other things a clear statement of the duties involved in the position, an outline of the qualifications that will be expected of persons for appointment, and a statement of the remuneration to be had. There are frequent instances in which competition has been entirely avoided by publishing uninformative and uninviting statements with respect to the positions open, in order that the examination might be limited to favorites who were fully informed.

In civil service various classifications of a general nature are used to define the status of individuals. These classifications are not uniform throughout the country. In some instances there are merely the classified service, the unclassified service, and the unskilled labor class, designating, respectively, those who are under civil service control, those who are removed therefrom by statute, and those who are required to register for employment. In other cases, there are the exempt class, the competitive class (or classified service), the non-competitive class (or unclassified service), and the labor class. In still other cities, there are only the classified and the exempt services. There is a certain tendency to

---

[1] Procter, *op. cit.*, 38, 39.
[2] The procedure for recruiting and selection of personnel is treated at length in Procter, *op. cit.*, Chap. VI.

CIVIL SERVICE 35

bring into the classified service all positions not specifically exempted by law or charter, which of course makes for simplicity. CHAP. III

So long as an unclassified service exists there is an inclination to retain the non-competitive examinations or pass examination, in which the candidate is required to have only sufficient qualifications to enable him to fill the position open. The non-competitive examination is also used extensively in making promotions. There is a growing feeling, however, that the non-competitive examination serves no useful purpose, and that all positions not subject to direct appointment without examination should be filled by competition. Non-competitive examinations

Competitive examinations are of two kinds—assembled and non-assembled. The assembled examination is provided for candidates that can be examined in considerable numbers at one place and at one time. The non-assembled examination is designed for candidates of special types—those who ordinarily would not submit to group examination; who, because of distance, it would be impractical to assemble; or, who, because of the special type of service for which they are examined, should be treated individually. Nature of examinations
Assembled and non-assembled

In preparing selective tests for most of the positions in public service, the following subjects must be considered in their relations to the specific duties of the employment sought: (1) education and training; (2) experience tending to qualify; (3) ability to perform the actual duties of the position; (4) executive or administrative ability; (5) personality; (6) citizenship, character, and habits; and (7) physical ability to perform the duties involved.[1] Examination designed to show qualifications

It is incumbent upon the civil service authorities to decide upon the best methods of securing information concerning the candidate in each of these subjects, and of determining the relative weight or value of each subject as bearing upon the qualifications. The values or weights given each subject should vary according to the qualities required for the several classes of positions in the city service. Therefore, the preparation of the weights, as well as the content of each examination must be done by persons familiar with the functions of the department, office, and position in which the vacancy to be filled is located, and with the technique of the trade or profession concerned.[2] Preparation and weighting of examinations

Civil service commissions do not agree with respect to the

[1] *Report on the Administration of Civil Service in Detroit,* prepared by the Detroit Bureau of Governmental Research (1921).
[2] *Ibid.*

Weighting experience

relative weights to be given to the subjects used in similar examinations. This is particularly true of allowances made for experience, education, and physical qualifications. Frequently experience is confused with general education, vocational training, and even physical condition. The best practice is to limit experience to experience in the occupation in question and in related occupations, and to vocational education. Experience should not include education that is not directly concerned with the occupation for which a candidate is being examined.[1] Some standard of experience must be set as the minimum qualifying condition of admission to the civil service examination. However, care must be exercised in applying this minimum, because in many instances the candidate who falls short in experience, may, nevertheless, possess other qualifications that would make him eligible for employment. In instances where experience is used only as establishing the minimum qualifying conditions for admission, weighting the subject is comparatively easy. The real difficulty arises when experience is used as a principal factor in the examination.[2]

Weighting education

The same difficulties arise with the weighting of education, although many civil service commissions consider education only as a qualifying condition. This means that a candidate must have sufficient education to fill the position. If he has additional education it may throw some light on personal characteristics, but should not count particularly, except as technical and professional education are taken into consideration in connection with experience.[3]

Weighting physical tests

A physical examination is, of course, necessary for all candidates, but the extent of this examination should depend upon the position for which the candidate is applying. A civil service commission should not admit to employment persons suffering from chronic illness, who cannot be expected to give a satisfactory day's service for a day's pay, or who will become an early charge on the retirement fund. In occupations requiring large physical strength, the physical examination should be of major concern, as, for example, with firemen, policemen, and laborers. The Civil Service Commission of the city of New York recognizes four distinct physical standards; namely, those requiring little, those requiring a high degree of physical ability, and positions in the fire and police service.[4] In the police service physical standard is, of course, an essential for which additional credit is given for

[1] Procter *op. cit.*, 135.
[2] *Ibid.*, 136.
[3] *Ibid.*, 139.
[4] *Ibid.*, 140.

a high grade. In the other occupations, the physical standard test is usually nothing more than a qualifying condition.

The examination of the candidate should be preceded by the submission of a written statement to include personal history, previous employments, education, references, etc. A careful investigation of this record will eliminate those persons morally or otherwise unfit for the public service. This preliminary statement and a physical examination should be pre-requisites of eligibility. A candidate should possess a high moral character, a proper education, and the physique necessary for the proper discharge of the duties of the position sought, or he should not be permitted to take the more detailed examinations. This is the fairest method of handling applicants for examination, both for the candidates themselves and for the public, and it reduces the labor of the examiners to a minimum.[1]

After the experience, education, physical condition, and character of candidates have been determined, the examiners may proceed to test the actual knowledge, mental ability, and personality of the candidates; this may be done by means of written, oral, practical, and psychological examinations, usually a combination of these methods as requirements dictate.

The written examination is the best practical method of determining what a candidate knows about the work of the position for which he is applying. At the same time it indicates the character of his fundamental education including his use of the English language. In the higher grades this written examination may be supplemented by a thesis, written outside the examination room, or in fact written prior to the examination. In many cases the written examination should be supplemented by an oral examination which will reveal more of the candidate's personality than can be developed by any other means.

One principal criticism of the merit system is that the element of personality in candidates is generally ignored. This need not, and should not, be the case, and the criticism arises from ignorance as to how examinations are actually conducted, or from the faulty procedure employed by some particular commission. The progressive civil service commission will use the oral examination as a means of determining whether the candidate possesses those in-

[1] *Memorandum to the Detroit Civil Service Commission re Rating of Examination Papers*, prepared by the Detroit Bureau of Governmental Research (1920).

38   PRACTICE OF MUNICIPAL ADMINISTRATION

CHAP.
III

tangible factors of personality that cannot be evidenced in the written examination.[1] The ability of personnel officials to judge men and women by personal appearance and particularly by physical characteristics has not been demonstrated; yet many qualities aside from intelligence may be learned through personal interview.[2] Authorities insist that some definite procedure be introduced into such oral examinations to prevent their resulting in nothing more than a general impression. A number of schedules of personal qualifications have been prepared, the following being indicative of their general character:[3]

>   Mental caliber, intelligence, "head"
>   Maturity, common sense, judgment, tact
>   Earnestness, industry, seriousness of purpose
>   Reliability, dependability, deportment, coöperation
>   Alertness, resourcefulness, initiative on the job
>   Energy, vigor, vim, pep
>   Leadership, executive ability, efficiency
>   Accuracy, neatness, skill, dexterity
>   Address, manner, appearance
>   General education, culture, refinement
>   Capacity for growth
>   Fitness for line of work chosen

Practical tests

If the position for which the candidates are endeavoring to qualify is of a mechanical character, it is feasible to give practical tests of ability. In many instances the best way to find out whether a man can or cannot do a thing is to have him try to do it, and then judge the quality of his output. These practical tests are particularly applicable to certain groups within the civil service in which men are asked to work with their hands. Such examinations are more expensive and require a longer period of time than do those of an academic character.[4]

Intelligence tests

For other groups, it may be desirable to give a psychological examination, and at the present time some emphasis is being laid upon the intelligence tests developed in the last decade. In

---

[1] Procter, *op. cit.*, 143, points out that the oral test is of largest value in connection with positions having contact with the public, and is of small use in conjunction with mechanical and clerical employment.

[2] See Katherine T. Omwake, "The Value of Photographs and Handwriting in Estimating Intelligence," *Public Personnel Studies*, III, 1-15 (January, 1925).

[3] From Charles H. Link, *Employment Psychology* (Macmillan, 1919), quoted by Procter, *op. cit.*, 144.

[4] *Ibid.*, 134.

certain instances these are supplemented by psychiatric examinations to determine the candidate's mental condition.[1]

Secrecy in examinations, that is the withholding of the identity of the candidate from the examiners to prevent any deviation from predetermined standards of rating for a person or persons whose identity is known, and the prevention of fraud by the use of a substitute for examination purposes only, is essential. As the merit system has developed the necessity has grown less, but as an insurance against criticism such safeguards should always be taken. A means of securing secrecy is by the use of identification sheets, which are given numbers called identification numbers. On these identification sheets the applicant's name, address, date of birth, and other intimate information are written by the person taking the examination. The identification number is also placed on the outside of an envelope handed to the applicants with the sheet, and after the sheet is properly filled in, it is placed in the envelope and the latter is sealed. This same identification number must appear on all examinations handed in by the applicant. The identification sheets of all applicants for any examination are collected, marked with the date and the examination for which the applicants are competing, and placed in security until all the examination ratings are made. At such time, the identification sheet is checked against the application, which is made out by the bona fide applicant, handwriting is compared, and such personal information as is asked on each is checked. Discrepancies are made the subject of investigation. After the eligible list in the order of standing has been made up, the identification sheets are secured, the envelopes opened, and the names corresponding to the identification numbers are placed opposite the numbers on the skeleton eligible list, which is then ready for promulgation. Any change in the ratings on the list so prepared should be made only after thorough investigation by the civil service commission.

The practice of rating examinations without having predetermined standards and scales of measurement is not only unsatisfactory to the examiners and the candidates, but is unscientific, inaccurate, and unfair. Before the examination papers are rated

[1] The Detroit Police Department, in coöperation with the Detroit Bureau of Governmental Research, recently gave intelligence tests and psychiatric examinations to 350 policemen and officers, the findings being later compared with their service records. An appraisal of this experiment will be found in L. L. Thurstone, "The Intelligence of Policemen," *Journal of Personnel Research*, I, 64-74 (June, 1922); and Jessie M. Ostrander, "One Hundred and Fifty Policemen," *Mental Hygiene*, IX, 60-78 (January, 1925).

40 PRACTICE OF MUNICIPAL ADMINISTRATION

CHAP. III

the examiners should be in strict agreement as to what will be considered as correct answers to the several questions, and the relative weight that will be attached to each answer. All papers should be rated independently by two examiners, the resulting mark being the average of the marks given. If there is a disparity of more than twenty percent between the marks given by the examiners on any question, the answers should be re-rated.[1]

The eligible list

The eligible list is made up of the candidates who have successfully passed the examination, in the order of their standing, and from this list names are certified to appointing officers upon request. Under the United States civil service law, the three highest names on the eligible list are certified, the appointing officer being allowed his choice. In event a candidate has been certified three times and not appointed, his name is arbitrarily dropped from the list. In many other jurisdictions only the name highest on the list is certified. Civil service authorities differ materially on the relative merits of these two methods. The most enthusiastic supporters of the merit system are usually in favor of certifying only the one name highest on the list, while others believe that civil service procedure is not so perfected as to insure the ablest candidate standing first on the list, and that the appointing authority should be left some discretion. Certainly, in many cases, the certification of three names permits the appointing authority to make allowances for personality and to make a selection more satisfactory to him. Some cases have been known in which the appointing authority has absolutely refused to appoint from the eligible list, preferring to do without the employee, or secure him by some roundabout means of promotion, rather than take a person who is distinctly distasteful to him. As politics become more and more eliminated from city government, it may be assumed that wider leeway in appointment will be allowed to the appointing officer. In fact, in Dayton, Ohio, and Kansas City, Mo., the entire eligible list is now submitted to the appointing authority for his selection.

Veteran preference

In this connection the question of veteran preference creates a distinct problem. Some civil service commissions, as in New York State, allow a small credit to the citizenship rating of any individual honorably discharged from the army or navy, the exact

---

[1] *Report on the Administration of Civil Service in Detroit* and *Memorandum to the Detroit Civil Service Commission re Rating of Examination Papers*, prepared by the Detroit Bureau of Governmental Research, 1920.

credit depending upon the amount and kind of service seen by the candidate. Some laws, however, as in Michigan, require that any veteran shall be given absolute preference, *i.e.*, that if he succeeds in passing the examination at all, he shall be placed at the head of the eligible list.[1] This practically means that nearly every public position will be filled by a veteran, who is not necessarily the best candidate. Such a system cannot be too strongly condemned. If additional rewards are to be given to the military because of their service, those rewards should be given with the full knowledge of the public that they are being given, and should not be paid in the indirect fashion of filling the public service with incompetent employees.

Every person appointed from an eligible list should be given a probationary appointment, usually from ninety days to six months, to determine his actual fitness for the job to which he has been assigned. The appointing authority should have the arbitrary right to dismiss such probationer during, or at the end of, this period by stating the reason for doing so to the civil service commission. The commission can then certify this person to another position for which he may be better fitted or drop him entirely from the list as the rules may prescribe. The probationary period furnishes a natural test of the person's capabilities in the job which he is trying to fill, and should be used more extensively and more carefully by the appointing authorities than it is at the present time. It is really a part of the testing process in which the appointing authority participates, and its existence refutes the criticism that these authorities have nothing to do with the selection of their subordinates.

Provisional or temporary appointments, usually effective for sixty or ninety days, are made by department heads when no eligible lists are available. This situation often arises because of the inadequacy of the examining staff, and as such such appointments are entirely proper. Occasionally it may be necessary to renew provisional appointments for an additional period.

However, temporary appointments should not furnish a means of circumventing the merit system. In many cases such appointments are permitted when there is no real need of them. Occasionally, upon a change of administration, commissions abolish all eligible lists, as they are entitled to do, opening the way for

---

[1] In 1921, such a proposal was defeated in the state of New York by a popular vote of 1,000,418 to 699,697.

42   PRACTICE OF MUNICIPAL ADMINISTRATION

CHAP. III

wholesale provisional appointments of persons acceptable to a new political régime. Obviously, a provisional appointee has a distinct advantage over other competitors in a later examination. Further, provisional or temporary employees are frequently continued on the roll by reappointment, and without examination, in spite of a time limit imposed by law or rule.

Exemptions

Attention should be directed to some of the other means by which the merit system is weakened or entirely defeated.[1] The possibility of violating the secrecy of examinations and the abuse of provisional appointments have already been mentioned. Another common abuse arises from the unwarranted exemption of positions from civil service, particularly when this exemption is within the power of the civil service commission. Frequently such exemptions are made, not because of the difficulty of securing proper candidates by examination, but to facilitate the appointment of political favorites. Too often higher grade positions are exempted, thus limiting the field of promotion of employees under the merit system. The abuse of exemptory positions from regular civil service and filling them by non-competitive examinations has been mentioned.

Tampering with examinations

Examinations are sometimes tampered with in the interest of favored individuals. A frequent practice is to advance the ratings of all persons, thus bringing certain candidates on to the list of eligibles. Other discreditable practices include the introduction of examination questions with which only certain candidates can be familiar; crediting experience gained as a provisional appointee; and nullifying eligible lists in order that examinations may be given to new candidates.[2]

Promotion and transfers

Promotions[3] and transfers should be subject to careful control by the civil service authorities, although too often they give small attention to these matters. Frequently, to bring about a transfer, the civil service commission is simply notified by the department head that the step has been taken. This is not the merit system, and such procedure is open to practically the same criticisms as are original political appointments. When vacancies of certain types

---

[1] *The Character and Functioning of Municipal Civil Service Commissions in the United States*, 25, 26.
[2] *Ibid.*, 27.
[3] Procter, *op. cit.*, 177, urges that a distinction be made between "promotion" and "advancement," the first term to designate a change in duties; the latter a change in pay without change in duties.

exist, examinations should be held by the civil service commission and restricted to public employees in the same line of service, assuming that a sufficient number are available to insure genuine competition. Only by this process of promoting from the lower ranks can the morale of public employment be maintained, and an incentive be provided for competent persons to enter public service.

Credit for length and character of service rendered in the occupied grade of employment should be an important element in every promotional examination. If such recognition is to be made intelligently, it is necessary that the civil service commission should compile a periodic appraisal of the employee's service as determined by his superior officer.[1] For these service records an officer should not be permitted to return a general statement of excellent, good, or poor service. These record forms should take cognizance of the qualities that make for effectiveness in the several kinds of service. Under such headings a number of ingenuous methods have been devised for securing accuracy of appraisal, and not infrequently it is possible to weigh the work and character of an employee against the work and character of other employees that have certain desirable or undesirable characteristics. In other words, if certain individuals can be selected as being excellent, good, fair, and poor in certain lines, the person being appraised can be weighed against these specific individuals.

Transfer means the moving of an employee from one department to another, but within the same grade of service and at substantially the same compensation. Such change in employment ordinarily results from agreement between a department head and an employee, the one seeking an efficient workman, the other more congenial work. Such transfers, when registered with the civil service commission, are of course desirable for all concerned. However, when positions are not classified and salaries are not standardized, transfers may be sought to secure the larger remuneration prevailing in certain departments. Such changes are really promotions, and should not take place without promotional examinations.

An essential feature of the merit system is adequate means for removing incompetent persons from public service, yet not

[1] Many authorities insist that rating schedules cannot be made of practical use.

permitting wholesale changes for political reasons. The merit system has been open to severe criticism because these ends have not been generally secured. Merit laws and regulations usually provide that removals may be made by giving notification of suspension to the employee concerned and filing charges with the civil service authorities. However, some laws provide further protection. Employees so removed are entitled to a public hearing before the civil service authorities, the removing officer must substantiate his charges to the satisfaction of the commission, and the employee under charges is entitled to legal counsel.[1] If the charges are not sustained, the employee is reinstated with compensation for time lost. In other instances, particularly where veterans are concerned, charges must be made and sustained before courts of record. Either procedure is distasteful to administrative authorities. The proving of some overt act may be relatively simple, but the reviewing authorities may feel that the punishment has been too drastic and order an employee's reinstatement after a period of suspension. In the more frequent instances of general incompetency proof is difficult indeed, and the administrative officer faces the judicial body and the attorney for the dismissed employee with no other evidence than a general opinion that the employee should be removed for the good of the service.

Unsupported opinions, challenged by the adroitness of a cross-examining attorney, will seldom be sustained by a civil service commission, and the disciplined employee finds his way back on the city payroll, with a feeling that he has been a victor over his superior officer. A general breakdown of morale results. The situation is aggravated by failure of appointing officers properly to prepare their cases, noting down specific instances of incompetency, with dates, and other information that might have a bearing upon the case.

Some authorities hold that these provisions go entirely too far in protecting employees and work a decided detriment to public service. It is urged that since the appointing authority must make his appointments from the eligible list, the chief cause of indiscriminate dismissals has been removed. Under these circumstances it may be sufficient to permit the appointing authority to formulate definite charges, the dismissal being complete after

[1] Procter, *op. cit.*, 34, states that "in perhaps eighty percent of the civil service jurisdictions throughout the country, administrative officers have the power to remove their subordinate employees, either absolutely or subject to certain restrictions."

handing these charges to the employee, with provision that he may have a public hearing upon them if he wishes. It is questionable whether such a practice would result in any general dismissal of public employees, and certainly public service would benefit by the elimination of a considerable number of persons who are generally incompetent, but cannot be charged with specific dereliction.[1] On the other hand, wise use of transfers would probably eliminate some of the necessity for dismissals. The civil service commission should facilitate transfers from one department to another, upon the initiative either of the employee or of the appointing officer, as a means of eliminating dissension. The labor turnover will be reduced and candidates given every opportunity to make good in the work selected.

The principal purpose of the merit system is to maintain ideal employment conditions in city government—conditions that involve securing competent workers, paying adequate compensation, providing opportunities for promotion, and forestalling situations that might lead to discontent. Of these, that of adequate compensation means something more than paying a living wage. It means also paying adequate compensation for each type of work performed, and the same compensation to all employees performing similar work. This is salary standardization. Naturally, such salary standardization is dependent upon a classification of positions in accordance with similarity of duties and responsibilities. In order to standardize salaries, every position must be analyzed as to duties, responsibility, and technique involved; the requisite minimum qualifications of education, training, and experience for satisfactory discharge of such duties must be carefully established; and a rate of compensation at least equal to the current local rate for similar work must be made effective. Further, it means that euphonious and misleading titles shall not cover departures from standard rates of pay, and that any departure from the standard rate, either by advancement within the grade or by promotion, shall not be made without demonstrated proof of merit or fitness.

A first step in the standardization of salaries and grades is to secure information from every public employee affected as to the

---

[1] It should be noted that the National Civil Service Reform League, which has had much to do with advancing the merit system, has consistently advocated the rules prevailing in the federal service and in the state of New York which give the department head complete and final jurisdiction in dismissals, excepting for a limited number of employees.

exact character of the work he performs.[1] To this end, cards are distributed to each employee on which he sets forth all of this information, and much more. These cards are assembled on a broad functional basis into classes or services,—as clerical, inspectional, etc. Taking clerical again, they are further arranged into groups as clerk, bookkeeper, accountant, typist, stenographer, messenger, etc. Finally each group is further subdivided into grades, ranging from the lowest, that is, the grade in which the simplest forms of clerical, bookkeeping, accounting, typing, etc., are done,—up to the highest forms done in each. Definitions of duties and responsibilities are prepared for each class or service, each group, and each grade, from a composite of all of the information sent in. Work done should be the sole basis of determination of these matters, with responsibility, etc., secondary. After work definitions and the qualifications of positions are set up, it is attempted to get the current rate paid for the same work and responsibility in representative employment in the locality. From these data, minimum and maximum rates of compensation, with intermediate rates, can be set up tentatively for each grade of work. After this, the problem of allocation of each employee to the proper group and grade must be solved.

Upon the completion of a new classification and the standard specifications for personal service, the legislative body has the task of considering it and of accepting or rejecting. If it accepts the specifications, it must establish the rates of pay for such services and enact an ordinance making them effective. Such a program contemplates a graded system, in which each grade may have a minimum and maximum rate of pay, with one or several intermediate rates. It is desirable to make provision for sufficient information concerning the actual performance of each individual before allowing the periodic increase in compensation. Furthermore, as the entire standardization of salaries is an attempt to secure a fairer control of payroll procedure, both for the employer and employee, the promotional procedure should be subject to an impartial regulation.

In order to make any plan of classification of positions and standardization of salaries effective, it must be administered by

[1] Adapted from "Public Employment in Detroit," *Public Business*, No. 89 (November 30, 1924). The methods of conducting such a standardization inquiry are set forth in detail in Procter, *op. cit.*, Chap. V.

an individual or group possessing all of the information concerning departmental functions, organization, and personnel. It is believed by some authorities that this group should have no affiliation with any department, and should not be a part of the body administering the civil service laws, although the ability and integrity of the commission might have a bearing on this point. It is the duty of such authority to analyze the necessity for all new positions, prepare definitions of positions, recommend salary rates, make current or periodic investigations of departmental practices to determine that employees are actually working in their classification as to group and grade, and to scrutinize payrolls in order to check against an individual being in more than one payroll division of the same department or in more than one department. This last duty is in addition to the check made by the civil service authority, which is essentially insurance against illegal appointment or promotion, and not properly an audit on duplicate payment.[1]

Another duty of the civil service commission is to maintain a record of properly appointed employees, in order to prevent fradulent employment. Usually all payrolls are submitted to the commission before being paid, and it is the duty of the commission to see that each individual is a properly qualified employee of the government and is working within his proper grade. This may be done by comparing such payrolls with a card index of employees, but it is more common to check each payroll with the preceding payroll on a sort of dead reckoning plan. In this way any additional names will be noted and their eligibility determined. Of course, this scheme is much easier than a positive check against a card index. Periodically, however, at some determined intervals, the payrolls should be checked back to the card index in order to discover any inadvertent errors that may have been made. This provision for payroll checking is most important, and constitutes the teeth of any civil service law. Without it, departmental heads may flout the law at will.

One of the conditions necessary to ideal employment arrangements is the retirement of superannuated employees, and of others incapacitated by accident or ill-health through no fault of their

[1] Reference may be made to the numerous classifications of titles and standardization of salaries that have been undertaken by the United States government, and the Dominion of Canada, the states of New Jersey and Pennsylvania, and the cities of Rochester, Detroit, Milwaukee, Chicago, New York, and numerous others.

48 PRACTICE OF MUNICIPAL ADMINISTRATION

<small>CHAP. III</small>

<small>Reasons for retirement systems</small>

own.[1] Such retirement involves the establishment of a pension system of some kind; and such pensions are common in the fire, police, and educational departments of cities. Recently, there has been a growing demand that the public provide means of retirement for all public employees, thus reflecting a sentiment which is becoming widespread in industry. Mr. Lewis Merriam states that the advantages are: "(1) the elimination from its active force of those who have lost their efficiency because of advancing age or long service; (2) the elimination of those who have lost their efficiency in earlier life because of accident or disease; (3) the improvement of the morale of the remainder; (4) the retention in service of the best of its employees, many of whom in the absence of such a system resign to accept positions elsewhere; (5) the attraction to the service of a higher grade of men."[2]

<small>Parties concerned</small>

With respect to the benefits of a retirement system, it may be said that three parties are concerned: the government in its capacity as employer; the employees because they are the persons directly affected; and the public because of less direct benefits and because it must pay part or all of the cost.[3] The interests are not identical, but may, nevertheless, in an ideal system be correlated.[4]

<small>Types of pension systems</small>

Retirement systems are of three kinds—wholly contributory, non-contributory, and partly contributory. In the wholly contributory plan, the fund is maintained principally by contributions or assessments from the beneficiaries themselves, augmented by interest and miscellaneous income, no contribution being made by the taxpayer. In such a system the employee entirely controls the retirement fund and the taxpayer gains whatever benefits accrue in efficiency of service without an additional tax burden. The disadvantages are many. The systems are seldom on an actuarial basis, and the employee who enters never knows the cost to himself at any future period, unless the contributions are specifically limited. In this event the time of dissolution because of the inability to meet obligations is advanced. If this limit is not imposed, the financial burden of younger employees is out of all proportion to that carried by older ones for the same benefits. The disastrous history of mutual associations that have started on a

<small>Contributory plan</small>

---

[1] Reference should be made to Lewis Meriam, *Principles of Governing the Retirement of Public Employees* (Appleton, 1918); and Paul Studensky, *The Pension Problem and the Philosophy of Contributions* (Pension Pub. Co., 1917).
[2] Meriam, *op. cit.*, 3.   [3] *Ibid.*, 1.
[4] The discussion of retirement methods is adapted from *Memorandum on Retirement Funds,* prepared by the Detroit Bureau of Governmental Research (1920).

weak financial and actuarial unsound basis has been essentially the same.

From the standpoint of the employee, the non-contributory retirement and pension plan is at first glance the most attractive. Certainly, older employees would favor this plan, since with but a short time to remain in service they consider some retirement provision by the city a proper due. Also, the younger employee, who lives in the present, wants all of his salary for personal and immediate needs. Retirement at some late period in life is so remote as to require no consideration or financial outlay on his part. More likely than not he considers his salary less than he earns and that an annuity is due for that reason. On the other hand, it is argued that in a non-contributory system, in which the governing authorities provide all the money, the result is a reduction of salaries and a tendency to keep the employee in a feudal system. Such a plan is autocratic in that there is usually a complete forfeiture of pension rights upon resignation or dismissal, and an unusual authority is obtained over the employee. Further, as the total amount of benefits increase, the tendency is to economize by lowering the individual compensation return. This system also removes incentive to thrift and increases the burden of taxation. The expense is frequently so large that the creation of an actuarial reserve is neglected, resulting in the pushing forward of a large burden upon future taxpayers, or the future amendment of the pension fund, to the detriment of employees.

In the partly contributory plan the financial burden is divided between the employee and the taxpayer. This is the mean between the two other systems; it combines social insurance with the principle that every worker must share in the cost of his protection. The benefits are mutual and each interested party has a voice in the management and control. It makes no inequitable distinction between the young and the old employee, is subject to actuarial analysis, and an actuarial reserve is possible without imposing an undue burden on either interested party.

With all of these retirement plans there are certain essential features that cannot be disregarded. These include the retirement of the employee at some particular time in his life with annuity; provision for the retirement on physical disability prior to the arrival of this date, such a pension to be pro-rated on the years of service; provision for pensions to the dependents of beneficiaries receiving disabling or fatal injuries in the line of duty; and some provision entitling employees to withdraw from service without losing all of their contributions to the fund. These essentials may be summed up as superannuation benefit, service benefit, death benefit, and disability benefit.

Two methods are usually in vogue for the creation of pension funds—assessment and actuarial reserve.

Under the assessment plan all benefits are paid annually as due from current revenue, which may include contributions from employees as well as from taxpayers. Such a system does not provide for any large reserve, and these reserves, if created, are in time wiped out by increased demands. Obviously, the assessment must increase largely as the age of the fund increases. As long as the city is growing in population and in number of employees the danger from the assessment plan is small. However, no city can expect to increase in size indefinitely. There comes a time when an undue proportion of employees reach the age of retirement, and at this point the assessments must be increased to care for the beneficiaries, or the amount provided must be decreased. The assessment plan has long since been discarded in the field of insurance, and for pensions it provides only a haphazard makeshift. It is unbusinesslike, as the real cost is unknown and future obligations are unconsidered. In times of economic stress, the assessment plan is liable to criticism.

The annual appropriations are successively larger and larger, and it has been proved by experience that under this plan the amount levied against taxes will be equal to the amount levied annually under the actuarial reserve plan within twenty years, and from this point mounts higher and higher annually and indefinitely. The plan is also inequitable as between the obligations imposed now and those placed upon the taxpayers of the next generation. Finally, it is not so easily adaptable as to give equal benefit to all employees. Embarrassment may be caused by questions arising as to the justice of the respective contributions of the city and the employees and as between the various classes of employees.

Under the actuarial reserve plan, a fund is established and at regular intervals stated sums are turned over to this fund. These sums, whether from the employer or from taxation, are all placed at interest, and, with the latter compounded, will be sufficient to meet all obligations as due. Under this plan the persons receiving the service pay all of the obligations incurred in respect to that service. It is absolutely equitable between one generation of taxpayers and one generation of employees to another; it is businesslike; and finally, it is adaptable to either a contributory or a non-contributory system. It may be argued that the calculation of an actuarial reserve is complicated, expensive, and dangerous. That an actuarial study is complicated, technical, and expensive cannot be denied. Periodic valuations to meet changes in personnel, compensation, etc., are, of course, necessary and the machinery of assessment must be kept up. These objections, however, are not particularly weighty, and all of them may be met by reasonably sound administration and ordinary common sense. An actuarial reserve is the only system that should be permitted in any pension fund, and every pension fund that has been created under any other system has ultimately fallen into difficulty.[1]

It has been customary for municipal employees, particularly those employed in large groups, to associate themselves together into welfare organizations. These organizations have an ostensibly social character, and sometimes they provide a small accident or death benefit through the payment of limited assessments; but they have as their real purpose influencing legislative bodies to secure additional pay and protection from removal. In the past ten years, there has been a tendency to attempt the complete unionization of such city services and the association of such local unions with the American Federation of Labor. The question of these unions was brought definitely to a head in the now famous police strikes of Boston and Cincinnati and the strikes of firemen in other localities. In each instance the strikes were beaten with steps taken to prevent the unionization of employees.

In the "uniformed" services, particularly fire and police, it is regarded that the employees are in the nature of a military branch of the government and owe a responsibility to the public which outweighs the right of private organization.[2] The question has not been so forcefully raised in other branches of the service. However, some charters absolutely prevent the city from recognizing a union, although no discrimination is shown against union

---

[1] It is estimated that over ninety percent of the pension funds in the United States were bankrupt because of their reliance upon the assessment system as opposed to the actuarial reserve.
[2] The constitution of the National Federation of Federal Employees provides "that under no circumstances shall this Federation engage in or support strikes against the United States Government."

men. While the recognition of unions is an accepted matter in some European countries, particularly England, American administrators have often taken a firm stand to prevent the unionization of city services, particularly firemen, policemen, and school teachers; and the future of unionization among public employees is with us a debatable matter.[1]

Political activity — Civil service regulations universally prohibit political activity on the part of persons holding positions under the merit system. Unfortunately the authorities are not always alert to enforce such rules, and the definition of political activity may have a very liberal interpretation. Similarly, employees are forbidden to pay national assessments or make mandatory contributions to party organizations for political purposes. Often such assessments are disguised as donations and are based on a definite percentage of salary. Such procedure is to be heartily condemned. Civil service employees should not be permitted to engage in political campaigns or to contribute financially to their conduct.

[1] Some authorities believe that unionization is on the way to accomplishment. In Chicago some services are from fifty to one hundred percent unionized. Probably more than one-half of federal employees are members of unions. For some statistics on unionization, see S. D. Spero, *Labor Movement in a Government Industry* (Doran, 1924).

CHAPTER IV

BUDGET [1]

The most important single task that falls jointly upon the administrator and the legislative body of a city is the preparation and authorization of appropriations. It is by means of these appropriations that the extent of city activities is determined, that public funds are allocated among these activities, and that the total necessary income is calculated. In every governmental unit some more or less regular processes are followed in preparing these estimates and having them approved by the legislative body, resulting finally in a legal authorization to incur liabilities for designated purposes. To the popular mind this final authorization, the appropriation act, is the budget; the processes by which the amount and character of the budget are determined form the budget procedure. Every government, in some fashion, correlates estimated income and estimated expenditure, authorizes the latter, and hence has a budget procedure and a budget.[2] The methods employed in this correlation and authorization may be

<small>Definition of budget and budget procedure</small>

[1] Brief monographs on budget-making, most suitable for the administrator, are A. E. Buck, *Municipal Budgets and Budget Making* (National Municipal League, 1925); and R. E. Taylor, *Municipal Budget Making* (Univ. of Chicago Press, 1925). A mass of literature on the theory and practice of budget-making has been published. The interested student should consult *Competency and Economy in Public Expenditures* (Annals, CXIII, May, 1924); F. A. Cleveland and A. E. Buck, *The Budget and Responsible Government* (Macmillan, 1920); *National Budget System* (Hearing before the Select Committee on the Budget of the House of Representatives, Washington, 1919); W. F. Willoughby, *The Problem of a National Budget*, and *The Movement for Budgetary Reform in the States* (Appleton, 1918); Charles W. Collins, *The National Budget System* (Macmillan, 1917); Edward A. Fitzpatrick, *Budget Making in a Democracy* (Macmillan, 1918); Réné Stourm, *The Budget* (trans., Appleton, 1917); *Public Budgets* (Annals, LXII, November, 1915); "Next Steps in the Development of a Budget Procedure for the City of Greater New York," *Municipal Research* (No. 57, January, 1915, New York Bureau of Municipal Research); S. Gale Lowrie, *The Budget* (Wisconsin State Board of Affairs, 1912). Numerous articles will be found in the *National Municipal Review*. Professor Taylor's book contains an extensive bibliography on the subject. Typical of illustrative budgets are those of the United States Government, the states of New York, Ohio, and Virginia, and the cities of New York, Detroit, Dayton and Kalamazoo.

[2] "In its simplest terms a budget may be deemed to be but a consolidated statement of the estimated revenue and expenditure needs of a government for a fixed period," W. F. Willoughby, *The Movement for Budgetary Reform in the States* (Appleton, 1918), 175.

54   PRACTICE OF MUNICIPAL ADMINISTRATION

Defects of ordinary budget procedure

orderly and informative, furthering social and economic conditions, or they may not be so. Hence the budget procedure and the budget may be either good or bad.

The fundamental defect of ordinary budget methods is lack of careful planning—the budget, *i.e.*, the appropriative ordinance, does not express a well-considered program of governmental activities in which an estimated cost of work to be done has been balanced with expected income, and the needs of each governmental activity have been weighed against the needs of every other activity, and from which "hobbies" and mere political desires have been eliminated. Such budgets usually consist of unrelated appropriation measures formulated with little or no attempt to support requests with understandable detail of proved needs. It is nobody's business to prepare a correlated financial program. Unintelligible estimates, reinforced by persuasive oratory, are submitted to one or more committees of the legislative body and finally appear as one or more appropriation bills having only casual relation to actual requirements. They are characterized by absence of thorough review before being considered by the legislative body; by "padding" in anticipation of perhaps ill-considered reductions; "log-rolling"; and a resulting waste of public funds or neglect of worthy activities.

Introduction of modern procedure

The formulation of the appropriation ordinance in accordance with an orderly and informing procedure, rather than in a haphazard and piecemeal fashion, was the second important reform in American administrative methods, the merit system of selecting employees having been introduced many years previously. In 1907 the financial estimates of the Health Department of New York City were prepared in accordance with plans formulated in conjunction with the New York Bureau of Municipal Research. In the years following, the budget estimates of the entire city government were made to conform to the experimental program, and by 1914 New York operated under a modernized procedure. With such modifications as were dictated by experience, the so-called segregated budget and its procedure were adopted gradually by a number of state governments, more cities, and finally, in 1921, by the government of the United States. However, many governmental units still operate under former methods, and in many instances in which changes in procedure have been made the improvement has been only partial.

This slowness of the American public, and of officials, to

appreciate and adopt modern budget methods attests the carelessness with which our governments, local as well as national, are conducted. For a number of years it was said ironically that the United States and Turkey were the only civilized nations without sound methods of appropriating for the needs of government. Yet the importance of the budget has been long understood by statesmen and political scientists. Gladstone, while prime minister of England, stated: "Budgets are not merely affairs of arithmetic, but in a thousand ways go to the root of prosperity of individuals, the relation of classes, and the strength of kingdoms."[1] Professor A. R. Hatton, at the time when modern budget procedure was first introduced in the United States, wrote: "The budget provides the means through which citizens may assure themselves that their effort which has been diverted to community ends is not used for private gain, is not misused nor frittered away, but is applied to the accomplishment of those purposes which the community approves, and is made to produce the maximum of results for the effort expended. . . . Above and beyond its relation to economy and efficiency in public affairs it may be made one of the most potent instruments in democracy. . . . No single change would add so largely to both democracy and efficiency as the introduction of proper budget methods."[2]

The proponents of improved budget procedure have been in substantial agreement as to general principles, but have differed somewhat as to details, and even as to definition of terms. In fact, there are nearly as many definitions of a budget and of budget procedure as there are writers upon the subject. Some of these definitions cover the appropriation act and the procedure antecedent to its formulation in one statement, requiring that the procedure conform to certain standards before a budget may be said to exist.[3] These differences are academic and do not concern the administrator. In a practical way, sound budget methods require (1) that the estimates of needs be submitted to the legislative body as a thoughtfully balanced program of work, prepared preferably by the administrator responsible for carrying out the program, and embodying his ideas of how best to meet community

Essentials of modern budget procedure

---

[1] John Morley, *Life of Gladstone* (Macmillan, 1911), I, 458.
[2] "Foreword," *Public Budgets* (Annals, LXII, November, 1915).
[3] A budget is "a plan for financing an enterprise or government during a definite period, which is prepared and submitted by a responsible executive to a representative body . . . whose approval and authorization are necessary before the plan may be executed." F. A. Cleveland, "Evolution of the Budget Idea in the United States," *ibid.*, 15.

needs; (2) that these estimates be correlated with available or expected income; (3) that the estimates be so stated as to be readily understood and examined by the legislative body; and (4) that the appropriation ordinance based upon the estimates be passed as a single measure and in such terms as will afford a maximum of control with a minimum of handicap upon the administrator.

Responsibility for preparing budget estimates

The budget estimates should be a thoughtful work program representing the most urgent opportunities and needs of a community, prepared and reviewed by some authority acquainted with departmental requirements. Such a program must be determined in accordance with accurate information of the efficiency of each governmental activity, the necessity of its continuance, its cost, and its desirability as compared with every other activity. This authority in a city government can be only the mayor or the city manager, and never a committee or committees of the city council. Such committees are unfamiliar with the detailed workings of departments, frequently have political axes to grind, and are not responsible in the public mind for the conduct of government. The actual assembly and initial review of the estimates in the preparation of what is called an executive budget are, of course, seldom done by the executive. The office of the controller or a specially organized budget bureau functions for this purpose, the executive reviewing the work and making such amendments as seem desirable.

This particular improvement in the preparation and submission of budget estimates has been expedited through its adoption by several hundred cities with city managers and by a few cities of the strong mayor type of government, both of which plans of organization place fiscal and administrative responsibility directly upon the executive. The chief administrative officer—city manager or mayor—prepares a financial program which he is willing to support, and presents it to the legislative body, thus theoretically to the people, for adoption or amendment.

In city governments more loosely organized, and in which administrative responsibility is shared by the mayor with other elected officials, as well as with independent and quasi-independent boards and commissions, it is desirable that the mayor, who in the mind of the public is largely responsible for city administration, should bring together the heads of the independent departments supported from public funds. Before this body he can present the current resources of the city and ask that they be properly apportioned. Here, by a committee of the whole, public needs can be correlated, absolute essentials approved, and the entire estimate, with supporting data, prepared for presentation to the legislative body. With such methods the chances of one activity of the city government being over-emphasized at the expense of others are lessened, and the temptation of the council to interfere with the detailed conduct of the departments is reduced.

The preparation of budget estimates by a responsible administrator or committee of administrators, independent of the city council, and the approval or disapproval of these estimates by the council itself, tend to place the responsibility for the government where it actually belongs, removing in some measure the burden of ineffectiveness and shifting responsibility which cities now bear.

It has been suggested that estimates so prepared by the executive or administrative branch of government should be subject only to revision downward by the legislative body.[1] However, such a proposition is at present illegal in practically all American cities, and draws its support from other than American municipal experience, if a number of New York cities and Boston be excepted. The public speaks through its elected representatives, and it appears absurd to deny to the public the right to amend, as it sees fit, any financial program presented by the administrative branch of the government. It should be sufficient that those responsible for administration present their work program for approval, and that the legislative body representing the public have the right to amend that program and assume the responsibility therefor.

In municipalities it is customary to set aside sums of money for special uses called funds. All obligations of a city pertain to some particular fund out of which they must be paid. These funds may be classified as (1) the current, operating, or general fund—the income of which is largely taxes, and from which are met the costs of current operation, and of a limited amount of permanent improvements; (2) the capital fund—consisting principally of the returns from the sale of bonds, and which is used entirely for permanent improvements; (3) the special and trust funds—consisting of gifts, dues, and specially levied taxes, which a city holds for specific purposes in its capacity as trustee; and

[1] The Maryland state budget law forbids increase of the executive estimates by the legislature unless additional revenues are provided. Any such plan can be easily circumvented by the legislative body, and finds little support among budget authorities.

58   PRACTICE OF MUNICIPAL ADMINISTRATION

CHAP. IV

(4) the sinking fund—consisting of resources secured largely from taxation and the interest on investments, and which are held for the amortization and redemption of the city debt.[1] Current incomes of utilities are commonly segregated as funds, though for current operation.

Continuing appropriations

Funds of a slightly different character occur through the practice of setting aside certain incomes within the current fund for the purpose of carrying out specific objects. This subdivision of current funds is sometimes done by ordinance, but more frequently by state statute or charter, usually indicating a minimum tax rate to be levied, or minimum income to accrue for the operation of certain city functions; commonly, health and education. Such continuing appropriations, when once made by the appropriating authority, remain in force from fiscal period to fiscal period without further specific authorization. Their usual object is to prevent a powerful minority from interfering periodically with the maintenance of activities accepted as necessary or desirable by the public; or from periodically trading support for such activities in order to secure a like support for less worthy projects. Continuing appropriations are sometimes expedient, yet violate the generally accepted principle of budget procedure, that the financial and work program of each activity should come periodically before the public for approval. Nowadays, these mandatory appropriations are usually so much less than actual needs that they are supplemented by general appropriations. As a result they do not seriously interfere with sound budget methods, although they do complicate the accounting procedure.

Modern procedure limited to operating funds

Progress in budget procedure has been limited largely to the current or operating funds of governments. This has occurred because such funds are raised directly by taxation and attract considerable public attention when they are apportioned to the several city activities. Also considerable planning and publicity are required before the final authorization to incur liabilities is approved by the legislative body. In fact, progressive budget making has been so long associated with these current or operating funds that when the term budget is used this fund is usually taken for granted. However, it is equally feasible to develop a scientific budget procedure to cover the other funds which are expended by governments. In fact, a movement is slowly developing to require

[1] Francis Oakey, *Principles of Government Accounting and Reporting* (Appleton, 1921), Chap. I.

a more careful planning prior to the expenditure of funds obtained from the sale of long term securities, and bond budgets have been widely discussed and seriously urged.

Bond budgets

On one occasion New York City presented a definite public improvement program with plans for its financing, but this proposal was discontinued after one year. St. Louis, Minneapolis, and Newark have made similar experiments. For many years Detroit has habitually presented at the beginning of the fiscal period a program of public improvements, or bond budget, in connection with the operating budget. Such portion of this bond budget as is required by law, or is thought expedient, is financed from the operating fund, the remainder by the sale of long-term securities. There is little doubt that in the near future, administrative authorities will present for public discussion and consideration their programs for public improvements over a fixed period. This period may not, and probably will not, correspond with the fiscal year, except in so far as such public improvements are to be financed from current funds rather than the sale of securities. On the contrary, the public improvement budget may be presented about the middle of the fiscal year, in order that its consideration may not be confused with the consideration of the operating fund budget, and it will cover probably a longer period than one year, inasmuch as many public improvements cannot be completed within that time.[1] Improvements by special assessment deserve similar treatment, which is more difficult to give, since such projects often originate through private initiative.

Sinking fund budgets

The requirements of sinking funds are usually carefully determined and appropriated in connection with the operating fund of a city, and necessitate no separate budgeting. This is because sinking funds normally secure their income—excepting the interest on investments—from taxation and from the earnings of public utilities, which must be formally transferred to the sinking fund before they can be used for the amortization and redemption of the city debt.

Trust fund budgets

There is need for annually budgeting special and trust funds which in some cities are of considerable importance. In this con-

---

[1] See *A Ten-Year Financial Program for Detroit* (The Report of the Mayor's Committee on Finance, Detroit Bureau of Governmental Research, June, 1925); and *A Million a Year; A Five Year School Building Program* (City of Minneapolis, 1916). See also, C. E. Rightor, "How Detroit's Ten-Year Financial Program was Prepared," *Nat. Mun. Rev.*, XV, 108 (February, 1926).

60   PRACTICE OF MUNICIPAL ADMINISTRATION

CHAP. IV

nection the budget estimates for retirement funds should contain other information than probable income and expense, and it is frequently desirable to have an actuarial statement, indicating the condition of these funds over a long period of years as correlated with probable demands upon them.[1]

Revenue and expense should be correlated

Perhaps the most severe criticism leveled at former methods of appropriation was the frequent absence of correlation between anticipated income and anticipated expense. Even were some effort made to secure a statement of anticipated income, in the absence of centralized responsibility, no one could be found willing to assume the duty of limiting departmental requests to within such estimates. Frequently the entire requests were allowed by the legislative body with verbal warning that income must not be exceeded, an admonition more honored in the breach than in the observance, unless supervisory control was provided.[2] Modern budget procedure has eliminated this source of extravagance.

Classification of revenues

In preparing estimates of available and expected income, it is expedient to classify them in accordance with some uniform schedule that will facilitate comparisons and accurate calculations. A suggested classification of income is as follows, although a briefer classification will be found suitable for cities of ordinary size.[3]

INCOME
    Taxes
        General property (specify)
        Poll
        Income
        Business (specify)
        Inheritance
        Miscellaneous

    Rights and Privileges
        Licenses
            Motor (specify)
            Business (specify)
            Professional (specify)
            Miscellaneous (specify)
        Permits (specify)
        Franchises (specify utility)
        Concessions (specify)
        Rents (specify)
        Royalties (specify)

---

[1] For a discussion of retirement funds, see Chap. III.
[2] This procedure is followed in the state budget of South Carolina.
[3] From A. E. Buck, *op. cit.*, 26.

BUDGET 61

    Services and Sales
        Fees
            Legal services
            Inspectional services
            Technical services
            Miscellaneous (specify)
        Sales of services and commodities (specify)

    Interest and Premiums
        Interest (specify)
        Premiums
        Discount

    Fines and Forfeitures
        Fines
        Forfeitures
        Penalties

    Grants and Donations (specify)

    Pension Assessments

PROCEEDS FROM SALES OF BONDS

PROCEEDS FROM SALES OF CAPITAL ASSETS

SPECIAL ASSESSMENTS [1]

Any classification of income should include all income. An outstanding weakness of governmental fiscal systems is the failure to control completely through the budget cash received and disbursed by certain units. This defect is not so prevalent in municipalities, as in counties, and particular state governments. In cities there is now a decided tendency to require that all cash be received and disbursed by the central treasury and be appropriated through the budget. Such control is generally so desirable that it may be dangerous to suggest that the plan is not uniformly so. However, in a few departments, particularly those of an institutional character, it may be feasible to permit of some trading not under budgetary and treasury control. To do so stimulates efficiency on the part of the administrative officer and often the more economical operation of the institution. For example, farm products may sometimes be sold, exchanged, and rebought to public advantage without the proceeds passing through the treasury.[2] If so, such transactions should be under definite accounting

Budgetary control of departmental receipts

---

[1] A. E. Buck now treats special assessments as a general revenue on the theory that they are being used more and more to meet current expenses.

[2] The budgetary methods of the states of Virginia and Pennsylvania are diametrically opposite on this point and should be studied by those interested.

Understandable requests

control, even though the money is not received by the treasury and is not appropriated by the legislative body.

After a conservative estimate of operating income has been made, and of other income if other funds be included in the budget, and it has been definitely resolved that the appropriation shall be kept within this estimate of resources, there follows the more detailed task of preparing the requests of the several departments, boards, and commissions found in a city or other governmental unit. These estimates of needs are the real basis of budget making, and upon their being prepared correctly depends the success of a budget. If the requests are presented on miscellaneous sheets of paper, salaries sometimes grouped by themselves, three or four of the larger items segregated, and the remainder lumped as miscellaneous expense, and these sheets are used as the basis for the appropriations of the following year, it is a budget as typical of the average American city or county as it is typical of what a budget ought not to be. If, however, some care and thought are given to the problem, these estimates will offer to the responsible authorities a statement of proved departmental needs, and to the public, a comprehensive idea of the work which the government proposes to do during the coming fiscal period.

Classification by department and activities

First, it is essential, in preparing estimates and making appropriations, that the needs of each activity performed by the several administrative departments appear separately, in order that the public, the appropriating body, and the administrator may be able to see readily what it is proposed to spend for each distinct work of the government. For example, within the specific objective of street cleaning there are the activities of brush brooming, machine brooming, street flushing, etc.; within the objective of police protection are foot patrol, mounted patrol, detective service, criminal identification, etc. Such activity estimates form the basis of unit costs accounts, since the proposed units of work are the only additional information necessary. Further, the activity estimates facilitate weighing the merits of all public work, consideration of the effectiveness of methods, and the distinguishing of needs from desires. Any budget procedure that does not provide that each activity stand separately and upon its own merits in the consideration of appropriations has neglected the first requirement of sound practice.

Classification by character

In order that any change in assets may be reflected properly in the balance sheet of the government, and that actual operating expenses may be known, it is desirable to separate the estimates of each activity into operating expense and capital outlay. In larger budgets this separation is frequently extended to include debt service and deficits, and is known as classification by character.

After the larger classification of estimates by character, it is desirable to make a further classification by objects of expenditure. If the budget making authorities are to give relative weight to the needs of each activity, these needs must be expressed in the same terms, and expenditures for requirements of the same character must be comparable. This classification by the kind of things to be purchased varies according to the individual ideas of budget makers, but in broad, general lines it usually follows the classification first developed for New York City. The designations are ordinarily personal service (salaries and wages), supplies, materials, contractual services, debt services, equipment, and acquisition of real estate. Some changes in the original classification are being made gradually, particularly in the supplies and materials groups, where sub-classifications by purpose are being discarded for those by character.[1] For example, designation as stable and veterinary supplies, or hospital supplies, is by purpose; food, forage, chemicals, or medicines, is by character. This detailed classification is of particular value, especially when the actual expenditures for similar items over recent periods is included in the estimates. The chief financial officer of a government is usually responsible for furnishing these data, which are easily secured by tabulating vouchers by mechanical means.

A suggested classification, by objects of expenditure is as follows:[2]

A. *Personal Service*
Personal service is direct labor of persons in the regular or temporary employment of the corporation.

1. Salaries
2. Wages
3. Special

---

[1] Such classification, solely by character, was first developed in connection with the Dayton budget of 1914, by the Dayton Bureau of Municipal Research.

[2] From the Budget of the City of Dayton, 1914. Numerous classifications are available that follow somewhat different lines. See also, President's Commission on Economy and Efficiency, *Outline of Classification of Objects of Government Expenditure on a Uniform Basis* (Circular No. 19, 1911). Some authorities maintain that this uniform classification is only valuable as an assistance to the purchasing agent in estimating quantities of supplies to be bought.

B. *Contractual Services*
Contractual services are activities performed by other than municipal departments, under expressed or implied agreement, involving personal service plus the use of equipment or the furnishing of commodities.

1. Communication
2. Contractual repairs
3. Hire of equipment
4. Insurance
5. Public utility services, (not otherwise specified)
6. Special service
7. Traveling
8. Other contractual services

C. *Sundry Charges*
Sundry charges include those outlays legally or morally obligatory upon the city as a public corporation and trustee.

1. Contributions
2. Debt service
3. Depreciation
4. Imprest cash
5. Pensions
6. Refunds and claims
7. Taxes

D. *Supplies*
Supplies are commodities of a nature which after use show a material change in, or an appreciable impairment of their physical condition; and instruments liable to loss, theft, and rapid depreciation.

1. Chemicals, drugs, and medicines
2. Clothing, dry goods, and notions
3. Food products
4. Forage
5. Fuel
6. Minor instruments
7. Oils and lubricants
8. Stationery
9. Other supplies

E. *Materials*
Materials are commodities of a permanent nature,—in a raw, finished, or unfinished state,—entering into the construction, renewal, replacement or repair of any land, building, structure, or equipment.

1. Lumber
2. Machine and metal materials
3. Masonry
4. Paints, oils, and glass
5. Other materials

BUDGET

F. *Equipment*

Equipment comprises the live stock, furniture, machinery, implements, vehicles, and apparatus necessary and useful in the operation of the corporation, and which may be used repeatedly without appreciable impairment of their physical condition, having a calculable period of service.

1. Furniture and furnishings
2. Live stock
3. Machinery and implements
4. Motor vehicles
5. Vehicles and harness
6. Miscellaneous

G. *Real Estate*
1. Lands
2. Structures

A typical example of budget estimates classified according to the foregoing plan, follows:[1]

Department: Water Supply
Activity: Pumping
Expense
  Personal Service

			Schedule	Expense	Appropriations
80 A-1 Salaries					
Chief Engineer (1)	$1,800 per yr.		$1,800.00		
Engineers (3)	1,350 ,, ,,		4,050.00		
Firemen (3)	900 ,, ,,		2,700.00		
Oilers & Wipers (3)	1,095 ,, ,,		3,285.00		
Janitor	900 ,, ,,		900.00	$12,735.00	
80 A-2 *Wages*					
Boiler Cleaners (3)	$3.00	313 days	939.00		
Steamfitter and machinist	$4.40	313 days	1,377.20		
Laborers	$2.00	1,760 days	3,520.00	5,836.20	$18,571.20
Contractual Services					
81 B-2 Contractual Repairs				2,500.00	
81 B-5 Public Utility Service				10,000.00	
81 B-6 Special Service				1,200.00	13,700.00
Supplies					
82 D-1 Chemical, Drugs and Medicines				250.00	
82 D-2 Clothing, Dry Goods and Notions				100.00	
82 D-5 Fuel				18,000.00	
82 D-6 Minor Instruments				500.00	
82 D-7 Oils and Lubricants				2,000.00	
82 D-8 Stationery				50.00	
82 D-9 Other				50.00	20,950.00

[1] From Dayton budget of 1914, *op. cit.*

66 PRACTICE OF MUNICIPAL ADMINISTRATION

CHAP. IV

Materials

83 E-2	Machine and Metal Materials	900.00	
83 E-4	Paints, Oils, and Glass	50.00	
83 E-5	Other	200.00	1,150.00

Capital Outlay
Equipment

84 F-3	Machinery and Implements	250.00
	Total	$54,621.20

Summary of requirements

In summary, modern budget procedure requires that budget estimates be segregated:

A. By fund—capital, operating, special, trust, and sinking.
B. By departments—police, health, welfare, etc.
C. By activity—for police, as to foot patrol, detective service, criminal identification, etc.
D. By character—for current expense or acquisition of assets. Sometimes debt service and deficits are also shown separately.
E. By object—for personal services, supplies, contractual services, equipment, etc., each of these being further subdivided as may be necessary.

The salary schedule

A further important feature in the preparation of the estimates is the presentation of a salary schedule carrying the number of employees of each class, with the rate of pay, or in case of labor, the total number of days or hours at each rate, with the rate per period, noting increases in each instance. This is more desirable than appropriating a lump sum of money for salaries, and later passing a salary ordinance which carries the rate of pay for each class of employees.[1] In connection with the statement of salaries and wages desired, it is of assistance to have a comparison with the conditions of the current year. At the top of the estimate sheets may be printed a summary as follows: request for salaries, existing conditions, net increase in salaries, net decrease in salaries, net added force, net reduction in force, net total increase, and net total decrease.[2]

Uniform budget stationery

It is of considerable help—in fact, it is almost necessary—that the department requests be presented to the budget authorities upon uniform stationery. Sometimes separate sheets are provided for each classification, but this is not essential. It is desirable, however, to have different sheets for personal service estimates, owing to the different character of comparative data wanted.

All estimate sheets should provide space for data somewhat as

[1] The Boston budget carries a separate personal service schedule.
[2] Used chiefly by New York City.

BUDGET 67

follows: code number of the proposed appropriation; title and rate of wage or price per unit; number of employees or quantity of supplies, etc.; the number of hours, days, or months; total amount of request; estimated balance at the end of the fiscal year; expenditures for corresponding items for the current and last two fiscal years; comparison with increase or decrease; estimated stock on hand by quantity, unit value and amount; allowance recommended by the executive; tentative allowance by the finance committee of the city council, and final appropriation. If such stationery is used properly with the assistance of the accounting officers, it presents to the budget authorities necessary information for the preparation of a sound financial and work program. Each increase or decrease in requests is shown, and is measured, not with the appropriation of the current and previous years, but in comparison with the actual expenditures over these periods.[1]

The budget authorities, both executive and legislative, now have before them, in detail, the monetary requests of the governmental departments. Here are the general work programs of each division, supported by the items of proposed expenditures. The budget authorities can weigh the value of one activity as against another; eliminate one portion of an activity without injuring the remainder of the work; and definitely provide that certain activities shall not be followed, and that the whole strength of a division must be concentrated upon others. Salary increases are definite, and explanations can be asked for each. Additions to the numbers employed must be accounted for and justified. Executives and their subordinates can be brought before the authorities and asked to explain specific requests, specific increases, specific needs, and specific programs, instead of generalities. Reductions in requests are more reasonable when it is possible to effect the reduction of a number of different items rather than of a grand total.

In larger budgets it is desirable to have much more information than has been specified. The essentials of such supplementary information may be stated as consisting of (1) a comparative balance sheet showing the assets and liabilities of the city; (2) an operation statement comparing the income and the expense of the present year with the year previous; (3) a surplus statement showing the net unexpended balance at the end of the year; (4) a

[1] In some budgets, notably those of Boston and the State of Pennsylvania, the original departmental requests are not published.

68   PRACTICE OF MUNICIPAL ADMINISTRATION

statement of the public debt indicating its relation to the condition of the sinking fund and to the debt limits of the municipality; and (5) a fund statement evidencing the actual unencumbered balances available for reappropriation.[1]

Publicity — Before the budget is considered by the budget authorities, it should be made available to the public in preliminary hearings. It has been aptly said that democracy in government is not as necessarily correlated with methods of representation as with the information which the public has concerning the acts or failures to act of its representatives.

Since the budget outlines nearly all public activities, there has been a marked tendency in the past ten years to popularize the preparation of governmental spending programs. Not only does publicity stimulate citizen interest in how public money is being spent, but the knowledge that people know what the government is doing will urge the conscientious official to a higher endeavor, and require of the careless one a minimum of effectiveness. It is equally desirable that the budget as finally passed by the legislature be in printed form, not only that public employees may have ready access to the authorization to incur liabilities, but also that citizens may secure a definite statement of the city's public program.

Formulation of the plan — Irrespective of the authority that may be responsible for reviewing and presenting the estimates to the legislature, and the fashion in which the estimates are prepared, the manner in which they are expressed in the appropriation bill is of signal importance. In respect to appropriations, budgets may be classified as of three kinds—lump sum, segregated, and allotment.

Lump sum appropriations — The term "lump sum" is ordinarily used to designate the large group of budgets in which appropriations are granted in aggregates, without endeavoring to make a separate appropriation for each governmental activity, or to segregate these appropriations by the character of commodity or services to be purchased. With the introduction of estimates classified by activity and character of proposed expense, these classifications are finding a place in the appropriation bill. The granting of lump sum budgets has one large advantage, in that it leaves a wide degree of judgment to the administrator, permitting him to operate freely within the limits of his appropriation and removing the handicap of legisla-

[1] "Next Steps in the Development of a Budget Procedure for the City of Greater New York," *op. cit.*, 80 *et seq.*

BUDGET

tive interference in the operation of departments. However, it is conceded by most authorities that this advantage is outweighed by the fact that the legislative body and the public have little or nothing to say as to the extent to which the various activities of the department shall be supported, and by the further fact that there are large opportunities for the misappropriation of funds for political purposes. These evils have been recognized so widely that not a single city of the first class in the United States uses a lump sum budget, and it is said all but one of the nine first class cities have adopted the functional, segregated budget.

The essentials of the segregated budget are separate appropriations to each city activity, further subdivided by the character of the proposed expenditure. This subdivision may be carried to any degree, but usually the group of salaries, wages, supplies, materials, equipment, etc., within each activity is made the primary unit of appropriation.[1] This style of budget tends to eliminate useless expenditure, but also hampers administrative discretion, and compels frequent transfers of funds. The idea of the segregated budget has been extended to many cities, and has perhaps been carried farther in detail than necessary to secure desired control. Recently there have been attempts to retain the advantages of the lump sum appropriation. Sometimes these advantages have been saved by making the detailed allotment within the activity advisory only, and allowing some authority, other than the legislative body, usually the mayor or city manager, to make transfers within an activity.

A newer development in this direction is the allotment budget, which is simply the lump sum budget, allotted to the spending department on monthly or quarterly periods. This periodic authorization should be made by the chief administrative officer upon satisfactory evidence of need, and assurance that the fiscal period will be completed without a deficit. The lump sum appropriation may be based upon as much detail as is used in compiling a highly segregated budget; or upon cost schedules showing the units of work done and proposed to be done with actual and estimated unit costs.[2] This method of budgeting assumes sufficient information upon which to base careful appropriations, plus care in making allotments. With these requirements satisfied the procedure af-

CHAP. IV

The segregated appropriation

The allotment appropriation

---

[1] The appropriation items in the Boston budget are much more itemized.
[2] This latter method is used in estimating the budgets of the Department of Water Supply and Department of Street Railways in Detroit, although no periodic allotment of the appropriation is made.

Appropriation ordinance

fords ample check on waste, yet allows a wide latitude of departmental discretion in making expenditures.[1]

Aside from whether the budget is of the lump sum, segregated, or allotment type, it is desirable that the appropriation bill be so worded as to make effective the proposals of the budget makers. While the particular phrasing of the bill may vary according to local legal requirements, there are certain provisions which experience has indicated should be made binding upon administrative officers.[2] It is of first importance that no expense be incurred by any authority unless an appropriation has been previously made authorizing the creation of the obligation, and to this end every contract or purchase order should bear the signature of the controller before it is valid. The estimated amount which eventually will become payable should be entered against the proper appropriation, and if that account is already fully encumbered, the contract should not be signed, or the purchase made.

The salary schedules which were part of the original estimates should be attached to and become part of each appropriation for personal services. The number of positions and salaries payable for each are thus fixed, and should not be increased except by action of the legislative body.[3]

There should be an absolute prohibition of the amendment of the appropriation act without action of the legislative body. In larger municipalities, notably New York, it is made impossible to transfer an authorization to incur liabilities for personal service to an authorization for other than personal service, and vice versa. This check is to prevent a department needlessly increasing its salary or wage roll after the publicity which attended the passage of the original budget.

Some appropriation ordinances carry the provision that no more than one-twelfth of the appropriation for salaries shall be spent in one month, nor more than one fifty-second of the appropriation for wages shall be spent in any one week. A glance at the payroll growth which formerly prevailed in New York and

---

[1] This entire procedure is clearly presented in "Next Steps in the Development of a Budget Procedure for the City of Greater New York," *op. cit.*, Chap. V.

[2] Adapted, with preceding paragraphs, from Lent D. Upson, "Budget Making for Small Cities," *Public Budgets* (Annals, LXII, November, 1915).

[3] This need not be true under the allotment plan, but it is customary, and probably good practice, for the legislative body to dictate salaries in detail, at least in cities. State budget procedure may deviate in several respects from methods set forth here.

BUDGET 71

elsewhere immediately before election time indicates the necessity of such a regulation in some instances. It is a feature, however, which is highly undesirable in smaller places. It is an unnecessary restriction upon public officers, and prevents seasonal variation in work programs. It will serve a good purpose only in instances where the budget allotments were made up for three months at a time.

A budget is essentially a plan, and is valuable only so far as the plan is adhered to by administrative officers, or is modified only after due deliberation. To compel such adherence certain budgetary controls have been established that are an integral part of any modern budget procedure. As yet, these controls are not entirely satisfactory, and the next steps in budget improvement must be toward their development. In the meantime, the most important control in common use is that obtained by encumbering appropriations with the estimated amount of purchase orders and contracts, before such proposed obligations will be valid; the encumbrance being removed when the actual obligation is paid and deducted from the appropriation. Conscientiously used, this procedure prevents appropriations being overdrawn and the incurring of charges for which no provision has been made.[1] Similarly, it is desirable that a salary and payroll schedule be a part of the appropriation ordinance, and that these rolls be examined by the civil service authorities to insure that only properly authorized persons are employed, and at the stipulated rates.[2] If an appropriation is ill distributed over the objects of expenditure, transfers should be permitted with the approval of the chief administrator and knowledge of the auditor.[3] If, however, the extent of activities is modified by transfers from one activity to another, or by supplementary appropriations, this action should be taken by the legislative body, since the approved plan of city operations has been modified.[4] Supplementary appropriations should preferably be made from a contingent reserve, or, as is done in some jurisdictions, by the creation of a deficit to be met from the revenues of the following year. This latter method must be used with care. The use of code numbers on all vouchers, to facilitate the charging of proper appropriations, has been mentioned.[5] The controller, himself, as an accommodation to a department, may

[1] See p. 139.
[2] See p. 47.
[3] See p. 69.
[4] See p. 70.
[5] See p. 67.

72 PRACTICE OF MUNICIPAL ADMINISTRATION

<small>CHAP. IV</small>

<small>The budget and other business procedure</small>

<small>Where present budget procedure fails</small>

<small>Next steps in budget procedure: Emphasize appropriations by activities</small>

connive in improper charges. In this event, the public is without protection, as no mechanical safeguards devised are a complete substitute for personal integrity. As a control on the propriety of departmental charges, it is expected that the auditors in the controllers' office will exercise diligence in detecting unintentional errors and intentional fraud.

Sound budget procedure cannot alone insure economical and efficient government. A budget is only one part of an entire business procedure which is essential to sound government. Happily the associated elements are being rapidly introduced, and modern accounting control over public funds, scientific purchasing of supplies, time and service records, unit and job cost accounting, and standards of accomplishment are finding a place in even the smallest governmental units.

Modern budget procedure has created definite fiscal programs and kept those programs within the limits of available finances; and it has afforded numerous opportunities for reducing minor items here and there, large in the aggregate, but not sufficient to affect the marked upward trend of city expenditures. The average city official, confronted with the budget, finds nothing in it that enables him to determine in a large way the value of the activities that are rendered the public, or in a lesser way the degree of efficiency with which such activities are conducted. Modern budget procedure, valuable as it is, does not entirely meet present requirements in a number of respects.[1]

In the further development of budget procedure it is important that the activity rather than function be made invariably the unit of appropriation. Neither legislators nor the public can measure administrative emphasis unless such activities are authorized and adhered to. For example, the frequent comparisons of police departments on the basis of area or population are almost worthless unless the relative strengths detailed to traffic, detective, harbor, sanitation, and clerical forces are known. Police departments are only illustrative and the same principle applies generally. This principle has been well understood since the beginning of budget improvement, but has not been well executed. City departments are not anxious to carry out segregation in any further detail than required, and there is a constant incentive to eliminate

---

[1] These concluding paragraphs are adapted from Lent D. Upson, "Half-Time Budget Methods," *Competency and Economy in Public Expenditures* (Annals, CXIII, May, 1924).

activity in favor of departmental appropriations. Also, the average city that definitely accepts an activity classification finds it obsolete in a few years unless efforts are made to keep it up to date.

The budget estimates should present a complete picture of what is hoped to be accomplished eventually by governmental means, and of how nearly that ideal is being reached with present resources. For example, health departments should state the practical minimum death rate that can be expected by governmental action, the cost in dollars to secure that minimum. Similarly, the percentage of the recreation problem being met should be known; and so forth. A request for an appropriation, whether to secure a low death rate, clean streets, or the use of playgrounds, has no quantitative value until compared with some other figure. To this end, a request should be accompanied by a statement of exactly what ideal is to be anticipated in that particular service, and what percentage of that ideal can be achieved through the appropriation requested. The ideal should then be open to the criticisms of those who may not be as enthusiastic about the project as the specialist in charge.

Administrative officers seldom amplify requests with definite statements of work to be done—*i.e.*, a specific number of visits by nurses to be made, of so many lives that will be saved, so many more miles of streets to be cleaned, and recreation provided for so many more children. These matters may be discussed informally and incompletely before the legislative body, but they are seldom set down in intelligible shape for public information. It was a great improvement in budget making when lump sum appropriations were detailed, using a uniform classification of accounts. The next big step in budget making may be putting these segregated items together again in terms of actual results to be secured.

Private business through the balance sheet and income and expense statement has automatic measures of its operations. Public business has no such automatic and definite measures. There is no profit or loss, and surpluses and deficits are not necessarily an indication that an administration has been good or bad, but only whether there has been a careful adherence to appropriations. The public balance sheet, when it exists, does not furnish even a rough criterion of efficiency and adequacy of services. Further, there is no competition in public business, which is the great stimulus to effective and wasteless operation in private business. Rarely is a

74   PRACTICE OF MUNICIPAL ADMINISTRATION

<small>CHAP. IV</small>

<small>Unit costs</small>

city in direct competition with private industry, and when it is, the operating figures are usually too obscure to permit comparisons. Therefore, an effective budget must be based upon unit cost figures so framed that comparisons can be made between years, between sections of the same city, and between similar cities. Ultimately, departments must support budget requests with statements of unit costs of work done, with proper comparisons, and the reason for decreases or increases.

<small>Interdepartmental services</small>

Accurate unit costs cannot be obtained unless proper consideration is given to the services rendered by one department to another within the same city, although students of budget procedure have arrived at no conclusions with respect to the proper treatment of such matters. Examples of such services are water and light furnished to city buildings, water provided for fire service, etc. Of a somewhat different character is interest on the capital investment used by a particular department, as well as overhead services such as purchasing, legal work, and general administration. Eventually, specific measurable services rendered by one department to another may appear in the budget, more as a means of insuring that these services will be measured and definitely known than for any other purpose. Intangible services will doubtless continue to be appropriated for as overhead activities. There is an inclination to emphasize the fact that the budget is not a document for determining costs, and hence need not contain an accurate and complete statement of all costs, but should be used only to facilitate cost keeping as an independent activity.

<small>Operation audits</small>

Every year cities spend thousands of dollars seeing that expenditures are not made unless properly authorized, in examining the additions of vouchers, and in assuring the public that their servants have been honest in the handling of cash. But scarcely a penny is spent for auditing operations, in checking the effectiveness of these honest expenditures, in indicating the amount of work produced, and in assuring the public that their servants have been efficient as well as honest.

<small>Operation reports</small>

Facts cannot be secured annually for the appropriation ordinance unless facts are currently available for administrative guidance. If the administrator knows daily the units of work and the unit cost of such work, he is in a position to check daily the operations of subordinates. He should have before him daily, monthly, and yearly consolidated statements of such operations which will permit him to modify his methods and meet the exigencies of occasions. Such consolidated reports, coming from every department and covering every activity of the city, will furnish a clear statement of the progress of departments from day to day, week to week, month to month, and year to year. Given to the press and to the public, these operating statements will furnish a control over expenditures at present unknown.

Such operating reports will also furnish somewhat adequate tests of effective government. Perhaps the next job for the applied political scientist is to set up certain definite standards which will enable us to take cities of comparative size and locations and evaluate the numerous activities of each, giving a proper ranking for each subject. Nothing will stimulate the public official more than to know that his work is being measured not only by the work he did last year, but the work similar officials have done in other communities.

In summary, budget procedure is designed to control the fiscal operations of government in two ways: first, by requiring that its programs be undertaken after mature thought; and second by requiring that these programs be carried out with economy and efficiency. To date, budget procedure has been concerned largely with only the first of these controls. Budget procedure now works during the few months that the preparation of the budget is actually going on; then it stops, leaving the most important evaluations unsecured. It is a half-time budget procedure. The next step is the development of budget procedure on a full-time basis.

CHAPTER V

REVENUES [1]

The expanding field of governmental action

As the already large and rapidly increasing list of public activities testifies, certain functions can be performed more effectively and with less expense by organized government than by the individual citizen. Hence the old principle that governmental action is justified only when protecting life, liberty, and property has been supplemented by a new theory based on the furtherance of social interest and public comfort. City activities no longer are only protective or monopolistic; and municipalities are advancing into the disputed sphere of competition with private initiative in the conduct of public markets, recreation facilities, port development, transportation, and similar enterprises. Nowadays a main, if not the ultimate, test of the propriety of governmental action seems to be ability to conduct an activity with efficiency and economy.

Definition of revenues

Before the numerous activities of government can be administered so as to produce satisfactory results, they must be financed by revenues to be devoted to municipal operations. Revenues "represent amounts of moneys or other wealth received by or placed to the credit of the local governments for governmental purposes, under such conditions that they increase the assets without increasing the debt liabilities or decrease the debt liabilities without decreasing the assets." [2] Practically each city treats as revenue

---

[1] There are no publications dealing completely with the subject of municipal revenues. Many general texts on public finance are available and a special treatise for cities, Arthur E. Buck, ed., *Municipal Finance* (Macmillan, 1926) is now being published. Reference to particular subjects are cited throughout this chapter. In addition, the student should be familiar with *The Financial Statistics of Cities Having a Population of over 30,000* (U. S. Bureau of the Census), and with the numerous studies of municipal revenues. For current reference, see the *Proceedings of the Annual Conference of Taxation* under the auspices of the National Tax Association; *The National Municipal Review* (monthly); and *The American City* (monthly).

[2] *Financial Statistics of Cities, 1923*, 14. Francis Oakey, *Principles of Government Accounting and Reporting* (Appleton, 1921), 292, defines revenues "as comprehending those receipts applicable to the current period which increase assets or decrease reserves without increasing liabilities or reserves, which do not represent the recovery of particular expenditures, and the sources of which are known or ascertainable."

the income that can be used legally to meet the costs of current operations, usually in conformance with the definition cited, but sometimes including the returns from the sale of assets, transfers from sinking funds, and loans.

The Census Bureau enumerates the sources of municipal revenues, as:[1]

1. Taxes, subdivided as follows.
    (a) General property taxes
    (b) Special taxes, such as those on bank stocks, incomes, inheritances, mortgages, corporations, etc.
    (c) Poll taxes, including all per capita taxes
    (d) Business taxes, whether in proportion to the volume of the business, or by reason of the nature of the business, etc.
    (e) Non-business licenses, such as those of automobiles, dogs, building permits, marriage licenses, etc.
2. Special assessments
3. Fines, forfeits, and escheats
4. Subventions or grants from the state and other units
5. Donations and gifts
6. Pension assessments upon policemen, firemen, etc.
7. Highway privileges, or payments by individuals and corporations for special privileges in the streets and public places
8. Rents of investment properties owned by the city
9. Interest on municipal funds
10. Earnings of general departments for services actually performed, goods delivered, etc., such as the sale of publications, copying of documents, etc.
11. Earnings of public service enterprises, such as water, gas, electricity, etc.[2]

In the following discussion of municipal revenues the sources are considered in the following order: (1) taxes; (2) licenses and fees; (3) miscellaneous; (4) sale of industrial products and utility services; and (5) floating debt—this last not being a revenue in a technical sense, since such loans must ultimately be liquidated from revenue.

The assessment and collection of these revenues is delegated to

---

[1] As summarized by William Anderson, *American City Government* (Holt, 1926), 536-537. For detailed statement, see *Financial Statistics of Cities*, 1923, 16-18.

[2] For an economic classification of revenues, see Harley L. Lutz, *Public Finance* (Appleton, 1924), Chap. IX. Oakey, *op. cit.*, 308-313, enumerates the general sources of revenue as (1) taxes; (2) licenses; (3) permits; (4) franchises; (5) privileges; (6) rents; (7) proceeds of sales of commodities and services; (8) fees; (9) fines, penalties, and forfeitures; (10) escheats; (11) grants and donations applicable to current needs; (12) interest, premium, and discount; (13) royalties; and (14) pension assessments.

78   PRACTICE OF MUNICIPAL ADMINISTRATION

CHAP. V

Responsibility for assessment and collection of revenues

many authorities. The principal municipal revenue, taxation on real and personal property, is assessed ordinarily by city or county assessing officials and collected by the city or county treasurer, although the state government may collect the taxes on certain types of property, such as utilities, and return all or a portion of the collections to the local unit. Income taxes are invariably assessed and collected by state authorities and pro-rated to the localities. License fees or special taxes are authorized by state law or local ordinance, and collected through a license division of the city treasurer's office, or more frequently by the city department responsible for the supervision of the activity licensed. Fees are assessed in accordance with rates established by ordinance and collected by the department performing the service paid for. The collection of miscellaneous revenues is usually allocated to the department through whose activities the returns originate. Public utility revenues and industrial earnings are assessed and collected by the utility or industry concerned. Trust funds are invested by the city treasurer or other trustees and the revenues collected by him or them. Floating debt, when in the form of unfunded loans from banking institutions, is authorized by the legislative body and negotiated by the controller.

The revenue of greatest importance to municipalities is that derived from the taxation of real and personal property.[1] State laws usually prescribe that for public needs, wealth shall be taxed according to its ability to pay, and indicate the method to be followed in measuring ability. Ordinarily for real property that measure is its "true cash value."[2] The machinery is established through the assessing authorities for locating each parcel of taxable property and determining its value for purposes of taxation.

Exemptions from taxation

Not all property within a city is taxable, exemptions being determined by charter or state legislation. Tax-exempt property normally includes all property owned by the city, county, state, and national governments; recognized religious organizations, if used for religious purposes; charity organizations; cemeteries; and educational institutions not for profit; such exemptions amount to about fifteen or twenty percent of assessed values. A limited amount of personal property is also exempt, sometimes to the amount of $500 for household furniture, tools of artisans,

[1] Reference should be made to "A Plan of a Model System of State and Local Taxation," *Proceedings of the Thirteenth Annual Conference on Taxation*, under the auspices of the National Tax Association (1919).
[2] There are exceptions to this rule that are noted on p. 91.

personal wearing apparel, and the household effects of certain soldiers.[1] In practice, little personalty in the form of furniture, apparel, or jewelry finds its way on the assessment roll, owing to the difficulty both of assessment and of collection. Another type of local exemption relates to property segregated to the state for taxation purposes.

Taxation is a state function, and the method of selecting local tax assessors is prescribed by state law. Sometimes these authorities are appointed by state authority; sometimes—too often, in fact—they are elected by the local communities—and sometimes they are appointed by the local city council or the chief executive of the city. There may be either a single assessing authority for each unit of government, or a board of assessors, although the former is more desirable.[2]

Frequently the county, rather than the city, village, or township, is the unit for the assessment and collection of taxes, the tax levy and returns being apportioned among the county and lesser governmental units in proportion to assessed value. The assessment and collection of taxes on certain types of property, such as utilities, is often undertaken by the state, the returns being distributed upon varying bases.

An ideal system of tax assessment involves a single authority for each larger unit of local government, the county preferably, except when a large city is concerned. Such authority should have a long, if not a permanent, tenure of office and be divorced as completely as possible from political considerations, and with adequate facilities for the periodic (preferably annual) appraisal of all taxable wealth. Such wealth falls into several natural classes, each requiring specialized treatment for proper assessment. These groups are (1) real property, including lands and buildings; (2) personal property, including the intangibles of corporations, unincorporated businesses, individuals, and estates; and (3) business enterprises. Proper assessment facilities also include engineering assistance to be used in connection with the appraisal of structures and for the drafting of subdivision plats and tax and land value maps.

Assessing authorities are gradually availing themselves of the standard assessment methods developed by the larger and more

[1] See p. 91.
[2] See "Report of the Committee on Method of Selecting Assessors," *Proceedings of the Ninth Annual Conference on Taxation* (1915).

80 PRACTICE OF MUNICIPAL ADMINISTRATION

CHAP. V

progressive cities, such as New York, Cleveland, Buffalo, Rochester, Newark, Baltimore, Washington, and Detroit; although a number of smaller cities also have brought their procedure to a high degree of effectiveness.

Elements of an assessing system

The following features are believed to present the chief elements of a modern and scientific assessing system:[1] (1) assessment at true cash value, of both real and personal property; (2) separation of the assessment of land and improvements; (3) the district, block, and lot system of indexing property holdings and office records; (4) preparation and publication of a land value map of the entire city; (5) tax maps showing the metes and bounds of all property within the limits of the taxing district; (6) the adoption of the unit-foot as a standard of quantity; (7) the adoption of an approved depth rule, corner influence rule, plottage rule, and other minor rules as may be necessary; (8) adoption of a standard building classification, with unit factors of building value; (9) adoption of rules of economic and structural depreciation of buildings; (10) a file record of all improvements upon each description; (11) collection and filing for current use of all pertinent information relative to property values,—as sales, record of deeds filed, building permits issued, etc.; and (12) for personal property, a personal return form to be filled out by each taxpayer; or, in event the form is not returned, the fixing of a reasonable assessment by the assessors. The more important of these elements are discussed in the following pages, but not in the order given above since it seems desirable to describe the method of placing property on the rolls before considering the methods of arriving at valuations.

Preparation of assessment rolls

To tax property, its value must be determined and placed upon the assessment rolls, a task performed by the assessors or their representatives. Such authorities must visit all real property at stated intervals and determine its true cash value. Personalty is placed upon the assessment roll from lists prepared by the owner or trustee.[2] The assessment rolls are made up annually and should carry a description of the property assessed, the separate value of the land, and the separate value of the buildings located upon it. The name of the owner does not appear unless a system

[1] See *Manual of Assessment* (City of Detroit, 1926); *Assessor's Manual* (Minnesota Tax Commission, 1926); and *Assessor's Manual* (Missouri State Tax Commission, 1924).

[2] Tangible property is also appraised by assessor or assistant.

of pre-billing taxes is operated. Personalty appears in a separate roll and is listed by wards under the name of the owner.

CHAP. V

Property placed upon the assessment roll must be indicated so accurately that it can be recognized by the taxpayer as his particular property, and described in such legal terms as to constitute a binding assessment. In the case of personalty this is easily accomplished by listing the goods taxed under the name of the owner; in the case of buildings by designating the land upon which they stand. But the satisfactory, and at the same time legal, description of land is a more difficult matter. In older cities the first settled portions were usually described by metes and bounds, *i.e.*, in lineal measurements from generally recognized points. Additions to this area were later made in the form of subdivisions of tracts, the plats of which were recorded with the proper authorities. Such property is usually described by lot and block within such and such recorded subdivision. These descriptions are matters of record, appear on both deeds and abstracts, and are used to describe the property when placed upon the assessment rolls.

Description of property for taxation purposes

It will be apparent, however, to any one familiar with descriptions of either type that they are of considerable length, and involve undue labor when copied on assessment rolls, collection books, and tax bills. Also, such descriptions are sometimes difficult to locate, and often, because there is no continuity in description, offer little security against duplication upon or omission from the assessment rolls. To overcome these difficulties the block and lot system of describing property for taxation purposes has been devised, and is in operation in New York, Baltimore, Washington, San Francisco, and other cities. Under this plan an arbitrary number is assigned each block in the city, the numbers being consecutive. Within each block, each separate parcel of land is also numbered consecutively. The description "lot so and so, block so and so" briefly describes any parcel of property within the city, eliminating the cumbersome descriptions; and reducing to a minimum the possibility of duplication or omission of property. In order that taxpayers and the assessors may easily locate any property by its longer description of record, indexes are prepared showing descriptions. By reference to this index the taxpayer can assure himself at any time that the description for purposes of taxation designates the property which he holds by title of record.

Block and lot descriptions

82   PRACTICE OF MUNICIPAL ADMINISTRATION

<small>Tax maps</small>

<small>Land value maps</small>

<small>Valuation of land</small>

The taxation description is seldom placed upon deeds or abstracts, unless as a mere memorandum, and property is of course transferred by its title of record.[1]

Essential to a complete assessing procedure are tax maps. A tax map is one showing the exact dimensions of every separately owned parcel of real estate in the city. In the thickly settled portions of the city where parcels are small, such maps should be on a scale of fifty feet to the inch; in other sections, the scale may be 200 feet to the inch. These maps serve as the basis for the preparation of the assessment rolls for the year, each separate parcel shown on the maps being checked with the rolls to assure that all property within the city is on the books for assessment, and that the dimensions of each item on the rolls are correct. Also, the assessors need these maps in their field work of examining property. They should be available for the entire city and be kept current by the engineering department of the assessor's office. Many cities have no maps of their own and use an insurance atlas as a rather unsatisfactory substitute.

To assist the property owners in understanding their land valuations and to enable them to make comparisons with other parcels of land as to uniformity and equity in assessment, a city should prepare land value maps. These maps should not be confused with tax maps, as they do not show the separate parcels of real estate, but only the boundaries of blocks. The value of the land per front foot on every side of each block is indicated, and in unplatted areas the value per acre. The front foot values shown must refer to unit values uniformly, and it is generally found expedient to use a depth of 100 feet as a standard. These maps should be open to public inspection at reasonable hours, and in large cities are sometimes published in book form for distribution. The value of such maps in promoting public understanding of and confidence in the system of assessing is evident. Excellent examples of these maps are to be found in New York City, Detroit and Cleveland.

It is the equitable assessment of land values that raises the greatest difficulties for the taxation authorities. Assuming that all property is on the assessment roll, and assuming that there is a sincere desire to make an equitable assessment, the question of value still remains largely one of personal opinion. There are, of course,

[1] See "Lot and Block Method of Describing Property for Taxation Purposes," *Public Business*, No. 35 (Detroit, March 1, 1919).

certain factors inherent in real estate which assist in formulating judgment as to value. These principal factors of value are location, utility, shape, and size. As to location and utility, land is valuable in proportion to its nearness to people who will pay to use it, and the most valuable lot in any city is that lot which is located so as to be accessible to the greatest number of people who will buy goods. The effects of shape and size are apparent. To be of greatest value, a parcel of land must be of sufficient size to meet business demands, and so shaped that it can be utilized fully; and recognition of these features in assessing is called plottage. There are other minor factors which help determine value, *i.e.*, transportation facilities, sunshine, street conditions, character of business done, social atmosphere, soil, grades, etc., as Zangerle and others have pointed out.[1]

A number of methods are used for determining the combined effect of all these factors and arriving at the resulting value in dollars per front foot or per acre.[2] Assessors occasionally endeavor to obtain a neighborhood expression of value, *i.e.*, allow the owners in each particular section to express their opinions of tax worth. With an assessor of unusual ability, this system has merit, but frequently it is open to criticism. If the expression of opinion is intelligent, the assessor is unlikely to get the truth, from design; if the opinion is not intelligent, it will naturally be inaccurate.

Analysis of sales in a neighborhood is an acceptable method of determining value, but only after due allowance has been made for difference in such factors as character of buildings, methods of payment, side of street, and size and usefulness of lot.

In arriving at a judgment of value by the sale price, allowance must also be made for urgent need or for personal inclinations, both of which frequently determine a price in excess of actual value. A growing merchant will pay an exorbitant price for the lot next to him in order to expand his business without moving; and sentiment will rebuy the old homestead at a price in excess of its ordinary utility. Nor can value be determined by the price received at a forced sale. Real market value, cash sale value, or fair cash value is the price demanded when the buyer is willing,

---

[1] See John A. Zangerle, *Principles of Real Estate Appraising* (McMichael, 1924), Chap. II; and Frederick M. Babcock, *The Appraisal of Real Estate* (Macmillan, 1924), Chaps. II-IV.
[2] Zangerle, *op. cit.*, Chaps. III-VIII; and Babcock, *op. cit.*, Chaps. V-VIII, and XII. For a suggestion as to the methods to be applied to each type of real estate, see Babcock, *op. cit.*, 325.

84   PRACTICE OF MUNICIPAL ADMINISTRATION

CHAP. V

Rentals and leases

Rules of assessment

Unit depth rules

but not compelled, to buy, and the seller is willing, but not compelled, to sell.

A less satisfactory, but frequently more available method of value is by the capitalization of rentals and leases. In the capitalization of rentals different rates must be used for different classes of real estate, and for real estate in different localities. In certain types of property, such as amusement places and garages, the rental is not a good index of value.

From such evidence it is possible to approximate the value of certain parcels of land throughout a city, and this information may be used to allocate values to neighboring parcels. But these values may not be assigned blindly—neighboring areas may be of different shapes and depths, may be of a size not best suited to the purpose, may be affected by corner influence, etc. Realization of these conditions has brought about the formulation of rules for applying known facts in the valuation of properties. At best these rules are empirical, as is evidenced by their lack of uniformity in important cities, but when intelligently used, they are helpful.[1]

The first of these rules has to do with the common unit of land measurement. Undeveloped territory is usually valued by the acre; industrial sites by the square foot; and residential and business property by the unit foot, *i.e.*, one foot front by the usual depth of properties in any particular city, often one foot by one hundred or one hundred and twenty feet, located in the center of a block.[2] Having arrived at the value of a unit foot in each block

[1] "I believe that while rules are useful and good things to have . . . there should be a trained mind, experienced in the neighborhood who applies the rules when and so far as they fit the actual facts found on the ground." Lawson Purdy, *Proceedings of the Seventh Annual Conference Under the Auspices of the National Tax Association* (1913), 283.

[2] John A. Zangerle, county auditor of Cuyahoga County in which the city of Cleveland is located, and Lawson Purdy, formerly chairman of the Board of Assessors of New York City, have made outstanding contributions in the solution of assessing problems and assessing property for purposes of taxation. Reference should be made to *Principles of Real Estate Appraising* and *Unit Value Land Maps* by Mr. Zangerle (1924); and *The Assessment of Real Estate* by Lawson Purdy (Supplement, *Nat. Mun. Rev.*, VIII, 509-527 (September, 1919).

Among other valuable publications are Alfred D. Bernard, *Some Principles and Problems of Real Estate Valuation* (United States Fidelity and Guaranty Company, Baltimore, 1913); Richard M. Hurd, *Principles of City Land Values* (Record and Guide, 1924); Frederick M. Babcock, *The Appraisal of Real Estate* (Macmillan, 1924); Stanley McMichael and Robert F. Bingham, *City Growth and Values* (McMichael, 1923); J. Ben Stoner, *Systems of Equalizing, Assessing, and Collecting Taxes* (Austin, Texas, 1924); and W. W. Pollock and Karl W. H. Scholz, *The Science and Practice of Urban Land Valuation* (Manufacturers' Appraisal Co., 1926).

Reference should also be made to the assessing manuals of St. Paul, Washington, Bridgeport, and Detroit; to the *Report on the Assessment of Real*

REVENUES 85

or street frontage, the assessor might determine the value of each lot by the simple process of multiplying the unit foot value by the number of front feet in each parcel. But this simple method would be grossly unfair because lots vary in depth, and in the business sections particularly a shallow lot is worth more proportionately than a deep one, because of accessibility.[1] The depth rules devised endeavor to estimate the distribution of value within a lot.

CHAP.
V

The 4-3-2-1 rule is to the effect that the first, or street, frontage to a depth of twenty-five feet of a lot 100 feet deep is worth forty percent of the whole; the second twenty-five feet, thirty percent of the whole; the third twenty-five feet twenty percent of the whole; and the rear twenty-five feet, ten percent of the whole. According to the Hoffman rule, the street-half of a lot 200 feet deep is worth two-thirds of the value of the whole lot and the Hoffman-Neill rule works out the relative value of intermediate depths. Other important rules are the Newark rule, the Pleydell rule, the Lindsay-Bernard rule, and the Somers rule. The application of several of these rules to lots 100 feet deep is shown in the table on page 86.[2]

Certain of these rules have been worked out in detail for different types of lots and there is a difference of opinion as to whether a single rule can be devised to apply to all real estate business frontage, wholesale district, and residence lots. For example, would the first twenty-five feet of a residence lot hold the same percentage of value as the first twenty-five feet of a business lot of the same length? Probably not.

The rules apply to inside lots and make no provision for the increased value of corner lots which comes primarily because of accessibility, but also because of light, ventilation, and general utility. It is difficult to formulate a rule for measuring corner influence, because of its lack of uniformity and there is wide discrepancy in the rules adopted by various cities. A corner lot in the shopping center may have unusual value because it attracts customers from several directions; a corner in the wholesale section may have no advantages over an inside location except that which comes from better light and ventilation; and a residence

Corner
lots

Property in the City of Rochester (Rochester Bureau of Municipal Research, 1921); and to Walter W. Pollock, "An Equitable Standard for Land Valuations," *Proceedings of the Seventh National Conference on Taxation.*

[1] It is usual for a city to employ two depth rules, one for lots of a standard size, and another for lots of unusual depth.

[2] For numerous other rules. some of them applying to a deeper lot unit, see Babcock, *op. cit.,* 278-281.

86 PRACTICE OF MUNICIPAL ADMINISTRATION

DEPTH RULES
ON 100 FOOT UNITS

Depth (Feet)	Somers Cleveland Detroit %	Davies- N. Y. %	4-3-2-1 %	Hoffman- Neill %	Martin- Chicago %	Dist. of Columbia (Richards) %
5....	14.35	12.60	9.40	17.32	14.95	22.36
10....	25.00	21.70	17.80	25.98	19.90	31.62
15....	33.22	29.20	25.60	32.98	24.75	38.73
20....	41.00	35.80	33.00	38.99	29.60	44.72
25....	47.90	41.70	40.00	44.44	34.35	50.00
30....	54.00	47.10	46.70	49.47	39.10	54.77
35....	59.20	52.10	53.10	54.12	43.75	59.16
40....	64.00	56.80	59.10	58.49	48.40	63.25
45....	68.45	61.30	64.70	62.67	52.95	67.09
50....	72.50	65.40	70.00	66.67	57.50	70.71
55....	76.20	69.40	74.90	70.51	61.95	74.16
60....	79.50	73.40	79.40	74.20	66.40	77.46
65....	82.61	77.10	83.40	77.74	70.75	80.62
70....	85.60	80.60	86.90	81.17	75.10	83.67
75....	88.30	84.10	90.00	84.49	79.35	86.60
80....	90.90	87.60	92.22	87.73	83.60	89.44
85....	93.33	91.00	94.22	90.90	87.75	92.20
90....	95.60	94.00	96.17	94.01	91.90	94.87
95....	97.85	97.00	98.10	97.03	95.95	97.47
100....	100.00	100.00	100.00	100.00	100.00	100.00
110....	104.00	106.00	103.76		107.90	104.88
120....	107.50	111.20	107.35		115.60	109.55
130....	110.50	116.20	110.60		123.10	114.02
140....	113.00	121.20	113.80		130.40	118.32
150....	115.00	126.20	117.00	117.00	137.50	122.48
160....	116.80	131.20	119.80		144.40	126.49
170....	118.40	136.20	122.60		151.10	130.38
180....	119.80	141.20	125.20		157.60	134.16
190....	121.00	145.20	127.60		163.90	137.84
200....	122.00	149.20	130.00	130.00	170.00	141.42
250....	126.05					
300....	129.25					
350....	131.90					
400....	134.20					
500....	137.85					
600....	140.55					

corner may actually be worth less than inside property because of its double liability to special assessments and its exposure to traffic annoyance. After examining many rules, Messrs. Lindsay and Bernard, in Baltimore, have suggested a rule for finding the minimum value of corner property, which involves the simple plan of treating a corner lot as two lots, one fronting on each street. The value of each lot is found as an inside lot, and these values, when added together, give the total value including corner influence.[1] Mr. John A. Zangerle, county auditor of Cuyahoga County, Ohio, in which the city of Cleveland is located, says that

[1] Bernard, op. cit., 52.

REVENUES

an examination of hundreds of important corners, comparing such assessment with the known values or capitalized leases, established to his satisfaction that the Baltimore method was not excessive or unjust. However, in deference to certain opposition, Mr. Zangerle makes a reduction of twenty-eight percent on such valuation, the corner influence being applied on the basis of the so-called Zangerle Curve.[1] Corner influence is ordinarily assumed to extend for 100 feet from the street intersection, although some authorities deny this, holding that the influence affects only the corner parcel regardless of size. Zangerle says: "The true test of a corner lot system must be that blocks of like size and units when added together will be identical in value with other blocks of the same area," and curves have been developed for extending the influence accordingly. An example of such a table applying a maximum of thirty-six percent of the side street influence to sixty feet of a corner is as follows:

DETROIT CORNER INFLUENCE TABLE

1 ft.	1.65%	21 ft.	24.93%	41 ft.	34.31%
2 ft.	3.25	22 ft.	25.67	42 ft.	34.53
3 ft.	4.80	23 ft.	26.38	43 ft.	34.73
4 ft.	6.30	24 ft.	27.06	44 ft.	34.91
5 ft.	7.75	25 ft.	27.71	45 ft.	35.07
6 ft.	9.15	26 ft.	28.33	46 ft.	35.21
7 ft.	10.50	27 ft.	28.92	47 ft.	35.33
8 ft.	11.80	28 ft.	29.48	48 ft.	35.44
9 ft.	13.05	29 ft.	30.01	49 ft.	35.54
10 ft.	14.26	30 ft.	30.51	50 ft.	35.63
11 ft.	15.43	31 ft.	30.98	51 ft.	35.71
12 ft.	16.56	32 ft.	31.42	52 ft.	35.78
13 ft.	17.65	33 ft.	31.83	53 ft.	35.84
14 ft.	18.70	34 ft.	32.21	54 ft.	35.89
15 ft.	19.71	35 ft.	32.57	55 ft.	35.93
16 ft.	20.68	36 ft.	32.91	56 ft.	35.96
17 ft.	21.61	37 ft.	33.23	57 ft.	35.98
18 ft.	22.50	38 ft.	33.53	58 ft.	35.99
19 ft	23.35	39 ft.	33.81	59 ft.	35.995
20 ft.	24.16	40 ft.	34.07	60 ft.	36.00

As has been stated it is held by some that residence corners have little or no additional value over inside lots, and that business property of a low value should take on a less percent of corner influence than business property of high value. In this connection, Mr. Zangerle has developed a table of partial corner addition, showing the percentage that should be added for corner influence up to values of $200 per front foot, above which value the usual

[1] Zangerle, *op. cit.*, 96. See also, Babcock, *op. cit.*, 307.

88 PRACTICE OF MUNICIPAL ADMINISTRATION

<small>CHAP. V</small>

corner rule prevails.¹ Babcock starts with the Lindsay-Bernard rule, but modifies it by the application of coefficients that decrease from the unit one in high class retail districts to .65 for residence property.²

<small>Irregular parcels</small>

The appraisal of angular and irregular-shaped lots, and property in curved lines or of trapezoid shape offers difficulties which have been met by the application of rules, based upon the valuation of plots in the form of right angled triangles. In valuing such properties it is customary to extend the boundary lines so as to form a rectangular plot, and secure the value of this parcel by the usual methods. Then, if the base of the triangular section rests on the street it is treated as a rectangle with one-half the depth of the triangle, and valued accordingly. This value subtracted from the value of the completed rectangle will give the residual value to be applied to a triangle, the apex of which rather than the base rests upon the street. The rule applying to triangular plats is not exactly equitable, but may be sufficiently so for practical purposes.

<small>Triangular plots</small>

By judicious use of these rules it is possible to assign values to many irregular parcels that can be cut into rectangles and triangles, and to value property having frontage on three streets.³

<small>Plottage</small>

Previous mention has been made of "plottage," which is the utility of land as determined by its size. Ordinarily a small parcel is not as usable as a larger one, and its value must be reduced accordingly.⁴ Rules have been developed to care for this reduction in value.⁵

<small>Alleys</small>

Alleys add to the value of business lots in particular, because of added accessibility, ventilation and light. If a lot "fronts" only on an alley, a unit foot value should be assigned, and the thoroughfare treated as a street. Otherwise, the Zangerle rule provides that one-half of the width of the alley be added to the depth of the lot as the circumstances require.⁶ The Babcock rule is more precise, and involves the addition of coefficients varying with the type of property, and allows for the ratio of alley width to the size of the property affected.⁷

---

¹ Zangerle, *op. cit.*, 106.   ² Babcock, *op. cit.*, 304.
³ When the lot is a trapezoid or composed of irregularities, block off into squares and triangles that are divisable into the lot, find the value of each according to accepted rules, and add up these values for the total value of the lot.
⁴ This is not always true, as a small plot may absorb value because of the use to which large neighboring plots are put.
⁵ Babcock, *op. cit.*, 308-312.   ⁶ Zangerle, *op. cit.*, 139.
⁷ Babcock, *op. cit.*, 313-316.

In assessing structures it must be borne in mind that a building is worth no more than the difference between the value of the land and the total value of the property.[1] If an improvement reflects the highest utility of the land upon which it is placed, the improvement is worth its cost of reproduction, less structural depreciation. If the highest utility is not reflected in the structure, it is obsolete. This element of obsolescence should be considered before the other elements entering into value are determined. Some authorities have endeavored to measure this obsolescence and establish uniform tables of economic depreciation.[2] However, uniform tables are difficult if not impossible of formulation since economic depreciation or obsolescence is most marked in cities and sections of cities of rapid growth, and what is fair in one instance is absurd in another. It may be concluded that if the improvements will not sell for their sound value plus the value of the land, or will not earn a fair return on their sound value plus the value of the land, economic depreciation or obsolescence has set in and must be allowed for.[3] Some assessing authorities deny this implication, largely on the ground that to allow for an absence of full use of a parcel of property is to open the door to graft and favoritism.[4]

CHAP. V

Assessing structures

Obsolescence

The following table of economic depreciation is summarized from Bolton by Bernard, and is only illustrative:[5]

TYPE	LIFE IN YEARS
Taxpayer (a cheap structure designed to earn taxes on a site while it is going to a higher utility.)	12–15
Hotels	15–18
Apartment houses	18–21
Store Buildings	21–25
Tenements and flats (distinguished from apartment houses in that features of maintenance such as heat, elevators, janitor service, etc., are lacking.)	25–27
Office and business buildings	27–33
Lofts and factories	33–37
Residences	37–44
Banks and institutions	44–50

[1] "Real estate is never the sum of the land plus the structural value of the improvements, unless the improvements are peculiarly adapted to the lot; that is, the utility of the lot is best served by the improvement erected on it." Bernard, op. cit., 65.
[2] See R. P. Bolton, *Building for Profit* (1922).
[3] Bernard, op. cit., 74.
[4] "It is a wide door for friends and a narrow door for foes." Zangerle, op. cit., 223.
[5] Bernard, op. cit., 72.

90 PRACTICE OF MUNICIPAL ADMINISTRATION

CHAP. V

Structural depreciation

After obsolescence it is necessary, to consider the difficult subject of structural depreciation. As an estimate of structural depreciation some authorities make an allowance of one percent a year for good brick construction and two percent a year for frame construction, and have found this procedure satisfactory.[1] Authorities have developed numerous tables covering the physical depreciation of buildings, but here again so many factors enter that categorical determinations are impossible. The following table of structural deteriorations is appended for illustrative purposes:[2]

Type	Life in Years
Cheap detached frame residences	30– 40
Good detached frame residences	40– 60
Ordinary brick residences	50– 75
Good brick and stone residences	100–150
Frame tenements	25– 35
Brick tenements and flats	40– 50
Good class apartment houses	50– 75
High class fireproof apartment houses	75–100
Cheap brick shops and dwellings	40– 50
Ordinary brick shops and dwellings	50– 75
Good brick and stone stores and offices	75–100
High class offices of masonry and steel	150–

Cost of construction

After consideration of economic and structural depreciation, the assessor naturally turns to the cost of construction as an index of value, assuming that this cost can be obtained accurately. As a rule, however, estimated costs must be secured by comparison with the cost of similar structures, making allowances for the varying grades of construction which are found. Numerous tables have been developed to assist the assessor, based upon both the square feet of floor space and the cubic contents of buildings. There are many types of structures and variations within the same general type.[3]

Appreciation

In recent years many buildings have appreciated largely in value because of increased construction costs. Assessors have been gradually taking these increased values into consideration, but not with sufficient rapidity to undo the inequality of assessment that exists between new and old construction.[4]

It is roughly estimated that personal property keeps pace with

[1] Bernard, op. cit., 76.
[2] Zangerle, op. cit., 226-227.
[3] These are given in detail with photographs of each type of structure in Zangerle, op. cit., Chap. XXXVIII-XL.
[4] See Zangerle, op. cit., Chap. XXXVII.

real estate in amount, yet the ratio of personalty taxes to real estate taxes is constantly decreasing, as will be noted on all assessment rolls in recent years. The cause of this decrease is obvious. Taxes on personal property cannot be collected, even when extreme measures are used to place it on the assessment rolls. To be sure, household furniture, stocks in trade, etc., which are physical, can be assessed. If the owners of such property are large holders the assessed taxes can be collected; many of the smaller assessments are eventually reported delinquent and uncollectible. But such property is negligible compared to the wealth of stocks, bonds, mortgages, and other evidences of ownership or indebtedness upon which it is often endeavored to collect taxes, although such taxes result in double taxation, and the tax is usually so high as to prohibit ownership if taxes are paid.[1] A four percent or five percent bond taxed at, say, two percent does not leave a return that justifies ownership. Some states have recognized this situation and have provided for small registration taxes on mortgages and bonds, after which such property is exempt from further payments. This practice is not widespread, and the impossible and unjust effort to assess personalty is still kept up in many communities.[2]

CHAP. V

Assessment of personalty

Recognition of the fact that not all property should be taxed alike has inspired a movement for the classification of property for purposes of taxation. Under this proposal it is probable that real estate would bear the brunt of taxation, on the grounds that it has permanent value, profits from unearned increment, and secures the greatest benefits from the operations of government. Structures would be taxed at a lower rate, as they rapidly depreciate in value; and their erection would be encouraged by this subsidy, if it may be so called. Personalty would be taxed least of all, for reasons already given. It is to be anticipated that this movement will develop rapidly as cities secure home rule in taxation. The scheme is already in operation in Pittsburgh, where the city tax on buildings is reduced each year until a value of fifty percent is reached. Minnesota has a fourfold classification with different rates of assessment for iron ore, household goods,

Classification of property for purpose of taxation

---

[1] Some assessors send a blank to every resident, or to every person listed in the telephone directory, placing an arbitrary assessment against those who make no return. These assessments are then increased each year until a protest results.

[2] Important exceptions are Minnesota, New York, Pennsylvania, and Massachusetts.

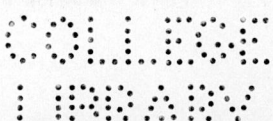

live stock and agricultural products and all other property. In 1918 the principle of classification of property for purposes of taxation was written into the constitution of Ohio; but the amendment was nullified by another amendment passed at the same time.[1]

Review of assessments

After the assessment has been made, opportunity is usually given for review by the assessing officers, or by the members of a special board of review, who listen to the protests of citizens. Not infrequently, errors of assessments are ascertained and corrected.

Equalization

These local boards of review serve to equalize assessments as between individuals in the same community only, and after local review, appeal may be had to state board, and finally to the courts. Most states have, for purposes of state taxation, a state authority responsible for review and equalization of assessments as between counties and cities. Otherwise grave injustice would be done larger communities which assess at nearly full value in order to increase the bonding limits.

The assessing manual

The procedure for assessing property in any locality, including the several rules adopted, constitutes a manual of assessment. All of the procedure used should be definite, and a matter of record. To this end, the manual should be printed and available for distribution among interested citizens.

Accounting control of taxes

When the assessment rolls are approved they are certified to the proper tax-collecting authority or authorities. Usually one such authority—for example, the county treasurer—collects the taxes of all the taxing units within a locality.[2] Such, however, is not always the case. In a few instances the total of assessed taxes belonging to any city is certified to the controller and set up on his books as an asset. Such procedure provides some control over the collection on taxes; but it is not usual.

Limitation of taxation

State legislation or charter provision frequently restricts the amount of taxes that can be levied in any one year for public purposes. These tax restrictions appeal to the taxpayer, who looks upon the municipality as a tax spending machine, and they may, if reasonable, check useless expenditure. But in the long run, the merit of legal restrictions is illusionary, because cities resort to every unsound expedient to circumvent them.

The favorite method of tax limitation is the prescription of a

---

[1] A discussion of the classification of property for purposes of taxation appears in the *Bulletins of the Constitutional Convention* (State of Massachusetts, 1918).

[2] For a discussion of the prebilling and collection of taxes, see p. 128.

fixed rate of levy for certain specific purposes or for all purposes. Mr. R. C. Atkinson states that there is usually no inherent reasonableness in the particular rates established, and the interior limitations are arbitrary and very often produce serious injustice as among the various levying districts subject to a single levy. Further the method of controlling expenditures by a flat tax limitation, when applied to the whole state, is too rigid, too mechanical, and does not result in protecting the taxpayer. The plan assumes that all districts are expending at about the same rate and neglects the fact that those districts which are comparatively new, but which are growing rapidly in population, such as the newer industrial centers, may have a scale of requirements—urgent ones too—entirely different from that of older and more slowly developing communities.[1] Another type of limitation restricts taxation according to the levies of the previous year, permitting the levy of each year to increase only a certain percent over the levy of the preceding year. Some legislatures have established the maximum per capita levy that may be made, as in Minnesota. Still another method of limitation is to permit taxpayers the right of appeal from all tax levies to a state board, which, free from local influences, examines the relative necessity of demands and makes a decision accordingly. This plan is in use in Indiana, but is open to the obvious criticism that control of local financial affairs is placed in the hands of individuals not conversant with the needs of a community, and that the principle of local autonomy is contravened.[2]

The principal results of rigorous tax limitations are the reduction of municipal expenditures below a standard of decency prevailing in cities of similar size; heavy increase in public debt owing to the issuance of deficiency bonds, or bonds for improvements that would be met ordinarily from current revenues; improper financial practices, including diversions of moneys from special funds to funds having more urgent need; and general failure to provide for the maintenance and repair of public property,

---

[1] For a straightforward statement of how such tax limitations have affected the cities of one state, see R. C. Atkinson, *The Effects of Tax Limitations upon Local Finance in Ohio 1911 to 1922* (Cleveland, 1923); also, "Tax and Debt Limit Laws," *Proceedings of Seventeenth Annual Conference on Taxation* (1924).
[2] Philip Zoercher, "Central Supervision of Local Expenditures," *Proceedings of the Seventeenth Annual Conference on Taxation*. See also, Frank G. Bates, "State Control of Local Finance in Indiana," *Amer. Polit. Sci. Rev.*, XX, 352-360 (May, 1926).

thus placing a burden upon future taxpayers for the benefit of immediate taxpayers. These studies of tax limits have forced the conclusion that they do not actually limit, and that they often encourage unsound financing. There is no effective way in a democracy of blocking a genuine popular demand for increased governmental service. The only sound method of securing a restriction on tax levies is by the establishment of a comprehensive and binding budget system, the enactment of bonding laws which will prevent unsound bonding, and the wide distribution among the electorate of the direct tax burden.[1]

Centralization of taxation authority

Centralization of fiscal and taxation authority is one of the principal tendencies of recent years, as manifested in the establishment of state tax commissions and the amplification of their powers. This centralization has affected taxation within municipalities in several general directions. First, there has been a tendency towards state supervision of local assessments, the central authority supervising and controlling the work of local assessing, thus depriving localities of considerable autonomy. In some states all assessments are subject to state review and are equalized as between governmental units, especially for purposes of state taxation. In this same connection the state authorities are assuming control of the assessment of utilities. It is clearly recognized that untrained local assessors are utterly incapable of evaluating the parts of a railroad or telephone system, and today such assessments are made primarily by state tax commissions or other central authority. This procedure has not brought about the elimination of all inequalities, but it has at least tended to substitute scientific knowledge and uniformity for ignorance in the taxing of these types of properties.

A second result is found in the control of the administration of special taxes, particularly taxes on inheritances, incomes, and gasoline, and other miscellaneous taxes. Sometimes the moneys collected in taxes are turned back to the city on some basis, but more often they are allocated, in whole or in part, to the use of the state. A last result is the establishment of central control over local expenditures and debt, through the examination of local budgets and central supervision of local finances and accounting. Examples of this control are found in the provisions of the Indiana law of 1919, already mentioned; the Ohio provision for the state supervision and control of public offices; the operations of the

[1] See previous citations.

REVENUES

county tax conservation commission in Portland, Oregon; and the laws of New Jersey and Massachusetts.[1]

Special taxes

The cost of current activities not secured from general property taxation is derived largely by licensing the conduct of certain private enterprises that require a measure of police regulation, or through the collection of fees for services that the city renders to private individuals. These special taxes[2] are of three types; (1) licenses for revenue, (2) licenses for regulation, and (3) fees.

Licenses for revenue must be authorized specifically by statute or charter provision, and except in Southern states are little used. In general, the idea of a special tax on certain occupations and trades has been repugnant to taxing authorities and to the public. When used, the more common imposts on trades and occupations are taxes on vehicles, merchants, telephone and telegraph companies, express companies, insurance companies and agents, lawyers, theaters, engineers, hotels, boarding houses, livery stables, architects, printers, brokers, agents, dairymen, bakers, mechanical trades, packers, bill posters, doctors, barbers, and others.[3]

Regulatory licences are a common source of city revenue. Such licenses are imposed, under the police power upon such businesses as require special police control. In theory the cost cannot exceed the additional public expense made necessary by the operation of such businesses. However, the courts are not inclined to inquire closely into the judgment of the legislative body on this point unless there is decided evidence of unreasonableness. Such regulatory licenses are employed to control the operations of vehicles for hire, transient merchants, scavengers, peddlers, pawnbrokers, second-hand dealers, auctioneers. pool and billiard rooms, dance halls, bowling alleys, and similar businesses.[4]

Fees are a payment to the city for services rendered and in which the benefit is to a particular individual rather than to the general public. In some instances a public benefit is also had, usually in the way of safety; but the larger service is to the individual. Public interest does, however, frequently dictate what shall be done for private individuals at a fee.[5]

[1] See Clyde J. Crobaugh, "Centralizing Fiscal Tendencies in State and Local Relations," *ibid.*
[2] Strictly speaking, a license is not a tax. A fee is a tax only when it exceeds the cost of the service rendered.
[3] McQuillen, *op. cit.*, III, Chap. XXVI. Francis Oakey, *op. cit.*, 300-301, defines and lists licenses, treating them as regulatory imposts.
[4] *Ibid.*
[5] Oakey, *op. cit.*, 305, for a definition and list of fees.

PRACTICE OF MUNICIPAL ADMINISTRATION

CHAP. V

Fees in lieu of salary

Collection of licenses and fees

As a source of revenue, fees are not exploited as generally as they should be, and cities frequently render special services without cost or at too small a cost. These special benefits include permission to make cuts in pavements, building inspection, elevator inspection, boiler inspection, etc. However, the demarcation between services of public and private benefit is not always clear. Citizens resent payments for which no little or no private benefit is received, and therefore the public usually assumes the cost of inspections and similar activities where the benefit is more general than individual—for example, the inspection of weights and measure, barber shops, restaurants, dairies, etc.

Formerly it was customary for municipal officers to receive fees in lieu of or as an addition to, their salaries. This practice is being done away with, as the citizen charged for a service, frequently not of his own seeking, resents making a payment not destined for the public treasury. Also, certain fees are so very productive that their retention by the public treasury is most desirable. To do otherwise is to over-pay an officer for his services, and make an office a prize for political intrigue.[1]

Licenses are issued ordinarily by a division of licenses in police or treasurer's department, although occasionally other departments function wholly or in part in this connection. Fees are usually collected by the department rendering the service charged for.

Accounting control over the collection of licenses and fees is secured in a number of ways. The usual method is the making of the receipt in duplicate or triplicate by means of carbon paper. This is thoroughly practical when the rate charged is uniform. Otherwise the copies held in the department can be altered easily by a clerk so minded. Another method is by the use of controlled stationery. In such cases receipts are treated as cash, and are charged to the issuing office. This scheme has not been widely used, owing to the possibility of theft, and to the extra accounting that it makes necessary. Where the charge is not uniform, a receipt with a staggered stub can be employed, the stub being so printed that when the receipt is detached the stub indicates the amount charged. A still more practical scheme, for both uniform and non-uniform collections, is the cash register. Registers are

---

[1] The sheriff of New York County is said to receive more than $100,000 a year in fees, and the clerk of Wayne County (in which Detroit is situated), more than $30,000.

available that will print the amount collected and the number of the clerk making the collection both upon the receipt issued the customer and that retained in the department, and upon a triplicate, if necessary. This plan furnishes a large degree of safety and an easy method of audit. Its drawback is the initial cost of installation.

The effectiveness of licenses and fees as a source of revenue depends upon the efficiency of the collection. With fees, collection is usually easy, since the service will not be rendered until the collection is made. Where a graduated fee is charged it is necessary to see that the amount of service is not understated. This is particularly true of the inspection of building plans; and the building department maintains a corps of field inspectors to see that plans are complied with, and that a sufficient fee has been charged.

In some instances fees are not collected until after the service is rendered, as, for example, cuts in pavements, where the work is done by the city for a privately owned utility. This is because the charge is not known until the work is completed. The collection of such charges depends upon the effectiveness of the controlling officer and the department doing the work. When such work is done with the authority of the controller, he retains a control that insures the work department reporting back a charge. The correctness of this charge depends upon the cost records maintained. Public utilities and contractors requiring frequent cuts in pavements will often make a deposit with the proper authorities, against which fees will be charged currently. Once a charge is reported, when a deposit is not made, its collection is a duty of the controller or the treasurer. A uniformed policeman is a most effective collector if the customary mailed statements are ignored.

Licenses can be imposed fully only through continuous inspection. When a license has been issued it is required to be exposed, or a metal tag is supplied indicating that the license for the current year has been paid. Such inspection is properly the function of the police.

The sources of miscellaneous revenues need only be mentioned. They are, chiefly, rents from leased properties, sale of materials, sale of property, fines, grants from other governmental units, leases of under-sidewalk space, payments for franchise privileges, gifts from individuals, uncollected minor claims, etc.

98   PRACTICE OF MUNICIPAL ADMINISTRATION

CHAP. V

Revenue from utility operation

A principal source of city revenue after property taxation is the income from publicly owned utilities and industries—revenue, however, that is more apparent than real. Generally the law provides that such income shall be used to pay operating expenses, provide betterments, and meet interest and debt retirement charges of the utility producing it. This is entirely proper. The patrons of a public utility are neither in theory nor in fact the entire citizen body, and to secure substantial revenue from such utilities for meeting the general operating expenses of a municipality is in fact taxation of a special class. On the whole, however, the complaint is reversed, namely, that publicly owned utilities are constructed from taxation or general bonds, and that the actual deficits of operation are met by taxation, though these deficits are frequently concealed or postponed. The justice of either argument is, of course, open to accounting determination, and one of the signs of healthy municipal progress is the adoption of sound accounting and financial methods in the construction and operation of publicly owned utilities.[1]

Revenues from industries

Municipal industries not in the nature of utilities are few, and their revenues are of small moment. The principal activities of this nature are municipal dance halls, bathing beaches, restaurants, refectories, etc. Most of these are only self-supporting and their finances are so planned. Occasionally cities operate major industries, such as factories in connection with prisons. The revenues from such activities may be substantial, yet they furnish only a small surplus towards the general operating costs of the city.

Collection of utility revenues

Utility revenues are so large, and are drawn from so many individuals, that their proper collection is a major accounting problem. Cities are interested principally in supplying water and electricity—charges for which involve measuring the consumption by many individuals, and the paying of relatively small sums by an equal number. In connection with controlling the revenues of these utilities, the administrator is essentially interested in seeing that a record is had of every establishment receiving service, so that each may be charged for services rendered; that the charges against such establishments are computed accurately; that the computed charges are recorded and billed correctly; and that the cash received actually reaches the city treasury. To be certain that these points are covered involves detailed utility ac-

[1] See Chap. XXXI.

counting with which the general administrator will not be immediately concerned.¹ {CHAP. V}

The operation of municipal industries involves not only the collection of cash receipts, but also production and sales. The administrator must know, among other facts, that purchases of raw materials and supplies are economically made; that the means of production are efficient; that no raw material, and none of the finished product, is lost during the manufacturing process; that sales are being made readily and at best prices; that the producing personnel is efficient; that collections are effective; and that the cash collected is reaching the treasury. All of these things, and others, can be assured through adequate industrial accounting procedure, too complex to be discussed here. {Collection of revenues from industries}

The collection of revenues from refectories and similar agencies presents questions of an entirely different type. Here the city buys finished products and disposes of them at a profit. The simplest method of control is to charge the agent with such goods at their retail prices and make proper credits for losses. For boating, bathing, and dancing privileges the self-recording ticket-vending machine is a help.

The last important source of municipal income is not a revenue at all, except in a limited sense. Such income is derived from temporary unfunded indebtedness, either as unpaid bills or actual borrowings. This floating debt usually occurs in one or more of the following forms: loans in anticipation of taxes, unsecured loans, authorizations in advance of tax levies, unpaid bills, and claim certificates. {Floating debt}

The fact that certain cities do not collect taxes in advance, thereby requiring that loans be made in anticipation of taxes, has been mentioned. Such loans are certainly legitimate, if not economical. The trouble is, however, that cities spend all of their accrued revenues and then borrow on next year's taxes to meet bills of the current year. Loans in anticipation of taxes are, of course, limited to such proportion of next year's taxes as the law permits, or that bankers will agree to furnish. The most desirable procedure is the collection of taxes in advance and the prohibition of borrowing with these taxes as a security. {Loans in anticipation of taxes}

Unsecured loans are of the same nature as loans in anticipation of taxes, except that such loans are not represented by collateral. {Unsecured loans}

¹ For a discussion of water revenues, see Chap. XXVIII.

100 PRACTICE OF MUNICIPAL ADMINISTRATION

CHAP. V

Sometimes such loans, made by agreement among local financiers, serve to tide over emergency situations, or pending the sale of bonds. In the latter instance they are entirely justified; in the former, only most urgent emergencies should be regarded as warranting such loans, and they should be retired by extra tax levies during the period immediately following.

Authorizations in advance of levies

Authorizations in advance of levies are made by practically every municipality. In such instances, departments are authorized to undertake activities not included in the current budget, but which will be included in the next budget. The funds are taken from the total of unexpended money remaining in the treasury, or money that may be borrowed. Such a system partly destroys the budget as a carefully prepared program, but it serves as a means of meeting emergencies when current authorizations have taken up all available funds. Of course, by this practice, one appropriating authority is attempting to pledge the conduct of a future one, which is legally impossible. But such pledges are usually made good, and since the debt is taken up in the succeeding year there are no marked ill effects.

Unpaid accounts

Every city will have some floating indebtedness in the form of unpaid accounts, which is entirely proper when the amounts are known and are represented by authorizations to incur liabilities and by cash in the treasury or anticipated revenues still uncollected. Unpaid accounts are vicious only when officials authorize expenditures in excess of income, leaving a heritage of debt to their successors. Such conduct is a lie to the public as regards the current expenses of the government; it handicaps the incoming administration and breaks down the credit of the municipality. Happily, cities—particularly the larger ones—are preventing such situations by limiting expenditure authorizations to income; and by accounting control they are preventing officials from incurring liabilities without adequate funds being available to liquidate them. When such courses are not followed voluntarily, they should be required by law.

When a city's finances reach a state where funds cannot be borrowed, either with or without security, claim certificates are a last resort. Ordinary bills can be left unpaid, but payrolls must be met in some fashion. This can be done by issuing negotiable claim certificates, sometimes bearing interest payable at some future time when money will be available. The public employee has a choice between resigning his position or accepting this paper,

REVENUES

trusting to the banks or trades people to cash it either at par or at a discount.

Trust funds are, of course, not a revenue at all, in the accepted sense of the word. Revenues may accrue to them, but the funds themselves must be applied to some specific object or objects. Such funds comprehend reserves for the refund of taxes, assessments and water rates paid in error, funds donated for special purposes, fire and police pension funds, together with other adjustments and payments of special nature. The task of keeping such funds intact is simple if public officials are properly inclined. Occasionally trust funds are borrowed as are sinking funds, with liability to similar defects.

The pressure of increasing costs has been commented upon. It has prompted many cities to seek new sources of revenue. Investigations looking to the discovery of new sources, and the greater exploitation of old ones, have been undertaken by nearly every large city and by many smaller ones.[1] Studies of this character have peculiar local applications, and deal largely with constitutional amendments extending to cities larger powers of local taxation or providing more equitable division of revenues between cities and other taxing bodies. Aside from recommendations modifying the powers of taxation on real and personal property, which are always of local significance, these investigations have led to certain recommendations which have common application to many cities, and of which the more important may be noted as follows: reduction in tax exemptions, larger interest from public funds, reduction in interest charges, increased returns from public utilities and industries, increased licenses, increased fees, wider use of special assessments, and more adequate payments for use of public property.[2]

One of the principal suggestions deals with the reduction of tax

---

[1] *Reports of the Joint Committee on Taxation and Retrenchment* (State of New York, Leg. Doc. No. 97, 1925, and Leg. Doc. No. 80, 1920); *Report of the Baltimore Tax Commission* (1923); *Milwaukee's Tax Problem* (Citizens' Bureau, 1921); *New Sources of Revenue for New Jersey Municipalities* (State League of Municipalities, 1921); *Some Phases of the Miscellaneous Revenue Situation in San Francisco* (San Francisco Bureau of Governmental Research, 1920); *Final Report of the Committee on Taxation of the City of New York* (1916); *Report of the Commission on New Sources of Revenue, City of New York* (1913); Lent D. Upson, *Sources of Municipal Revenues in Illinois* (Univ. of Ill., 1912); and C. E. Merriam, *Municipal Revenues in Chicago* (City Club of Chicago, 1906).

[2] Dr. Luther Gulick has truthfully said that the result of these studies indicates that there are no new sources of revenue: merely a further development of old ones and of new economics.

102   PRACTICE OF MUNICIPAL ADMINISTRATION

CHAP. V

Limiting of tax exemptions

exemptions on real property, and urges that the properties of fraternal and benevolent organizations, private sanitariums and hospitals other than free and public hospitals, church property other than the buildings used for worship and religious instruction, and private schools which charge for instruction, be placed on the assessment roll and required to bear their share of the expense of state and local governments. The exempting of church, hospital, and similar property from taxation may be considered in the light of a contribution by the people to these benevolent organizations and purposes, and if the people intentionally and knowingly release the holders of such property from taxation, for the purposes in hand, there is certainly no reason why objection should be entered.

There is some question, however, whether the taxpayers generally understand just what this exemption means to them. For instance, it is estimated that if the exempted property in New York State were taxed for state purposes on the same basis as other property it would contribute one-third of the entire expenses of the state; in other words, if this property were not exempted each taxpayer in the state would have one-third less tax to pay. Certainly a more business-like and more open way of making public contribution to these objects of benevolence would be to collect taxes from them for all real estate which they hold, and to make contribution through municipalities or the state of such sums as it might be desired to allot to each of them. One desirable result of this, it is anticipated, would be to remove the opportunity (now taken advantage of in many cases) for organizations to secure the advantages of exemptions through subterfuge or favoritism.[1]

Larger interest on public funds can be secured by the elimination of the practice of allowing the city treasurer to receive interest on such funds as a perquisite of office, a practice that still prevails in a limited number of localities. Where this usage has been abandoned, it is essential that the city receive the maximum rate of interest on daily balances of all kinds.[2]

Reducing interest payments

Akin to the proposal to secure increased interest is that to reduce interest on the public debt. It is suggested that there be a semi-annual collection of taxes, thus saving interest paid on

[1] See Research Report No. 64, *Tax Burdens and Exemptions* (National Industrial Conference Board, 1923).
[2] See Chap. VII.

temporary loans issued in anticipation of taxes and diminishing tax delinquencies by permitting property owners who are unable to pay the whole tax to pay at least half and go in arrearage for the other half. Some cities do not collect any of their taxes in advance, but borrow money to pay running expenses until the tax is collected, the interest on such loans, of course, being added to the tax levy.

CHAP. V

The possibility of the larger utilization of publicly owned utilities and industries as an added source of current income is discussed more fully in another place.[1] Cities are more and more socializing industries as well as utilities, and it is reasonable to expect that an increasing amount of net revenue will come from these sources, particularly through the sale of land secured by excess condemnation.

Utility revenue

A review of licenses levied in municipalities indicates general tendencies, but no uniformity in scope. Licenses are not popular, and it is generally conceded that the charge for licenses imposed should be regulated by the cost of police supervision. Yet such supervision is made necessary by an increasing number of private activities, and it is proper that they should bear its cost.

Licenses

One of the first results of financial pressure is the development of special assessments to cover the cost of work formerly done from general operating funds. In some instances street repair and street cleaning, as well as street lighting, are paid for by this means. The practice is not general, however, and it is more common to find that street oiling, street sprinkling and flushing, special boulevard lighting, and activities of localized benefit are paid for by this method. Somewhat akin to this are the charges made for snow removal, vault cleaning, street cuts, etc. As the limit of taxation is reached, further recourse must be had to this type of municipal financing.

Special assessments

Fees serve only to reimburse the municipality for costs actually incurred, but there has been a marked tendency to undercharge for services. Practically every commission which has investigated city revenues has recommended that the fee system be revised in order that an adequate return may be secured.

Fees

Cities have large sums invested in leased or idle real estate, the return upon which is notoriously inadequate. Unused city lands are rented on long term leases for small sums, and few cities in the country charge at all for space used on highways.

Public owned **real** estate

[1] See Chap. XXXI.

If public service companies are so regulated as to earn only a fair return on the actual capital invested, this neglect to collect for rent of streets is perhaps justified. Unfortunately, this ideal condition seldom exists. Where business houses are using sidewalk spaces for areaways and where no public benefit can possibly accrue, the absence of a fair rental is absurd. Indeed, these corporations not only fail to pay rent but insist that long use has given them a property right in the street. Chicago has undertaken to collect rental for sidewalk space at the rate of two percent per year on the valuation of one-tenth of the assessed value per square foot. Other cities have drafted similar regulations based annually on the tax value of the property used. Sidewalk space is only one of the important privileges that might be granted with compensation. Others include the right to use public property, either upon or below the street, whether for electric signs, bay windows, switch tracks, or car tracks.

These are some of the more important sources from which new revenues may be obtained. Local conditions differ, and there are sources of revenue peculiar to different localities which, under study, may be discovered and developed. The principal sources of increased returns, however, must be industries, licenses, special assessments, and charges for services rendered.

CHAPTER VI

DEBT [1]

In municipal governments public improvements of a permanent character are ordinarily secured through indebtedness represented by bonds. These bonds are promises to pay certain specified sums of money at the end of a stated period, interest at a definite rate being payable annually or semi-annually during their life. Occasionally such bonds are given directly to the contractor in exchange for the improvement secured, but usually they are sold to investors and the proceeds applied to that purpose.

Municipal bonds are of four main kinds: general bonds, utility bonds, mortgage bonds, and special assessment bonds. Improvements of general benefit, serving the interests of all citizens, are usually financed through the sale of general bonds, so named because they are secured by the "full faith and credit" of the city. The property of the city government and of all citizens is pledged as security and the sums necessary for interest and principal payments are raised by general taxation. The interest and retirement charges on bonds issued for certain utilities may be paid from the earnings of such utilities, but the faith of the city is the essential security, and, so far as the bond purchaser is concerned, public utility bonds do not differ from general city bonds. If the public and private assets of the municipality do not secure such utility bonds, they are secured by a mortgage on the utility itself, and are known as mortgage bonds. Bonds so secured are seldom issued.[2] Public improvements benefiting the property of a limited number of citizens are commonly financed by the sale of special assessment bonds. These bonds are a lien, first upon the property benefited by their issue, and then ordinarily upon all property, public and private, within the city.

Classification of bonds

[1] Helpful texts on bond procedure are Lawrence Chamberlain, *The Principles of Bond Investment* (Holt, 1911), and Fraser Brown, *Municipal Bonds* (Prentice-Hall, 1922). The extent of municipal indebtedness will be found in the *Financial Statistics of Cities* (U. S. Bureau of Census); and the annual compilation of city debt made by C. E. Rightor of the Detroit Bureau of Governmental Research, and published in the *National Municipal Review*.

[2] Mortgage bonds may be issued legally by Detroit for transportation purposes, and by Los Angeles to finance housing. Two million dollars of such bonds have been issued by Bay City, Michigan, to secure a filtration plant.

106   PRACTICE OF MUNICIPAL ADMINISTRATION

<small>CHAP. VI

Methods of financing permanent improvements

The general purpose of bonds</small>

Bonds are issued as a means of distributing the cost of an improvement over a period of years substantially equal to the life of the improvement, and over all persons benefited. Such improvements include trunk sewers, water works, lighting plants and other public utilities, bridges, parks, extensive public buildings, and the acquisition of valuable lands. Except in instances of general emergency, such as the preservation of public safety from the effect of flood, fire, epidemics, etc., bond issues are expedient only when large immediate burdens would be thrown upon the taxpayers of any one period were important improvements to be paid for currently, and the improvement is to be enjoyed over a long period of time. Bonded debt should not be incurred for current expenses or trivial improvements, and when incurred, should be liquidated during the life of the improvement it represents.

<small>Detailed purposes for which debt may be incurred</small>

It is difficult to define the purposes for which public debt may not be entered into, and for that reason state laws and city charters frequently set up definitely the objects for which loans may be authorized, and designate the number of years for which bonds may run before being retired.[1]

In event the life of the bond is not prescribed it is sometimes provided that a competent authority shall certify the estimated life of each issue of bonds, and such bonds shall not run for a longer time.[2] The following purposes and years of life of bond issues are illustrative only:[3]

For funding floating debt	1 year
For departmental equipment	5 years
For emergencies involving public safety and health	5 years
For pavements	15 years
For buildings	20 years
For sewers	30 years
For water mains	30 years
For parks	50 years

<small>Types of bonds</small>

Municipal bonds issued as evidences of debt are further distinguished by the method used in transferring ownership and paying interest. On these bases, there are three types in general use, *i.e.*, registered, coupon, and convertible coupon. Coupon bonds

---

[1] On this subject the legislation of New Jersey is considered as a model. Reference should be made also to the laws of Massachusetts, Ohio, and South Carolina, and the model bond law published by the National Municipal League.

[2] New York City now requires the controller to certify to "probable life of the improvement."

[3] Massachusetts Municipal Finance Act of 1913.

DEBT 107

are payable to bearer and have negotiable interest coupons attached. Title to such securities is conveyed without formality, and the interest is easily collected. The principal disadvantage is liability to loss by theft or fire. Where a more permanent investment is desired, registered bonds, payable to a particular individual who is registered as the owner on the records of the municipality, are preferred. Such bonds are not negotiable and can be transferred only on the books of the city, after proper endorsement upon the bond. Interest is payable to the registered owner, usually by mail, and without production of the bond. Such bonds have the advantage of being safe from accidental loss, and interest is paid without difficulty. Convertible coupon bonds are issued in order that the security may be attractive to all customers. These bonds are issued as coupon bonds, but upon presentation to the proper authorities may be converted into registered bonds. There is really a fourth type of bond which is convertible and reconvertible at pleasure, but such securities are seldom issued because of the expense of printing new bonds when converted from the registered to the coupon type. However, some dealers in municipal securities state that such bonds would be advantageous. Prevailing practice is to issue registered or convertible coupon bonds.

<small>CHAP. VI</small>

After the city council has authorized by resolution the incurrence of debt, the proper city authority, usually the controller or treasurer, proceeds to sell bonds to the amount authorized. Such a bond sale must be advertised for a stated period, and the time and place of the sale set forth specifically. Sales are advertised in the leading financial papers and magazines, but greater dependence is placed upon direct negotiations with banks and financial syndicates. Sealed bids are received, accompanied by a certified check for a prescribed percent of the amount of bonds bid upon. The bids should be opened only in the presence of the proper city authorities, such of the public as appears, and the representatives of the financial institutions interested. After the amount of each bid is read aloud, and memorandum made of it, the offers are essembled and the bonds awarded to the highest bidder. Such offers are always subject to examination and approval of the bonds for legality.

<small>Procedure in sale of bonds</small>

Bids may be for the face of the bonds plus a premium, especially if the interest rate has been set by the city, the amount of the premium determining the highest bid; or in amount of

<small>Methods of bidding</small>

108   PRACTICE OF MUNICIPAL ADMINISTRATION

CHAP. VI

bonds that the city must deliver for a stipulated sum, thus eliminating the premium feature; or in terms of an acceptable interest rate, stated in quarters of a percent, and possibly plus a premium, the best bid being determined by correlating the lowest rates of interest with the highest premium. This latter method of bidding is being generally prescribed by cities, as it returns to the treasury substantially the face amount of the bonds sold. The premium plan of sale usually results in an excess return, an actual borrowing in excess of the authorization. The method of bidding in terms of the amount of bonds to be paid for a stipulated sum is relatively new, but has advantages that highly recommend it.

Collusion in bidding

Very rarely it is expedient to dispose of bonds at private sale, but under all ordinary circumstances municipal authorities should make every effort to insure that bonds are sold under actual competitive conditions. No self-respecting public officer will invite the criticism that justly follows a non-competitive sale. The practice of some bond buyers of submitting bids prearranged with competitors, and later distributing the bonds among all bidders in a combine, is well known. The only real safeguard against this subterfuge is to solicit bids from responsible dealers who will not resort to questionable methods. The selling authority should be authorized under the law to refuse to accept any bids if, in his judgment, the city's interests require such a course.

Marketability

Municipal bonds normally command a ready sale because of security of principal and interest, marketability, and tax exemption. As a result the rate of interest is low; and during a period of high federal income taxes the bonds are eagerly sought since they are exempt from taxation.

Sales below par

Frequently a low rate of interest is prescribed by statute, which is not an unmixed blessing. Under such restrictions, in times of scarce money, cities frequently resort to subterfuge in order to sell bonds bearing rates of interest abnormally below the prevailing market rate. The most common practice is a sale below par, by which procedure the interest rate can be automatically adjusted. When such sales are prohibited by law, or by a desire to maintain the superficial credit of the city, a high sales commission can be given to the bank or brokers disposing of the bonds, which amounts to the same thing. Or an agreement for abatement of interest can be made by which the city undertakes to pay interest on the bonds sold, although the proceeds are not

DEBT 109

immediately turned over to the municipality. Similarly, by a deposit agreement the city may engage to leave the proceeds on deposit for a definite period and at a low interest rate, with the bank buying the bonds, thus allowing the purchaser to profit by the difference between the interest rate on certificates of deposit or daily bank balances and what the funds will bring as short-time loans in the open market.

What has been said should not be interpreted in opposition to the frank sale of bonds below par by a municipality. Such sales are usually forbidden by statute, but perhaps unwisely so. Bonds purchased at par plus a premium must be sold above par by the banks and bond houses. Such re-sales are relatively difficult. It is argued by the bond distributors that money could be bought cheaper by a city if it disposed of its bonds at a few points below face value.[1]

Recently there has been a movement for smaller denominations in bonds—$50 and $100 in place of, or in addition to $500 and $1,000 bonds; and for the sale of bonds directly to citizens. The "baby bond" has never been well established in municipal practice, because the low rate of interest is not attractive to the small investor, and their sale directly to citizens has met with indifferent success. The idea of directly interesting a large number of citizens in their communities through ownership of city securities is itself excellent. But, for obvious reasons, municipal bonds are not readily absorbed by persons of small means. In addition, attempts at disposal "over the counter" antagonize the large bond dealers, who are expected to buy the greater proportion of important issues, and it is not yet a practical municipal policy.

Sales over the counter

The sale of municipal securities to the sinking fund is desirable because a careful purchase of a city's own securities is an excellent method of debt retirement. However, the authorities should beware of the specious argument that this end can be accomplished by the immediate cancellation of such purchases. When a city's own bonds are bought attention must be given to maturities and the annual requirements of the sinking fund. No good purpose is served if a city must throw a mass of bonds, possibly with undesirable maturities, on the bond market in order to secure ready cash for the sinking fund. Some states require that all bonds be

Sales to the sinking fund

[1] This is the argument of the bond broker; some authorities hold that cities have suffered unnecessary losses by this procedure.

110 PRACTICE OF MUNICIPAL ADMINISTRATION

CHAP. VI

offered for sale to the sinking fund commission before being publicly sold.

Frequently the sinking fund is used to purchase bonds, the legality of which is in question. Such a practice removes immediate difficulties, but evades the law, and may involve trouble for a later administration, should it be necessary to sell such bonds in order to secure cash for the fund. The possible results on the credit of the city, with bonds falling due, a depleted fund, and an amount of illegal bonds as assets, can be imagined.

Term, serial, and annuity bonds

The most fundamental differences in municipal bonds occur in the various provisions for redemption, a feature, incidentally, of small concern to the ultimate investor. When all of the bonds of an issue mature after a designated period of years, they are called term bonds, and are retired by the use of a sinking fund. Serial bonds are those retired by paying off a predetermined and equal, or nearly equal, amount of the entire bond issue each year. Annuity bonds require serial retirement of the principal, but with such payments gradually increasing as the interest payments decrease, the total always being substantially the same.[1]

Redemption by sinking fund

A sinking fund is a financial arrangement whereby term bonds are redeemed by setting aside annually a certain sum which is invested and allowed to accumulate until the various contributions, together with their earnings, are sufficient to retire the debt upon maturity. If, therefore, it were possible to determine the earnings of the fund in advance and there could be an absolute guarantee that the annual instalments would be provided from revenue, the sinking fund would form a reasonably satisfactory method of extinguishing debt. Unfortunately, however, these conditions, upon which the successful administration of sinking funds depends, are not always met, and can only be approximated at best by most careful computation and skilful financing, adjusting the sinking fund instalments each year to the earnings of the previous fiscal period. If a sinking fund is maintained the annual calculation is simplified by the use of annuity tables found in many accounting texts.[2]

So many difficulties have been experienced in sinking fund administration that the sinking fund method of debt redemption

[1] A brief article, "Methods of Borrowing—Sinking Fund *vs.* Serial Bonds," appears in *Bulletins for the Constitutional Convention* (Massachusetts), II, 157-170. See also, Laurence I. Hewes, and James W. Glover, *Highway Bonds* (U. S. Dept. of Agriculture, Bulletin No. 136), 14-24.

[2] For examples, see footnote p. 111.

has fallen into considerable disfavor.¹ Legislative bodies frequently fail to make sufficient annual appropriations to meet sinking fund requirements, either deliberately, or because revenues for all purposes are inadequate. Anticipating that at some future time there may be sufficient revenue to make up the deficit without direct taxation, one administration passes the shortage along to the next, which, in turn, rather than meet not only its own but its predecessor's obligations, finds it easier to allow the deficit to continue.² Frequently, officials, seeing that there is sufficient cash in the aggregate of the various funds to meet any one maturing loan, do not realize that a deficiency in a sinking fund exists. They fail to appreciate that there may not be enough money to meet the requirements of all of the several loans at their maturity—a condition demonstrated only by an actuarial calculation showing the requirements of each separate bond issue at a given time.³ Shortcomings of sinking fund plan

Furthermore, the sinking fund method creates temptation to engage in public improvements in advance of needs. This results from the delusion that a sinking fund has some mysterious efficacy whereby a debt can be paid without the burden being greatly felt by the present or future generations. The annual requirements by the sinking fund method for liquidating debt, if interest charges are ignored, seem to be less than if the debt is retired by the serial method; but it is a fallacy to close one's eyes to the significance and costliness of the interest burden carried over a long period of years. Temptation to extravagance

The presence of large amounts of cash in a sinking fund at certain periods is a constant temptation to borrow for current expenses with the intention of returning the loan later. The undesirable possibilities of such a practice are evident. To restrict this practice, as well as to insure interest earnings, some laws pre- Borrowing from sinking fund

[1] Some of these difficulties are enumerated in *Report of a Special Investigation Relative to the Sinking Funds and Serial Loans of the Cities and Towns of the Commonwealth of Massachusetts* (Bureau of Statistics, 1913).

[2] In 1911, the City of Peoria, Ill., was still carrying refunded Civil War bounty bonds for which no sinking fund had ever been provided.

[3] The mathematics applicable to bond calculations will be found in the several books dealing with the accountancy of investment, including Hewes and Glover, *op. cit.*, 35-73; E. H. Turner, *The Repayment of Local and Other Loans* (Ronald, 1913); E. Z. Sprague, *The Accountancy of Investment* (Ronald, 1918); and H. L. Rietz, A. R. Crathorne, and J. C. Rietz, *Mathematics of Finance* (Holt, 1921). Very extensive tables are found in J. W. Glover, *Tables of Applied Mathematics in Finance, Insurance Statistics* (Wakr, Ann Arbor, 1923).

When in 1925 a statute was enacted in Michigan placing all sinking funds on a sound actuarial basis, there was scarcely a governmental unit that did not readjust its sinking fund, usually to care for an existing deficit.

112   PRACTICE OF MUNICIPAL ADMINISTRATION

CHAP. VI

Purchase of illegal securities

Difficulty of calculating sinking fund requirements

scribe the maximum of cash that may be held in the sinking fund.

Practically every city has occasional issues of bonds, the legality of which may be in question and which could not be sold in the open market. The sinking fund authorities may connive in the purchase of such securities by the sinking fund as a means of circumventing the legal safeguards that have been thrown around the incurrence of public debt.

Another source of difficulty is failure to correctly calculate sinking fund requirements. This error is frequent, creating a deficit or surplus in the fund, either of which is undesirable. A deficit may occur because of practices already mentioned, or because interest earnings have been overestimated. A surplus in the sinking fund usually arises because of too large annual instalments,[1] because of an underestimate of interest earnings, because payments are made into the fund at the beginning of the fiscal period rather than on the anniversary of the date of sale, because of premiums received by the fund, and because of real estate sold or other allocated revenues credited to the fund. The presence of either a surplus or deficit in the fund during the life of the bonds effects a change in the required amount of current annual contributions. When a sinking fund is maintained it is a safe plan to calculate the annual and cumulative interest and amortization requirements of each bond issue based upon the assumed earning rate of the fund. This calculation should show the amounts supposed to be in the fund at the end of each regular fiscal period. With such tabulations available, and maintained currently as new bonds are issued, it is relatively simple for the administrator to check the condition of the fund at the beginning of each fiscal period. Any surplus or deficit can be adjusted by increasing or decreasing current payments into the fund.[2] When term bonds are outstanding for which no sinking fund levy has been made, future sinking fund contributions should be upon the

[1] In Dayton, Ohio, the city council formerly appropriated annually the total of each bond issue divided by the number of years of its term, thus entirely ignoring sinking fund earnings. The Detroit charter requires that three-quarters of the total of each bond issue divided by the years of the term be annually appropriated. The result is a deficit on short term, and a surplus on long term bonds.

[2] By state law, all governmental units in Michigan must annually report the condition of sinking fund bond issues outstanding to the state treasurer. The treasurer maintains a current record of the adequacy of each fund. The forms used for this purpose will be helpful to any administrator responsible for sinking fund operations.

basis the years the bonds have yet to run, or if that period is impractical, the bonds should be refunded for not more than a ten-year period.

CHAP. VI

Recently there has been some public discussion of the moral and legal rights of sinking fund authorities to sell sinking fund assets for purposes of reinvestment. Occasions arise when a switch in holdings may result in a higher rate of interest or the securing of a substantial premium. Some authorities hold that securities should be sold only when cash is required for retirement purposes, finding legal objection to any other procedure. It would appear, however, that a business administration of a sinking fund which obtains the highest rate of return consistent with safety is to be endorsed.

Reinvestment of sinking fund assets

Serial bonds are so issued that an equal amount of bonds matures each year, this amount being determined by dividing the amount of the issue by the number of years for which the longest bond is to run.[1] Thus while the annual principal payments are equal, the payments for interest are constantly reduced and the total interest charges are less than for an equal amount of term bonds, for reasons that are discussed later. The maturity of serial bonds should begin within two years of the date of issue, and the maturities should be in substantially equal annual instalments. Cities sometimes violate this principle by arranging serial bond maturities in other than equal amounts and at other than annual periods, or by deferring the first maturity for a considerable number of years. Such bonds are called "deferred serials," or derisively, "jumping serials," and should be treated as term bonds. The serial bond has the merit of simplicity since certain bonds mature each year, and it is only necessary that current funds be made available to pay the instalments maturing and the interest due.

Serial redemption

Much has been written for and against the proposition that serial bonds are less expensive to the taxpayer than are term bonds. The arguments and tables presented are often specious since they fail to consider certain modifying circumstances. For example, it is often assumed that a sinking fund cannot earn at a rate equal to that paid on outstanding securities. Authorities

Cost of sinking fund vs. serial redemption

[1] The Bureau of Municipal Research of Philadelphia reports that of twelve cities in the United States with a population of over 500,000 according to the 1920 census, Philadelphia is the only one that does not issue serial bonds, and that twenty-nine of the thirty municipalities that issued $500,000 or more of bonds in January, 1926, issued only serial bonds in that month.

in cities still having old-fashioned three and one-half percent bonds outstanding know better than this; and many cities invest sinking fund cash in special assessment bonds, paying six percent interest, although the general bonds outstanding carry only four and one-half. It is also assumed that the average life of a serial issue is much less than that of a term issue, and that the interest payments must be proportionately less. Such calculations ignore payments into the sinking fund. The actual difference in the life of the two types of issues is not large. The situation can be best presented by indicating the exactions from the taxpayer, for both principal and interest payments with each type.

From the numerous calculations of the relative cost of term and serial bonds, financial authorities have deduced certain general principles that should guide in the issuing of bonds. First, as the sinking fund earning rate decreases, the saving on serial issues naturally increases. Second, the average annual cost of a serial bond for any given term is less than the average annual cost of a term bond for a like period. As the period lengthens, the difference in average annual cost of the two types of bond increases.

COMPARATIVE COST OF A·$1.00, 4%, 20-YEAR BOND SOLD UPON A SINKING FUND, SERIAL, AND ANNUITY BASIS,—SINKING FUND ACCUMULATED AT 4% ANNUALLY

Sinking Fund Bond

Year	Principal	Interest	Total
1	$ .033582	$ .04	$ .073582
2	.033582	.04	.073582
3	.033582	.04	.073582
4	.033582	.04	.073582
5	.033582	.04	.073582
6	.033582	.04	.073582
7	.033582	.04	.073582
8	.033582	.04	.073582
9	.033582	.04	.073582
10	.033582	.04	.073582
11	.033582	.04	.073582
12	.033582	.04	.073582
13	.033582	.04	.073582
14	.033582	.04	.073582
15	.033582	.04	.073582
16	.033582	.04	.073582
17	.033582	.04	.073582
18	.033582	.04	.073582
19	.033582	.04	.073582
20	.033582	.04	.073582
Total	$ .671640	$ .80	$1.471640

Average Life, 11.79 Years.

DEBT

Serial Bond

Year	Principal	Interest	Total
1	$ .05	$ .04	$ .09
2	.05	.038	.088
3	.05	.036	.086
4	.05	.034	.084
5	.05	.032	.082
6	.05	.030	.080
7	.05	.028	.078
8	.05	.026	.076
9	.05	.024	.074
10	.05	.022	.072
11	.05	.020	.070
12	.05	.018	.068
13	.05	.016	.066
14	.05	.014	.064
15	.05	.012	.062
16	.05	.010	.060
17	.05	.008	.058
18	.05	.006	.056
19	.05	.004	.054
20	.05	.002	.052
Total	$1.00	$ .420	$1.420

Average Life, 10.5 Years.

Annuity Bond

Year	Principal	Interest	Total
1	$ .033582	$ .040000	$ .073582
2	.034925	.038657	.073582
3	.036322	.037260	.073582
4	.037775	.035807	.073582
5	.039286	.034296	.073582
6	.040857	.032724	.073581
7	.042492	.031090	.073582
8	.044191	.029390	.073581
9	.045959	.027623	.073582
10	.047797	.025784	.073581
11	.049709	.023873	.073582
12	.051698	.021884	.073582
13	.053765	.019816	.073581
14	.055916	.017666	.073582
15	.058153	.015429	.073582
16	.060479	.013103	.073582
17	.062898	.010684	.073582
18	.065414	.008168	.073582
19	.068030	.005551	.073581
20	.070752	.002830	.073582
Total	$1.000000	$ .471635	$1.471635

Average Life, 11.79 Years.

Third, the decrease in the average annual cost for any period exceeding thirty-five years is so small that it is doubtful whether the issue of any type of bond for a longer term is ever justified. Fourth, the annual interest cost on any term bond is greater than

116   PRACTICE OF MUNICIPAL ADMINISTRATION

<small>CHAP. VI</small>

<small>Annuity bond retirement</small>

the total average cost of a serial bond (both interest and retirement charges) for any period over forty-one years.

It should be pointed out that serial bonds are not entirely equitable, since the interest payments during the early years are much greater than at later periods when the outstanding debt is largely reduced. This partially nullifies the purpose of bonding, which is to distribute the charges equitably over the period in which the improvement will be enjoyed. However, annuity schemes have been devised by which retirements of principal gradually increase over the life of the bond issue, while the interest payments decrease. By careful computation a sum consisting of interest plus principal can be determined which will be equal for each period. It must be added, though, that such a system has lost the virtue of simplicity and is not in general use. In spite of all objections, the serial plan of debt retirement is rapidly displacing the sinking fund method, and in some states is made mandatory by law.

It may be said in justification of issuing term bonds, that the maintenance of sinking funds offers the only real competition to the organized bond buyers and serves a useful purpose in helping to keep down the rate of interest. Professional bond buyers in general prefer the serial bond because of its resale possibilities. Sinking fund bonds are usually bought by long term investors and are not as frequently resold. Also, term bonds may at times find a market at a more favorable rate of interest than serial or annuity bonds.

<small>Stabilized bonds</small>

Recently, some consideration has been given to the issuance of stabilized bonds in which the payment of both interest and principal is based on an index of commodity purchasing power rather than on actual dollars borrowed. Such bonds provide that the interest and principal shall be paid in a specified amount in dollars in event the commodity index does not vary by a certain percentage from that prevailing at the time of purchase. Should the commodity index vary, the interest rate and the repayment of principal is varied accordingly so that the lender of money actually receives a return equal to the buying power that he advanced. It is reported that these bonds have been issued by at least one American industrial company and that a number of other companies are utilizing commodity indexes as a means of stabilizing wages.

DEBT

Municipal practice with respect to lost and destroyed bonds of the non-registered type is not uniform. Often no provision is made for their replacement. In some instances state law provides that upon evidence that a security has been lost or destroyed, a new security may be ordered issued by a court of competent jurisdiction, the recipient posting sufficient surety to protect the corporation.

As cities have been gradually shifting from the sinking fund to the serial plan of bond redemption, both because of simplicity and because of the saving in interest effected in the latter plan, some consideration has been given to further economy through the adoption of a pay-as-you-go program.[1] Pay-as-you-go means the payment for public improvements out of current taxation, rather than by the issuance of bonds. Its advocates point out that in spite of popular opinion to the contrary, every public improvement, no matter how financed, must sooner or later be paid for by taxation. The issuance of bonds merely postpones the day of reckoning—a moratorium purchased at the cost of all accumulated interest. When a thirty- to forty-year bond is issued, the taxpayer is ordinarily required to furnish two dollars for debt retirement and interest purposes for every dollar received from the original sale of the bond. Most large and growing cities issue bonds in considerable quantities and at reasonably regular periods, one important public improvement coming after another. In other words, there are few cases in which exceptional amounts of money are needed at any specific time. Under these circumstances, worthy projects can be budgeted and undertaken with regularity by the levying of taxes; and in this way the public might be saved the vast sums of interest now running against municipal securities. Of course, there are cases in which a city needs a very large sum of money to carry out important projects immediately. However, such a need probably could have been avoided had requirements been foreseen and apportioned properly over a period of years.

The arguments advanced by the opponents to the pay-as-you-go plan are similar to those presented against the issuance of serial bonds. After the usual statements that each generation should bear the cost of public improvements from which it benefits, which

---

[1] The arguments, pro and con, on the pay-as-you-go plan have been brought out in detail in a number of articles by different writers, appearing in the *National Municipal Review* during the year 1924.

118   PRACTICE OF MUNICIPAL ADMINISTRATION

<small>CHAP. VI</small>

incidence can be secured only through the issuance of bonds covering the life of the improvement, it is pointed out that a dollar in the pocket of the taxpayer is worth more than the same dollar in a sinking fund, or paid out for the liquidation of the cost of permanent improvements. It is urged that in the private enterprise, a dollar earns an unusually large return and that rather than remove this dollar from its private activity to purchase public improvements, it is wiser for the city to borrow the money at the low rates of interest that usually go with municipal securities.

<small>Fallacy of the argument</small>

This argument is sound if every dollar paid in taxes would otherwise be engaged in profitable private business. But it will not do to assume this. Many private dollars are engaged in unprofitable business, and many other private dollars are in no business at all, but are lying idle in the bank or the cracked china cup in the cupboard waiting for the tax-paying day to come around. It is questionable whether the average tax dollar is being withdrawn from lucrative private business, paying some phenomenal return, and put to work paying for public improvements when money for the same purpose can be secured at four or five percent. The most pertinent objection to this position is evidenced by carrying the argument to its absurd conclusion. On the theory presented, it would be wise for a city to collect no taxes for current expenses, but rather to borrow for both operation costs and permanent improvements. Theoretically, the taxpayer could well afford to pay the small rate of interest charged on this money and keep his tax dollars actively engaged in a profit-making business. Were such the case, it would not be long before the debt of a city would exceed all of the tangible wealth in it and the interest and principal charges would far exceed the ability of the public to pay taxes to meet them.

<small>Pay-as-you-go in New York and Chicago</small>

The pay-as-you-go scheme was brought to the fore in New York City shortly before the World War. At that time the banks of the city prevailed upon the municipal authorities to adopt the pay-as-you-go plan for non-revenue-producing improvements. It was decided that the transition would be made over a period of four years, one-quarter of the public improvements being financed from taxes the first year, one-half the second, and so on. Revenue-producing improvements were to continue on a bond basis. However, before the plan could be put in effect, the war made delay necessary and the city has now discarded the plan. Chicago has been notably on the pay-as-you-go plan with respect to school building, and the debt of this city is still one of the lowest of the large municipalities.

There is little question that the pay-as-you-go plan should be adopted, particularly for recurring improvements such as school buildings, fire stations, street improvements, and other improvements of this nature, which cost moderate sums of money and recur year after year.

The difficulty of making the transition from the bond to the pay-as-you-go plan arises from the amount of taxes that must be levied at any particular time. If a city could declare a construction holiday for a few years, such a transition might be made, but such a step is seldom possible. Also, the pay-as-you-go plan contemplates a budgeting of public improvements over a definite period of time, and the raising each year of an amount of taxes sufficient to carry its share of the public improvements. Unless public opinion in a city is pretty well convinced of the desirability of this move, it is relatively simple for an administration to issue bonds for public improvements, make an impressive showing for the administration with respect to the tax rate, and saddle the burden upon the future.

However, the rapid increase of public debt is turning the attention of the taxpayers to the subject, and it is to be assumed that the next few years will see more and more cities giving attention to pay-as-you-go proposals. It, like many other advances, is based upon the education of the public to an appreciation of its own best interests. Without definite commitment to a pay-as-you-go policy, many cities pay for minor public improvements from current revenue, and this is particularly true of public utility improvements. Ordinarily the operating surplus of publicly owned utilities may not be turned into the general fund of a city, and perforce is invested in means for rendering better service.

The past ten years has witnessed a remarkable increase in the debts of municipalities. The causes of this increase are too numerous and complex to justify lengthy discussion at this point. It will be sufficient to recall to the administrator the substantial increase in all wealth during recent years, a certain proportion of which increase may justifiably be expended by government; the improved standards of living that have made necessities out of improvements that were once luxuries; the decreased purchasing power of the dollar that throws all comparisons out of joint; and finally, the inclination of cities to engage in revenue-producing activities. In the last analysis, it is immaterial whether a utility

120 PRACTICE OF MUNICIPAL ADMINISTRATION

CHAP. VI

Limitations on bonded debt

is publicly or privately owned, so far as the evidences of debt are concerned.[1]

The growth of taxation and indebtedness has naturally directed attention to methods by which they may be controlled. Limits are usually placed on bonded debt, either by state statute or charter. Frequently these limitations not only govern the gross debt, but operate to control the amount of debt that may be incurred for specific projects, such as schools, public utilities, general improvements, etc. The limitations run as high as ten percent of the assessed valuation, but in a majority of cases are about five percent, with frequent exceptions by which self-supporting utilities, special assessments, and debt incurred for emergencies are placed outside of the limitation. Mr. R. C. Atkinson, of the Ohio Institute, who has given considerable study to the limitations of taxation and debt, states that the method of limiting debt to a percentage of the assessed valuation is most common, although other limitations, such as regulations as to the purposes for which bonds may be issued, restrictions upon the terms for which bonds may run, requiring that all bonds be of the serial type, and requiring popular authorizations for the issuance of certain types of bonds, are provided.[2]

Need for limitations

The general desirability of some type of debt limitation is generally recognized; otherwise the demand for public improvements would frequently raise the local debt beyond the limit of wisdom and jeopardize public credit, or impose unfair burdens upon future taxpayers. Without such regulations a city might issue an excessive amount of bonds, extend the life of the bonds beyond the life of the improvement, or fail to make adequate provisions for the retirement of bonds.[3] The basing of public debt upon taxable values is open to some question, because it applies with equal force to municipalities of every size. In this way it is open to the same criticisms as is a uniform limitation on tax rates for all cities, regardless of their needs. As a result, large cities, which have an extensive demand for public improvements, are prompted to increase their assessed values in order to provide

---

[1] For the present debt situation of the more important cities of the United States see previous citations. In examining these comparisons it should be remembered that the real test of indebtedness is not the amount, but the wisdom of the permanent improvements represented by the debt.

[2] R. C. Atkinson, "Tax and Debt Limit Laws," *Proceedings of the Seventeenth Annual Conference on Taxation* (1924) 151.

[3] *Ibid.*, 153.

additional borrowing power. This works a decided injustice in case such real estate is taxed for state and county purposes without some means of equalization. The average large city will find its real estate assessed at nearer one hundred percent of its true value than is country property. In consequence the city pays far more than its share of state taxes on realty.

The principal factor, however, in controlling the debt of the more important municipalities is not local limitations, but rather the limitations that are imposed by the state in which the securities of such cities must be sold. Most small cities having a limited debt find a ready local market for their securities in their immediate vicinity. However, the larger cities, with a heavy public debt ranging upward from $100 per capita, must look for a market in localities that are in a position to absorb large issues of securities. These localities are particularly the states having surplus wealth available for investment—Massachusetts, Connecticut, New York, and Pennsylvania particularly. In these states are found large savings banks, insurance companies, and estates that are making investments in municipal bonds. All of these states rigidly prescribe the character of investments that may be made by these institutions, and in doing so place certain qualifications on the municipal bonds that may be bought, including a maximum ratio of debt to assessed value. In determining this limitation, exemption is usually made of bonds issued on behalf of self-supporting water works, and money or securities in the sinking fund, etc. Cities which look to New York as a market for their securities are not so much interested in their own bond limitation as they are in the so-called New York seven percent law.

There are certain public improvements, such as street paving, lateral sewers, and sidewalks, which benefit certain individuals more than the general public. The cost of such public works is usually distributed between the public and the individuals concerned. The public's share is raised by the issuing of bonds or by general taxation; the remainder is assessed against the specially benefited property and is paid in cash or in a series of instalments with interest. When payment is made in instalments, the public assumes responsibility for the indebtedness, and usually issues bonds for the entire amount, but the individuals concerned pay interest on these bonds, and eventually retire them by payment of charges which are placed upon their tax bills, over a period of

122 PRACTICE OF MUNICIPAL ADMINISTRATION

CHAP. VI

For benefits received

Purpose

from four to ten years, sometimes longer. This system is one of special assessment.[1]

When private property is improved by the special assessment method there is an assumption that the assessment will not exceed the benefits received, otherwise there would be a taking of private property for public use without compensation. However, the method of measuring the benefit must be determined by the legislative body of the city, and, unless palpably unjust, is usually upheld by the courts.

The specific purposes for which special assessments may be used are controlled by state and local legislation. In a general way, the improvement must be of a public character but with a local application. Special assessments are usually authorized for opening, widening,[2] grading, curbing, and paving streets;[3] construction and maintenance of sidewalks; street parking; planting and maintaining shade trees; street widening and alteration; street sprinkling; street cleaning; construction of sewers; street lighting equipment and operation; laying water pipes; and acquisition of parks. Many public improvements and most current activities have such general benefits that the local benefit is usually overlooked and the cost is met by general taxation. The increasing cost of local government and the limits on general property taxation may, however, induce municipalities to undertake such activities as street cleaning, rubbish removal, garbage collection, etc., by means of special assessments.[4]

---

[1] The outstanding book on this subject is Victor Rosewater, *Special Assessments* (Columbia University, 1898). See also, Eugene McQuillan, *Municipal Corporations*, V, 4323, for the law of special assessments.

[2] In many cities it is a practice to assess from seventy-five to eighty-five percent of opening and widening streets against the abutting property, or in assessment districts arbitrarily laid out by the council. Most of these widenings and openings are designed to take care of increased traffic, which is detrimental to residential property. However, benefits in both residential and business districts are measured by the same standards.

[3] In some cities the cost of laying the first pavement is charged against the abutting property and the re-paving, re-surfacing and repair is paid by the city at large. Other cities charge from twenty-five to fifty percent of the re-paving and re-surfacing to the abutting property. Most cities apportion paving costs against the abutting property according to the frontage, and do not consider the shape of the parcel nor the use for which the property is restricted. This practice sometimes becomes confiscatory, particularly in the paving of side streets to relieve traffic.

[4] The extent to which special assessments are used for improvements in a growing city is seen in the data from Detroit. In 1925, this city, with a total of 389,246 parcels of property, levied special assessments on more than 57,238 of these parcels as follows: street paving, 30,828 parcels, $8,603,456.04; alley paving, 12,852 parcels, $1,164,526.16; street openings, 13,558 parcels,

In establishing the boundaries of the assessment district and determining the extent to which each property located within the district is benefited, the legislative body usually acts upon the advice of its engineers and assessing officers. Because a property is exempt from general taxation, it does not follow that it will be relieved from special assessments. In practice, however, religious and educational institutions, and properties of the national government, are exempted from such taxes by express statutory provision.

<small>CHAP. VI</small>

<small>Property subject to assessment</small>

The method of apportioning the cost of improvements may be prescribed by law; otherwise the legislative body may adopt any reasonable plan. The more usual methods are: (1) according to the value, without regard to improvements, (2) according to frontage benefited, (3) according to area, and (4) according to the exact cost of the work done in front of each property. Frequently, to prevent the assessment of improvements out of all proportion to the value of the property benefited, some restriction may be imposed, limiting the assessment to a proportion of the value of property assessed. If the benefit cannot be secured within this proportion, the remainder must be met by general taxation. In frequent practice this proportion is based upon the valuation before the improvement. Perhaps a sounder plan would be a proportion of the value after the improvement is made.[1]

<small>Methods of apportionment</small>

Not all of the cost of the improvement need be borne by the benefited property owners. Occasionally, for an important project, such as a street opening and widening, as much as fifty percent of the cost is borne by the city at large. On smaller projects, it is customary for the city to pay for property exempted from assessment, street intersections, or a fixed percentage of the cost estimated as sufficient to compensate for such charges.

The proper authority—usually the legislative body of the municipality, but sometimes specially authorized boards or commissions —will authorize a public improvement by resolution outlining the benefited district. The owners of benefited property should have adequate notice of the proposed improvement and assessment, and public hearing upon the project be allowed. Usually assessments are made after the improvement is completed and its cost

<small>Mechanics of special assessments</small>

$2,965,610.86; sidewalks, $394,625.99; tree planting, $50,680.25; total, $13,178,899.30.

[1] Otherwise, the general taxpayers may create values for private benefit. In an instance that came to the attention of the writer, a city constructed expensive street improvements into otherwise inaccessible land of little value. Assessments were limited to one-third of the value of the property before the improvement, so nearly its entire cost was paid by general taxation.

124   PRACTICE OF MUNICIPAL ADMINISTRATION

CHAP. VI

is known. Occasionally, assessments are made upon estimate before the contract is let. This practice has resulted almost inevitably in over- or under-assessments, usually the former. The task of making the necessary rebates is enormous, and, where the amounts are small, prompts evasion of the law by the authorities. It has also been charged that when assessments are made in advance upon city engineering estimates, contractors are placed to advantage in preparing their bids. The preparation of the assessment after the work is completed involves the difficulty of paying the contractor as work progresses. If he has to wait until the work is concluded, this inconvenience must be charged for and added to the contract price. Certain cities make no efforts to obviate this difficulty, while others maintain a rotary fund for the purpose.

Cash and deferred payments

After the work has been completed, or the proper estimate of cost has been made, the special assessment division of the city—usually in the public works department or controller's office, but preferably the assessor because of his knowledge of property values, estimates the assessment upon each parcel of property benefited. The property holder is allowed to pay the entire amount within a specified time, or the charge is placed as a lien against the property to be paid in annual instalments, along with the general property taxes. In this latter event, special assessment bonds are issued to cover the amounts unpaid.

Payment of contractor

Frequently the special assessment bonds issued to cover the unpaid portion of special assessments are given to the contractor in payment for his contract. Such a procedure results in increased bids for the improvement by the contractor to cover his inconvenience, and in the peddling of these bonds at a discount in order to secure ready cash. The most satisfactory procedure is for the city to issue bonds in lieu of deferred payments, sell the bonds, and pay the contractor in cash. When such a procedure is not legal, cities can arrange for the sinking fund to assume all special assessment issues, or for a bank to do so, thus insuring the contractor payment in cash.

Organization for debt control

As has been indicated, the issuance of bonds for public improvements involves not one city authority, but several. Projects first originate in the department immediately concerned, and are approved by the chief executive and the legislative body of the city, authority to issue bonds being formally given. The actual issuance and sale is an activity of the controller or treasurer. At this point, if term bonds are issued, sinking fund authorities must make provision for the retirement of the bonds, computing the annual sinking fund and interest charge and requesting adequate appropriations for the same. The sinking fund authority is usually a commission of from three to seven members. Sometimes these members are appointed by the chief executive or the legislative body; more often the commission is made up of certain city officials ex-officio, including the mayor and all financial officers. The detailed duties of the commission are transacted by a secretary, the city controller ordinarily filling this position in addition to his regular duties.

CHAPTER VII

TREASURY [1]

Custodial distinct from auditing authority

The collection, custody, and disbursement of public funds are proper activities of the office of the city treasurer, an accounting control of these fiscal activities being held by the auditor. In early governments, the combined custodial and auditing duties were exercised by a single individual, the treasurer not only receiving and disbursing funds, but making any required accounting for his stewardship. Thus, the early treasurer was an important officer, upon whose ability and integrity rested the financial well-being of the government. The creation of the office of auditor, which appears early in American city governments, made the treasurer a purely custodial agent whose transactions were subject to check by a second and independent authority. Apart from connivance with the accounting official, the only opportunity for substantial defalcation on the part of the treasurer is an actual physical absconding with funds. As a result, the duties of the office are routine and mechanical, calling for no more than ordinary discretion, through requiring attention to important details.

Position of the treasurer in American city government

In American city government, however, the office of treasurer has retained much of the glamour of its former greatness. Under these circumstances it is not surprising to find that the city treasurer is often elected—almost always so in loosely organized municipalities. Independence of the treasurer from control of the spending authority is supposed to safeguard funds, although actual protection is not secured in any such manner. Under city-manager organization, practice runs to the other extreme, and the financial duties of both custody and audit are frequently centralized in a single authority. In this situation, public funds should always be safeguarded by periodic, if not continuous, audits by some agent independent of those in power. The most suitable method of selecting the treasurer is appointment by the chief ad-

[1] See Martin L. Faust, *The Custody of State Funds* (National Institute of Public Administration, 1925); New York Bureau of Municipal Research, *Handbook of Municipal Accounting* (Appleton, 1913), Chaps. VIII and X; and D. C. Eggleston, *Municipal Accounting* (Ronald, 1914), Chaps. IX, XI, and XVI.

ministrator of the city; and other means than independence of position should be relied on to insure the safety of public money.

While the general duties of the treasurer are those of collection, custody, and disbursement of money,[1] there is no uniformity as to organization for these purposes, much depending upon how far these activities, particularly the collection of revenues, are shared with other city, county, and state authorities. In many communities the duties of the treasurer are essentially custodial. He receives money collected by other governmental agencies, sees that such sums are properly cared for, and disburses them upon proper warrant. The actual collection of revenues is left to the different departments with which such revenues originate. No definite principles have been laid down with respect to how far the treasurer should be concerned with the collection of revenues. Certainly there are many minor revenues which it is impracticable for his office to collect. One would scarcely expect a citizen paying a minor fee into a department to appear at that department to have the fee calculated and the proper warrant drawn, and then visit the treasurer's office in order actually to pay the amount charged. Such procedure would involve so much routine as to be ridiculous. In case of large sums of money, it would appear reasonable for citizens to obtain warrants or bills from the proper departments and make payments at the treasurer's office. In this way the opportunity for defalcation would be reduced and accounting control over such payments would be easier to maintain. On the whole, however, it may be assumed that minor collections will be made by practically every city department and that the treasurer will continue primarily as a depositary of public funds.

The principal exception to this rule is the collection of taxes. In some jurisdictions, of course, tax collection is assumed to be a state function and taxes are collected by county authorities, rather than by the city. However, more frequently, tax collections are made directly by the city treasurer, at least in the case of taxes levied for the municipality. In certain cities, as Philadelphia, the receiver of taxes also collects water bills, a procedure of doubtful wisdom. In event the treasurer collects taxes, it is necessary to set up annually extensive machinery for preparing, distributing, and collecting many thousands of tax charges—several hundred thousand in large cities. In addition, provision must

[1] Ordinarily it is desirable that all money received by a city pass through the treasury. For a discussion of this subject, see Chap. IV.

128   PRACTICE OF MUNICIPAL ADMINISTRATION

CHAP. VII

be made for recording delinquent taxes and for the sale of property upon which taxes remain unpaid.

The methods used for collecting taxes in American cities are archaic, and similar business practices would not be tolerated in the collection of charges made by privately owned utilities. As a rule, the owner of property is compelled to appear at the tax collection office, describe his property, and pay the bill when presented. This procedure involves standing in line, sometimes for hours, first to secure the tax bill, and second to make the payment. If a taxpayer owns a number of pieces of property, he will usually prepare a list of descriptions and present it to the collector by mail and receive the proper bills in the same manner. However, the smaller property owner seldom does this. Owners of property who live out of town must make application to the collector for tax bills, which involves keeping careful account of the pieces of property of which they are owners.

Pre-billing of taxes

A preferable plan is that of pre-billing taxes and the mailing of bills to all property owners. The principal difficulty involved in this procedure arises from the fact that the assessors take no account of ownership, assessments being made against specific pieces of property and not against individuals. This situation can be remedied in part by placing the name of the last owner upon the roll, the tax collector making every effort to keep the rolls up to date. This may be done from the record of transfers filed with the county recorder of deeds, and by making such corrections as come to his attention through the return of tax bills that cannot be delivered properly, and by changes that may be indicated on bills returned by former owners. This system of pre-billing does not necessitate as much detail as a method of ledger control, which involves opening a ledger account with each property owner, making additions and deductions as transfers occur, and rendering to the taxpayer annual accounts of his liability to the community. The pre-billing of taxes has been very successful in the cities in which it has been tried. It is a satisfaction to the taxpayer to know that his bill will be mailed to him in ample time for payment without further attention on his part, and statistics indicate that the amount of delinquent taxes is decidedly reduced by this method.[1]

[1] Pre-billing is used in a number of larger cities, including Detroit, Boston, and Baltimore.

TREASURY

Pre-billing also facilitates the installment payment of taxes which is popular with both large and small taxpayers. Such payments, however, increase the costs of collection and reduce the interest earnings on city deposits.

<small>CHAP. VII</small>

<small>Installment payments</small>

Taxes normally are collected in advance of the year on which they apply. When based upon real estate they are relatively easy of collection, as taxes are a lien upon the property involved and the property may be sold to liquidate the claims of the municipality. When taxes become due, a limited period is provided for payment to the proper authorities, and sometimes a small discount is allowed for promptness. After this period of grace, a penalty in the form of interest accrues over a definite period, usually not to exceed one year. It is then customary to sell the delinquent taxes at public auction, the buyers being largely a professional group, who invest in these securities. The exact procedure followed in the sale of delinquent taxes varies in different states. Always, however, a penalty (sometimes reaching 100 per cent of the tax) is assessed, and there is a given period during which the property may be redeemed by dealing either with city authorities or with the persons purchasing the delinquent taxes. After a stated period, it is customary to give a tax title to the purchaser, either directly by the municipality or by some court of record.

<small>Collection of taxes</small>

<small>Collection of delinquent taxes</small>

Numerous abuses have grown out of this system of collecting municipal taxes, but only a few citizens are affected by tax sales procedure, and consequently public opinion is slow to bring about a reform of methods. A person who has failed to pay taxes on property because of neglect or force of circumstances, or because payment has been made in error on the wrong piece of property, is forced to pay unreasonable penalties to the purchaser of the delinquent taxes, or if a brief period of time has elapsed, the title of the property may have passed to others, at perhaps a small fraction of its real value.

<small>Abuses in system of collection</small>

Some authorities have suggested that modern tax sale laws should require that a graduated, progressive interest or penalty rate be imposed on delinquent taxes. This penalty should begin at a minimum of about ten per cent and reach a maximum of say fifteen per cent after four or five years. Always during the penalty period the property owner should have the right to redeem his property by paying the delinquent taxes and accumulated penalties directly to public officers.

<small>Modern tendencies in collection</small>

While it is not desirable for a city to issue tax titles directly, there must be some means of eventually enforcing a claim arising from the purchase of delinquent taxes. It is suggested that the law should provide that after the elapse of a reasonable period of time, possibly six or eight years, foreclosure proceedings may be brought in some court of record to liquidate all accumulated claims. Such proceeding would be a judicial and not an administrative act. In consequence full justice would be done the property owner as well as the purchaser of the tax title. In the end the property would be sold at approximately its full value and a marketable title secured.[1]

Under this system the owner has an absolute right to redeem delinquent taxes by direct payment to the city treasurer until some competent court has foreclosed this right of redemption. This eliminates the absurdity of an owner being limited to one or two years after a tax sale for redemption of the property and then being required to negotiate a settlement with some private tax buyer, perhaps located in another city. So far as competition at delinquent tax sales is concerned, provision should be made that the tax buyer shall bid on the delinquent tax plus a rate of penalty to be enforced.

A few cities, notably Philadelphia, do not sell delinquent taxes, the arrears being handled by the city itself in a department of arrears. This practice is never satisfactory. However just the penalties, officials are constantly being importuned by citizens to have them released. In consequence, the city does not actually receive its delinquent taxes promptly and a large amount of them are taken off the books because of action by the legislative body. At the same time, it is necessary to build up an expensive arrears department to handle these accounts.

Interest on funds in the custody of the treasurer is one of the sources of municipal revenue frequently neglected in smaller communities. This arises from two causes—first, some cities do not take the trouble to secure a proper rate of interest on deposits; and second, public funds are often handled in such a manner that an adequate return is impossible.

---

[1] This method of enforcement by simple tax foreclosure is a common procedure in the eastern states of the country, and universal in New York and New Jersey.

These suggestions for improving the methods of collecting delinquent taxes were made in a memorandum submitted to the Council and City Treasurer of Detroit by Mr. Charles H. Wiltsie of Rochester, N. Y.

TREASURY 131

Too frequently cities are required by charter or state law to divide their money into a number of separate funds. Some distinction should be made between general tax money, money from the sale of bonds, and money to be devoted to the sinking fund; and these should be kept in separate accounts. But it is absurd to divide the general revenues of the city into a number of different funds, each for a specific purpose. When such divisions are made it often happens that money in one fund is temporarily exhausted while ample money is available in another. As a result, it is not at all unusual to see a city borrowing large sums of short-term money at a high rate of interest when it has on deposit in the same institution ample funds receiving little or no interest. The solution of this difficulty lies in keeping practically all public money in one fund, the auditor maintaining separate accounting for each of the proper divisions. In this way the temporary exhaustion of one fund can be made up by short-term borrowing from a fund in which there are ample means.

CHAP. VII

Deposit of funds

In some cities it is customary to borrow from taxes when there is ample money on hand, in order to carry on public construction work that would ordinarily be met by the sale of bonds. In this way, the sale of bonds can be postponed to meet a more satisfactory market. This procedure is not generally recommended, as there is no saving in the long run, but it may be necessary at times when the financial authorities are entering into negotiations which may mean a low interest rate. Borrowing from sinking funds is not recommended, and these should always be kept separate from other funds. On the whole, however, the city controller can maintain an adequate control over public moneys devoted to specific purposes without depositing these moneys in separate accounts. To do otherwise would be as absurd as for a householder, instead of maintaining a single bank account, to maintain a dozen bank accounts, one for each particular item to which he had budgeted his income.

Public funds on deposit in local and foreign banks should always earn a substantial rate of interest and be protected by a surety bond.[1] In smaller cities these earnings are sometimes prevented by connivance among banks. In these instances, if the administrator can overcome political pressure he is usually able

Interest on deposits

---

[1] Such bonds are not only a direct protection to deposits, but insure a thorough investigation of the bank by independent interests.

132 PRACTICE OF MUNICIPAL ADMINISTRATION

CHAP. VII

to get a bid from out-of-town banks which will bring the local depositories to reason. Depositories are usually named by the city on a competitive basis, the amounts deposited having a direct relation to the combined capital and surplus of each bank. The contracts are let for a fixed period of time, although occasionally indeterminate contracts are entered into which can be annulled by either party upon reasonable notice. Bids are taken upon three types of funds: sinking funds, reserve funds, and checking funds. It is obvious that a checking account should receive a lower rate of interest than funds that will not be drawn upon for a considerable period of time. Also, the bank holding a checking account is compelled to undertake all of the bookkeeping that goes with the numerous checks that are issued by a municipality. The usual procedure is to let one or two banks act as checking banks, the balance of the funds being placed on reserve deposit to be drawn upon only as necessary. When occasion requires, considerable sums of money can be transferred by official check from the reserve fund to the checking fund. Funds inactive for a number of months should be invested in certificates of deposits. Sinking funds are usually kept on deposit only to meet bonds and coupons falling due, or pending investment in securities, and some state laws prescribe the maximum amount of sinking fund cash that may be kept on hand. Larger municipalities usually keep certain sinking fund moneys on deposit in the banks of the larger centers, such as Chicago and New York, in order to meet obligations presented at these points. Frequently, city bonds are made payable in New York. It is unusual for the correspondent bank to pay interest on deposits, it being assumed that any interest earned on such deposits are in a sense a compensation for handling bonds and coupons.

Payrolls

One of the important activities of the treasurer's office is the meeting of the numerous payrolls received from the several city departments. This task involves not only the preparation of checks for regularly salaried civil service employees, the payment of whom may become a fixed routine, but also the preparation of checks and cash for the large number of wage earners whose employment is irregular and who must be paid on the job, and frequently paid in currency. The preparation of payrolls is discussed in another section,[1] inasmuch as the city treasurer deals with these rolls only after they have been prepared and certified by the de-

[1] See p. 147.

TREASURY

partment head and approved by the city controller and the civil service commission. When presented to the treasurer, these rolls represent a completed period of work, usually two weeks for wage earners. As they have had to be approved by several departments, they are presumably several days in arrears when actually received by the treasurer's office. It is then his duty to draw the checks necessary to meet the rolls as expeditiously as possible, and distribute these checks to the proper persons. When checks are used, it is customary to pass them down to sub-department heads, who become responsible for their distribution to the persons concerned. This plan is simple, but it furthers any scheme of payroll padding that may be on foot, inasmuch as the treasurer's agents do not see the person who actually receives the check. This situation may be avoided by having the employee call at the treasurer's office for his check, as is done frequently with employees who are distributed widely over the city, and whom it would be difficult to pay off on the job. The drawback to this plan is that employees frequently take half a day to go to the city hall and get their check and return to duty. When this is done by hundreds of employees, once every two weeks, the amount of time lost to the city becomes considerable.

When employees are paid in currency, as must be done on all emergency work, and in some instances with day labor, it is customary for the payroll clerks to go directly to the job with the cash made up in envelopes. In such cases, the signature of the employee is required on the payroll as a receipt for this envelope. Proper protection of course, must be given to the payroll clerks, and they usually perform their activities in an armored car. In cases of purely emergency work, such as snow removal, where the employees must be paid off daily, it is necessary for a representative of the treasurer's office to appear personally on the job. The men are paid off in currency without the preparation of a payroll, but upon the time records of the superintendent in charge of each job, taking the signature of the employee or more often of the superintendent as a receipt of payment. Or payments may be made by the department concerned from imprest cash later reimbursed by the treasurer.

The question of whether all employees, particularly those on wage rates, should be paid by check or currency is gradually being resolved in favor of the check system. In other days it was alleged that the cashing of such checks was a hardship on the em-

134 PRACTICE OF MUNICIPAL ADMINISTRATION

CHAP. VII

ployee, who not infrequently spent some portion of his pay in a saloon in order that the check might be cashed by its proprietor. However, with the gradual increase in the standards of living, the establishment of branch banks and of savings accounts by wage laborers, the necessity of paying off in cash has gradually decreased.

Records

While the duties of the office of treasurer are routine and perfunctory, certain records must be maintained that require careful and accurate bookkeeping. Among the most important are records showing receipts by funds, disbursements by funds and depositories, complete records of accounts receivable, whether they be from taxes, special assessments, or miscellaneous sources, and records of cash deposited and withdrawn by fund and depositary. The treasurer must be in a position to report daily the total cash on deposit in the various depositories of the city and to check the monthly statements from banks and the computation of interest accruing to the city on average daily balances. Some of these tasks are laborious. When the treasurer collects general city taxes and special assessments, detailed records must be kept of the condition of all tax and assessment rolls, showing accounts receivable by parcels of property and total receivables by fund. In the larger cities this routine requires considerable clerical help, and its cost becomes an item to be reckoned with in the compilation of the annual budget.

CHAPTER VIII

ACCOUNTING [1]

A modern city is a great business corporation, employing thousands of men and women; owing vast properties, equipment and supplies; borrowing large sums of money on its credit; securing larger sums through its powers of taxation—all for the purpose of engaging in extensive and diversified activities for the benefit of the community. The collection and disbursement of large sums of money, the ownership of property, and the responsibility for debt should be facilitated and safeguarded by the maintenance of proper records indicating the character and result of all financial transactions. Considering the many centuries during which organized government has existed and has exercised its elementary function of acquiring and expending money, it might be expected that a science of governmental accounting would have reached a high degree of development. Exactly the contrary is true. Neither as a means of preventing fraud and waste nor as a source of information upon which to base administrative action are the accounting records of most American cities equal to those to be found in any private enterprise of equal magnitude.

The importance of accounts

Today, many municipalities concern themselves only with cash receipts and cash disbursements. They permit departments to incur liabilities without the authorization or knowledge of the accounting authorities, and maintain no control over publicly owned properties. In consequence, liabilities may be incurred in excess of appropriations and will be liquidated from funds belonging to another fiscal year, or the appropriations themselves will be in excess of the actual income of the city, creating a deficit eventually

Defects in municipal accounting

---

[1] Important references on municipal accounting are Francis Oakey, *Principles of Governmental Accounting and Reporting* (Appleton, 1921); D. C. Eggleston, *Municipal Accounting* (Ronald, 1914); and New York Bureau of Municipal Research, *Handbook of Municipal Accounting* (Appleton, 1913). Official city accounting manuals are also valuable, particularly John M. Walton, *Manual of Accounting, Reporting, and Business Procedure of the City and County of Philadelphia* (1917); Herman A. Metz, *Manual of Accounting and Business Procedure of the City of New York* (1909). For current reference, see *Proceedings of the National Association of Comptrollers and Accounting Officers* (annual); and *Journal of Accounting* (monthly). Lloyd Morey, *Introduction to Government Accounting*, and *Manual of Municipal Accounting* are now being published by the Wiley Accounting Series.

136   PRACTICE OF MUNICIPAL ADMINISTRATION

CHAP. VIII

represented by floating or unfunded debt. Income, the earning for a definite period derived from taxes levied, licenses issued, rentals of property, etc., is seldom correctly treated. All governmental income for each fiscal year should be accrued and established in the records of that year irrespective of the date collected. Appropriations made upon the basis of expected income would limit expenditures, prevent deficits, and also prevent losses in the collection of amounts due. This last is particularly true of the income from rents and leases on record in a division of the government having charge of public property but having no connection with the collection of public money. When public property is not controlled, not only are movable goods diverted from public use, but even real estate may pass into private hands without adequate compensation.[1]

Development of modern accounting methods

Recognizing these defects, efforts made by New York, Philadelphia, Cleveland, Detroit, and other cities, and particularly those with the city manager form of government, have resulted in sound accounting systems being completely or partially installed, and in the use, when possible, of mechanical equipment for accounting purposes. These systems have been modeled closely upon those common to better managed private businesses, and with such additional controls as are made necessary by the public character of city business. In few instances have all desirable details been completed.[2]

Purpose of accounting

The purpose of such modern accounting methods is to record in detail the results of all business activities, in order that at any time there may be obtained a complete picture of the fiscal condition of a city and of the financial transactions that created that condition. Thus the integrity of financial transactions is maintained, and what is of equal importance, a basis is provided for

[1] An example of the failure to allocate income to the proper financial period was found in Dayton, Ohio, in 1912, when, during financial stress, the liquor licenses for two years were included in the budget of one, simply because they were paid for the new year a few days before the old fiscal year closed. This same city for a period of six years incurred a deficit averaging $60,000 a year because departmental heads were permitted to create liabilities without regard to expected income for the fiscal year, and because the total appropriations exceeded the total expected income. Similarly, the rentals on valuable real estate remained uncollected for several years, and other leased real estate that should have been reappraised periodically for the purpose of determining proper rentals went unappraised because of the lack of proper financial records.

[2] For initial work in this field credit is due Mr. Herman A. Metz, formerly controller of New York City, and Mr. U. L. Leonhauser. Mr. Metz's conception of the need for improvement in municipal accounting methods prompted him to finance the preparation of the *Hand Book on Municipal Accounting*, prepared for the New York Bureau of Municipal Research by Mr. Leonhauser.

official and public judgments as to the safe-guarding of public property and the effectiveness of public endeavor.

<small>CHAP. VIII</small>

The first requirement of a modern accounting system for a municipality is its centralization under a single responsible authority.[1] The reasons for this requirement can be easily understood. In event departments are permitted to collect income and incur liabilities on their independent responsibility, the financial authorities secure a knowledge of such transactions only when payments are made to or from the treasury. Under these circumstances no financial records maintained by the financial officer can be complete, or will permit of an accurate statement of assets and liabilities, of income and expenditures, or of the relation of the authorizations to incur liabilities to liabilities actually incurred—or, in more technical language, of a balance sheet, operating statement and appropriation statement. Only when every transaction affecting a city's finances is reported instantly to the financial officer can accurate records be maintained, and such knowledge can be had only when complete accounting control is centralized in his office. It is difficult to say where responsibility should be located for the centralized accounting control maintained by a city. This uncertainty arises because the chief accounting officer of a municipality is usually given two distinct duties that are more or less mutually antagonistic—*i.e.*, record keeping and auditing.

<small>Centralization of control</small>

<small>Location of centralized control</small>

A large proportion of the efforts of the accounting office of a city is devoted to the routine recording of financial transactions and the preparation of reports reflecting these transactions for the use of administrative officers and the public. This duty comprehends the installation of a proper accounting system and procedure using mechanical equipment and the preparation of prompt and accurate reports—obligations that imply subordination to the chief administrator of the city, in order that complete and timely coöperation may be required. Otherwise the administrator may be handicapped in securing information necessary to the proper execution of his duties. On the other hand, it is usually the duty of the accounting officer to audit all expenditures made by the municipality, requiring that such expenditures be strictly in accordance with the appropriation ordinance which is the authorization to incur liabilities as passed by the legislative body, and in conformance with the charter of the municipality and the laws of

<small>Dual character of duties of accounting officer</small>

---

[1] This does not mean that the detailed asset and liability records of publicly owned utilities need to be centralized.

the state under which the municipality operates. In the exercise of this responsibility, the accounting officer does not represent the administrative authorities, but the legislative body and the public, and it is desirable that he conduct himself with independence and recognize no obligation to the administration whose accounts are being examined.

Here then are duties of two distinct kinds—record keeping, for which the accounting officer should be subordinate to the chief administrator of the city; and auditing, for which the accounting officer should be independent of all expending branches of the government, and responsible to the public only, or its representatives, the legislative body. It is this dual nature of accounting responsibilities that creates uncertainty as to where the accounting responsibility should be lodged in a city organization, in order to secure both efficiency and safety. Many governmental units have accepted one horn of the dilemma and elect the accounting officer. In such instances this official may be a handicap to efficient administration by refusal to coöperate with the administrative authority, and by furthering his own political advantage at the expense of his colleagues. Some cities, notably the large number of city manager municipalities, have placed greater emphasis upon bookkeeping than upon auditing activities depending on independent audits, and here the auditor or controller is frequently appointed by the city manager.[1] A compromise solution of the problem is found in the selection of the auditor by the legislative body. However, the results of actual experience suggest selection by the chief administrator, at the same time providing for some periodic independent audit of a city's fiscal transactions. Such audits may be made by state authority at the expense of the municipality, or provision may be made for an independent outside audit by a private accounting firm.

Regardless of differences of opinions as to the most desirable method of selecting the accounting officer of a municipality, there is substantial agreement as to the fundamental characteristics of the accounting system this officer should maintain. A city is concerned with the transactions and conditions resulting from: (1) income accrued and liabilities incurred; (2) property owned and

---

[1] For the appointing authority of the city manager in these cities, consult R. T. Crane, *Loose Leaf Digest of City Manager Charters* (National Municipal League, 1923).

ACCOUNTING

funded obligations outstanding; (3) estimated revenue and offsetting appropriations; and (4) cash received and cash disbursed.[1]

<small>CHAP. VIII</small>

Control of cash receipts and disbursements is, of course, necessary, and should be secured from the records of the treasurer, but it is agreed that such a statement is of little value in determining policies, fixing responsibility, and indicating results. Practical accounting methods would control the creation and accrual of income, acquisition and maintenance of property, the bonded debt, the appropriations or authorizations to incur liabilities, and the actual liabilities which result from the delivery of commodities or performance of service. With this information, those essential documents—a balance sheet, an income and expense statement, and an appropriation statement—can be prepared. If these documents are properly amplified and used, there is reasonable assurance that the fixed assets of the city will not be lost sight of, that income due will be collected, that appropriations will not be exceeded, and that the city will be operated in accordance with a sound financial program. This system is known as the accrual method as opposed to the cash method of accounting.

<small>Accrual vs. cash accounting</small>

Accrual accounting establishes control over income when the amount is known, as of taxes levied for a specific year, or of rent for a month or other known period. In general the classes of income to be treated in this way are rents, licenses, assessments, taxes, water rents, etc. There are certain classes of accruals which create accounts receivable and are immediately liquidated by reason of the accrual to the city being coincident with the cash payment, as, for example, licenses and permits of an incidental character, paid for in cash at the time they are applied for, minor sales, and fines and penalties paid in cash when imposed. However, the accounting for all classes of income would be the same, except that with income of this character, the sole problem relates to the completeness with which they are collected and the probability of actual receipts being turned into the city treasury.

<small>Control of income</small>

With respect to liabilities, it is desirable that accrued liabilities for a fiscal period, include all actual operating expenses for that period, and ignore liabilities incurred for the previous year, but which will be liquidated in subsequent periods. To accomplish this, progressive governments not only limit the authorizations to expend by the actual income for a given period, but insure that

<small>Control of liabilities</small>

[1] Oakey, *op. cit.*, Chap. I.

140 PRACTICE OF MUNICIPAL ADMINISTRATION

Control of property

Control of appropriations and estimated income

administrative officials do not exceed this authorization. Contracts or orders for supplies, materials, and contractual services may not be entered into except with the authority of the central accounting office, which in each instance encumbers the proper appropriation with the estimated or actual amount of the liability. When the actual amount of the indebtedness becomes known the encumbrance is adjusted, if necessary. The appropriation balance always represents a residue available for the creation of liabilities. This procedure is as important for bond accounts and special assessment accounts as for general operating accounts.

However, accounting control should not end with the payment of the actual liability, but be extended to include control over assets, as lands, buildings, equipment, stores, and any other property owned, used, or managed. The ownership of such property should be safeguarded by perpetual inventories under control of the accounting office, and subject to periodic check. When possible, vouchers should indicate whether a charge is for current expense or whether it augments the property of the city, and as an additional check, monthly statements of additions to, and deductions from property should be required of officials having property within their control. Coincidentally there must be accurate control of, and statements reflecting the condition of, the sinking fund, and of funded debt outstanding.

Previous mention of encumbrances indicates the necessity of controlling appropriations, and commitments against appropriations in the form of contingent liabilities upon uncompleted contracts and orders against which deliveries have not as yet been made. For this reason appropriation accounting is valuable as a means of showing authorized appropriations, contingent liabilities, and net balances unencumbered and available for further creation of liabilities, as well as the actual or anticipated income for meeting these liabilities. The statement of appropriation balances enables the financial officer to be informed currently as to liabilities coming due and the means at hand for meeting them. If cash will not be available because of inaccurate estimates of income or excessive expenditures, there is still time to make necessary corrections. The accounts receivable should be analyzed monthly, showing income overdue, as a check on the current flow of cash into the treasury, for the payment of current liabilities. Such statements are essential to efficient administration.

The foregoing outline may appear technical and uninteresting.

ACCOUNTING 141

The details of accounting are, of course, technical, and no general administrator will be expected to be so completely a jack-of-all-trades as to be able to direct the activities of a city and also devise and maintain its accounting system. Accountants can be employed for that purpose. But every administrator should be able to read, understand, and find interesting the accounting record of his activities as it is placed before him, and be able to judge the completeness of that record. Such ability implies a knowledge of general accounting principles as applied to governmental affairs. The administrator must know that a mere control of public money received and spent is incomplete; that with such control must also go control of the amounts owed to a city and of the amounts the city owes to others; of the property of all kinds owned or managed by the city; and of the authorization to create liabilities, and of the means by which it is expected to finance those authorizations.

CHAP. VIII

Summary

A detailed discussion of the records and procedure necessary in an adequate municipal accounting system would be too extensive and technical to merit consideration in other than an accounting manual. The brief summary which follows and which is digested with some modifications from a memorandum prepared by the New York Bureau of Municipal Research will be sufficient to familiarize the student with the terminology and principles involved.[1] Municipal accounting requires the use of certain original documents, registers, and subsidiary records, which when posted through a general journal and general ledger permit the preparation of the financial statements and records of operation essential to proper administration.

Summary details of modern municipal accounting procedure

Money does not come into the possession of a city, nor is it paid out by any public official, without some original record being made of the transaction. The income of a city is derived largely from approved tax assessments that are duly collected, from charges of one kind and another for which bills are rendered to persons charged, and from certain transactions, coincident with cash payments, for services rendered and privileges granted. The total of all such income has been estimated in connection with the preparation of the budget, and upon this estimate is based the authorization to incur liabilities made in the appropriation ordinance. Authorized expenditures have their origin in requisi-

Original documents

[1] This is an unpublished document, and deals in detail with definitions, records, and procedure.

142 PRACTICE OF MUNICIPAL ADMINISTRATION

tions drawn on a storeroom, in purchase orders, contracts, and payrolls, which are duly approved on vouchers, and paid by warrants on the city treasurer. So the original documents upon which an accounting system is based are the appropriation ordinance and other acts of the legislative body, contracts, requisitions, purchase orders, payrolls, invoices, warrants, tax rolls, and documents reflecting other income.

Registers

These original documents must be gathered and properly classified before they can serve as a complete basis of control and information. The numerous requisitions, purchase orders, contracts, and payrolls must be entered in respective registers; the vouchers in a register of accounts payable; the warrants drawn on the treasury in a register of warrant-checks; the documents reflecting income in a register of accounts receivable; and the cash actually received and paid out in a register of receipts and disbursements.

Subsidiary records

From these original documents and registers certain subsidiary records can be prepared—*i.e.*, appropriation ledger, claimants ledger, expense ledger, property and equipment ledger, and the

Statements

cash book. The totals of these registers at the end of each month, or other period, may be posted through the general journal to the general ledger; and from the general ledger and subsidiary ledgers may be prepared the balance sheet, statement of income and expense, statement of receipts and disbursements, and statement of appropriation balances, all of which are essential to the proper control and understanding of the city's financial transactions. Because the administrator must be able to use effectively the financial statements that will result from a proper system of accounts, it is desirable to discuss these statements somewhat in detail.

Balance sheets

The balance sheet is a summary statement showing at a certain time on the one side the estimated values of property and the amounts due from debtors, and on the other, the amounts due to creditors, including bonded debt, the difference between the two being calculated in order to show the approximate surplus or deficit.[1]

Income and expense statement

The statement of income and expense should show for the period stated the income accrued from the levying of taxes and assessments, and from charges for privileges and services; the cost of operation and maintenance of the several departments; and

[1] Oakey, *op. cit.*, Chap. IX.

the excess of income over expense, or the excess of expenses over income.

From the appropriation ledger as controlled by the general ledger, there should be prepared periodically a statement of appropriation balances, which will indicate with respect to each appropriation the amount of the original appropriation as modified by transfers, the total amount of actual expenditures charged, the amount of the unexpended balance, the amount of reserve for contracts and orders, and the amount of the unencumbered balance. Copies of this statement should be submitted to the administrative officers of each department immediately following the end of each month. This statement must be accurately and promptly prepared. If it is not, the separate departments will be tempted to maintain sufficient accounting procedure of their own to provide this information which is so necessary to their proper administration.

It is desirable, if all of the essential data required by the administrative officials are to be available, that an adequate classification of income and expenditures be established. Such a classification forms the framework of the accounting structure, and upon it the value of the whole accounting system largely depends. This classification should be constructed so as to permit of the segregation of income and expenditures according to the functions or activities of each department, and should be subdivided under each activity according to the character of the income received and the expenditure made. In other words, municipalities should show the income and expense segregated for each unit of government. The principal functional titles as used by the Bureau of the Census, and in accordance with which municipal reports are requested, are as follows: (1) general government; (2) protection to persons and property; (3) conservation of health; (4) sanitation or promotion of cleanliness; (5) highways; (6) charities, hospitals, and corrections; (7) education; (8) recreation; and (9) miscellaneous; the actual detailed classification of accounts should permit the arrangement of all financial transactions within these groups.

The purposes of such a system of accounts as has been outlined with be furthered if the accounts have been codified in accordance with some definite method, somewhat as follows: (1) current assets; (2) capital assets and bond accounts for construction; (3)

144 PRACTICE OF MUNICIPAL ADMINISTRATION

CHAP. VIII

sinking fund and special trust assets; (4) current liabilities and reserves; (5) sinking, special and trust fund liabilities, and reserves; (6) funded debt; (7) income accounts; (8) expense accounts; and (9) appropriation accounts. Each of these groups may be further amplified and subdivided into subsidiary groups as occasion requires.

Separate group accounting

Usually cities maintain a number of separate accounts, such as bond accounts, sinking fund accounts, trust accounts, and special assessment accounts, each having its own peculiar assets and liabilities. To merge these accounts in a general balance sheet would allow a surplus in one account to cancel a possible deficit in another account, and would be anything but good business.

Statutes require separate cash accounts

Because of ignorant and vicious legislation that confuses appropriations with cash, cities generally are required by statute to split up their cash into numerous subsidiary funds, earmarking them for specific purposes. This plan was originated to insure certain amounts of money being spent for particular purposes, such as police and education, on the theory that the common sense and good judgment of those in actual charge of a city government are not to be trusted. The scheme usually results in certain activities receiving cash out of relative proportion to their needs, and in resort to subterfuge to redress the inequality. It means also that if cash is available in one fund, but not in another, the deficiency cannot be made up legally by temporary borrowing from the affluent fund, but such borrowing must be from banks at an interest rate usually greater than that received on deposits. This absurdity persists in most cities—borrowing money from banks in which large sums of public money restricted by statute for specific purposes are already on deposit.

Depreciation and appreciation

In preparing the general balance sheet and consolidated balance sheet found in ordinary municipal reports, small consideration, if any, is given to depreciation. On the asset side of the statement are placed all public improvements at their original cost or at assessed valuation, while on the liability side appear the bonds outstanding. Nor are governmental accountants entirely agreed as to the proper treatment of appreciation and depreciation with respect to assets acquired by a city. It is believed, however, that depreciation on buildings, other structures, and equipment should be considered; and the rates established and allowed by the Federal service for income purposes may be used for the purpose of calculating the annual amount.

ACCOUNTING 145

Accounting authorities usually divide the assets of a city into a number of groups somewhat as follows: first, assets realizable and remunerative, such as public utilities; second, assets realizable but not remunerative, such as parks; third, assets neither realizable nor remunerative, such as street paving; and fourth, assets in the form of equipment, furnishings, and fixtures.

CHAP. VIII

Forms of assets

In the first of these groups in particular, which includes public utilities and industries such as water plants, electric light systems, gas plants, street railways, paving plants, etc., depreciation is an item which cannot be ignored.[1] Depreciation is the reduction in value of property due to wear and tear, age, physical decay, inadequacy, obsolescence or supersession, but not made good from charges to maintenance. The loss in value due to wear and discarding because of inadequacy is as much a cost of operating a public utility or an industry as are the wages of employees or the cost of supplies that enter into a service. Only when such valuation losses are included in the operating statement is it possible to get a true statement of the cost of operation and of the unit cost of the work that results from this operation. Only when such charges are deducted from the assets of a utility or industry does the balance sheet actually present to the management and to the public the true condition of affairs.

Realizable and remunerative

Few cities consider appreciation or depreciation in connection with assets of the second group, of which parks and playgrounds are examples, or even record such assets in the financial records. To prepare a balance sheet, the items are not all taken from the general ledger, but the financial officer will secure from the assessors or engineering department a rough estimate of the value of such properties and place them in the balance sheet as given. Or, frequently, such assets are kept on a mere memorandum record from which the balance sheet entry is made. However, it is desirable that every piece of public property shall be under absolute accounting control and appear in the balance sheet at accurate value, even though a city is organized for service and not profit and surplus. There is no valid reason why such properties should not be carried in the general ledger at true value (as nearly as that value can be easily estimated) and carried into the balance sheet in an orderly way.

Realizable but unremunerative

The third class of assets, which includes streets and possible

[1] With respect to public utilities, reference may be made to the discussion of depreciation in Chap. XXX.

sewers that require a capital outlay in their acquisition, should be controlled by proper accounting records. However, since they cannot be sold it may be argued that there is no real purpose in carrying them in the balance sheet or depreciating them as they wear out. On the other hand, a purpose is accomplished in indicating to the public the amount of property owned by a municipality compared with the outstanding debt. A reasonable period of life should be assigned to public improvements of this nature, and they should be written off at this rate, using depreciation methods outlined.

These same conclusions are true with respect to the fourth group of assets, composed of machinery, furniture, fixtures, and equipment. In certain activities it is necessary to make a charge for depreciation in order to obtain the true costs of operation. Machinery and equipment used in street repair, street construction, street cleaning, garbage and refuse removal, and other similar work, in which unit costs are desirable, should certainly be carried on the books of the city and depreciated at an acceptable rate. Other furnishings and fixtures must be carried on the property books in some orderly manner, to the end that they may not be lost. It is customary in some cities when buying equipment to charge the same to expense, in which case such articles are written down to a nominal value immediately. Another practice is to carry such property at its full value on the books until it is destroyed, sold, or replaced. In such instances replacements are not treated as adding to capital assets. It may be good practice to charge very minor equipment as an expense item, placing it under proper inventory control so that it may not be stolen, but certainly all other equipment should be carried at original values, deducting the amount of depreciation in total on the balance sheet.

Records of unit and job costs are essential to proper administration, although they are usually the last information which an administrator secures and are frequently the least reliable. It is possible to determine over a given period the actual cost of any activity of the government and the income which such activity has earned. If in addition accurate records are maintained of the amount of work performed, measured by some unit which is standard from city to city and over period to period, the problem of determining unit costs becomes largely one of simple division. The administrator is in a position to learn from month to month,

ACCOUNTING

for example, the unit cost of cleaning streets, collecting and disposing of garbage and refuse, making inspections, caring for the sick, feeding horses, running automobiles, and so on for every activity or method of performing services. Comparisons may be made and division heads may be required constantly to reduce their costs or to furnish an adequate reason for not doing so.

The job cost applies to the cost of accomplishing some particular task, such as erection of a building, the installation of equipment, or the repair of particular highways. For example, while it is desirable to know the cost per square yard of paving or repairing streets of a certain character during a given period, it may be of equal importance to know the cost of such work on a particular street, or on each block of a street. Multiplying the units in a job by the unit cost gives only an average job cost, and an administrator who can give instantly the unit cost of performing the work under his jurisdiction may be stumped when asked to say exactly what it cost to pave several blocks on a particular street, or to remove garbage from some particular section of the city. To obtain an accurate statement, an account must be kept for each job of charges on account for supplies and materials furnished on order or from stores, for payrolls directly involved, for equipment used, for depreciation, and finally for a proportion of overhead administrative expense. This last item can be prorated on a percentage basis determined by actual experience only temporarily until all work of a like character is completed and the exact ratio of charges is determined. Job costs are not justified except on special work of some magnitude, on work in which conditions are such that unit costs will be quite erroneous, or when necessary to ascertain cost of a service to citizens to be charged.[1]

In preparing budget estimates, salaries and wages for each activity should be schedulized, increases in force and in rates of pay being plainly indicated. Each position is usually given with the salary rate, the number of employees, and the total salary paid. Salary rates are ordinarily predetermined by a salary ordinance which should be enacted after salaries are standardized. It is then customary for the civil service authorities to examine each payroll to be sure that each employee has been properly inducted into service and is working in the proper grade and at the proper rate. Attached to the payroll is a certification, to be signed by the of-

[1] See J. P. Jordan and G. L. Harris, *Cost Accounting* (2d. ed., Ronald, 1925).

148 PRACTICE OF MUNICIPAL ADMINISTRATION

CHAP. VIII

ficial in charge, usually under oath, that the persons named have actually worked for the period indicated. These safeguards are usually sufficient to prevent unauthorized payments to salaried employees.

Payroll padding

Day labor payrolls are more difficult to control, particularly as only the skilled trades are ordinarily under civil service. Where civil service regulations prevail, the checking procedure is the same as for salaried employees. Frequent payroll defalcations arise from foremen certifying to the names of persons who have been released from city service, and whose names are still retained on the civil service list; from adding the fictitious names of non-existent persons to the roll; and from certifying to more hours of work than has been done, in each instance arranging with a confederate for the collection and distribution of the spoils. Such payroll padding can be best prevented by a daily, or even more frequent, examination of the foreman's roll by a payroll clerk, who should make the check at unexpected times. When daily rolls are properly certified by the foreman, and by the clerk who assures himself that the persons certified were at work at least when he made his check, they become the basis of the weekly roll from which payment is made. Such rolls are sometimes paid in cash by a paymaster at the point where the men are at work, each person signing the roll. It is recommended, however, that payments be made by check. Payroll manipulation is a prevailing form of petty grafting, and the administrator can expect its frequent recurrence. Industries suffer from this evil as much as do city governments, although the most elaborate precautions are taken, and employees can be better controlled because located in a limited number of places. Public officers abate the abuse only through constant vigilance and judicious rotation of the supervisory forces.

Service records

Service records are in use in only a few public departments, but are being rapidly extended as the value of unit costs for administrative purposes is appreciated. Inspectors are usually required to report daily on the number of inspections made; nurses report visits; policemen report arrests and violations of ordinances noticed; street cleaners report the number of yards cleaned; wagon drivers the number of loads moved; etc. It may not be long until bookkeepers, clerks, and stengraphers will be required to measure and report on a standard day's work. When such a point is reached, budget estimates can be based upon units of work done and to be done, rather than upon departmental guesses and oratory.

ACCOUNTING 149

Governmental accounting is the recording of financial transactions in such manner that accurate information is available to administrators and to the public. Auditing is an examination of such transactions and accounts to insure their legality and correctness. Even when municipal records were of the simplest character, audits were made to assure that moneys were properly spent, and sometimes all claims were published in local newspapers with the idea that public scrutiny might detect errors of accident or intention. One of the oldest institutions in local government is the office of controller or auditor. It is a function of this office to inspect each claim presented to determine whether the proposed expenditure has been properly authorized, whether it is in accordance with law, and whether the sum is correct, and to refuse approval of questionable accounts. To be assured that proper entries of approved vouchers are made, that proper warrants are drawn upon the city treasurer, and that legal disposition is made of all income accruing to the city, the controller or auditor is assumed to make a periodical examination of all municipal accounts and to report the findings to the proper municipal authorities and to the public. This examination is called an audit and is made at occasional intervals throughout the year as circumstances require. Hence it has acquired the name of a continuing audit. Lately, certain cities have adopted the practice of having an independent audit made by public accountants either annually or semi-annually. These audits are frequently called continuing audits, although they are usually made at regular periods. Such audits usually duplicate work already performed by city officers, but have a large value inasmuch as the check is impersonal, and because these private auditing firms have done much to stimulate the installation of more adequate accounting methods and procedure. There is some danger, however, from the fact that few private accountants are conversant with the conditions inherent in the accounts of a governmental unit as distinct from the accounts of private business, and as a result the reports of audits may be unintentionally distorted. Further, accounting firms may color their reports with the intent of currying favor with the administration for which an audit is made.

Some states, notably New York, New Jersey, Ohio, Massachusetts, Wisconsin, Indiana, and Iowa, exercise a control over the methods of accounting and the nature of expenditures of local governments. In Ohio a semi-annual or annual examination of all

CHAP. VIII

Audits

State control and audit

such accounts is made by the state auditor at the expense of the local community and the resulting reports are referred to the local authorities. There is a decided difference of opinion as to the value of this state supervision, with the preponderance of evidence somewhat in its favor. The accounting methods employed by local governments, and particularly by the smaller villages, school boards, and townships, are notoriously faulty, and an outside check is of unqualified advantage. However, it is doubtful whether this state control has worked any great good to larger cities. The state representatives are not always qualified for their duties; they have sometimes been able to detect only the most obvious derelictions or inconsistencies; they have at times insisted upon a rigidity inconsistent with efficient city operation; and improvements in accounting systems and procedure have often been installed only over their opposition. Sometimes the reports of state audits have been modified for purely political reasons, to condemn or favor a local official at odds with or in the favor of the state administration. The examinations have been of value in checking the misappropriation of money, and criticism must be directed to the methods of administration rather than to the principles involved. If such audits were entirely free from political bias, if the interpretations of the law were more uniform and reasonable, and if the state auditing authorities made a greater effort to insure the installation of modern accounting methods, their value would be unquestioned. Perhaps a happy solution would be to permit cities under state financial control to choose between an audit by state authorities and one by private accountants. Competition might stimulate a higher character of service on the part of both.

Audits ordinarily indicate the actual receipts and disbursements, and sometimes the income and expense, during the fiscal year, of the governmental division examined. This fiscal year does not necessarily correspond with the calendar year, but is an arbitrary period of twelve months which is used by municipalities as a measure of their yearly activities. In most instances, it begins January and ends December 31, or begins July and ends June 30. In some cases the fiscal year varies from this rule, the determining factor being the dates when large payments of taxes are anticipated. It is usual to place the beginning of the fiscal year immediately after or immediately before such payments, since the budget becomes effective at the beginning of the fiscal year and it is desirable that funds for its financing be available. Otherwise, the locality must resort to short-time loans made in anticipation of taxes.

It is currently believed that citizens are concerned not so much with the total cost of government as with the character and quantity of services rendered for that cost. Unhappily, neither the public nor the administrators are able to learn the exact quantity of services secured for money expended; nor are they able to compare the quality and unit cost of such services from one year to the next or from one city to another. Only the most thoroughgoing budget procedure delineates the fundamental activities performed by a city government, and rarely does it embody a statement of the number of units or the unit cost of services performed as compared with previous budgets. In consequence, no person is in a position to judge the actual quality and quantity of public work, and in the main, people must rely upon general and frequently erroneous, impressions.

Probably the next important step in the science of public administration will be the development of periodic departmental reports indicating the quantity and unit cost of work done over a comparable period, and correlating these reports with the budget procedure. In this way the administrator may judge as accurately as does a manufacturer the quantity and cost of the work for which he is responsible, and the legislative body can consider requests for appropriations in terms of proposed units of work and unit costs rather than in general terms of men and materials.

There are certain public activities, the results of which cannot be easily measured. Possibly such activities are fewer than is supposed; and in cases where the product cannot be evaluated some estimate of efficiency may be secured by measuring the operations of the machinery that produces the product. But as yet the development of operating reports is in its infancy. Health departments, however, have gone far in this direction. Not only do they enumerate the activities performed, patients visited, attendance in clinics, and conditions inspections, but the results of this work can be deducted from the death and morbidity rates by groups of people and nature of diseases. The police have developed daily reports setting forth the operations of each activity and the results accomplished as measured in arrests, complaints of crimes, property stolen, property recovered, and accidents, etc., compared with the previous day, and summarizing the total to date for the same period for the year previous. These reports of different health and police activities may, in turn, be consolidated into daily reports for chief departmental administrators and form the groundwork for consolidated monthly and yearly reports. Public works, street cleaning, refuse removal, and similar activities should be next to be subjected to this procedure. Such reports, eliminating detail in the process of consolidation, must eventually be received from every department and appear as a consolidated report in the hands of the chief administrator, who from the important elements indicated may determine what more detailed reports should be reviewed. These consolidated city reports indicating the salient features of government operations will in turn furnish the fundamentals of a report to the public which will eliminate useless statistics and be comparable for a city from period to period and with the similar reports from other cities.

CHAPTER IX

PURCHASING[1]

A city not only purchases supplies, materials, and equipment, but also real estate, contractual services, and personal services. The purchasing of personal services is so distinct a problem that a special branch of the government—the civil service authority—is provided for that purpose. The buying of real estate is ordinarily consummated either by condemnation proceedings or by direct negotiations between the department concerned and the owner, always subject to the approval of the legislative body. With respect to the purchasing of contractual services, common practice varies, but there is an inclination to leave to the several departments the task of contracting for telephone and telegraph service, automobile repairs, electric power, and similar services in which both personal service and materials are involved. Or the legislative body may take the task of purchasing these articles out of the hands of the departments and enter into direct negotiations with the utilities, or other parties concerned. These eliminations restrict a consideration of city buying to the acquisition of supplies, materials, and equipment for ordinary city departments, and in considering purchasing and storing it is usually understood that only these three groups of goods are involved. *The scope of city purchasing*

Until the last fifteen years, the purchasing of these goods was entirely a departmental activity, and it remains so now in probably more than half of the cities of the country. Considering the *Departmental responsibility for purchasing*

[1] Important studies of purchasing and storing include Arthur A. Thomas, *Principles of Government Purchasing* (Appleton, 1919); H. B. Twyford, *Purchasing and Storing* (Van Nostrand, 1918 and 1924); John C. Dinsmore, *Purchasing Principles and Practices* (Prentice-Hall, 1922); and William A. Prendergast, City Controller, *Report Submitting Plan of Proposed System for the Central Purchase and Distribution of Supplies for the City of New York* (Merchants Assc. of New York, 1913). An instructive book for purchasing agents, dealing with principles rather than procedure, is Helen Hysell, *The Science of Purchasing* (Appleton, 1922). A recent article containing data on the extent of centralized purchasing is Russell Forbes, "Centralized Purchasing in Governments of United States and Canada," *Competency and Economy in Public Expenditures* (Annals, CXIII, May, 1921). Reference should also be made to the *Annual Proceedings of the National Association of Purchasing Agents*.

154   PRACTICE OF MUNICIPAL ADMINISTRATION

CHAP. IX

casual development of governmental organization, this division of responsibility among so many individuals is not surprising. Further, this prerogative of personal buying has been held so tenaciously by departments because such independence extends the personal influence of the department officials concerned, needed goods can be bought promptly without routine, and favored brands and patented articles can be specified when desired. Governmental departments normally wish to do their own purchasing, and the process of cutting off the privilege of doing so and of centralizing responsibility in a single purchasing authority has been introduced largely because of the serious abuses developed under the departmental system.

Abuses of departmental purchasing

The principal abuse of departmental purchasing is the buying of goods in small quantities and often at retail prices, which if bought in the aggregate could be secured at wholesale. With this abuse are associated additional shortcomings: the absence of uniform trade customs; the neglect of helpful records; the lack of specialized knowledge on all types of goods; the favoring of trade-marked and well-advertised articles; and the tendency to favor friends.

Not infrequently, buying is done through brokers who actually have no stock in trade except their familiarity with government procedure and their friendship for governmental officials. The invariable consequences of such decentralized responsibility are extravagance on the part of officials, and the purchase of inferior goods at high prices.[1]

Introduction of centralized purchasing and scientific purchasing methods

These abuses are not peculiar to city government, but have prevailed to an equal or greater extent in private business. But with the growth of private industry, managers undertook to develop some methods of purchasing that would eliminate the evils

[1] A comparison of prices paid for certain selected articles of the same quality by Dayton, Ohio, before and after the introduction of scientific purchasing methods is as follows:

Article	Before	After
Floor oil	$1.25 per unit	$ .12 per unit
Typewriter ribbons	.75 "	.25 "
Carbon paper	3.00 "	.65 "
Paper clips	.80 "	.23 "
Flash lights	2.50 "	.95 "
Second sheets	1.00 "	.28 "
Cup grease	.10 "	.03½ "
Rubber bands	4.00 "	1.26 "
Rough soap	8.75 "	4.50 "

incident to indiscriminate buying by a number of miscellaneous agents.[1] It was concluded that a solution lay in the centralization of purchasing authority in a single individual who could be held responsible for developing scientific methods, and honestly and effectively administering the activity. The plan and procedure developed by important industries were soon copied by governmental agencies and adapted to their purposes, with only such changes as were made necessary by the legal restrictions thrown about public buying.[2]

Location of purchasing authority

The location of the centralized authority differs in various jurisdictions. In many cities the purchasing agent is the head of an independent department and is appointed by the mayor or city manager. In other instances, and particularly in small municipalities, the purchasing duties may be assumed directly by, or by a subordinate of, the city manager, the auditor, or the city clerk. In any event, the actual purchasing officer should be chosen for his ability and experience, and should be retained so long as competent.

Advantages of centralized purchasing

Centralized purchasing should mean quantity buying at wholesale prices. If, under the centralized plan, purchasing continue in "dribs and dabs," a principal advantage is lost.[3] When goods are bought in quantities firms become interested which otherwise would not be concerned, and the increased attractiveness of public business to competitors largely eliminates favoritism. The letting of such contracts will be observed by vendors throughout the community, and any evidences of irregularity will bring instant protest.

Wholesale buying

Next in importance is the advantage of expertness which centralization makes possible. A departmental buyer may be an expert in one, or at best a few, lines; centralized purchasing permits an expert buyer to be provided for every trade group. Specialization in buying must result in lower prices for a better selection of goods.

Expertness

The standardization of specifications that should be corollary to centralized purchasing provides for standardization both as to

Standard specifications

[1] For a discussion of this development, see Thomas, *op. cit.*, 10-20.
[2] Cincinnati was one of the first American cities to adopt this principle of centralized purchasing, the procedure being installed about 1911. For nearly fifteen years this procedure, or some other procedure based upon it, has been used as a model by cities seeking to improve their purchasing methods.
[3] This is most important. Centralized purchasing has often broken down because of repeated small orders by departments.

156   PRACTICE OF MUNICIPAL ADMINISTRATION

CHAP. IX

quality and use. One of the essential duties of the central purchasing agent is to determine the desirable ingredients of every supply and material used by the city, and to buy these ingredients rather than fancy names and packages. Similarly, the goods most suitable to each use should be determined upon, and purchases restricted accordingly.

Thorough inspection

Incident to wholesale buying is wholesale delivery, usually at a central warehouse from which goods can be distributed to departments in quantities needed. This central delivery provides proper control and inspection of deliveries, with a complete and adequate audit.

Prompt payments

Another advantage that usually attends centralized purchasing is the expediting of payments. Prompt payment reassures the vendors and may reduce bids. Also substantial cash discounts may be taken by the city, which would not be availed of under other methods.[1]

Disadvantages of centralized purchasing

The principal complaint lodged against centralized purchasing by departmental officials is directed against the delay between the placing of a requisition and the actual delivery of the goods required. This complaint may be partially eliminated by the maintenance of a central storehouse for a limited selection of articles in common use, and from which deliveries can be made almost immediately. This does not mean that any large part of the many articles purchased by a city should be stored—only those in common use. Otherwise there is danger of over-purchasing and the establishment of large inactive inventories.

Delay in deliveries

It is customary for purchasing departments to accumulate orders and to buy certain kinds of commodities upon fixed days, usually once each week. To do otherwise results in buying trifling quantities, and in vendors having to follow the purchasing proceeding every day. However, buying each trade group one day a week means that a city department must maintain a close check on supplies on hand, and make weekly requisitions for goods required. Some time must elapse for the purchasing procedure to be carried out—the soliciting of bids, placing of orders, and final delivery—with the result that a department may receive goods some days after the actual requisition. Departments which are lax in their control of supplies may be handicapped by failure

[1] Centralized purchasing usually involves an absolute control of unpaid bills by the auditor, and this control is often advanced as a principal reason for the installation of a purchasing department. The same control could be secured under departmental purchasing.

PURCHASING 157

to secure immediate deliveries, thus necessitating emergency purchases, with attendant difficulties.

CHAP. IX

Another principal cause of complaint is the absence of definite limitations on the jurisdiction of the purchasing agent. Is the purchasing agent a mere order clerk, or is he also a judge of necessity and quality of goods requisitioned? In a thoroughly established purchasing organization and procedure, it is to be expected that specifications will be provided to govern the quality of all goods purchased for ordinary use. However, the determination of definite specifications is frequently neglected, and there is conconstant bickering between the purchasing agent and the departments with respect to the quality of goods bought. Also when a department presents a requisition for supplies, materials, or equipment, specifying qualities which in the judgment of the purchasing agent are unnecessary for the purposes to be served, the purchasing agent will often assume to modify the request, or enter into negotiations with the department for such modification. Or a department may request what appears to be excessive quantities, with the same outcome.

Conflict of jurisdiction

There is no common practice among cities with respect to conflicting jurisdiction between the purchasing agent and the departments, but there is a tendency to overcome the difficulty by making the purchasing agent solely an ordering department. In other words, this official is under compulsion to fill the requisitions furnished to him by the departments, leaving to other branches of the government, primarily the auditor, the problem of determining whether a department is ordering supplies in unnecessary quantities and unsatisfactory qualities.

Some criticism also arises in connection with the purchasing of technical articles. Certain departments of a city government must buy, on occasions, technical apparatus and special supplies which they, rather than the purchasing agent, are best equipped to secure. Difficulty may be avoided, however, if the purchasing agent will realize his limitations and, while acting as an order clerk, place the responsibility for the determination of specifications and the solicitation of vendors upon the department concerned. Some charters go so far as to state specifically that technical articles in certain departments shall be bought only with the coöperation of the department concerned.

Technical articles

Ordinarily, the state law, the city charter, or a municipal ordinance determines the essential restrictions thrown about purchas-

Restrictions governing purchasing

158   PRACTICE OF MUNICIPAL ADMINISTRATION

<small>CHAP. IX</small>

ing for the proper protection of vendors and taxpayers; frequently all three regulate the matter.[1] A usual provision found in law is that competition shall be upon open specifications, and that the award shall be made to the lowest responsible bidder. There are certain favorite devices for nullifying apparently open specifications—some single detail may involve a patented article controlled by a favored company, either preventing bidding by competitors or forcing so high a price on the completed article that actual competition cannot prevail; the specified period for delivery may be so short that only a favored company can get into large-scale production in the time allowed; a favored vendor may be notified of an impending purchase, and every legal effort made to keep this knowledge from competitors; or unusually severe specifications may be provided, a favored vendor knowing that compliance will not be required, and regulating the amount of his bid accordingly.[2]

<small>Open specifications</small>

<small>Lowest and best bidder</small>

The requirement that the contract shall go to the lowest responsible bidder is a clause open to discretionary determination. Certainly a vendor that has defaulted on deliveries, or whose dealings with a city have shown evidences of moral turpitude, can be excluded by action of the purchasing agent, the chief executive, or the legislative body. Sometimes, however, unjust discrimination may be made in favor of a strong, well-established company on the grounds that its financial condition will insure full compliance with any agreements entered into. Moral and financial responsibility on the part of vendors is expected.[3]

<small>Fidelity deposits</small>

To insure compliance with contracts, it is customary for municipalities to require a certified check or a cash deposit to be given by each bidder when bids are submitted. This initial deposit should be only a small percentage of the amount of the bid. In event a bid is accepted, the initial deposit should be increased to an amount at least sufficient to safeguard the city from default on a rising market. It should be borne in mind that these deposits are a formality not ordinarily required by private corporations in making purchases, except on highly important transactions, and they add to the cost of public business. For this reason the

---

[1] "The legal restrictions with which purchasing is commonly hedged about in governments constitute the most destructive feature of government as opposed to private purchasing." Thomas, *op. cit.*, 44.

[2] For years New York City specified and paid for a grade of oats which was never sold in the New York market.

[3] Award to the lowest and best bidder implies full publicity of bids. Yet occasionally the best bid can only be secured when bids are secret—particularly on articles controlled by a combination.

PURCHASING

restrictions should be as reasonable as possible. Checks accompanying rejected bids should be returned promptly.

Invariably some legal limit is placed on the value of goods that may be bought by a purchasing agent without public advertising, formal competition, and approval of the resulting contract by the legislative body. Such limitations usually apply only to purchases of over $500 or $1,000. This formality is frequently protested by both city departments and purchasing agents, but has protected the interests of the public, and of vendors, on innumerable occasions. A vendor who feels that he has been discriminated against can appeal to the city council, and even to the courts, before the proposed contract in question has been actually signed. This regulation is occasionally avoided by repeated purchases that are just under the prescribed amount.[1]

It is customary to exclude all public officers from bidding upon articles purchased by the city. This requirement has merit as applied to salaried employees, but if it eliminates corporations in which non-salaried members of commissions may be interested, it works a hardship both to taxpayers and the officials. If purchasing is safeguarded by open specifications and bidding, there is little danger in permitting non-salaried officials to be interested in contracts which do not concern their particular departments.

When a city enjoys the talents of prominent business men on its boards and commissions, without compensation, it should not penalize this service by preventing firms in which such officers are interested, either as stockholders or as officers, from bidding on public contracts of every kind in which the officials are not directly concerned.[2]

Further restriction in the purchasing of public supplies is found frequently in regulations applying to the character of labor utilized in the production of such supplies.[3] Many states have regulations governing the use of materials produced by prison

---

[1] It is alleged that a building in City Hall Square in New York City was built without competition on orders to a contractor that were just under the amount requiring advertisement and open competition.

[2] Sometimes this restriction on officials is carried to a ridiculous extent. In the city of Cincinnati some years ago, upon a change in administration, a member of the service commission was ousted because a corporation in which he was a minor stockholder had sold material to the city through the purchasing agent, probably without the official's knowledge, and certainly with small benefit to him.

[3] During the period when there was national regulation of materials made by child labor and appearing in interstate commerce, a purchasing agent had to assure himself that the supplies used by the city were not made in contravention of national law.

160 PRACTICE OF MUNICIPAL ADMINISTRATION

<small>CHAP. IX</small>

<small>Procedure for centralized purchasing</small>

labor, and cities are not allowed to purchase such supplies in competition with that produced by free labor.[1]

The procedure of centralized purchasing originates with the issuing of a requisition upon the purchasing agent by the department desiring goods.[2] These requisitions state the quantity and quality of goods wanted, and are prepared in duplicate upon uniform blanks, the original being transmitted to the purchasing agent. Should the amount of the requisition be sufficient to require advertisement and open competition, the purchasing agent will proceed with publication, and also send requests for bids to interested vendors. If the amount involved is small, informal bids will be solicited by writing or by telephone, or the requisitions will be held until a day set for purchasing goods of a particular type—an advisable practice. These purchasing days become known in advance to all vendors, and they can put in an appearance to submit informal bids on all accumulated requisitions. Purchases made without formal competition are known as open-market orders. Formal bids are submitted preferably on uniform stationery, and upon a date indicated are opened and tabulated; or, if informal and secured by telephone, they should appear on a memorandum of informal bids, with a list of vendors invited to bid.

<small>Price agreements</small>

It is usual for a city to enter into a contract for articles that are purchased in large quantities, or needed at regular intervals; or, in the absence of a contract, to have a price agreement with vendors, such price agreements having been established by competition. These price agreements form a catalog of authorized bids which stand for a definite period, or until canceled, either by the purchasing department or by the vendor concerned. In such instances, it is not necessary to solicit bids to fill a requisition, but the order may be sent directly to the firm with which a contract or a price agreement rests.[3]

<small>The order</small>

When the price to be paid for an article has been determined, the purchasing agent is in a position to issue an order on the vendor. However, under modern accounting methods, before the order becomes valid it must be sent to the chief financial officer of the city, in order that the particular account to which it is to be

---

[1] The subject of legal restrictions is discussed in detail by Thomas, *op. cit.*, Chap. III.

[2] See F. X. A. Purcell, *Purchasing for Large Cities* (Municipal Engineers of the City of New York, Paper No. 82, September, 1913).

[3] See "Continuing Agreements in City Purchasing," Extracts from a paper on "A Central Purchasing Agency for the City of New York," by W. V. S. Thorne, reprinted in Thomas, *op. cit.*, Appendix 3.

charged may be encumbered and certification made that funds are available from which the purchase can be made. The order is then sent to the vendor, memorandum duplicates being retained by the purchasing agent, and also sent, to the department concerned, to the inspector of purchases, and to the accounting department of the city. The purchasing agent's copies are filed alphabetically by vendor and by order number. The use of these files is supplemented by a separate card index of purchases.

The procedure outlined cannot be entered into by a department in every instance in which it requires supplies. It is possible for a machine to break, and the repairs must be secured immediately in order that the regular operations shall not be handicapped; an automobile may be stalled on the road for the want of gasoline, in which case a supply must be secured from a neighboring oil station; or through oversight some requirement must be met instanter. Under these circumstances, it should be provided in the purchasing procedure that the necessary purchase may be made directly by the department, a memorandum of such a purchase being submitted to the purchasing agent on a special form. The purchasing agent should go through the regular procedure of sending a confirming order to the vendor involved, properly indicating that the purchase made was an emergency one, and that delivery has already been effected. The abuses of emergency purchasing are reduced to a minimum under the centralized plan, as goods likely to be required are maintained in stock.

One of the difficulties in purchasing is to insure that supplies are delivered in accordance with specifications—in other words, to see that a city gets what it buys and pays for. Inspection insures the proper delivery of quantity and quality of goods and facilitates promptness in delivery. The first step in the adequate inspection of supplies is, of course, the existence of specifications that definitely describe what the city expects the vendor to deliver. Secondly, there must be available for the purchasing agent means of determining whether or not the supplies delivered conform to these specifications. Where very technical specifications are involved, the proper inspection of commodities can be secured only through the use of a testing laboratory with facilities for making chemical and physical analysis of all kinds. In the instance of other supplies, where general descriptive specifications are sufficient, inspection requires merely the presence of some person for the purpose of checking quantities and general examination.

It is to be anticipated that the purchasing department will have a reasonable corps of inspectors available for inspection of deliveries of large quantities, and for all deliveries made at a central storehouse. In other instances the inspectors must be persons delegated to this duty in the departments to which supplies will be delivered from time to time. In connection with inspection it is customary to have correct lists upon which inspectors can note any shortages that appear, and also proper facilities for recording partial deliveries when the deliveries are made over a considerable period of time.

Specifications

One of the important duties of the centralized purchasing authority is the establishment of uniform standards for supplies, in the form of definite written specifications, or by the adoption of actual standard samples. The absence of uniform standards is unfair to the dealer and is likely to prove costly to the city, because it precludes real competition. Lack of clear understanding by vendors as to the exact desires of the purchasing agent means the submission of bids upon various qualities or grades of a commodity by respective bidders, possibly resulting in the placing of a contract with the lowest bidder for an inferior article. Vendors interpreting the indefinite specifications to mean a higher grade commodity lose the contract, and unfairly so. For cities to purchase articles by specifying trade names is to discourage competition because of discrimination against other trade marks. The "or equal" clause added to trade name specifications in order to eliminate discrimination works to the disadvantage of the city, because where such equality does not exist the burden of proof rests on the buyer.

Benefits of standardization of use

Corollary with the preparation of standard specifications for supplies is standardization of the use to which such supplies are put. A review of the purchases of any city will reveal many instances in which goods of superior quality are used for inferior purposes. One does not dress in broadcloth to dig in ditches, and a city should not purchase high grade goods for low grade use. Such standardization of use is of course difficult to accomplish because of the personal likes and dislikes of officers, and it must be done with their coöperation. Once established, however, it means not only economy in buying, but also the elimination of dozens of brands of articles used where one or two would be sufficient. The result is concentration of purchases, with obvious savings.

PURCHASING

The benefits of standardization of quality are these:[1] the article is used which experience has shown to be the best for the purposes; quantity buying is facilitated because the number of different articles bought is reduced; stock is reduced by the elimination of needless variety; emergency purchasing is curtailed; surpluses arising from the disapproval of goods on hand by new officials is done away with; favoritism in buying is avoided; the work of purchasing and inspection is simplified; accounting and auditing is made easier; and finally, comparisons of prices is facilitated.

The authorities responsible for the standardization of supplies in New York City have suggested that responsibility for standardization should rest, not with the purchasing agent alone, but rather with a committee on which the more important city departments making purchases are represented, and before which important vendors and manufacturers can be called for consultation. This committee can bring together the best experience of the city, and at the same time develop a coöperative enterprise that will have the complete support of all of the operating units concerned. The first problem of a standardization committee is the selection of articles for which the standardization of specifications will be made, and the number of grades or varieties of each article necessary to meet the precise needs of the departments.[2] The competent purchasing agent can say immediately what articles are of the most importance and which involve the largest amount of money, and the departments themselves can indicate the varieties needed. Such a method is better than establishing some scientific classification of supplies and materials, and taking up a single class at a time. Having determined the class of items and varieties to be standardized, specifications of similar articles used by other large purchasers, and the specifications adopted by the numerous scientific societies and governmental agencies engaged in this work should be examined and tentative specifications prepared accordingly. In this connection, it is necessary that the articles actually specified be used in current commerce, be produced in quantities sufficient to give the city an advantageous price, and not be so unduly precise as to limit competition. Following the preparation of the specifications, means should be found for their constant

CHAP. IX

Benefits of standardization of quality

Procedure for standardization

[1] As enumerated by Thomas, *op. cit.*, 134.
[2] New York City in 1910 analyzed 50,000 vouchers, obtaining a classification of 18,000 items purchased by departments, as a basis for standardizing the purchases of supplies through specifications.

164   PRACTICE OF MUNICIPAL ADMINISTRATION

CHAP. IX

Supply control

revision to meet changing conditions on the part of either the purchasers or the vendors. The tentative specifications should be finally adopted only after an experience period has proved their practicability.[1]

Although there has been criticism of the plan of establishing city stockrooms under the control of the purchasing department, the present tendency is in this direction. The confusion, duplication of inventories, and unnecessary expense of each department maintaining its own stock will be evident upon a little thought. While each department has specialized requirements, many of them use large quantities of the same supplies and materials. If each organization operates its own yards and warehouses, the total inventories in storage will be unnecessarily high, hauling will be done from the departmental stock instead of from the nearest available supply, and each department will use its own discretion as to the proper time and the proper amounts to buy. An alternative is the establishment of supply depots at suitable locations over the city, and under the entire control of the purchasing department. Goods can be stocked in conservative accordance with the requirements evidenced in the budget, purchases can be made when the purchasing agent, by special study, thinks the markets most favorable, and all charges paid for from a rotary fund. Upon presentation of a bill of materials for each job, goods will be released from the nearest supply and the appropriation of the department charged accordingly.

Stores record

A central storehouse necessitates the keeping of an accurate account of goods received and disbursed. This may be done through a perpetual inventory, such inventory to be in the form of bin records or stores ledgers, or both, each having its advantages for certain articles. When stores are delivered to a department, it should be charged something in excess of the actual cost price; this excess is to take care of the usual wastage through loss and breakage. This percentage of overcharge should be adjusted periodically to meet actual conditions.

A centralized store system does not necessarily mean the exist-

---

[1] In New York City it was found serviceable to call in not only the department heads in the final stages of the preparation of specifications, but also representatives of manufacturers and large dealers, in order that these persons might state their opinions on the tentative specifications and thus facilitate securing the best qualities at the most reasonable prices. Bids were taken on tentative specifications and upon the specifications that they superseded in order that test prices could be determined. For a more detailed statement of the New York procedure, see Thomas, *op. cit.*, Chap. VIII.

ence of a storehouse in which large quantities of goods used by the city are kept for distribution. It may mean merely a recorded control of the distribution of supplies purchased by the city, no matter where the supplies are kept. Frequently, these supplies are retained by the vendor, to be delivered only upon order of the purchasing agent.

The principal objection to a centralized storehouse is the possibility of the city overloading on supplies and having large sums of money invested in goods that may become obsolete, or on which there is a slow turnover at best. This is, perhaps, an argument not so much against the central storehouse as against incompetency on the part of the purchasing agent. No one would argue that a central storehouse should keep constantly on hand all of the thousands of articles that a city may purchase. Rather it should start in a small way, dealing in those articles which cannot be easily delivered from vendors at a wholesale price.

The matter of used equipment raises an interesting point with respect to the duties of the purchasing agent. Primarily he is looked upon as a buying officer. He should also be considered a selling officer for salvaged material and as exchange center for the departments of the city government. Each department finding itself in need of equipment should be required to communicate with the purchasing department to determine whether such equipment is available in some other unit of the government. Similarly, every department having supplies or equipment to dispose of should register such material or equipment with the purchasing agent, or deposit it in the central storehouse. In this way it is possible for the surplus goods of one department to be utilized by another, with substantial savings.[1]

Because centralized purchasing has been subject to such violent criticism by both vendors and departments, it may be well to summarize from the foregoing discussion the points at which this service has failed. In many instances the difficulty lies at the door of the purchasing agent, who often is unfamiliar with the requirements of his job, and who does not have sufficient understanding and moral courage to break down the illogical procedure that he inherits. If the purchasing agent is a mere order clerk,

---

[1] The recent activities of the United States Budget Director have forcefully emphasized the savings that are possible by such an interchange, and at the same time have indicated the deliberate waste of one department buying goods in the open market in which another department is selling substantially the same article because found unnecessary.

buying minute quantities of supplies as they are requisitioned by the departments, ignoring the benefits of standardizing both use and quantity, and placing no control over inventories, then the real benefits of centralization are thrown away. Such purchasing adds only red tape and delay to the ills of the former individualized methods, aggravating rather than helping an already bad situation.

CHAPTER X

MOTOR TRANSPORTATION [1]

The control of publicly owned motor equipment is a function of city government made necessary by the wide adoption of motor vehicles for municipal uses and the large resulting expense. It is doubtful whether the many diversified services of modern municipal government could be rendered satisfactorily but for the almost complete motorization of practically all branches of city service. The administrative officer finds that the use of the automobile facilitates the personal supervision of the numerous activities within his jurisdiction, provides rapid transportation for men and equipment to and from jobs far distant from the city hall, or other headquarters, permits the tripling and quadrupling of results from inspectors and others required to make personal visits to work or persons, and practically supplants horsedrawn vehicles with speedy, large capacity trucks for long distance hauling, and at material reduction in costs. Also, much of the city's special equipment such as fire apparatus, street sprinklers and sweepers, ambulances, and buses, are motor driven. The great extent to which private industry has found motor vehicles an economical instrument of production justifies their wide adoption by municipal governments.[2]

The wide adoption of motor equipment

With the general adoption of motor equipment, each department of the city government considered its transport problems and facilities as separate and distinct from those of all other departments, acquiring the machines requisite to its needs, and

Abuses of decentralized control

---

[1] For a thorough discussion of this subject see Percival White, *Motor Transportation* (McGraw-Hill, 1923). Certain chapters of interest will be found in Roy Hauer and George H. Scragg, *Bus Operating Practice* (International Motor, 1925). For current reference, see *Motor Transport* (monthly), *Automotive Industries* (monthly), and *Motor Trucks* (monthly).

[2] Russell Forbes, research secretary of the National Association of Purchasing Agents, writing in the *American City*, XXXI, 359-362 (October, 1924), states that in 1911 motor trucks were used in only 85 of our cities, and that a total of only 387 were then in operation. In 1920 the number of trucks in use had increased to 7,840. In 1923, over 16,000 were in use in 3,895 cities. The 16,000 trucks represented an investment of almost thirty-one and a half million dollars. This does not include other motor equipment now widely employed.

168 PRACTICE OF MUNICIPAL ADMINISTRATION

CHAP. X

insisting upon a separate administration of them. This procedure immediately developed the inherent weaknesses of decentralized control. Departments that needed an automobile for only a small part of each day bought cars, with the result that an unnecessarily large investment was made in motor equipment. The type of cars purchased was dictated by the whim of the department concerned, regardless of the type most economical for the use involved. Officials, impressed with their own importance, found a ready outlet for that emotion in the purchase of expensive cars, establishing precedents soon emulated by department heads of equal rank. Elegant cars called for professional drivers, who, if not allowed by the city council, were surreptitiously drafted from competent employees already on the payroll of the department concerned. Such cars, of course, were used in transacting city business, but official junkets sometimes called for their being driven halfway across the continent. Often, too, they served all of the transportation needs of both the official and his family, both in and out of working hours. Certain equipment was duplicated by branches of the city government, although it stood idle for a considerable part of the year; for example, trucks used for rubbish collection in the summer were seldom available for snow removal in the winter. The maintenance and repairs were either cared for by a separate organization in each department or at private garages at high prices.

An analysis of the problem

Administrations having any business sense at all were not long in appreciating the increasing importance of automobile purchase and maintenance as an item in the city budget; also the fact that these automobiles were a gross extravagance as long as they served private as well as public purposes, and were bought and operated under unbusiness-like methods. Analysis of the situation suggested that what a city government required was the efficient and economical transportation of persons and things, and that the automobile could be made an effective instrument to that end, as measured in the number of units of work that could be produced and the costs for each unit. But the production of low cost transportation units involved reducing both capital investment and operation expense to an absolute minimum. No more cars should be purchased than necessary to the transportation needs of a city; the investment in each car must be the least possible consistent with the type of service required of it; and the car, once bought, must be made to produce the greatest possible mileage at the least possible cost, and be used only in public business of requisite importance.

As usual, low unit costs could be secured only by large scale production, and large scale production could be secured only by a consolidation of transportation service under expert supervision. As a result, a number of larger cities undertook to standardize motor equipment to exact needs, and place the operation and maintenance under centralized control.[1]

Solution found in standardization and centralized control

It will be apparent that the same type of motor vehicle, operated under the same conditions, cannot be made to serve all city purposes. The mayor of a great city cannot be expected to drive personally his own car on public business or use an open car of the most inexpensive class for the entertainment of distinguished visitors. Important executive officers are entitled to automobiles of quality and character compatible with the dignity of their office, and ordinarily to the services of a professional driver. Less important officers may prefer cars of the same kind, although for all practical purposes a moderately priced vehicle of low maintenance cost will serve equally well. An even less expensive automobile may be adapted to the numerous uses of many minor city employees whose chief requirement is a speedy and inexpensive method of transportation without undue emphasis upon comfort or æsthetic qualities. Some cities standardize their passenger cars into three classes,—*i.e.*, light, medium, and heavy, which appear to meet all principal requirements. A special make of car is selected as best fitted for each class of service, on the basis of appearance, dependability, and economy. When such selection has been made after mature consideration of requirements and of the merits of competing manufacturers, it should be adhered to regardless of the pressure that will be brought each time a number of cars are purchased. Trucks are standardized in a similar manner.

Standardization of vehicles

Advantages of standardizing types of vehicles for the several city purposes come not only from a reduction in initial investment, but also from reduced cost of maintenance. When a city has in use a large number of automobiles of a similar make, it is possible to purchase repair parts in quantities at wholesale prices, to have these parts on hand without the duplication that would be

---

[1] In 1924, according to Mr. Russell Forbes, 31 cities had undertaken some type of centralized control of motor equipment.

170   PRACTICE OF MUNICIPAL ADMINISTRATION

necessary with a number of diversified makes of machines, and to permit the speedy familiarity of garage mechanics with the repairs necessary on the cars in use. With the standardization of machines and repair parts goes also the standardization of supplies, such as oil, gasoline, and other requirements of current operation.[1]

Centralized control of vehicles

The second essential to economical motor transportation is control of maintenance and operation, which can be secured only through the unification of authority with respect to this service. The supplying of transportation must be entrusted to a single agency of the government created for that purpose. As to personal qualifications, the individual responsible for this activity should be reasonably familiar with the mechanics of automobiles, and understand the work necessary to be done on machines, even though he does not undertake that work himself. Of more importance, his authority should be so definite, and his tenure of office so secure, that he can contend successfully with the heads of other departments who will continuously importune him for more service than is actually required, and continually criticize the character of the service rendered, since it will be always less satisfactory in the opinion of the departmental executive than that provided by the departmental ownership and operation of cars.

A centralized garage

To secure complete control of transportation, the title of and responsibility for all city cars should rest in the transportation department, and their operation and maintenance should be under its control. Such control implies a central garage where publicly owned cars, with the exception of certain special equipment noted later, are stored and repaired, and from which cars can be dispatched as required for departmental use.

Maintenance

Cars in continual use will be driven by the employees using them, being taken from the garage in the morning and returned at night. Employees having only intermittent use for cars can obtain them upon call when desired. Under this system all cars are in the garage when not in actual service, and subject to current inspection as to mechanical condition, and needed minor repairs can be made immediately. Drivers, upon returning cars to the garage, should make note of any needed repairs made evident by the day's driving. The availability of a few reserve cars

[1] It is reported that in Norfolk, Virginia, during a single year, there was saved in wholesale discounts on repair parts alone an amount equal to the payroll of the gaarge. In Houston, Texas, the operation of the municipal garage is estimated to have saved $20,000 a year.

permits all cars to be repaired promptly, and maintained continually in good operating order.

Centralized storage permits all supplies to be placed under control, and the cost charged to the account of each car. When the same cars are checked out in the morning and checked in at night to the proper persons, record can be made of mileage operated and of supplies issued. In this way it is possible to maintain proper cost records for each car, including depreciation, supplies, repairs, and tires; the total mileage secured for a period; and the total cost per mile.

Incidentally, a saving in the cost of supplies can be made by quantity buying. Tires, oil, and gasoline in quantities are always to be bought at liberal discounts from retail prices. Gasoline purchased in tank car lots, and issued from a central filling station, can be secured at a saving of several cents a gallon. It is also possible to make agreements with private filling stations throughout the city and environs to furnish gasoline and oil, using the coupon plan of payment.[1] Supplies, such as gasoline, oil, tires, etc., should be tested in a city or private laboratory, with supplementary road tests.

With cars under control at night, it is possible to reduce joy riding and the unauthorized use of cars to a minimum. Incidentally, there is an opportunity of educating car drivers to the proper use of the equipment placed in their hands. When a car has a frequent record of repairs due to accidents and abuse, it is proper for the person in charge of the garage to call the attention of the superior departmental officer to an apparent inefficiency on the part of the driver involved. The suggestion has been made that professional drivers be employed upon a wage bonus system. The repair records of the machines serve as the base of determining the additional wage. This system has proved an economy, due to the improved condition of machines, but is somewhat difficult of administration.

For the better control of vehicles while away from the garage mechanical devices have been perfected that tell a practically complete story of movements made. These instruments are largely utilized on trucks and automatically register the time of starting, periods in motion, periods standing, speeding, etc. In most business the average running time of trucks is less than three hours a day, the balance of the time being spent in loading, unloading,

[1] Unless complicated by a gasoline tax for which a municipality is not liable.

172 PRACTICE OF MUNICIPAL ADMINISTRATION

Motor despatch

or other inactivity. A truck is useful only when in motion, and information as to idle time permits the administrator to reduce this loss to a minimum.

As has been indicated, one of the excessive costs of the city operation of motor cars arises from the capital invested in vehicles that are not in continuous use. This waste can be eliminated by centralized motor despatch, however unpopular such service may be to officials who would prefer complete control of a car. Under this plan, officers having only occasional use for an automobile are loaned a car with or without a driver when needed. A city can well afford to supply a car and driver to officials having only occasional use for transportation, rather than buy cars and place them at such officers' entire disposal, even without drivers. Under this system, the officer in need of a car telephones the despatching bureau and the first available vehicle is placed at his disposal for whatever length of time required. Actual hourly and mileage cost can be determined for this service, and the department charged accordingly.

Taxicab service

After serious attempts to place the motor vehicles of the city of Pittsburgh under control, that municipality entirely discontinued the supplying of motor passenger vehicles for the occasional use of departments. As a substitute, an agreement was entered into with certain taxicab companies by which service is rendered to proper officers upon demand, payment being made in the form of a service order. Books containing a number of blank trip orders are furnished to the departments and officers entitled to them, and when properly filled out, are accepted by any taxicab company as cash. These service orders are transmitted monthly to the city for collection. Careful records are kept by the motor authorities as to the cost of rides, and all records are checked to prevent abuses which might creep into such a system. It is reported that this system in Pittsburgh has worked a considerable economy in the city's expense of automobile transportation, and has enabled the city practically to eliminate the investment in vehicles of this kind. Doubtless its inauguration would be resented by those officials accustomed to having control of their own vehicles, and it is entirely possible that a too rigorous enforcement of regulations might cause employees to use up valuable time walking or on street cars when they should be riding in automobiles.[1]

---

[1] A complete discussion of this plan will be found in the pamphlet *How Pittsburgh Solved Its Official Transportation Problem*, by the Adoption of

In the smallest of municipalities, owning and operating only one or two, or at the most a few, machines, the use of such cars for private as well as public purposes is often looked upon as a perquisite of office in lieu of salary, and openly recognized as proper. In such instances, it is the practice for the city to provide the car, plus a suitable allowance for operation and maintenance, no accounting being required for this appropriation.

<small>Operation subsidies for city-owned cars</small>

There is a recent tendency, in departments responsible for inspection and similar services calling for the fairly constant use of automobiles, to require inspectors and other employees to furnish their own cars. Maintenance is provided on a mileage basis from daily records submitted. These records are occasionally checked on city maps to prevent fraudulent charges. This plan might be extended profitably to many officials having part-time use for an automobile. A public employee driving his own car will give it care not ordinarily extended to public property. Or maintenance may be allowed as a lump sum which is the general practice of public service corporations.

<small>Operation subsidies for privately owned cars</small>

Some city-owned automobiles cannot be made subject to centralized control. Certain vehicles are subject to emergency use, as, for example, those of the water and health departments. In other instances, in which a car is in almost constant use throughout the day and its driver is far removed from the central garage, to require storage of the car would be folly. The loss of time on the part of the municipal employee entailed by going for and delivering the car each day would be considerable. Such cars may be placed under substantial control by the issuance of special permits to be secured for other than centralized storage, and the agreement that inspections and reports on such cars be had at regular intervals.

<small>Exceptions to centralized control</small>

It cannot be expected that cars used in the police and fire services will be placed under the control of the transportation authority. These cars are for special service and must be available instantly to the officials and employees using them. Fire department cars, in particular, have chassis and engines of special construction for fire fighting purposes, and not infrequently are combined with pumping and hoisting facilities. These types of vehicles require specially trained mechanics for their care, and no

Public Taxicab Service, by J. C. Slippy, chief accountant of the mayor's office, and distributed by the Yellow Taxicab Manufacturing Co., Chicago, Ill. The author states that this service was inaugurated only after heroic efforts had been made to place the motor vehicles of Pittsburgh under control.

one has ever seriously considered the removal of their control from the department in which they are lodged.

Also, it may be questioned whether the vehicles required by a single large department specializing in some particular service should be placed under centralized control, *e.g.*, a street cleaning department using a large amount of special equipment, in addition to numerous trucks, trailers, and tractors. Probably, in a large city at least, these vehicles can be taken care of in a garage provided by the particular department involved to greater advantage than would arise from transferring their control to a single central garage. However, there are instances in which the central garage maintains a jurisdiction over such special departmental garages, insuring unified methods of repairing and operating, and comparable cost records.

One of the irritating abuses arising from city ownership of motor vehicles is the use of such vehicles for private purposes. Such abuse is especially possible when motor vehicles are stored in some public garage or in private garages owned or controlled by the drivers. When cars are not under control, the correspondence columns of the newspapers will contain numerous letters from irate taxpayers, inquiring why a vehicle known to be city owned is running about the city at night, or is seen far in the country on a Sunday or other holiday. To prevent such misuse of public property, it is customary for all city owned cars, with the possible exception of a few executives' cars, to be labeled in large letters, with the name of the city, the number of the car, and the department to which it is assigned. In this manner, when a city car is seen either on or off its regular beat of duty, it can at least be recognized. Certain departments, however, object to the complete lettering and numbering of city vehicles, especially departments having night and sometimes country work or subject to emergency calls. Public criticism in these instances can be largely obviated by additional lettering, indicating that the car is a special service or emergency car. Even the numbering and lettering of cars will not completely stop their private use. City chauffeurs have been known to have special coverings made, which upon occasion can be dropped over the city's lettering, and other subterfuges will be resorted to, such as throwing a robe or other material over the number, or so besmearing the lettering with oil or dirt that it cannot be recognized. The difficulty can be overcome completely only when every publicly owned car is in a central garage during the hours when it is not occupied in public service.

In addition to physical control, it is necessary to have a financial control over cars owned and operated by a city. The records involved are not complicated, and their efficiency depends only upon the accuracy with which they are maintained. It is customary for the transportation authority to maintain a ledger account for each car owned. This ledger account indicates the make of the car, the model, year produced, original cost, license number, factory serial number, motor number, any other data that will be of assistance in identifying the machine, and the department to which assigned. On this record can be added charges for repairs, additional equipment, accessories, tires, parts, oil, gasoline, other supplies, and depreciation. These entries are made from garage repair tickets and service tickets, on which are entered the car number, hours of labor, and supplies used. Periodic reports can then be prepared, showing the monthly and yearly operating cost of each car, the car and tire mileage, and similar information that may be of value in determining the utility of the particular car, the care with which it is driven, and the cost of the service secured from it. Certain garages also keep a record of tires separately by number, indicating the make of tire, size, date of purchase, miles of service, and cost of repairs, in order to determine the relative value of the different tires on the market.[1]

In calculating the cost of vehicle operation, depreciation cannot be ignored, it being as essential a cost of operation as are gasoline and repairs. A car is lessened in value with each mile driven, and although this cost is not paid for at that immediate moment, it must be met ultimately in the purchase of a new vehicle. The principle of charging for depreciation does not vary, although the method of handling the subject does. A depreciation reserve or sinking fund is used to replace a motor vehicle after its period of economic use is ended. The item is considered as a fixed charge when calculated on a yearly basis, but as a variable charge when calculated on a mileage basis. The amount to be written off in either case depends upon the proportion of the total investment which is to be replaced by the funds so established. The

---

[1] An example of desirable operating records will be found in the *National Standard Truck Cost System*, adopted by the National Team and Motor Truck Owners Conference.

usual practice is to subtract the value of the tires from the total cost of the vehicle and thus arrive at the sum to be amortized.

When depreciation is calculated as a fixed charge, the estimated life of the vehicle is usually decided upon by the person responsible for the garage operation. The total amount to be depreciated divided by the number of years of the life of the vehicle will give the depreciation charge per year. When depreciation is calculated as a variable charge, the life of the vehicle is estimated in miles, and the amount to be depreciated is divided by this figure. The result is a depreciation charge per mile which, multiplied by the mileage of any period, will determine the reserve to be set aside for that period. In any statement of cost this depreciation loss must be included, although a city may not actually set aside the cash necessary to replace the vehicle. In this latter instance, the new vehicle is not charged to capital, but is treated as a replacement and is a charge to operating expense.

Repair contracts

What has been said with respect to the centralized control of motor vehicles is by no means equally applicable to all cities. There are many smaller municipalities in which the maintenance of a publicly owned garage and repair crew would be folly. The most feasible alternative is a contract with a private garage for the storage and repair of city machines.

Automobile insurance

Fire and theft insurance of a group nature can ordinarily be secured on city cars at a low rate, particularly if the cars are so distinctively marked as to minimize the possibility of thievery, but this course is recommended only for small communities. The liability of a city for damages done to persons and property through the operation of publicly owned cars raises a separate question. A city is not legally responsible for damages committed by automobiles operated by certain departments, such as the department of health, police, and fire. However, a moral obligation exists, and it is ordinary practice for a city to grant relief to persons so damaged. The greater number of municipal vehicles are operated by departments undertaking proprietary activities, such as street cleaning, garbage removal, etc. A city is completely liable for damages done by vehicles so operated. Under these circumstances it would seem wise for every municipality to make provision for liability insurance, although few do so, and the insurance companies have not yet developed policies applicable to city owned vehicles.

CHAPTER XI

LAW [1]

In certain respects, the relations of the legal advisor of a city government to the legislative and administrative branches are similar to those of the principal financial officer. Both pass frequent judgment on the legality of proposed acts, and in doing so exercise a dual control over the official conduct of their associates. However, the opinions of the legal authorities are advisory only, while those of the financial authorities are frequently mandatory. On the other hand, both officers perform routine duties only casually related to other activities of the government. The first of these functions requires an independence and freedom of opinion inconsistent with subordination to even the chief executive of a city. The second function is purely administrative, as administration has been defined, and should be controlled by the chief authority responsible for administrative policies.

The dual responsibility of the legal advisor

Thus, the duties of the legal advisor are both quasi-judicial and ministerial. The giving of legal advice to the legislative body and to city departments, either directly or through the chief executive, is a quasi-judicial activity. Acting as attorney in litigation for a city, serving so far as may be necessary as prosecutor of municipal ordinance violations, and the preparation of routine legal documents are ministerial or administrative functions.

Duties of the legal advisor

Legal advice is worthless if it is influenced by the desires of the authorities soliciting it. If a city council, a mayor, or a city manager is in a position to say to the attorney of a city that opinions with respect to the legality of proposed actions must be satisfactory or else an advisor will be secured who is more amenable, then the office of city attorney ceases to be a control upon illegal actions by such public officers, and the public is without the protection to which it is entitled. It may be concluded from this that the position of city attorney should be filled by election, or perhaps through appointment by the legislative body of

Methods of selection

[1] The standard references on municipal law are John F. Dillon, *Commentaries on the Law of Municipal Corporations* (5th ed., 5 vols., Little, Brown, 1911); and Eugene McQuillin, *A Treatise on the Law of Municipal Corporations* (8 vols., Callaghan, 1911).

the city, rather than by the mayor or city manager. If elected, the city attorney is in a position of complete independence and may exercise such check upon the actions of the legislative and executive branches of the local government as the law and his conscience dictate. If appointed by the legislative body, which is in turn elective, the relation of the attorney to the administrative offices of the city is one of complete independence. Although subordinate to the legislature, it may be assumed that this department will exercise a legitimate control over administrative functions. It is for this reason that in many municipalities the city attorney is an elective officer, and in many city manager charters is made either elective or appointive by the city council.

<small>Relation to administration</small>

<small>Quasi-judicial duties</small>

However, this independence of the administrative authorities may be a constant source of discord and maladministration. The sphere of city authority under state law, particularly in home rule communities, is vague, city charters are drafted loosely and frequently stand in opposition to state law, and the codification of municipal ordinances is undertaken so seldom that it is questionable whether a single large city in America could conduct its affairs properly under a strict interpretation of the law.[1] A city attorney, so minded, probably could prevent any aggressive action on the part of an administrator in the interests of citizens and taxpayers, by finding some technical reason why such action would be illegal. This is not an argument for the violation of law in the interests of effective government, but an argument for the sensible interpretation of law in that interest. If the state law, a city charter, or a city ordinance specifically forbids certain acts to be undertaken, then it is incumbent upon the administrator to refrain from such action, and upon the city attorney to advise that such action cannot be undertaken legally. But where there is reasonable doubt as to the legality or illegality of a desirable course of action fully sanctioned by those responsible for the administration of the city, and such action is without apparent detriment to anyone, it is sometimes advisable to proceed. It may be assumed that if any citizen's rights are invaded, he will have recourse to such legal protection as is given him by law, and the

---

[1] The Bureau of Municipal Research of Philadelphia has pointed out that there has not been a codification of the ordinances of Philadelphia since 1789, and that these ordinances would fill 35,000 printed pages. Many of the ordinances that have not been repealed prescribe restrictions on city departments no longer necessary and generally ignored. For example, it is provided that every automobile must be examined by the Bureau of Boiler Inspection before being operated on the streets.

courts have established the general policy of requiring close observance of delegated powers on the part of cities. Or in some instances the city may deliberately make grounds for a friendly suit which will determine the legality of its conduct.

Where financial interests are involved, the necessity for sound advice in these respects is apparent. Frequently the expenditure of large sums is involved and activities are embarked upon, which, if later proved unlawful, will result in considerable loss of money. It is important to note that in connection with the giving of legal advice, the relation of a city's attorney to a city is similar to that existing between attorney and client, and no redress is to be had should the advice given prove faulty. It is usual, however, in cases of major importance for test cases to be brought, and an adjudication to be made by the court of the doubtful issues before any considerable sums are risked. These suits are most often mandamus, or injunction, proceedings by some officer of the city against the officials concerned. Frequently, too, taxpayers bring these proceedings against the city and its officers.

The ministerial or administrative duties of the department of law include several classes of work: ordinances are drafted, contracts and leases drawn, deeds and abstracts examined, violators of municipal ordinances prosecuted, condemnation proceedings instituted, and the usual work of defending the city or of prosecuting claims in its behalf undertaken.

Of these duties perhaps the most important is that of representing the city in litigation either directed against the corporation or instituted by a city against other parties. Such suits are numerous, and a competent city attorney can earn his salary many times over by exercising sound judgment as to when a case should be settled out of court; and, when a case goes to court, by representing the city with an ability and preparation equal to that presented by the attorneys for the opposing litigant.

In these respects the service rendered by the city attorney's office in many cities is frequently ineffective. The official is often a political appointee, and his assistants young attorneys at a moderate compensation, to whom the office offers an excellent opportunity to extend acquaintanceship and to learn the practical details of court procedure. The office is crowded with requests for opinions originating with the legislative body and the heads of departments, and becomes so involved with work that the young attorney of the city finds himself in court ill prepared and opposed by some leader in the legal profession whose interest in the case at hand is large, from the point of view both of personal gratification and of compensation. These cases against the city range all the way from suits by individuals who have injured, or think they have injured themselves, on defective sidewalks, to great corporations which find themselves at odds with the municipality in respect to the proper execution of contracts. Incompetent service is seldom cheap, and this is particularly true of legal services. One good-sized damage suit lost through incompetency would pay the entire cost of an adequate legal staff. Also, the public utility corporations, with which cities find themselves in frequent conflict, do not scruple to employ the best talent available, and also to retain other talent in order to keep it from falling into the hands of the enemy.

Public utility litigation

The relations of the legal department of a city to public utility litigation are so important as to merit special attention. Rate regulation and the relation of public utility services to franchises, expired and unexpired, usually involve such substantial issues and sums of money that they eventually find their way into court. Rate cases often involve some constitutional question as to whether a given rate is confiscatory or represents a fair return on a fair valuation, and a large number go to the state supreme court and the Supreme Court of the United States. The controversies become mixed ones of politics, fact, and law, and the details of auditing and of securing engineering data should be supervised by the legal advisor. Too often, legislative or executive action is taken for political reasons without facts and without consultation with the legal department. As a result, the legal advisor is required to institute or defend suits which cannot possibly be won by the city, or the final settlement of a controversy is delayed when the municipal interests could have been preserved. Since a defective legal position is practically the only point at which private interests can successfully attack, a well-defined and carefully laid out legal plan is absolutely essential to accomplish any advance in municipal service at the expense of private business interests. Legislative and executive leaping without looking has caused more municipal setbacks and defeats in this field than any one thing.

Suits against a city

In considering the subject of damage suits against a city, it must be remembered that a municipality exercises both governmental and proprietary functions. At least it is a common rule of law that such distinction exists, difficult as it may be for the citizen and sometimes for the courts, to determine whether an activity belongs in one or the other group. A city is liable for damages arising from the wrongs of its officers committed in connection with proprietary functions; it is not liable when such wrongs are committed in connection with governmental activities, although the officer is personally responsible. These doctrines grow out of the ancient maxim that "the king can do no wrong," which meant originally that the king was not privileged to do wrong. The expression has now come to mean that a government is incapable of doing wrong so long as it carries on purely governmental functions. However, in these latter days, cities have undertaken what is known as proprietary functions, *e.g.*, the collection and removal of rubbish, supplying of water and other public utility services, etc., and it is in these fields of service that a city is liable for damage arising from the neglect of its employees. For example, a citizen may be run over by a garbage wagon and secure damages from the city; he may be run over by a fire wagon and not secure damages. One of these activities is a governmental function; one is not so governmental. But it is hard to perceive the difference between them,[1] and there is a tendency on the part of the courts to enlarge the proprietary field.

When suits are brought against public employees for their torts, such actions are frequently defended by the city's legal representative; or the legislative body may appropriate money to provide counsel, as in the case of police officers who are frequently sued for exceeding their authority. The chances of collection, even in case damages are allowed, are not very good.

Of course, when a city engages in public transportation, whether by street railways, subways, or motor buses, numerous personal injury cases will arise, and in such instances it is almost imperative that there be established a claim department which can specialize in the adjustment and prosecution of this particular type of litigation, just as is done by transportation utilities when privately owned.

In the discussion of police, courts, and correction in other chapters of this book [2] appear detailed statements concerning the offenses that may be committed against the citizens of a municipal-

---

[1] This subject is considered at length in Thomas H. Reed, *Municipal Government in the United States* (Century, 1926), Chap. VIII; Joseph Wright, *Selected Readings in Municipal Problems* (Ginn, 1925), Chap. XI; and W. B. Munro, *Government of American Cities* (4th ed. Macmillan, 1926), Chap. VI.

[2] Chaps. XIX, XXI, and XXII.

ity, the means by which justice is administered to the offenders, and the correction that is applied to them. It is sufficient to say here that a large part of the activities of local courts are devoted to the application of justice to persons who have violated the ordinances of the city, that is, to misdemeanants. The largest part of these misdemeanors consist of traffic violations, and a considerable share of the complex and extensive machinery that has been built up for the administration of justice in its various branches is devoted to the prevention of over-parking, violation of traffic signals, speeding, and other offenses that can be committed with an automobile. There are other misdemeanors, although many of them are prosecuted under state law rather than municipal ordinances. Within the municipal group are to be found the numerous offenses related to obstructing highways in one manner and another, failure to maintain proper sanitary conditions, and the numerous groups of prohibitions to be found in the code of city ordinances and designed to further the amenities of urban life. Unhappily, in American cities, these many regulations are frequently more honored in the breach than in the observance, although they constitute a part of the code by which true liberty is secured. It is annoying to be prevented by city ordinance from throwing rubbish into an alley or being prevented from parking one's car in front of a fire hydrant. Yet the fact that other persons are prevented from doing exactly these things mean greater liberty for everyone. This is liberty within the law, as opposed to license without law.

It is a part of the city attorney's duty to coöperate with the police and the courts in enforcing these regulations; although most of these cases are handled directly by the latter authorities without action by the city's legal advisors. Each morning in the courts of a large city will be found hundreds of ordinance violators who are appearing before the judge without jury, without prosecutor, and with scarcely the semblance of a trial. The word of the police officer with respect to the charge is heard, usually the offender is asked to state his side of the case, and the verdict of the judge is rendered instantly. When several hundred cases are heard by a single judge in an hour, there is little opportunity for that careful administration of justice so much to be desired. Theoretically, the city attorney or an assistant is present at these court sessions, but in larger cities he is seldom there unless the case is of considerable moment. In cases where an ordinance violation assumes the dignity of a formal trial, the city attorney's office

LAW 183

will have someone present to represent the interest of the municipality.

In court, ignorance of the law is not an excuse for law violation. However, the maintenance of public order is more dependent upon voluntary law observance than upon law enforcement, and to be observed laws must be known. For this reason provision is usually made for the publication of municipal ordinances either in a newspaper of general circulation, or, in large cities, in the official organ of the municipality. Such publication, valuable as it is, is totally inadequate. Departments that are particularly interested in the enforcement of certain ordinances, particularly those of a regulatory nature, should make provision for their periodic publication in leaflet form, and their distribution to householders. In addition, there should be frequent codification of all ordinances with amendments in order that they may be easily accessible to the public. Too often this collection, revision, and codification of ordinances is neglected by cities for years at a time; many obsolete and unenforceable regulations remain as law; and frequently the administrative officer as well as the citizen is in a quandary as to which particular legislation is in force.[1]

Mr. Edward D. Greenman suggests that in an exemplary municipal code the subjects should be arranged by chapters, articles, sections, subdivisions, etc., and present a classification which can be contracted or expanded to suit the needs of the various cities. Smaller cities can devise a code with the simplest method of classification, while larger cities will need a more elaborate and detailed one. All municipal codes should be divided into two divisions, namely, (1) administrative ordinances pertaining to the control and management of city departments, and (2) regulatory ordinances affecting the life, property, welfare, and conduct of the citizens.[2] This division has the merit of setting off the regulations under which the administrator works in a separate section of the code, thus conserving the time and energy of such officers.

In practice, there is a wide variation in the methods by which the legal advisors of the city are chosen. In a few cities this official is an appointee of the mayor or city manager; in most communities he is elected by the public or by the council. It may be assumed generally that the duties requiring independence on

[1] See footnote on page 178.
[2] "Codification of Municipal Ordinances," *Municipal Index, 1925* (American City), 39-43. This is a detailed discussion of the subject, and includes an outline for a model code.

the part of the city attorney are less important than those requiring dependence and coöperation with the administrative offices. For this reason, in principle, it may be stated that the city attorney should be appointed by the chief administrative officer of the community, whether he be mayor or city manager. The subordinate offices of the department are frequently protected by civil service, their tenure being during good behavior. This is as it should be, because even an attorney of such small experience or limited ability as to be willing to accept a civil service position in a city government may develop such ability and such familiarity with the particular subject with which he is required to deal that his retention in office over a long period of years is highly desirable.

The scope and magnitude of duties determines the size of the organization. In larger cities a department of law is created with an administrative head and several assistants. In small cities the department is less pretentious, and often only the part-time service of some practising attorney is required. In the larger communities one employee may be assigned to the preparation of ordinances and the drafting of interpretations required by the legislative body and the chief administrator; another may be in charge of the ordinary damage suits brought against the city; another, responsible for condemnation cases. The numerous branches of a city's legal activities makes different types of mind, if not different training desirable.

In addition to the personnel immediately attached to the city attorney's office, in a large city there is need for legal advice in a number of the more important departments. It is also customary for the police department, and the department of education, to have attorneys of their own. Sometimes these officers are employed independently of the city attorney's office, but it is to be preferred that special individuals be delegated to these particular services by the office. In highly important litigations it is customary, too, for the city to employ legal talent of a special character to assist its regular legal advisors. Such a course is desirable, but in larger cities is occasionally abused for purposes of patronage.

In addition to definite legal work to be done, a large city necessarily must have some one in its legal department who can advise the numerous poor citizens who constantly visit its offices to seek redress from private or public wrongs. Frequently, a few moments, conference will prevent a private disaster or expose situations which would promote injustice or frauds. In other words, there should be developed in a legal department a certain social service instinct, even though other agencies, such as legal aid bureaus, exist to take care of such cases. A large number of unfortunate citizens will seek the law offices of a city for advice and help, and indifference to such requests lessens the applicants' faith in government.[1]

[1] On this subject, see *Legal Aid Work* (Annals, CXXIV, March, 1926); and *Growth of Legal Aid Work in the United States* (Bulletin of the U. S. Bureau of Labor Statistics, No. 398, January, 1926).

CHAPTER XII

PLANNING [1]

A modern municipality should secure to its citizens those physical improvements that will facilitate transportation, promote comfortable and hygienic living and further the æsthetic character of the community. Such improvements are not the result of casual individual effort but come from the consistent scientific direction of city growth. In the opinion of Mr. Walter Blucher [2] this direction should comprehend control of (1) street layout; (2) traffic; [3] (3) platting of subdivisions; (4) parks, playgrounds, and playfields; [4] (5) local transportation facilities, including rapid transit; (6) water front development; (7) public buildings; (8) water mains; [5] (9) sewerage; [6] (10) housing; [7] (11) zoning, and (12) landscape and beautification.

Planning and re-planning Complete control of physical developments is only possible in a new city and in the new areas of an old one. With few exceptions the older sections of present-day municipalities, like Topsy, "just growed." These sections can be replanned to meet modern requirements, but such replacing can be carried out only in a limited way and when conditions become intolerable. Important streets may be opened and widened, but a community is never rebuilt on new lines unless some disaster, such as fire or earthquake, makes such action feasible.[8]

[1] Numerous books, pamphlets, and magazine articles are available on the many phases of city planning. Theodora Kimball, *Manual of Information on City Planning and Zoning* (Harvard Univ. Press, 1923), has a most valuable bibliography. Among general references, see Nelson P. Lewis, *The Planning of the Modern City* (2d ed. Wiley, 1923); Frank B. Williams, *The Law of City Planning and Zoning* (Macmillan, 1922); Charles M. Robinson, *City Planning* (Putnam, 1916); Thomas Adams, "Modern City Planning," Supplement, *Nat. Mun. Rev.*, XI (June, 1922), and John Nolen (ed.), *City Planning* (National Municipal League, 1916). For current reference, see *Proceedings of the National Conference on City Planning* (annual); *City Planning* (quarterly); *Journal of the Town Planning Institute of Canada* (bi-monthly); *Housing Betterment* (quarterly); and *Journal of the American Institute of Architects* (monthly); *The American City* (monthly).
[2] Secretary of the Detroit City Planning Commission.
[3] See Chap. XX.   [4] See Chap. XVII.   [5] See Chap. XXVIII.
[6] See Chap. XXVII.   [7] See Chap. XIII.
[8] Paris undertook considerable replanning without such incentive; on the other hand, London, after the great fire, refused to follow Wren's plan. Tokio, after its recent disaster, adopted a compromise re-plan.

PLANNING

<small>CHAP. XII</small>

Such part of the planning authority as is not delegated to specific operating departments ordinarily rests with a city planning commission.[1] Such official commissions are an outgrowth of voluntary groups of citizens organized for the purpose of suggesting city plans. These suggestions indicated the feasibility of planning, and gradually induced its adoption by public authorities. However, early city planning commissions, whether official or voluntary, undertook to prepare a city plan, and then ceased to exist. This was a mistake, and nowadays permanent commissions are usually appointed.[2] "The city is not a static thing to be made complete, according to model once for all, but a growing and changing organism. Not only must the plan be prepared but it must be enforced on forgetful and sometimes unwilling city officials and property owners, and added to or modified as the growth and change of the city demands. All this requires the watchfulness and study of a planning executive—a duty which the commission that prepared the plan, if a proper one, is best fitted to perform. The planning commission should therefore, from the start be a permanent one."[3]

<small>The city planning commission</small>

A city planning commission is ordinarily composed of from five to fifteen citizens appointed by the mayor or council, and who serve without pay. However, there are instances of ex-officio membership and of commissions made up of the heads of city departments, with a few laymen added. A planning commission usually has authority within the incorporated area of the city, and control of real estate platting over a peripheral area, which generally extends from three to five miles outside.

Valuable as such planning control may be, it is insufficient for large communities having large outlying developments. To plan for such metropolitan areas, there must be a regional planning commission, or close coöperation between the commissions of the several communities.[4] Almost inevitably small municipalities will be incorporated in a neighboring large one, or so completely or partially surrounded by the principal city that no physical line of demarcation is in evidence. Physically, such contiguous cities are one, their street systems are continuous, and their tran-

---

[1] It is reported that the first permanent official planning commission was appointed in Hartford, Connecticut, in 1907.
[2] Frank B. Williams, "The Law of the City Plan," *Nat. Mun. Rev.*, Supplement, Vol. IX, 661-690 (October, 1920).
[3] *Ibid.*, 673.
[4] See Frank B. Williams, *The Law of City Planning and Zoning* (Macmillan, 1922).

188   PRACTICE OF MUNICIPAL ADMINISTRATION

CHAP. XII

sit facilities and utility services are often furnished from the same source. If the planning and replanning of these areas are uncorrelated serious obstacles to well-rounded development will arise.[1] Sometimes the county can be used as the administrative area for planning, especially when it is almost entirely urban; and under any circumstances the county authorities should control real estate plattage in villages too small to have a planning commission. Also there are many general county features, such as parks, highways and sewerage, that are subject to orderly development. This is particularly true when a county contains cities of any considerable size. There are as yet only a few such planning commissions in this country, most of them voluntary bodies; but regional planning promises to assume more and more importance.

Powers of the planning commission

Mr. Frank B. Williams has enumerated the several types of planning authority as (1) the giving of general advice to the legislative body and to city officers; (2) the giving of such advice as a prerequisite to action by these authorities; (3) the giving of advice that may be overruled by more than a majority vote of the legislative body; and (4) absolute control of the character of improvements, subject to such limitations as may be imposed through the financial authority of the city council. Mr. Williams's discussion of these powers is summarized in the next few paragraphs.[2]

General advice

Planning commissions, including those that are given additional powers, naturally have the right to prepare a plan for a city and environs and present that plan to the appropriate legislative bodies and other authorities, as well as to the private interests concerned. This right, limited as it may be, is useful in so far as a competently prepared plan will appeal to the common sense of a community. In the long run it may be expected that many features of such advisory plans will be followed out, although sometimes materially modified. Voluntary commissions have seldom had more than advisory powers, and occasionally official commissions have but little more authority.

Advice as a prerequisite to action

More recent planning legislation has provided that city planning authorities, in addition to giving general advice, shall report on certain specified matters before any other public authority may take final action upon them. This advice may be ignored,

[1] The planning of Boston and its suburbs is controlled by the planning authority of the metropolitan district. For a discussion of the problems and government of metropolitan areas, consult Thomas H. Reed, *Municipal Government in the United States* (Century, 1926), Chap. XVIII.
[2] *Nat. Mun. Rev.*, op. cit., 675-676.

PLANNING

but if it is, there is full knowledge on the part of the public and other officials that expert information and suggestion have been disregarded. Fortunately, a custom has grown up in many communities of having all public projects referred to the city plan commission before final action is taken, even though specific legislative requirement on the point does not exist.

A few laws and ordinances provide for such a report as a prerequisite to legislative or administrative action on specific projects, and further provide that this advice may be overridden only by a specific vote of the legislative body. This provision is not general, and its advisability is somewhat in question.

Advice that may be overridden

In a limited number of instances, the planning authority is given power not only to plan but actually to carry out a city's policy in respect to public improvements. This erects the city plan commission into an actual board of public works, subject only to such financial restrictions as may be imposed by the legislative body. Such an arrangement is not advisable.

Absolute control

Frequently, city plan commissions have authority to pass upon all projects of an artistic character, in order to protect the city not only from itself but from the misguided ideas of private donors of art objects. Authorities hold that in large cities the art commission and the city plan board should be distinct, since different qualifications for members are desirable.

Control of art

Regardless of the powers conferred upon the planning authorities, it is not expected that the individual members will possess an expert knowledge of city planning. It is, therefore, incumbent upon the commission to employ a consultant, permanently if possible, to collaborate with other city authorities. This expert should be employed in making the preliminary survey, and in fact during the entire working out of the plan. When a permanent city planning executive cannot be employed, the temporary consultant should undertake this work in conjunction with the city engineer, since it is extremely important to have someone on the job who is familiar with local conditions and who can be responsible for the continuous development of the plan and its adjustment to meet unforeseen circumstances.[1]

Expert advice

In large cities there should be a properly qualified city plan executive with a reasonably permanent tenure of office. This officer is necessary "to keep the plan constantly alive, and to estab-

Type of executive

CHAP. XII

---

[1] Thomas Adams "Modern City Planning," Supplement, *Nat. Mun. Rev.*, XI, 157-177 (June, 1922). This is an excellent brief discussion of the methods of city planning.

lish such contacts with city officials and private bodies as will promote the carrying out of the various portions of the plan for which they are responsible. The qualifications of such a man must include personality and evident capability such as to insure the confidence and support of administrative officials, council members, and the public generally; familiarity with the provisions of the city plan and the reasons back of them; technical ability to make such adaptations of plan features as may become necessary in the changing conditions of a growing city, and forcefulness of character, sufficient to prevent unwarranted changes or abandonment of particular features where such action would impair the essential value of the plan as a whole. The appointment of such an executive coincident with the adoption of a city plan by the city plan commission is a most important step for insuring the success of the work." [1]

Survey

Intelligent city planning must be based upon accurate facts as to the physical character and future requirements of the community, and the first act of a planning commission must be the collection of data relating to street layout and use, nature and location of underground structures, distribution of population, character and use of transportation facilities, public spaces, industries, topography, etc. These data may be supplemented by aerial maps, which are of value for visualizing the natural features and the densities of building.[2]

Interpretation of data

When all available data have been interpreted by persons conversant with the technique of planning, recommendations will evolve, both for replanning existing conditions, and for preventing unwholesome developments in the future. These recommendations, particularly as they relate to replanning, may constitute a program to be worked toward over a long period of time. Certain of them because of financial limitations or the opposition of property owners may never be realized. But at least the ideal will be before the public and its representatives, and whatever progress is made represents complete gain.

Changing nature of city plan

Under any circumstances the planning body should not feel that its work is completed with the framing of a plan, rather it should consider that it has barely begun. The plan must be constantly changed to meet changing conditions; errors must be corrected; and the public must be constantly educated to the advan-

---

[1] Glenn Phillips, "City Planning," *Government of Cincinnati and Hamilton County*, 400.   [2] Adams, *op. cit.*, 162-163.

PLANNING

tages to be realized. Too many practical, as well as beautiful, city plans have been made and printed only to collect library dust, because the authorities responsible for them failed to vitalize the results of their efforts. The successful city planner must impress his ideas upon the commission; so in turn the commission must convince the public of the practicability of the plans proposed, and of the necessity that they be materialized.

The city planner is first concerned with the street layout, of which there are two general types—regular and irregular. The regular or "gridiron" plan to which American cities are thoroughly addicted, probably results from our land surveys and mile interval roads, with which every student from the middle west, at least, is familiar.[1] The gridiron has been generously criticized for its monotony, its disregard for topography, and the inability of traffic to "cut crosslots." The plan does have the merit of simplicity, affords the maximum use of land, and when sensibily modified with radial and curvilinear roads will continue as the foundation of street design.

The irregular or radial plan consists of a central point from which thoroughfares radiate; or there may be several points with connecting radial streets.[2] A city seldom adopts the pure radial plan; what it does is rather to superimpose radial streets upon a network of parallel and perpendicular streets, this providing more direct routes from one section of the city to another, and a relief from the monotony of the regular system. The combined radial and gridiron layout, giving reasonable consideration to topography, is most satisfactory. The intersections of diagonal highways with gridiron streets must be given careful treatment to avoid waste areas and dangerous and inconvenient traffic points; and a scheme of radial and curvilinear streets can be carried so far as to be more picturesque than convenient.[3]

Street layout with respect to width, direction, and the removal of dead ends and dangerous intersections is determined essentially by traffic requirements. On the basis of traffic carried streets may be classified as through, major, and minor streets, although this

---

[1] There is evidence that Egyptian cities were so laid out, as were the Roman camps that served as the origin of so many European municipalities.

[2] L'Enfant's plan for Washington is an excellent example of the compound radial built upon a gridiron of secondary streets.

[3] For a valuable discussion of street layouts, including widths, intersections, and grades, see Herbert S. Swan and George W. Tuttle "Land Subdivisions and the City Plan," *Nat. Mun. Rev.*, Supplement, XIV, 7 (July, 1925).

192   PRACTICE OF MUNICIPAL ADMINISTRATION

Street ornamentation

division is sometimes amplified. The titles are sufficiently descriptive so that definition of each is unnecessary. In laying out these streets, odd widths are no longer in vogue, consideration being given to the number of traffic lanes that must be accommodated. Each lane requires approximately ten feet of width, and provision must be made for multiples of two. The modern street is therefore forty, sixty, eighty, one hundred, or one hundred and twenty feet wide.[1]

The subject of street layout cannot be divorced from street ornamentation, which has not received deserved attention. Too often the selection and care of shade trees has been left to private initiative, with casual consequence or none at all. Satisfactory results can be obtained only when the city assumes responsibility for the selection, planting, and care of trees, assessing the cost upon the benefited property owner when necessary, and requiring official approval of the type and size of trees planted when such improvement is made by the property owner. Authorities have designated three general types of tree planting: the over-arching type designed to form a canopy over a street; the avenue type for producing vistas; and the decorative type used for forming decorative lines along the façades of buildings. These types of planting are applied to the several classes of streets—business streets, formal business avenues, residential streets, parkways and boulevards, and outlying roads of approach, as the nature of the street effect desired and the possibilities of plant growth under existing conditions dictate. The selection of the species of trees for planting purposes, the method of planting, the protection of trees from injuries, disease, and pests are problems that must be left to the park authorities, operating in conjunction with the city plan executive.[2]

Naming of streets

The official naming of streets is the function of the legislative body of a city, although actual selection of street names should be made by the city plan commission, which can give thought to the several problems involved. Mr. N. N. Wolpert, one of the few writers on the subject, suggests certain considerations that should be given.[3] First, the designation of alley, lane,

---

[1] See *Proposed Super-Highway Plan for Greater Detroit* (Detroit Rapid Transit Commission, 1924).

[2] For a detailed discussion of these questions, see T. Glenn Phillips, *City Tree Planting* (Detroit City Plan Commission, rev. ed., 1914).

[3] See N. N. Wolpert, "Observations on the Naming and Marking of Streets," *American City*, XXXIII, 620-622 (December, 1925).

road, avenue, and boulevard must not be indiscriminately applied to thoroughfares. Frequently the term avenue is used to indicate thoroughfares running in one direction, while the term street is reserved for those running at right angles. This is a suitable distinction if it can be generally applied. In other jurisdictions the word avenue is used to designate residential thoroughfares, while the term street is reserved, in general, for the business or main trunk highways. A "place" is usually a street only two or three blocks in length. The terms "terrace" and "road" are not in general use, and are usually reserved for thoroughfares of an unusual residential character.

In American cities, particularly those that have had a rapid growth, the designation of street names has been left largely to private initiative, and particularly to real estate operators who have chosen names within their subdivisions to suit their fancy. In consequence, it is common to find that continuous thoroughfares bear two or three different names in their progress across the city; that names are frequently duplicated; that names are chosen that have no historical or other significance, often being those of families interested in the property developed; and, what is most important, that the names do not give the stranger any indication as to location within the city. Numbering streets is of course a simple procedure which indicates location, but it has a monotony that is undesirable. There has been a tendency in recent years toward naming streets in alphabetical order, using two or three words beginning with A for streets near the center of the city, then progressing through the B's, and so on. Or streets may be appropriately named after the states in the Union if they are arranged in alphabetical order. Sometimes the names of the Presidents are used, in which case they should be arranged chronologically. Similarity of names should be avoided so far as possible.

Cities employ a variety of ways of displaying street signs. Mr. Wolpert urges that some standard plan be employed throughout the community, but that the most important consideration is that street signs of some kind be actually used and located where they can be seen. The amount of time lost by delivery wagon drivers and citizens in locating streets when street signs are absent would pay many times over that small sum necessary to mark every thoroughfare in a community. The method of displaying signs varies. A preferable plan is to have the signs erected on a post or standard on two diagonally opposite corners. If this is not possible, the signs may be attached to poles, or even houses. The most desirable sign indicates the name of the street in letters sufficiently large to be read easily from passing vehicles, with the name of the cross street appearing in smaller letters above, or below, and so placed as to be illuminated by the street lights at night. Some cities stencil the name of the street in black or white on the right hand corner of each street intersection. This system is appreciated by motorists, who are thus enabled to distinguish cross streets without difficulty.[1]

In planning mass transportation consideration must be given to the use of street railways, rapid transportation in subways or on elevated railroads, and motor busses.

Electric street railways, although a development of the older "horse cars," have been perforce superimposed on a street system already established. The administrator had no alternative but to place this slow, noisy, and dangerous means of transportation on through streets that were already over congested. The street railway was faster than its predecessors, the horse-car and horse-drawn omnibus, and relatively inexpensive of construction and operation. It served well, and still serves well, as a method of mass transportation, and no proven substitute has been offered. For the time being, at least, the city planner is concerned with the routing of cars so as to add as little to the congestion as possible, and in the newer sections to require sufficient street widths to accommodate both rail and rail-free traffic.[2]

At the present time the motor bus is the only competitor of the street railway, and the ability of the motor bus to care for mass transportation has not been demonstrated. The capital required for bus lines is small per unit of the transportation furnished; they have practically the same operating speed and costs as street cars, and can go around traffic rather than through it. If they could care for rush hour patronage their substitution for street railways would be rapid. Perhaps they can do this, and a controlled test on the thoroughfares of some large city is awaited with interest. In the meantime busses are effective as "feeders" to rail lines, and as a means of transportation in residential sections.

Street cars and busses are slow and of limited capacity, making some form of rapid transportation desirable in the largest cities,

[1] Wolpert, *op. cit.*
[2] See Chap. XX.

although there is danger of over emphasizing its necessity. This transportation may take the form of electric trains operating on elevated tracks or in subways. The former is the less expensive to construct, but is unsightly, dirty, inconvenient and noisy, even with ballasted road beds of the newer type. On the other hand, subways are of enormous cost, cannot be operated at an ordinary rate of fare,[1] and are only to be constructed by the wealthiest communities. The determination of the extent and routes for rapid transit are matters for specialists in this field, if lines are to be built and operated at a minimum of cost and additional congestion not to be piled on that already existing. The local planner can, however, prepare the way for subways ultimately to be built, by seeing that all main streets are one hundred and twenty feet in width. In this way the expensive underpinning of heavy buildings, which is otherwise necessary when excavations are made, will be avoided.[2]

Water front

The planning of the water fronts and their approaches is of importance in most cities, since practically all municipalities of over 200,000 population are either located on the sea or have access to it. The construction of docks and piers should be taken for granted, although actually, little has been done in the way of port development, and the prosperity of many cities is reduced, because shipping cannot load and unload goods. Such facilities as are available are seldom correlated with the steam and street railway systems and with industries. In consequence merchandise must be trucked at heavy cost through city streets, adding to existing congestion.

Parks and playgrounds

During the last two generations cities have become interested in the acquisition and maintenance of parks and playgrounds, primarily because the free open spaces disappeared before advancing building. Central Park, located in the heart of New York City and acquired in 1857, was not the first instance of park purchase, but was the first case of a city setting aside a considerable portion of its area for such purpose. Since then practically every important city has acquired parks and playgrounds as places of recreation for citizens. There are rather well-defined principles that should guide the city planner and the recreation authorities in

---

[1] The New York subways are not self-supporting; and those in Boston are so only by a high rate of fare in both subways and street railways.
[2] Outside the city limits of Detroit, streets 200 feet in width are being planned, so that subway tracks may be brought to the surface without interfering with other traffic. See citations, p. 192.

196   PRACTICE OF MUNICIPAL ADMINISTRATION

Civic centers

the location and development of these spaces, and they are discussed at length in another place.[1]

The planning of public and semi-public buildings provides an opportunity for the combination of utility and attractiveness. The city hall and other buildings devoted to government should be situated so as to be reasonably accessible from all parts of the city. Occasionally these structures are located as a civic center in which are brought together the important public buildings of the city and county, as well as the post office, public auditorium and union railway station. Cleveland has done more in this development than any other community.

Art groups

A variation of the idea is found in the art center, in which the library, the art museum, and possibly a university or other educational buildings are located. The architectural treatment of such a group is naturally different from that of the civic center, and in location, accessibility is perhaps not as important as is the possibility of æsthetic treatment.

Buildings scattered about city

The sites of library branches, elementary schools and police and fire stations should be determined not by ward politics, but by the possibility of serving the maximum number of people most conveniently. Library branches and schools could well be located on the same plot of ground, or even in the same building, but it is seldom done. Police stations and fire houses should seldom be grouped under the same roof, because the factors determining their location are widely different.

Buildings demanding special location

Municipal and private hospitals should be located outside of heavy traffic zones, in order to avoid noise and confusion. The house of correction, the poorhouse, garbage loading stations, incineration plants, and other public structures to which nobody wants to be neighbor must be located at various points throughout the city, but the problem of placing them most advantageously without offending residential districts is a perplexing one. Had cities been planned from the beginning, large open tracts could have been provided for these unwelcome, although necessary, institutions and utilities.[2]

Fountains and sculpture

American cities have grown so rapidly that comparatively little attention has been given to their artificial adornment. Stabilization of growth will doubtless be followed by this sort of artistic development. Portions of some streets may be used for ornamentation; and small areas are often found at street intersections

[1] See Chap. XVII.
[2] See Munro, *op. cit.*, 86, 87.

PLANNING 197

which can be treated in an artistic manner. Some of the more recent bridges and viaducts have been built for beauty as well as practicability.

CHAP. XII

The garden city movement, dating from the latter part of the last century, began as an economic and sociological, rather than as an æsthetic, conception.[1] The principle is one of coöperative town building in which unearned increment plays no part.[2] Undeveloped land is purchased upon which to build the city; industries and citizens are attracted by low rentals and improved living conditions. The city is scientifically planned—factories are properly located; about twelve houses are allowed per acre, to prevent over-population of the area, and frequently a limitation is placed upon the total population; the street plan is conveniently laid out; a setback is required in front of each residence; and a garden space is allowed to the rear. Around the city there may be an agricultural belt, to be cultivated, or to serve as a permanent park system separating the city from other communities.

The garden city movement

Little has been accomplished in the way of developing distinctly garden cities in America. More space has been available for city development, and many cities largely enjoy the advantages of the garden city without being incorporated as such. Several American efforts have failed because the practical aspects of the problem have been overlooked.[3]

Garden cities in America

The indiscriminate use of city area means that the municipality is a mere collection of structures and business activities rather than an orderly arrangement designed to further the well-being of all inhabitants. In newer sections, privately imposed restrictions have been widely employed for the protection of property values, particularly in high grade residential districts. Such con-

Zoning by private restrictions

---

[1] See Ebenezer Howard's *Garden Cities of Tomorrow*. The first garden city actually realized was Letchworth, England, about thirty-five miles outside of London. The original area purchased was about 4,000 acres, but it was later increased to near 5,000. The company was capitalized at $1,500,000 in small shares, that the factory worker might invest in the project. The rate of return was limited to five percent, the unearned increment being retained by the corporation to prevent speculation in real estate. The land being the property of the corporation, the resident did not own his property, but was granted a long-term lease. It was found that houses could be leased for about two dollars per week, a rate much lower than was possible in the ordinary city. The success of the first experiment was sufficient to warrant starting a second, Melwyn, at the close of the World War; and others are now in prospect.

[2] In the new capital city of Australia, unearned increment is being retained by the state.

[3] For an account of the garden city movement, see Ewart Culpin, *The Garden City Movement Up-to-date* (Garden Cities and Town Planning Assoc., London, 1913).

tractual restrictions have proved satisfactory only in the absence of more general restrictions imposed by law, and as a means of enforcing details of construction and use that cannot be governed by general law. Perpetual restrictions are frequently modified by changing conditions, and are accordingly nullified by court action; and the restrictions on neighboring property may be so lax as seriously to affect more highly restricted areas. The average life of contractual restrictions is estimated at from fifteen to twenty years, and older sections of a city are seldom restricted at all.

Zoning by general law

In consequence of this failure of private restrictions, or of the absence of any restrictions, buildings are constructed on the entire lot areas, thereby robbing neighbors of necessary light; they are built to any height regardless of street width, resulting in acute traffic congestion; and business structures intrude into exclusive residence districts, destroying property values. Zoning by general law is a process designed to end these evils through dividing a city into districts or zones, regulating the height, bulk, and arrangement of buildings, and also the use of buildings and premises, within such zones.[1]

Regulating the height of buildings

Laws governing the height of buildings differ widely in various cities. In New York the height is based upon the width of the street, there being districts in which the building heights may be two and one-half, two, one and one-half and one and one-quarter times, and also one time the width. After reaching the prescribed height it is necessary to set back the building at the rate of one foot for every four feet of additional height. Some cities allow buildings to be constructed on the street line to a height of 250 feet, compelling them to be set back if they go higher. Other cities set an arbitrary height above which no building will be allowed to go. Probably the best plan of procedure is to establish a reasonable height according to the width of the street and then require a setback upon exceeding that height. Such a regulation provides adequate light and air and relieves the monotony of an even building line by the creation of a distinctive style of tall building architecture. However, the real purpose of bulk zoning is not to create

---

[1] For excellent photographs illustrating the need of zoning in cities, see *A Building Zone Plan for Detroit* and *Zoning and Its Application to Detroit* (Detroit City Plan Commission, 1919 and 1922).

In 1916 there were zoning ordinances in effect in six cities; in 1926, 436 cities had such ordinances, among them forty-seven of the sixty-eight municipalities of over 100,000 population.

distinctive architecture, but to limit building to the traffic capacity of abutting streets.¹ CHAP. XII

Provision for the proper distribution of light and air between lot owners can be furthered by regulating the proportion of lot area that may be occupied by structures. Some buildings may properly occupy the entire lot, while others would be more valuable, as would their neighbors, if a portion of the lot were preserved to admit light and air. Height and area districts do not need to be coterminous and frequently are not. Area districts are usually designated by letters of the alphabet, commonly A, B, C, D, and E. The A districts may be warehouse and industrial districts in which the building may well cover the entire lot. The E district is that for detached residences where the building should not cover more than thirty percent of the lot.² Regulating the area of buildings

Should zoning stop with the creation of height and area districts, it would be possible for buildings of an undesirable nature to encroach upon residential areas. There would be nothing to prevent garages, stores, and small factories being built in the midst of fine residences, detracting from their value. Consequently, use districts are created which need not correspond with the other zones established, and usually do not. The types of district should be so few in number that their necessity may be established before the courts. Best practice at present dictates areas restricted to heavy industry, light industry, business, and residential purposes. It is not necessary to enumerate the various structures and activities that pertain to each district, as the designating names are fairly explanatory. As a general rule, any occupancy of a more restricted district is permitted within a less restricted one.³ Use zoning is also necessary to the successful handling of mass transportation. Regulating the use of property

A city zoning ordinance prevents the construction and use of buildings that do not conform to the regulations only after the ordinance has been passed, and it is doubtful if the courts would uphold retroactive regulations. Nonconforming buildings unless they constitute absolute nuisances, must be tolerated until the buildings have depreciated to the extent that their demolition is necessary. Any other policy means the appropriation of property without due process of law. When the time comes to alter a building Nonconforming buildings

¹ Edward M. Bassett, ''Zoning,'' Supplement, *Nat. Mun. Rev.*, IX, 315-341 (May, 1920).
² *Ibid.*, 323.
³ *Ibid.*, 324-325.

200 PRACTICE OF MUNICIPAL ADMINISTRATION

CHAP. XII

materially, the changes should not be allowed unless the character and use requirements of the district are met. Thus, it may be a number of years before a city can be completely zoned according to the letter of the ordinance.[1]

Who should prepare a zoning plan?

The question of who should prepare the zoning plan is one that each city must settle for itself. Sometimes the city plan commission, or more often a special zoning commission is utilized. In either case the commission should hold frequent hearings, secure the suggestions of property owners, and enlist the coöperation of civic organizations, chambers of commerce, improvement associations, taxpayers' associations, etc., to the end that the plan may have general acceptance and support.[2]

The law of planning and zoning

The authority wielded by any municipality in city planning and zoning must be specifically granted by state law. In planning, the state has the power to take private property for a public use by eminent domain if necessary, or by other means less ruthless. Zoning is undertaken under the police power of the state, which regulates private property in the interest of the health, safety, and morals of the people. The courts are also showing a tendency to uphold zoning regulations serving convenience and æsthetic values.[3]

Acquiring property for public use

City planning requires the government to take over a considerable quantity of private property, which is usually secured in one of three ways. When land is subdivided for residential purposes space must be left for streets, and it is usually dedicated to the city as an inducement to provide pavements and public utility services. This control of subdivision platting by a city within its own limits, and by the county in suburban areas, is one of the most powerful forces for successful city planning and should be utilized to the fullest extent by the public authorities. By this means the newer portions of a city can be planned as a part of a well thought out plan without the large expense of purchase or condemnation. To this end, there should be an established policy with respect to the acceptance of subdivisions, set forth in rules regulating street, sidewalk, and roadway widths; block length and widths; the extension of existing streets and the carrying of streets to the property line; dead end and offset streets; the enlargement of street intersections and curves; the deflection of streets within the block; alleys and public utility easements in the rear

Dedication

---

[1] Bassett, *op. cit.*, 326-327.
[2] *Ibid.*, 327-328.
[3] *Ibid.*, 327; and Frank B. Williams, *The Law of City Planning and Zoning* (Macmillan, 1922).

of lots; street grades; the width and depth of lots, and the relation of lot side lines to the street; reserve strips; and other similar factors.¹

CHAP. XII

In the older and already developed sections of a city, property for street widening and openings must be acquired by purchase or condemnation, as must be practically all land for playgrounds, parks, and the sites of public structures. Occasionally wealthy and public-spirited citizens will donate properties for parks and playgrounds; but no municipality can depend alone upon the generosity of its citizens for these facilities, and citizens can scarcely be expected to give sites for sewage disposal plants or for other unromantic uses. The practice of cities with respect to the purchase of needed properties varies. Where possible, many municipalities prefer to enter into direct negotiations with owners, the price being fixed by unbiased expert appraisal. Often public spirited citizens will purchase properties privately and hold them at no advance in price until the city can acquire them. However, since venal office holders have utilized their advance information to purchase property to be later acquired for public purposes, or have connived with citizens to mulct the city in transfers, some cities require that all properties be taken by condemnation.

Purchase

The right to acquire private property for public purposes, usually called the right of eminent domain, is inherent in sovereign governments and may be delegated to their agents. In the United States the owner of private property is protected by the constitutional provision that the exercise of this right must be in accordance with due process of law, and the states have set up elaborate procedures to safeguard private interests against public exactions. The details of these procedures are unimportant here; their variation from state to state is large. However, there are certain common features. For example, the property must be taken for a public purpose, the necessity of that purpose must be established, and the compensation paid must be adequate —all of these points to be determined through judicial process in a competent court.

Condemnation

At times it is desirable that more land be acquired by a munici-

---

¹ Herbert S. Swan and George W. Tuttle, "Land Subdivisions and the City Plan," *Nat. Mun. Rev.*, Supplement, XIV, 435-462 (July, 1925). The City Planning Commission of Akron, Ohio, has adopted interesting regulations governing the plotting of land. See *Public Works*, September 18, 1920. Also *Regulations and Requirements for Laying Out, Platting and Subdividing Land* (Wayne Co., Mich., Board of Auditors, 1925).

Excess condemnation

pality than is absolutely required for public purposes. This acquisition of more land than needed is known as excess condemnation.[1] The principle is relatively new in America and has encountered the decided opposition of the courts unless specific constitutional authority exists. Excess condemnation was first used in the United States as a solution of the remnant lot problem incident to street widenings and openings. Small and odd-shaped lots are often created by these improvements, which alone are of no value to the owner, and hence must be paid for by the city, although title does not pass. If these remnants could be acquired by a city, they might as a single holding be of some use and be disposed of accordingly. Of equal importance is the need of protecting the beauty of an improvement from the unsightly use of left-over parcels of land. When the public acquires a property and improves it, the adjacent areas immediately have an enhanced value. By excess condemnation this enhancement can be taken by the community that has created the increment. This last procedure is still somewhat distasteful to American communities, and taxpayers have an inherent distrust of the business ventures of a government.

Setbacks

Recently, cities have been endeavoring to reduce the difficulties of street widening by establishing setback lines on certain thoroughfares. Under this plan a street line is created, beyond which new construction is not permitted to encroach, except by the erection of temporary buildings. At a feasible time the land so vacated is taken and compensated for and the street widening accomplished at a minimum cost.

Rear lot condemnation

As a further means of reducing the cost of street widening in business areas, cities are experimenting with rear lot condemnation. Under this plan relatively inexpensive property to the rear of that affected by a widening is condemned, the alleys relocated, and the business structures moved back to allow for the street improvement.

Public control of private property

So far this discussion has been limited to the public acquisition and development of property. However, if the city is to be well planned it is necessary to control the development of private

---

[1] See R. E. Cushman, *Excess Condemnation* (Appleton, 1917); Frank B. Williams, *Law of City Planning and Zoning* (Macmillan, 1922); "Excess Condemnation," *Bulletins for the Constitutional Convention,* II, 107-123 (State of Massachusetts, 1917); "Eminent Domain and Excess Condemnations," *Constitutional Convention Bulletins* (State of Illinois, 1920); and *Report on Excess Condemnation* (Chicago Bureau of Public Efficiency, 1918).

property. To a certain extent, this can be done under the police power. The practice of zoning, already discussed, represents the most comprehensive planning by the authority of the police power. Other uses of this power for the protection of health, safety, and morals of the people are found in the application of building codes, housing regulations, factory laws, etc.[1]

One distasteful aspect of the modern city is created by the presence of advertising billboards. The courts have not permitted the regulation of advertising signs for æsthetic reasons only.[2] The most that can be said of such advertising is that it is inartistic, and up to the present time a person cannot be deprived of property solely because it is ugly. When billboards are so constructed or located as to affect the health, safety, or morals of a community they may, of course, be regulated; and some day such authority may be extended to æsthetic features. Advertisers have recognized that billboards, properly placed, artistically designed, and well constructed cannot be severely criticized, and have shown a tendency to coöperate with public authorities to these ends.[3]

The practical city planner will give serious attention to the financing of the plan. Idealists can vision the city of the future with broad thoroughfares, splendid public buildings, and picturesque open spaces. However, the immediate and urgent need is to plan with respect to financial possibilities. Legal limitations on taxation and debt, and public ideas as to governmental economy, establish very real barriers beyond which it is impossible to proceed. There are three means by which city improvements can be financed—taxation, the sale of bonds, and the levy of special assessments for benefits conferred—and in recent times there has been a decided tendency to emphasize the use of the last named method. The continuance of this tendency, coupled with the judicious use of other means, will permit the plan to move slowly toward completion through the years. "Rome was not built in a day"; nor can a great modern municipality be planned and replanned, built and rebuilt in a few years—perhaps not in several generations.

[1] See "Public Control of Private Real Estate," John Nolen (ed.), *City Planning* (National Municipal League, 1916).
[2] See p. 219 for a discussion of changing tendencies.
[3] For a more complete discussion of this subject, see Chap. XIII.

CHAPTER XIII

SAFETY [1]

The need of safety engineering

The complex character of modern city life is better evidenced by the activity of safety engineering than by any other public undertaking, unless it be traffic control. Nothing is more typical of today's civilization than tall steel buildings housing enough people to make a small city, with basements cluttered with machinery, express elevators, sanitary plumbing, and flaunting electric signs, all of them of possible danger to human life. Under these conditions, it becomes desirable for the community to protect itself against the defective construction of buildings, faulty construction and operation of elevators, defective electric wiring, fire hazards (including inadequate exits from buildings), dangerous boilers and machinery, and hazardous signs and billboards. This protection is designed essentially for citizens in their homes and in public places, and although it covers the construction of manufacturing buildings and their ordinary appurtenances, it does not include special industrial machinery. Most industrial states have enacted laws compensating workmen for industrial accidents, requiring safety devices on extra-hazardous machinery, and prescribing sanitary working conditions. This industrial safety is primarily an activity of the state government, although the local health authorities exercise a coördinate jurisdiction in enforcing health regulations.

Authorities responsible for safety

The local enforcement of other safety conditions is frequently distributed among a number of different authorities—plumbing, housing, and smoke abatement with the health officer; investigation of suspected arson, with the police; use of inflammable liquids, explosives, and other fire hazards, with the fire department; and

---

[1] Formal material on the control of building construction is not abundant. A wealth of informal data with respect to the organization of building departments and their administrative problems will be found in the *Annual Proceedings of the Meetings of Building Officials Conference*. Also, reference may be made to the *Report on the Administration of the Bureau of Buildings, in the Department of the City of Rochester, N. Y.* (Rochester Bureau of Municipal Research, 1921); and to the surveys of building departments made by various bureaus of governmental research.

SAFETY

the construction of buildings, elevators, and signs and the operation of elevators, boilers, and steam-actuated machinery, with a building department. Only in larger and more fully developed communities are all phases of public safety, except those relating essentially to health and police, entrusted to a single authority dealing with buildings and safety engineering. Such a safety department is ordinarily in charge of a single individual known as the superintendent of safety engineering, superintendent of building construction, or some other appropriate title. In many cities the position is filled by competitive examination, since not only must the occupant have the personal qualities of tact, courage, and administrative ability, but he must be technically trained in diversified phases of construction engineering.

<small>CHAP. XIII</small>

<small>Superintendence</small>

No safety ordinance can be so complete as to cover every possible situation. Exceptions dictated by common sense, if not in strict accord with the technical phases of the law, must be allowed. Hence certain discretionary authority must be lodged with the safety authorities. For this reason, one ordinarily finds a number of citizens connected with the department in an advisory capacity—sometimes as a board of appeal to which decisions of the administrative officer can be taken for final adjudication, and sometimes as a commission, having this appellate authority, but also responsible for the administration of the department, the technical officer acting as the immediate subordinate in charge. It is preferable that the citizen board should have only appeal duties, the administrative officer being directly responsible to the chief executive of the city, and that the membership of the board should be distributed among the architectural and engineering professions concerned with building construction.

<small>Adjudication</small>

On the staff of the building department must be trained engineers for the examination of plans and of special types of construction, artisans for the inspection of more simple construction, electric wiring, and plumbing, and properly trained persons for the inspections involved in associated activities such as control of elevators, signs, inflammable liquids, and smoke.

<small>Inspection</small>

The regulation of the construction of buildings and their appurtenances is a proper exercise of the police power of the state, preventing the use of private property in a manner inimical to the welfare of the public. Ordinarily such regulations are expressed in a state statute prescribing certain minimum building standards throughout the state, with more severe standards for cities of con-

<small>The building code</small>

<small>Definition and purpose</small>

205

206 PRACTICE OF MUNICIPAL ADMINISTRATION

CHAP. XIII

siderable size when special legislation is not prohibited by the state constitution. In addition, larger municipalities enact their own codes embracing details that cannot be covered by general state law.

Indirect effects

Such a building code is simply an ordinance, or number of ordinances, which because of effect upon the community are of special importance. Although the primary object of such codes is to prevent fires, protect persons and property from loss due to structural failures, and promote public health through abatement of unsanitary conditions, code authorities emphasize the indirect influence upon private property. The code has a relation to the type of structures built, the use and value of land, the rate of insurance, the ownership of homes, and the interests of manufacturers of materials and of the skilled trades that utilize them.

Preparation of the code

In their general principles, building codes of different cities do not vary greatly. Nevertheless, each city should draft its own code, formulating the details with reasonable regard for prevailing construction practices, availability of particular building materials, regulations of the fire underwriters and other similar national organizations, and the character of local prejudices. Such a code can be prepared best by a group of citizens selected for the purpose from the architectural and engineering professions, with proper representation of the authorities dealing with health, fire protection, and city planning. Advice should be solicited from the numerous trades affected, not forgetting the humble householder whose pocketbook, as well as safety, is involved.

Code must be reasonable

The problem of building costs is by no means of least importance in the consideration of a proposed building code. To design buildings and equipment that will be fire and accident proof is solely an engineering matter. But it is not practicable for all people to live and work in fire and accident proof structures. For this reason, building regulations must be a compromise between what is technically desirable and what is practically possible, without unduly restricting home and industrial building. In this same connection, it must be remembered that trades and industries are not always unselfish in respect to the regulations urged by them. Electrical contractors and journeymen may ask in the name of safety for a restricted, and possibly impracticable, number of openings on each electric circuit; plumbing installations may be hedged about with restrictions that are in nowise necessary to public health;[1] the clay and steel products manufacturers will desire a maximum of fire-proofing; asphalt-roofing producers will wrangle with the lumber interests in an effort, and perhaps a proper one, to outlaw wooden shingles; and amidst all of these, and many other conflicts, the code writers must hold an even balance, with a keen eye to carefully disguised special privilege, formulating an ordinance that best serves the public.

A complete building code—or better, the several building codes—must be very detailed, covering restricted areas in which only fireproof buildings may be erected, especially hazardous buildings, building materials, structural strength, fire escapes and fire hazards in public and semi-public buildings, sanitation, electric equipment and wiring, heating and ventilating, steam plants and steam actuated machinery, elevators, signs, billboards, and numerous other features. This means that a code must specify the qualitative arrangement of materials in buildings according to their height, size, and occupancy; qualitative and quantitative requirements as to materials; procedure to be observed in erecting and destroying buildings; and restrictions pertaining to projection into public ways. Because of varying conditions of climate, typography, industry, and available materials, it is doubtful whether a single uniform code applicable to cities of all classes can be drafted although the so-called Hoover codes are an attempt in this direction, and a model code has been drafted by the **National Board of Fire Underwriters**.[2]

Mr. Frank Burton is of the opinion that the greatest drawback of present building codes is not their lack of uniform requirements, but the difficulty of ascertaining the requirements in any particular case.[3] Construction requirements are so scattered

---

[1] *The Report for 1918,* Division of Health, City of Toledo, quoting a health survey of the city made in 1916 by the United States Public Health Service, called attention to the injustice of the elaborate system required under the plumbing code, and submitted a simplified but entirely adequate system of plumbing for small houses.

[2] *Building Code Recommended by the National Board of Fire Underwriters* (4th ed. 1922). Typical sections of codes have been prepared by the Bureau of Standards of the U. S. Department of Commerce which are available for the guidance of cities, among them *Recommended Minimum Requirements for Plumbing in Dwellings and Similar Buildings; Minimum Live Loads Allowable;* and *Recommended Minimum Requirements for Masonry Wall Construction.*

[3] An able paper on "The Construction of a Building Code," by Mr. Frank Burton, Commissioner, Department of Buildings and Safety Engineering, City of Detroit, is published in *Proceedings of the Ninth Annual Meet-*

through the ordinary code that it is necessary for an architect or engineer to review nearly every page in order to obtain all of the regulations pertaining to even a small unimportant building, and practically to commit a code to memory before drawing an important plan. This difficulty is aggravated when effort is made to practise in a city with which a designer is not familiar. It has been suggested that the present difficulties with codes could be minimized, not through uniformity of requirements, but through uniformity in arrangement of subjects and of the requirements for each type of structure, so as to be readily accessible to the practising architect without undue expenditure of energy.

Suggested outline of uniform code

Eliminations

From a code so arranged would be eliminated those provisions not directly related to building construction, since they usually affect particular trades, and an intimate knowledge of them, on the part of the architect, is not required—for example, elevator construction, electric wiring, plumbing, and boiler and heating requirements; and also those provisions applicable to certain classes of structures that are not buildings in the ordinary sense of the word—for example, roller coasters and similar amusement devices, and possibly grain elevators, coal pockets, and other engineering constructions. The code proper would contain subject matter arranged somewhat in the order of the following paragraphs.[1]

Administrative organization

Every code should have an introductory chapter dealing with the methods of administration, procedure, enforcement and penalty; and this is the best place in a code to insert the special provisions regarding the handling of dangerous buildings. It is particularly essential that the methods of enforcement should be effective and workable.

Definitive and descriptive provisions

Immediately after a description of the administrative procedure, provision should be made for the definitions of such words as it may be necessary to use in an unusual fashion and for the definitions of all words which have no exact meaning according to ordinary standards. There is no object in including definitions of words

ing of the Building Officials Conference (1923), 31-39. A paper by the same author on "Some Legal Aspects of Building Codes and Their Enforcement" appears in *Proceedings* of the same conference (1924), 95-103.

[1] Frank Burton, *op. cit.*, 32 *et. seq.* These paragraphs are summarized from the paper mentioned, with modifications made with approval of the author. Much important material has been omitted, and the complete paper should be consulted by any one concerned in the preparation of a building code.

For a model code outline following a somewhat different order, see a paper by Dean C. C. Williams, Department of Civil Engineering, University of Illinois, before the Kansas School for Water Works Superintendents, April, 1922, *Kansas Municipalities*, VIII (October, 1922).

which already are clearly and accurately defined in ordinary dictionaries, but the writer of a code should make sure that he is using words in their accepted sense, for wherever arguments come up in the interpretation of a code, the courts will refer to a dictionary and accept the meanings given, often in spite of the fact that the word is quite commonly used with somewhat different sense.

CHAP. XIII

In the laying out of fire limits, care should be taken that the boundaries are established for good reason and not as a matter of real estate promotion or politics. So long as the fire limits include those districts of the city where goods of great value are stored, or where factories and warehouses, whose loss would be a vital matter to the city, are located, such fire limits are valuable. Too often politicians seek to extend the fire limits into some districts or omit them from others, with the view to acquiring special privileges for certain property owners, and this often destroys the value of such limits. It is peculiarly necessary in regard to fire limits that the questions pertaining to rebuilding, altering, and adding to existing buildings be clearly stated and carefully thought out, as these questions give much more trouble than those relating to new buildings.

Fire limits

Types of construction may be designated by name or by number, and should include fireproof, mill, ordinary, and frame construction, and it may be wise to add some other types, as, for example, pressed steel construction, if not classed as fireproof. It is important that the description of each type of construction should be as complete and systematic as possible, and the sections dealing with different types of construction should be arranged in an identical manner. Starting with walls and foundations, the code should proceed to partitions, stair and elevator enclosures, columns, floors, roofs, pent houses, spires, and other roof construction, bay windows, porches, cornices, etc., endeavoring to include every detail or element of a building which the ordinance is intended to govern. All through the discussion of types of construction the materials to be used should be specified as accurately as possible, and it is unwise to state that the materials will be subject to the approval of the department, unless it be impossible to make a more accurate statement and be just.

Types of construction

The next logical step is to establish the classification of buildings according to their occupancy, and this classification should be based upon similarity of requirements from a building code standpoint. This is probably the most difficult feature in the arrange-

General classification of buildings

ment of a systematic building code, and there will be a great diversity of opinion on this subject. It is suggested that first, all buildings be divided into those occupied only during the daytime, and those occupied both during the daytime and night, *i.e.*, buildings containing sleeping rooms. Then divide the first group as follows: (1) buildings in which the material factor is predominant and in which the human element of occupancy is secondary, as factories, warehouses, power houses, and similar buildings, except those having some exceptionally high element of fire risk; (2) buildings of the same class, but having an element of exceptionally high fire risk, such as garages, paint shops, storage rooms for inflammable substances, dry cleaning establishments, rag shops, and possibly stables, since this class of buildings should be more severely restricted, and popular opinion now demands a high degree of fire protection for dumb animals; (3) buildings of a semi-public character in which the material element is important, but secondary to the human element, to include retail stores, offices, business colleges, and other buildings of this nature, and very small assembly halls and meeting rooms; (4) buildings of a public nature, in which the human element only is to be considered, and in which the question of the material element, that is, the cost of construction, can be made entirely secondary—for example, here place public administration buildings, auditoriums, dance halls, lodge halls, churches, schools, and possibly minor theaters having no stages for movable scenery; (5) buildings used as major theaters with stages for movable scenery. By this arrangement it is possible to make increasingly severe requirements for each class of buildings, although certain special provisions must be made for those in class 2, especially as regards type of construction.

Buildings used for dwelling purposes should be grouped into two additional classes, one relating to multiple apartments, and one to single and two family dwellings. Multiple dwellings should be further classified into (1) dwellings of three or more apartments, hotels, boarding houses, boarding schools, dormitories, etc., with say about ten or more sleeping rooms; (2) hospitals, sanitoriums, and similar buildings, housing persons who are partly disabled from sickness or other cause; and (3) jails, prisons, insane asylums and other buildings of detention, where the inmates are entirely helpless as regards escape. In each of these sub-classes the restrictions as to the type of construction should be increasingly more severe, so that while four-story apartment houses might properly be of ordinary construction, hospitals, beyond two stories, should be fireproof, and places of detention should be fully fireproof regardless of how small they may be.

CHAP. XIII

The class containing single and two-family dwellings should contain all of those small dwelling houses and dormitories having less than ten sleeping rooms, and the requirements for this class of occupancy should be made very lenient.

Single and two-family dwellings

The code should devote an entire chapter to each class of buildings, and one section to each of the most important features. These sections should be so arranged that sections of the same number in each chapter would pertain to the same subject regardless of the class of occupancy of the building. The sections in each chapter should be somewhat as follows: (1) type of construction, starting with the smallest and lowest buildings in the classification and stating what types of construction may be used, going progressively to the larger and larger buildings, eliminating one type of construction after another until only fireproof construction is left; (2) mixed occupancy, dealing with those restrictions regarding mixed occupancy, which will be necessary to make the code intelligent and workable; (3) exits, which vitally affect the layout and general arrangement of a building, and concerning which the present rules are often illogical and so burdensome as to be ridiculous in some cases and quite inadequate in others; (4) stair and elevator enclosures and other types of vertical openings through floors; (5) restrictions as to location on property and fire protection afforded by sidelines, court walls, etc.; (6) fire walls and limitations of areas within fire walls; (7) fire protection apparatus, including all of the requirements as to stand pipes, sprinkler systems, and similar matters; (8) miscellaneous details of construction which the code governs, but which find no place in the systematic arrangement suggested; (9) exceptions to general restrictions; (10) retroactive provision; and (11) alterations of existing buildings to new use.

Details of construction

The remainder of the code may properly deal with (1) excavations and foundations; (2) masonry construction; (3) steel; (4) concrete; (5) timber; (6) street and alley encroachments; (7) the procedure in building operations, pertaining to obtaining and posting permits, construction of sidewalk covers, guards around excavations, the planking of steel frames, guarding elevator and stair wells during construction, and similar features important to the building construction superintendent; and (8) specifications as to

Other elements of construction

212 PRACTICE OF MUNICIPAL ADMINISTRATION

<small>CHAP. XIII</small>

<small>Special codes</small>

details of construction, containing the standards governing fire doors, chimneys, moving picture booths, etc.

The foregoing outlines make no mention of electrical wiring, boiler construction, and similar subjects. The inclusion of these subjects in the one general code has never been successful, and in some states is frowned upon by the courts on the grounds that the building code proper affects real property, while the regulation of wiring and boilers relates to the use of personal property. It is a more desirable procedure for a city to adopt the special codes proposed by the technical organizations wherever they have been tried out and found practical. The electrical code of the National Fire Protection Association is now standard under the procedure of the American Engineering Standards Committee. It has been adopted by nearly all important cities of the United States, and its adoption by local ordinance is much better than an attempt to draft local codes as parts of such local ordinances.[1] The boiler code of the American Society of Mechanical Engineers, known as the A.S.M.E. code, is now used in nearly all states of the Union except Massachusetts, and is far superior to any local code. The adoption of these national codes is desirable, not only because of the care with which they have been formulated, but because of the adverse effect of local codes upon the taxpayers. Electrical apparatus, boilers, etc., manufactured in one city, are used throughout the country. It would be difficult, as well as expensive, for citizens to purchase such equipment according to special order and design, instead of specifying the American standards applying.

<small>Zoning</small>

The code outlined does not include the control of character and use of buildings except within the fire limits. These subjects are closely allied to safety and welfare, but are more properly treated under the discussion of city planning.

<small>Organization for enforcing the code</small>

The enactment of a building code is only the first step in securing structural and engineering safety. The enforcement of the code must be delegated to a competent authority, independent of the political pressure that will be brought by those interests desiring modifications of the law for their benefits; otherwise, little good will result.[2] In addition to competent supervision and facil-

[1] This code has been issued in some fifteen editions over a period of thirty years. To maintain the code abreast of the times there is a permanent national committee representative of all interests concerned, and also an electrical field engineering service to assist municipalities and others in the use and necessary development of this code as the art rapidly advances.

[2] In Boston on January 15, 1919, a molasses tank collapsed, resulting in fourteen deaths, sixty persons injured, and large adjacent property damage.

ities for interpreting debatable provisions of, and allowing reasonable exceptions to, the law, provision should be made for an engineering staff competent to examine the technical building plans submitted and an inspectional force adequate to see that the approved plans are conformed to.

Persons desiring to construct or remodel buildings of any character, install heating or power equipment, or erect signs upon buildings, should be required to obtain a building permit from the safety engineering authorities. This permit should be granted only after plans or sketches have been submitted, examined, and approved as conforming to the code, affidavit has been taken as to the estimated cost, and the proper fee paid. A majority of building projects are of such small importance that it is not necessary to require the submission of detailed plans to the building department. Some arbitrary limit of cost is fixed, say at $1,000 to $2,000, within which only rough sketches are required. These sketches, and the application, will ordinarily be examined when presented, so that the builder will suffer no delay. The department should, however, reserve the right to require detailed plans if conditions appear which are out of the ordinary.

<small>Submission of plans</small>

The plans of more pretentious buildings should be presented in detail, and should be prepared by registered architects and engineers. Many states now require the examination and registration of members of these professions, and important buildings and appurtenances should not be designed by people who cannot qualify accordingly. Such plans should be left for examination, and should be in duplicate, one to be returned when properly approved, the other to be retained in the files of the department for reference. If the department, after examining plans, will refuse to give advice on incomplete or inaccurate construction details, or to act in any way as a designing agency, incompetent private designers

<small>Examination of plans</small>

The findings of the court of inquiry are pertinent, in so far as they suggest the very prevalent public negligence in relation to building conditions. The court said: "The chief blame rests upon the public itself. This single accident has cost more in material damage alone than all the supposed economies in the building department. Laws are cheap of passage, but costly of enforcement. They do not execute themselves. A good law poorly administered is worse than a poor law well administered. A public, which, with one eye on its tax rate, provides itself with an administrative equipment fifty percent qualified, has no right to complain that it does not get a 100 percent product, and so long as it accepts political influence as the equivalent of scientific attainment in positions which demand such attainment in a high degree, so long it must expect breakdowns in its machinery. . . . It is no part of the business of this court to find a scapegoat to order for an indifferent or niggardly public. . . ."

214   PRACTICE OF MUNICIPAL ADMINISTRATION

CHAP. XIII

will soon disappear. In Massachusetts, as a further safeguard on engineering requirements, the petitioner for a permit is required to make an affidavit that all requirements of the building code have been complied with. The examination of important plans requires time, and there will be criticism if the actual construction of a building is delayed on this account. In New York City this difficulty is circumvented by issuing a foundation permit in advance of the permit for the superstructure.

Approved plans, with any correspondence relative to them, should be given a filing number and preserved for reference. The files may be catalogued by character of structure, name of owner and contractor, or location. This last basis is best, an index of street and numbers affording a simple and immediate reference.

Inspection of construction

The number and character of the inspections varies with the type of building, ranging from the almost continuous and technical inspection required on a monolithic reinforced concrete structure to the few inspections necessary on a steel frame building. The inspections are by the several regulated trades, such as construction proper, electric equipment and wiring, heating and ventilating, and plumbing. Prompt inspection is necessary to prevent expensive delays in construction, and to expedite matters the contractors usually notify the authorities as to when work will be in a proper condition for inspection.

Buildings

For inspection purposes a city is laid off in districts of requisite size for each type of inspection, and an inspector is assigned to each district. At daily intervals each inspector receives a work sheet containing the inspections to be made, as compiled from the office records of construction under way and from notices of inspections requested. Each day there is added to this record a report on each inspection made, which is ultimately transferred as a permanent record to an inspection file geographically arranged. It is not practicable to file these reports with the original plans, since inspections continue for many years after a building is completed. The inspection reports and the approved plan can be correlated easily when necessary.

Appurtenances

In addition to construction inspection, there must be periodic examinations of elevators, heating and ventilating apparatus, power plants, refrigerating machinery, etc., supplementing that given by the underwriters for insurance purposes. A list of such equipment requiring current inspection is maintained in the department, and a sufficient number of inspectors is assigned to cover

SAFETY

everything at proper intervals. A record of such examinations is filed in the department, and notice is posted on the premises as to the date of inspection and the conditions found.

CHAP. XIII

A certain amount of inspection is necessary on older buildings to determine changes in use that may affect safety, to locate deterioration of structural parts with age, and to secure compliance with newer regulations governing fire escapes, proper exits, and enclosure of stairs and elevators. A portion of the inspection force should be delegated to reinspection work only, and not permitted to make any inspections on new buildings; otherwise when the department is busy reinspection work will be put into the background. The inspection of new work is pleasant and easy, and will absorb the attention of the entire inspection force if there is no restraining influence. The inspection of sanitary and housing conditions is properly an activity of the health, rather than the building, authorities.

Old buildings

The proper and economical administration of the building department requires that inspections be made sufficiently often to safeguard the interests of the public, but with no unnecessary frequency. Too frequent inspections only irritate the contractor and furnish an excuse to the inspector for finding trivial derelictions that will justify his job to his superiors. The proper number of inspections for each type of construction is a matter to be determined by the person in charge of the department.[1]

Number of inspections

It is one matter to require that building plans conform to code standards, and quite another to compel specific performance in the actual construction. The inspectors, if honest and competent, will report deviations from the code to their superiors in the department. What action shall be taken? To be sure, the head of the

Enforcement of requirements

[1] The practice of typical cities in this respect is indicated by the following tabulation taken from the *Report on the Building Department of the City of Rochester* (Rochester Bureau of Municipal Research, 1921), 35:

	Indianapolis	Detroit	Columbus	Rochester
Cost $1 to $2,000				
New work	2	2	1	2
Alterations	1-3	2	1	2
Cost $2 to $10,000				
Dwellings	3-4	4	3	4
Commercial	3	2	3	5
Alterations	3-5	2	3	6
Cost $10,000 and up, per unit of $10,000				
Dwellings	5	6	4	3
Commercial	5	4	4	4
Alterations	5	4	–	5

department can proceed to secure a warrant for the arrest of the offending builder and appear in court against him, and after the usual legal delays and annoyances the offender may be fined or censored. But this handicaps the work of the department, compels inspectors to spend time in court rather than in the field where they belong, and makes unnecessary enemies of persons who may have violated the code either unintentionally or because of the chicanery of subordinates or sub-contractors.

The first proper step in enforcement is a warning by the inspector that the code is being violated and a follow-up inspection to determine whether the warning has been heeded. Ordinarily, such action is all that is necessary. Some cities, *e.g.*, Portland, Ore., adopt the more formal plan giving a written notice to the responsible parties, and in case correction does not result within a reasonable time, serving a second notice designating a number of days within which compliance with law must be had. If proper action is not taken, a warrant for the arrest of the offending builder is secured. In Jacksonville, Fla., in addition to warning, a notice is placed on the job to the effect that part of the work has been condemned as not being in accordance with law. Such notice immediately brings the wrath of the owner upon the contractor. Other cities, as New York and Toledo, issue a blunt stop order through the inspector when a contractor is found proceeding without a permit or in other violation of law. Such stop orders are backed by arrests if necessary. In Minneapolis a person starting work without a permit is compelled to pay a double fee.

Licensing of builders

As a means of further controlling code violations, a few cities have experimented with the licensing of building contractors. The results have not been satisfactory except as a means of controlling manufacturers and vendors of materials whose activities cannot be readily controlled by inspection. The application of the plan is limited by legal considerations, and by the fact that the revoking of licenses results in the involuntary idleness of employees, and in unpopularity with the public.

Fees

Practices for determining the amount of the fee for the approval of plans and subsequent inspection of construction differ. Many cities base charges upon the type and cubic content of the structure to be erected. Other cities collect a fraction of a percent of the estimated cost of the building. The latter practice is conducive to underestimates and perjury, and if the rate varies with the type of structure is difficult of application in those of com-

SAFETY

bined use, such as buildings with stores below and flats above. Some cities use a combination of these plans. Under any plan, the department should be self-supporting, on the theory that the service rendered is largely of particular rather than general benefit.

With industrial development, increasing attention has been directed to the damages arising from the unrestricted production of smoke, particularly in the business sections of cities. The soot poured out of the stacks of factory buildings, heating plants, and locomotives, not only is an annoyance but causes large monetary losses by the destruction of materials exposed for sale, by requiring the continual cleansing of buildings inside and out, and by the destruction of shade trees. The effect of smoke on internal lighting is also important. With smoky air and rainy weather which washes the soot down upon the window pane, it is estimated that within a few days fifty percent to seventy-five percent of light is excluded. Newer medical science is also coming to believe that one of the great dangers of smoke comes from excluding the ultraviolet rays of the sun.

The purpose of all ordinances regulating smoke is to prevent the "emission of dense smoke" within the confines of the city. What constitutes "dense smoke"? To determine the degree of density, certain arbitrary standards are set up, based upon the grayness of glass having a capacity to cut off a certain percentage of light from a flame having a lighting power of sixteen candles. The instrument used is called an umbrascope. One thickness of gray glass of sufficient capacity to cut off sixty per cent of such light may be taken as the basis of a scale, and four thicknesses of such a glass is designated as a degree of darkness equal to that of dense smoke. The Ringlemann chart[1] is also used, this chart consisting of various lattice works of black lines drawn on white paper. Difficulty has been found in checking readings for the Ringlemann chart with those made from the umbrascope, and it is concluded by some authorities that the former is of little use in practical work. With some means of calculating density, the smoke inspector is able to examine the emissions of smoke from the stacks under survey and determine the degree of conformance with law. Regulations and ordinances ordinarily do not absolutely prevent the emission of dense smoke at all times. The density of smoke will range according to the chart, and it is usual to provide

[1] Published by the U. S. Geological Survey.

218   PRACTICE OF MUNICIPAL ADMINISTRATION

CHAP. XIII

that smoke of the maximum density may be emitted for a few minutes during each hour, grading down to a point where a very considerable number of minutes is allowed to smoke of a minor density.

Regulation of boilers, etc.

There is considerable difficulty, however, in the enforcement of such smoke regulations. To be sure, convictions can be obtained from time to time, but they are insufficient to secure the abolition of the smoke nuisance. Therefore, the smoke prevention ordinances go much farther than regulating the density of smoke. They deal with boilers, flues, stacks, coal, and manner of firing, and attempt to prescribe heating apparatus which will not produce smoke. Further, the efforts of the smoke inspector are, in a majority of cases, confined to enforcing these construction regulations and to instructing building owners and operators in methods of scientific firing so that smoke may be eliminated.[1]

The enforcement authority

The abatement of the smoke nuisance has been allocated in most instances to the health authorities, on the assumption that smoke constitutes a menace to health; and the enforcement of regulations concerning the emission of dense smoke has been confined to the prosecution of the violators. However, with developments in the construction of grates, boilers, and stacks, and scientific methods of stoking, it has been realized that more can be done to abate smoke through securing the proper construction and use of furnaces and their accessories than by the difficult enforcement of regulations against the emission of smoke. The control of furnace structure is properly a function of the authority of the city having to do with building construction, and for this reason smoke abatement has frequently been transferred from the jurisdiction of the health authority to the building department.

Billboard regulation

As long as public safety is involved, the regulation of billboards, electric signs, and other advertising structures is a reasonably simple matter under the police power.[2] Municipal ordinances

---

[1] A compilation of a number of ordinances on smoke prevention will be found in *The Manual of Smoke and Boiler Ordinances and Requirements in the Interest of Smoke Regulation* (Public Service Committee of the Smoke Prevention Association, 1924). A study of the police powers in connection with such ordinances will be found in Lucius H. Cannon, *Smoke Abatement: A Study of the Police Power as Embodied in the Laws and Ordinances and Court Decisions* (St. Louis Public Library, 1924). See also, John B. C. Kershaw, *Fuel Economy and Smoke Prevention* (Van Nostrand, 3d ed., 1925). An interesting study of a particular city is *Some Engineering Phases of Pittsburgh's Smoke Problem* (Bulletin No. 8, Mellon Institute).

[2] See Howard L. McBain, *American City Progress and the Law* (Columbia Univ. Press, 1918) for a discussion of billboards from the legal standpoint.

SAFETY

may require permits for the erection of such signs, compel them to be erected in accordance with structural safety, inspect them periodically, and levy a reasonable tax upon them. When signs are erected upon the ground, where the possible damage from collapse is small, the methods of construction may still be regulated so as to insure complete safety and prevent the boards from being a cover for nuisances and crimes.

Such regulation, however, is not adequate from an æsthetic sense. Serious objection to billboards is not made when they are located in the business section of the city, and frequently their lighting is a welcome supplement to that provided by the regular methods. The principal complaint comes from signs and billboards placed indiscriminately throughout residence sections. The rights of private property stand in the way of solving this particular problem. The courts have referred repeatedly to the unsightliness of billboards, but no higher court has sustained a billboard ordinance predicated solely upon æsthetic grounds, and numerous courts have declared that legislation for æsthetic purposes is wholly beyond the scope of the police power. However, it is probable that, in the course of time, American courts will reverse their earlier decisions and openly include æsthetics among the objects for which regulations may be imposed.[1] In Pennsylvania billboards are being attacked on the ground that they interfere with safety in driving, since the driver cannot read billboards and watch the road at the same time; and a bill was introduced into the state legislature of 1925 proposing to place under state control all advertising signs erected along state highways.[2]

The assignment of street numbers is a proper activity of the building department, although it is often done by the engineering service of the city. Every city adopts some definite plan of num-

For the æsthetic point of view, see C. M. Robinson, *Modern Civic Art* (Putnam, 1918), 152 *et seq.*

[1] The Supreme Court of Maryland remarked in 1908: "It may be that in the development of a higher civilization, the culture and refinement of the people has reached the point where the educational value of the fine arts, as expressed and embodied in architectural symmetry and harmony, is so well recognized as to give sanction, under some circumstances, to the exercise of this police power even for such purposes." (Cochran *vs.* Preston, 108 Md. 220). In a Philippine decision of December, 1915, a statute authorizing the removal of billboards was upheld upon the express ground that the police power may be exercised for æsthetic purposes. The court argued, furthermore, that offensive sights are in the same category as offensive noises and odors (Churchill *vs.* Collector of Internal Revenue, 14 Official Gazette of the Philippines, 383). Quoted by McBain, *op. cit.*, 89.

[2] Horace McFarland, "A Proposal to Control Bill Boards," *Nat. Mun. Rev.*, XIV, 337 (June, 1925).

220 PRACTICE OF MUNICIPAL ADMINISTRATION

bering, as a convenience to citizens and visitors, and as a necessity to the postal authorities. These numbering systems are essentially similar, and are based on the assignment of a number for each given number of lineal feet, usually ten, along a street, the even numbers being assigned to the right hand, and the odd numbers to the left-hand side. Two base lines, usually one north and south, and one east and west, are established and all numbers are allotted from these bases as zero. In this way, a given number will indicate in a general way the distance from the base, and will be parallel to all other similar numbers throughout that side of the city. This system is far preferable to that of beginning each street as a zero base, resulting in a total confusion of numbers. Some smaller cities, particularly when laid out in small square or rectangular blocks, assign one hundred numbers to each block. By this plan, the distance of a given number in blocks from the base line can be known exactly; but the numbers involved become too unwieldy for use in a large community. A variation of this plan that may be used by cities with numbered streets calls for placing the number of the nearest cross street before each house number, the two being separated by a hyphen.

Cost of building control

As with many municipal activities, the authorities responsible for the control of building construction generally complain of inadequate financial support. Even though the department is made self-supporting, or practically so, through the imposition of fees, city councils are frequently reluctant to put the fees sufficiently high to provide for the reasonably thorough examination of plans and inspection of work under construction and the reinspection of old work. The importance of the duties of building departments varies with different communities, as does the thoroughness with which the duties are performed. In consequence, the yearly expenditures for building control in the cities of the United States ranges from five to sixty cents per capita. It is advanced by some authorities that a yearly expenditure of less than twenty cents per capita does not produce worth-while results, and that an expenditure in excess of twenty-five cents per capita is unnecessary. Others believe that a per capita cost of fifteen cents will produce good results. Amount of construction done and not population, however, should determine inspection expense, and between the limits of expense just indicated lies a more precise figure to be determined by the particular requirements of the municipality, assuming that a maximum of service is given for the money spent.

SAFETY

With respect to efficient service, the activities of a building department are of a character that may be measured with a precision not possible for all city functions. To be sure, the results of building control as evidenced in unsafe buildings, fires, and accidents are not as appreciable as are morbidity and mortality rates when applied to the work of a health department; but the efficiency of even plan examiners and building inspectors can be gauged as exactly as can the efficiency of visiting nurses and food inspectors.[1]

Measurement of service

The work of plan examiners and engineers is relatively most difficult of appraisal, because in addition to checking plans of varying complexity, time must be spent in consultations with architects, engineers, and builders. It is practicable, however, to require a daily statement from each plan examiner and engineer as to the amount and character of work done. Such statements can be used to weed out the most inefficient of the staff, and the mere recording of each day's work inspires a friendly rivalry and stimulates a maximum of activity.

Plan examiners and engineers

The work of inspectors may be divided into office work, transportation, and inspection, and is more easily measured. The daily service records of the inspectors should indicate the amount of time spent in the office, and office visits should be limited to one a day. When in the office, inspectors have an inclination to stay there, are dilatory in the preparation of their reports, and are interrupted by telephone calls and visitors. One of the first problems of departmental procedure is that of getting inspectors into the field at as early an hour as possible. The service records should also indicate the time spent in transportation to each job and the time spent on each inspection. The number of daily inspections that will be accomplished by inspectors varies with the type of work inspected, distance to be covered, method of transportation, and to some extent the season of the year.[2] In Detroit building

Inspectors

Work required of inspectors

---

[1] An informing paper on "Efficiency in a Building Department," by H. E. Plummer, inspector of buildings, Portland, Ore., appears in the *Proceedings of the Tenth Annual Meeting of the Building Officials Conference* (1924), 59-80.

[2] H. E. Plummer, *ibid.*, 65 *et seq.* Tables of inspection requirements prepared by the building department of Portland, Ore., are based on the following estimates:

Type of Inspection	Inspections per Permit	Daily Inspections per Inspector With Auto	Daily Inspections per Inspector Without Auto
Buildings	2.75	25	18.5
Electrical	2.70	20	15.3
Plumbing	2.20	16	12.0

222 PRACTICE OF MUNICIPAL ADMINISTRATION

CHAP. XIII

inspectors average twenty-four to twenty-five inspections per day; electrical inspectors, twenty-two or twenty-three; and plumbing inspectors, twenty-one to twenty-two. Some authorities hold that an average of from twelve to fifteen inspections on approved alterations and new work are sufficient to constitute a good day's work. Administrative authorities concerned with the personnel of a building department must have these data for sound conclusions: the average number of inspections necessary to each type of permit; and the average number of inspections that reasonably may be expected from each inspector of each type of construction. With a knowledge of the actual or estimated number of permits of each character over a given period, it is a simple matter to calculate the number of inspectors necessary to perform the work required.

These data of number of inspections should be translated into cost per inspection by dividing into the total cost of inspections. This will give a net cost. The gross cost should be secured by dividing the total cost of operating the department by the number of inspections made. These figures should be compared over periods of years in the same cities, and with similar data from other municipalities.

Use of automobiles

It will have been noted that the number of inspections is materially increased by the use of the automobile. In Portland, Ore., it has been calculated that the use of automobiles reduces the cost of inspections from twelve to fourteen percent. In Detroit, an inspector with a car makes one third-more inspections than a man on foot. In that city, municipally owned cars cost about $95 a month for operation. However, this cost is reduced by allowing $50 a month to each inspector who owns his own car, deducting two dollars for each twenty-five miles less than 625 miles run per month. The inspector must be relied upon for the mileage record, but by occasionally checking the distance between jobs, dishonesty is reduced to a minimum.[1]

Consolidation of inspections

Examination of any city budget will indicate the large number of different inspections of private activities made by representatives of the city—of sanitary conditions by the health department, of safety engineering by the building department, of defective sidewalks and streets by the public works department, of commercial amusement by the recreation department, of fire hazards by the fire department, and of all of these conditions by the

---

[1] On the whole, however, a flat allowance each month is preferred to the mileage basis. See Chap. X.

police. At first thought it might appear that economy would be served and annoyance eliminated by consolidating certain of these inspections. However, the requirements to be met are so diversified that it is questionable whether any such plan can be satisfactorily materialized.[1]

[1] In 1921 the Detroit Bureau of Governmental Research made a study of the inspection situation in Detroit and concluded that consolidation was not feasible. It is reported that an experiment in consolidated inspection is under way in Chicago, but the results are not yet available.

CHAPTER XIV

FIRE [1]

Property loss by fire in the United States has been increasing, and in 1924 amounted to $535,000,000, accompanied by more than 15,000 deaths.[2] These losses, affecting costs of production, insurance, and taxes, occurred despite increased facilities for fire protection and the increased construction of fire-resisting buildings.

[1] The National Fire Protection Association, the National Board of Fire Underwriters, and the Underwriters Laboratories have prepared many useful pamphlets on the subject of fire prevention and fire protection. Valuable books on the subjects are E. F. Croker, *Fire Prevention* (Dodd, Mead, 1912); and E. U. Crosby, H. A. Fiske, and H. W. Forster, *Handbook of Fire Protection* (7th ed., Van Nostrand, 1924). *The Cyclopedia of Fire Prevention* (4 vols., American School of Correspondence, 1912) is still of value. Current information should be obtained from the *Quarterly* and other numerous publications of the National Fire Protection Association; *Fire Protection* (monthly); *Fire Engineering* (weekly); and the *Firemen's Herald* (weekly); *The American City* (monthly).

[2] See yearly statements of the National Board of Fire Underwriters. The data for 1924 are classified as follows:

Strictly Preventable Causes

Defective chimneys and flues	$ 20,838,162
Fireworks, firecrackers, etc.	639,131
Gas, natural and artificial	3,819,274
Hot ashes and coals, open fires	5,365,914
Ignition of hot grease, oil, tar, wax, asphalt, etc.	1,740,418
Matches—smoking	29,045,007
Open lights	3,332,191
Petroleum and its products	11,183,421
Rubbish and litter	1,576,433
Sparks on roofs	15,931,342
Steam and hot-water pipes	419,586
Stoves, furnaces, boilers, and other pipes	18,658,248

Partly Preventable Causes

Electricity	14,091,789
Explosions	3,064,198
Exposure (including conflagrations)	69,030,839
Sparks from machinery	7,499,600
Incendiarism	1,662,987
Lighting	10,922,660
Miscellaneous known causes	6,470,790
Sparks from combustion	6,533,542
Spontaneous combustion	16,110,945
Unknown causes (probably preventable)	180,373,441
Total	$428,298,226
25% to cover unreported losses	107,074,556
Grand total	$535,372,782

FIRE

They are all the more startling when compared with those of European countries. As compared with American cities, European municipalities spend little for direct fire protection, and their fire-fighting equipment is decidedly inferior in both quantity and quality. Yet fires are successfully controlled and the annual loss from this cause is reduced.[1] However, in considering relative per capita losses it is well to remember that property located in the United States has a higher value expressed in dollars than if located abroad, and that the per capita ownership of property is much greater in this country. Nevertheless, Europe possesses a decided superiority in the control of fire, which is due to a number of causes. The buildings of European cities are constructed largely of fire-resisting materials, and conflagrations are usually of minor and localized significance. In America, construction is principally of wood, due to the abundance and comparative low cost of timber. Also because of the inflammable nature of buildings, fires once under way here are difficult to control and frequently result in widespread conflagrations. A contributing factor is found in the strict regulations of European authorities with respect to building construction and fire prevention, and the amenability of European populations to law. Happily, in larger cities at least, sensible efforts in behalf of fire prevention as well as fire protection are being made, fire hazards are being eliminated, and so-called fireproof or fire-resisting structures are taking the place of less permanent buildings in more congested areas. A building is fireproof only when its neighbors are fireproof, and it will take several generations or more to accomplish the practical fireproofing of American commercial and industrial districts.

Organized efforts to protect cities against fire were first evolved by the Romans, who introduced formal fire departments independent of the military and the police, and with a personnel both well trained and equipped. The Middle Ages, however, depended

[1] The following tabulation of the per capita annual losses of the several important countries indicates the unnecessary fire waste that is taking place in the United States.

Country	Per Capita Loss
Holland	$ .11
Switzerland	.15
Italy	.25
Australia	.25
Germany	.28
France	.49
Great Britain	.72
United States	4.75

226 PRACTICE OF MUNICIPAL ADMINISTRATION

CHAP. XIV

entirely upon the efforts of volunteer firemen and soldiers using the primitive pail as their equipment. At the beginning of the seventeenth century the hand pump engine was developed, but the invention was not placed in immediate general use.[1]

Early American practice

The early ordinances providing for fire protection in American cities forbade the use of wooden chimneys and provided for the purchase of leather buckets and ladders. In most communities citizens were compelled to take certain precautions against fires, provide water pails and ladders, and go to the rescue of their neighbor's property in event of conflagrations. For many years this volunteer service was the only protection provided, largely because fires were infrequent and easily controlled. Later, volunteer fire service became somewhat formalized and carried a considerable degree of social distinction. The volunteers affected dashing apparel and paraded the streets on holidays and gala occasions, and in time their organizations came to wield decided political influence; sometimes the members were rewarded with pensions, jury exemption, and civil service advantages.[2]

Mechanical improvements

The fire departments of the nineteenth century were well organized and equipped, and the gradual introduction of mechanical appliances, including the steam fire engine, made a permanent, trained personnel necessary.

Need of modern fire protection

Modern development in fire protection methods has been coincident with the increase in the number of fire hazards. Congestion in population and in building construction has made intolerable buildings of combustible material in the business section of a city, and has made certain restrictions necessary when such buildings are constructed in other districts. Also, the present-day activities that may be carried on in city buildings increases the danger of fire, and such buildings as schools, theaters, and tenements, because of their use or occupancy, must be given added protection. The ease with which fire is produced and its general use creates innumerable hazards of which a simpler civilization was ignorant—those of machine friction, inflammable liquids, modern heating, transmission of electricity and gas, and strange chemical reactions.

Reducing physical hazards

Modern fire departments are confronted with the problem not only of extinguishing fires, but of decreasing by every possible

---

[1] For the historic development of fire protection, see John Kenlon, *Fires and Fire Fighters* (Doran, 1913).

[2] Boston organized the first volunteer company under municipal control in 1678, and imported a hand engine from England.

means the hazardous character and use of buildings. Construction where economically practicable must be of fire-resisting materials; provision is made for reducing the chances of fire; dangerous occupancy is regulated; certain equipment for extinguishing fires and giving of alarms is installed; and appliances are provided for the escape of occupants. In most cities, all buildings are constructed in accordance with a building code which controls the details of building, taking into consideration location, use, and size. In certain areas of high value, only fireproof constructions are allowed.[1] The constant inspection of certain buildings is intended to secure compliance with law as well as to educate owners and occupants to the advantages of proper precautions.

<small>Causes of fire</small>

It is difficult to determine the exact causes of fire since the origin of each blaze is usually destroyed before a determination of cause can be made. Consequently the statistics of fire causes compiled by cities are often erroneous. Frequently no investigation is undertaken, the owner or occupant of the property ascribing a cause in which you may be sure no element of carelessness enters. The only way to secure reasonably accurate data of the causes of fire is a thorough investigation of each case by qualified persons.

The complexity of modern urban life has introduced so many fire hazards that no attempt can be made to enumerate them all.[2] Among the more important causes is the heat produced by various lighting and heating devices; short circuits in the transmission of electric power; the friction incident to the operation of machinery; the use of explosives, oils, gasoline, volatile lacquers, products having a nitro-cellulose base, and other inflammable liquids; and the presence of materials liable to ignition by spontaneous combustion. Dwellings are subject to fire danger from furnaces and stoves, electrical appliances, smoking, matches, and lightning.

<small>Carelessness a cause</small>

While these agents may be the immediate causes of fire, often only carelessness permits them to do so, and it is estimated that more than half of the fires in American cities are the result of neglect. Smokers are careless with cigarettes and matches, fireplaces are unscreened, gas jets are placed in the proximity of combustible substance, oily clothes are piled so as to ignite by spontaneous combustion, rubbish is allowed to accumulate, electrical appliances are misused, and buildings are constructed with little

---

[1] This feature of fire protection is discussed in Chap. XIII.
[2] Crosby-Fiske-Forster, *Handbook of Fire Protection*, Chap. VII, enumerates practically every cause of fire.

Arson

regard for fire risks. Control of this moral hazard would be the largest single advance to be made in fire prevention.

The malicious firing of a structure is known as arson, and is a well-organized business in some cities. In periods of depression, the criminal business man or manufacturer will destroy his property for the insurance with which to settle with creditors, as is evidenced by the increased number of fires during such times. Other individuals make it a business to over-insure and then burn at a profit. The pyromaniac sets fire to property at the urging of a diseased mind, and certain criminal individuals burn property for revenge. Suppression of arson rests in part with the insurance companies, since over-insurance is the most frequent instigation of this criminal act. Failure of insurance agents to value property correctly when insurance is asked, and to amend values as business changes dictate, is responsible for over-insurance and the temptations that go with it.

Although there may be moral certainty of arson in a given case, it is not easy to secure the conviction of the culpable. Connection with the origin of a fire is easily concealed, and at the best only circumstantial evidence exists. Not only must a motive be established, but there must be actual proof of the overt act before a complete case is made against the suspect. Necessary proof in cases of arson results from long and detailed investigation by detectives especially trained in this sort of work, and has prompted a number of cities to establish arson squads to work in conjunction with the fire department.[1] In large municipalities, the detectives assigned to an arson squad devote their entire time to the investigation of suspicious fires, or at least make such cases their major assignment. Firemen are required to make a preliminary investigation of the origin of a fire immediately upon arrival. If a blaze appears of incendiary origin, or there are grounds for suspecting such origin, uniformed police are placed in charge of the premises, and the arson squad is summoned. If sufficient evidence exists, the suspect is placed under arrest, pending further investigation. When the facts do not warrant summary action, subpœnas are served upon the owners and other witnesses, and a formal inquisition is held. These methods are proving effective in dealing with suspected arson.

Almost all large cities have a separate department for fire

[1] In some jurisdictions these duties are assumed by a fire marshal who responds to all alarms.

protection which is headed by a civilian commissioner, or occasionally directly by a professional fire fighter. In a few instances the board system of control still prevails, the fire chief being the direct agent of the board. In commission and city manager cities the police and fire departments are often brought into a single department of public safety under civilian direction, professional officers being in subordinate control of the separate branches. The wisdom of unifying the general direction of two widely different functions is an open question. Casual observation may suggest that the two departments have much in common, since both have a uniformed, disciplined personnel, with high physical requirements. As a matter of fact, these qualities are the only ones that the two departments do have in common, and many important differences separate them. The science of fire fighting and the science of policing are, or should be, highly specialized, requiring vastly different training and temperament both for the administrative head and for the rank and file. Seldom has one person a complete knowledge of and keen interest in both. Almost invariably, with a single civilian director in charge of both departments, policing will be neglected to the advantage of fire fighting, or vice versa. Separate departmental organizations are best in all cities.

<small>CHAP. XIV</small>

<small>General organization for fire protection</small>

The fire-fighting activity requires the largest part of the personnel and equipment of the fire department and is always organized upon a semi-military basis. Fighting fire requires a thoroughly disciplined and highly organized force. The smallest unit is the company, consisting of the small number of firemen who man a single piece of equipment. These groups constitute engine companies, ladder companies, rescue companies, high pressure hose companies, etc., each under the command of a captain or a captain and a lieutenant. The several companies stationed in a district make up a battalion, under the command of a battalion chief, who in turn is directly responsible to the fire chiefs or his assistants.

<small>Fire-fighting division</small>

The fire districts vary in size according to the wealth, congestion, fire hazards, and physical features of the territory. Topography is often a governing feature in the layout of districts, which will be arranged so that apparatus does not need to climb steep hills, cross railroad tracks, or drawbridges. Districts are naturally smaller in high value sections. Stations, of which there may be one or more in each district, serve as shelters for the various pieces of apparatus, and as dormitories for the men on station who

<small>Fire districts and stations</small>

230   PRACTICE OF MUNICIPAL ADMINISTRATION

man the equipment. No fixed rule can be made as to the number of stations in each district, as this feature is governed by the necessity for different types of apparatus and ease of access to the area served. The motorization of fire apparatus has made it necessary to relocate fire stations in many instances, to reduce their number, and to increase the size of districts, because of the greater area that can be covered by modern equipment. It is now believed that the limit of distance for motorized apparatus on first alarms should be one and one-half miles for residential districts (slightly more in sparsely settled sections), and about three-quarters of a mile in the congested and high value areas.

Stations are constructed to house one or two pieces of apparatus, usually an engine and a ladder company. Some authorities believe that it is desirable to have only one company in a station, but this is a question of finance and administration to be determined by the conditions in each particular city. The design and construction of stations should harmonize with surrounding buildings, and a fire station in a residential section should conform to the architectural treatment of the neighboring dwellings, so far as standardized plans will permit. This feature has been given decided consideration in recent years.

Apparatus

In recent years there has been a marked development of fire-fighting apparatus. Pumping apparatus operated by internal combustion engines supplanted the steam pumping engine; chemical fire extinguishers were improved, including the carbon tetrachloride and "foam" type for fighting fires on which water is ineffective; and larger cities completely motorized their equipment, which is less expensive to maintain and faster in reaching fires. Gas masks and helmets now enable firemen to enter buildings, and to fight fires under conditions that would have been intolerable a few years ago. Fireboats, of the tug type, are equipped with powerful pumps and used to extinguish fires in property more easily and rapidly accessible from the waterside.[1]

Types of apparatus

Pumping engines are necessary in small cities where the water plants are of limited capacity, and in large cities in all districts having high buildings or low water pressure. The modern pumping engine, or pumper as it is generally called, is operated by an internal combustion engine, and is capable of delivering 750 to 1000 gallons of water a minute at about 100 pounds pres-

[1] See Harry J. Corcoran, "Selection, Care and Operation of Fire Fighting Equipment," *Municipal and County Engineering*, LXX, 209-216 (April, 1926).

sure.[1] The automotive pumper is considered more reliable than the steam pumper and has practically supplanted the latter, although the new equipment weighs from 16,000 to 21,000 pounds, and can be used only on well-constructed roadways. To meet this difficulty, light weight engines called "suburbanites" are now being made. These machines will throw a minimum of 350 gallons of water a minute and can operate over unpaved highways.

CHAP. XIV
Pumpers

Ladder trucks are of several types, the quick-raising aerial apparatus being used primarily in large cities. To secure rapid elevation, this ladder is operated by spring, electric, or air hoist. The ordinary ladder truck may also include a chemical tank, connected with 250 feet of one inch hose. This equipment is known as a combination service truck, and is used on all small fires. Considerable additional equipment is carried including axes, buckets, burst hose jackets, crowbars, deluge sets (Siamese joints for uniting several water lines into one stream), forcible entry tools, hand pumps, life nets, etc.

Ladder trucks

Triple combinations, so-called, consist of a combination pumping engine, chemical tank, and hose body. This machine is in general use in cities of small and medium size, and is considered by some authorities as desirable for congested areas.

Triple combinations

Hose wagons have a capacity of at least 4,000 feet of hose usually in two sizes. Water towers are heavy, expensive pieces of equipment used only in a few of the largest cities. All cities now require stand pipes in new buildings of over a certain height in order to place water on the top floors. The water tower is nothing more or less than a movable stand pipe erected in the street, designed to pour water onto a fire that is too high or too hot for hand lines to reach.

Hose wagons and water towers

A rescue wagon is equipped with special rescue equipment, such as life nets, pulmotors, gas masks, restoratives, and acetylene torches for cutting metals. Its purpose is to aid in the escape of people from burning buildings and to give first aid to those injured. Such wagons are manned by a rescue squad of eight or ten firemen and respond to all first alarm fires in congested districts. If the services of the rescue squad are not required, the wagon returns to its station; or in serious fires, the crew is assigned to assist the other companies.

Rescue squad

The maintenance of automobile equipment requires a repair

Maintenance

[1] Many cities hold their displaced steam pumpers in reserve, equipped with tractors as motive power. Some firemen still believe this equipment is more powerful and more reliable than automotive engines.

232   PRACTICE OF MUNICIPAL ADMINISTRATION

<small>CHAP. XIV</small>

<small>Amount of equipment</small>
shop and the employment of a considerable number of skilled mechanics, auto repairmen, electricians, painters, and machinists.

The amount and type of equipment used by a city is influenced by the recommendations of the National Board of Fire Underwriters, which sets up standards in connection with insurance ratings. The several stations constituting a downtown district may contain six or seven engines, two or three ladder trucks, several hose wagons, an aërial ladder truck, and a water tower. The equipment for a residential district may be one or two engines and one ladder truck. The total equipment is dependent upon the number of stations, in turn determined by the size and hazards of the city.

<small>Medical</small>
The medical bureau is an important adjunct to the rescue squad as well as to the fire-fighting force generally. The medical staff attached to the bureau renders first aid both to fire fighters and to citizens injured in connection with fires, and responds to second and third alarms. In addition, the staff cares for all ordinary cases of sickness and accident in the organization, and by a careful surveillance of the health needs of the personnel increases its general efficiency.

<small>Telegraph or alarm system</small>
The central telegraph station has been called the heart of the fire department, and for its protection is often housed in an isolated fireproof building devoted exclusively to the purpose. Alarm boxes connected with the central station are distributed over the city at short intervals, although telephones are also used extensively for notification of fires—a practice not generally approved by fire authorities except in conjunction with the regular alarm system.

<small>The alarm</small>
In a modern fire alarm box the transmission of the alarm results from the manipulation of a lever revealed by opening the alarm box door or window. Boxes in which the sending of the alarm is automatic with the opening of the door or the turning of a handle cannot be used because of the facility with which false alarms are turned in. The number of the box calling is registered in the central telegraph station, and the call is repeated a number of times. This number is usually relayed three times to all stations throughout the city, which procedure enables the entire force to know where fires are located, and what may be expected of the companies not immediately summoned.

<small>The "running card"</small>
Each piece of equipment is numbered and a schedule is prepared for each box alarm indicating the number of the apparatus that will respond to original and succeeding alarms. This is called

FIRE

CHAP. XIV

a "running card" and a complete set covering all alarm districts is maintained in each station. When a company responds to an alarm, the remaining alarm districts for which it is responsible are obviously left unprotected. In consequence, as a company or companies within a district respond to an alarm, the running cards of the remaining companies are automatically moved up—*i.e.*,

6743   Alameda & Kenneth

1st	2nd	3rd	4th	5th	1st	2nd	3rd	4th	5th	1st	2nd	3rd	4th	5th	1st	2nd	3rd	4th
ENGINES					LADDERS					H. P.					RESCUE			
40	43	39	35	21	18	17	15								2			
44	24	47	17	28														
					CHIEFS					W. T.					F. B.			
					9	4	10											

6743   1-1-25

second alarm assignments become first alarm assignments—to meet the new situation. This rearrangement may require companies to move from their stations to stations more centrally located. The succeeding alarms following the first are put in by the firemen for the purpose of calling more equipment. The final alarm, usually the third, fourth, or fifth, depending upon the size of the city, summons the maximum of equipment to any alarm district. The quantity of equipment that will respond to an alarm of fire is determined by the nature of the hazards in the immediate vicinity. An alarm in the high-value area will bring many pieces of apparatus, while an alarm in a sparsely settled residential district may call out only a single piece of equipment designed to deal with small conflagrations.

Fire routes are arranged, and kept practically clear of standing vehicles so that there may be no unnecessary delay in the response of apparatus. Even though called, no equipment will leave a station until the first alarm has been verified by the second sounding or "round of alarm." By the second round, however, the doors of the station should be open, drivers and tillermen on their seats, motors started, and the apparatus manned. Before the

Fire routes

234 PRACTICE OF MUNICIPAL ADMINISTRATION

CHAP. XIV

Fighting the fire

third round of alarm is completed—at least in the daytime—the equipment should have left the station.

Two to three minutes is the maximum time allowed a company to reach the most remote fire on its "running card." The first company commander arriving upon the scene takes charge of operations and directs the procedure, until the arrival of the battalion chief, whereupon that official assumes charge. If a fire is in a high-value area, or involves an industrial section, lines of hose are laid and connected with hydrants or pumpers; ladders are erected; and water towers are placed in position.

With small blazes, proper precautions to prevent unnecessary damage are taken, and while hose is connected and made ready for use by the first arriving company, water will not be used if chemical extinguishers will serve.

The fire-fighting procedure follows a definite routine enjoined on each company, but the actual technique of extinguishing the blaze will be determined by the command officer in accordance with certain established principles of fire fighting as modified by the exigencies of the occasion. The battalion chief, or the chief of the department, if he is present, must in a very brief period of time survey the burning structure both inside and out, determine the nature and location of the fire, its probable direction of travel and its possible communication with adjoining property, the structure and occupancy of the building, the length of time firemen can remain inside or in proximity to the building, the amount of apparatus at hand and the amount that may be necessary to stop the fire, etc. The chief must also determine the quantities of water that should be thrown upon the fire and whether the high pressure system can be used without danger of collapsing the building or of destroying an excessive amount of stock. Neighboring buildings must be protected by forming a water screen between them and the conflagration. Certain apparatus will be assigned to the direction of the battalion chiefs, and the points of attack for which they will be responsible will be indicated. When the fire is "stopped," the various pieces of apparatus return to their stations, and the other stations are notified and their responsibility for other than their first alarm territory ceases.

Police coöperation

The police department should coöperate closely with the fire department in establishing fire lines, in maintaining order in the vicinity of a fire, and expediting the movement of apparatus. When an alarm is turned in, the police department should be notified immediately, and at least one policeman should report in response to every alarm.

To reduce fire department costs, it is necessary to utilize every company as much as possible. In the congested areas companies respond to fires frequently, but in other sections equipment and men may be idle most of the time, answering only a few alarms each month. To overcome this difficulty some cities have adopted the plan of reducing outlying companies to skeleton strength, but with a concentration of large squads of firemen in strategically located stations. These latter squads support the outlying companies on every alarm, arriving in ample time to be of service in case of a serious fire. This program keeps a maximum number of men busy for the maximum amount of time.

It is estimated that seventy percent of fire loss is due to damage from smoke and water. This difficulty is being met by the development of salvage activities within the fire department, or privately as an adjunct to it. In some cities the National Fire Underwriters' Association maintains a salvage corps which responds to alarms, particularly in business and mercantile districts. These salvage companies cover counters and stock-shelves with tarpaulins, rescue valuable records, and divert the flow of water from upper floors by means of channels contrived with tarpaulins at stairways or through holes in ceilings. In some cities, the service hook and ladder trucks carry these tarpaulins, and certain firemen may be detailed to salvage duty. However, effective salvage work can come only from more or less specialized training, and with men working in a distinct organization.[1]

A report should be made of each fire, large and small. Separate operating reports are usually made by each company, the officer in charge securing the general data on origin, loss, etc., and preparing the consolidated report for headquarters. This consolidated report indicates the number of pieces of apparatus responding, the number of hose lines laid, the time required to lay them, the time spent in extinguishing the fire, and any other data pertinent to a full understanding of the situation. The report should be made out promptly and turned over to the administrative division, as a permanent public record.

Municipal fire departments usually respond to fires outside the city limits, when requested to do so by proper authorities, and

[1] C. A. Crosser, "Report on Toledo Fire Department," *Toledo City Journal*, X, 91 (February 28, 1925).

236 PRACTICE OF MUNICIPAL ADMINISTRATION

Out of town fires

in emergencies companies will even run to neighboring cities. A charge is usually made for such service. Frequently, adjacent suburbs will contract with a large city for all fire protection at an established cost per run.

Effective fire-fighting requires a large amount of water under pressure.[1] This pressure usually ranges from twenty-five to forty-five pounds per square inch at street level, and supplies streams of sufficient strength in residential districts. In high-value and industrial areas, pumpers must be used or the water taken from an independent high pressure system.

High pressure systems

A high pressure service consists of a separate water system gridironing the high value district and from which water may be taken at a pressure of from 125 to 150 pounds per square inch. Powerful streams can thus be concentrated on a fire at great heights without the use of pumping engines. In a few cities this high pressure water is secured by gravity, while others take their supply from the water front, the mains being fed by fireboats. This latter method has disadvantages and is eventually supplanted by permanent pumping stations. The mains are kept full of water but not under pressure, since this can be secured in less than a minute. The pumping station is usually a fireproof structure removed from the zone of conflagrations, and should be able to furnish from 10,000 to 20,000 gallons of water per minute at a maximum pressure of 300 pounds. High pressure hydrants must be distinctly marked so that no errors will be committed in making hose connections.

Recruiting the force

The larger fire departments are under civil service regulations, and firemen are selected by competitive examination. The work of a fireman is largely physical, but he must exercise certain intelligence and alertness, and the physical examination should be supplemented by mental and intelligence tests.

Training

At one time newly appointed firemen were put to work without preliminary training and this custom continues in smaller communities. In recent years training schools have been established in many cities in which student firemen receive from fifteen to thirty days' instruction, in the use of fire-fighting appliances, fire prevention, rescue work, the technique of extinguishing blazes of different origins and in different types of structures, etc.

Firemen are also required to keep fit by drill work at regular

---

[1] Yet fire departments use only a fraction of one percent of the water pumped by a city.

FIRE

periods, usually in connection with company drills. Many cities have drill instructors, trained in up-to-date methods of fire fighting, including ventilation, salvage, resuscitation, and similar subjects with which the ordinary company or battalion commander is not likely to be familiar. This plan makes training uniform throughout the department, which would not be the case were instruction given by company commanders.[1]

CHAP. XIV

Drill

Even with drill requirements and routine station duties, firemen have much idle time. Someone has said that a fireman's life consists of five parts idleness, three parts drudgery, and two parts heroism. The proper disposition of idle time has not been dealt with in a satisfactory manner. One solution is to make the departmental drill more intensive. Diagrams of all the important risks in a district could be studied and the best method of fighting fires in each building determined. In addition, every fireman could be trained in methods of fire prevention, and given a knowledge of the combustibility of various materials, the hazards of different businesses, etc. Such an educational program should indicate to the officers the men of superior ability and facilitate their promotion, to both individual and departmental benefit.

Promotions are made largely from the ranks, both efficiency and seniority being considered. Maintenance of discipline, including determination of guilt and imposition of penalty, is usually an obligaton of the chief, although there is a tendency to provide for disciplinary boards on which the ranks are represented. When under formal civil service, it is difficult to dismiss members of the force except as the result of preferred charges and a formal hearing. In any event, firemen once appointed, should be secure in their positions as long as efficient and well behaved.

Promotions and discipline

It is recommended that firemen be retired from active duty upon reaching sixty-two years of age, except in unusual cases.[2] This saving clause enables the department to profit by the accumulated experience of the higher officers who are free from manual labor. Firemen are usually pensioned, the rules providing that members may retire if disabled while on duty or after twenty to thirty years of service, if over a certain age. Pension funds may be provided by taxation, assessment upon members, or a combination of these methods.[3]

Retirement

Pensions

It has been common practice for firemen to do continuous duty

[1] C. A. Crosser, *op. cit.*, 91.
[2] National Board of Fire Underwriters.
[3] For a discussion of pensions, see Chap. III.

238 PRACTICE OF MUNICIPAL ADMINISTRATION

CHAP. XIV

Time off and on

for a specified number of days at a time, being allowed one day off in seven, one day off in five, and recently one day off in three. Such systems precluded any reasonable amount of home life and are a sad commentary on the public opinion that permitted it to continue. The platoon system was devised to remedy this evil and now operates, in some form, in a majority of American cities. Under the two platoon system the force is divided into equal groups each working a shift of either a ten-hour day and a fourteen-hour night, or twenty-four hours on and twenty-four off. The two platoon system is advantageous to the fireman and appears only reasonable, although it necessarily increases the size of the force and the cost of departmental operations. Also, with twenty-four hours of leisure, firemen are inclined to engage in incidental occupations or employment, a procedure disapproved by those in authority. The three platoon plan, providing an eight-hour shift, three sets of firemen coming on duty within a twenty-four hour period, is required by charter in Toledo, but has never been put in force. Considering the nature of the duties of firemen, this plan is nothing more than an imposition on the taxpayers who unwittingly permit it to exist.

Meals

Under the system of continuous duty, men were allowed a definite time off for meals, which obviously reduced the man-power at meal time. The best regulated platoon systems do not allow time off for meals, but permit the men to prepare their own meals and eat in the station houses. This program places the entire effective fire-fighting force on duty at all times.

Fire prevention

Fire prevention is of sufficient importance to merit a separate bureau in the department, manned with a specially trained personnel. This bureau should work in conjunction with the authorities controlling the construction and use of buildings, and the inspection of plans and construction for compliance with a city's building code is properly the duty of this authority. However, the fire prevention squad will find a profitable field of labor in inspections designed to bring older buildings within the requirements of the code, prevent violations in new buildings that originally met requirements, insuring the presence of fire extinguishers examining fire exits, use of standing room in theaters, etc. In some cities, this bureau tests all scenery of theaters, requiring that it be fire resisting. Inspections to detect hazards in both business and residential areas is a very important factor in fire prevention, and is most significant in reducing the number of fires. Many cities assign a fireman to all large gatherings to insure law enforcement.

A remedy for indifference with respect to fire-prevention measures lies in popular education as to its importance and in the development of greater personal responsibility. The schools provide excellent media for the spread of this anti-fire propaganda, and circulars, newspaper articles, and public addresses certainly leave some impression on the adult mind. Some jurisdictions establish a fire-prevention day or week, during which special instruction is given in fire-prevention and in protecting human life from fire.

As a practicable method of reducing fire hazards in congested business sections, every city of consequence has established fire limits within which it is unlawful to construct, or remodel to any great extent, a structure not of a fire-resisting character. This regulation is enforceable under the police power of the state.[1]

Increased fire protection and materially reduced insurance rates are secured for larger buildings through the use of automatic sprinklers, and automatic electric alarms. Hazardous buildings are equipped with such apparatus, and schools, hospitals, and other public buildings are also making such installations. A sprinkler system consists of pipes fastened to the ceilings of a building, the pipes having sprinkler heads at close intervals, sealed with a fusible material melting at a relatively low temperature. As the solder melts under heat, levers are released and the water is discharged against a deflector, covering a floor area of about 100 square feet with a fine spray.[2] The automatic alarm is used principally where the accidental letting go of a sprinkler head would damage valuable goods. It consists of a network of wires which expand under heat, completing an electric circuit. The modern sprinkling device is also equipped with an alarm located either in the watchman's quarters or in the nearest fire station. There are other means of private fire protection, such as periodic patrol, but they are not so elaborate nor as efficient.

The cost of fire protection in American cities is large but necessary. The width of streets, height of buildings, number of inflammable structures, water supply, area, topography, platoon system employed, rates of compensation, and numerous other fac-

[1] For a more detailed discussion, see Chap. XIII.
[2] Crosby-Fiske-Forster, *Handbook of Fire Protection*, Chap. XXIX, discusses automatic sprinklers and rules for their installation.

240 PRACTICE OF MUNICIPAL ADMINISTRATION

CHAP. XIV

Cost of fire protection

tors determine this item of the budget in any city. Cities of more than 30,000 population in the United States are probably spending over $100,000,000 a year for the general conduct of fire departments.[1] In 1923 fire-protection cost ranged from $1.50 to $4.00 per capita, the principal item, salaries of firemen, running from $1200 to $2400 each a year.[2]

Insurance

Fire insurance is devised to spread fire losses among many persons instead of allowing unduly large risks to be borne by a single individual, the rates paid being designed to cover the collective loss by fire over a given period of time. These rates vary, and are determined both by the hazard of each particular property insured and by the general hazard of all property within a particular city. It is, therefore, necessary to measure these hazards, and these tasks are assumed by the local inspection bureaus and the National Board of Fire Underwriters.

Rating general hazards

The National Board of Fire Underwriters is responsible for measuring the general hazards of cities. The board is an organization of approximately 180 stock fire insurance companies, and its purposes are to promote good practices by all companies, to maintain the stability of individual companies by reviewing their risks, to prevent arson, to promote engineering standards, to furnish statistics on fire insurance, and particularly to rate the ability of cities to protect themselves against fire. This rating is based upon prevalence of inflammable buildings, water supply, climatic conditions, fire protection, etc. All cities are classified into ten groups, based upon standards formulated from a study made of conditions in 500 cities. The sum of the maximum points of deficiency that a city may have totals 5,000 and is divided in accordance with the following relative values:[3]

Relative Values

	Points
Water Supply	1,700
Fire Department	1,500
Fire Alarm	550
Police	50
Building Laws	200
Hazards	300
Structural Conditions	700
	5,000

[1] In 1917, these cities spent $52,000,000. *Statistics of Fire Departments* (Bureau of Census, 1918).
[2] Statistics compiled by the St. Paul Bureau of Municipal Research.
[3] *Standard Schedule for Grading Cities and Towns of the United States* (National Board of Fire Underwriters, 1916).

FIRE

Cities and towns are classified by the relative number of points of deficiency in fire defenses and physical conditions as follows:

First	Class	0 to 500	points of deficiency
Second	”	501 to 1000	” ” ”
Third	”	1001 to 1500	” ” ”
Fourth	”	1501 to 2000	” ” ”
Fifth	”	2001 to 2500	” ” ”
Sixth	”	2501 to 3000	” ” ”
Seventh	”	3001 to 3500	” ” ”
Eighth	”	3501 to 4000	” ” ”
Ninth	”	4001 to 4500	” ” ”
Tenth	”	4501 to 5000	” ” ”

Such classification is valuable not only for insurance purposes, but also as a means of inducing cities to increase their protection in order to secure lower insurance rates. The requirements for first and second class ratings are extremely exacting, with the result that there are no cities in the first class and only a few in the second. A city must determine for itself whether it is economically justifiable to make the necessary expenditure to advance its classification, as the physical features of the city and its climatic conditions may make the realization of some requirements excessively expensive. A report on every large city, which describes existing conditions and offers recommendations as to how improvements can be made, is published at intervals.

The examination of individual properties to determine a proper rate is the task of the local inspection bureau maintained by the fire insurance companies operating in a particular territory. Such a bureau examines, when necessary, each property insured, and rates it in accordance with the so-called Dean schedule, which has been adopted in a number of states, and the use of which is being rapidly extended.[1] This schedule is based upon the fundamental assumption that there are three types of building construction—frame, brick, and fireproof. It assumes a one-story building 1,000 square feet in area of each type of construction, located without any fire protection whatsoever, and assigns a unit rate of one to each. On the basis of actual experience with fire losses, this unit of one can be increased by some definite coefficient for each additional story and any additional space added. It is evident that these bases can be arranged in the form of a table which will apply to all such buildings in a community without fire protection. However, cities have fire protection, and, as has been explained, are arranged in ten classes according to the number of points of de-

[1] A. F. Dean, *Analytic System for the Measurement of Relative Fire Hazard* (printed by J. V. Parker).

ficiency from standard. Again, knowing the element of risk of these three types of construction in the cities of each class, it is possible further to modify the schedule by this coefficient. This makes schedules available for the three types of construction, for any height of building, with any floor area, in any classified city.

Scheduling buildings

It will be pointed out, however, that certain other elements in addition to height and area enter into the fire risk of buildings. These hazards are exterior walls, foundations, roofs, ceilings, stairs, chimney stacks, breeching and stove pipes, fireproofing, exterior additions, occupancy, etc., the hazards being modified slightly for each type of construction. It is possible to examine any given building with these hazards in mind and make proper additions or deductions in accordance with a definite schedule of allowances. In larger cities all buildings are periodically scheduled by the local bureau and the results made available to fire underwriters. These schedules will indicate that a certain percentage must be added or subtracted from the unit risk as indicated in the Dean schedule designed for the building.

Basic rates

So far, then, the schedule is merely an abstract percentage to the unit one and nothing has been said about the actual rate to which these coefficients shall apply. The basic rates are established by the local inspection bureaus for each state. These basic rates apply to all types of buildings, and when multiplied by the proper coefficient, found by examining the Dean schedule, will indicate the rate to be applied in any given instance. The loss experience of different communities varies, which fact demands different basic rates. The basic rates represent the amount charged on $100 worth of insured property on the standard one-story structure having an area of 1,000 square feet. A table is constructed according to this basic rate and compiled by use of the Dean schedule, which shows the rate charged on any structure in any class city.

The resulting rate table

The problems of the administrator

In general, the administrator should assure himself of two facts: first, that the scheduling of buildings by the local inspection bureau is done accurately and without favoritism; and second, that the basic rate applied to a city is proper, providing only a fair return to the insurance companies.

CHAPTER XV

HEALTH [1]

For a number of centuries the public has recognized that certain diseases can be communicated from one person to another and has made organized efforts to reduce such communication to a minimum. Particularly during the plague periods of the Middle Ages, diseased persons were quarantined by the military, their domiciles placarded, and various additional precautions taken, some of which are now known to have been without effect. The crude methods of disease prevention were employed without knowledge of the means by which contagious and infectious diseases are communicated, and it was not recognized that animals, insects, food, and water are disease carriers of importance. In connection with personal quarantine, some official efforts were made to eliminate nuisances objectionable to smell, on the assumption that there was a vague connection between objectionable odors and disease. Such efforts, coupled with a hurried burial of the dead, constituted the principal official health work until recent times, and were supplemented with the individual use of charms, vile smelling chemicals, and pungent herbs.[2] Not until the middle

The beginning of public health work

---

[1] For a brief statement of health organization and administration it is difficult to add to the summary of C. E. A. Winslow and H. I. Harris, "An Ideal Health Department for a city of 100,000 population," Section II of the *Report of the Committee on Municipal Health Department Practice* of the American Public Health Association in coöperation with the U. S. Public Health Service (Public Health Bulletin No. 136, July, 1923); and "A Proposed Plan of Organization of Community Health Work for a City of 50,000 population," in *A Health Survey of 86 Cities* by the Research Division of the American Child Health Association (1925). These statements should be supplemented by the several separate sections appearing as Section I of the first report, and Section II of the latter study. For the details of administrative procedure, consult J. Scott MacNutt, *Manual for Health Officers* (Wiley, 1915). Many health surveys of individual cities are available, including the outstanding study, *The Cleveland Health and Hospital Survey* (Cleveland Hospital Council, 1920). For a guide to making such studies, see Murray P. Horwood, *Public Health Surveys* (Wiley, 1921). For current reference, see the *Proceedings of the American Public Health Association* (annual) and *American Journal of Public Health* (monthly).

[2] "This day . . . I did in Drury Lane see two or three houses marked with a red cross upon the doors, and 'Lord have mercy on us' writ there; which was a sad sight to me, being the first of that kind that, to my remembrance, I ever saw. It put me into an ill conception of myself and my smell, so that

244   PRACTICE OF MUNICIPAL ADMINISTRATION

The germ theory of disease and the progress of isolating disease germs

of the nineteenth century did the control of disease become an accepted public activity delegated to a single health authority.

The past fifty years have marked the establishment of public health work on a sound foundation, and with results that have justified the increasing expenditure of public funds for this purpose. These modern activities started with the propounding of the germ theory of disease, which serves as a place of beginning for the work of disease prevention and cure. This work has progressed rapidly, with the help of medical practitioners, both public and private. In 1877 Pasteur published his first paper showing that fermentation was caused by living organisms, establishing the basis upon which the germ theory of disease is predicated. It became known that innumerable minute organisms, of which there are perhaps 1,500 different kinds, variously known as germs, microbes, bacteria, and bacilli, exist in the air and upon nearly all substances. These organisms serve both useful and harmful purposes. They are the cause of the numerous fermentations by which cheese, yeast, vinegar, and alcoholic beverages are secured. Other similar organisms, less than 100 in number, are of a pathogenic character and are the source of disease when they enter the human body. These disease germs may be introduced in food or liquids, through the bites of insects, directly through abrasion, or by contact with discharges of the mucous membrane. For example, typhoid and certain other bacilli are carried by water, milk, or solid food; yellow fever is transmitted by the bite of the yellow fever mosquito; mucous membrane discharges are responsible for the spread of diphtheria, measles, scarlet fever, whooping cough, and common colds. These bacteria multiply rapidly, particularly when food and temperature are suitable to their growth, increasing largely by division. Such division is always made within a few hours, sometimes within twenty minutes, so that the number of the organisms increases enormously by geometric progression.[1] Beginning with the work of Pasteur, there have been many advances in this field. From the discovery of the organism of leprosy

I was forced to buy some roll-tobacco to smell and to chaw, which took away the apprehension.'' From Samuel Pepys, *Diary*, in which are mentioned numerous measures of plague prevention. ''A Doctor of Medicine'' in Rudyard Kipling, *Rewards and Fairies*, is also of interest.

[1] See H. W. Conn and J. Harold, *Bacteriology* (Williams and Wilkins, 1924); and W. H. Park, Anna W. Williams and Charles Krumwiede, *Pathogenic Micro-Organisms* (Lea and Febiger, 8th ed., 1924). See also, Paul H. DeKruif, *Microbe Hunters* (Harcourt, 1926); and for the life of a great physician in this field, Marie D. Gorgas and Burton J. Hendrick, *William Crawford Gorgas* (Lea and Febiger, 1924).

HEALTH

in 1879, through the isolation of the cause of yellow fever in 1919, the work of isolating the organisms that are responsible for some of the more common and malignant diseases is still continuing.

With this knowedge at hand, modern health authorities must concern themselves with the development of measures that will prevent the spread of communicable disease organisms, and with the identification of the particular organisms that cause diseases, in order that ailments may be properly diagnosed and steps taken toward their cure. Health authorities have therefore concentrated their labors on quarantine, so that diseases may not be transmitted from one person to another; disinfection, so that the houses and the personal property of persons infected cannot serve as a means of transmission; the elimination of certain carriers of disease bacteria, such as rats, mosquitoes, and flies; the protection of food from contamination by requiring that the conditions under which it is handled and produced are sanitary and that the persons handling it are free from infection; the development of individual immunity through the building up of general health; and the conquering of infection by the artificial introduction of serums and vaccines into the bodies of individuals, so that they will have an increased resistance to disease. The development of serums and vaccines has gone on with such a pace that smallpox, diphtheria, typhoid, rabies, tetanus and possibly scarlet fever and measles may be considered as susceptible of complete elimination.[1]

The resulting relation of government to public health is twofold, involving both prevention and cure, with greater emphasis on the former. The cure of disease is essentially an individual matter in which there is large personal incentive on the part of the persons afflicted, it being to their own interests to promote rapid recovery. However, it is not always to their immediate personal interest to prevent the spread of disease to other persons. Without the pressure that comes from an organized community, an individual taken by disease which is communicable may, through indifference or ignorance, transmit that disease to a large number of other persons; or an ignorant individual may maintain sanitary conditions

[1] For an excellent brief discussion of this phase of public health and hygiene, see W. B. Munro, *Municipal Government and Administration* (Macmillan, 1925), II, 258-273; and Part II of J. Scott MacNutt, *Manual for Health Officers* (Wiley, 1915). An extended treatise is Herbert H. Waite, *Disease Prevention* (Crowell, 1926). A historical development of public health work is published in the Jubilee Volume of the American Health Association, *A Half Century of Public Health*, edited by Mazyck C. Ravenel (American Health Association, New York City, 1921).

246   PRACTICE OF MUNICIPAL ADMINISTRATION

CHAP. XV

that are a menace, not only to his own health, but to the health of the community. The state, then, in its program of disease prevention finds it necessary to make a certain amount of provision for the cure of disease, particularly in persons who would otherwise be a menace to their neighbors. It is now accepted that every city should provide some official organization empowered to act in this field of prevention, and to function in the cure of disease so far as cure acts as a preventive measure.

The results of modern health work

Taking advantage of scientific advances, including the determination of the specific nature of many diseases, the use of vaccines and serums, knowledge of the means by which certain diseases are transmitted, the curability of some diseases by the use of the x-ray and radium, as well as general education of the public in the prevention of disease, and the building up of individual immunity to disease, has resulted in a material reduction of sickness and death and in a lengthening of the average period of human life.[1] The results of this work are best indicated by certain statistics accumulated by the New York City Department of Public Health.[2] In 1891, in that city, 241 out of every 1,000 babies born died before they were a year old, *i.e.*, nearly one-fourth. Now, only seventy-one out of every 1,000 die, or only one-fourteenth. Malaria, in 1870, accounted for twenty-seven deaths per 100,000 of population. Now deaths are rare. Smallpox, in 1872, caused a mortality of 124 per 100,000 of population, which contrasts with the fact that not a death from this disease has occurred in New York City in the last nine years. The death rate from tuberculosis in 1871 was 406 per 100,000 population. In 1921 it had been brought down to eighty-nine per 100,000. Had the rate of 1871 prevailed during 1921, there would have been 23,350 deaths instead of 5,143. Forty persons per 100,000 of population died of typhoid fever in 1870; in 1921, this rate had fallen to two persons per 100,000. In former years, the death rate from scarlet fever was about 100 per 100,000 and today it has been reduced to five per 100,000. In 1869, measles caused the death of sixty-two out of every 100,000 population, and by 1921 the rate had fallen to three per 100,000.

[1] Dr. Aleck P. Harrison, "The Organization of a City Health Department," *Texas Municipalities*, VII, 78-83 (July, 1920).
[2] Quoted by the Ohio Institute, Columbus, O., as of the year 1921. Interesting graphs illustrating similar data will be found in the pamphlet of Louis I. Dublin, *Some Problems of Life Extension* (Metropolitan Life Insurance Co., 1924).

HEALTH

The carrying out of measures for the furtherance of public health is based, first of all, upon specific authority conferred by the constitution and legislation of the state. But in many of its aspects it rests simply upon the exercise of police powers. Police powers are derived from the well established principle of common law that no person may use his property in a way to injure any other person; and under this power the public assumes the right to regulate the conduct of citizens in such a way that their acts or delinquencies do not work material injury to others.

<small>CHAP. XV</small>

<small>Source of health authority</small>

The control of public health is primarily a state function. Many activities undertaken by a municipality are for the convenience and benefit of its own citizens; but public health has a broader scope than mere city boundaries. Disease germs do not respect city charters and artificial territorial lines, and for this reason it is necessary that the state government prescribe minimum health standards and regulations for the entire area under its control. Usually the state legislature enacts a health code detailing these minimum essentials and delegating their administration to a state health authority. Local communities create their own health authorities as prescribed by law and enact such additional health regulations as are sanctioned by state law and city charter, and appear needed in particular localities. In a larger way, such local health authorities represent the state authorities, and therefore act in a dual capacity, being instrumental in the enforcement of both local and state regulations. Always, such local authorities are subject to certain supervision by the state, and the latter may not only enforce a minimum of health regulation, but may actually assume direction of situations that have got beyond local control. Because local health authorities so represent the state, they ordinarily exercise an authority not common to other city departments. Under the police powers, they can perform acts that would not be sanctioned on the part of other city officers; and in certain emergencies they may expend funds without the usual control of the municipal legislative body.[1]

<small>Health control a state function</small>

The health authorities of a community ordinarily operate in both administrative and legislative capacities, and occasionally exercise quasi-judicial powers. Administrative duties comprehend a responsibility for the enforcement of health regulations promulgated by the state and the local governments. Legislative power is involved in the enactment of regulations having the effect of

<small>Organization of the health authority</small>

[1] See J. Scott MacNutt, *A Manual for Health Officers*, Chaps. I-III.

248 PRACTICE OF MUNICIPAL ADMINISTRATION

CHAP. XV

Selection of the board

law, and suitable to situations not covered by other legislation. Judicial authority is involved when decisions are made as to the scope of local powers, and as to the extent that police power shall be exercised.

For these reasons, it is customary for a municipality to have the health authority lodged in a health board. Such boards of health may be elective, but almost universally are appointed by the mayor or the city council, or are of an ex-officio character. Ex-officio boards may include all of the members of the city council, the mayor, and heads of certain important departments, or they may be only an unofficial advisory board of physicians. In some cases, the character of the membership of appointive boards is prescribed by law, the personnel to consist of a certain number of physicians, engineers, laymen, nurses, and others. There has been a recent tendency to dispense with boards and lodge the health authority in a single executive, responsible only to the mayor or city manager. This executive may be supported by an ex-officio or appointive board acting solely in an advisory capacity. On account of the legislative and judicial authority reposing in the health authorities, it is believed that provision for an appointive board to exercise this authority is in accordance with sound organization. The tenure of the members of appointed boards will vary, but the terms of office should not all expire at the same time, thus preventing a continuity of policy.

The health officer

In cities employing the board, rather than the single appointed executive plan, the detail of actual administration and the carrying out of the health measures should rest with a health officer appointed by and responsible to the board. The health officer should have administrative ability, plus thorough technical training, and, according to prevailing opinion, should be a physician. A medical education is useful, but there has been a recent tendency to appoint trained health officers who are not necessarily doctors of medicine. Specialized courses in public health work, including biology, sanitation, and kindred subjects, have been established in a number of universities, leading to a certificate or degree in public health, and graduates are finding increased opportunities in professional work.[1]

On the administrative side, a health officer is responsible for

---

[1] See Allen W. Freeman, "The Health Board and the Health Officer," *Report of the Committee in Municipal Health Department Practice*, Chap. I; and *A Health Survey of 86 Cities*, Chap. II.

conducting a department of government employing persons of diversified training who are in constant contact with the public. Aside from technical training, an essential qualification of a health officer is ability to direct employees and to deal with the public. This public may be ignorant of the necessity for public health regulations, and the task of the health officer becomes one of education, of appealing to enlightened self-interest, and, in extreme cases, of compulsion. In such circumstances, the value of tact cannot be overestimated. A health officer who rides roughshod over popular good will will very shortly find himself in difficulty with influential citizens and with those branches of the government which are particularly responsive to political situations. On the other hand, the modern health officer must not go too softly, making public welfare subservient to political expediency, and relaxing regulations because they are offensive to powerful personages in the community.[1] Somewhere will be found a happy medium of conduct that will secure a large degree of public coöperation and conformance, and at the same time preserve the department from assaults that would eventually destroy its usefulness. The health officer should have available a sufficient number of competent employees so that he need give little attention to office routine, but can devote his time and energy to developing public contacts and inspecting the field activities of his organization. It must be assumed that an office requiring the peculiar qualifications necessary to successful health administration will be filled without regard for political considerations, preferably by civil service, and for a tenure dependent only upon capable administration. The compensation of the office should be sufficient to secure and retain competent full-time direction.

To carry out successfully a thorough program of public health service, the activities of a health department should be directed along somewhat the following lines:[2,3]

[1] McNutt, *op. cit.*, 14-16. The readers of Sinclair Lewis, *Arrowsmith* (Harcourt, Brace, 1925) will recall the extremes of health administration pictured in the arbitrary methods of Martin Arrowsmith, as opposed to the yielding conduct of Dr. Pickenbaugh.
[2] The activities here outlined are suggested by the American Public Health Association, the particular wording, with slight modification, being taken from the New York Bureau of Municipal Research, *Survey of Norfolk*, 331 et seq.
[3] The discussion of these several services in the following pages follows closely the program recommended by C. E. A. Winslow and H. I. Harris, "An Ideal Health Department for a City of 100,000 Population," *op. cit.*, 247-271; and "A Proposed Plan of Organization of Community Health for a City of 50,000 Population," *A Health Survey of 86 Cities*, 557-614.

250   PRACTICE OF MUNICIPAL ADMINISTRATION

CHAP. XV

1. *General administration,* including the correlation of all health activities; preparation of the budget; selection of employees; maintenance of records and reports; issuance of licenses and permits; care of buildings and stores; and all other activities which relate to the department as a whole.
2. *Keeping of vital statistics,* including the issuance of birth and death certificates; and the collection and compilation of data relative to births, deaths, and diseases.
3. *Control of communicable diseases,* including notification and registration of diseases; the provision of quarantine; the study of epidemiology as it relates to the protection of food and water supplies; the provision of immunization against diseases through the administration of the various serums and antitoxins of proved value; and the prevention of diseases of animals which are communicable to man.
4. *Promotion of child hygiene* by means of prenatal work among expectant mothers; the supervision of midwives, maternity hospitals, day nurseries, and other institutions for the care of children; the medical inspection and supervision of the health of school children; and the issuance of employment certificates.
5. *Control of occupational diseases* through notification and registration of diseases; the physical examination of workers; and the inspection of premises to prevent industrial hazards.
6. *Supervision of milk supply* by the inspection and scoring of dairies and places where milk is handled or sold; the establishment of milk standards; etc.
7. *Supervision of food products,* including their production, handling, and sale; the inspection and condemnation of animals slaughtered for food purposes; and the control of public food markets.
8. *Provision of laboratory service* for the detection and prevention of disease; and the determination of such facts relative to food, water, air, etc., as may be necessary for adequate health supervision.
9. *Public health education* through publications, lectures, exhibits, etc.
10. *Control of nuisances,* including the investigation of complaints; the prevention of health hazards by reason of unsanitary conditions of yards and premises; the extermination of rats, flies, mosquitoes, and other creatures which carry disease; and the prevention of nuisance arising from promiscuous spitting, use of common utensils, common towels, etc.
11. *Supervision of hospitals and dispensaries* in so far as such control may be legitimately exercised by the health department.
12. *Supervision of the construction and occupancy of buildings* from the health standpoint.
13. *Supervision of water supply and sewage disposal,* in so far as it affects the community health.
14. *Supervision of the operation of public conveniences,* such as public baths and comfort stations.

Vital statistics

The proper operation of a health department is impossible without the information that is made possible by the collection, tabulation, and interpretation of statistics of morbidity and mor-

HEALTH

tality. These data not only tell the health officer about conditions existing in his community, but point the way for modification. Because of their importance and because their treatment is a medical as well as a statistical problem, the activities having to do with vital statistics should be located entirely within the health department and operated independently of other public agencies. The compulsory reporting of certain social and disease data must be secured through adequate legislation and should include the registration of marriages, births, deaths, and all cases of communicable diseases. Periodically these data should be tabulated and such correlations be made as will indicate the relationships of disease, death, sex, age, districts, and nativity. Some authorities also maintain that the health department should maintain a continuous record of each child from birth through school until a work certificate is granted, although this practice is by no means universal. Every department should also record information with respect to all persons selling, manufacturing, or handling food products; as well as a record of inspections made, conditions found, and dispositions made of complaints of all kinds. It has been suggested that the bureau of vital statistics may also function in some respects as a research staff, making studies of mortality and morbidity and such other problems of public health as may guide the health officer in his work.[1]

The most important feature of disease prevention is the control of communicable diseases including scarlet fever, measles, diphtheria, typhoid fever, tuberculosis, smallpox, chickenpox, etc. These diseases should all be reported to the health authorities by the attending physician and every case investigated by a public health nurse. More serious diseases, such as diphtheria, smallpox, and scarlet fever, should be seen by a medical officer and specimens taken for laboratory diagnosis and verification. In every case there must be quarantine for a reasonable time,[2] accompanied by the disinfection of all infected discharges, and a cleansing of both person and habitation at the termination of the case. A good scrubbing with soap and water is most effective for this last purpose, fumigation now being used only when insect borne diseases

---

[1] See Louis I. Dublin, "Vital Statistics," *Report on Municipal Health Department Practice*, Chap. XVIII; and *A Health Survey of 86 Cities*, Chap. III.
[2] See the model health code prepared by the Committee on Model Health Legislation of the American Public Health Association, *American Journal of Public Health*, XI, 259 (March, 1921).

are involved. Some authorities urge that tuberculosis and venereal diseases, because of their peculiar character and necessarily different treatment, should be controlled by separate divisions of the department dealing with communicable diseases. This segregation is probably feasible in large communities but is not concurred in by some health officers on the grounds that in smaller cities it will require too many specialists.

Hospitalization

In cases where persons infected with communicable diseases cannot be properly cared for at home, or where there is danger of the spread of disease to others, it is usual to provide some form of hospitalization. In smaller communities, arrangements for space suitable for isolation can be made with private or semi-public hospitals, at a per diem per patient. In larger cities, the health authorities should construct and maintain contagious disease hospitals. Such hospitals take the place of the old-fashioned pesthouse employed during the unenlightened days when the proper care of contagious disease was unknown. In addition to the isolation and care of contagious disease cases, provision must be made for the detection and control of carriers of all infectious communicable diseases.

Serums and vaccines

Recently there has been a large development in the use of serums and vaccines for both disease prevention and cure, and one of the most important duties of every health department is to provide these supplies free, or at a low cost. Frequently, supplies are located in designated drug stores and police stations where they may be obtained by physicians. Smallpox immunization has been known for more than a century and a half, while immunization against typhoid fever, diphtheria, scarlet fever and measles is comparatively recent. Smallpox vaccination has removed that former scourge from the group of important diseases, and present occasional outbreaks are the result of official or public neglect. In most states smallpox vaccination is compulsory, although enforcement is handicapped by religious and hygienic propaganda on the part of certain groups. Health authorities usually enforce smallpox vaccination at the time a child enters school. Upon exposure, unvaccinated children and adults may be quarantined, although it is customary with children only to require that they remain away from school for the quarantine period. The administration of toxin antitoxin for diphtheria and of serum for scarlet fever is ordinarily optional, but effort is made to persuade parents to utilize the former or permit the health authorities to do so.

Immunization for scarlet fever and measles is as yet in the experimental stage. The control of typhoid carriers is so complete that immunization is unusual unless persons are entering areas in which the quality of water, milk, or food is questionable.[1]

CHAP. XV

The first organized interest in the prevention and cure of tuberculosis came from volunteer philanthropic agencies, and these organizations have continued their activities both in education for the prevention of tuberculosis and in the conduct of tuberculosis nursing and dispensaries. In consequence, many but not all, health departments have been content to leave these activities in semi-public hands. Large cities, however, have ordinarily taken over the purely medical side of tuberculosis work, largely leaving to private agencies the conduct of educational propaganda against the disease. The control of tuberculosis is as essentially a public activity as is the control of any communicable disease, and regardless of the policy that may be followed, health authorities must not be relieved of the responsibility of making certain that the machinery for controlling the disease is operating efficiently.[2]

Control of tuberculosis

In spite of requisite legislation it will be found difficult to compel the reporting of cases of tuberculosis by physicians, and in fact many cases will exist that are not properly diagnosed or in which no medical attendance has been secured. However, the health authorities should bend every effort to secure as complete reporting of this disease as is possible and should enter into coöperative arrangements with social workers and others, with a view to learning of cases that have been brought to the attention of these persons. Probably from seven to nine active cases of tuberculosis exist to every death in the community and the effectiveness of the reporting may be measured accordingly.[3] Because cases of tuberculosis are not always properly diagnosed the health authorities should make available to private physicians facilities where proper diagnosis can be made.

Once a case of tuberculosis is known to the authorities they should take steps to see that the infected person is properly taken care of at home, or in an institution, both for the welfare of the

---

[1] See Allen W. Freeman and W. Thurber Fales, "Control of Communicable Diseases," *Report on Municipal Health Department Practice*, Chap. III; and *A Health Survey of 86 Cities*, Chap. IV.
[2] See C. E. A. Winslow and Gertrude F. Baker, "Tuberculosis," *Report on Municipal Health Department Practice*, Chap. IV; and *A Health Survey of 86 Cities*, Chap. V.
[3] For a study of the incidence of tuberculosis, see Framingham Monograph No. 10, *Final Summary Report* (National Tuberculosis Association, 1924).

individual and as a means of insuring that the patient will not become a menace to others. Frequently it is desirable to establish tubercular clinics where treatment may be given ambulant cases and where persons who desire may receive a thorough diagnosis. In any event, the family of the infected person must be educated in methods of home treatment and in the means of proper disinfection in order that the spread of infection be made impossible. While it is recognized that tuberculosis in the early stages can be successfully treated in the home, sanitariums or hospital facilities should be provided for all advanced cases and for those cases where proper home facilities are lacking. It is sometimes urged that all cases should be hospitalized for at least a short time in order to inculcate good health habits.

An important part of anti-tuberculosis work should be provision for suitable employment and living conditions for arrested cases. In this activity the coöperation of employers and welfare organizations must be secured. If persons recovering from this disease could have proper home environment and treatment, and suitable work could be secured for them, a large amount of eventual hospitalization could be avoided. Finally, the health department should provide the usual machinery of open air schools and free camps, which can offer facilities for children who are undernourished, for contact cases, and for other persons who are not so advanced as to require home or institutional care.[1]

The control of venereal disease presents a special problem to the health officer because of social questions involved. Many states have legislation requiring the reporting of all such cases, but it is frequently more honored in the breach than in the observance. As a compromise, some health officers permit attending physicians to report cases by number, withholding the name and address, a procedure which is reasonably satisfactory so long as the patient takes proper precautions to prevent the infection of others. In many instances, however, after a few treatments the patient ceases medical treatment, although still uncured. In consequence, the health department has no assurance that the reporting of the disease means the suppression of the source of infection.

One means of control that is efficacious is the examination and segregation of prostitutes. In larger communities the health de-

[1] See Philip P. Jacobs, *The Tuberculosis Worker* (Williams and Wilkins, 1923); and the annual *Transactions of the National Tuberculosis Association*.

partment should maintain hospital facilities where these persons can be hospitalized immediately upon discovery. Any such procedure, however, requires the complete confidence of these persons in the health authorities, and will bring the latter in frequent conflict with the police department if the police insist that all known facts be communicated to them. Obviously, the health departments must decline to coöperate with police authorities in any such manner.

However, the greater portion of venereal disease cases are problems of home treatment in which the principal elements involved are early discovery and thorough medication. To this end, some cities maintain venereal disease clinics where treatment is either free or at a small cost. In conjunction with all of these activities the health department should carry on a thorough educational campaign and should within its limits encourage movements for the suppression of vice.[1]

Child hygiene should include work in connection with both infants and public school children. The beginning of infant work is in the pre-natal clinics for the medical examination and instruction of expectant mothers, particularly in those sections of the city where the standard of education and intelligence is such that instruction is desirable if children are to be safely brought into the world and given a reasonable chance of life afterwards. Some large cities even provide obstetrical care through hospitalization and obstetrical nursing for mothers not otherwise in a position to secure proper care. In any case there should be a licensing and supervision of midwives, restricting the practice of the profession to competent persons, along with the universal administration of silver nitrate in order that blindness from venereal disease may be prevented. Some cities provide infant welfare stations in certain districts where medical advice may be given to mothers with respect to their children and milk or diet formula dispensed at cost or free as circumstances require. Some authorities have gone so far as to suggest that every child from birth to five years of age should be visited by representatives of the health department to insure that it is receiving proper care and that the department should maintain a current record of all children from birth through to school age. Such procedure may be highly de-

[1] See Mary A. Clark, "Venereal Disease Control," *Report on Municipal Health Practice*, Chap. V; and *A Health Survey of 86 Cities*, Chap. VI.

256   PRACTICE OF MUNICIPAL ADMINISTRATION

CHAP. XV

Health work in schools

sirable but raises the question as to what point free public health service shall cease and proper care be left to the initiative of the individual.[1]

The desirability of health activities with school children and the extent of such activities is discussed in the chapter on education.[2] In this field, however, there is a continual question of jurisdiction —shall the work be done by the health or by the educational authorities? There is no categorical conclusion. In certain emergencies, if not at other times, the health of school children is closely related to the general health of the community, and it is entirely within the province of a department of health to prescribe and enforce the precautions necessary to safeguard the city. On the other hand, health education, to be successful, must be a part of the regular school curriculum. Probably the best solution of the problem is a coöperative arrangement between the two authorities by which a health program can be agreed upon and carried out as the respective budgets of the two authorities will best permit, adequate arrangement being made for the care of private and parochial schools.

The principal elements of a complete program of health supervision for school children involves two factors: first, daily examinations by the teacher and then by a school nurse of all children apparently suffering from colds and fevers or having other indications of communicable disease; and second, the periodical physical examination of all children for the detection of physical defects.

Experience indicates that the teachers will be more than ordinarily careful in referring suspected cases to the school nurse and that the school nurse is quite competent to determine what cases should be sent home for parental and perhaps medical observation. Both the nurse and the teacher will err on the side of safety and with any reasonable suspicion of illness the best place for the pupil is at home and in bed.

The physical examination requires more thorough treatment. Originally it was believed that each pupil should be examined each year by a physician with respect to general health, nutrition, cardiac and lung conditions, vision, hearing, teeth, etc. It is now felt that three such physical examinations are sufficient—one at entrance, one at about eight years of age, and one finally at about

[1] See Ira V. Hiscock, "Infant Hygiene," *Report on Municipal Health Practice*, Chap. VI; and *A Health Survey of 86 Cities*, Chaps. VII-IX.
[2] Chap. XVI.

HEALTH

fourteen.¹ A complete report on the physical condition of every child should be made known to the parent and the school nurse should undertake such follow-up work as seems necessary to bring about a correction of the defects found. In no case should parents be urged to utilize the clinics established by the city until there is an indication that they will not use the private medical resources at their command. Some cities do provide school dental clinics, but it is not recommended that the municipality extend its services beyond this point.²

CHAP. XV

Most communities provide that children upon reaching fourteen or sixteen years of age may be allowed to work provided family circumstances make it necessary and if certain continuation classes are attended. It is particularly desirable that these young children should not be permitted to undertake work beyond their strength. Before issuing working papers every applicant should be given a thorough physical examination and all the examining physicians should have a clear understanding of what constitutes sound health and normal development and should do their examining in accordance with standard requirements which will be the same for all.³

Working papers

Accident prevention is essentially an obligation of the state government rather than of the municipality, and is taken care of through current factory inspection by that department of the state government which is entrusted with the interests of labor, supplemented by the work of the safety committees in the several factories, and of interested civic organizations. In the same way, certain occupational diseases are matters of state rather than of local control. However, it is entirely proper that local health departments should undertake the careful investigation of indus-

Control of occupational diseases

---

¹ Certain selected children should be examined regardless of age. These will include the children greatly under weight and others recommended for examination by nurse or teacher.

² Ira V. Hiscock and W. T. Fales, "School Health Supervision," *Report on Municipal Health Practice*, Chap. VII-a; and *A Health Survey of 86 Cities*, Chap. X. See also, *Health Education, a Program for Public Schools and Teacher Training Institutions* (Report of the Joint Committee on Health Problems on Education of the National Education Association and the American Medical Association, New York, 1924); *Health Through the School Day* (Educational Bulletin No. 5, National Catholic Welfare Conference, Washington, D. C., 1924); and *Annual Report of Conference on Health Education and the Preparation of Teachers* (U. S. Bureau of Education and the American Child Health Organization); *Transactions of the American Child Health Organization* (annual); and the numerous publications of the Children's Bureau of the U. S. Department of Labor.

³ See Bessie Bunzel, "Working Paper Procedure," *Report on Municipal Health Practice*, Chap. VII-b.

258 PRACTICE OF MUNICIPAL ADMINISTRATION

CHAP. XV

Public health nursing

Supervision of milk supply

tries in which occupational diseases may be anticipated and should take such steps to reduce the incidental morbidity and mortality; although coöperation should be expected to exist between the local and state authorities.[1]

There is scarcely any activity of the public health department which does not involve the use of nursing service. The nurse serves in every branch,—child health work, visitation of cases of communicable disease, assists in clinics of all types, follow-up work in the homes, etc. Since public health nursing covers practically all public health activities, two distinct policies naturally result with respect to nursing organization. Some authorities believe that the best practice is the establishment of the nursing service as a separate activity for each function. Under this system the nursing districts of the city are large and several specialized nurses operate in the same district but in different fields. Others are of the opinion that generalized nursing is best, the districts being smaller and one nurse made responsible for practically all nursing service in the area.[2]

Milk plays a highly important part in modern diet and is so easily a carrier of disease that its production and distribution must be given careful supervision by the health authorities. This work is ordinarily undertaken by a division of food inspection, one branch of which is devoted to the subject of milk.

Until recent years the public authorities having to do with the quality of milk were of two distinct opinions as to the best method of procedure. Some believed that milk of a high grade could be best secured by careful inspection of dairies and distribution plants, grading them according to predetermined standards [3] and forbidding by proper legislation the distribution of milk within the city that was not produced under sanitary conditions.

[1] New York City maintains a clinic for occupational diseases and under the direction of Dr. Louis J. Harris, has undertaken numerous studies of the subject. See a number of reprints and monographs written by Dr. Harris and published by the Department, particularly *The Opportunities Which Industrial Hygiene Offers to the General Practitioner and to the Public Health Officer; Occupational Causes of Ill-Health; Industrial Hygiene; Clinical Types of Occupational Diseases*, etc., etc.

[2] C. E. A. Winslow and Margaret R. Burkhardt, "Public Health Nursing," *Report on Municipal Health Practice*, Chap. X; and *A Health Survey of 86 Cities*, Chap. XIV. A standard work on the subject is Mary S. Gardner, *Public Health Nursing* (Macmillan, 2d ed., 1924). For clinics consult Michael M. Davis, Jr., and Andrew R. Warner, *Dispensaries* (Macmillan, 1918). In Dayton, Ohio, the experiment with generalized nursing has produced excellent results and should be studied by any person interested in the subject.

[3] Sample standard score cards are provided by the U. S. Department of Agriculture.

HEALTH

Others believed that the most practical plan of milk control was through proper pasteurization coupled with a reasonable amount of inspection to insure that distribution plants were maintained in a sanitary condition. In small communities the periodic inspection and grading of dairies is entirely possible at a reasonable expenditure of money. In large communities the milk supply is received from many dairies scattered over a large area, sometimes located in several states. To inspect these plants properly would require an expenditure of money beyond the reasonable means of the average community. Under these circumstances it is probably wise to require a careful pasteurization which should be defined by law and made mandatory by frequent inspection, and the quality of milk should be checked by frequent chemical and bacteriological examinations. In all events the cattle producing all the milk supply of a city should be tuberculin tested since it is estimated that a considerable percentage of tuberculosis is of bovine origin.[1]

In addition to the control of milk supply most health departments undertake a supervision of foods and drugs, the standards of the Federal Pure Food law having been adopted by a number of states. Food regulations usually comprehend the licensing of all establishments where food products are sold such as restaurants, bakeries, groceries, candy stores, markets, soda fountains, fruit stands, and some provision for their periodic inspection. Some health authorities, however, restrict their activities to places where food is consumed upon the premises and endeavor to require the proper sterilization of all utensils used. In this connection effort has been made, with more or less success, to inspect all food handlers to insure freedom from communicable disease. Health authorities usually provide that food offered for sale which is to be consumed by the public without cooking shall be protected from dirt by proper screens or other enclosures, although stringent regulations will meet the vigorous opposition of dealers.[2]

One of the great difficulties met in this branch of health work is the proper control of meat supply. Meat which is provided by larger slaughtering establishments and subject to inspection by

---

[1] Seven percent of all tuberculosis in humans, and as much as thirty-three percent in that of children under five years of age.
See Ira V. Hiscock, "Milk Inspection," *Report on Municipal Health Practice*, Chap. XII; and *A Health Survey of 86 Cities*, 205-210. Also, *Proceedings of the International Association of Dairy and Milk Inspectors*.

[2] See Ira V. Hiscock, "Food and Drug Inspection," *Report on Municipal Health Practice*, Chap. XIII.

260   PRACTICE OF MUNICIPAL ADMINISTRATION

CHAP. XV

the United States government creates no problem. The real trouble arises with the small slaughtering houses in every community which are difficult of regulation because the amount of slaughtering does not require the continuous services of an inspector. Some cities have endeavored to meet this situation by providing a public abattoir for local slaughtering, and excluding from the city all meat not inspected either at this abattoir, or elsewhere under the Federal law.[1]

Laboratory service

Adequate laboratory facilities for the bacteriological examination of disease cultures and for the chemical and bacteriological examination of milk are absolutely necessary for the successful operation of any health department.[2]

Nuisances

In a city nuisances frequently arise from the improper treatment of privy vaults, stable manure, rubbish, garbage, and places fostering the breeding of mosquitoes and rats. For the control of these sources of disease the health authorities must retain a squad of sanitary police, preferably uniformed, to investigate promptly all complaints and undertake the regular and systematic inspection of unsanitary premises and conditions. If possible, these nuisances should be eliminated, but if that is not practical, efforts should be made to see that their possible annoyance is reduced to a minimum. Sometimes proper control of garbage and sewage will bring the health authorities in contact with other departments and require an amount of diplomatic action that will tax the ingenuity of the health officer. So far as private citizens are concerned with the maintenance of nuisances it is not anticipated that the authorities will secure a maximum of action through legal prosecutions. Sanitary police should be selected because of their ability to accomplish results through persuasion, and legal action should be taken only as a last resort.[3]

Housing

To some extent there will be a conflict of jurisdiction between the health authorities and those authorities having to do more particularly with the control of building construction. The building code of the state ordinarily deals with safety requirements and provides that buildings be built in such a manner as to minimize the danger of loss by fire and accident. These purely structural

[1] See Charles Thom and Albert C. Hunter, *Hygienic Fundamentals of Food Handling* (Williams and Wilkins, 1924).
[2] See Ira V. Hiscock and Margaret S. Hiscock, "Public Health Laboratories," *Report on Municipal Health Practice*, Chap. XI; and *A Health Survey of 86 Cities*, Chap. XII.
[3] See Ira V. Hiscock, "Sanitary Inspection and Sanitation," *Report on Municipal Health Practice*, Chap. XIV.

HEALTH

requirements should not be enforced by the health authorities, but should be administered by a special department empowered to pass on building plans and inspect the construction of buildings. On the other hand, in conjunction with such construction, the health authorities will be interested in securing a minimum height of ceilings, the proper lighting of hallways, and ventilation of bathrooms and hallways, provision for water supply, sewer connections, sanitary appliances and plumbing—matters that may be dealt with in a separate housing code. In some jurisdictions all of these matters are left to the safety department which is made responsible for enforcing all provisions relating to building construction. The approval of the health department may be required on all building plans although this scheme places an unnecessary annoyance upon those engaged in building. Perhaps the health authorities are most interested in the use to which buildings are put after they are constructed. Most housing codes prescribe the minimum amount of sleeping space that may be allotted to lodgers and provide that certain sanitary provisions must be made for their comfort. These are conditions that cannot be controlled through the mere inspection of construction plans, but must be regulated through periodic inspections of structures used for hotel and lodging purposes. Incidentally, such inspections are not as simple as they sound and compliance with housing regulations is a difficult matter to secure.[1]

The ordinary small city will not furnish general hospital service. Care of the sick in institutions is one of the oldest of human charities, and for more than 1500 years the maintenance of hospitals has been an activity of the church and of associated religious organizations. An activity so deeply rooted in religious organization and continuing over so many years cannot be easily destroyed in favor of general community action; nor is there need that it should be. For this reason, in every community of any size there are hospitals, supported and operated by religious, semi-religious, or charitable organizations, and supplemented by private institutions organized for profit. These institutions are usually sufficient to take care of the general hospital requirements of a small city, for both health and charity purposes, and the ordinary municipality finds it more expedient and economical to contract with such organizations for such care. These hospitals themselves do a large amount of charity and health work,

[1] Hiscock, *op. cit.*

262 PRACTICE OF MUNICIPAL ADMINISTRATION

CHAP.
XV

and very few of them can be considered as entirely self-supporting. Contracts with such institutions usually run for one year and provide that all cases referred by the health and charity departments of the city shall be taken care of at a per diem rate in wards. This situation does not mean that as a city increases in size and responsibility it is not necessary to have some form of municipal hospitalization.

Contagious disease hospitals

Very few private or semi-private hospitals are adequately equipped to handle contagious cases. For this reason, it is essential that the community, by general action, provide for a contagious disease hospital. Originally, such hospitals were devoted almost entirely to the cure of such diseases as smallpox and were known as pest-houses. They were ramshackle affairs, located in isolated sections of the country adjacent to a city, and only a minimum of attendance was given to the victims who found themselves placed in them. However, with the development of medical science and the increase in knowledge of the means of preventing the spread of contagious diseases, cities have built complete hospitals for all contagious diseases, of which smallpox is only one, and these institutions are so equipped and so managed that the possibility of infection being transmitted from the institution to other patients, to the attendants, and to the public is far less than would be the case were the patients isolated in their homes. Larger cities can be counted upon to supply special hospital facilities for tuberculosis, although these are frequently supplemented by private organizations interested in preventing and curing this disease.

The numerous accident and emergency cases which occur every day in a city are taken care of in a general city hospital, if one exists; and every hospital naturally furnishes some emergency service, even though it does not specially aim at this type of aid. If the patient and his family are without means, he is kept in the hospital until recovered. If they have means, they are supposed to pay an amount sufficient to cover the services rendered.

Hospital beds

The exact number of hospital beds that should be provided in a city, either by public or by private effort, cannot be stated categorically. Health authorities, however, feel that the ordinary municipality should have six beds per 1,000 inhabitants. The division of these beds among contagious, surgical, medical, and tuberculosis cases is a matter for local determination.

Hospital organization and administration will not be discussed

HEALTH

here in detail, because it is decidedly technical and is not an ordinary function of the municipality. The administration of a hospital is in many respects kindred to the administration of a hotel. The manager, known as the superintendent of the institution, cares for a large number of guests, supplies them with the conveniences of a hotel in the way of light, heat, food, and bedroom equipment, with continuous attendance in the way of nursing service, and with medical attention from regular physicians and internes. The superintendent is responsible for the operation of a building, having under his direction nurses, doctors, etc.; and the problem is one not of medicine, but of business administration. For this reason, there has been a tendency in recent years for hospital superintendents to be men who have had training in the operation of hospitals, recruited from individuals who have ability and an interest in this activity, rather than men taken from the medical field. This does not mean that a doctor may not be a good hospital superintendent, but only that a good hospital superintendent need not be a doctor.[1]

It will be noted that municipally owned and operated hospitals have a dual function. On the one hand, hospitals are established and operated for the purpose of controlling disease, such as contagious disease hospitals and tuberculosis sanatoriums. On the other hand, the community is required to furnish hospitalization for a large number of charity cases and for emergency relief cases. The two have no logical connection. From the community standpoint, one is a health matter, the other a charity matter. The health authorities will insist that contagious hospitals and hospitals that have to do with the prevention of disease should be administered by the health authorities, in order that their work may be correlated exactly with the other work of the health department. Equally, on the other hand, the charitable authorities of the community will insist that hospitals dealing with charity and emergency cases should be operated by the charity authorities for exactly the same reasons. Therefore, in some larger cities we see two sets of hospitals, side by side, administered by entirely different organizations. One is not prepared to say that

CHAP. XV

Hospital organization

Control of hospitals

[1] See Frank E. Chapman, *Hospital Organization and Operation* (Macmillan, 1924); W. M. Cole, *Cost Accounting for Institutions* (Ronald, 1913); Wm. V. S. Thorne, *Hospital Accounting and Statistics* (Dutton, 1918), and Edward A. Fitzpatrick, "Inter-relationships of Hospitals and Communities," *Modern Hospital*, Vol. 24, 133-144 (February, 1925). For current reference, see the *Proceedings of the American Hospital Association* (annual) · *Hospital Management* (monthly); and *The Modern Hospital* (monthly).

264   PRACTICE OF MUNICIPAL ADMINISTRATION

CHAP. XV

this is an incorrect situation. Nevertheless, it is not conducive to the correlation of the work of the different types of hospitals. For this reason some authorities insist that all of the hospitals in a community having a public character should be unified under one authority. This authority may be a separate, distinct hospital commission, or a superintendent who will be independent of both the health and charity forces of the city. Or, if this is not feasible, the hospitals may be unified in the health department, giving such service in a charitable way as may be necessary.

State medicine

A serious problem of hospitalization that may or may not have any direct connection with public health has to do with the high cost of illness and the practical impossibility of the so-called middle class affording competent medical attention. The indigent are not only cared for, but often receive the attention of the best physicians and surgeons in the public hospitals and clinics. The wealthy, of course. receive proper medical treatment, because they can afford to pay for it. But there is a very important group of citizens in between that can afford to pay and desire to pay a moderate amount for medical care, which amount, however, is insufficient to cover even reasonably good attention. This is a serious situation, and a solution appears impossible at this time. Hospitals are expensive to run, and either the patients or the taxpayers must pay for their operation. Possibly the public will eventually maintain municipal hospitals, in which patients may pay for service but use doctors of their own choice, the charges being moderate and deficits being made up frankly by taxation.

But if the state is to subsidize hospitals, how much farther may it go in promoting the health of individuals in a field that has little or nothing to do with the general public health? Is it one thing to prevent the spread of communicable disease, and quite another to repair the teeth or perform an operation for an individual at public expense because that individual is without sufficient funds? Or is it a proper function of government to undo to a limited extent the inequalities created by the economic system? No answer to these questions is proposed.[1]

Health education

If there are limits to the amount of money and effort that must be spent by the public on behalf of the health of individuals over and beyond such action as is necessary to prevent the spread of disease, then it seems desirable that the health authorities should

[1] See W. Thurber Fales, "Expenditures of Health Departments," *Report on Municipal Health Practice*, Chap. II.

undertake an educational program that will eventually bring about an individual appreciation of the need of health. To this end many health departments have a particular branch devoted to the question of health publicity. Periodic bulletins are prepared of different matters, ranging from those that may have an appeal to any citizen to furnishing detailed reports on morbidity and mortality designed particularly for those persons with a medical training. Occasionally special reports are issued on the control of communicable diseases, infant hygiene and like subjects. In addition, the health authorities make use of the press, lecture platform, schools, churches, and similar agencies as a means of general health education warning against certain prevailing conditions.[1]

In the chapter on the budget there was some consideration of the feasibility of developing standards by which the long-sought efficiency and economy of public work could be measured. It is curious that in public health, one of the more recently undertaken public activities, these standards have been brought nearer perfection than elsewhere. Certain of these standards are, indeed, rudimentary and obvious; the merest novice in public affairs can examine the morbidity and mortality rates of a city and determine the health standards that prevail, although a really adequate interpretation involves, of course, taking careful account of climate, water supply, types of population, migration, etc. The health authorities have gone further, and the American Public Health Association has prepared detailed standards that the more skilled administrator can apply in determining the rating of a city as compared to other municipalities.[2] It is hoped that this example will prove profitable to less progressive municipal departments.

Measuring the results of health work

[1] See George Anundsen, "Public Health Education," *Report on Municipal Health Practice*, Chap. XVII; and *A Health Report of 86 Cities*, Chap. XIII.
[2] *Appraisal Form for City Health Work* (American Public Health Association, 1925).

CHAPTER XVI

EDUCATION [1]

Professor Bode opens his *Fundamentals of Education* by stating that "the usual procedure, in most of our human affairs, is to do the things that need to be done and afterwards to construct a theory in order to explain just what was done and why it was done."[2] The author goes on to say that we become interested in theory, only after the results of practice fail our expectations; and the formulation of a theory helps to determine the causes of such failure.

The functions of education So, in discussing the administration of education it seems desirable to state first the accepted reasons as to why we have formal education at all, although the average reader will have some definite notions of his own. S. A. Courtis says that "Education is to be conceived as a process of social heredity which results in the integration of personality and the maintenance of a progressive social order."[3] In other words, in a democracy it is the function of education to provide for both the needs of the individual and the needs of society, keeping the one in balance with the other.[4] This means that education must develop the physical, mental, and moral resources of the individual so that each citizen may be equipped to earn a livelihood, to make the social adjustments necessary in our civilization, and to appreciate the wealth of our cultural heritage. The community, then, in the interest of its general and particular well-being, must make, and has made, education both free and compulsory.[5]

---

[1] Standard manuals on school administration are Ellwood P. Cubberley, *Public School Administration* (Houghton Mifflin, 1922); and Strayer, Engelhardt, McGaughy, Alexander, Mort, and others, *Problems in Educational Administration* (Columbia University, 1925). An outstanding school survey is *The Cleveland School Survey* (Cleveland Foundation, 1918). For current reference consult *Journal of the National Education Association* (monthly); *Research Bulletin of the National Education Association* (bi-monthly); *American School Board Journal* (monthly); and the numerous educational journals.

[2] Boyd Bode, *Fundamentals of Education* (Macmillan, 1922).

[3] Quoted by Arthur M. Moehlman, *Public Education in Detroit* (Public School Pub. Co., 1925), 216.

[4] Complete statements of the philosophy of education will be found in Bode, *op. cit.*; John Dewey, *School and Society* (Univ. of Chicago Press, 1915); and J. Crosby Chapman and George S. Counts, *Principles of Education* (Houghton Mifflin, 1924).   [5] Munro, *op. cit.*, 330.

EDUCATION

Formal education, at best, is a relative rather than an absolute thing, and facilities and efforts must be applied to its purposes in the order of their importance. Not all persons have the ability to acquire, or the time to devote to the acquisition of, the full benefits of educational effort. Neither is the state as yet in an economic position to provide maximum educational opportunities were each citizen ready to utilize them. Because so large a proportion of American youth gives only a few years to formal school work, that work must, after the basic fundamental subjects are completed, cover first of all the pupil's economic requirements, followed by civic and cultural needs, in the order named.[1]

In this industrial age in which extreme specialization of training and effort is necessary to insure personal success, as well as common progress, it is essential that the public schools place in the hands and heads of young men and women the means of economic production. A mere knowledge of reading, writing, and arithmetic is insufficient. Means must be taken to determine the native ability and inclinations of each youth, and to train these qualities with a view to the greatest usefulness in life. Out of such usefulness will come the wealth and leisure necessary to the fullest development of cultural values.

Next to economic requirements stands training in citizenship. Not only has life grown more complex, requiring a fineness of social adjustments unnecessary in other generations, but community effort has come to play a most important rôle in that life. Government grows increasingly complex. The services rendered to citizens are extending in number, importance, and cost. It is essential to wise control that the public know, understand, and evaluate these services. Information must come largely from reading and digesting press accounts of public matters. It is a happy evidence of the ability of democracy to meet the problems that it itself creates, that the school system of America is continually raising its standards, compelling a wider and larger attendance, and increasing its facilities. It is confidently expected, not only that illiteracy will be eliminated but that at no distant date a majority of citizens will receive a high school education or its equivalent. Such extension of education is necessary if it is true, as James Madison observed more than a century ago, that "Popu-

Chap. XVI

Need of industrial training

Democracy requires popular education

---

[1] This does not mean that education to meet economic requirements does not have social significance, nor that meeting individual needs in the order given necessarily upsets the balance between the individual and social functions of education.

268 PRACTICE OF MUNICIPAL ADMINISTRATION

CHAP. XVI

Cultural requirements

Scope of public education

Source of educational authority

lar government without popular information or the means of acquiring it, is the prologue to a farce or a tragedy." [1]

It is not sufficient that education prepare the individual for making a livelihood and for living in modern society. Such living would be mere existence were there no appreciation and enjoyment of the riches of morals, art, literature, and science. Within its limits, the modern school trains the appreciation and makes available the tools with which the rich cultural assets of the age can be utilized.[2]

The scope of public education has grown from teaching children reading, writing, and arithmetic, to the furnishing of a complex system of instruction which, in all of the larger cities and many of the smaller ones, includes regular day classes in the kindergarten, elementary, intermediate, and high schools, vocational training, normal school education, junior or full college courses, and in some cases specialized professional courses in medicine, engineering, and other subjects. Moreover, there is summer and evening instruction in practically all of these branches for both juveniles and adults and in a special way, continuation classes are maintained for the education of boys and girls who are working but are required by law to attend school a certain number of hours each week. Also, special education is provided for the anemic, the physically defective, the blind, the crippled, the deaf, children with defective speech, the retarded, and incorrigibles. Corollary to these educational activities, the education authorities are further expected to conduct a parental school for unruly children, to provide school baths, to promote health by examinations, clinics, and recreation, to furnish lunches for anemic and undernourished children, to supply free transportation for the physically handicapped, and frequently to establish free evening lectures for adults.

Schools originated through community effort under state sanction. Local management in time passed from citizen meetings to an elected board of trustees, and more recently the tendency has been for these school trustees to restrict their field to questions of development and policy and to place the authority and responsibility for management with an experienced superintendent.[3]

---

[1] G. Hunt (ed.), *Writings of James Madison*, IX, 104.
[2] Munro, *op. cit.*, 329-330.
[3] E. P. Cubberly, *Supplementary Report on the Organization and Administration of School District No. 1 in the City and County of Denver*, (1916). See also, *Public School Administration*, Chaps. I and II; and E. P. Cubberly

EDUCATION

Of late years, and more particularly since 1900, the state, in order to raise educational standards and managerial efficiency, has curtailed local powers and increased the amount of control by the county or the state itself. Affirming that education is primarily a state function, such action has been sustained by the courts. Thus school districts and school authorities may be said to act under delegated state authority as provided by statute.[1] Such statutes, in general, outline the authority of the educational district, prescribe the minimum scope of education, establish the qualifications of teachers, and require certain financial and statistical reports. In addition, many states in order to equalize somewhat educational opportunities between rich and poor sections, and especially to aid backward school districts, grant state money to primary school districts prorated in accordance with school population, and also subsidize high schools and libraries.

Paralleling the increased interest in, and regulation of, education by the state, the national government has of late years displayed activity in this field. As yet, its concern has been evidenced largely by investigations and reports on educational problems and conditions, and by acting in an advisory capacity to state and local officials. A bureau of education is maintained in the Department of the Interior, and a movement to create a separate Department of Education appears to be slowly gaining strength, with the support of many educators.[2] On the analogy of state subsidies to education, it is proposed that Congress grant money for educational purposes to the states. Objections to this proposal are made on the grounds that the money would be provided principally by the richer states which need no aid, and that federal regulation and control would follow such subsidies. In the field of vocational and agricultural education Congress has already provided financial grants to the states on a parity basis, and has aided in the rehabilitation of disabled veterans.[3]

The extent of local autonomy that should be exercised by school districts is an open question. While each district faces problems and requirements peculiar to itself, there is need for general uniformity in the qualifications of teachers, in budgeting and account-

and E. C. Elliott, *State and County School Administration* (Macmillan, 1915), 3-18.
[1] Cubberly, *op. cit.*
[2] The Curtis-Reed Bill. See Dorothy K. Brown, *Federal Aid to the States* (National League of Women Voters, 1926).
[3] The Smith-Hughes Bill.

ing procedure, in the compilation of statistics and reports, and in the general courses of elementary study. The evident desirability of such uniformity suggests that the state should legislate and supervise in a general way, permitting every community to exceed minimum requirements and to progress through experimentation.[1] General regulations should, and sometimes do, apply to parochial and private schools as well as to public institutions, but are seldom well enforced.

Interdependence of school districts

The taxpayers of any community naturally desire expenditures to benefit themselves. For that reason, it is customary to limit free education to persons actually resident in a school district, and to charge tuition to others desiring to take advantage of the facilities provided. However, it must be borne in mind that no community can limit the benefits of its school system to its own inhabitants. Children who receive a splendid education in one city may migrate to another and ignorant immigrant workers come in to take their places. No community lives unto itself alone, and it is to the advantage of every community to have its neighbors maintain high educational standards. Occasionally cities, and particularly villages, not enjoying complete educational facilities provide for the educating of a part of their children in contiguous cities, paying tuition on a cost basis.

The relation of the school system to the city government

The school district may be entirely dependent on, partially dependent on, or entirely independent of, the coterminous, or practically coterminous, municipality. This situation arises because of the existence of two opposing theories of the relationship between the city and the school district. One theory considers public education a phase of local government, and places the power to review school budgets and to levy school taxes with city authorities. It is maintained that a more independent relationship promotes extravagance and tends to prevent the proper correlation of education with other vital community services. Or this dependence may be modified by permitting some official body of the community, such as a county budget commission, a special school budget commission, or a town meeting, to exercise certain financial restraint over the educational authorities.[2]

The opposing theory considers the school district an independent governmental agency operating under state supervision. It

[1] Munro, *op. cit.*, 336-337.
[2] *Know and Help Your Schools,* I (American City Bureau, 1921).

holds that educational authorities should be elected directly by the people, and should be in nowise limited by the city government in the determination of their own budget, and the levying of their own taxes. Taxes so levied, however, may be certified to the regular city officials and collected with the taxes of the city proper. It is urged that a community is best served when the school authorities control educational policies and expenditures, untrammeled by irresponsible, and frequently unsympathetic, influences.[1]

To carry into practice the philosophy and objectives of public education organization is necessary, not as an end in itself, but as a means to an end. Educational organization, or any organization, for that matter, may be expressed in terms of the functions of planning, executing, and testing plans and results, *i.e.*, legislation, execution and appraisal.

Educators are agreed that the legislative authority in educational matters should rest with a board of education.[2] There are no absolute standards with respect to the relationship of the board of education to the other authorities in municipal government. Apparently the public believes there should be a degree of separation sufficient to minimize political influences, yet has not fully decided to make education a distinct function, with an independent local organization. The existing situation has removed political considerations to an extent, and the members of boards of education are consistently of a higher type than city councilmen.

The members of school boards should have little concern with party politics, and when elected should be chosen at large on a non-partizan ticket. About four-fifths of all cities elect board members, and four-fifths of these elect at large.[3] Elections are held annually or biennially, and terms are usually arranged to overlap, preventing inexperienced control and sudden changes in policy. In some cities the mayor is vested with authority to appoint school board members, on the theory that qualified representation of all classes will be had, and members will be secured who could not be induced to make an election campaign. This conclusion should

[1] *Ibid.*
[2] Cubberly, *op. cit.*; and Arthur E. Moehlman, *Public School Finance* (Rand, McNally, 1926).
[3] All data with respect to the organization of school boards, method of selecting members, term of service, and compensation are taken from the pamphlets *Know and Help Your Schools,* covering an investigation of 372 cities.

272 PRACTICE OF MUNICIPAL ADMINISTRATION

CHAP. XVI

be correct in both theory and practice, but too often the appointments have been made for political purposes and with little regard for education needs.

Term of service

The length of term varies from one year to life, averaging about three years. About one-half of the cities have three-year terms and one-fourth have four-year terms.

Only one city in seven pays salaries to board members, and in those that pay, the ordinary salary is $150 a year, a few allowing as much as $500 a year. A notable exception is San Francisco, which pays $4,000 a year to appointive members. Even a small salary attracts inferior personnel, which accounts for the general practice of making no provision for paying members. In many large communities the work of the school board has so expanded

Compensation

that the payment of a salary may seem justified. However, both paid and unpaid school boards have been usurping the duties of school superintendents and business managers, and the proper remedy lies in delegating more work to the professional staff, rather than in compensating board members. With proper organization, only a few hours of attention a week should be required of board members. Paying school board members only encourages interference in matters beyond their proper province.[1]

Organization

Usually with a large board elected by wards and sometimes with small boards elected at large, numerous standing committees are created such as judiciary, teachers, textbooks, course of study, finance, real estate and buildings, janitorial service, sanitation etc. This organization easily becomes and often is, a "patronage and plum" proposition. When board members are of small caliber and uninformed on school matters, they are prone to encroach on the prerogative of the superintendent, who becomes superintendent in name only. There is no more reason for standing committees in education than in private business. This fact is being increasingly recognized, and school boards and other public legislative bodies are now in the main transacting their business in committees of the whole. This is particularly true of small boards which can easily waive formalities. When special committees are required they can be created but they should terminate when their specific objective is accomplished.[2]

[1] Munro, *op. cit.*, 334.
[2] *Ibid.*, 334. An analysis of the proceedings of the Detroit Board of Education,—a small board of high character, by the way—for the six months ending June 30, 1925, showed that out of 615 items of business considered, 462, or seventy-five percent, were matters relating to detail; 44, or seven percent,

EDUCATION

CHAP. XVI

The executive

The expansion of the educational program and facilities has been paralleled by modification in organization. Out of the position of secretary to the school board, to whom increased responsibility was progressively delegated, there has evolved the position of school superintendent,[1] who is now generally recognized as the manager of the school system, responsible for all routine operations. Under this arrangement, the board of education establishes general policies, and the superintendent is responsible for the administration of these policies. It should be recognized that the superintendent of schools must be a trained professional educator, well paid, serving with reasonable assurance of continued tenure of office, and responsible for the following executive functions: (1) technical administration; (2) instruction; (3) child accounting; (4) personnel management; (5) finance; (6) research; and (7) public relations.[2]

Business administration

This authority of the superintendent has grown gradually at the expense of the board, which at one time employed teachers, erected schools, and directed technical administration, and has developed almost without opposition except in the field of business administration. Here, school boards presumed that the educator was unfitted to act. Therefore, in most educational organizations the superintendent has been relieved of business matters by the creation of the position of business manager, independent of the superintendent and directly responsible to the board. However, the superintendent is responsible for the efficient working of the school plant and must have buildings, building equipment, and supplies when and where required. The business department is organized for the purpose of furnishing these essentials, and in the interest of correlating the material and educational requirements of the school system, it is highly desirable that the business department be made subordinate to the superintendent. The business manager should be responsible, under the direction of the superintendent, for constructing, maintaining, and operating buildings; purchasing, storing, and distributing supplies; and account-

The superintendent and the business manager

---

were of an inspectorial nature; and 109, or eighteen percent, were policy determining. But of these policies, there was only one that dealt with education—the formation of a military company in one of the high schools.

[1] In 1870 not a single school superintendent had been employed in 24 of the 37 states forming the Union. Today there are over 2000 superintendents, Cubberly, *op. cit.*

[2] School superintendents maintain a national organization for the discussion of their particular problems known as the Department of Superintendence of the National Education Association.

274   PRACTICE OF MUNICIPAL ADMINISTRATION

CHAP. XVI

The business manager

ing and auditing. Such scope of duties makes the position of business manager of unusual importance. The incumbent not only must be an able business executive, but also must have an appreciation of educational problems and be able to coöperate wholeheartedly in their solution.[1]

Selection of teachers

In times when teaching was less a profession than a part-time or auxiliary employment the selection of teachers was made personally by the board of education.[2] Teachers were poorly trained, or had no training at all, and selection was based largely on friendship and local residence. This situation changed when state laws were enacted requiring that elementary and high school teachers possess a certificate of competency issued by the state authorities. Such certificates are given to persons completing prescribed courses in educational institutions and having certain teaching experience. Pending the securing of experience, temporary certificates are issued. In some states oral and written examinations and observation of classroom teaching are required before a permanent certificate can be secured. With the development of these state minimum standards and the increased administrative responsibility of superintendents, the selection of teachers has been in many instances delegated by the board to the professional staff. When only a few teachers are to be appointed and the superintendent is able to give the selection of each teacher his personal attention, they should be made after inquiry into the professional training, record of work, and personality of the applicant. The board should have authority to refuse concurrence in the recommendations of the superintendent, but not to appoint unrecommended candidates of its own choosing. This informal and direct method of teacher selection has many advantages. In cities where numerous teachers are hired each year, written examinations are sometimes held followed by personality interviews with eligible candidates. Although practically every large city and many small ones have normal schools, particularly for training elementary teachers, it is recognized as unwise to limit appointments to local talent, and little emphasis is now placed on the appointment of home-trained teachers. The interchange of ideas and the

---

[1] Report on the *Organization and Administration of the Business Department of the Detroit Board of Education*, prepared by the Detroit Bureau of Governmental Research (1916). See annual *Proceedings of the National Association of Public School Business Officials*.

[2] See E. E. Lewis, *Personnel Problems of the Teaching Staff* (Century, 1925).

EDUCATION 275

making of new contacts is so desirable for teachers that it is to the best interest of the community to make selections without reference to residence, or even to prefer non-residents.¹

Teachers are usually appointed for one school year, and their contracts must be renewed annually by the board upon recommendation of the superintendent. This periodic reopening of the question of employment stimulates the injection of politics and favoritism into teacher selection which is not to the best interest of the school children, the teachers, or the taxpayers. At the other extreme at least one city, San Francisco, has established a life tenure for school teachers after a limited period of probation. This solution does not help the situation. Life tenure means discharge only after a judicial adjudication of charges, and any one familiar with the difficulty of securing a discharge by a hearing before the less formal civil service commission can appreciate the difficulty of discharging a teacher in any such manner. A far more desirable practice is the annual appointment of teachers during several probationary years, after which the appointment continues unless some definite action is taken by one of the parties concerned, there being no binding contract to annoy the superintendent in instances where the services of a teacher should be discontinued.²

In an effort to meet the need for teachers, many communities have provided some sort of normal school education for high school graduates. Unfortunately, the character of this training, as a rule, has not been high. At the same time, the graduates of these training institutions afford local politicians an excellent opportunity to insist that home town girls be given the preference in appointments, regardless of actual qualifications. The local normal school has its place, but its graduates should be compelled to meet the graduates of other schools in open competition.³

For many years teaching was one of the poorest paid professions.⁴ A large number of girl graduates of high schools elected teaching as a satisfactory stop-gap pending marriage, and received the requisite training, when any was required, in local normal schools. As these teachers usually lived at home, their economic needs were small, and a low salary scale prevailed. However, in recent years, due to the increased demand for teachers arising from

¹ See Cubberly, *op. cit.*, Chap. XIV.
² *Ibid.*, Chap. XIV.
³ *Ibid.*, Chap. XV.
⁴ See Arthur E. Moehlman, *Public School Finance* (Rand, McNally, 1926).

the rapid expansion of school systems, the opportunities open for well-paid employment in social service and in business, and the establishment of higher state and city standards for teaching, the over-supply has been eliminated and more adequate salaries have been provided. This increased compensation has perhaps attracted more able individuals into the profession; at least it has helped to keep many of the best of those already in.

The rate of compensation is usually based upon the grade of instruction given, and sometimes on training and experience of the teachers. A minimum salary for beginning teachers within a particular grade is usual, and a small yearly increase is given until the maximum is reached, after a number of years of teaching. In most instances, these annual increments are mandatory in case the teacher is retained in service. In other cases, the increases are not mandatory, and it is incumbent upon the superintendent to appraise the service of the teacher and recommend promotion or adjustment. In some few instances, an examination is a prerequisite for promotion from one grade to another, or from one type of position to another. Other plans for salary increase involve recognition for studies that may be undertaken during vacation periods, and for demonstrated teaching ability. Although the principle is difficult to apply, promotion and increased compensation should be based entirely upon efficiency, with relatively small weight given to seniority. Such plans, however, require an evaluation of services which the superintendent and his subordinates are seldom in a position to make, pending the development of tests of teacher efficiency that will be fair and easy of application. If pay and promotion were based upon ability to teach, a higher grade of instruction would undoubtedly be forthcoming. Present difficulties of applying the principle of compensation based on merit retard its full adoption, but many cities, in their salary schedules, allow for preliminary and additional training. These changes in methods of remuneration are part of the whole movement to change teaching from a semi-amateur to a professional status.[1]

Administration of instruction
The traditional plan

In the old type school the pupils were in one room all day, except for recess, learning reading, writing and arithmetic, and a smattering of history and geography, from one teacher. This organization required that each pupil be in a room with the same teacher for a term, followed by promotion to another grade, another room, and another teacher. With the expansion of the cur-

[1] Cubberly, *op. cit.* Chap. XVI.

riculum embracing science, civics, physical education, manual training, cooking, sewing, etc., a natural development was the adding of special rooms to the old type schools to provide for the teaching of these new subjects. Under these conditions, when the pupils went to the special rooms, the regular rooms were unoccupied. As a result, school costs rose and brought protests from taxpayers, who criticized the building and use of the extra space for teaching "frills."

Then came the platoon, and later the modified "Gary" or work-study-play plan. These plans permit the accommodation of more pupils by full-time utilization of the special rooms. When a class goes to the auditorium or gymnasium, for example, another class takes the room vacated. Each class has its "home room" and its home room teacher who instructs in the traditional fundamentals of reading, writing, arithmetic. Other subjects are taught in special rooms, including the auditorium and gymnasium, by specialists, who teach the same subject to several classes. In the upper grades specialization of instruction is complete.

The platoon system has been introduced concurrently with an enrichment of the educational curriculum which aims at filling school work with varied interests and opportunities for self-expression and development, rather than solely training the faculties in preparation for adult use. The advantages of the platoon organization and theory include greater interest by the pupils as demonstrated by school popularity, relative absence of behavior difficulties, broader range of subjects covering physical and social as well as mental expression, and a material reduction in building and instruction costs for service units rendered. The principal objections to the platoon system arise from the fact that a child does not have the continuous attention of one teacher, that some time is lost in moving to and from classes, and that these moves make the pupil "nervous." To date, the opponents of the platoon system have not proved convincing.[1]

The traditional school period comprises eight years in ele-

[1] A thorough study of the platoon school will be found in Charles L. Spain, *The Platoon School* (Macmillan, 1924). Special reports of interest are *The Majority and Minority Reports of the Special Committee Named to Investigate Platoon Schools* (Proceedings of the Milwaukee School Board, May 6, 1924); *The Report on Detroit Platoon System by A Committee of Nine Chicago Classroom Teachers Who Visited Detroit Schools* (Chicago Teachers' Federation, March 3, 1924); Charles L. Spain, "The Platoon School in Detroit," *Detroit Educational Bulletin*, January, 1923; and "The Platoon School," Report of Detroit Federation of Labor.

mentary school and four years in high school, followed perhaps by four years in college. The compulsory school age usually ends at about the conclusion of the eight years of elementary work. In consequence, there has been a sharp break between the attendance of the elementary school and that of the high school, only a small minority continuing in the latter. Largely because of this situation, some cities have divided the school program into three stages by placing the last two years of elementary work and the first year of high school work in intermediate schools, or junior high schools, in accordance with what is commonly called the 6-3-3 plan as opposed to the traditional 8-4 plan. A pupil, after six years of elementary instruction, has not finished his compulsory school period and continues work in the intermediate school. The natural tendency is to finish this course, and, having received one year of high school education, there may be an inclination to continue through high school. This system also permits a better design of buildings to meet curriculum needs. The six-year elementary school can be built without special equipment needed in the intermediate school, and the same principle applies to some extent to differences between intermediate and high schools.

In recent years there has been a tendency to raise the compulsory school age, by state law, to eighteen years, or until completion of the high school or its equivalent. It does not follow that school work must be done exclusively until the pupil is eighteen years old, children over sixteen or other suitable age being permitted to work, provided they attend school a number of hours a week up to a usual maximum of eight. This attendance must be during the hours of a working day and not on Saturday afternoons, and such attendance at school must be considered a part of the number of hours minors are permitted to work. This is called the continuation school, and is often designed for vocational education. The results have not been very satisfactory.

Not only in the continuation school, but in high and even intermediate schools, there is now a distinct tendency towards vocational education. The school authorities realize that only a minor fraction of elementary school children will finish high school, and that only a small proportion of high school graduates will go to college. Many pupils will drop out because of economic pressure, and many more because of sheer mental inability to keep going. These pupils enter a highly specialized industrial and commercial life, and with only a general educational equipment suited for more elementary conditions, are at a disadvantage. It is only natural that those responsible for educational policies should try to prepare the pupils to cope with every day affairs. For that reason the high schools are providing facilities for training in stenography, bookkeeping, printing, and certain of the trades. An attempt is made to learn the aptitudes and abilities of the pupils even before they enter high school, and to guide their study into lines of future usefulness.

<small>CHAP. XVI</small>

This situation raises the question of vocational education versus general education. Higher compulsory standards for general education make for a more intelligent citizen body and for a nation better fitted to govern itself. It is probably true that vocational education produces men and women better equipped to begin their industrial or commercial life and is of general economic benefit. But which of these two aims, general education or vocational education, should be dominant? Will the continuation and trade schools endeavor to turn out thinking men and women, or merely vocationally proficient men and women? Will vocational education develop intellectual, ethical, and physical capacities as well as the technical ability of the individual? These questions cannot be answered from present-day experience.

<small>Vocational education</small>

Early public education included only elementary instruction. Hence arose the Latin grammar schools, private institutions preparatory to college. As a protest against this academic type of education there were established academies teaching both classical and non-classical subjects, and out of the academy evolved the modern public high school. The high school has been a formal intitution with highly academic courses, although recently there has been a gradual modification to conform with present-day conditions. However, a direct control of high school standards and curricula results from the establishment of certain entrance requirements by the universities. Under ordinary conditions, no local educator would conduct a high school, with respect to courses or scholarship, in such a fashion as to prevent its graduates entering at least the state university without examination.

<small>High schools</small>

Today the educational systems of cities include not only elementary and high school instruction, but in many there have been established junior colleges giving two years of college work, and in some, complete colleges or universities.[1] This, in spite of the

<small>Collegiate instruction</small>

[1] Municipal colleges or universities are found in Toledo, Portland, Ore., Akron, Cincinnati, Detroit, and New York.

fact that many states maintain one or more state universities towards which these same city taxpayers contribute. While the junior college appears generally accepted, some educators question whether its work should be expanded to a four-year course.[1] Probably all universities are receiving a registration in excess of that which they are really prepared to receive, and are not equipped, in either faculty of plant, to maintain high standards of advanced education. Much of the instruction in "collegiate fundamentals" could be given equally well or better in municipal junior colleges. The classes would be smaller, the instruction more intimate, the discipline more severe, and the expense much less to the public and to the students. Possibly many universities will ultimately eliminate freshman and sophomore classes and require that these groups be provided for in local institutions. The universities can then devote two years to advanced education, to be followed by specialized professional work.[2]

All year schools

It has also been urged that with the establishment of junior colleges and the elimination of the first two years of college work in the universities, the time spent in the elementary schools and high schools might be more profitably used. If a more thorough and rapid education could be given in the elementary school the student would be prepared to take the last two years of college work in the university at an earlier age, and enter the professions several years earlier. Such procedure would require that the elementary school system eliminate useless repetition and discard the traditional nine or ten months school year. The short school term came into being when America was largely rural, and children were required to help plant, cultivate, and harvest crops. Gradually, a three months school term has been expanded to the present "year" of thirty-eight to forty weeks. Concurrently with this change, school teaching has become a profession instead of a part-time job incidental to some "regular" occupation.

School teachers now receive pay comparable with that of other professions and have about eighty days of vacation per year, aside from Saturdays and Sundays. Children are required to attend

---

[1] In fact, some believe that there are definite limits to free education. It is questioned by them whether special educational privileges should be given at general expense to those who can afford to spend extra years in school. Perhaps university students should be required to pay the full cost of their education at the time of receiving it, or possibly after graduation.

[2] Munro, *op. cit.*, 343, suggests that the "junior college is only a half-way station on the road to a full four-year college course." If the universities discontinue the first two years of instruction, it may be a logical terminus.

school from the age of, say, six to sixteen, or for about ten years, during which time only about half of each year is spent in actual school attendance. The educational standards are being constantly raised. The school world wants children to attend school until they are eighteen, or at least until they have completed high school. Furthermore, the educational requirements for entrance in the industries and professions have been constantly increased. There is, however, a practical limit to the amount of time to be devoted to preparation for a vocation. By continuing school twelve months per year, with reasonable vacations for both children and teachers, it would be possible for practically all children to finish high school by the time they are sixteen, completing the present twelve-year course in ten years. This would give every child that enters industry a fundamental training, and would allow those entering the professions to begin their advanced training two years earlier.

In such a program, the school year might be divided into, say, five terms of ten weeks each instead of a school year of two terms of twenty or less weeks each. This smaller unit of school time would be of advantage in that a child would lose less time in case of failure to be promoted. The lengthening of the school term also would eventually increase the capacity of the schools by twenty-five percent, and the increased use of the school plant would reduce per pupil costs. All-year schools have been urged recently for Chicago, and there is an increasing demand for summer schools everywhere. On the other hand, their home city, Newark, N. J., doubts the value of all-year schools after years of testing.

In recent years educational authorities have given serious attention to the subject of adult education, supplementing classes in citizenship and English with general cultural and vocational instruction to adults, particularly in night schools. This work has been ably seconded by the public libraries. These institutions are rapidly realizing their possibilities as a means of adult education, and their opportunities for meeting the requirements of adults who have no need or inclination to participate in the more formal instruction provided by the school system. The public library must, of course, cater to the expressed wishes of the community in its selection of books; at the same time the modern trained librarian is placing all possible emphasis on the circulation of fiction having distinct literary merit and upon books of a non-fictional character. In fact, over one-half of the books circulated by the modern public library are of this latter class. Branch libraries are established throughout the community and, what is more important, subsidiary branches are placed in places of community gathering, such as factories, schools, recreation centers, etc. In addition, the public library endeavors to reach certain groups who have special library needs that cannot otherwise be met, such as the blind, technical societies, business men and public officials. In all of these activities the library has not neglected its opportunities as supplemental to the school, and school branch libraries make available to children, as well as adults, the book resources of the community.[1] In consequence of this relationship it sometimes happens that library trustees are appointed by the board of education, but more often they are selected by the chief executive of the city or are elected by the public. It is sometimes suggested that adult education would be furthered if the library were distinctly an adjunct of the educational system and a direct responsibility of the educational authorities.[2]

Educational research is developing tests for the evaluation of educational methods and results. Endeavor is being made to establish units and standards of measurement to apply to school systems, individual schools, classes, and pupils to determine the efficiency of the work being done.[3] This means the substitution of standardized measurements for personal opinion as the only criterion of pupil progress. These comparative measurements indicate that there has been continual advance in both the methods and results of education, and should allay the criticisms of those who lack understanding of and faith in the schools of today.[4]

[1] Munro, *op. cit.* 344, perhaps rightly does not take so favorable a view of library progress.
[2] In the field of library administration, consult A. E. Bostwick, *The American Public Library* (Appleton, 1923); J. C. Dana, *Library Primer* (Am. Lib. Assoc., 1920); J. L. Wheeler, *The Library and the Community* (Am. Lib. Assoc., 1924); and the current magazines, *The Library Journal*, and *Public Libraries.*
[3] See Cubberley, *op. cit.*, Chap. XIX; Chas. L. Spain, *The Platoon School* (Macmillan, 1924); Stuart A. Courtis, *Why Children Succeed* (Detroit, Michigan, 1925); *Standard Tests, ibid.;* and W. S. Monroe, J. C. DeVoss, and F. J. Kelly, *Educational Tests and Measurements* (Houghton Mifflin, 1924).
[4] To many the school appears to be full of frills—housed in monumental buildings which are equipped with machine shops, gymnasiums, auditoriums, swimming pools, and playrooms, all unknown in a former day, and perhaps of doubtful utility. The most frequent charge is that present day graduates do not write legibly or spell and figure as accurately as did the graduates of several generations ago. Happily, an opportunity has been presented recently to test the truth of this charge. In 1845, under the direction of the Board of Education of Boston tests were given to the school children to determine the efficiency of the educational system. This test consisted of 109 questions in

Under this program, group measurements are sometimes given pupils at the beginning and end of each semester, so that children may be roughly grouped according to educational progress. These group tests have shown the necessity for the individualization of instruction, and the same general methods that are now coming into use in teaching writing, certain phases of arithmetic, and reading should be developed and used for all branches of scholastic instruction.

Educational tests

Group intelligence tests are usually given pupils once or twice when they first enter school, and this rating continues unless there is some reason to reëxamine because apparent intelligence varies from that indicated by the educational tests. These tests permit a grouping into several classes, each to receive a somewhat different character of instruction. Individual intelligence tests are given to children who are outstandingly different from the general group.[1]

Intelligence tests

In accordance with the usual age-grade system, the first grade is started at six years, *i.e.*, between the sixth and seventh birthday, and the pupil remains in each grade one year. Accepting this as standard, the age-grade situation of all school children, in a specific school or city, may be compared with the theoretical situation based on uniform progress. Such studies disclose wide variation in over-age and under-age in the different schools, and in the different grades in the same schools. Obviously, over-age of any considerable percent is tremendously costly to a city if the pupils stay in school. However, over-age probably shortens school life on account of discouragement of the pupils and actually reduces instruction costs. For the pupils who remain, the years lost in the elementary school are lost beyond recovery and may preclude professional training. An analysis of the local situation should show how to minimize the problem and reduce the wastes.

Pupil progress over-age and under-age

The causes of retardation are numerous. Children may not start attending school young enough; the school environment may be so unsatisfactory as to impede rather than stimulate study; the history, geography, grammar, philosophy, astronomy, and arithmetic, the questions being divided equally between those calling for memory and skill and those calling for thought. Recently these questions and the results of the examination were made available for comparative use. The tests were somewhat modernized and were applied to some 40,000 school children scattered throughout the United States. The result indicated a decided superiority on the part of the modern education. See O. W. Caldwell and S. A. Curtis, *Then and Now in Education, 1845-1923* (World Book Co., 1923).

[1] The mental aspects of the unusual child are discussed by W. H. Burnham, *The Normal Mind* (Appleton, 1925), Chap. XV.

course of study suitable for the average child may be quite unsuited to the numerous variations from over-age; the course of study may not be adjusted so as to permit the normal progress of pupils; no provision may be made for "catching up" by pupils out of school on account of illness or for other reasons; promotion may be annual instead of semi-annual or quarterly, thus retarding a slow pupil over the entire year; promotion may be denied for a long period when only one or two subjects are involved;[1] special instruction may not be provided for pupils who are behind in one or two subjects; and, most important, poor teaching is a frequent, though seldom admitted, factor. Usually retardation in the elementary schools is at a minimum in the first grade and gradually increases until checked by the withdrawal of over-age pupils who have passed the period of compulsory attendance.[2]

Paralleling the problem of the retarded child is that of the unusually able pupil who is kept back with the average. If his interest is to be held, this child needs a course suited to his abilities. The difficulty is that the educational system has ordinarily attempted to place all children in a lock-step suitable only for the average child, thereby failing to provide for the quick learners or the slow learners.

Times of promotion — In recent years educational authorities have been experimenting with a number of devices to meet this situation. These include less rigid enforcement of the administratively convenient system of keeping a child in the same grade in all subjects, individualized instruction embracing special instruction for both the slow and rapid students, and frequent promotion intervals to enable the slow to be retarded for only a minimum period of time and to enable the rapid to proceed with less restraint. Among the examples enumerated by Cubberly are classes for non-English speaking students, supplementary classes to fit for high school those who are not fully prepared, over-age classes for the retarded, ungraded classes for pupils who are at a disadvantage in the grade and who need extra help, summer schools for those who desire to make up back work or to move forward more rapidly, disciplinary classes for refractory children, parental schools for the incorrigible, open air classes for tubercular and anemic children, schools for the crippled, schools for those with speech defects, classes for the deaf, classes

---

[1] More progressive systems employ subject promotion and restoration or opportunity classes.

[2] See Leonard P. Ayres, *Laggards in Our Schools* (Russell Sage Foundation, 1909).

for the blind, classes for morons, classes for epileptics, classes for specially gifted children, industrial classes in the upper grades for those desiring vocational training, trade schools for instruction in the fundamentals underlying the practice of the more common trades, special art schools particularly for adult instruction, schools in home making for domestic science instruction, and neighborhood schools organized to study and meet the needs of both pupils and parents.[1]

<small>CHAP. XVI</small>

State laws compel school attendance from the age of six or seven to now generally seventeen or eighteen, though sometimes less. To enforce this law, the attendance department takes an annual census of school children and employs truancy officers. The census enumeration is also often the basis for the distribution of state subsidies to elementary schools. In addition to census taking, it is the duty of the census department to keep on record all of the children enumerated and, so far as possible, to insist that they be in school. This is done by following up all cases of unwarranted absence as they are reported, by picking up children on the streets, by coöperating with employers in the enforcement of child labor laws, and by checking attendance records against the school census records which are or should be maintained by the attendance department. The old-fashioned attendance officer and his methods are now being supplemented by the visting teacher, on the theory that the child in school cannot be guided properly by police methods. All of the factors that enter into the development of the child—home, neighborhood, and environment—must be thoroughly understood, and treatment based on the findings. To do this requires a person of training and skill, who can appraise situations and apply whatever measures are necessary—in short, the application of a high type of social case work. Also there is being introduced into the school census the idea of a continuous check of all school children within certain sections through exchanges of data between adjacent districts. These records involve the transfer of a child from one school to another, even when the transfer is outside of the district. By this means, a superintendent of a school system is notified of children transferring to his jurisdiction, and the attendance department is in a position to check them up in case of non-appearance.[2]

<small>Enforcing attendance</small>

<small>School census and truancy</small>

A frequent political slogan is "a seat for every pupil." In

[1] Cubberley, *op. cit.*, Chap. XVIII.
[2] See Arthur B. Moehlman, *Child Accounting* (Courtis Standard Tests, 1924).

Half-time sessions

cities of rapid growth it has been difficult to make such provision, particularly in the lower grades, even though generous use has been made of temporary portable schools. It is still a moot question whether pupils, particularly in the lower grades, do not receive as much benefit from a half-day session as from a full-day session.[1] However, parents are not inclined to have their children about the premises either in the afternoon or morning if they can be cared for in the schools, and this is, oddly enough, one of the most insistent arguments for a whole-day session. But a social problem is also involved. In congested and poorer districts children are better off in school under supervision and training than in aimlessly running about the streets.

Health work in schools

Closely related to pupil progress is pupil health. Educational requirements must be based upon the abilities of healthy children in continuous attendance at school. Lessened abilities or intermittent absences because of ill health place a costly burden upon the system. Further, in justice to the children in their charge the educational authorities should prevent, so far as possible, the spread of communicable diseases which the daily bringing together of large numbers of persons facilitates. Health education is also as essential to human well-being as is training in the more conventional subjects. The school system is therefore concerned with child health from three distinct angles.

Every child should be given a thorough physical examination upon entering the school system, and periodically thereafter. Such examination will reveal any constitutional defects that will make special educational facilities necessary, or that can be corrected by the proper attention of the parents. In event parents do not have the means to secure treatment, use should be made of limited free dental and medical clinics, within or without the school system. All pupils within the system should be inoculated against smallpox and diphtheria. Progress is being made in the prevention of measles and scarlet fever, and shortly inoculation against these diseases may be mandatory. Examination of pupils may be either independently or in coöperation with the municipal health authorities.[2]

Teachers should be on the alert to discover indications of communicable disease, and all pupils appearing at school with

---

[1] A study in Detroit indicates that part-time children do not do as well as those on full time. See *Effectiveness of Half-Time Sessions*, Detroit Educational Bulletin, *Research Bulletin* No. 11 (February, 1926).

[2] See Chap. XV.

fevers and colds should be segregated and seen by the school nurse before being permitted to attend classes. Children who are apparently undernourished should be given the attention of the school nurse, and attempts made to remedy the home conditions that make this situation possible. Some school systems find it necessary to maintain nutrition classes and to provide school luncheons for certain children either free or at a nominal charge. Health education including recreation should be a part of every school curriculum. It is frequently undertaken in conjunction with the work of the American Red Cross, local anti-tuberculosis societies, public and private recreation groups, and similar organizations.[1]

CHAP. XVI

The recreational authorities ordinarily utilize the facilities provided by the board of education in the way of school buildings and school grounds, for both juvenile and adult recreation. Sometimes serious disagreements result because school janitors resent the additional work of opening buildings and keeping them lighted and cleaned, and occasionally property is damaged. For these reasons, and because the educational authorities desire to undertake a complete program of education, there is an inclination to place under boards of education the recreational activities that require the use of educational property. Such a program should be examined with care before being undertaken. A result is the creation of two public agencies for carrying on recreation, and as the use of school property is necessary to a comprehensive recreational program, the withdrawal of this property puts the recreational authorities at a distinct disadvantage. It is recognized that play is a means of education, and a distinction should be made between teaching children to play and providing for the leisure time of adults and children. It seems a proper function of the schools to teach play, but the leisure time problem deserves consideration by a department which has no other problem. Although there may be friction between recreational and educational authorities over the use of school buildings, it should be easier to work out a plan for the joint use of buildings by two departments than to correlate two distinct recreational programs.[2]

Education and recreation

Cities spend for school buildings more than is spent for any

[1] See Thomas D. Wood and Hugh G. Powell, *Health Through Prevention and Control of Diseases* (World Book Co., 1925); *Report of the Cambridge Health Education Conference* (1924), and *Report of the International Health Education Conference* (1923), both published by the American Child Health Association (New York); Luther H. Gulick and Leonard P. Ayres, *Medical Inspection of Schools* (Russell Sage Foundation, 1925).

[2] See Chap. XVI

288 PRACTICE OF MUNICIPAL ADMINISTRATION

Standardization of building design

other permanent improvement. At a time when the course of study was much simpler than it is now a school building consisted simply of classrooms. At the present time, it is usual to add auditoriums, gymnasiums, swimming pools, special facilities for manual training and domestic science, and other special features, which mean a highly complex school structure. The simpler form of school could be designed by practically any architect; the more modern school requires a highly specialized one. Unfortunately, boards of education are in many instances accustomed to distribute the building of schools among local architects with small regard to their special ability. As a consequence, the architect may design, without a proper knowledge of school needs, a building of fine appearance but unsuitable for school purposes and unnecessarily expensive to operate. When such distribution of work occurs, the school authorities find it difficult to profit by the mistakes they have made in the past or to benefit by the progress made in school design. Not only does modern school architecture require a standardization of classrooms, flue spaces, hallways, and other space so that there is a minimum of space which is not in actual full-time use, but the buildings must also be designed so that additional units can be added at a minimum expense.[1] Nearly all large cities —New York, Chicago, Philadelphia, Boston, Cleveland, St. Louis, Pittsburgh, Milwaukee, Minneapolis, and others—maintain technical architectural departments to plan and supervise the construction of school buildings. The experience of these cities indicates that best results accrue from the maintenance of such a department in the school organization. Such organization lends itself to the correction of mistakes and the pursuit of a continuous policy of improvement. If an architectural department cannot be created, an architectural staff should be employed to collaborate with the outside architects.[2] The procedure followed in the actual construction of school buildings does not differ from that employed in any public construction work and is discussed in another place.[3]

Engineering and janitorial service

The engineering and janitorial service of a school system creates a problem that is seldom met to the satisfaction of the supervisory

[1] It is equally necessary that buildings be located in line with the growth of population, and with a maximum of accessibility. This is a problem in itself.
[2] A. L. Weeks, "School Building Construction," *Government of Cincinnati and Hamilton County, Method of Securing Architectural Services and Planning of School Buildings,* and *Architectural Services in Eight Cities,* prepared for the Detroit Board of Education by the Detroit Bureau of Governmental Research (1918 and 1919).
[3] See Chap. XXIV.

staff. This service in large cities sometimes calls for engineers with first class licenses capable of handling heating and ventilating plants, engineers holding combination engineer and janitorial positions, firemen and coal passers, janitors who are responsible for the heating and cleaning of schools, and for their subordinates, assistant janitors, and janitresses. This division of the service is usually directed by the business manager and frequently is placed in direct charge of a superintendent of property or a superintendent of janitorial and engineering service. One principal difficulty arises because frequently these janitors and engineers are employed by reason of political influence with members of the board of education. Under such circumstances they recognize little subordination to the supervisor of the property or business manager, and even less to the principals of the schools. Even when appointed purely upon a merit basis, there is sometimes a division of authority between the school principal and the engineering-janitorial force. The engineering-janitorial force is presumed to report to the business manager or some technical member of the educational staff and is not directly subordinate to the principal, yet in the last analysis this function of the schools is to assist in education, and frequently derelictions on the part of the janitorial or engineering force have a decided effect upon the usefulness of the educational facilities. While it is not recommended that janitors and engineers be made subordinate to principals, it is believed that all of these employees should be amenable to minor discipline from the principal, who also should report periodically on the condition of the building in accordance with a definite rating scale. Some cities, for moral effect, style janitors as custodians, and provide janitor training courses to improve their work.[1]

The assignment and compensation of engineers and janitors also affords an opportunity for favoritism and for increased expense in the operation of schools. The most satisfactory plan appears to be to have the janitors and engineers paid upon exact units of work done. The amount of work required of engineers, firemen, and janitors in the heating and cleaning of certain individual schools may be measured and the compensation adjusted accordingly, ranging from a minimum which provides a living wage to a proper maximum.

[1] *Organization and Administration of the Engineering and Janitorial Service of the Detroit Board of Education,* prepared by the Detroit Bureau of Governmental Research (1917).

290   PRACTICE OF MUNICIPAL ADMINISTRATION

CHAP. XVI

Efficiency

In addition to compensation on the basis of units of work, it is necessary that there should be some measure for compensation based on efficiency. One factor which aids greatly in measuring the efficiency of an engineer is the amount of coal he uses in meeting the heat and power load, the most efficient engineer being the one who maintains the required standard of heat and power with a minimum consumption of fuel. While the construction of a building is a factor to be reckoned with in keeping it heated at a required temperature, the matter of coal deliveries is something that needs close inspection and supervision if inequalities in coal consumption are to be avoided. The only satisfactory method of treating this problem is to provide a careful calculation of the heat loads of the various schools such as may be scientifically computed by heating engineers, against which the coal consumption will be checked.[1] In some instances, Cincinnati, for example, the schools are heated and cleaned on a contract basis.[2]

Maintenance of school plants

As a rule, the business manager makes use of a staff of carpenters, painters, and plumbers to undertake whatever minor repairs and installations are necessary. During the summer months, when the schools are closed, this force is augmented to overhaul the buildings more or less thoroughly. In addition to frequent visits to school buildings, the manager should make a complete examination of every building in the system once each year, noting all repairs and maintenance work necessary, estimating the cost of such work, and submitting these estimates to the board for its consideration. Such annual overhaul lessens depreciation and keeps the plant in prime condition.[3]

The annual requirement of supplies for the school system

[1] Heating and ventilation provide perplexing problems of school administration. See C. E. A. Winslow, *Fresh Air and Ventilation* (Dutton, 1925); *Report of New York State Commission on Ventilation* (Dutton, 1923); and J. R. McLure, *The Ventilation of School Buildings* (Teachers College, Columbia Univ., 1924).

[2] Biennial competitive bids are requested for the labor necessary for cleaning and heating school buildings, the fuel and supplies being furnished by the board. A mechanical engineer and a chief janitor are employed to determine whether the equipment is kept in good condition and is properly operated, and whether the heating and cleaning of buildings are in accordance with specifications. In addition, the principals file reports when occasion requires. The Cincinnati board of education claims that it is well rid of the heating and cleaning problem, and believes that it receives less expensive service than could be secured otherwise.

[3] In Henry Steffens, Jr., "Business Procedure of the Board of Education," *Government of Cincinnati and Hamilton County; Report on the Maintenance of School Property*, and *Report on the Organization and Administration of*

EDUCATION

should be determined from requisitions prepared by the principals, and upon estimates made by the manager based upon past experience. The various department heads, with the superintendent, can decide the kind and type of supplies required for the subjects taught. Specifications arranged by trade lines should be prepared and forwarded to prospective bidders, after which the bids can be received, tabulated, and presented to the board of education for its action. In this respect, the system of purchasing of the boards of education does not differ from centralized purchasing for a city, although the educational system is seldom included in such centralized purchasing. Such educational supplies, except in special cases, should be delivered to general storerooms to permit proper inspection as to quantity and quality.

CHAP. XVI

Purchase of supplies

Requisitions for educational supplies should be presented to the business manager only after approval by the department heads, and in case of special items, by the superintendent. The business manager, however, should not interfere with educational policies. He should take possession of excess supplies found in schools upon his inspection trips, and some system should be installed for controlling the use and consumption of supplies by allowing a fixed quantity and kind per pupil per grade per subject. The same principle may be applied to the assignment of textbooks, which will reduce the possibility of purchasing and storing excess volumes. To make this control effective, it is merely necessary to agree upon the average relative requirement in accordance with the money available per pupil per grade for each subject taught. Requisitions should then be controlled automatically and filled on the basis of attendance reports. Under this system, the department heads and principals would be relieved of considerable routine record work which arises when supplies are not automatically controlled. Also, requirements should be met promptly, and the control placed with the business manager, who is held responsible for all supplies. Visible stock records of all supply items should be kept and periodic inventories taken.

Control of supplies in storerooms

The budget and accounting procedure of an educational system does not differ essentially from that used in other branches of

Budget and accounting

Centralized Purchasing, prepared for the Detroit Board of Education by the Detroit Bureau of Governmental Research (1917).
On the subject of building insurance, see William T. Melchior, *Insuring Public School Property* (Teachers College, Columbia Univ., 1925); also Chap. XXIV of the text.

292 PRACTICE OF MUNICIPAL ADMINISTRATION

CHAP. XVI

municipal government. To summarize, the budget should be prepared by the superintendent upon estimates submitted by his subordinates and should represent a work program, and expenditures should be balanced by the anticipated income and reviewed by the board of education. The accounting principles should be based upon an accrual system, consideration being taken of the accruing revenues and obligations, and should provide a journal and ledger reflecting both the operating condition over any given period and the balance sheet as of any given date.[1]

Schools have gone farther in some instances than many other branches of city government in methods of cost accounting. In recent times, systems have been introduced for the keeping of cost records of all school activities. This is done on the basis of per pupil-hour and per subject taught. When set up to include a proper distribution of all administrative expense, as well as expense of textbooks and teaching costs, the detailed cost of conducting any course on a per pupil-hour basis is shown, which, when totaled for classes and schools, will give the cost of instruction in each subject and the cost of operating each school.[2]

Cost of education

Since a word has been said with respect to the limits of free education, the subject should be supplemented with something concerning the cost of education in the United States. The individual cost of education in some large cities may appear unusually high. However, it should be borne in mind that this country in 1922 spent only a billion and a half dollars for public elementary and secondary instruction. This figure is, of course, relative and should be measured against a national wealth of more than 350 billions, an average yearly income of 65 billions, and expenditure for luxuries of over 17 billions, of amount in savings accounts of more than 17 billions, and a total of all governmental costs in excess of 9 billions. The personal and public results of education have been so often discussed in detail that they need not be repeated here. It is of interest, however, to note that the states which rank highest in public school efficiency are also the states which rank highest in the annual income of those persons that are gainfully employed, in the average savings accounts of such persons, in more general interest in public affairs, in the intelligence scor-

[1] See *A Uniform Financial Procedure for the Public Schools of Michigan* (Bulletin No. 4, Part I, Michigan State Teachers Association, 1924).

[2] General forms for budget and cost accounting procedure of schools have been prepared by the United States Bureau of Education.

ing of army drafts, and in the production of men and women in leadership.¹

It is of interest to note that the educational authorities have developed units for measuring educational efficiency, although much simpler than those now being formulated for public health work. This standard of measurement, known as the Ayre's Index, is based on ten points including the percent of school population attending school daily, average days attended by each child of school age, average number of days schools were kept open, percent that high school attendance was of total attendance, percent that boys were of girls in high schools, average annual expenditure per child attending, average annual expenditure per child of school age, average annual expenditure per teacher employed, expenditure per pupil for purposes other than teachers' salaries, and expenditures per teacher for salaries.²

Measuring educational efficiency

¹ *Research Bulletin* of the National Education Association, I, No. 4, and II, No. 4 (September, 1923, and September, 1924). Also B. F. Pittenger, *An Introduction to Public School Finance* (Houghton Mifflin, 1925).
² *Ibid.*

CHAPTER XVII

RECREATION [1]

Origin of public recreation

In the small and medium sized cities of a few years ago, there was no occasion to provide recreation facilities by community effort. Outside of the congested area, there was room for play on any quantity of undeveloped land, and the groves and open places in the neighborhood of every city furnished picnic grounds and playgrounds. City boys found no great difficulty in getting beyond the urban limits, in finding neighborhood creeks and rivers in which to swim, forests and fields in which to range for birds' nests and collectors' specimens, and vacant plots for games. The idea of directed play, and of education through play, had not arisen. Recent urban growth and development of the transportation facilities furnished by electric street railways and motor vehicles, however, have pushed the undeveloped land of cities far beyond the actual urban centers, and have made it difficult for the average city boy to profit from the out-of-doors life enjoyed by the youth of a generation ago. In place of woods, meadows, and brooks, he must ordinarily find his recreation in streets and alleys and in pool rooms and dance halls. Under these conditions, public welfare requires that the city provide, even at considerable expense, play spaces and directed play facilities that a less complex society enjoyed free of cost.

Purpose of recreation

The manner in which the members of a community spend their leisure time reflects to some extent the moral character of that community. The working hours of the people are automatically

[1] A thorough study of public recreation will be found in the *Cleveland Recreation Survey Report* (Cleveland Foundation, 1920). This report, in seven sections, covers delinquency in spare time, school work in spare time, books and citizens in spare time, the sphere of private agencies, commercial recreation, public provision for recreation, and the community recreation program. Other texts valuable to the administrator are: Playground and Recreation Association of America, *The Normal Course in Play* (Barnes, 1925); W. P. Bowen and E. D. Mitchell, *Theory of Organized Play*, and *The Practice of Organized Play* (Barnes, 1923); Clarence Rainwater, *Play Movement in the United States* (Univ. of Chicago, Press, 1922); H. S. Curtis, *Practical Conduct of Play* (Macmillan, 1915); Joseph Lee, *Play in Education* (Macmillan, 1915). For current reference, see *Proceedings and Bulletins of the Playground and Recreation Association of America; Playground* (monthly); *Parks and Recreation* (monthly); and *The American City* (monthly).

taken care of. The use made of leisure time, however, largely determines their plane of living. Regarded in this light, the effects of a program of wholesome public recreation are of more than casual importance.

Philanthropic motives alone have not been responsible for the club houses, tennis courts, ball fields, garden plots, and other recreational facilities provided employees by progressive and far-sighted corporations. Evenings and holidays spent by employees in wholesome diversion have been found wonderfully productive of good morale. No less benefit accrues to a community as a whole if its inhabitants use their leisure hours in wholesome recreation. A proper and adequate program of recreation on the part of a city government means a decreasing of juvenile delinquency, a breaking down of race prejudice, assimilation of the foreigner, education through play, a building up of the health and physique of the people, the development of community spirit and civic pride, and the safeguarding of citizens against harmful commercial amusements.

Such a recreational program does not mean that a city must supply the actual entertainment or amusement to every one. It means that the city should furnish certain facilities and a staff of play leaders to stimulate and guide the people of the community to a utilization of the best forms of leisure-time employment. Not all persons in the city require this stimulus; nor are all dependent upon the city's initiative to enjoy wholesome recreation. But neither do all parents depend upon the medical inspection in the public schools for the discovery and correction of physical defects of children, which inspection has nevertheless brought immeasurable benefit to the community in health returns.

The actual duties of a public department of recreation are to provide certain recreational facilities to care for the leisure time of both juvenile and adult citizens, to supervise such recreation, to act as a clearing house for recreation having its origin in private associations, and to regulate commercial amusements undertaken by private initiative.[1] Proper recreational work should cover every field of wholesome activity which groups can enjoy. This means that a city must make provision for parks, boulevards, playgrounds, beaches, bath houses, skating rinks, golf links, tennis courts, ball

[1] This chapter largely summarizes the discussion and recommendations found in the *Report on the Organization and Administration of the Detroit Recreation Commission,* prepared by the Detroit Bureau of Governmental Research (January, 1919).

grounds, indoor facilities, summer camps, and garden plots. It means utilizing not only the usual public places such as schools, libraries, parks, playgrounds, and community centers erected specifically for recreational purposes, but also all existing facilities in the community which offer an opportunity for recreation. Advantage should be taken of private social settlements, hospitals, and other institutions of a similar nature, and even industrial plants where physical facilities are provided and an established clientele is to be found. In this manner, all groups, of all races and religions in the community—some of whom do not frequent public places—can be reached.

Scope of recreational activities

The general scope of public recreational work should include the work of clubs in recreational centers, recess and after-hours work with school children, playgrounds, gardening, summer camps, bath houses and bathing beaches, art extension, concerts, supervision of athletic contests, and recommendation of licenses for amusements.[1]

Community center work

Community center, or recreational center, work means the building up of juvenile and adult clubs which, during the daytime or evening, enjoy recreation in the community recreation centers provided. The recreational activities undertaken include athletics, debating, dramatics, dancing and games, gymnasium work, manual arts, sewing, knitting, etc. The work does not differ materially as between children and adults. It is the frequent practice of the recreation authorities not only to organize the activities but to furnish the leaders for each individual phase of the work, demanding only that the people of the neighborhood attend the centers. The groups are not required to assume responsibility for organizing themselves into self-governing clubs. To carry out such a program on a large scale would be financially impracticable for any city, even were it desirable.

On the other hand, it is possible to provide a maximum of recreation and social intercourse if the organized efforts of the respective communities are enlisted. Considerable interest has been shown of late in the organization of community associations, and in their efficacy as agents of socialization and democratization, the latter naturally involving Americanization of foreign people touched by such organizations. It is urged that social groups should be

---

[1] Consult *Layout and Equipment of Playgrounds, Community Drama, Rural and Small Community, Home Play, Community Recreation, Community Music*, pamphlets edited by the Playground and Recreation Association of America.

organized into small democracies, with the community center as the capital, which should thus become the focus of social and extra-occupational life of the community affected. This involves the organization of the people of the community into an association with a board of directors and officers to conduct this social democracy, to outline its policies, and to decide upon its activities.[1]

It is questionable whether the policy of erecting expensive buildings in various sections of a city for such community centers, as is done in some cities, notably Chicago, could be duplicated satisfactorily in most communities. Certainly the recreation authorities should use every facility within the community before separate buildings are erected, making all possible use of school buildings, social settlements, parish houses, churches and branch libraries.

Although the recreational authorities are usually vested with authority to supervise and manage outdoor and indoor recreational facilities, it is a question of how far this work must be undertaken with children, under these auspices. If it is true that children must be educated to play and, conversely, must play to be educated, it follows that every child should receive the benefits of this method of self-improvement and should be taught to play, or taught through play, by the educational rather than the recreational authorities. That this theory is recognized, and is being put into practice more and more, is evident by the enriched curriculum of the school, which often is providing a daily period for some form of play or physical education. This is particularly true under the platoon type or, as it is sometimes known, the work-study-play plan of organization. There remains, however, the problem of providing for the leisure time of the child, and in those cities where the school authorities do not assume this as their function it remains for the recreation department to be the agent through whom provision shall be made for the proper enjoyment of the leisure time of the children. It seems, therefore, that the proper division of function between the schools and the recreation department, in cities where the latter exists independently of the schools, is for the recreation authorities to provide facilities where the child can apply in its hours of leisure out of school that which it has learned in school. Under these conditions of conflicting theory and jurisdiction, it is necessary to have close coöperation between the edu-

[1] This is the plan of the United States Bureau of Education. While the proposal is most applicable to rural communities and small towns, a modified form of social center adapted to city conditions is quite practical.

cational authorities and the recreational authorities and a sensible adjustment of the programs of both. Where the educational authorities do not include a reasonable amount of directed play in their own curricula, it is doubtless proper to continue the activities now undertaken with juveniles by the recreation department.[1]

Playgrounds

Investigation indicates that only a small proportion of the total number of school children go to playgrounds and recreation centers for recreation, but rather play in the streets and alleys and vacant lots adjacent to their homes.[2] Since thousands of children must be given places in which to play with safety and comfort, it is necessary that there should be close coöperation between the recreational authorities and those responsible for city planning in arranging play spaces. New streets, new subdivisions of property, and all other construction of a public and semi-public character should be arranged so as to provide ample spaces for children to play safely and near home. Such play spaces should not relieve parents of responsibility for their children—responsibility which they are duty-bound to exercise, and toward which the whole social program is tending by emphasis upon the integrity of the family.

A number of large play spaces are necessary, although caution must be exercised not to over-emphasize large and costly recreation fields at the expense of numerous and important smaller areas. The play learned by the children at school will be given expression in these smaller play spaces; so that supervision, though desirable, will be absolutely necessary only in the larger centers to which children come from a considerable distance, and where there is danger of the "bully" and of undesirable behavior generally.

Large playgrounds without direction are no considerable asset to a community. If facilities for recreation are not provided, the property becomes more or less useless. Play areas require proper surfacing to endure hard use; shelter buildings for changes of clothing; toilets and washrooms; supervision and protection for smaller children; and stimulating leadership for the youths and older girls. Mr. T. Glenn Phillips, in discussing this feature of direction, suggests in substance that the unsupervised playgrounds in many American cities eventually become the resorts of loafers and bullies, who misuse the play equipment until it must be removed. Directed play not only provides good bodily exercise but

[1] For a plan of city and educational coöperation in the conduct of recreation, see Jay B. Nash, "Organizing a City's Play and Recreation Assets," *American City*, XXXIV, 475-479 (May, 1926).

[2] In some cities little used streets are blocked off for play purposes.

teaches fair dealing through coöperative effort. Competent play leaders should be secured to stimulate and to follow up with organized groups the use of the play facilities of the larger parks and playgrounds by the young men and women who need and seek recreation out of business hours.[1]

The work on playgrounds covers usually a period of two or three months during the summer season, and constitutes a most evident, yet really smaller, part of the year-round program of the recreational authorities. It is important, however, because all school children during this period have a large amount of leisure time. Larger playgrounds are under supervision, usually from morning until dark, daily except Sundays. Most of these have at least two leaders, a man and a woman, although smaller playgrounds may have only one leader. Attendance at the playgrounds will be found heaviest during the late afternoon and early evening.

An adjunct to the playground is the home and school garden. During periods of industrial depression, and particularly during the war, when there was a desire to stimulate food production, cities have laid emphasis upon the development of home and vacant lot gardens. Some cities have continued this program and have gone so far as to solicit from owners the use of vacant lots, plow them free or at a nominal charge, and turn them over to citizens who desire to make a garden. Prizes are given for the best gardens, both at home and on vacant lots, and there is usually an annual exhibit of the production of these gardens. Dayton, Ohio, in particular has had notable success with this form of recreational work. In addition, some effort has been made in the direction of stimulating the interests of urban bred children in gardening through the schools, where schools are located on large areas some part of which is tillable. Also a city may make use of some centrally located property which can be tilled in small plots by school groups. These gardens have proved of very large interest to school children, although vandalism sometimes nullifies the efforts made. School gardening work can also be extended to include canning clubs, and so be closely coördinated with domestic science work in the schools.

In every large city provision for numerous camps is made by various philanthropic organizations; and, of course, for the wealthy there are innumerable camps where children may safety be sent.

[1] T. Glenn Phillips and George Huttenloch, "Parks," *Government of Cincinnati and Hamilton County*.

The camps of the recreational authorities should be for the type of child who can pay only a moderate amount and whose parents cannot afford to go into the country with the whole family. A city should have available a permanent camp, largely on a self-supporting basis, where both juveniles and adults can find accommodations at reasonable cost. Such camps will be under continuous supervision, and the attendance scheduled in an orderly manner.

Bath-houses

Bath-houses are usually partly self-supporting, and are operated on an all-year-round schedule in congested districts where the sanitary conditions are not particularly high grade. As a rule, both swimming pools and shower baths are provided, and, except in a few instances where persons are not able to pay, a charge of a few cents is made for both adults and children. For this charge, the bather should be furnished with soap, towels, swimming trunks, and locker. These institutions have met with indifferent success.

Bathing beaches

The operation of summer bathing beaches and swimming pools offers another problem. A bathing beach should be made entirely self-supporting. With any kind of attendance, this can be done at a nominal charge. Bathing beaches should be well located, maintained in a sanitary condition, and well equipped, so that they may be enjoyed with a minimum of inconvenience by citizens. They are meant not as a charitable proposition, but as a form of recreation that cannot be provided satisfactorily upon a commercial basis.

Art extensions and exhibits

An interesting and valuable phase of a recreation department's work is involved in art extension, talks in the art museum, community singing, and neighborhood homeland exhibits which promote an appreciation of art through direct contact with material available in the city. The recreational authorities should inaugurate such activities when there is no other agency whose legitimate function it is to do so.

The extent to which art work can be carried on depends upon the art resources of the community. In some instances this work can be well organized by the authorities responsible for the art museum. Where this is not possible, it is entirely proper for the program to be undertaken by the recreational authorities with the idea of making art exhibits available to school children and of conducting educational discussions of art in that connection. This activity may be carried on by means of walk-talks, in which classes of school children and others are taken to exhibits and given lectures on the work exhibited there. In this connection, there is a possibility of neighborhood exhibits of home articles of artistic value, supplemented with objects from a museum. The articles exhibited, many of which may have been brought from Europe, should be furnished by the people of the neighborhood. Aside from any artistic value the exhibits may have, they are an excellent means of Americanizing and assimilating foreigners into the community. It makes them feel themselves a greater factor in the community because they have something to contribute.

Many cities offer band concerts in parks and play spaces during the summer months, and occasionally a symphony orchestra is employed. This form of recreation is always popular, particularly with park users, and in recent times provision has been made for the broadcasting by radio of a single band concert to a number of different parks. At least before the introduction of the radio, some recreational authorities found it feasible to promote high grade concert courses for citizens during the winter. Most of the concerts offered by private individuals on a business basis are too costly to be attended by thousands who would appreciate the opportunity to hear good music. Recreational authorities themselves have financed such ventures or have induced public spirited citizens to do so; and the concerts, while more than self-supporting, furnish recreation to many at a moderate cost.

The recreation department can, of course, be counted upon to organize certain special events which are of city-wide interest. These include track meets, field meets, winter sports, aquatic sports, kite flying contests, marble playing contests, pageants, and similar events.

The aim of the city in stimulating competitive athletic leagues is to raise the standards of sportsmanship, to furnishing facilities and to supervise this sort of recreation. Every city has a number of baseball leagues, basket ball leagues, and hockey, soccer, and tennis organizations which find in the facilities offered by the city an opportunity to satisfy their demand for competitive recreation. Such facilities are provided to some extent by private organizations, particularly on a commercial basis. However, the demand for public baseball diamonds, basket ball courts, and tennis courts will exceed the supply. It is, therefore, desirable for a city to make provision for facilities for these games, and at the same time to exercise a wholesome control over them; and a city usually has available a number of baseball diamonds and other facilities which are allotted to private recreational organizations at specific

302   PRACTICE OF MUNICIPAL ADMINISTRATION

CHAP. XVII

times and long in advance of their use. Frequently, leagues are organized which will take over baseball diamonds and tennis courts for an entire season, at a particular hour. This is one of the most important forms of recreational activities, since it involves small expense on the part of the city and has the advantage of stimulating individuals to take care of themselves through private initiative.

Recreation at cost

Certain types of public recreational facilities, such as moving pictures and dances,[1] which compete in a way with private commercial recreation, should be largely self-supporting. There is no question about furnishing concerts or other appropriate recreation free to those confined in hospitals or eleemosynary institutions, but there should be a limit to the free entertainment of this nature furnished to the general community. The community is its own master, and if it wishes to provide recreation for itself on the community plan, the cost to be met by taxation, nobody can deny it such a policy. However, it is believed that more appreciated entertainment and recreation can be furnished on a communal plan, if the beneficiaries will pay directly the nominal sum necessary to finance such ventures. It seems feasible, for instance, for the recreational authorities to furnish a community center, with a moving picture machine, an operator, and films for an evening, at cost price, which will be met by the dues or contributions of the organized centers.

Supervision of commercial recreation

Commercial dance halls, moving picture theaters, theaters, pool and billiard parlors, and other pleasure resorts furnish recreation to the greatest proportion of the population of a city, and will continue to do so. In a few cities the recreational authorities are given the responsibility of enforcing proper standards in these private activities. Private dance halls and other amusement places are commonly licensed, and these licenses are issued by the police department upon the recommendation of the recreational authorities. It is the general practice for representatives of the recreational authorities to visit dance halls and other places of commercial recreation upon notification that an application for license has been made, and for these representatives to ascertain the nationality and general conduct of the people attending, the type of dancing or other recreation, and any other pertinent social conditions that may have a bearing upon the issuance of the license. Upon the

[1] Small cities frequently hold pavement dances.

RECREATION 303

basis of this investigation, the recommendation of the inspectors is made. _{CHAP. XVII}

Usually there is a follow-up during the year, particularly if any criticism arises concerning the operation of the commercial recreation; and upon recommendation of the recreational authorities, licenses may be canceled as provided by law. In many cities these functions are delegated to the police department, which acts as censor. The coöperation of the police department should, of course, constitute a part of the plan of supervision of commercial recreation; but the task should not be delegated exclusively to the police.

In the foregoing discussion public recreation has been treated independently of the use of parks,—which areas include large informal spaces, improved boulevards, and small plots frequently located in the heart of the city, or in the residential sections.[1] Such open spaces were provided long before organized recreational facilities of cities were developed. Even the oldest communities were in the habit of setting aside, or if necessary acquiring, parcels of land which might be enjoyed by the public. No definite recreational facilities were necessary. The park was kept planted with trees, the grass mowed, walks maintained, and facilities for enjoying the park in the way of seats were installed, but beyond this the ordinary city did not go until recent years. At the present time, there is a tendency to provide band concerts and facilities for holding picnics, in the way of ovens, benches, tables, etc.

The justification of a park system is the relaxation it provides and the emphasis upon recreation is becoming stronger each year. As Mr. Phillips puts it: "Fine natural surroundings do not comprise the total equipment for modern parks. If they are to attract crowds sufficient to justify their existence, they must have other facilities for outdoor recreation—smooth lands for informal games, tennis courts and baseball fields, shelters and band stands, play equipment, and drives."[2] For educational purposes zoölogical gardens and arboretums may be established.

The park system of a city, including its boulevards, is maintained essentially for recreation; it would seem that this use by

---

[1] The first large area acquired for park purposes is said to be Central Park in New York City in 1858 although this statement is disputed.
[2] T. Glenn Phillips and George Huttenlock, *op. cit.*

the public should be controlled and directed by the authorities having charge of recreation policies. Any other direction and control may mean that parks become merely a matter of landscape artistry, with city life largely left out. Such a unified control would mean that the recreational facilities of the parks would be more extensively developed. The purely mechanical processes of park maintenance should in nowise be impaired by this consolidation. This unified control is by no means prevailing practice, and will require a new public concept of recreation.

Parks are not all of the same character. First, there is the small tract of land set apart either as a playground or as a space where the public can enjoy trees, flowers, and quiet. Sometimes band concerts are provided, but the means for recreation are usually limited. Second, in addition to these plots, located at intervals throughout the city there must be large parks kept essentially in undeveloped condition with portions to be used as playfields, picnic grounds, and places of general recreation. These larger parks are a more recent development, and have grown out of the transportation facilities provided in the last generation. There was small need of large parks removed from the center of the city when no means were available for getting to them. Now, however, with the development of the street railway and the automobile, these parks, even though a number of miles from the city proper, have a substantial place in the city's recreational program, and are used very freely by citizens.

Where a park system is developed embracing several semi-urban parks, it is frequently desirable to connect them with a continuous boulevard as a means of automobile recreation. The public finds little satisfaction in riding over city streets, constantly alert for pedestrians and traffic, but may find considerable diversion in a boulevard system miles in length, and connecting a number of recreation spots. Such a boulevard running through congested or residential sections if properly landscaped may furnish a continuous playground and park place for the use of the public.

Tourists camps are not exactly parks in the accepted sense of the word, yet have most of the characteristics of parks. Such camps, as maintained by many cities located on main trunk roads, are situated on the edge of the city adjacent to the highway. Like parks, the areas should be attractively wooded, and of inviting appearance. Unlike parks the principal purpose is not recreation, but the business of affording temporary shelter for tourists. To this end the camp should be properly lighted and policed, and provided with shelters in event of storms, hot and cold water, bathing and washing facilities, camp stoves, etc. In the better camps a nominal fee is charged for camping privilege.[1]

One important problem of park administration is the control of refreshments and incidental amusements. These activities may be undertaken directly by the municipality but will involve the recreational authorities in all of the annoying difficulties of food purveying. More often concessions are let to private individuals. In such event the department has dismissed one set of troubles to acquire another involving equitable leasing, responsible character of concessionaires, quality of service rendered, and prices charged. In a choice of two procedures, both of which are unsatisfactory, probably the lesser evil will be found in public ownership and operation.[2]

It is stated by some authorities that one-tenth of the area of a city should be in playgrounds and parks. This, however, depends considerably upon the distribution. It is folly for a city to place all of its play area in a single park, more or less inaccessible to a considerable proportion of its citizens. The development of a recreation system for a city is a science in itself and should be committed to persons who have made a special study of the subject. Playgrounds must be carefully located according to the distribution of the population that is to use them. Parks must be located with consideration to congestion and the need of breathing spaces in a congested community. Larger parks, for full recreational purposes, must be so located as to be accessible to several sections of the city, and properly placed with respect to street car lines, automobile highways, etc. It is desirable that boulevards connecting such parks be located so as not to become thoroughfares for commercial vehicles or other vehicles designing to go to a specific part of the city, but rather with the idea of furnishing a purely recreational facility.[3]

---

[1] See *Auto Tourist Camps,* compiled by the Civic Development Department of the Chamber of Commerce of the United States (June, 1922); and P. J. Hoffmaster, ''The Tourist Camp Site, Equipment and Maintenance,'' *American City,* XXXII, 401-406 (April, 1925). For bibliography, see *Municipal Index 1925,* and *ibid.,* 1926.

[2] See Bulletin No. 12, American Institute of Park Executives, *Concessions and Privileges in Public Parks* (1915).

[3] W. T. Lyle, *Parks and Park Engineering* (Wiley, 1916), is standard except as the automobile has come into common use since its publication. For design of parks, see H. V. Hubbard and Theodora Kimball, *Introduction to the Study of Landscape Design* (1917). For current reference, see the publi-

Supervision of recreation

It is customary for recreation to be in charge of a recreation commissioner or superintendent appointed by the executive head of the city, although a recreation board so appointed is sometimes found, the superintendent being appointed by and subordinate to this board. In either case, the executive should be in full charge of all facilities and activities and responsible for the general program of recreation. The more immediate supervision of recreation raises a number of questions. Public recreation divides itself into a number of activities: adult and juvenile, winter and summer, night and day, indoor and outdoor, and male and female. Along what definite division of these activities shall the recreation work be organized? If, for example, the division is along the line of sex, there results a vertical arrangement of work and of supervision which creates a division of responsibility and a duplication of labor for practically all recreational activities. Such an arrangement is illogical from the point of view of the results to be accomplished and unnecessarily complicated from the standpoint of organization and administration. On the other hand, to enlist the interest of adults in public recreational facilities is a problem quite different from organizing playgrounds and play centers for children. Each group is sufficiently distinctive to require individual attention, which attention can be given satisfactorily only when responsibility is definitely located.

It is believed best, therefore, that principal activities be made the unit of organization and that each branch of the several activities be assigned to supervisors. The entire responsibility for each activity would be placed with one person subordinate to the superintendent, and each person so responsible would control all directors and play leaders, whether male or female, within the unit. This suggested division of labor and responsibility for supervision involves separate control of children's playground activities and of amateur athletic activities. In each activity the supervisor of playgrounds would be in charge of the work of all directors and play leaders and assistant supervisors of playgrounds, whether male or female. Under this arrangement, one person would be in charge of a whole activity and of every person connected with it.

It may be assumed that a play leader or play director, in addition to being technically proficient, should have a broad social

cations of the American Institute of Park Executives including *Parks and Recreation* (monthly).

viewpoint and be qualified to build up community interest. Play leaders are social workers as well as play directors. For this reason, in addition to certain minimum educational requirements, the play leader should have certain training in physical education or teaching, and should have spent some time in the study of theory and practice of play development. Sound health and a reasonable proficiency in simple physical exercises should also be taken for granted.

CHAP. XVII

Qualifications of play leaders and directors

The work of a recreation department is varied and requires a versatility of accomplishments to do it at all effectively. Social dancing, folk dancing, athletics, gymnastics, study clubs, dramatic clubs, and efforts to conduct successfully community centers for adults are a few of the tasks exacted of the same person. During the winter a day's program may include organized recess play with small children, dramatics and games with larger children, and a social dance for adults. When the warm weather arrives, outdoor games, athletics, and general playground activities, including manual work, are to be directed. Obviously, broad qualifications must be exacted from one individual.

Part-time vs. full-time employees

The plan of securing these qualifications by hiring year-round employees has three defects: first, it is not reasonable to expect one person to be adequately proficient in all branches of the work undertaken by a recreational program; second, because of the small salaries paid, coupled with limited opportunities for advancement, it is difficult to get well-qualified play leaders and directors, particularly men on a full-time schedule; third, with a full-time staff throughout the year, emphasis may be placed upon merely doing things to keep the staff busy.

To remedy these defects, it is suggested that the recreational authorities will do well to employ part-time workers for the special activities of evening recreation centers, afternoon centers, etc. This plan does not preclude employment by the year of workers whose work may touch all activities. Every city has a large number of professional persons, school teachers, social workers, and others with adequate training and experience, who are not available for whole-time service, but are available under a part-time plan.[1] Further, part-time employment of workers for particular branches would tend to encourage a more vigorous prosecution of all parts of the recreational program, because persons employed

[1] Social and philanthropic agencies will frequently donate the part-time services of play leaders.

308 PRACTICE OF MUNICIPAL ADMINISTRATION

CHAP. XVII

by the year know that work will be found for them in some branch or other, should their original assignment meet with failure. Payment for seasonal workers should be based upon the number of sessions served each week. It is recognized that this plan of part-time employment is more complex than one of continuous employment and necessitates a more thorough planning of a program.

Recreation records

It is believed that daily reports from play leaders and directors in charge of centers or playgrounds should be required. The reports should indicate the nature of the activity carried on, attendance classified as to men, women, boys, and girls, and the kind of work done each day. In addition, there should be assignment records of the workers maintained, showing every center in which they worked and the kind of work they did.

Cost of recreation

Compared with the cost of education and police protection, the cost of recreation is very small. Reports from various cities in the United States show that the cost each time a person participates in public recreation ranges from five to twenty cents. One large city for the past four years has had an average cost of five and one-half cents per person attendant at its recreational activities. The amount of money a city should appropriate for recreational purposes varies according to local conditions, *i.e.*, density of population, availability of park or playground space, topographical conditions, etc. Some authorities feel that a fair estimate of the budget for a leisure-time program in any city should be approximately one percent of the total budget of the municipality.

CHAPTER XVIII

CHARITIES [1]

In the United States the public has not taken kindly to the extended intrusion of municipal government into the field of public charity, *i.e.*, charity administered by some local governmental agency. Unlike education, that was once a private, and is now almost completely a public activity, municipal charity continues as substantially a matter for private endeavor.[2] The reasons for this indifference on the part of local government are numerous. Because of the large outlay of capital required and the small number of cases to be found in any local community, the state has generally assumed institutional responsibility for the insane, feeble-minded, epileptic, blind, deaf and dumb and occasionally for alcoholics, and dependent children. In a similar way the county government ordinarily provides for mother's pensions and for indoor institutional relief for the aged poor. This leaves to the city and township government and to private charity the almost universal necessity of providing for outdoor poor relief, and usually for the relief of dependent children, vagrants, and care of the sick. In these last fields there is an evident willingness of private philanthropy to carry the burden, and possibly the proper administration of non-institutional charity requires a personal element that up to the present at least is impossible to the formal, legalistic and bureau-

The government and charity

---

[1] A standard reference on charities is Amos G. Warner, *American Charities* (Crowell, 3d ed., 1919), first published in 1894. Much has been written on the subject, but the public administrator will find of particular value H. W. Odum and D. W. Willard, *Systems of Public Welfare* (Univ. of North Carolina Press, 1925); James Ford, *Social Problems and Social Policy* (Ginn, 1923), Chaps. XXIV-XXV; Robert W. Kelso, *History of Public Poor Relief in Massachusetts* (Houghton Mifflin, 1922); M. F. Parmelee, *Poverty and Social Progress* (Macmillan, 1916); and Edward T. Devine, *Misery and Its Causes* (Macmillan, 1911). For current reference, see the *Proceedings of the National Conference of Social Work* (annual); *The Survey* (bi-weekly); and journals for specialized branches of charity work.

[2] This statement refers to municipal charity in a restricted sense. Mr. W. J. Norton, secretary of the Detroit Community Fund, points out that in larger cities social welfare activities often considered as charitable are financed on about the following basis: forty-five percent by clients, mostly in private institutions; thirty percent by taxation; and twenty-five percent by voluntary contributions to private agencies.

CHAP. XVIII

The need for charity

cratic character of government. Local government does perform certain charitable activities, but in a limited way and with evident reluctance.

Organized society cannot entirely escape responsibility for the fundamental economic needs of its members. From the beginning of time some portion of the population has been in want for one or more of a number of causes. In primitive civilization with the communal ownership of property, this individual want was reduced to a minimum unless it became merged with the general poverty of the entire community brought on by war, pestilence, or failure of food supply. During the Middle Ages, however, the situation underwent a marked change. With the decay of the feudal régime and the inauguration of the enclosure system a large poverty-stricken class sprang up. Relief was administered entirely through private gifts, and monasteries, guilds, and endowed hospitals doled out indiscriminate alms to both the vagrant and to the worthy poor, a practice that steadily increased the number of applicants. No attempt was made to solve the problems of relief because the aid was given not so much to rehabilitate the needy as to save the soul of the giver. Ultimately, the number of sturdy beggars became so numerous and the burden of their support so exasperating that foreign vagrants had to be warned from communities, and local ones put to work. This segregation of professional vagrants from the meritorious needy of the immediate community induced the idea of public responsibility for relief resulting in compulsory tax contributions by individuals. This development in the various boroughs later culminated in the English Poor Law of 1601, providing a weekly grant to paupers to be raised by taxation.[1]

Charity in early America

Many of the settlers of New England came from small English boroughs where the burden of the poor taxes had fallen heavily. This, taken with the fact that the ordinary necessities of life were none too plentiful, made the first Americans rather chary of fostering mendicancy. "Stern measures were taken by the watchful selectmen, first to avoid the burden, and second, when finally charged, to carry as little of it as possible. To be relieved at all, the needy must have been in direct want for the necessities of life and relief when given was such as merely to sustain life."[2] At first the poor were auctioned off in single lots to individuals, while

[1] Stuart A. Queen, *Social Work in the Light of History* (Lippincott, 1922).
[2] Robert W. Kelso, *History of Public Poor Relief in Massachusetts* (Houghton, Mifflin, 1920).

a little later they were let out in lump contracts to one caretaker with no provision for classification and segregation. Institutions grew up slowly and outdoor relief was given only in case of dire need.

The results of this neglect of public charity were not so harsh as might appear. In a country predominately rural and agricultural the needs of charitable relief were not great. An agricultural community may not possess large wealth, but it seldom wants for the necessities of life. The common causes of want met in an industrial society do not prevail to any extent in a rural one. Even the loss of the principal bread winner did not result in complete destitution. Ordinarily, the home remained, the family was kept intact, and the wife and children could wring at least a meager living from the soil, the forests, and the streams.

With the development of modern industrial life the need of relief to certain individuals became accentuated. To be sure, more wealth exists, and many persons enjoy greater material comforts than were possible in a simpler civilization. At the same time many more persons are several stages removed from the direct production of the necessities of life. They live in homes of which they are not the actual owners; do not work for themselves; and have no economic interest in the tools of production. Few of these industrial workers receive in return for their labor more than is necessary to maintain a decent standard of living, and when a surplus is received, it is seldom preserved for the periods of distress that may be anticipated. In city life there is small possibility of having needs cared for by the relatives or friends of the person involved. Citizens do not have the same acquaintance with and interest in their neighbors as in rural communities, and in consequence persons may suffer direct want without that want being known or appreciated by others in the community. Existing under these circumstances a number of factors may create an economic situation requiring outside intervention to relieve the most acute distress.

The factors that create the need of relief are simple to state and difficult to analyze. For mental or physical reasons an individual may be unemployable; sickness, accidents, or old age may remove the chief means of family support; or unemployment may arise from causes far beyond the remedy of the individual affected—economic depressions, fires, wars, etc.[1]

[1] See Warner, *op. cit.*, Chaps. II-III.

312 PRACTICE OF MUNICIPAL ADMINISTRATION

CHAP. XVIII

The resulting policy

The public and individual conscience will not permit individuals to suffer absolute want without amelioration, and the public authorities must take cognizance of elementary requirements and provide for them from the common purse. Aside from sheer fundamentals, however, the public is content to leave charity to the well-meaning and generous impulses of the individual citizen acting through the private charitable or ecclesiastical organizations. In consequence, in every great city, there are scores of charitable groups dealing with different requirements—direct relief to individuals, care for dependent children, homes for the aged, nursing and medical service for the sick, securing employment for the unemployed, temporary shelter for destitute men and women, aid to delinquent girls, training for the physically handicapped, educational instruction to those who cannot secure it through the regular channels provided by the municipality, training for the blind and handicapped, education for the specially gifted in music and arts, hospitals of different types, clinics for the medical treatment of the different classifications of persons and for different types of diseases, certain kinds of recreation, and settlements for the stimulation of higher ideals on the part of those who do not receive the advantages of the best homes and environment. In fact private benevolence runs its course from the giving of food and shelter to those in actual need of the physical requirements of life to providing higher educational advantages for youths who would not otherwise receive them; from what is known as absolute charity to the philanthropies dealing with social, political, and cultural improvement.[1]

The plan of governmental activity

Obviously, because of policies developed out of historical precedent and practical experience, a city government cannot be concerned in all of these different types of charities and philanthropies. Many of these ventures are experimental and may well be left to individual benevolence. However, communities cannot neglect to provide the absolute necessities of life for their citizens who for the time being cannot secure those requirements. This is a broad general statement of public policy, and the extent to which any given community may actually be involved depends entirely upon its economic resources and its social conscience.

---

[1] In more than 250 cities in the United States, funds for these activities are raised locally in a single united campaign. These funds are distributed by a community fund, community chest, or similar organization. A national association is maintained, The American Association for Community Organizations, 215 Fourth Ave., New York City.

CHARITIES

Today, the most common charity on the part of a city government is outdoor relief, *i.e.*, individuals and families in need are given direct relief in the form of food, clothing, fuel, and rent in proportion to their immediate requirements. Relief takes this form because it has been found socially more expedient and less costly to keep a family together during a period of distress than to separate it by placing its members in institutions. Cases of need that are called to the attention of the authorities are investigated, or should be, by competent persons who can determine the course of action that should be taken in each case. Usually a specific allowance is made to families, depending upon their size and condition. Rent will be paid to a certain amount, orders for groceries and clothing will be supplied in accordance with actual requirements, and such fuel and other commodities will be given as is necessary to subsistence. This relief must be continued as long as the necessity exists, and it is therefore incumbent upon the social worker in charge of such cases to take every step possible to relieve the circumstances which are creating the situation.

The aged cannot always be cared for in their homes because in many instances they have no homes, or the maintenance of a home would be a large expense in proportion to the benefits received. Most communities maintain, through the instrument of private charities, satisfactory homes for the aged to which cases such as these may be referred by the city authorities, particularly when the individual or friends can pay for some part of the support provided. In addition, provision of a sort must be made by the community in the almshouse.

The ordinary institution for the poor not maintained by outdoor relief is the almshouse. Sometimes the almshouse is operated by the municipality, but more often it is a county institution. It is primarily an institution for the care of persons who cannot be immediately restored as self-supporting members of society. Unfortunately, in the past institutions of this kind have been on the whole poorly administered, and provided poor food and bad treatment. The reason for this disgraceful state of affairs was due largely to the fact that such institutions were often the plaything of politics.[1] Superintendents were chosen on a basis of political patronage rather than of ability; inadequate appropriations were

---

[1] Johnson Alexander, *The Almshouse* (Russell Sage Foundation, 1911), and Harry C. Evans, *The American Poorfarm and Its Inmates* (Des Moines, 1926).

314   PRACTICE OF MUNICIPAL ADMINISTRATION

CHAP. XVIII

made; and no classification or segregation of inmates was practised, with the result that many almost unthinkable conditions existed. The insane, feeble-minded, diseased, old and young, male and female were frequently thrown together in the same institution and forced to live together under the most intimate conditions. These conditions did not always exist, but were so often the case that almshouses have received a very bad reputation in the United States. As a result, individuals will permit themselves to be committed only as a last resort.

Temporary homes for children

A discussion of indoor relief would not be complete without some word about the care of homeless children.[1] It is the concensus of opinion that children should not be confined in institutions unless such procedure is absolutely necessary.[2] It is important, however, that some provision be made for their care until they can be properly placed with some good family. In this connection the city should provide a temporary home for the children with the idea that they shall be kept there only until suitable homes can be found. It is on this latter phase of the work that all effort and thought should be expended. Most often private and religious organizations undertake this service, investigating the character of homes for child placement, paying all or part of the board of children in these homes, and currently examining the circumstances of children so placed.

Municipal lodgings

Most communities make some provision for the care of transient individuals who are seeking work and are without means of providing themselves with food and lodging. Occasionally these institutions are operated by private charity, but often they are maintained by the municipality. Where a city does not actually have a municipal lodging house, the police station is ordinarily open for such purposes. A bed is provided upon demand and usually a single meal and sometimes two are given. In the better organized lodging houses provision is made for baths, for the fumigation of clothes, for the writing of letters, and for other comforts. In such institutions it is anticipated that reasonably

---

[1] H. W. Odum and D. W. Willard, *Systems of Public Welfare* (Univ. of North Carolina Press, 1925); Sophie V. Theis, *How Foster Children Turn Out* (New York State Charities Aid Association, 1924); R. R. Reeder, *How Two Hundred Children Live and Learn* (New York Charities Publication Committee, 1910); and Homer Folks, *The Care of Destitute, Neglected, and Delinquent Children* (Macmillan, 1902).

[2] Institutional care is sometimes necessary. The Hebrew Sheltering Guardian Society has issued a valuable manual outlining the supervision of children. See Leon W. Goldrich, *A Manual for Cottage Mothers and Supervisors* (1925).

cheap meals will be provided and every means taken to see that the transient worker has an opportunity to secure a job. Relief will be granted for a very limited period of time and sometimes a small charge is made for the facilities given. If a person is financially unable to meet any charges at all, opportunity is given to do a small amount of physical labor in return for the benefits received. In communities where municipal lodging houses exist beggars can be turned away from kitchen doors and panhandlers refused alms with a clear conscience.

One group of individuals who cannot be helped by the ordinary facilities of outdoor relief or ordinary institutional care are the sick. A large number of persons who are ill and who cannot afford medical treatment can of course be treated in their homes. For this reason it is customary for cities to make available to indigent persons the services of a number of physicians, and sometimes nursing service. However, many such persons have such meager home facilities that hospitalization is the only satisfactory means of promoting recovery. To care for these patients, cities either maintain their own hospitals or let contracts to private hospitals for the care of public patients on a per diem basis. Municipal hospitals have been more or less subject to misuse, and oftentimes patients are sent to them who should rightly go to other institutions. The fact that clean beds, good food, and ample supervision are ever in readiness constitutes a considerable temptation to malingering.

In a modern community many individuals, and particularly the poor and ignorant, find themselves in difficulties where only recourse to law or at least to some intelligent individual familiar with the law, can be of aid. There are continually questions of unpaid wages, difficulties in the purchase of homes, fraud in connection with minor purchases, and the illegal exactions of individuals who threaten trouble for one reason or another. These cases can usually be settled very quickly by persons who are familiar with the legal rights of individuals and the means by which these rights can be enforced. Any public administrator who has been long on his task will have a keen appreciation of the number of cases drawn to his attention that require justice. Particularly the foreign populations look upon the city and officialdom as the proper avenue to secure redress for injuries. The answer is found in a legal aid bureau staffed with competent attorneys. Sometimes these legal aid bureaus are operated in connection with the corporation counsel's office or by a lawyer in the welfare department, but more often by private philanthropy.[1]

Employment agencies

Often cities maintain municipal employment agencies for the purpose of securing positions for persons in need. Or such institutions may be operated in conjunction with state or United States agencies of the same character.

In connection with the age-old problem of unemployment it has been advocated by a number of economists that every city maintain a sort of reserve of employment by undertaking public works during periods of depression. Unfortunately, cities do not attempt such relief on any large scale. Such a program would be helpful, but it must be borne in mind that, even under the most extraordinary impetus, public work will employ only a very small part of the persons thrown out of work by a serious economic upheaval.

Coördination bureau

Social work on the part of municipalities involves a coördination with the social work of private agencies, since only a small proportion of charitable work is actually done by the public. Public welfare officers must understand thoroughly what other agencies are doing, and these numerous highly specialized activities must be correlated with the more rudimentary work of the municipal authorities. The foundation of this correlation is the confidential clearing house of cases that is ordinarily maintained in every city by some private agency or occasionally by the welfare department, and made possible by the coöperative efforts of all charities. A complete record of charity cases is secured by requiring that every organization giving relief of any kind report all facts concerning the case to the confidential exchange. Such a record provides data for a scientific study and treatment of all cases; and prevents an unwarranted duplication of activities on the part of different agencies. Were it not for such clearing houses it would be possible for the professional mendicant to secure continuous charitable aid by running from one institution to another.

Social research and prevention

The purpose of welfare work should be to build a ladder upon which the individuals in distress can climb back to a normal relationship with the balance of society, and not merely to hand out bread, fuel, and shelter continuously to individuals in need. The administrator will not be as much interested in the giving of relief,

---

[1] See *Legal Aid Work* (Annals, CXXIX, March, 1926); and *Growth of Legal Aid Work in the United States* (Bulletin of the U. S. Bureau of Labor Statistics, No. 398, January, 1926).

CHARITIES 317

although a temporary situation must be relieved, as he is in eliminating the causes that may have created the distress. For that reason the giving of relief must be in the hands of persons who can properly study and analyze each case and prescribe and apply such remedies as will reëstablish upon a self-supporting basis the persons involved.[1] In some instances the distress will be remedied by the mere securing of employment; in others illness must be eliminated even though it requires long institutional care to effect a cure; sometimes it may be necessary to give a trade education, particularly to handicapped individuals, such as the blind and the lame; and sometimes tools and equipment may be secured which will permit the person involved to become a self-supporting unit. Under any circumstances the social worker must make every effort to find a solution of the case which will relieve the community from the necessity of giving relief. This may involve learning of the whereabouts, apprehending, and bringing back deserted husbands and requiring them to properly support their families; legal difficulties may be straightened out to the benefit of all persons concerned; relatives or friends may be found who will actually undertake the care of distressed individuals involved; and if the persons are not citizens of the city they may properly be returned to their own communities for care. No small part of the work of a municipal welfare organization in a large industrial city will be the providing of railroad fare and incidental expenses to return to their own homes persons who have become stranded while looking for employment.

Many uninformed persons interpret charity as the actual giving of material relief. This is an outgrown ideal, and one that has made many difficulties for public and private relief giving. Of course, immediate needs must be met, amply, sympathetically, and with a minimum of "red tape" and investigation. But true charity is the service that helps the person in distress to help himself; that injures the pride and self-respect of individuals the least; and enables the persons relieved to become self-reliant members of society. The efficacy of the dollars spent for charity should not be measured by the relative amount that is spent in material relief, but rather in the amount that is spent for constructive

[1] See Mary E. Richmond, *Social Diagnosis,* and *What Is Social Case Work?* (Russell Sage Foundation, 1917 and 1922); Richard C. Cabot, *Social Work* (Houghton Mifflin, 1919); Ada E. Sheffield, *The Social Case History* (Russell Sage Foundation, 1920); and Sophonisba P. Breckinridge, *Family Welfare Work in a Metropolitan Community* (Univ. of Chicago Press, 1924).

service. If society made more effort in the direction of rehabilitation, it would be saved a substantial portion of the income that is now devoted to continuous doles to the unfortunate. The slow process of changing ideals is the old story of interesting the public in the prosaic fence at the top of the precipice rather than in the clanging ambulance at its foot.

Subsidies to private agencies

In some communities the coöperation between public and private charities goes so far as to involve public subsidies to private agencies. This procedure is sound if under proper control. It is possible, however, that by utilizing political pressure a private organization may secure subsidies out of all proportion to its requirements, and to the detriment of well-rounded social work in a community. On the other hand, it is sometimes more feasible for a city to employ private agencies to undertake its charitable work than to do it itself. In a small community having a general relief organization, the city can very properly make an appropriation to that organization covering either investigation and relief, or sometimes only relief, leaving the question of investigation entirely as a responsibility upon the private organization.

Industrial compensation

As modern industrial civilization has caused no small part of the existing need for charity, at the same time it is making halting steps to eliminate the more obvious causes. In industrial communities we find common law doctrines of fellow servant and contributary negligence discarded, and their places being taken by industrial compensation for accidents and death received in ordinary employment, sometimes through the medium of state insurance and sometimes through insurance carried by the employer. This is known as employers' liability.

Health and unemployment insurance

In recent years there has been a decided agitation for health and unemployment insurance that will provide practically every wage earner with protection. These last two efforts, however, have made little progress in American cities. Foreign students familiar with unemployment, health, and accident insurance in their own countries are amazed when visiting American cities to see the general prosperity of American industrial workers unaided by public funds.

Old age pensions

The movement for old age pensions has also made some progress and with the spread of education along these lines we can expect it to be taken more seriously in the near future. For many years the pensions that were accorded Civil War veterans provided substantial care to a large proportion of aged American citizens.

However, a new generation of citizens are now reaching old age and some provision must be made for them.

A number of industrial states provide pensions to widows with dependent children, and to the blind, usually administered by the courts.

It is difficult to state categorically the type of welfare organization that should be maintained by a municipality. In many city-manager cities a department of public welfare is established and is responsible for relief, employment, social research, and investigation, legal aid, parks, recreation, and similar social activities. In such instances charity constitutes but a separate division of the larger subject of welfare. In other instances a charity superintendent may be appointed by and report to the chief executive. Occasionally a citizens' board intervenes between the executive and the director of the department, but it is questionable whether such a board serves any useful purpose.

CHAPTER XIX

POLICE [1]

Responsibility for law enforcement

The maintenance of law and order is often compared to a three-legged stool, its supports being the police, the prosecution, and the courts. In truth, there is a fourth support, *i.e.*, correction, but the methods of present-day correction are so unscientific and its results so nearly negligible that its place in law enforcement is often discounted. In the public mind the chief administrator of the city is often held solely responsible for the proper conduct of all of these activities. The citizen does not know, or at least seldom realizes, that this responsibility is distributed among a number of entirely independent authorities—that law enforcement devolves upon city police, county sheriffs, state police, and United States marshalls and agents; that prosecution is an obligation of the city attorney, the county prosecutor, and the United States district attorney; that justice is administered by city police courts, county or other state courts, and United States district courts; and that incarceration of offenders may be in city, county, state, or national institutions. These many authorities may be, but more often are not, concerned with entirely different offenses; and there must be a complete and sympathetic coöperation among them if their common purpose is to be achieved.

Police function

The police department is the one division of law enforcement over which the city administrator has reasonably complete control and for whose operations he may be held responsible. It is charged

[1] See Raymond B. Fosdick, "Police Administration," *Criminal Justice in Cleveland* (Cleveland Foundation, 1921), and his two books, *European Police Systems*, and *American Police Systems* (Century, 1915, 1920); C. F. Cahalane, *Police Practice and Procedure*, and *Policeman* (Dutton, 1914, 1923); Leonard F. Fuld, *Police Administration* (Putnam, 1910); Elmer D. Graper, *American Police Administration* (Macmillan, 1921); Bruce Smith, *State Police* (Macmillan, 1925); Arthur Woods, *Crime Prevention* (Princeton Univ. Press, 1918), and *Policeman and Public* (Yale Univ. Press, 1919). For studies of particular police departments, see Arch Mandel, "Police," *Government of Cincinnati and Hamilton County* (1925), 236-262; C. A. Crosser, "How Your Police Department Functions," Supplement, *Toledo City Journal* (January 30, 1926); New York Bureau of Municipal Research, *Survey of San Francisco* (1916), 159-272; and surveys of other cities. For current reference, see *Police Journal* (monthly); *Police Magazine* (monthly); and *Sheriffs, Police, and Peace Officers Review* (monthly).

with the repression of anti-social conduct as defined by law, including the preservation of life and property from the depredation of individuals, as well as the care of injured and distressed persons, the abatement of nuisances and unsanitary conditions, the control of traffic, the issuance of licenses, and frequently the inspection of weights and measures. Following the English theory, the police power in the United States is strictly limited to law enforcement and the preservation of public peace. Legally, the police have little more authority than any citizen; actually they exercise rather arbitrary powers, subject only to the restraints imposed by liability to prosecution and actions for damages, and by the censure of the courts and public opinion. The American police are in the unfortunate position of having to exercise more power than is conferred by law if they are to work effectively. For this reason, their authority to use personal discretion should be increased and the character of personnel improved so that this discretion will be wisely exercised.

In the development of the police function, one of the oldest of municipal activities, are reflected all stages of the organization of municipal government in the United States—the struggle for home rule by cities, and the changes from decentralized administration by council committees, through the period of boards and commissions, to the single-headed departments of today. Above all, the story of political methods, which has been the shame of American city government, will be found in full detail in a review of police department history; and today police department progress, compared with that of other municipal activities, furnishes a striking exhibit of political blight.

The early American settlers naturally copied English police methods, which meant following the "watch" system, and later Sir Robert Peel's metropolitan plan for London. Each town had its duly elected constable, who was the single police officer and jailer. As the communities grew the number of constables was increased, one to each ward. The safeguarding of citizens and of property was performed by the night watch, which in the beginning was an unpaid service, made obligatory upon every citizen. When their turn came, citizens able to afford it hired substitutes, who frequently were irresponsible loafers, and sometimes ruffians.

Early in the nineteenth century the night watch became a paid body, but conditions were little better than under the old system, as the force was recruited largely from men with regular daily occupations who supplemented their income by serving as night police. Under this plan, police protection was provided only at night. Each ward was an independent unit for administration, and political qualifications were the basis of appointments. The next step in the development of police departments was the creation of a day force independent of the night watch, the personnel (varying with the city) being appointed by the mayor or council, or elected directly by the voters in each ward. This dual police force proved ineffective, failing to meet the needs of the growing and sometimes turbulent cities.

Beginning with New York in 1844, the watch system was abolished in the larger cities, and unified police forces under a single head were organized. In 1844 the New York legislature passed a law establishing a police force of eight hundred men in the metropolis, under the direction of a chief of police appointed by the mayor. This did not mean, however, an immediate metamorphosis from a loosely organized, inefficient band, into a uniformed, well-disciplined, and competent police force. Ward politics controlled the appointments; the spoils system had full sway. In spite of strenuous efforts by various cities, the police refused to wear uniforms, because it was considered un-American and undemocratic. Discipline was almost unknown. The police were powerless to cope with crime increase in the growing cosmopolitan cities. To remedy the situation, the New York legislature enacted a law in 1857 creating a metropolitan police force for New York and Brooklyn, under a board appointed by the governor. This act, patterned upon Sir Robert Peel's famous Metropolitan Police Act adopted for London in 1829, ushered in the modern uniformed, centrally controlled police force in American cities. This was the beginning of real protection, and by its effective work the Metropolitan Police of New York gained the confidence and support of the public. Other American cities adopted the plan in rapid succession.

While the ineffectiveness of the urban police furnished a plausible excuse for the state government to inject itself into police administration, the real reason was a desire to secure political control of the police department. Up to this time police administration was a purely local affair, but the New York act of 1857, copied by other states, introduced state control through appointment of the police boards by the governor. This was the source of much bitter strife between the city and state governments until home rule in police affairs became the general practice. The notable exceptions to home rule today are Boston, Baltimore, Kansas City, and St. Louis.

The presumption in favor of state control is the removal of the police establishment from local politics. It is argued that the governor, disinterested in the local political situation, will make appointments on the basis of merit and the service to be rendered rather than for the advancement of any political faction. Boston is usually cited as an example of the superiority of state control; but on the other hand there are the less impressive examples of Kansas City and St. Louis. There is nothing inherent in state control to insure, nor in local control to prevent superior police administration. The belief that partizan political considerations do not enter into local appointments by governors is a delusion, and when they do so they have the added disadvantage of being more difficult of correction by the municipality. With the strenuous efforts necessary to maintain non-partizanship in municipal government, it is essential that every taint of politics be eliminated from local administration. Another undesirable feature of state control is the practically mandatory demand by an outside authority for appropriations for its support of the police department. The city pays the bill, and it should have complete control of its expenditures for police protection.

In the early history of city government in this country the various municipal functions were administered and supervised by council committees. With the growth of cities and the increased complexity of administration in the nineteenth century, administrative supervision by council proved inadequate, and there were created independent administrative boards. This system, passing through the stages of partizanship, bi-partizanship, and non-partizanship, spread throughout the country in the administration of all departments, and it is only in recent years that it has been largely abolished.

While boards may be useful in exercising quasi-judicial functions or in promulgating policies, they have proved ineffective as administrative bodies. This is particularly true in police departments, where satisfactory administration demands promptness and dispatch in making decisions. Police boards, even though composed of citizens of the highest integrity and ability, cannot acquire, through their periodic meetings and casual contact with the department, the intimate knowledge essential to competent and productive administration. Furthermore, differences of opinion colored by personal hobbies and biases as to emphasis of the various police activities inevitably arise in a group of independently thinking men, and make it difficult for the chief of police to know what to do. This, together with the fact that members of boards tend to inject themselves into details of administration, makes for confusion and misunderstanding. The prevention of crime is a science which demands constant study and application, which, however, is impossible under a plan by which the administrative heads are on duty only a fraction of the time, and with whom the position is incidental.[1]

Today the general practice in the larger cities is to have a single commissioner, a civilian, appointed by the mayor, as the administrative head of the police department. In the smaller cities the chief is, as a rule, the head of the department, reporting directly to the mayor or city manager, without having a civilian commissioner as an intermediary. It is not generally apparent to the public why a civilian is necessary to the management of a police organization, but failure to appreciate this need is due to ignorance of the responsibilities of the position. And, judging by the character of administration, this ignorance is shared by police heads themselves. The backwardness which characterizes police administration in this country arises largely from the lack of continuing management by competent leadership, which was supposed to have been supplied by the commissioners of police drawn from the ranks.

If the functions of the police comprised only the patrolling of streets and other routine duties, the problem of securing properly qualified heads would not be difficult. Many capable officials could be found who had risen from the rank of patrolman and who would meet the requirements of such a position. The function of the police is, however, more than that of a glorified watchman. In addition to being a business enterprise spending large sums of money, the police department is the direct crime prevention agency, and is concerned with a social problem that is interrelated with all the social and economic conditions in the community. This country has barely begun to approach the social problem rationally, applying to it what scientific knowledge is now available. An inherently difficult situation is aggravated by the unprecedented growth of population and wealth and a remarkable heterogeneity of population.

[1] See Chap. I.

Obviously the task of combating crime calls for superior abilities, together with training and education. The head of a police department must have a broad social viewpoint, the capacity to grasp the relationship of crime to other social problems and conditions, and ability to win the intelligent coöperation of all the social forces in the community. It is a position that calls for tolerance and a sympathetic understanding of the various races making up the population. The commissioner must also have that most important quality, the power to investigate, analyze, and test like a scientist, so that new knowledge may be applied and older methods may be adapted to changing conditions. While many police chiefs have proved themselves men of large native ability, their background and training has limited their viewpoint. The habit of following a routine for many years, from the position of patrolman upward, often disqualifies them for handling large administrative duties, or adapting themselves to a position that calls for the qualifications of a suitable police commissioner.

Nowhere in municipal administration are the fruits of political methods so evident as in the operation of police departments. The position of commissioner has always been, and continues to be, a political one, the incumbents changing with almost every change in administration.[1] Even when competent men are selected, apply themselves to their task, and become useful, they are removed from office to make way for untrained successors. Improvements made by one commissioner are often abandoned by the next one, merely because they have been introduced by another administration. This periodic change is not as serious in other departments, because professionally qualified men may be secured to administer health departments, public works departments, and legal departments. But the only opportunity for receiving training in police administration is in the police department. There are no schools in this country, as there are in Europe, for the training of police heads.

Immediately subordinate to the commissioner of police is the chief or superintendent. As a rule, he is a man who has come up from the ranks, having entered the service as a patrolman, although in a few cities the police chief has sometimes been appointed from outside the department. The chief is the technical

---

[1] According to Fosdick, *op. cit.*, London has had seven police commissioners in ninety-one years, the last three serving for fifteen, thirty-nine, and seventeen years respectively. Detroit has had ten commissioners in twenty-five years, with an average term of about two and one-half years.

326 PRACTICE OF MUNICIPAL ADMINISTRATION

CHAP. XIX

head who carries out the policies laid down by the commissioner and attends to the details of the operation of the department. Chiefs of police usually have no permanent tenure of office, and they often change with changes in administration. This absence of even a permanent technical head multiplies the difficulties of police administration in this country.

Organization of the department

Police departments are composed of two main divisions, the uniformed force and the detective force. The function of the former is the prevention of crime by patroling city streets and handling traffic. The detective force is primarily concerned with following up complaints of crime and apprehending offenders after the commission of the crime. The chief of police is the head of both divisions. The uniformed branch is by far the larger, and in many ways more important. The unit of administration of this branch is the patrol post, or "beat," covered by the patrolman, who is the lowest ranking officer. Next comes the sergeant, who supervises the patrolmen. The lieutenant, next in rank, is usually in charge of the detail work in the precinct station house, under the direction of the precinct commander. Inspectors, next in rank to the chief, are employed in larger cities as supervisory officers of a number of precincts.

Precincts

For purposes of administration, cities are divided into large districts called precincts, under the command of an officer, usually a captain, who is responsible for the preservation of order in his territory. The activities of the precinct are carried on from the police station, to and from which the patrolmen assigned to that district report. Each station has a number of cells for retaining prisoners arrested in the district. Since the introduction of the motor vehicle in police work, the tendency has been to reduce the number of precincts by increasing their size, because it is now possible to reach the farthest boundaries of the precinct within a few minutes in case of calls, and patrolmen in automobiles can reach their posts within a correspondingly short time. In the larger cities a number of precincts are combined into inspection districts, under the supervision of inspectors.

Each precinct has one commander, or captain, assisted by three lieutenants, one for each eight hours of the day, who attend to the detail work in the station house, receiving complaints, registering arrested persons, meeting the public, keeping the records, and answering the many inquiries received. The lieutenants also supervise the patrol.

The patrol post, or beat, has been from the earliest day, and still remains, the basic unit of police department organization. Each precinct is divided into these smaller units, in accordance with its size and character, and to each is assigned a patrolman. In the business and congested sections the beats are smaller than in the more sparsely settled districts. Also at night, when the greater number of patrolmen are on duty, the posts are smaller than in the day. The beat may be a number of city blocks, but is preferably one continuous street plus a half block in side streets. This system permits more thorough patrolling, and the officer may be more readily located by a citizen or by another officer or called by the signal lamps. The fixed post, by which an officer is always on duty at a definite location, alternating in patrol with another officer, has been found effective in congested areas; but as a rule it requires more men than can reasonably be afforded.

CHAP. XIX

Patrol posts

In this matter of patrolling, police departments give evidence of failure to adapt themselves to new conditions. Foot patrol is still the prevailing method, and patrol beats often remain unchanged year after year, regardless of change in character. In locating fire apparatus and in arranging the "runs," the character of the districts as to fire hazards are carefully considered; in distributing a corps of public health nurses, health departments, on the basis of records, appraise the health hazards of the various districts in the city; but police departments have done little to base the distribution of the force on any carefully worked out plan of establishing the "crime hazard" of the various districts.

The greater frequency with which a patrolman can cover every part of his beat, the more effective is he as a crime prevention force. But inasmuch as the amount of territory that can be properly kept under surveillance is extremely limited, the ability of the patrolman to prevent crime, particularly when on foot, is limited. Foot patrol is useless except in congested sections where the beats are small enough to be covered with sufficient frequency. On large beats it is only a fortuitous coincidence that brings the patrolman to a spot where he is needed. If, however, he has the means of arriving quickly and unexpectedly in any part of his beat, he may be of real preventive value. The introduction of the automobile and motorcycle in patrolling, while too gradual, is increasing the protective power of the police and is making up for deficiencies in the number of patrolmen usually available. Foot patrol will cover about nine miles per shift; automobile patrol will

Defects of patrol

cover about thirty miles. From the records it must be concluded, however, that would-be criminals do not seem to be deterred by fear of being caught in the act.[1]

A number of cities have experimented with the plan of establishing patrol booths in their outlying sections, from which point of vantage two men, as a rule, equipped with motor vehicles, operate. Except when responding to emergency calls, one officer remains in the booth to receive telephone calls, while the other patrols the vicinity. Help can be had, almost immediately after a call comes in, by the citizens in the district limits covered by the particular booth. This method of patrol and emergency protection has met with varying success. Some cities find that with the required number of booths strategically located good police protection is secured. Others prefer patrol and emergency service working out of a limited number of precinct stations, with small patrol booths placed only on highways near the outskirts of the city. The officers stationed in these booths are used to close all avenues of escape for criminals who have committed a crime in the city, or to apprehend those who are escaping from a neighboring municipality.

Mounted patrol

Mounted patrol has been used to some extent, but is being discontinued except as an aid in parades and in the regulation of traffic. Mounted patrol is expensive to maintain; the officer can easily be seen and heard by miscreants; and sometimes he must give more attention to his horse than to the observing of conditions.

Auto patrol

A number of cities have been experimenting with bicycle, motor cycle, and automobile patrol, particularly as operated in conjunction with the patrol booth, with an inclination to adopt the last type. A large territory can be covered in not a very thorough way, but unusual opportunity is afforded to investigate suspicious automobiles, pick up dangerous traffic violators, etc.

Signal system

Patrol is supervised by sergeants, who make regular rounds of their territory and report on the conditions found. Further control over patrolmen is secured by the requirement that they shall call up their precinct stations at regular intervals, usually every hour. At such times they also receive special instructions to take care of assignments that have arisen since they left the station house for their tour of duty. In this connection larger cities make use of a special police telephone and signal system. The

---

[1] Occasional patrol is valuable for the enforcement of certain regulatory ordinances.

POLICE

signals are distributed at convenient intervals throughout the city and are operated from police headquarters. By means of automatic flashing lamps the police of one precinct or the entire city can be called to the telephone to receive emergency orders. These signals are equipped with a telephone and are also used for regular police reporting.

Platoons

Police work is usually divided into three shifts, or platoons, of eight hours each. The men are transferred periodically from one platoon to another, so that an officer is not continuously on night or day duty. As a rule the force is not divided into platoons of equal size, the platoon on duty from 7 a.m. to 3 p.m. or 8 a.m. to 4 p.m. being the smallest. The greatest number of men are on the night shift. There is large variation among cities as to the arrangement of platoons and the number of men on duty and on reserve. Some cities still retain a two-platoon system, which is unsatisfactory because the men are on duty or reserve for very long hours.

Selection of personnel

Selection of personnel by police departments means practically selection of patrolmen, because as a rule appointment as patrolman is the entrance to all positions in the department. And herein lies the clue to the lack of progress, and to the usual low standard of performance, by the police in American cities. Popular opinion notwithstanding, a patrolman's job is not a sinecure nor one of set routine. A patrolman must, in so far as he is able, preserve order on his beat, and prevent the commission of serious crime as well as of minor infractions. He must do this without infringing on the rights of citizens, and with as much tact as possible. Violations of sanitary regulations, street obstructions or dangerous and defective conditions which need correction, unlighted street lamps—all must be noted and reported. He must be prepared to give first aid to injured persons and be of general assistance to persons in distress on his post. He is the protector, the guide, and the counselor of the people in his jurisdiction, and at a moment's notice must decide whether the laws are being violated and whether persons are subject to arrest. Particularly in the foreign districts of the larger cities, he stands for the government, and upon his conduct largely depends the civic attitude of the people. His is a position requiring physical courage, initiative, diplomacy, alertness, resourcefulness, a sense of justice, and the highest integrity. When he faces danger he usually does so alone, without the stimulus offered by admiring crowds or a holy cause to spur him on. In one city a veteran of many battles in the World War resigned his position on the police force after a brief experience, because he found that searching dark alleys alone at night was quite different from entering a battle under stress of excitement.

Examination In most large cities patrolmen are selected on the merit system but usually they have only a common school education and are recruited for the most part from the ranks of labor, largely from unskilled trades.[1] The qualifications are standard throughout the country—good physical condition, minimum height of five feet eight and one-half or nine inches, ability to read and write, United States citizenship, residence in the city, and good character. The entrance examination consists of a medical examination and a written test designed to show the applicant's knowledge of the city and his ability to read and write. In addition, an investigation of his character is made. The Detroit police department, which is not under the jurisdiction of the civil service board, once experimented for a short time with psychiatric examinations, every applicant being given a standard intelligence test and an examination by a psychiatrist.[2]

Effects of merit system Successful candidates are appointed as probationers for three or six months, during which time they may be dropped by the head of the department without right of appeal to the civil service authorities. After the probationary period has been passed, however, members of the department, if discharged, may appeal their cases to the civil service board, which, after due trial, the officer being represented by counsel, affirms or reverses the decision of the department head. While the merit system has been designed to eliminate the spoils system and all its attendant evils, it frequently goes to the other extreme of making it unusually difficult for the police department to rid itself of incompetent officers, because the undesirability and unfitness cannot always be proved; also, the usual types of examinations given both for orig-

[1] See Fred Telford and F. A. Moss, "Suggested Tests for Patrolmen," *Public Personnel Studies*, II, 112-145 (July, 1924).
[2] These tests were discontinued by a succeeding commissioner. For a discussion of results in Detroit and elsewhere, see Arch Mandel, "Getting and Keeping Good Policemen," *Nat. Mun. Rev.*, XII, 299-302 (June, 1923); L. L. Thurstone, "The Intelligence of Policemen," *Jour. Personnel Research*, I, 64-74 (June, 1922); Edward M. Martin, "An Experiment in New Methods of Selecting Policemen," *Nat. Mun. Rev.*, XII, 671-681 (November, 1923); "An Aptitude Test for Policemen," *Jour. Criminal Law and Criminology*, XIV, 375-410 (November, 1923); and Jessie M. Ostrander, "One Hundred and Fifty Policemen," *Mental Hygiene*, IX, 60-73 (January, 1925). See also Chap. III.

inal appointments and for promotions are not designed to disclose the qualifications necessary for the various positions. In the cities where the merit system is used for original appointments it is also, as a rule, used in promotions.

This uniform standard of qualifications for entrance to the force, together with the practice of limiting eligibility for all positions to members of the department, has seriously retarded police progress. Within a police department there are many distinctive lines of duty, which require varied types of ability. For example, the two major classifications are the patrolman and the detective, the one enforcing the law by patrolling the city, the other by investigating and ferreting out the perpetrators of crime. Two distinct types of ability are required. Yet the same requirements are set up for both types, so far as admission to the force is concerned, and no man can become a detective without having the exact physical qualifications of a patrolman, or without having served in that position. Civilians known to be highly competent as investigators will not be hired in that capacity. On this point Chief August Vollmer, of Berkeley, has this to say: "Where is there a business concern that compels applicants for various vacancies in the organization to submit to the same physical and mental examination; where the janitor, clerk, salesman, engineer, department head, superintendent, and manager are all compelled to answer the same questions, measure up to the same physical standards as to health, height, weight, age, and sex, and all commencing their employment at the same occupational level and at the same pay? Where is there a business concern that limits the selection of men for technical positions to employees holding inferior positions in the same establishment?" If police departments are to develop as they should in the function of crime prevention, they will require a type of ability and training able to coöperate with other local social forces—a thing which cannot be secured under present employment conditions.

Private corporations have found it profitable through personnel departments to match the job to the man. Why cannot the same methods be applied to police departments? Where civil service examinations do not apply, the department can have its own personnel division; and in cities where selection and promotion are under the jurisdiction of a civil service department, the latter should adapt its methods to produce the desired results. The ordinary civil service procedure does not do this, either in selection

332 PRACTICE OF MUNICIPAL ADMINISTRATION

CHAP. XIX

Training of recruits

or promotion. Detailed service records giving successes and failures must be maintained in order to judge a policeman's fitness for the assignment he may have or for promotion.[1] At the present time, if supervising officers and detectives are secured who are qualified for their positions, it is largely a matter of chance.

An attempt is being made by police departments to train recruits in their duties before they are assigned to active service. The first real police school in this country was established by the New York Police Department in 1917, giving a two months' course of daily instruction in the duties of policemen. Other cities have schools for shorter periods, but they are not organized upon as elaborate a basis as that of New York. The subjects taught in the schools are rules of evidence, laws and ordinances, criminal identification, handling of prisoners, first aid, report writing, local geography, and methods of police operation by the case method of study. In addition to lectures from officers of the various branches of the service, the prosecuting attorney and judges are often called in. While the schools are rudimentary, they are an improvement on the old method, which was to equip a successful candidate with his uniform and paraphernalia and send him out to patrol a beat after a few days' tutelage under a sergeant or older patrolman. Smaller cities having only a few recruits a year operate a school only when a class can be assembled which is large enough to make the effort worth while. Or these communities sometimes send their recruits to the police school operated in a large neighboring city—a plan that has mutual advantages and is deserving of encouragement.

No city has any system of instruction for persons promoted to the office of sergeant, lieutenant, captain, and inspector. It would be difficult to imagine the lack of effectiveness in a modern army that drew all of its officers from the ranks of private soldiers and provided no means of military instruction for them. The police are an army fighting an unknown and invisible enemy, and their officers are secured under exactly the conditions stated. It has been suggested that every patrolman appointed to be a sergeant, or at least every sergeant made a lieutenant, should be required to show a high degree of intelligence and should be provided with a

[1] For an interesting schedule to determine fitness for promotion, see Solon E. Rose, "A Rating Form for Policemen," *Kansas Municipalities*, X, 26-27 (February, 1924).

thorough course of instruction in the science of policing, sociology, political science, economics, law, and similarly related subjects.

CHAP. XIX

Policemen are paid anywhere from $1,380 to $2,500 a year, depending upon the city and the length of service. In addition, two weeks' vacation is usually allowed and some provision made for sick leave. Practically all larger municipalities arrange for a pension after a long period of service or if injured in the line of duty. The department usually furnishes all special equipment, but in all but a few cities the men are required to provide their own uniforms.[1] Ordinarily, detectives receive slightly higher pay than patrolmen. *Compensation of personnel*

Although numerically very much smaller than the uniformed force, the detective division is a major branch of the department and is as essential to crime reduction as the uniform service. While primarily detectives seek to apprehend offenders after the crime has been committed, their knowledge of the underworld and of the ways of criminals makes them an effective force in crime prevention. Furthermore, the reputation of a detective bureau has a wholesome or opposite effect upon the operations of professional criminals in a city. *Detective force*

Because of the nature of the work, the detective bureau should be made up of the pick of the police force. If however, this happens, it is generally an accidental circumstance. Since the only entrance to the police department is through the position of patrolman, the elementary standards set up for applicants for admission to the police force govern the standards of ability available for all other positions in the department. Therefore the detective force, from the head down, is recruited from the uniformed division, from which, presumably, the men most fitted for the work are selected either by civil service examination or assignment. Where the former practice is followed the position is a permanent one after the probationary period has been served, and removal or transfer can be made only according to the civil service regulations. This method of selection and consequent tenure are serious handicaps. On the other hand, continual shifting of personnel merely because of shifts in administrative heads has equally serious drawbacks. Detectives are not specially trained, but frequently they *Selection of force*

---

[1] For a discussion of current practice on all of these points, see W. C. Beyer, "The Hire of Firemen and Policemen," *Competency and Economy in Public Expenditures* (Annals, CXIII, 235-247, May, 1924).

334 PRACTICE OF MUNICIPAL ADMINISTRATION

CHAP. XIX

Chief of detectives

serve an apprenticeship as plain clothes men in a precinct or as a member of a special squad working in plain clothes.

The position of chief of detectives is assigned directly by the head of the department or upon the chief's recommendation, the incumbent serving at the pleasure of the appointing officer. Changing administrations may see changes in the head of the detective force, seriously limiting the effectiveness of the bureau.

Detective divisions are organized in various ways. In some cities the whole detective force is centralized in one bureau at headquarters; in other cities the decentralized plan of having detectives operate from each precinct under the direction of the precinct commanders is followed. There is also the combination of a major centralized force at headquarters with branches in the various precincts, or in specially created detective branches, all operating under the direction of the head of the bureau at headquarters. In some cities the headquarters and branch plan is followed, in addition to which each precinct has its own plain clothes men. The latter are assigned to complaints originating in the precinct, but if a major crime is involved, members of the regular detective force are also assigned to it. The headquarters branch is usually divided into a number of squads handling specialized phases of the work—homicide, Italian, vice, narcotic, pawn shop, pickpocket, and automobile squads. The last named in many cities are practically bureaus in themselves. The plan of centralized or decentralized detective divisions is not fixed in any city, changes being made from one to the other, according to the policy of the head of the department. Arguments are advanced for both plans, but there seems to be no logical reason for a completely decentralized detective division. A precinct boundary does not limit the territory in which a criminal operates.[1]

Criminal identification

The method of identification of criminals originally adopted by police departments in this country and Europe was the Bertillon system, which originated in France and consists of very intricate measurements of the offender. In recent years a second method of identifying by fingerprints has also been introduced.[2] Smaller cities have adopted neither system, although photographs of criminals are sometimes taken by local photographers. The larger cities

---

[1] Chief August Vollmer believes that the regulation of vice, gambling, narcotics, and liquor should be handled by a separate division of the police, and independently of crime suppression.

[2] More progressive officials are also undertaking identification by the characteristics of the crime committed.

use both methods; but it is being recognized that the fingerprint, which is simpler to operate, is also the more accurate and satisfactory. Until concerted action is taken by all cities to adopt the fingerprint system alone, both methods will be used, although it is an inconvenience and an expense. The tendency is toward discarding the Bertillon system, and it is probable that this will take place within a few years. Under present conditions, with the ease of traveling all over the country, successful combating of crime requires a national clearing house for criminal records, so that no matter where a criminal may be apprehended his identity can be established. Up to 1923 a National Bureau of Criminal Identification, inadequate for the purpose, was operated in Washington by the International Association of Police Chiefs. In 1923, through the efforts of the latter organization, the federal government established a national clearing house in the Department of Justice.

With the advent of the automobile the problem of controlling and regulating traffic has become an important phase of police departments' functions. While it is an essential service that must be rendered, diversion of from ten to twenty percent of the force and of the funds of police departments to traffic control has seriously handicapped the primary functions of police, namely, the preservation of law and order. To enforce traffic regulations has meant either detailing men from their regular duties or increasing the personnel of the department. Where the latter measure has not been possible, it has meant the subtraction of men for traffic duty from a force already inadequate for crime prevention. And even in those cities where additional policemen are available, the crime prevention function suffers, because the public, by its failure to regard the expenditures for traffic control as separate from those for the old line duties, denies sufficient funds to meet the need of a growing city for increased crime prevention facilities.

In addition to directing traffic at intersections, police officers are detailed to the painting and installing of signs, marking pavements, lecturing in schools, and carrying on elaborate safety campaigns. Larger cities maintain accident prevention bureaus to investigate every traffic accident reported. Traffic control, however, involves more than merely stationing policemen at intersections or installing automatic signal systems. It is a problem that must be solved by rational city planning and other means, because the cost of regulating traffic by employing policemen at all heavily traveled intersections is prohibitive. If the public, however, in-

336 PRACTICE OF MUNICIPAL ADMINISTRATION

CHAP. XIX

Policewomen

sists on making it necessary to have itself watched and regulated it will have to pay the bill or suffer the consequences.[1]

Over one hundred cities in the United States employ policewomen, the larger ones having substantial bureaus. In New York and Detroit the head of the policewomen's bureau is a deputy commissioner of police. The duties of policewomen are somewhat different from those of policemen and reflect the changing point of view as to the functions of a police department. The emphasis of policewomen's duties varies from city to city. In some cases, it is placed on patrolling streets to protect girls and visiting dance halls, theaters, and other places where young people congregate; in other instances, in addition to these activities, equal attention is given to protective work with girls. In the performance of the latter function, policewomen's bureaus act as social agencies, doing social case work themselves or utilizing the private social agencies of the community in an effort to prevent delinquency or to rehabilitate girls and women already entered upon a delinquent career. The greatest value and the most successful work of the policewomen is, of course, with the young girl whose habits of delinquency have not become too firmly fixed. In a few cities, every female arrested is placed in charge of the policewomen and interviewed by them, and in so far as possible a complete history of her life, her social condition, and her environment is obtained by investigation. All of this information is presented to the court, so that a more intelligent disposition may be made of the case. In short, the emphasis is shifted from the offense to the offender, where it should be. The cause of anti-social conduct is sought, and measures are taken to prevent repetition by removing the cause.[2]

Weights and measures

The supervision of weights and measures may be assigned to a special police detail, may be in charge of a separate department of the government dealing with this subject, or may be a duty of the department in charge of public markets. Practice is not sufficiently uniform to indicate the preferable procedure. A discussion of the matter appears in another place.[3]

Licenses

Nor is there uniform practice among cities with respect to the issuance of licenses, and this activity may be found located in

[1] See Chap. XX.
[2] See Chloe Owings, *Women Police* (Hitchcock, 1925).
[3] See Chap. XXIII.

almost any one of a number of departments, or may be distributed among several departments. Considerable may be said in favor of placing this responsibility with the police. Licensing is undertaken as a police measure and is justified on that ground alone. In theory at least, the municipality is not so much interested in the financial return as in the character of control afforded. This control is essentially an obligation of the police. Under these circumstances, it would appear that the police should have final decision as to who will and who will not receive licenses, and subject to proper supervision, as to when licenses should be revoked. If made responsible for issuing licenses, the police should investigate the moral character of each applicant, maintain a thorough record of complaints against establishments, and give such current supervision as is desirable.

Police departments have no physical manifestations of their work, of results achieved or failures suffered. The only means of knowing what is or is not being accomplished is by means of adequate records. Without definite knowledge as to whether crime is increasing or decreasing, in which crimes and in what districts the increases are taking place, the head of the department cannot intelligently formulate policies or administer the department. Progress of public health departments in their fight against preventable disease has been due in no small measure to the assembling and study of accurate vital statistics. The reverse is true of police affairs.

The many complaints of major and minor offenses received by police departments—in the smaller cities hundreds and in the larger ones many thousands—are assigned to detectives to investigate and to clear up. These assignments are usually made, though not in all cities, by giving the detective a written statement of the complaint. The problem for the head of the detective division is to supervise the handling of each of these individual complaints, and to see that they are not set aside and forgotten. This requires follow-up devices which detective bureaus usually do not have. Spectacular crimes can, of course, be followed carefully enough by the head of the bureau. But it is impossible to keep track of all the minor cases by memory, which is what is being attempted. Progress made on each case ought to be recorded, so that the current status is available to the head of the bureau without the necessity of calling upon the particular detective working on the case,

338   PRACTICE OF MUNICIPAL ADMINISTRATION

CHAP.
XIX

who is the only one under the present prevailing systems that can furnish any of the details. When this lack of records is brought to the attention of the police heads, the usual rejoinder is that policemen are not college graduates or "bookkeepers," and that if they spent their time keeping records no work would be accomplished. On the other hand, how police departments can function properly without adequate records is a mystery. This deficiency of records in police departments is probably due to the fact that police heads have found no urgent need for them, and this failure to appreciate the need and value of records is, in turn, due to the inability of the average police official to use or interpret them.

What adequate records entail

An adequate record system entails careful and complete entry of all matters brought to the attention of the department—crimes, missing persons, vice conditions, accidents, fires, etc.; a system to enable the various divisions and bureau heads to follow up the disposition of all complaints and dispositions, so that the chief and commissioner may with facility know currently what the conditions are in the city, what the department was called upon to do, and what has been accomplished.

Such records must originate with a report of performance of individual policemen. A memorandum book should be furnished each officer by the department, and this book should be periodically examined by a precinct officer. In this book should be recorded the exact time and place of meeting supervisory officers when on patrol, complete data on all arrests, notation of street lamps not burning, dangerous pavements and sidewalks, building permits, time of making reports, and any other facts that may be required or useful.

A somewhat similar record covering the operations of the precinct station should be maintained as the police blotter. This important record should indicate daily all business transacted by the force, assignments of men, delinquencies, complaints by citizens, property received, etc. As an adjunct to the blotter there should be a complete notation of all arrests, with supplementary information.

From these records, the central office can prepare the consolidated daily report picturing the entire operations of the department, complaints received classified by type of offense, arrests made, disposition of arrests, property stolen, property recovered, etc., so accumulated as to be comparable with similar previous periods. Consolidated monthly and yearly reports follow naturally.¹

The crime-prevention methods of the police departments are still essentially those of the monitor. The policemen are assigned to patrol definite districts, or beats, and are held responsible for the enforcement of law and the maintenance of order on the beats under their jurisdiction. In addition to the patrol, the police can prevent crime by continued vigorous efforts to keep a city free of known criminals and undesirables through persistent cleaning up of "hang-outs" and notorious resorts. Even this is becoming less effective, however, through the ability of criminals, by the use of automobiles, to enter a city, accomplish their object, and be miles away while the police are gathering details of the crime. When it is realized that within a few minutes a robbery can be staged and the escape of the robbers practically assured, it is surprising that there are not more crimes of this type.

The police force must still be considered the direct crime prevention agency of the community, but its present methods must be extended and improved, and it must also assume a greater responsibility for the prevention of criminality by closer and better coöperation with other forces in the community. It is already doing this in the field of juvenile delinquency and in the handling of women offenders through policewomen. Mr. Arthur Woods, former police commissioner of New York, recognizing the social causes responsible for crimes, initiated counteracting measures, and Chief August Vollmer, of Berkeley, a student of criminology, is applying preventive methods. To do this requires no change in forms of organization; but it calls for a different viewpoint and a change in the type of administration.

Too much emphasis cannot be placed upon the need for a scientific approach to police organization and administration. Failure at this point has been the outstanding weakness in this field and is largely responsible for the ineffectiveness of the fight against crime. Divorce of police affairs from politics, and continuity of administration by qualified police commissioners, are at once the first steps and the most urgent needs, but they cannot be achieved without intelligent, wholehearted, and continuous public support. The newly created national bureau, organized as a division of the

---

¹ For a detailed statement of desirable records and examples of record forms, see New York Bureau of Municipal Research, *Survey of San Francisco* (1916), 159-272.

Department of Justice at the behest of the police chiefs of the United States, may promote scientific study of the problem. At the present time, however, it is practically impossible to secure accurate data on crime in this country because of varied nomenclature and general lack of reliable records. Progress in every other field of public or private affairs is predicated on exact knowledge of the elements involved in a given situation; and there is no reason to suppose that police departments are exceptions to the rule.

CHAPTER XX

TRAFFIC [1]

Traffic congestion has very likely been a vexatious problem as long as cities have existed. Even ancient and medieval cities must have found difficulty in accommodating pedestrians, sedan chairs, pack horses, wains, coaches, and military cavalcades in their narrow and crooked streets. However, such congestion probably involved nothing more serious than crowding worthy citizens against the wall, and an occasional street bawl. Modern large cities, and particularly the cities of the United States, are confronted with traffic problems that by no means can be compared with those of earlier communities. The ever-increasing density of street traffic, both pedestrian and vehicular, has resulted in a tremendous increase of street hazards and impedance of free movement. Overloaded streets at certain hours are a commonplace in all large cities, and the driving of private vehicles a burden. The manufacturers of motor vehicles are realizing that the long threatened "saturation point" may be a physical rather than an economic one. Cars will not be purchased if there is little convenience to be gained by their use.

These same motor cars have become the leading agency of accidental injury and death by violence. In 1925 the loss in the United States due to highway accidents amounted to 23,900 fatalities, 600,000 serious injuries, and $600,000,000 worth of property destroyed. These figures represent an increase of about eighty

Results of congestion

Loss of life

---

[1] Miller McClintock, *Street Traffic Control* (McGraw-Hill, 1925), covers the subject in detail. See also *The Automobile, Its Province and Problems* (Annals, CXVI, November, 1924) Parts 6 and 7. Current information will be found largely in the reports of the National Conference on Street and Highway Safety; The National Safety Council; The Educational Committees of the National Highway Traffic Association, etc. Traffic surveys of more than ordinary interest are McClellan and Juntersfeld, Inc., *1925 Transportation Survey of the City of Washington, D. C.;* and Technical Advisory Corporation, *City Plan of Cincinnati.* Also consult the *Regional Plan of New York and Its Environs* (Russell Sage Foundation); and *Traffic, Transit, and Transportation* (Chamber of Commerce of the City of Newark, 1926). For current reference see *The American City* (monthly), *The Electric Railway Journal* (weekly), and *Engineering News-Record* (weekly). A valuable recent report is *The Traffic Problem* (Metropolitan Life Insurance Co., 1926).

341

342 PRACTICE OF MUNICIPAL ADMINISTRATION

CHAP. XX

Economic loss

percent over those of 1917.[1] The majority of these accidents result from carelessness or recklessness on the part of motorists and pedestrians.[2] Yet with the increasing dependence on motor vehicles, relief must be secured in a way that will not interfere unduly with the movement of traffic. Fortunately, with the improvement of the mechanical character of automobiles, better regulation of their use, the education of the public as to attendant dangers, and the licensing of drivers, the number of motor fatalities per 100,000 of motor vehicles is being reduced. For example, in 1917 there were 190 fatal accidents for each 100,000 motor vehicles registered. In 1922 this figure had been reduced to 106. In the meantime the total registration of motor vehicles multiplied three times, or to a total in excess of 15,000,000. However, the total number of deaths caused by automobiles is increasing.[3]

Apart from the question of deaths and injuries due to traffic accidents is the economic loss resulting from the retardation and suppression of traffic. These losses arise from the unprofitable use of time and equipment, waste of fuel, and the more expensive types of transportation that must be used to avoid delays. The cost of congestion has been estimated for 1925 at about $2,000,000,-000.[1] To this economic loss must be added the personal inconvenience and annoyance caused by the over-crowding of city streets.

[1] *Second National Conference on Street and Highway Safety.*

[2] "A study of the types of accident which are most numerous is illuminating. Out of nearly 3,000 cases reported to the National Automobile Chamber of Commerce, instances where automobiles struck pedestrians are at the top of the list. Next come collisions between automobiles and street cars. The deadly railroad crossing is fourth, and collisions between automobiles and stationary objects fifth. Far behind come cases wherein cars have run down bicyclists, and, finally, those in which for one reason or another an automobile has turned turtle.

"The list of causes assigned to these accidents is also worth noting. Fast driving comes first, and violating the rules of the road second. Inattention is listed as third, and fourth and fifth are inexperience and confusion—conditions which of course frequently occur together. Intoxication, which so often appears in newspaper headlines as a reason for accident, is at the foot of the list, being responsible for only about one-third as many disasters as speeding.

"Among physical conditions, fog, snow and rain are the chief causes of trouble. Skidding, which is closely allied to at least two of these, is next, and then follow: defects in vehicle, blinding lights on approaching car, inadequate street lights, road defects and confusion resulting from the dimming of headlights. In cases where the pedestrian is held responsible, jaywalking by adults leads all other causes. Then comes improper use of streets by children, confusion on the part of pedestrians, intoxication, physical disability of the pedestrian (the driver of the car having erroneously assumed that his victim can leap out of the way), and stealing rides by boys." *The New Republic* (July 7, 1926), 189.

[3] *Public Roads,* VI, 265 (February, 1926).

TRAFFIC

When highway traffic becomes so great as to preclude the free movement of vehicles, introduces extra accident hazards, and causes economic losses we have "traffic congestion."

CHAP. XX

Such congestion is traceable to four general causes: first, the concentration of population in small areas, made possible by the construction of tall buildings and the centralization of industrial interests; second, certain poor physical characteristics of streets which retard the progress of vehicles and pedestrians; third, the large use of automobiles as a means of transportation, with the augmented space requirements per passenger unit carried, and, lastly, the increased movement of citizens due to broadened business and recreational interests.[1]

General causes of congestion

In addition to the fact that present streets were designed to accommodate a minimum of slow moving vehicles, they were planned particularly to accommodate a population living and working in buildings averaging two stories in height.[2] Today these same arteries must care for the masses of people working in skyscrapers and large industrial establishments, and living in huge apartment houses. Some office buildings alone have a daytime population equal to that of a small city.

Twenty years ago it was a mark of distinction to own a carriage or motor car; today it is an exception for a family not to own one, and in industrial communities there is one automobile for every four or five persons. This motorization of the great majority of families requires a street capacity greatly in excess of that now available in most of our cities.[3] This means that modern communities must rebuild the facilities of an older generation, so that they will serve our changed transportation needs, in so far as is practicable. The change in traffic demands and the loads on our highways have amounted to a revolution, and street systems formerly adequate are now woefully inadequate and becoming more so every day.

The more immediate or physical causes of congestion are numerous. They include narrow streets, made more narrow by the parking and storing of vehicles at the curb, dead-end and offset streets, "bottlenecks" in streets, steep grades, the overloading of focal points and main arteries, the development of concentrated

Immediate causes of congestion

---

[1] See McClintock, *op. cit.*, 1-5.
[2] As one engineer puts it: "We have built forty-story cities on a street plan designed for a three-story town." Quoted by McClintock, *op. cit.*, 3.
[3] Some authorities estimate that street provision must be made for an ultimate registration of one car or truck for every three persons.

344 PRACTICE OF MUNICIPAL ADMINISTRATION

Streets

business, industrial, and amusement centers, the mingling of fast and slow vehicles, "cruising" taxicabs, the mixing of rail and free-wheel vehicles, and indiscriminate pedestrian use of cross walks and sometimes of other space designed for vehicular traffic.

Of these various factors, inadequate street width is the most important. The present day demand on street space for curb loading, parking, and storing has removed from effective use two traffic lanes on streets where these uses are permitted. On most streets this means one-half of the area. As has been said, streets were not planned to care for the amount of traffic now poured into them. They are not wide enough for a sufficient number of traffic lanes; little provision has been made to facilitate or by-pass through traffic;[1] traffic from several streets may be forced into a single street of relatively narrow width; an otherwise satisfactory highway may have a narrow section, or "bottleneck;" dead-ends and awkward offsets exist that slow up traffic movement and create confusion and hazards; and grades are often so steep that streets that could otherwise be used for the relief of congestion are avoided.[2]

Concentration of population

Traffic is further congested by the centralization of business and amusements. The density of population of business districts has increased at a rate far out of proportion to the increase in the city as a whole, and has resulted not only in increasing street loads but in causing peak loads at "rush hours" when men and women are going to and from work or seeking amusement in such areas.

Vehicles of varied character

Another cause of congestion comes from the presence of vehicles of different characteristics. Highways must accommodate both fast and slow moving units. Variation in speed between a passenger automobile and a horse-drawn vehicle or heavy commercial truck has a disastrous effect upon free movement since the slowest moving vehicle in a traffic lane reduces all other vehicles in that lane to its own speed. In this connection, taxicabs, when "cruising,"[3] aggravate the problem in many important streets. In addition, there is a constant interference between rail and free-wheel vehicles due to the obstruction of one by the other. A street car must remain on its tracks and cannot turn out for trucks and vehicles which insist upon using that portion of the street. At the same time, in most communities vehicular traffic must stop for

---

[1] *I.e.*, routing such traffic around the congested areas.
[2] For a discussion of street design, see Chap. XII.
[3] By "cruising" is meant covering a beat over and over again at a relatively slow rate of speed looking for passengers

street cars taking on or discharging passengers, and the presence of safety loading zones creates a permanent or temporary bottleneck at nearly every such stopping place. However, since about eighty percent of movement to and from centers of congestion is by mass transportation units, impedance and restriction to use of private motor cars is warranted and usual. Certain street areas of dense load must be recognized as paramountly required for mass transportation and restricted largely to the use of street cars, busses, and pedestrians.

Add to all this a constant movement of pedestrians in the streets either as "jay-walkers" or on cross walks when the signals are against them, and one has an idea of the traffic confusion met with in cities.

The only theoretically adequate solutions appear to be either the building of two-storied streets, subway or elevated, or complete decentralization of housing, business and industry. Both are impossible of complete realization. However, much relief can be afforded along the following lines: first, the decentralization or by-passing of traffic away from highly congested areas; second, the physical improvement of streets to ease the movement of traffic; and third, traffic regulation, including the licensing of drivers. Too often cities take a short-sighted view and bend their energies upon one, or at best two, of these solutions. Proper remedy to the traffic situation in any city requires a comprehensive survey and analysis of all the elements of the problem.[1]

One means of greatly relieving the traffic situation would be to eliminate pleasure cars and through traffic from the congested area at times when the whole area is demanded for use by pedestrians, mass transportation units, and commercial vehicles. In this connection it must be recognized that the traffic flow is unevenly spread over the day. In the morning a major part of the traffic is moving in from the residential sections to the business center. In the evening "rush hour" the movement is reversed, and, if anything, concentrated into a shorter period of time. Similarly, there is a marked seasonal fluctuation in northern cities, where many drivers put up their cars for the winter. Fortunately, some leveling of peak loads has been brought about by industries, business houses, and officers "staggering" their hours of employment in realization of the fact that it is almost physically impossible for everybody to be at work exactly at the same hour in the morning

[1] McClintock, *op. cit.*, Chap. 2.

346   PRACTICE OF MUNICIPAL ADMINISTRATION

or to leave at exactly the same hour in the afternoon. Large industries may arrange their working periods so that their employees arrive and leave their place of business over a reasonable period of time. Offices may open and close fifteen minutes earlier or later than the regular conventional hour, with a decided effect upon the facility with which their employees are transported to and from their homes.

Zoning

The zoning programs undertaken by many communities, and being considered by practically all of them, have as one of their main features the distribution or decentralization of office buildings and stores over a wide area so that narrow, inadequate streets will not be chronically overloaded. Cities can also relieve their congested sections by building important public structures at points somewhat removed from existing foci. In a similar way, the moving of large retail stores and the development of new shopping centers may have a decided effect upon the number of people that need to enter the highly congested area.

By-pass highways

A further means of traffic relief is the construction of by-pass highways. When improved national and state highways were first proposed, every city made a bid to have its main thoroughfares linked into such routes. It is now recognized that such connections are a detriment rather than a benefit; that the number of purchases made by tourists passing through a city amount to little; that problems of health and morals are created by the presence of the modern motor gypsy; and finally that the increase in congestion and the problem of its relief overbalances any immediate benefit. As a result, cities are now promoting by-pass highways whereby through traffic will be deflected away from areas of congestion. Such by-pass highways may be supplemented by tourist camps properly controlled that will accommodate those tourists who really wish to stop and patronize the city's business institutions.[1]

Crosstown routes

Crosstown and belt line streets connecting one important section of the city with another without passing through the congested area are now recognized as eminently desirable, and are supported by the business interests. It is realized in part that a passing vehicle is not necessarily a potential customer, and that the presence of a large number of vehicles in a business street obstructs trade rather than benefits it. Even cities with radial street layouts,

[1] See p. 304.

TRAFFIC

which ordinarily facilitate traffic, have been compelled to provide loops that will relieve congestion at focal points.

Intelligent action with respect to facilitating the movement of traffic through improvements in the physical characteristics of the overloaded streets, is almost always necessarily predicated on a careful traffic survey. The detailed technique of such a survey is tedious, and it is perhaps sufficient to indicate some of its more salient features. Such a survey should include a study of all the elements of traffic flow so that the administrator may have a clear understanding of the movement of persons and commodities over the streets of a city, and of certain specific factors such as volume, origin, character, and destination of the traffic; the growth and distribution of population and the distribution of the ownership of vehicles; standing vehicles; the street plan; and the location and cause of street hazards.[1]

Street paving is probably one of the first improvements that should receive the attention of the public officer. Vehicles, and particularly automobiles, avoid badly paved streets. Frequently an unexpected amount of relief is secured by the proper paving of heretofore little used highways. In this connection it is sometimes desirable to remove street car tracks and re-route street car traffic so that an entire highway may be reclaimed for vehicular use.

There is, of course, a decided difference in the running and acceleration speeds of street cars and automobiles. On the other hand street cars stop at practically every intersection,[2] and it is usually unlawful to pass them if they are taking on or discharging passengers.[3] In consequence, a line of automobiles will form behind the car and move with it rather than with the traffic signals, or will file past it at a reduced rate of speed. It has been estimated that the elimination of street cars on four-traffic-lane streets increases the vehicular capacity of the street by at least fifty percent. However, this increase of vehicular traffic should not be confused with that of passenger capacity, since street cars require

---

[1] See *Transportation Survey of Washington, D. C., 1925.*

[2] Particularly in downtown areas. In the residence districts of many cities the "skip-stop" plan is employed, or more logically, the stop at every third street intersection.

[3] Practice varies. Some cities permit vehicles to pass, accepting the hazard to passengers in lieu of that which comes from vehicles speeding to pass the street car before it stops. Generally vehicles may pass standing cars at intersections at which an officer or automatic control is located.

a much smaller road area per person carried than does the ordinary automobile.

After the elimination of car tracks, where possible, and the improvement of pavements, comes the matter of traffic lanes. Unfortunately, in days gone by streets were laid out arbitrarily with various street widths. It is now realized that street capacity is measured not so much by linear width as by ability to accommodate two, four, or six lines of moving vehicles. Traffic lanes require ten feet each, and must be in an even number. For this reason nearly all cities are engaged in street widening—in cutting back the vacant space between the sidewalk and the curb; in moving sidewalks and shade trees back to the private property line; and often in condemning strips of private property for widening purposes. This process is expensive, particularly so, when private property already built upon must be taken. Cities are now experimenting with the establishment of setback lines, rear lot condemnations, and other devices that will permit the ultimate widening of streets without enormous cost.[1]

The practice of arcading sidewalks has not been extensively undertaken in this country, but is a measure that must be given serious consideration in the near future. Minor alteration of buildings so as to permit sidewalks being set back on private property can often be accomplished at small expense, leaving the entire upper portion intact and changing but little the display features of the store fronts. Such an elimination of sidewalk and curb space places the entire width of the street at the disposal of vehicular traffic.

In connection with street widening, consideration must be given to streets that vary in width. In many instances streets will be found which suddenly narrow, expanding again after a short distance. The traffic on such streets is eventually restricted by the bottleneck thus formed. The elimination of bottlenecks is usually essential, and on heavily traveled streets is imperative, regardless of cost. What can be done to remedy the bottleneck effect of safety zones, and particularly of the raised safety zone, is still an open question. These zones are a decided deterrent to the free movement of traffic, particularly when the city ordinances prevent vehicular movement to their left. Some cities have avoided the difficulty by widening the streets at these points so that the paved area is not restricted. This relief is possible in only a limited

[1] See Chap. XII.

number of instances and does not obviate the necessity of vehicles modifying their direction of travel.

Offset streets present a problem similar to that created by bottlenecks. These situations arise from the careless planning which prevails when real estate developers are permitted full control of their planning without consideration of community interests. The immediate problem of the real estate promoter is to secure a certain number of lots from a given area of ground, and his problem is often made easier if he can entirely ignore the connection of the new streets platted with the streets that are already in existence. Offset streets create not only traffic congestion but unusual traffic hazards. Where such streets exist it is often necessary to condemn all or portions of corner lots in order to permit a degree of straightening, or if this is not feasible it is sometimes possible to move back the curb on opposite sides of the street so as to make a more direct approach. Streets that cross one another at right angles cause a delay in traffic, but this delay is reduced to a minimum and the hazard is much less than in many streets that enter a main thoroughfare at a lesser angle. It is possible, however, to facilitate traffic on diagonal streets by a proper set back of the curb which will facilitate the right hand turn of vehicles. Streets entering at a diagonal can also be arranged so that the entering flow of traffic will interfere at a minimum with the lines of new traffic already established. This arrangement of diagonal streets entering at different angles is not a matter of guesswork but of mathematical measurement, and should be given careful study by some one familiar with traffic control before modifications of existing conditions are undertaken.[1]

Sharp curves in streets are also a traffic hindrance because they do not correspond to the deflection of an automobile from a straight line when rounding a curve at ordinary rates of speed. Such curves should be modified.

Grades frequently serve the same purpose by slowing up all traffic at a particular point and thus preventing the full use of the street up to and beyond the grade. Steep grades, which are frequently slippery at certain times of the year, are also a decided deterrent to street use. Motorists will instinctively route themselves around any street on which they are compelled to ascend or descend a steep hill.

[1] See Herbert S. Swan and George W. Tuttle, ''Land Subdivisions and the City Plan,'' *Nat. Mun. Rev.*, Supplement, XIV, 435-462 (July, 1925).

350   PRACTICE OF MUNICIPAL ADMINISTRATION

Traffic regulation

Traffic regulation, important as it is in itself, should be undertaken after or in conjunction with certain broad efforts to cause a deconcentration of traffic and the elimination of all possible physical obstructions. As has been said, cities too often emphasize traffic regulation without considering the other elements which contribute to the reduction of congestion. It has been said that traffic control consists in passing by artificial regulation through existing streets, generally of inadequate capacity, with safety to both passengers and pedestrians, a larger volume of traffic than the streets would accommodate were the movement of vehicles and pedestrians left uncontrolled.[1] Much of the present regulation unduly interferes with traffic by extending the use of stop and go signals beyond required hours, by installing automatic or manual stop and go signals where warning flashers only are needed, by failure to synchronize traffic movements, by permitting or requiring street cars to stop at too frequent intervals, and in other ways.

Parking

The greatest impedance to the free use of streets is caused by stopped, loading, or parked vehicles. It is because such practices are necessary, and at the same time very inconvenient, that the regulation of standing vehicles becomes a very serious problem. A vehicle in the street has a right to stop as well as a right to move, but the demand for street use for moving vehicles must be given precedence over that for stopped vehicles; and hence the least beneficial use of streets, i.e., parking, is commonly curtailed in congested districts. A stopped vehicle standing at the curb all day occupies space that might be utilized by a thousand moving vehicles. Also, if streets are widened at great expense and then turned into spaces for the storing of vehicles during the day, no particular advantage has been gained. When parking restrictions were first placed in effect merchants objected for fear of customers being driven away. It is now recognized that when the space in front of places of business is used merely for the storage of vehicles, such interference with the loading and unloading of passengers is a greater handicap.[2] In large cities the rational solution perhaps is to prohibit parking on certain "mass transportation" streets, where street car, bus, and pedestrian loads are heavy. This pro-

---

[1] 1913 Report of the London Traffic Branch of the Board of Trade.
[2] See *Vehicular Traffic Congestion and Retail Business* (U. S. Dept. of Commerce, Trade Information Bulletin No. 394, April, 1926). See also for a treatment of principles involved "To Park or Not to Park," *The American City*, XXXV, 461-464 (October, 1926).

hibition should not prevent motor cars from stopping to discharge and receive passengers. On streets having a lighter load use, limited time parking should be permitted, to allow a citizen to transact business in the shops and offices of the business section. This time period should be uniform over large areas, an hour being recommended.[1]

In connection with parking, some cities are experimenting with the prohibition of parking on the side of the street carrying the burden of traffic during the morning and afternoon hours, respectively. In theory this should work very well, but in actual practice it requires an undue amount of education to get people to comply. Many cities are now prohibiting parking on main arterial streets in the hours of acute congestion, particularly between four-thirty and six-thirty. At all events, parking privileges must be limited and regulated if the traffic demands on highways are to be met.

After the removal of street obstructions of all types, perhaps the most important question that confronts the administrator with respect to traffic regulation is its speed. On the subject of speed control a great amount of nonsense has been perpetrated at the expense of both the pedestrian public and the automobile driver. In the early days of the automobile the speed of horse-drawn vehicles was ordinarily the guide of municipalities in determining speed limits, and often in travelling through the country one runs across villages at the entrance of which warnings are posted that a speed of eight or ten miles an hour is the maximum permitted.[2] With the rapidly increasing number of accidents due to the use of motor vehicles, it is only natural that many people should immediately consider speed as one of the principal causes. Of course many accidents are the result of machines moving at an excessive speed and being unable to stop when difficulty arises. In many more cases, however, the accident is due to the machine not being under control and has no connection whatsoever with a particular rate of speed; or the accident may be entirely beyond the control

---

[1] If parking regulations are not enforced by regular patrol they are useless, and short-time parking, i.e., five or ten minutes, is purposeless, because it cannot be controlled.

[2] Village speed regulations frequently apply solely to the unwary stranger, and are designed for revenue only. A disgraceful situation is created by the numerous small communities that secure a substantial proportion of their incomes by fining tourists for minor traffic infractions, and by the rural constables and justices of the police who secure a dishonest livelihood by the same process.

352   PRACTICE OF MUNICIPAL ADMINISTRATION

CHAP.
XX

of the driver regardless of speed. Gradually realizing these facts, cities are approaching the problem of speed from two angles. Either particular areas are designated in which certain speeds will be permitted—for example, fifteen miles per hour in the congested business sections and twenty miles per hour in residential sections; or a definite maximum rate of speed is fixed and supplementary legislation enacted against reckless driving. Under certain circumstances, a speed of twenty-five miles an hour or greater with the machine under proper control may be perfectly safe.

When rates of speed are fixed too low to facilitate the maximum movement of traffic, the police ignore violations and tolerate an arbitrary speed limit which must be reached before an arrest will be made. No definite conclusions can be made as to what is the proper rate. It has been conclusively proven that the greatest amount of traffic is not borne by a street where the machines are operated at high speeds. The reason for this is obvious when one considers the amount of space that must intervene between fast moving machines if they are to be kept under control. In other words, the slower the rate of movement of machines, down to about twelve miles per hour, the larger the number of vehicles that can be put through a given street area within a given time.[1] At present there is a tendency to prohibit reckless driving, interpreting some specific rate of speed as prima facie evidence of recklessness in case of an accident, and to place the entire responsibility for safe driving upon the driver and the police officer.[2]

Speed controls

The best control over reckless driving is brought about through the use of uniformed motorized patrols. The old practice of taking these men out of uniform leads the offender to feel that he is being apprehended by some disreputable trick and destroys whatever moral effect might come from the presence of a recognized authority. It is believed nowadays that no self-respecting administrator will resort to trick cars and trick officers with the idea of apprehending the offender through these disguises. Reckless driving cannot be eliminated unless the patrol officer is in full uniform

---

[1] This rule holds only when the traffic saturation point has been reached.

[2] However, it should be noted that the National Conference on Street and Highway Safety, during its last conference, after long debate decided upon definite limits as follows: fifteen miles per hour for congested districts; twenty miles per hour for residential sections; and thirty-five miles per hour for the open country.

TRAFFIC

serving a constant notice to all who pass that the road is under regular surveillance. Some cities, and particularly villages, have indulged in speed traps, timing the passage of automobiles over a certain section of the road. This again is only a means of apprehending offenders and not of preventing the offense. Fortunately, in some states there is a tendency to remove the main state highways from the control of local officers and to place them under the jurisdiction of competent state police.[1]

As a means of reducing accidents, and at the same time expediting the flow of traffic on main arteries, many cities have recently instituted the so-called "stop-street" or "through street" plan. Investigation shows that the major portion of all accidents occur at street intersections where two automobiles dispute the right of way. At first, rules were put into effect that automobiles approaching from the right should have the right of way. However, no automobilist was ever sure that the person approaching from the cross street was going to obey this regulation. The faster moving vehicles would ordinarily take the right of way and accidents resulted. In fact, any such regulation is usually worse than no regulation at all. Then came the stop-street provision, which is usually limited to principal thoroughfares and provides that every machine entering that street shall come to a full stop. This regulation has come into vogue only within the last two years and its use has spread rapidly. As yet, however, its effectiveness requires confirmation over a longer period. Too often, drivers operating on the principal highway assume that because it is a through street it becomes a speedway and that pedestrians and automobiles attempting to cross it have no rights whatsoever. On streets in which a signal system can be used at convenient intersections the stop-streets will, of course, work satisfactorily, since an opportunity to cross will be given at each turn of the signals. The stop-street should not be looked upon as a cure-all for certain traffic problems, or installed where unnecessary.[2]

To eliminate the difficulties that pedestrians have in crossing through streets, Los Angeles has passed an ordinance giving every

---

[1] The police and the courts are gradually realizing that the offense to be regulated is that of reckless driving, regardless of how that dereliction may be defined in law. A legal rate of speed may be reckless under many traffic conditions; a high rate of speed may be safe under others.

[2] Too many stop-streets slow up traffic. A preferable substitute is a warning sign that the motorist is approaching a heavily travelled thoroughfare.

354 PRACTICE OF MUNICIPAL ADMINISTRATION

Automatic control

pedestrian in the residential section the powers of a traffic officer. The pedestrian has only to raise his hand and stop all traffic while crossing a street. The practicability of such regulation is open to question.[1]

Examining the problem of traffic regulation in the light of the definition given earlier, the chief object of the administrator should be to keep a steady stream of vehicles moving through the street. This is, of course, not possible in any absolute sense because of the necessity that other vehicles cross the traffic stream, and traffic entanglements will arise at intersections unless they are under proper control. It has been customary, therefore, to station traffic officers with semaphores at prominent intersections, who at intervals stop traffic in one direction and permit traffic in the opposite direction to flow past. Such a provision results in a minimum of traffic confusion and delay, but the financial outlay of such control is large. Under these circumstances it is only natural for the administrator to look for some mechanical apparatus that can be substituted for the policeman. This has been found in the centrally controlled stop and go signal system, employing colored lights.[2]

The platoon system

Such a system provides for traffic lights which are automatically controlled from a traffic tower or central headquarters, and which move traffic over a given number of blocks at regular intervals.[3] As a rule, these lights are synchronized so that traffic will move for four or five blocks without a stop and then into another area. Frequently, the synchronization can be such that a machine moving at a normal rate of speed can start in the downtown area and move a long distance into the residential section without being stopped at all. This is called "progressive operation." It must be borne in mind, however, that this kind of regulation provides

Individual timing

for a wave motion of traffic. During the interval when traffic is blocked large street areas are not in use. At the same time a uniform period of stop is required at each cross street regardless

---

[1] The legality of the Los Angeles ordinance has also been questioned.

[2] These lamps may be suspended overhead, located on pedestals in the center of the street, or similarly on diagonal corners. The last two plans are preferable, choice being determined by the width of the street. Some authorities object decidedly to obstructions in the center of heavy traffic streets and also to diagonal corner signals, believing that the best method is a four-way signal suspended in the center of the intersection or four one-way signals placed at the corners. See K. W. Mackall, "Operation and Control of Traffic Signal System," *The American City*, XXXV (November, 1926).

[3] Few cities have tested the results of automatic control by actual surveys of conditions before and after installation.

of the amount of traffic.¹ On this account, the wave-like motion of traffic is being questioned by some authorities, and there is an inclination to synchronize each individual light on the basis of the amount of cross street traffic that may be moving. This is known as "coördinate operation."

Recently a form of rotary traffic control has been patented and is in experimental use.² This plan involves the maintenance of four signal lamps at each intersection, one on each corner. When one of these lamps is at "go" the remaining three are at "stop." This permits the traffic on the open street to proceed in three directions, left turn, straight ahead, and right turn without interference from vehicles coming in the opposite direction. After a proper interval the street to the right is opened and the others closed. If the student will draw a rough diagram of a street intersection with arrows indicating the movement of traffic as described, certain of the advantages of this proposal, particularly on streets where a left hand turn is required, will be apparent. The lamps at a number of adjacent intersections can, of course, be synchronized.

To date, automatic signals have not been as effective in decreasing accidents as was hoped. Many cities employ a three-color lamp—red, green, and yellow—the yellow being an indication that the signal is about to change, affording time for traffic making a turn to do so, and allowing the street intersections to be cleared.³ Unfortunately, many drivers have interpreted the yellow signal as a warning to speed up their machines in order that they may get across before the stopped traffic can be started. In consequence there have been many accidents. There seems now to be a tendency to adopt only the two-light signal, red and green, sometimes so equipped that the lights in all directions go red at certain intervals giving the intersection time to clear. This system of permitting all lights to go red is also useful in cases of fire. One of the principal objections to the automatic signals which arose in the early years of their use was that fire trucks, police wagons, and ambulances would uniformly disregard the signals and be a prolific cause of accidents. However, if all lights can be thrown to danger along a fire route, this difficulty is avoided.

[1] In a properly operated system the timing of the lamps should be modified a number of times a day to accommodate traffic changes.
[2] This plan was developed by H. E. Young and E. S. Taylor. See *Engineering News-Record* (May 27, 1926), 858.
[3] Either right or left turn, although most cities permit a right turn without waiting for the "go" signal, providing the vehicle has come to a stop.

356 PRACTICE OF MUNICIPAL ADMINISTRATION

CHAP. XX

Left turns

Another difficulty of expediting traffic arises from the left-hand turn. A driver making a left-hand turn must cut across two lines of traffic and in doing so obstructs one line which has the right of way. For this reason, in many cities left-hand turns in congested sections are prohibited. This has the advantage of moving traffic rapidly, but it frequently requires a vehicle to add to the general congestion by going several blocks out of its way before it is permitted to make a turn. Ordinarily, in making a left-hand turn the driver is required to go directly to the center of the street, making the turn immediately if traffic will permit, and if not, waiting until the intersection is clear. Some cities require the driver to go to the extreme edge of the street before making the turn, a practical plan only on controlled intersections.

One-way streets

Most cities make use of one-way streets, a street in which traffic moves in one direction only. Very narrow streets, particularly those twenty feet or less in width, should be made one-way streets, as should narrow thoroughfares on which a single street car line is placed. All such streets should be prominently marked, and adjacent streets should be provided which will carry traffic in the opposite direction.

Segregation of vehicles

A street will discharge the maximum amount of traffic when all vehicles in that street are moving at a uniform rate of speed. Unfortunately, this situation rarely, if ever, exists. Slow-moving vehicles are mixed with rapid-moving ones, and these slow-moving vehicles create the bottleneck which delays the balance of traffic. For this reason it is often provided that slow-moving vehicles shall keep close to the right curb and that rapidly moving vehicles shall keep to the left. This regulation is difficult of enforcement, and, where possible, cities provide certain through streets upon which slow-moving traffic, particularly trucks and heavily laden vehicles, are prohibited.

Regulation of drivers

In addition to the regulation of vehicles, there must be some control of drivers to insure reasonable competency. State laws or city ordinances ordinarily provide that every person regularly operating a motor vehicle shall satisfactorily pass an examination given by designated authorities—usually the police. This examination is in two parts—physical and informational. The successful applicant must be physically capable of operating a machine, *i.e.*, have proper use of hands and feet, be able to distinguish colors, and read traffic signs easily. He must also be familiar with the current traffic code. In the near future, it may be expected that

TRAFFIC

such examinations will include a test of mental ability, particularly speed of physical reactions to mental stimulus.[1] Provision is made for the suspension of the driving license of chronic or serious traffic offenders, and driving without a license means serious difficulties.

Control of taxicabs

The general control of taxicabs is not easily secured. Being almost constantly on the road, drivers chafe at traffic regulations. Competition for business is usually keen, and a certain type of taxi driver is a notorious violator of more serious laws in an effort to secure illicit profits. As a means of regulation taxicabs are always required to have a license in addition to that required of ordinary motor vehicles, and drivers are examined and licensed by the police or other authorities. Locations on a public highway at which taxicabs may stand while awaiting call are designated by the council and these locations are open legally to any passenger vehicle for hire. In actual practice, however, the taxicab companies agree among themselves as to the occupants of these stands. Such agreements are necessary if peace and order are to be maintained, and when not entered into voluntarily, the police will in an extra-legal fashion designate the locations that the several companies are to occupy.[2]

Traffic codes

Ordinarily, city traffic is governed by both state and municipal codes, one supplementing the other. These codes are usually rather complex and somewhat confusing to the vehicle driver. This is particularly true for the reason that there is no uniformity in the traffic codes of cities and the cross-country traveler is constantly liable to difficulties with the police of strange cities, and is likely to slow down traffic if he shows a proper desire to be cautious. Efforts are now being made to draft a reasonably uniform code that will be adopted nation wide by important municipalities. Much has been done in this direction by the National Conference on Street and Highway Safety, and it may be expected that the model code now under consideration will be generally accepted.

Traffic department

Traffic regulation is ordinarily an activity of the police department. There is no particular reason why this should be so, except that in the early days a few policemen were assigned to the task,

---

[1] In some jurisdictions an actual driving test is given. On the whole, the examinations are superficial, and at best cannot eliminate the driver whose defect is a moral one. The most reckless motorists are usually "good" drivers.

[2] Jitney cars create a problem because of the large area of street occupied per passenger carried. More progressive cities have barred this type of vehicle.

358   PRACTICE OF MUNICIPAL ADMINISTRATION

CHAP. XX

which has now grown to one of the major jobs of the police department. There is little relation between traffic control and the apprehension of ordinary offenders, and no doubt the sensible direction of traffic requires an entirely different attitude of mind and training from that necessary to the police officer engaged in other branches of public protection. Possibly it would be better part of wisdom to create a department devoted exclusively to traffic matters and entirely separate from the regular police administration.

Accident investigation

Traffic control is not complete if it does not provide for thorough investigation of every accident. Usually this work is undertaken by a separate bureau within the traffic department. This bureau should have officers on detail constantly, who, upon being notified that an accident has taken place, will immediately be dispatched to the scene. Here, such officers can secure the names and addresses of persons who have been involved, learn the details of the case, and may apprehend the person who is obviously at fault, or arrange for informal examination of the parties involved at a convenient time.[1] Such investigations not only serve as a means of locating guilt, and punishing drivers who have been at fault, but indicate the causes of accidents, so that they ultimately may be eliminated.

Violation bureaus

One of the innovations that has become necessary in order to control the increased number of traffic violations is the violation bureau, or clearing house for complaints of traffic violations. In the early history of traffic control, violators of every kind were brought before the regular police court authorities for trial and punishment. This procedure cluttered up already congested courts and made a farce of this particular branch of the administration of justice. On mornings devoted to traffic cases in a large city, hundreds of offenders would be in court, with numerous police officers. Frequently, an offender would spend the morning, and sometimes an entire day, waiting for trial, which usually resulted in a plea of guilty and the imposition of a small fine. Officers were taken away from their regular duty and frequently compelled to appear at times that were highly inconvenient to them.

As a result, some police departments have installed a police bureau which takes the place of the regular court in the punish-

[1] The most nimble-minded party to an accident will usually demand that the other be arrested regardless of the circumstances, knowing that the defendant has a hard time in traffic courts. The writer saw this trick worked by a trio of bandits, its success being marred by the arrival of pursuing officers.

ment of minor offenses. It is recognized that such a procedure is largely extra-legal and has no established place in law, yet at the same time it is accepted generally because of the pressing necessity of some alternative to a more formal judicial hearing. As ordinarily organized, the police bureau keeps a record of all notifications to appear because of violations. At the bureau the offender may tacitly admit his guilt by paying a small fee, varying according to the nature and number of the offenses. The notices given the offender state that unless payment is made within a limited period a regular summons will be issued and the offender will be brought to court for a more lengthy procedure. Most traffic violators will prefer to appear at the bureau, pay a nominal fine, and dismiss the whole matter without demanding a formal trial. As a result, officers are more willing to keep a full check on traffic violations, since they are not compelled to appear in court against the violator, and a more thorough control of traffic is had.[1]

The principal difficulty with violation bureaus is that a number of cases can be "fixed" by knowing somebody in authority. It is an unfortunate reflection upon American justice that in almost every city a person who knows an alderman, the mayor, a high police officer, a clerk in some of the courts—or even knows somebody who knows one of these individuals—can have his ticket torn up. Probably there is no cure for this situation except the gradual development among police authorities of a high standard of rectitude, based on the perception that special favors to citizens merely break down law, destroy the morale of the force, and add to the problems of the department.

[1] For a discussion of traffic courts, see p. 374.

CHAPTER XXI

COURTS [1]

Responsibility for administration of justice

The procedure and results of the administration of justice are determined by laws, jurisdictions, and personnel usually far removed from the control of the municipal administrator. In fact, it is difficult to indicate the lines of demarcation between justice as administered by cities and by other governmental units—by counties, by the state, and by the national government. The courts are usually either state or national institutions, but practically, the administration of justice very much concerns the municipality, and agencies employed and paid by the city are actively engaged in it.

Nature of offenses

In the interest of such clarity as may be obtained in this maze of law enforcement, it is necessary to enumerate the character of offenses that can be committed and locate the respective jurisdictions that deal with them. Legal derelictions, of course, vary in each community, depending largely upon the terms of state laws. In general, however, offenses may be roughly designated as against public peace, public health and morals, persons and property. A suggested detailed classification is as follows: [2]

> Offenses against the safety of the state—treason, sedition, desecration of the flag, impersonating an officer, etc.
> Interfering with the administration of justice—perjury, contempt of court, interfering with an officer, resisting an officer, concealment of crime, etc.
> Disorderly conduct—disorderly acts, loitering, etc.
> Drunkenness

---

[1] See *Criminal Justice in Cleveland* (Cleveland Foundation, 1922), including the sections by R. H. Smith and H. B. Ehrmann, "Judicial Administration"; A. M. Kales, "Legal Education"; M. K. Wisehart, "Newspapers and Criminal Justice"; Alfred Bettman and Howard F. Burns, "Prosecution"; and Herman M. Adler, "Psychiatry and Medical Relations"; and R. H. Smith, *Justice and the Poor* (Carnegie Foundation, 1919). Raymond Moley, ed., *The Missouri Crime Survey* (Macmillan, 1926), is a state-wide study of criminal courts in felony cases. Current reference should be made to the *Journal of Criminal Law and Criminology* (quarterly); and the *Journal of the American Judicature Society* (bi-monthly).

[2] From an unpublished study of 250,000 arrests made by the Detroit Bureau of Governmental Research.

Begging and vagrancy
Gambling offenses—gambling and operating gambling rooms
Violating regulatory statutes relating to vehicles, drugs, immigration, interstate commerce, health, plumbing, food, labor, game, post office, etc.
Illegal sale of liquor
Simple dishonesty—simple larceny, grand larceny, larceny from the person, theft of automobile, etc.
Dishonesty by fraud—embezzlement, removing contract property, receiving stolen goods, false pretenses, forgery, larceny by conversion, extortion, counterfeiting, etc.
Offenses against persons with violence—robbery, assault and battery, carrying concealed weapons, felonious assault, threats, careless use of fire-arms, kidnapping, abortion, etc.
Murder—murder, manslaughter, assault to murder, etc.
Destruction of property—malicious injury, arson, etc.
Offenses against morality—prostitution, adultery, pandering, bigamy, etc.
Family neglect—non-support, abandonment, etc.

These offenses arise out of violations of national, state, and city laws. Certain acts may be a violation of only one set of prohibitions, while others may violate all three. For example, failure to clean a sidewalk may be contrary to a city ordinance; excessive speed with an automobile may violate laws of both city and state regulating speed; and the selling of intoxicating liquors may violate city, state, and national regulations. The courts can deal only with offenses over which they have specific jurisdiction; enforcement officers, however, and particularly city police, are really state officers, and are concerned with violations of both state and city laws, and with many national laws the violation of which is also a state offense. Enforcement officers of the state, *i.e.*, city police, deputy sheriffs, and state police, ordinarily coöperate closely with national agents, and persons apprehended by one of them are turned over to the proper authorities. *Jurisdiction of law enforcement officers*

For judicial purposes, offenses are of three general types—misdemeanors, felonies, and treason. Misdemeanors are minor offenses violating a city ordinance or a state law; felonies are more serious offenses violating a state law. Misdemeanors are punished by a small fine, or possibly confinement for a short time in a corrective institution; felonies are punished by heavy fines or confinement for a longer period in a state institution, or both. Treason need not be considered in this discussion. *Misdemeanors and felonies*

For the trial of misdemeanor cases that arise from the viola-

362 PRACTICE OF MUNICIPAL ADMINISTRATION

CHAP. XXI

Misdemeanant courts

tion of city ordinances, and state laws, the states have invariably permitted cities to set up courts of limited jurisdiction known generally as police courts, which usualy are not courts of record.[1] The number of justices in these courts ranges from one to several, depending upon the population of the community. These justices are usually elected, although in some instances they are appointed by the mayor or city council. Salaries and other expenses are ordinarily paid by the city.

Felony courts

Felony cases are seldom tried in city courts, but rather in the tribunals organized for a county or larger area. These courts are known by a variety of names, e.g., courts of common pleas, circuit courts, county courts, district courts, etc., and usually have both criminal and civil jurisdiction. The judges are chosen by the voters of the judicial district which may be a city, but more often a county, or several counties. They receive a relatively higher compensation than police justices, and usually serve for a substantially longer term.

The breakdown of law enforcement

The serious situation with respect to crime in this country has been ascribed to diverse causes, many of them social, such as city life with its love of luxury, the lack of religious education and home training, unassimilated foreign populations, etc.; some governmental, such as the lack of progress in police methods, failure of correctional means, lack of directness in judicial procedure, and not least, the complexity, ambiguity, and impertinence of the law, with consequent lack of respect for it. Particularly at the doors of the courts is thrown the charge that technicalities, delays, unwise treatment of offenders, absence of coöperation with the police and prosecuting authorities, and other abuses are making efforts of law enforcement futile.[2] To understand the degree of justice with which this charge is made it is necessary to examine the procedure under which courts operate, whether handling misdemeanant or felony cases.

Judicial procedure: The complainant and warrant

Judicial procedure begins with the issuance of a warrant calling for the arrest of a person suspected of an offense. To be sure, a great many people accused of misdemeanors appear in court upon a written summons of the police, but do so only because to demand a warrant would involve them in legal routine which they desire to avoid if possible. A warrant is obtained by the police prosecutor,

---

[1] I.e., no permanent, legal record is made of the testimony.
[2] Wellman makes the point that much delay is due to lack of knowledge of law on the part of attornyes.

or by other complainant appearing before a judge and charging that a misdemeanor or a felony has been committed, this charge being in the nature of a complaint. The judicial authorities must decide that there are reasons for believing that an offense has been committed, and such decision may require an investigation by the judge or by the staff of the prosecutor. Upon satisfactory information, the complaint will be attested and a warrant will be issued.

CHAP. XXI

The warrant is turned over to the police, whose duty it is to apprehend and arrest the persons named. The arrest may involve the actual taking of the person to some place of incarceration where he may be held until taken to court; or, if the charge is a misdemeanor, he may be merely notified to appear in court at a designated time. Persons may be formally arrested without a warrant only when apprehended in the act of committing an offense, or when under suspicion of certain offenses of a grave nature. Even in such cases a warrant must, or should, be secured immediately after arrest. This does not mean that police departments do not arrest many individuals each year, and hold them for investigation or lodge some minor charge against them until an investigation of their character can be made. These actions on the part of the police are, however, extra-legal and apply largely to persons who are not in a position to protect themselves. Since "floaters," "bums," and itinerant workers are notoriously frequent offenders and this is the class mainly harassed by such action, this extra-legal police activity is not often criticized by the public.[1]

The arrest

It is seldom necessary to admit misdemeanant cases to bail. If a warrant is issued, or the offender is in court upon a summons, he is almost immediately thereafter brought to trial. The arraignment, plea, and trial all take place in one procedure, unless time is necessary for the accused to prepare for trial. If a continuance of the case is allowed, the accused is ordinarily released on personal recognizance.

The trial of misdemeanant cases

In misdemeanor cases the city is represented by a member of the corporation counsel's staff, or is supposed to be. In fact, such officer is usually present in court but takes part in trials only as required in exceptional cases. In many states a jury trial is not permitted and the process is very informal. A number of persons appear before the judge in procession: the complainant—officer or citizen—is present; a few questions are addressed to the accuser

[1] See John B. Waite, "Protection from the Police," *Atlantic Monthly*, CXXXVIII, 162-168 (August, 1926).

and the accused; the judge renders his decision; and sentence is pronounced if the accused is found guilty. If the accused is dissatisfied with the verdict or sentence imposed by the judge he may ordinarily, within a limited time, take an appeal to a higher court.[1]

If the person arrested is held by the police for a serious offense, he should be taken before the court without delay. It is then the duty of the judge to inform the prisoner of the nature of the offense with which he is charged, to ask him concerning his innocence or guilt, and to fix the amount of bail if the offense is a bailable one, all of which constitutes the arrangement. The right to bail may be denied for murder, where the guilt appears to be clear, and for certain other serious offenses. The amount of the bail must be reasonable, its object being to permit the accused person liberty and yet insure his presence to answer any prosecution growing out of the charge on which he is accused.

The mere issuance of a warrant, followed by the arrest, arraignment, and fixing of bail, is not sufficient to bring a person accused of a felony to trial. There must be sufficient evidence to warrant a trial, and the presence of this evidence must be determined by judicial examination. In most states this examination is conducted by a grand jury to which the prosecutor presents the evidence on behalf of the state, the accused not being allowed to appear or to present witnesses. If the evidence indicates that there is reasonable grounds for suspicion of guilt, an indictment is brought. This indictment is followed by a new warrant and a new fixing of bail, and in due time the case will be set for trial.

Some states have done away with indictment by grand jury. At the time of arraignment, the accused is asked whether or not he desires an examination. At this examination no testimony is introduced on behalf of the defendant, as the proceeding is designed chiefly to determine whether the state has sufficient cause for making the charge against the accused. In some jurisdictions, after the examination—or after the arraignment, if examination is waived by the defendant—a formal accusation is drafted by the prosecuting attorney which is known as the information, and which corresponds to an indictment by the grand jury. After the filing of this formal accusation with the courts by the prosecuting

[1] See John F. Dillon, "Municipal Courts," *Commentaries on the Law of Municipal Corporations* II, 1115-1136; and Eugene McQuillin, "Actions to Enforce Police Ordinances," *A Treatise on the Law of Municipal Corporations*, Chap. 26.

attorney the defendant is again required to appear before the court and to enter a plea of guilty or not guilty of the offense charged. At this time the court must again fix the amount of the bail required, and a new bond must be entered into if the accused is to be allowed his freedom until the time of trial. CHAP. XXI

The trial in felony cases is a proceeding in which formal determination of a person's guilt or innocence is made, the process being in entire control of the judge. The prosecuting attorney represents the people prosecuting the claims of the state, and the prisoner is represented either by counsel of his own selection, or, if financially unable to employ counsel, by counsel selected for him by the court. This selection may be made from the local bar; or the business may be handled regularly by a retained officer usually called "a friend of the court," or public defender. A jury is selected by lot from a jury panel, comprising a group of persons ready for service, previously called by the court for that purpose. It is the duty of the jury chosen to listen to the evidence presented by the witnesses and to the law governing the case as propounded by the judge, after which it must return a verdict of guilty or not guilty. In cases where the jurors fail to reach a unanimous verdict the entire trial is disregarded and a new jury impaneled, and the case is retried as before. Trial

After the verdict, the jury is discharged, and if the prisoner is found guilty he is remanded to jail to await sentence by the court. The sentence is within the discretion of the judge, tempered by definite provisions of law defining the maximum, and in some cases the minmium, punishment for the offense committed. The convicted person has a right of appeal to higher courts on points of law in the case, involving exclusion of evidence, the instructions given by the judge to the jury, the validity of the procedure, etc. No question of fact can be reviewed by a superior court. The state has not the right of appeal, and when a jury finds the accused not guilty, the verdict is final. Sentence

This entire procedure governing the adjudication of misdemeanors and felonies is so disorganized and ineffective, that criminal judicial procedure and criminal courts have been brought into general disrepute. The abuses complained of include an absence of uniform organization and procedure in the courts, lack of competent prosecution, and a breakdown of the corrective processes. Some of these criticisms may well be discussed in connection with Disorganization of the courts

CHAP. XXI

the remedies suggested. With respect to misdemeanors, the trials are ordinarily in the hands of elected police justices. As cities have grown, the number of justices sit in a single building, but more often they are scattered over the city. Obviously, there is no general direction of their activities—they may not attend assiduously to their duties; they may permit practices in the way of bail or release of prisoners which are not in accordance with public policy; and always there is a difference of opinion among them as to procedure, which makes the work of the police difficult, and as to the proper severity of sentences, which creates decided vagaries in what may be called justice. The situation is not much better in courts dealing with felony cases. The judges of these courts usually sit in a single building, but seldom have unified direction. All of the criticisms that can be brought against police justices may, in most jurisdictions, be brought with equal force against the judges of the superior criminal courts.

Unified courts

For these reasons efforts have been made to improve judicial procedure, and to secure unified misdemeanant and felony courts for important municipalities. Such courts would have original jurisdiction over all offenses committed within a city's boundaries except violations of national laws, and would also have original jurisdiction in all state civil cases. Thus all cases involving city ordinances or state laws would be adjudicated in a single court, with provision for appeal to higher authority. Detroit is the only American city having a city court with this combined jurisdiction over misdemeanant and felony cases, but without civil jurisdiction. A number of other cities, New York, Chicago, and notably municipalities in Ohio, have unified municipal courts with combined misdemeanant and petty civil jurisdiction.

In every instance there is assumed to be a chief justice who will assign cases for trial, and who in conjunction with the other members of the court will establish regulations and build up a procedure which will govern the actions of the court and secure uniformity in the sentences that are imposed. There is only one court instead of a considerable number. Judges are, under the most favored scheme of organization, assigned by the chief justice to the specialized divisions of the court such as felony, domestic relations, traffic, etc., and it is the duty of each judge to perform such additional duties as may be prescribed. The general policy and procedure of the court as a whole is established by the majority of the judges, while the continuing assignments in each division makes for further uniformity. In short, the court is a coherent organization which can be operated as an administrative unit and for whose operation responsibility is definitely located.¹

Coupled with the unification of the courts must go such changes in legislation as are necessary to correct present glaring defects in procedure. One of the most serious of these is delay. There is delay between the arrest and the indictment, between the indictment and the trial, in the trial itself, and between the trial and the execution of the sentence if the accused is found guilty. Delay in disposing of criminal cases tends to defeat the purpose of law-enforcing agencies. The sentence may be severe or lenient, but it is imperative that it be quick and certain. When months, and sometimes years, elapse before a defendant is brought to trial, witnesses disappear, the circumstances become vague in the minds of those concerned in the case, pressure of public opinion lapses, and the acute interest that is needed to bring the defendant to justice is lacking. As delay works so well to prevent conviction of the guilty, there is every inducement for a defendant to obtain bond from professional bondsmen and defer trial as long as possible. Such a situation encourages an attitude of indifference, and even of contempt, on the part of criminals. Therefore, the first step in the improvement of criminal procedure is the expeditious disposition of cases.

Another source of delay may be actual connivance on the part of the clerk of the courts. Ordinarily there is no current control of cases by judges. The defendant is arraigned, the plea taken, and the prisoner released on bond or returned to jail. It is the duty of the clerk of the court to set the cases for trial, selecting those that he believes are ready, giving preference to the oldest cases, or those in which the defendant is in jail. If a clerk so desires, he can postpone a case almost indefinitely and it will be dragged along unless something occurs to bring it to the attention of the court or of the prosecuting attorney.

A reasonable remedy for delay is to make the presiding judge of the court responsible for the calendar covering all cases. If the court contains separate divisions the head of each branch

---

[1] Two studies of the unified criminal court in Detroit have been made by the Detroit Bureau of Governmental Research and published as *Public Business*, Nos. 63 and 72. See also, American Judicature Society, *Bulletin 4A and 4B* (1914); C. R. Woodruff (ed.), *A New Municipal Program* (National Municipal League, 1919), 228-250; and Herbert Harley, "The Model Municipal Court," *Nat. Mun. Rev.*, III, 57-67 (January, 1914).

should assume this duty. The date for trial should be set in the appropriate docket, and this docket should be before the presiding judge at all times. Each day he should call up for trial the cases set for that day and assign them to their respective judges. If the prosecution or the defense is not ready to proceed with the trial, and if an adequate reason is furnished and is accepted by the presiding judge, the case may be postponed to a definite docketed date. It is important to stress the fact that continuances should be discouraged by refusal to accept the trivial excuses commonly offered in criminal courts. The docket of the presiding judge is also an effective current control of cases and keeps them from being overlooked.

Expeditious work on the part of a court should be reflected by reducing to a minimum the time prisoners are confined in jail. It is not a question of how many persons there are in jail at any particular time awaiting trial, but rather of how long those persons remain in jail before their cases are disposed of. Persons remain in jail awaiting trial when they are ineligible to bail, or are unable to provide a bond, and, not infrequently, valuable witnesses are incarcerated because there is no other sure way of retaining them. When a suspected offender is kept in jail for months at a time awaiting trial, he is being punished for an offense for which he has not yet been found guilty, and in event that his innocence is established the state has enforced a punishment that is unwarranted.[1] Modern justice should take every reasonable step to provide speedy trial for persons accused, and particularly for those who, because of the nature of the offense or the lack of personal resources, find it impossible to be released on bail.

The professional bondsman is usually an unscrupulous parasite preying upon the ignorance and terror of arrested persons. Such a bondsman may indeed serve a useful purpose if he furnishes a bond at a reasonable fee and terminates his services at this point. But frequently, in addition to charging outrageous fees for furnishing bonds that are not always protected by satisfactory collateral, the bondsman is in league with the shyster lawyer who mulcts the victim as much as possible. Also he is a notorious corruptor of jailers and police officers. Every modern court must wage continuous aggressive fight against the nefarious practices of these court hangers-on.

[1] No action can be against the state for such imprisonment.

The professional bondsman has been aided and abetted by the laxity of public authorities in dealing with the bonding situation. To some extent, the professional bondsman exists because he knows that it will be nobody's business to enforce the collection of a bond in case of default. The chances of such enforcement are meagre, and if actual efforts of enforcement are made certain subterfuges may be resorted to to prevent collection. Collection on defaulted bonds is usually an obligation of the prosecutor's office. But this office may be too busy to undertake collection, or defalcations may not be called to its attention by the officers of the court. In some jurisdictions bonds do not become a lien upon real estate that may be offered as security. In such instances it is relatively a simple matter for the bondsman, upon learning of the default, to transfer ownership of the property, and thus prevent collection by the state. In some cases professional bondsmen offer one piece of property on different bonds outstanding at the same time or present property which is worth far less than the bond required.

In addition to legislation providing that bonds shall become an immediate lien upon property, the matter of bond procedure should be put in the hands of a bond bureau operated in conjunction with the courts. It should be the business of this bond bureau to scrutinize all property offered in security of bonds, keep an accurate record of such security in order that it may not be accepted on bonds in excess of its value, notify the proper authorities in case a bond is defaulted, and press for rapid action looking to the collection of defaulted bonds. At the same time, the officer in charge of the bureau should visit the jail daily and inform prisoners as to the proper procedure for securing bonds and of the fees that should be paid. Such actions will perhaps do more to prevent the evil of professional bondsmen than any amount of moralizing on the subject or of judicial scoring of professional hangers-on in the court.

Associated with bond releases are the evils of releases by court order. On many occasions the police take into custody persons who should be released upon their own recognizance and not be compelled to spend hours or days in the police station. The police often fail to use sound judgment in these cases, and judges must be importuned by friends to order the release. A judge cannot always refuse these requests, nor should he. But the release system can be easily abused. It is one thing to release the ordinarily well-behaved citizen who may be apprehended for the first time in his life, and quite another to release the professional gambler and prostitute immediately after arrest. These latter ilk frequently have releases awaiting them at the police station even before they themselves arrive, and certain types of court hangers-on may carry a sheaf of such releases signed in blank to be used as occasion requires. It is difficult to lay down any set procedure for the use of releases, but public opinion can at least penalize the judge who abuses his powers and prostitutes his high office to abet anti-social conduct.

The shyster lawyer

The shyster lawyer is close kin to the professional bondsman. The professional cards of both are in the hands of subsidized bailiffs and turnkeys, who pass them on to the ignorant who have fallen into the clutches of the law. These vultures promise everything, take everything, and do as little as possible. Occasionally an irate judge will compel part of an outrageous fee to be returned, but more often such cases never reach the attention of the bench.[1] A community is rightfully indignant, when it pays any attention to the matter at all, at the practices of professional bondsmen and shyster lawyers; but it must remember that it is itself directly responsible. Arrest and the thought of jail appears to most persons a most overwhelming calamity. Ignorant of court procedure, they turn to the first person who seems to know the mysteries of the law and offers to help them out of their predicament. The service furnished, however, expensive and inefficient it may be, is one that the community fails to render.

Public defender

Courts dealing with both misdemeanors and felonies have before them a large number of people who are ignorant of the law or who are not financially able to secure the services of a legal advisor. If these persons are able to pay at all, the shyster lawyer will be on hand to secure exorbitant fees for his services. In cases of major importance the court is expected to appoint an attorney at the expense of the state if the accused cannot supply one. This prerogative on the part of the court often degenerates into a petty graft, certain attorneys being rewarded for political services. To avoid both of these situations, some jurisdictions provide a public defender whose business it is to defend any

[1] "There are three golden rules in the profession. First, thoroughly threaten and terrify your client. Second, find out how much money he has, and where it is. Third, get it." Arthur Train, *The Confessions of Artemas Quibble* (Scribners, 1924).

accused person who is without means to secure competent legal services.¹

The defendant is not alone handicapped with respect to legal advice. The state may be in an even worse position. But the results are not so serious. The prosecutor is frequently defeated in the proper exercise of his duties by the general lack of organization in the felony courts and by the lack of coöperation between the judiciary and the prosecution. Cases are often assigned on the morning of the trial, with a result that the prosecutor must present his case without opportunity for preparation. This is prejudicial to public interest, but it is common in many jurisdictions. Also, cases may be transferred from one judge to another without notice to the prosecuting attorney. The prosecutor is often compelled to proceed with trial prepared only by hasty conferences with the police officers in charge of a case and a hurried reading of the testimony taken at the preliminary examination. This clearly places the state at a decided disadvantage in a criminal trial and subjects the official prosecutor to the handicap of meeting a well prepared counsel for the defense without himself having an opportunity to become equally well prepared.

A further shortcoming of judicial procedure is the lack of authentic information by the court with respect to the offender. An important adjunct of the modern court is facilities for investigation and probation. Able and properly directed investigators should interview practically all persons convicted before sentence is passed. In addition, the circumstances surrounding the committing of the offense and the family history of each person as far as it can be obtained should be secured and presented to the trial judge. This information is apart from police records which are normally introduced during trial. If the circumstances of the offense and the history of the offender seem to warrant further information before the most equitable disposition can be made of the case, the case should be continued for a day or two, or for such time as is necessary to obtain a complete history through a more thorough investigation. Such further investigation may include an examination by the psychopathic clinic. Only when the

¹ See M. C. Goldman, *Public Defender* (Putnam, 2d. ed., 1919); and R. H. Smith, *op. cit.*, Chaps. XIV-XV. For additional references, consult A. Mabel Barrow, "Public Defender, a Bibliography," *Journal of Criminal Law and Criminology*, XIV, 556-572 (February, 1924). More recent articles appear in *Legal Aid Work* (Annals, CXXIV, March, 1926); and *Growth of Legal Aid Work in the United States* (Bulletin of the U. S. Bureau of Labor Statistics, No. 398, January, 1926), Chap. XI.

372 PRACTICE OF MUNICIPAL ADMINISTRATION

CHAP. XXI

Psychopathic clinics

facts so obtained are at hand can a judge make such disposition of the case as is most desirable, from the point of view both of the individual and of society.[1]

There is a growing recognition in judicial circles that a large amount of crime results from mental or nervous diseases, and that punishment cannot be imposed properly until the mental condition of the offender is known. The means of acquiring this information is through use of the psychopathic clinic. This is a medical clinic where persons are examined as to their mental condition, mental equipment, and nervous stability. Psychiatry, like other branches of medical science, has gradually developed through research and experience, and its application has been widened until today it is applied generally where there appears to be a predisposition to abnormal conduct. There is nothing unusual about the application of psychiatry to persons accused of crime, although Detroit is the first American city to do so through a permanent clinic in connection with felonies. Philadelphia, Boston, and Chicago have psychopathic clinics as subsidiaries of their courts trying minor offenses, and fifteen or twenty juvenile courts in various cities have such clinics. Psychiatry was applied to offenders for many years in Europe before it was taken up in the United States.

Importance of psychiatry

Every year hundreds of thousands of men, women, and children are arrested and tried for acts contrary to the laws established to govern conduct. The causes of such anti-social actions are many and complex, but it has been definitely ascertained that knowledge of the personality of the offender is not only essential to an understanding of the causative factors but absolutely required in order that an intelligent disposition can be made of the offender —a disposition that will offer the greatest chance of correction and the least chance of recidivism. The personality of the offender is the ground on which outside causes germinate, and it contains the roots of all his actions even when it is not of itself the preponderant causation. The science of psychiatry and psychology reveals through a highly developed technique the mental caliber, motivations, and reactions requisite to explain conduct.

Futility of ignoring personality

For centuries, organized society has sought methods of preventing crime. Capital punishment has been imposed for even minor offenses; torture has been frequently resorted to; and in-

[1] The subject of probation as a form of punishment is discussed more fully in Chap. XXII.

carceration has been a usual course—all in the hope of deterring others by example and reforming the offender by punishment. However, crime has continued, and the repetition of offenses is notoriously chronic. Experience has proved that the modern methods of incarceration in a prison, even where the physical conditions and the care are good, does not restore all, or any considerable proportion, of offenders as normal and conventional members of society. In short, such disposition of offenders has been of limited benefit to society and of less benefit to the prisoner. To make the punishment fit the crime and not the criminal, has proved futile.

Sometimes during the course of the offender's progress through the court, the judge may, if he sees fit, refer him to the psychopathic clinic for examination. The complete examination consists of three steps. First, as thorough a social history as possible is obtained by probation investigators, through interviews with family, friends, neighbors, employers, and through correspondence with former associates in other cities. Secondly, an examination by standard methods is made by the psychologist to determine the "intelligence quotient." The last step is a psycho-medical examination by the psychiatrist to find out whether the "patient" is suffering from any mental or nervous disease, and to complete the personality analysis. At the conclusion of this examination, the psychiatrist makes a diagnosis, just as any physician does after getting the history of a patient, and recommends a form of treatment to the judge. This recommended treatment may be institutionalization in a prison, reformatory, hospital, or feeble-minded home; or it may be probation. The treatment prescribed is, of course, limited by the practicability of carrying out the plan for the particular patient. The character of the offense committed is considered merely as a symptom, just as fever is considered in other diseases. A patient may have a temperature of 104 degrees and require only slight medication, while another patient may have a temperature of 100 degrees and require confinement in bed for an extended period. The report of the diagnosis, and the recommendation based on it, is submitted to the judge by whom the case was referred; and he may follow the recommendations or not as he sees it.

A properly organized system of municipal justice will provide an organization for the effective handling of women offenders, where such cases may be heard and disposed of separately and at different hours from those of men. The judge of this branch of the court, should by employing the aid of the women's probation officers and psychopathic clinic, have a complete knowledge of the history of each offender. Each case can then be given adequate consideration and be disposed of with the idea of constructive benefit to the defendant. Unfortunately, the facilities for executing these sentences in a satisfactory manner in the case of women offenders are usually limited.

Another feature of municipal justice that should be emphasized is the use of a night court. Before such a court should be brought all persons arrested after prisoners are taken by the police to the regular daily sessions of court. This prevents persons arrested spending a night, or even a day and a night, in police station houses before being taken to court the following morning, and restricts the activities of the professional bondsman. Also, during the night court session bonds may be signed for the release of prisoners, thus preventing in many cases prisoners staying in jail over night because a judge is not available to accept bail.

The fatalities and the permanent injuries inflicted upon hundreds of persons every year by vehicular traffic is evidence of the serious consideration that must be given this problem. Accidents have been mounting year by year—accidents that are due, in the main, to carelessness and to lack of consideration of the rights of others. Rigorous law enforcement is required for the safety of the public, and the courts can play no small part in this remedy. But more than perfunctory handling of the violators of traffic laws is needed. Under the ordinary court organization in a city, hundreds of traffic violators are tried each morning, and of necessity cases cannot be handled separately or with any degree of consideration. To meet this problem, it is necessary that a branch of the municipal court specialize in traffic cases, pursuing a firm, uniform policy, and placing increased penalties on repeaters.

Reduction of traffic accidents is a matter of education as well as punishment. With the establishment of traffic courts, not only should the seriousness of offenses be impressed upon the offenders by relatively severe fines and paroles, and by frequent sentences to a correctional institution, but in addition to this the judge may take advantage of this favorable opportunity to emphasize to offenders by thoroughgoing explanation the reasons for the necessity of obeying all traffic regulations, however trivial they may be. The work of a traffic court should serve two purposes—to inspire respect for the law by not allowing anyone to escape with impunity, and to educate the offender to see that regulations are based upon reason.

CHAP. XXI

In most communities juveniles under a certain age are not tried or incarcerated with regular offenders, but their cases are examined by judges presumably peculiarly qualified to deal with children and in separate courts created for that purpose. The hearings in these juvenile courts are quite informal as compared with tribunals in which the trials of adults are held, and the trial of a juvenile compares somewhat closely with the informal investigations made by probation officers. The judge examines the offender, listening to the statements of the accuser, of parents, and of investigators who have studied the case. At the conclusion of the hearing, decision is rendered. This decision may involve the placing of the offender under the restraint of parents or guardian, or sentence to a parental school or to the state reformatory. This last measure is coming to be adopted only as a final recourse.[1]

Juvenile courts

The socialized treatment of juvenile offenders raises the query as to the desirability of similar procedure in connection with adults. The law makes as arbitrary distinction between juveniles and adults, determined only by physical age. Yet modern psychology shows that physical age has only a relative control over the acts of various individuals. An adult may be a man in years but a child in mind. Under these circumstances, it would seem sensible to apply the same methods of treatment to childish-minded adults that are applied to childish-minded juveniles, due regard being given the stronger emotional nature of adults and their more intrenched habits. If this were done, trials would assume a much less formal character, and the punishment would probably be more fully suited to the individual than at present. This does not mean—and this should be emphasized—that the treatment would be less severe than at present. But it does mean that a person who, because of his mental state, is in fact a habitual criminal will be treated as a habitual offender, rather than merely be given some brief sentence for some dereliction in which he has been apprehended.

This discussion has centered around criminal courts, largely because this is the phase of the judiciary that has to do with the

[1] See *A Symposium, The Child, the Clinic, and the Court* (*The New Republic*, 1925); Miriam VanWaters, *Youth in Conflict* (*ibid.*); and Roger Baldwin and Bernard Flexner, *Juvenile Courts and Probation* (*Century*, 1914).

376 PRACTICE OF MUNICIPAL ADMINISTRATION

CHAP. XXI

Other municipal courts

conduct of individuals as it relates to society as a whole. However, it should be borne in mind that the civil requirements of a community come to some extent within the purview of the administrator. The courts for the trial of civil cases of a minor character are presided over by justices of the peace, who are ordinarily elected at large in a city or by districts within a city. The same criticisms that have been applied to the disorganized character of the criminal courts apply with equal force to these justice courts. It is in these courts that the poor man finds justice in his civil relationships. Unfortunately, many abuses have grown up in connection with the use of constables, elected court officers of the justice courts, with the political character of the court, and with other features too numerous to mention in detail.[1]

Court records

One of the problems of criminal courts is to prevent the clogging of machinery with trivial cases that, with a little attention and advice by authorized persons other than judges, can be settled

The clerk

without trial. In this class of cases are neighborhood quarrels and domestic squabbles in which the first thought of the aggrieved individual is the securing of a warrant to have somebody arrested. Frequently there is danger of issuing warrants unjustly unless the representations of persons seeking the warrant are investigated. To solve these two problems, a few courts have established facilities for investigation. Official investigators examine all requests for warrants and make recommendations accordingly to the judge. In domestic relations difficulties and in neighborhood quarrels the investigators are able, by intervention, to settle numerous cases out of court without the issuance of warrants. In certain of these cases, investigation and settlement should be followed up by reports to various social agencies of the city, to the end that greater constructive results may be obtained.

To a considerable degree, the work of the court depends upon the accuracy of the records kept and the accessibility of the information bearing upon the transactions of the court. Records of all classes of work in a court should be centralized under a single individual (generally known as the clerk); and he should be responsible for the numerous subordinates who have distinct assignments, with respect to the records maintained.

The records kept by the clerk's office begin with the files which contain, by number and name, all official papers concerning each

---

[1] See *Growth of Legal Aid Work in the United States,* Chap. VIII; and R. H. Smith, *op. cit.*

case. Starting with the first papers entered in the files, a calendar is made, which gives the record of the development of each case from the moment it makes its appearance in the court to its disposition. The value of this record lies in the fact that it furnishes ready information on each case at every stage. The entries on the calendar are naturally made from the files and from a record which is kept of the action of each judge with respect to each case. It is extremely important that every precaution be taken against the loss of any file or of any papers from a file. References are being continually made to the files, and their availability is a matter of importance to the efficient running of the office. It is not uncommon for papers to be deliberately abstracted to prevent further action or to delay action by the court. To correct this situation it is, as has been said, essential that a single individual be made responsible for their keeping. No files should be removed without the knowledge of this clerk and without a memorandum being made of issuance.

The docket is a record of cases set for trial. It must be prepared by some competent individual acting under orders of the court, and should contain full information relative to court records, reports of probation officers and other investigators, notices of requests for continuance, lack of witnesses, proper notification of officers, and any other causes that might delay the sessions of the court. With the docket before him, the judge can be forewarned and delay can be avoided by substituting cases that are ready for trial. There should also be a bond record giving all available information with respect to bonds, amount, bondsmen, and the final disposition of the bond. This record should be checked periodically in order that action may be taken upon defaulted bonds.

In addition, an important means of controlling the work of the court may be secured through a register of cases so arranged that the chief justice, or the chief clerk, can see at a glance how many cases are pending, what stage they have reached, and how long they have been in court. If desired, this record may be substituted for the calendar.

Whenever the structure of a governmental institution is changed, presumably for the better, all the benefits that appear are ordinarily attributed to the change in organization. Considerable danger lies in such a habit of mind, because it leads the public to be easily persuaded to believe that, the machinery being improved, good results will automatically follow. This is particularly true with respect to judicial organization, where great emphasis has been laid upon disorganized structure. Undoubtedly, improved court organization will be responsible for the expeditious handling of cases, and will make possible more effective administration of justice. But improved organization without judges anxious to operate it is of doubtful value. Judges must be selected who will bend every effort to conduct a court for the community's welfare; and in this they must have the coöperation of effective police action and prosecution. To these ends, an alert interest on the part of the public is absolutely essential. Occasionally it is desirable to organize this interest in such agencies as the Chicago Crime Commission, the Cleveland Crime Commission, the Missouri Association for Criminal Justice, and the National Crime Commission. But in any case, sustained public interest is a prime requisite.

CHAPTER XXII

CORRECTION [1]

When an authority to which a person is subject finds him guilty of the violation of established law or custom some form of punishment ordinarily follows. In civilized society this authority is the state; the law consists of common law, municipal ordinances, and state and national statutes; and the punishment is that prescribed by law and imposed by a court of competent jurisdiction.[2] {The genesis of punishment}

Early judicial theory considered practically every offense as a tort committed directly against some individual, the punishment for which was a matter of personal vengeance—an affair of the offended person, his relatives, and his friends. Gradually custom and law prescribed certain limits upon the retaliation that might be indulged in and commuted certain injuries into payments of cash or kind. Finally, as the public became conscious of injury by private feuds, the state assumed responsibility for determining guilt and imposing punishment. It was necessary that this transition be made. Personal reprisals were too harsh to be tolerated by a society that pretended to any degree of civilization. {Vindictive punishment}

---

[1] Frederick H. Wines, *Punishment and Reformation* (rev. ed., Crowell, 1919); John L. Gillin, *Criminology and Penology* (Century, 1926); Edwin H. Sutherland, *Criminology*, (Lippincott, 1924); Louis N. Robinson, *Penology in the United States* (Winston, 1921); and C. R. Henderson, *Cause and Cure of Crime* (McClurg, 1914), are outstanding works on the subject of correction. *Correction and Prevention* is the general title of four valuable volumes prepared for the Eighth International Prison Congress under the direction of C. R. Henderson (Russell Sage Foundation, 1910). Burdette C. Lewis, *Penal and Correctional Treatment*, appears as a part of the *Cleveland Crime Study* (Cleveland Foundation, 1922). The *Modern Criminal Science Series* issued under the auspices of the American Institute of Criminal Law and Criminology (Little, Brown) contains the principal works of the great criminologists, *e.g.*, Gross, Lombroso, Tarde, Aschaffenburg, Ferri, and others. For current reference, consult the *Proceedings of the Congress of the American Prison Association* (annual); Publications of the Prison Association of New York; *Journal of Criminal Law and Criminology* (quarterly); and the *Journal of the American Judicature Society* (bi-monthly).

[2] Crime is an intentional violation of duties imposed by law, which inflicts an injury upon others. Criminals are persons convicted of crime by competent courts. Punishment is suffering inflicted on the criminal for the wrong-doing done by him, with a special view to secure his reformation.—Declaration of Principles, American Prison Association, affirmed in 1870, and re-affirmed in 1919.

Distinction between civil and criminal offenses

With this change there came a gradual distinction between offenses considered as against the state rather than against the individual, and those that would not be so considered. Offenses became either civil or criminal. In this latter group are found certain offenses against public peace and order, against public health and morals, against persons, and against property. Other offenses, such as breach of contract, some forms of libel, and indebtedness are not considered as criminal but as civil or private wrongs. Redress through the courts involves restitution rather than punishment.[1]

Punishment for deterrence and example

With the development of the idea that certain offenses were committed against the state rather than against the individual, and with the intrusion of the state into the processes of determining guilt and inflicting punishment, there naturally followed a somewhat different attitude with respect to punishment. As regards an individual, society should not hate, should not entertain passions, and should not obtain satisfaction by wreaking vengeance. Punishment by the state cannot properly be vindictive; it is rather a means of social protection used to deter the individual from a repetition of the offense, and by example, to deter other members of society from committing a like dereliction.

These theories of deterrence were a long step forward, but when carried to what appeared to be their logical conclusions they required indulgence by society in revolting cruelties. Even in comparatively recent times English law has imposed the death sentence for more than forty offenses, many of which are now considered somewhat trivial.[2] The theory of deterrence also called for corporal punishment, and for making public spectacles of it. To a certain extent, it is now recognized that brutality by the state brutalizes its members, and that deterrence from crime comes from other elements than severity and publicity of punishment. However, the classical or legalistic theory of severity of punishment for its deterrent effect is still held in a somewhat modified form in England, Canada, and Germany, and its results are often quoted in its favor.[3] In these countries the corrective process submerges the individual's welfare in that of society, holds him strictly re-

[1] Munro, *op. cit.*, 223.
[2] It is said, perhaps with some foundation, that this severity was necessary because England had a very small and disorganized police force.
[3] "As year by year the criminal laws were relieved of further absurdities, the number of convictions (in England) for serious crimes kept falling.

sponsible for his acts, and punishes him in order that others may not follow his example.[1]

New theories of correction involve the individualization of punishment, recognizing that the responsibility of the individual is affected by social conditions, heredity, mental deficiency, and other forces over which the offender has little or no control. This is the determinist, or individualistic conception of punishment assumed to prevail in Italy and France, and appearing in America.[2] In accordance with this thought, society now takes proper measures to protect itself against the offender, negatively, by isolation, to prevent anti-social conduct by the offender in the immediate future; and positively, by means of correction, so that the offender may become rehabilitated and reinstated as a useful member of society. This change does not mean that punishment as a deterrent to others has been entirely abandoned. Rather, it assumes a position of less importance, since it by itself has failed to produce desired results. It is believed that to punish a criminal in excess of his just deserts, in order to deter some potential criminal from committing an offense, leaves the offender with the feeling that

Punishment for protection and correction

Thus, in 1859 for each 100,000 of population there were 13.4 persons sentenced to convict prisons for the higher crimes. Ten years later (1869) this number had dropped to 9.1; in 1874 it had dropped to 6.6; in 1889 to 3.3; in 1899 to 2.5; and, according to the latest available statistics (1923), it is now but 1.26 in 100,000." Lawrence Veiller, "Where American Justice Failed," *World's Work*, LI, 499-509 (March, 1926).

[1] See Charles C. Nott, Jr., "Coddling Criminals," *Scribner's Magazine*, LXXIX (May, 1926).

[2] "Admitting for the sake of argument that the crime wave exists, is more drastic punishment the way to curb it? Ever so many highly respectable people nowadays are saying that it is. Yet one weak point exists in their chain of argument which we think has not been pointed out. If punishments are made more drastic, you must not only make sure that potential criminals know this has happened: you must also make sure that potential criminals have enough intelligence to think ahead and weigh the increased risks they now run. On this matter of their ability to perform such a feat in logic, the National Committee for Mental Hygiene has some interesting facts to contribute. More than 8,500 prisoners, in eleven states, were recently given careful tests. Of these one-twentieth were found to suffer from some definite and serious mental disease, such as dementia præcox or paranoia. Another eighth were mentally defective, and an eighth more were what are called 'borderline cases.' Nearly another fifth were psychopathic persons, described as being defective to a degree which seriously impairs their moral sensitiveness, although their appearance is sufficiently normal so that judges and juries usually hold them to be 'sane' and responsible. In other words, more than half of these prisoners are mentally abnormal, which raises two interesting questions. Would increased severity of punishments be any deterrent to such individuals? Do any punishments, no matter how drastic, ever prevent their committing crimes?" *The New Republic*, XLVI, 314 (May 5, 1926).

382   PRACTICE OF MUNICIPAL ADMINISTRATION

CHAP. XXII

society has more than settled its score and that future offenses will only balance the scale.¹

Essentials of individualistic punishment

Under this individualistic theory, punishment should be certain, speedy, and corrective. Certainty of punishment is probably a far more effective deterrent than severity, as is indicated both by experience and a knowledge of psychology. To be a corrective measure, punishment must be speedy so that it may be connected with the mental attitude of the offender at the time of the offense. Otherwise, a new set of emotions is built up in the offender's mind through the lapse of time, personal justification for a crime is created, and the punishment inflicted becomes, for him, not an accepted correction applied by society, but a wrong for which there is a right to retaliate when the opportunity presents. Real correction is obviously to be desired if recidivism is to be prevented and society correspondingly protected.

Means of punishment employed

Out of this corrective and protective policy of punishment has evolved the following methods for the disposition of criminals: suspended sentences, fines, probation, parole, pardons, and incarceration with definite and indeterminate sentences. Before discussing them directly, however, it may be well to say a word in general about their use by the courts.

Lack of emphasis on proper disposition

A court has two very important functions to perform. First, it must adjudicate the case against the accused; and second, if the accused is found guilty it must impose punishment. The breakdown of the first of these processes has been mentioned in another place.² The latter phase of the court's work has been equally unintelligent—so much so that it has even been suggested that the imposition of penalties be removed from the jurisdiction of the court and placed in possibly more competent hands.

In making their decisions, judges have usually had to depend entirely upon their own limited knowledge of the offender and the offense. However, isolated attempts along two lines are nowadays being made to aid the courts by providing them with information about the criminal. First, an effort is made to appraise the

---

¹ See Sanford Bates, "What May Be Done to Forward the Judicious Application of the Principle of Individualization of Punishment by the Judge Who Assigns the Penalty to be Inflicted on the Offender," and John R. Oliver, "Criminology and Common Sense," *Journal of Criminology and Criminal Law*, XVI (February, 1926). See also Raymond Saleilles, *The Individualization of Punishment* (Little, Brown, 1911); William Healy, *The Individual Delinquent* (Little, Brown, 1915); and J. O. Stutzman, *Curing the Criminal* (Macmillan, 1926).

² See Chap. XXI.

offender himself through the operation of a psychopathic clinic which gives authentic facts as to mental capacity, attitude toward society, and general mental and physical condition; second, by the investigation of probation officers to present salient facts concerning the offender's educational, social, moral, and industrial history —in all, a general summary of past and present environment. This information is necessary if the court is to make a proper diagnosis, prescribe the type of treatment which will best safeguard society, and at the same time, as far as is consistent with public policy, meet the needs of the individual. Best American thought considers that much progress in the prevention of crime will come from a more systematic study of the offender. Experience has demonstrated that emphasis on the offense and disposition without considering the offender has been futile. This does not necessarily lead to greater leniency.[1] It involves intelligent handling of the crime problem; in individual treatment of the delinquent, whether it be with greater leniecy or greater severity.

The first punishment in the hands of the judge is the suspended sentence, which should be used with great discretion. Suspension implies that society finds the offender guilty of the offense but foregoes further punishment. It is used frequently in the case of minor offenses, particularly misdemeanors when no wrongful act was intended, or when certain mitigating circumstances are present, such as suffering undergone by the offender previous to his trial. In other words, the person is technically guilty, but no one is seriously injured and the ends of society are served by dismissing the incident. The suspended sentence may also be used in connection with some felonies in which the extreme youth of the offender makes it undesirable to continue any contact with the formal correctional system. However, with the development of the probation system the suspended sentence in felony cases has become less desirable.

The fine is a left-over of a period when every offense was considered an act against the individual and could be compensated by the payment of cash or goods. Nowadays fines may be imposed in lieu of prison sentences or in conjunction with them. Ordinarily, the imposition of a fine is reserved for minor offenses for which it is thought that incarceration will serve no good purpose, or it is used as an alternative to a prison sentence. In event of

[1] Under this proposal a chronic misdemeanant might be given an indeterminate sentence that would result in life imprisonment.

non-payment, the time served in prison may be commuted correspondingly. Unfortunately, this system practically results in imprisonment for debt. Very few states allow an individual to be imprisoned for an unpaid debt to another individual, yet every state and every city imprisons persons for debts that cannot be paid to the community itself. In consequence, poverty is penalized by imprisonment while wealth escapes. It has been suggested that this situation could be remedied if judges took the wealth of offenders into consideration in determining the amount of fines, and if impecunious persons were allowed to pay such fines on the instalment plan out of current earnings. The latter practice should be particularly applicable to employed persons, and to persons with families who would be allowed to continue in their employment and family support. This plan would also save many individuals from the stigma of serving in a correctional institution, would preserve their families from want, and yet serve every needful purpose for which a fine is imposed. In default of this proposal a reasonable opportunity should also be given prisoners who have the option of paying fines to raise the money before they are transferred to the correctional institution.

Probation

Probation is the process by which an individual convicted of a crime is permitted, for purposes of reformation, to resume a normal life in the community under the supervision of an officer designated by the court. Under the old principle of fitting the punishment to the crime, the offender was overlooked, the aim of the law being to approximate the severity of the sentence to the degree of the offense committed. Such a sentence usually took the form of isolating the offender in an institution for a definite period of time, with the hope that the deprivation of liberty, the unpleasantness and even hardships of restricted living, would, while punishing the crime, deter the individual from continuing his anti-social conduct when released, and by example deter others from anti-social conduct. Probation is a distinct move towards fitting the punishment to the needs of the offender, ignoring to a degree the exemplary value of punishment.

How probation operates

Having been placed upon probation, the probationer is usually interviewed by a probation officer, his problem discussed, advice and counsel given, and definite instructions prescribed as to his conduct during the probation period. The probationer is then required to report to his probation officer at regular intervals. The outstanding weakness of the probation system in most cities lies

CORRECTION 385

in the fact that there is not an adequate supervision of probationers. Real supervision means positive constructive work with each individual probationer by a competent probation officer. It entails familiarity with the probationer's manner of living, his friends, leisure time pursuits, employment, home life, domestic relations, etc. Such knowledge can be gained only through repeated visits to the home and neighborhood of the probationer and through the establishment of confidence by the probation officer.[1]

CHAP. XXII

Supervision of probationers

Knowing—if he does—all about the probationer, the officer is able to call into play the necessary forces in the delinquent and in the community which will help him readjust himself for normal living. Probation is a play of personality upon personality. Successful results can be obtained only through intensive work with each individual, and by creating the feeling in the probationer that his welfare and his conduct are the principal interests in the officer's life, and that the latter is not only an official of the court but even more a friend ready to help at all times. Merely reporting to a probation officer every week or month for the purpose of having his presence recorded on a card and to be asked a perfunctory question or two cannot reform an offender. At the most, it may only cause him to behave properly during his period of probation. In the last analysis, the efficacy of probation rests upon the extent to which the court avails itself of the system as a means of reclaiming offenders, the degree to which the judges interest themselves intelligently in the machinery of the probation department and follow the cases on probation, and the judgment used by probation officers. Only by these means can the system of probation be an effective adjunct to the administration of justice.

It is recognized, however, that society must be protected against irresponsible and anti-social individuals, and that, for the safety of the community, offenders who will not respond to the benefits of probation must be disposed of in another fashion. Incarceration implies commitment to an institution for a period of time determined by the judge in accordance with law. At the outset, there is a segregation of prisoners in accordance with the nature of the offense. Minor offenders, *i.e.*, misdemeanants, are ordinarily committed to a local workhouse operated by the municipality or the county; major offenders, *i.e.*, felons, are ordinarily committed to the custody of the state and placed in one of the several state

Alternatives to probation

Incarceration

---

[1] See *Methods of Supervising Persons on Probation*, and *Manual for Probation Officers* (New York State Probation Commission, 1918).

prisons that are maintained for felons. The municipal administrator presumably will have little or nothing to do with the treatment of felons by the state prison authorities. However, it is desirable that these officers be familiar with the modern theory of segregation of prisoners in order that in a modified way the same general principles may be applied in local institutions.

Segregation

Proper segregation means that first-time offenders convicted of minor offenses be kept in a special institution for these types, and that the hardened offenders sentenced to long terms be sent to an institution particularly adapted to their requirements. At the same time, some efforts have been made in the direction of segregation according to mental condition, as is seen in the establishment of institutions for the criminal insane, and in the psychopathic examinations that are given to state prisoners, followed by efforts to segregate psychopathic cases from the balance of offenders. Such a segregation of prisoners is a step in the direction of classification in accordance with both the nature of the offense and the character of the offender.

Pardons

The use of executive clemency, or the pardoning power, varies in accordance with state laws. It may or may not be possible for the governor to pardon offenders confined in state institutions, or for the mayor to pardon offenders confined in municipal institutions. Or this privilege may be applied to only a part of the offenses for which offenders are incarcerated. A pardon is ordinarily used when it is believed that the ends of justice have been served and that an injustice will be done if the prisoner is compelled to remain any longer in an institution. Evidence may arise to indicate that the convicted person was innocent of the offense; the judge or jury may themselves suggest a pardon on the grounds that excessive sentence was inflicted; or the conduct of the individual in prison may be such as to indicate that he has reformed, and that the ends of society will be best served by returning him to civil life.

The indeterminate sentence

If the object of the penal system is punishment and nothing more, it may be argued that a hardened criminal, by a sentence of a given number of years, expiates the crime committed and is entitled to his freedom. But if, as we have seen, the aim is to protect society and to rehabilitate the offender, little can be said for the procedure that imprisons the offender for a definite period, and later releases him, perhaps uncorrected, to resume his evil practices. While perfect justice cannot be expected from any human instrument, it seems exceptionally fallacious to expect a judge to determine during the course of a trial the amount of treatment an offender requires. Yet the law imposes upon the judge in most instances the responsibility of determining, within the limits laid down by statute, how many days, weeks, months, or years are necessary to make the offender regret his act and to afford him sufficient training to warrant his return to the responsibilities of citizenship. While the state's facilities for intelligent supervision and treatment of offenders remain inadequate, it is important that at least a minimum sentence be fixed by the courts, and possible errors are minimized by the possession of facilities such as psychopathic clinics and social investigating machinery.

CHAP. XXII

However, the indeterminate sentence relieves the court of this responsibility and leaves with the criminal and those who have supervision over him the determination of the period of incarceration. The extension and intelligent use of such sentences is to be hoped for, and any law applying particularly to habitual offenders should provide accordingly. With the best of facilities, it is seldom possible to prophesy the exact period of institutional treatment necessary in a given case. Also by means of the indeterminate sentence the criminal can be compelled to coöperate in his own reform; or failing that, society can be sure of permanent protection.

Paroling is the practice of releasing offenders from correctional institutions before the complete expiration of the sentence imposed, and placing them under the supervision of a parole officer. The law assumes that the corrective processes will not have been completed until the minimum of the sentence is served. But after a prisoner has completed this minimum sentence, he ordinarily becomes eligible for parole. Most states provide for a parole officer, or a parole board, to whom all such cases are brought upon recommendation of the prison warden. A prisoner who has served his minimum sentence, and who has conducted himself properly within the institution, may be recommended to the parole board for parole. In such cases it is customary for the prisoner to report currently to the parole officer during the balance of his sentence, and if he violates this sentence by disregarding the regulations that are laid down for him by the parole officer he may be apprehended and returned to the prison to serve all or part of the balance of his term, ordinarily losing such deduction for good

Parole

conduct as may have been allowed. The plan is particularly applicable in cases of indeterminate sentences.

Recently there has been much criticism of the parole system. This has arisen, not because parole is unsound in theory, but because there has been a breakdown in its administration. Occasionally prisoners have been paroled for money payments or for political reasons; or because of crowded prison conditions; or without a knowledge of the circumstances surrounding the offense for which commitment was made; or with too little study of the mental processes of the offender and of the environment to which he is to return. The merits of the system are evidenced by the large numbers of paroled prisoners who have benefited by its processes. Unfortunately, an occasional parole case returns to a life of crime and brings the entire procedure into disrepute.

<small>Misdemeanant parole</small>

Parole does not ordinarily apply to short term offenders, and it has been thought that misdemeanants would be serving such short terms as to make parole of little consequence. However, many misdemeanants receive sentences up to a period of six months and might well be eligible for parole.

<small>Partial parole</small>

Dayton, Ohio, has developed an interesting experiment in the direction of what may be called partial parole. In instances where a misdemeanant is the sole support of his family it is believed that the ends of society are sometimes served if he spends only his leisure time within the confines of the correctional institution. Such offenders are allowed to continue their regular employment outside of prison, leaving in the morning and returning at night, their compensation being duly collected by the institution and turned over to the family. A man may be permitted to pay a fine in the same fashion, when it is not paid on the instalment plan, or when it does not seem advisable to bring him entirely under custodial care. It may be anticipated that this form of incarceration will be extended in other institutions to certain types of offenders.

<small>Purpose of municipal prisons</small>

The municipal prison has as its function the carrying out of the sentences of the court, to the ends that society may be protected from future anti-social conduct of the offender, and that the offender may be so far rehabilitated so as to be a useful citizen. The responsibility of the prison executive for achieving these objectives is complete, in so far as it is possible under the sentences given. The value of his work must be judged primarily from the effectiveness of the correctional treatment, which should involve classification, personal diagnosis and special treatment for each group of prisoners, character building, employment, and vocational education, proper health measures, and general physical rehabilitation.

The person directly responsible for the management and operation of the prison is the warden. In some communities he is selected directly by the chief executive, but more often he is the appointee of a board of prison commissioners, who are in turn appointed by the chief executive. It is believed that prison management would be equally effective were the warden or superintendent directly responsible to the chief executive, but custom has approved the use of prison boards and they continue in many jurisdictions. Too often it is assumed that any one is good enough to run a prison, and wardens are chosen without regard to fitness, unless it is in the field of political activity in behalf of the appointing authority. Too, prison management often attracts a type of person, who, in the opportunity to domineer over the helpless, finds an outlet for unconscious feelings of physical or mental weakness.[1]

Or, if some judgment is used in the selection of a warden, the qualifications emphasized are those necessary in connection with the management of the prison factory. Some day it may be more completely realized by the public and by their representatives that the purpose of a prison is not primarily to produce goods, but to produce men, and that the qualities of the prison warden should be such as to make him as great a corrective

---

[1] ". . . a certain type of man is almost irresistibly drawn to seek the position of prison warden or prison guard. Frequently—and this is a fact too often overlooked—such men are either physically weak or else they are mental cowards, obsessed in either case by a tormenting sense of inferiority, for which they seek and find compensation in a calling that gives them almost unlimited control over the minds and bodies of their less fortunate fellows. These are the brutal, domineering prison guards, to whom physical suffering is meat and drink. They expand, they grow fat in an atmosphere of cringing obedience. And those prisoners who cannot or who will not cringe, these they "break." The merely physical "breaking" may not be beyond repair, but some prisoners are broken mentally forever. The very tone of voice, in which such guards address the average prisoner, is an insult. An insult that the prisoner is almost powerless to resent; and if he does show resentment, he knows that he is playing directly into the hands of his tormentor. When one has heard and seen such things, as one often must hear and see them without comment or criticism, one understands why prisoners, who pass through the hands of such men leave prison either broken or useless, or else filled with a bitterness of soul, a desperate rebellion against authority that is naturally and logically transferred to society and its laws."—John R. Oliver, "Criminology and Common Sense," *Journal of Criminal Law and Criminology*, XVI, 559 (February, 1926).

390 PRACTICE OF MUNICIPAL ADMINISTRATION

CHAP. XXII

influence within the prison walls as possible. If he is to be such, he must be able to handle men, to inspire their confidence, and to urge them to the best endeavors within their possibilities; also sufficiently broad-minded to realize the trend of modern penology, yet with an absence of sentimentality. Unfortunately, the profession of warden is not sufficiently recognized and the educational machinery for training wardens is very inadequate.[1]

Classification of prisoners

An essential practice in the management of prisons is the classification of prisoners into more or less clearly defined groups, each of which requires major treatment of a different kind. The obvious considerations in such classification are, first, that confirmed offenders should be securely jailed, and second, that new offenders should be handled with a special care. The grouping, however, should further provide for such separation as may be made desirable by personality studies of the mental and physical characteristics of the individual, social environment, education, etc. Misdemeanants may be divided roughly into an honor group which would include only those who would be considered by probation authorities as good probation prospects, who have satisfactory records, who constitute no social menace, and who would not be benefited by institutional life; a middle group including those who would be considered fair probation prospects and who have only fair records; and a low group including those for whom institutional treatment appears eminently desirable. This custodial group includes those whose records and other characteristics, such as ability to adjust in institutional life but not in a competitive society, indicate a custodial problem or a need of close supervision. In the custodial group special consideration must be given to chronic alcoholics, whose records, history, and personality show that repeated intoxication is the common factor in their cases, although this group will include many who are committed on other charges than drunkenness; and to drug addicts, whose difficulties arise largely from a dependence upon drugs, although the most common charge lodged against them is petty larceny.

Habitual offenders

The practicability of giving long terms to misdemeanant recidivists is a question not only of judicial policy and of institutional facilities, but also of law. Long terms or indeterminate sentences are of greatest importance, not only that constructive work may be done with these persons, but also with a view to deterrence. It

[1] It is reported that in England even prison guards are required to make a formal study of their occupation.

is a notorious fact that the imposition of long sentences quickly becomes "under-world" news and that drug addicts and other habitual offenders of certain types will not go to cities where long terms are the rule.

Prison housing has always followed rather closely the prevailing theory of punishment.[1] As a rule, the early prisons were heavy masonry structures constructed for some other purpose, but turned into prisons because they afforded a sure means of confinement. Imprisonment was then largely a matter of indefinite incarceration or of detention prior to execution. With the conception of imprisonment as a practical means of punishment, larger institutions were necessary. These buildings were designed to secure the prisoners and provided for solitary confinement in tiers of cells without proper heat, light, ventilation, or other sanitary necessities. Eventually it was demonstrated that solitary confinement was both inhuman and economically impracticable, and new prisons were constructed to facilitiate the classification of prisoners and to provide opportunities for employment and recreation.[2] Always there was solitary confinement in part, and the individual cell remained the dominant feature, although sanitation and comfort were given proper treatment.[3]

Cities are principally concerned with the housing and treatment of committed misdemeanants, and in this connection care should be taken not to over-emphasize the penitentiary type of prison developed for more serious offenders.[4] Present-day opinion urges that short term petty offenders should be provided with as nearly the housing of normal individuals as proper regard for the safety of the community will permit.[5] Any analysis of misdemeanants in a municipal prison will indicate that a large majority of them formerly lived in rooming houses, boarding houses, and cheap hotels. The institutional parallel to these places is dormitories rather than individual cells or rooms. The process of rehabilitat-

---

[1] See F. H. Wines, *Punishment and Reformation* (rev. ed., Crowell, 1919); and Louis N. Robinson, *Penology in the United States* (Winston, 1921).
[2] This was the Auburn as opposed to the Pennsylvania plan, the relative merits of which were vigorously debated some years ago.
[3] *Prisons and Prison Building* (Rogers and Manson, 1918); and Hastings H. Hart, *Plans and Illustrations of Prisons and Reformatories* (Russell Sage Foundation, 1922).
[4] The following discussion of the housing, employment, and discipline of misdemeanants summarizes a study made by the Detroit Bureau of Governmental Research, *A New House of Correction* (July, 1924).
[5] Many small cities use the county jail as a place of incarceration, or make arrangements with a neighboring municipality to provide workhouse facilities.

ing the minor offender and of equipping him to fulfil his functions as a normal law-abiding citizen will be made more difficult if during incarceration he is kept under abnormal conditions. After all, the custodial feature has been enormously over-emphasized as a factor in the evaluation of reform institutions. If, with misdemeanants, a few escapes take place, while at the same time a greater number of men are prepared to assume a proper place in society, there can be no question but that the community has been served to a better advantage, both economically and socially, than if there were no escapes and no rehabilitation. Also, the records prove that misdemeanants that escape will in the large majority of cases be recaptured, or will shortly be resentenced for a subsequent minor offense. This does not mean that provision for secure confinement is not needed. In receiving institutions there should be a section devoted to secure yet comfortable quarters where offenders may be confined until proper classification has been determined, and solitary cells should be provided in all institutions for the confinement of dangerous cases and as a means of punishment for the unruly.

<small>Barracks *vs.* room and cell plan</small>

The trend of much authoritative opinion with respect to housing is from cells to rooms for long-term state felons, and to barracks or rooms for short-term misdemeanants. By the term "barracks" is meant one-story separate buildings, each to house from thirty to fifty men, and containing a sleeping ward, a small social room, and baths and toilets. There is a distinct difference from penitentiary construction, both in the amount of privacy in sleeping and during leisure hours. Privacy during leisure hours is not customary in the outside life of the misdemeanant group, nor does it aid in the adjustment of the individual to the group. Privacy "to afford opportunity for meditation" actually means affording an opportunity for augmenting the disorganization of personality which is nearly always present to a greater or less degree. Nor should prisoners be given a higher standard of housing than they are accustomed to in private life. Also, while the housing should be decent and comfortable, the prisoner must be made to look forward to the completion of his term. This is especially true with chronic drunkards, drug addicts, vagabonds, and the shiftless dependents, who, if the surroundings are too agreeable, acquire the "institutional habit," and return again and again to enjoy the hospitality of the correctional institutions. The use of dormitories is successful with these groups and should be preferred by both management and inmates.

The bulk of a workhouse population may be expected to consist of chronic misdemeanants, alcoholics, drug addicts, and miscellaneous offenders, who will be a relatively mature group, whose greatest social need is for human contact and group activity. Their failure in society has been due to their lack of adjustment as individuals to society. Their greatest need is for group work and group play. This is evidenced by their very low sense of social responsibility, their need for adjustment in work, their abuse of leisure time, their non-participation in voting, failure to belong to any societies, poor family relationships, etc. These considerations seem to make dormitory housing preferable to any other arrangement.[1]

The problem of handling these groups of misdemeanants is one of supervision rather than of custody, and supervision of barrack units is simple. A spirit of competition and rivalry is easily fostered; natural racial and color cleavages are easily cared for; the oppressive penitentiary atmosphere common in the cell-block type of institution is eliminated; and the increased social equality and sense of freedom elevates the tone of prison management and increases the likelihood of moral improvement. The plan permits the segregation of prisoners into suitable small groups and classes, to each of which a particular method of treatment likely to be most helpful can be applied. Also, barracks lend themselves to the principle of pliability, permitting future alteration in the system and adaptation to changes in penal methods. The testimony of many prison wardens is that when the more incorrigible and perverted classes are segregated in cell-type buildings, the large remainder, particularly of misdemeanants, may preferably be handled in barrack dormitories.[2]

A municipal institution must find employment for its inmates, both to reduce the cost of operation and because of the salutary effect of hard labor upon offenders. Officials must therefore turn either to industry or to agriculture as a means of employment. In the older type of prisons it has been customary to establish indus-

[1] These characteristics of inmates are taken from the previously cited study of the Detroit House of Correction made by the Detroit Bureau of Governmental Research.
[2] Opinion is not unanimous, but in reply to inquiries assent to this position was given by a number of outstanding prison administrators.

tries for the manufacture of brushes, chairs, clothing, or similar products requiring relatively unskilled workers. Or, prisoners are hired to contractors on a per diem basis. This last method of employment has fallen into disrepute and disuse in all but most backward communities. It is objectionable because of the inhuman conditions under which prisoners are often required to live and work, because of the competition of prison-made goods with those manufactured by free labor, and because prison contractors frequently pay the state much less than the prison labor is worth, becoming wealthy by the exploitation of unfortunates. Objection to the direct use of prison labor in manufacturing processes has been met to some extent by restricting the output to public uses. However the fact remains that although these industries do not compete directly with private enterprises they eventually reduce their market.

Regardless of all this discussion, however, from the economic and physiological standpoint, it would be utter folly to allow prisoners to remain idle. Progressive wardens throughout the country have demonstrated time and again that about the worst treatment for the prisoner is to keep him continually behind prison bars, and that with proper supervision he can be induced to work industriously and intelligently. Work is more important for those in institutions than for the civilian. To place a man in confinement without work is to make him less capable of honest endeavor when he is released from prison than he was before he went in. But work done under a constant rule of force and fear by men who are confined when not working produces the least possible amount of good results.

If self-control, self-discipline and the spirit of coöperation are not developed in the prisoner, he, when released and the pressure of force is removed, will almost inevitably resume his anti-social attitude and activities, and will be at least as great a social and economic liability to the community as he was before serving the sentence. The benefits derived from work depend almost entirely upon the environmental and social characteristics of the institution. Purposeless work is not itself beneficial; purposeful work is an aid to be used in conjunction with a well-rounded scheme of physical and mental rehabilitation.

Vocational training

Under an ideal plan of handling chronic misdemeanants, the sentences would be sufficiently long—whether fixed or, preferably, indeterminate and coupled with the parole—as to permit of a corrective and educational treatment not now possible. Definite goals of attainment could be established for each prisoner which, in addition to good conduct, must be reached before his case would be heard for parole.[1] These goals might be of a twofold nature, industrial and academic. In this connection it would be advisable to make an analysis of all men entering a municipal institution on the basis of industrial ability and adaptability, and to include psychological tests as to mentality and vocational guidance tests correlated with work history. These tests would serve to divide the unskilled, or those having no ability for trade training; the semi-skilled, capable of limited trade training; those of average trade ability; journeymen or high grade clerical workers; and those of foreman grade or higher. Industry should be organized to provide training for each of these grades,[2] and progress in trade training should be satisfactory before the prisoner could be heard for parole. The same method should be applied in the academic school.[3] Such a work classification seems to be freer from institutional artificiality, as compared with life outside, than any other, and is undoubtedly the most practical help that can be extended to the men. It has the advantage of definite goals of attainment which should inspire prisoners to their best efforts, and the tests limit the goals to the realm of practicability. This type of training is, of course, very costly.

It would be useless to attempt to enumerate the various trades which might be taught in a penal institution. In fact, the teaching of any particular trade is not so much at point as the importance of acquainting the inmate with the use of tools. However, some limitations must be made, and these should be governed by dominant industry in the community.[4] In this connection it becomes very essential that every effort be made to keep the methods taught abreast of the best practices in private industry.

On the other hand it is more or less impossible to deal satis-

---

[1] The procedure outlined here is that employed in the New Jersey Reformatory, and made possible by the indeterminate sentence and parole laws of the state.
[2] In the New Jersey reformatory this classification has proved to be of the greatest service.
[3] For example, if it is found, when a man enters, that his educational level is in the second grade and by tests it is shown that he has mental abilities sufficient to let him reach the fifth grade, the fifth grade accomplishment should be required.
[4] In Detroit, for example, the House of Correction attempts through its furniture factory to acquaint inmates with the use of tools cognate with those used in the automobile industry.

396 PRACTICE OF MUNICIPAL ADMINISTRATION

CHAP. XXII

Prison farms

factorily in an industrial way with short-time offenders. Complicated manufacturing processes are impracticable when the employers have an average labor turnover of a thousand or more percent per year, which is bound to occur with the short-term sentences that are now imposed upon misdemeanants.[1] The only alternative is the use of the prison farm, which has come into high favor as a method of employing not only misdemeanants but the more serious offenders as well. Agricultural work is not used so much as a matter of trade training as for its therapeutic value. Few of the inmates will ever make use of the knowledge so gained, yet the general mental and physical rehabilitation resulting may be of large value.[2]

Payments to prisoners

It has been aptly said that when the average man is placed in prison an even more severe punishment is imposed upon those innocent persons dependent upon him. Not only are they stigmatized by the prison sentence, but they have lost their natural means of support. For this reason, it is frequently necessary for the charitable branch of the city government immediately to undertake the care of those dependent on the person incarcerated. In this connection one of the notable improvements that has been made in prison procedure has been the payment of prisoners for the work which they are compelled to undertake. This pay may amount to a substantial sum and is turned over to the dependents of the prisoner when such payments are necessary for their maintenance. If no dependents exist, or they are not in need of aid, a small stipend is given which is allowed to accumulate to the credit of the prisoner and is given him upon the expiration of his sentence. This sends him out into the world with a small amount of money which may last while he is re-establishing himself in society. As an incentive to good behavior, some part of these payments are ordinarily allowed a prisoner, during his confinement, to be used for minor luxuries which are not ordinarily included in the prison routine.

Prison education

No modern prison is complete without educational facilities, even for short-term offenders. After provision has been made for productive work during the ordinary working day, opportunity

---

[1] In 1924, the average commitment to the Detroit House of Correction was twenty-nine days, meaning an annual labor turnover of in excess of 1200 percent.

[2] The use of prison farms is no guarantee of sound penology. For a study of revolting conditions on state penal farms, see Carl C. Jensen, "Our Convict Slaves," *Atlantic Monthly*, CXXXVII, 591-603 (May, 1926).

for study should be provided during the period between dinner and "lights out." Such work will ordinarily be undertaken by the educational authorities of the community on request. It is not expected that so much can be accomplished with short-term offenders, but the school can provide excellently for those having reasonably long terms, so that the prisoner may at least obtain the rudiments of an elementary education. The use of motion pictures should prove very helpful in this connection, due to the lack of imagination which seems to characterize prisoners. Prisoners who have the means, either directly or by earning within the prison walls, are often permitted to take correspondence courses along the lines in which they are particularly interested.

The old time prison was a place of horror, and unfortunately too many prisons still remain so.[1] Not only are prisoners punished by the loss of liberty, but life is further made rigorous for them by poor food, unsanitary quarters, hard work, stern discipline, prevention of conversation among themselves and deliberate cruelties not uncommon when one group of men is placed in absolute domination of another. Modern tendencies, however, are in the direction of humane treatment of offenders, on the ground that denial of freedom is a sufficient punishment. Cruel and unusual punishments for violations of rules are not inflicted, and the rules themselves have become more lenient. Men are permitted to talk with one another, to take part in social activities within the prison walls, and to conduct themselves in somewhat the same manner that they would in civil life. Under such circumstances, discipline becomes a matter of rewards rather than one of punishment. A man who conducts himself properly within the prison is allowed certain privileges; if he does not so conduct himself those privileges are withdrawn. It has been demonstrated that this treatment is more effective as a corrective, and the prisoner when released does not carry with him a rancor to be vented upon society.

Recently there has grown up a belief among persons more or less unfamiliar with prisons that these institutions are becoming sentimental in their treatment of prisoners, and that some individuals would prefer to be in prison than outside. Of course there are individuals and groups that have been in prison so much that they cannot adjust themselves to civil life and when once released take the very shortest course to get back again. However,

[1] See articles in the *Atlantic Monthly* for April, August, and October, 1920, by Frank Tannenbaum.

it is questionable whether a single recidivist was ever created by humane contact within a prison, and it is a certainty that many such have been created by inhumane treatment. Modern penology aims primarily at the criminal and thus at the source of crime. It recognizes fully the right of society to protect itself, and it provides for that protection by a treatment of the offender that may be even more severe than that now prevailing. But in this treatment it considers every law-breaker as a delinquent whose personality (including heredity), and social, physical and mental condition must be taken into account. The prison should be no longer an instrument of revenge—a place where excessive labor, poor food, and cruel treatment prevail as a matter of course. It is recognized that punishment is inherent in imprisonment and that deprivation of liberty by itself may be sufficient to vindicate the established order; and that to do constructive work, emphasis must be placed basically and continually on reformatory influences.

CHAPTER XXIII

MARKETS [1]

As compared with European municipalities, provision for public marketing has engaged little of the energy of American cities.[2] Economic pressure—the difficulty of winning a sheer livelihood by the mass of European peoples—has instilled a frugality and indifference to petty inconveniences that does not prevail among the more fortunate citizens of the United States. As long as financial means permit, most American housewives will prefer to patronize the corner grocery with its facilities of credit, telephone, and delivery, or the neighborhood chain store, to the less pleasant alternative of trudging to a public market with basket on arm, and haggling over supplies, even though better in quality and at a somewhat reduced price. By the same token, the public has continued relatively indifferent to the waste of farm and orchard products because profitable markets cannot be found for them, and to the excessive prices made necessary by slipshod methods of production and preparation for market, by the absence of storage facilities, by unnecessary middlemen and more middlemen, by expensive trucking and other transportation, and by the luxury of grocery stores and small markets that exist in far too large numbers for the population they serve.

Public indifference to problems of food distribution

This wasteful situation cannot continue forever. Farmers and orchardists, suffering from almost continuous economic depression, and impressed with the quantity of their products that finds no market at all, or is sold at prices in great disparity with those

The opportunity of the producer

---

[1] Much that has been written on public markets does not correctly reflect present day opinions on the subject. For reference purposes, however, see the following: J. W. Sullivan, *Markets for the People* (Macmillan, 1913); *Report of the Mayor's Market Commission of New York City* (1913); *Municipal Markets* (Annals, XLVIII, July, 1913); Clyde L. King, *Lower Living Costs in Cities* (Appleton, 1915). Reports on market conditions are available for several cities, including New York, Chicago, Detroit, and Minneapolis.

[2] In 1918, there were 237 public markets in 228 cities of over 30,000 population. New Orleans reported 19 markets and Baltimore 11. Newark has recently erected a market costing $5,000,000. For detailed discussion of these markets see U. S. Bureau of Census, *Municipal Markets in Cities Having a Population of Over 30,000* (1918); National Municipal League, *Public Markets in the United States* (1917); New York State Bureau of Information, Report No. 29, *Municipal Public Markets* (Albany, 1917); and *Report of the Mayor's Market Commission of New York City* (1913).

finally paid by the consumer, are slowly seeking a way out. Agricultural colleges and various farm organizations are teaching the advantages of crop diversification, of better production and preparation of produce for market, of planning market production more accurately to meet market requirements, and of coöperative methods of marketing. The rural food producer, notoriously inadept at united action, is finding that only through such a program is it possible for him to receive a greater portion of the final price of his product.

The opportunity of the consumer

Urban population has increased at the expense of the rural food-producing groups, the consuming population increasing and the producing population decreasing. This urban population finds itself concerned not only with foodstuffs raised at constantly increased distances from the points of consumption, but also by inadequate facilities for storage, by excessive costs of transferring from the point of city arrival to the points of final distribution, and by repeated handlings of produce, each at an added expense. With the question of an adequate and economical food supply becoming more urgent, many cities are happily directing attention to the part they must take in the solution of the problem. Under average conditions, cities can improve the situation by the construction and operation of public farmers' markets, beginning, where necessary, with simple curb markets, and gradually extending to wholesale and terminal facilities.

Source of supplies

Most large cities have two general sources of supply for fruits, vegetables, poultry, and eggs, which make up the bulk of the perishable farm produce received. The major portion arrives by rail and boat from distant shippers and is handled first by the group of merchants known as car-lot receivers, or jobbers.[1] The car quantities are distributed, mostly in large lots, to wholesalers, who in turn supply the retailers. The minor portion is styled "home-grown," and is trucked into the city from near-by points. This supply usually goes to a wholesale and retail public farmers' market, if one exists, or is left with the wholesale and commission merchants to be sold. In some places the producers, through lack of proper marketing facilities, are forced to peddle their produce

[1] The term "jobber" as used in this discussion, is synonymous with the "car-lot receiver." The term "wholesaler" is construed to mean the smaller dealer who buys mostly in less-than-carload lots from the car-lot receiver or jobber and sells to the retailer. In some cities, particularly in the East, usage gives exactly the opposite meaning to these terms. Thus in New York City wholesaler is synonymous with car-lot receiver, while the jobber is the smaller dealer who takes care of the needs of the retailer.

from store to store or to consumers, a slow and unsatisfactory method of disposal.

In cities of small and medium size, the functions of the car-lot receiver and the wholesaler are more or less combined. In the large city, greater specialization has been found necessary, especially in the handling of the car-lot supply. The following diagram will help visualize the main channels of distribution in larger cities, and at the same time will show the complexity of the problem

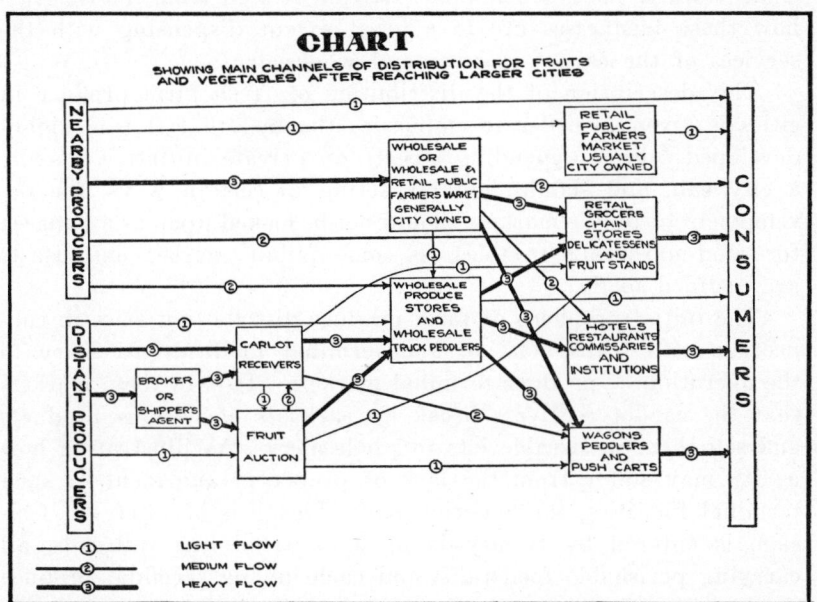

of furnishing a large urban population with fresh farm produce every day.

The heavy lines indicate the flow of the bulk of the daily receipts of farm produce. It can be seen that while short and direct routes between producer and consumer are open, nevertheless most of the produce takes the longer route and passes through several hands. This is due to the ever-increasing demand of the public and of the distributing agencies themselves for uniform and convenient service involving credit, delivery, and well graded and standardized goods in great variety in and out of season, and in small day-to-day quantities. While wholesalers, retailers, and consumers wish to buy in small quantities and in great assortment, the trend is for producers to sell in large quantities and specialize on fewer crops. These circumstances necessitate a marked division in the functions of the city agencies of distribution, and furnish an explanation of the number of middlemen found in the business. While some of these middlemen may be unnecessary in the food distribution industry, the general system seems to fit existing conditions, and probably will be changed only as economic conditions change. As an instance of such change, the development of the chain store is the best example. It can be seen from the diagram how those businesses are to a great extent dispensing with the services of the car-lot receiver and wholesaler.

This description of the distribution of fresh farm produce in cities is given in order to emphasize the fact that it is a highly developed service depending largely on private initiative. While a city can, and should, aid marketing in certain ways, the development of public markets should not be looked upon as a panacea for food-marketing troubles, as some public market enthusiasts are inclined to do.

The initial problems of farm produce distribution arise in connection with transportation and terminal facilities necessary to the operation of produce terminal markets. It is in these markets that the car-lot receivers break up carloads of various products and sell them in sizeable lots to wholesalers. As illustrating how a city may suffer from the lack of proper arrangement of such terminal facilities, the experience of Chicago is of interest. Chicago is entered by twenty-six or more trunk-line railroads, all carrying perishable foodstuffs, and each having terminal produce yards originally located wherever space permitted. The stores of car-lot receivers were situated in a congested high-rent district on South Water Street, along the Chicago River and bordering the "Loop" district. Practically all produce had to be trucked from the various railroad yards through the congested section of the city to these wholesale stores and then sold and distributed throughout the city. Oftentimes trucks of produce would be delayed from one to three hours in getting through the "Loop" district alone. Frequently the same type of product from the same shipping district would arrive the same day in three or four yards, all consigned to the same firm. In countless ways, the costs of trucking, car inspection, sales work, delivery, etc., were increased, in addition to constantly mounting rentals, all because of the lack of a well-planned central produce terminal or primary market;

and the consumer paid the bill. For fifty years there were repeated movements to develop such a terminal. But, on account of conflicting interests and jealousies among the members of the produce trade and the railroads involved, all plans failed. Finally the city forced a change in 1924 by condemning the South Water Street produce district in order to improve the riverfront. In 1925, therefore, the produce trade formed an organization which, with the coöperation of the transportation lines, has developed fairly satisfactory facilities at a cost of around $17,000,000.

<small>CHAP. XXIII</small>

New York City is confronted with a similar problem on which the Port of New York Authority has been working for a number of years. The solution involves such a staggering sum of money, and a practical plan is so difficult to devise and agree upon, that definite physical results have not been obtained.[1] In a large measure, this situation can be laid to the failure of the produce trade, the railroads, and the city government to realize long ago the vital importance of economical distribution of perishable food for the city, and of the development of a plan capable of expansion to meet the needs of an ever-increasing population. To a lesser extent, Philadelphia is faced with the same problem, as is practically every other large city in this country and abroad.

<small>The problem in New York and Philadelphia</small>

It is not argued that a city should build municipally-owned produce terminals, although certain conditions may warrant such action. But every city, in conjunction with the produce trade and the transportation lines, should take the necessary steps to plan for the development of privately owned produce-terminal facilities as the need manifests itself. There can be no doubt that such planning will save large sums for most growing cities.

Location is a vital factor in connection with the construction and operation of a wholesale produce terminal. The ideal site would be on a belt railway line that intersects all or most of the trunk lines entering the city, and with ample ground for expansion. If a considerable part of the perishable food of the city comes in by boat, the best location would be a combined water and belt line railway terminal. If such a terminal must be located on a trunk line, it is important that such railway be obligated to switch to the terminal promptly, and at a reasonable charge, cars coming over other roads. The layout of a modern terminal should

<small>Location of wholesale produce terminal</small>

---

[1] See New York City, Department of Public Markets, *Municipal Wholesale Terminal Markets and Their Relation to the Food Problem;* Cyrus C. Miller, "Municipal Terminal Markets," *Journal of the National Institute of Social Sciences,* July, 1916.

404 PRACTICE OF MUNICIPAL ADMINISTRATION

CHAP. XXIII

include a "hold" yard, an adequate delivery or "team track" yard, a cold storage unit, and warehouse and storage facilities for the car-lot receivers, and a fruit auction. It is not within the province of this discussion to outline a detailed arrangement of these facilities, but the project is large and worthy of the most careful study by the administrator concerned.

Wholesale produce districts—the secondary market

On leaving the primary market, the bulk of produce in any large city moves to the wholesale produce districts, where the needs of the retailer are taken care of. In smaller cities this specialization is not necessary or practical to any extent, but in large cities experience has shown that the car-lot receivers and the primary terminal cannot satisfactorily handle the retail and hotel and restaurant trade, due to lack of space, multiplicity of accounts, the restricted kinds of produce which the average car-lot receiver sells, and numerous other reasons.

Wholesale produce district logical location for municipal wholesale farmers' markets

Probably the largest wholesale district will be located within easy trucking distance of the downtown business center; for a large proportion of the receipts of perishable fruits, vegetables, and poultry products goes to the hotels, restaurants, and stores of the downtown district. While such a secondary produce market is purely a private development, it is of interest to the municipal administrator, since the ideal location for a municipal wholesale and retail farmers' market is in conjunction with it. Sometimes the farmers' markets are located first and the wholesale district grows up around them. This shows the natural relation and mutual helpfulness of the two, since under such an arrangement a retail buyer can get his entire requirements of perishable products, both home-grown and shipped-in, quickly and conveniently. Both the public market and the private wholesale district attract trade which is likely to be mutually beneficial. Hence, although the two are competitive in a "trade" sense, the advantages of close relationship more than offset any resultant losses.

Not practical for cities to buy and sell

So far as the cities of this country are concerned, the interest of the municipal government is in practically all cases limited to the furnishing of market facilities in the way of buildings, grounds, or street curb space, and the renting of such facilities under proper regulations to either producers or dealers in food products, or both. A few experiments have been made where the city or state authorities involved have offered a selling service on a commission basis to producers who desired to send their products to a municipally-owned market, but who could not conveniently come in themselves to act as salesmen. So far as is known, all of these attempts have resulted in practical failure and have been discontinued. Such a service on the part of a city appeals as being both desirable and practical to many persons who are acquainted with the problems of food distribution. But experience shows that the resulting troubles have overwhelmed any resulting advantages. Students of both marketing and municipal government will generally agree that a city is not on safe economic ground in entering into either buying or selling operations in this field except in cases of emergency.

Existing public markets owned and controlled by municipalities may be divided roughly into two classes—inclosed and open. Municipally-owned markets of the inclosed type, wherein market stall facilities are rented to retail dealers in fruits and vegetables, meats, fish, dairy and poultry products, etc., are going out of fashion. Whereas they once played an important part in the food-distribution system of many cities, most of them are now of minor importance, due to the rise of chain-store systems, the betterment of independent food stores, the competition of privately-owned public markets, and generally poor management. The practical failure of Newark's new $5,000,000 market bears out this contention.

It has been believed that such retail markets, being publicly owned, could reduce stall rentals and the general cost of doing business, with consequent lower prices to the consumer. In addition they have offered the advantage of a large assortment of foodstuffs under one roof, from which the consumer might select. It is possible that, if properly managed, such markets might yet offer appreciably lower prices, particularly on meats, which chain stores do not handle to any extent. But studies have shown that very few public markets of this character really do sell foodstuffs any lower than, if as low as, competing chain stores. The chain store has a location convenient to the housewife and a large buying power, advantages with which the small stall keeper in a public market finds it difficult to compete. Under such conditions, there seems little reason for the average city to spend money, always needed badly for other more essential and unquestionable activities, to develop an institution that only offers a service which is now more efficiently and economically undertaken by private enterprise.

In the case of cities which have retail markets, or determine

CHAP. XXIII

Construction

that their special conditions warrant building and operating them, certain conclusions apply. Such a market is a food department store and should be located only where other types of department stores can succeed. This restricts the location to the downtown shopping center preferably, or at least to well developed subsidiary shopping and business districts. The building should be economically constructed, as undue ornateness adds to the investment and must be reflected in increased stall rentals if the market is to be self-sustaining. A high standard of sanitation should prevail throughout. Refrigerated, glass-enclosed counters, adequate refrigeration rooms, equipment which can be easily and thoroughly cleansed, and good ventilation are essential. The sections devoted to the sale of live poultry, and possibly fish, should be walled off from the balance of the market with glass partitions. The best existing public market buildings, privately as well as publicly owned, should be studied by the architect employed, as both design and equipment are of a highly specialized nature. In this connection, the advice of a consulting expert in market design and management should be obtained if possible.

Operation

A competent, experienced manager is essential to the success of such markets, and he must be free from political interference. Stall and other rentals should be set to return an income at least sufficient to cover the cost of conducting the institution when all the charges are assessed against it that a private institution of the same nature would have to pay. If the business will not bear such a scale of rentals, the market is not justified from any point of view. Management measures must insure that dealers in the market conduct their business on the basis of big volume with small margin of profit, and honest dealing. This requires absolute control of tenants through short stall leases and unhampered ability on the part of the manager to dispossess stall holders whose conduct and business methods do not make for the success of the institution. Delivery and credit service at the expense of the individual dealer has been found a poor policy. In some markets coöperative delivery systems have been found useful, but the most successful ones are of the "cash and carry" type.

The popularity of an inclosed retail public market for dealers is generally enhanced by a retail farmers' market held two or three days a week, along the adjacent street curb, or under sheds on adjoining property. While this feature involves competition for certain of the dealers, it is so valuable as a means of attracting consumers that the market dealers themselves are usually heartily in favor of it. In fact some markets would find it hard to continue without the "farmers' line" outside.[1]

A few cities of medium size have for years had municipally-owned inclosed retail market houses, the space in which is rented almost exclusively to farmers for use on two or three days a week. This is a service to the producer and consumer which it is not desired to criticize; but it is safe to say that the economic value of such a market to either farmer or consumer is relatively small, due to the comparatively meagre amount and restricted variety of produce which can be distributed in that way. The money value of such market properties is usually large in proportion to the limited use and service given. Old markets of this type in certain smaller cities have considerable sentimental value to the group of families that have been in the habit of using them for many years. They give a protected place to buy fresh country produce direct from the producer, and are of some service to smaller producers who do not have a good outlet for their miscellaneous products and whose time is not particularly valuable on the farm. As a rule, however, most cities as well as their surrounding rural communities, will be better served by a farmers' market of the open-shed type which is both wholesale and retail in character.

Without doubt, the most practical field for municipal endeavor, so far as public markets are concerned, lies in the establishment and proper management and control of farmers' markets in which the selling is done partially at wholesale to retail grocers and hucksters, and also at retail to consumers. Such a market may be held uncovered along a street curb, or it may be placed inside the property line either with or without overhead covering. Preferably, it should be off the street and provided with well designed sheds. If the market is in a city with cold winter temperatures, a certain unit of the shed structures, of sufficient capacity to accommodate stall renters who sell during the cold season, should be provided with rolling steel or other type of doors so that it may be inclosed when weather conditions require.

CHAP. XXIII

Municipal retail market houses for producers not generally recommended

Municipally owned public farmers' markets of the open or shed type best for most cities

[1] For further discussion of inclosed retail dealers' markets, see G. V. Branch, *Retail Public Markets*, in Year Book, Separate No. 191, U. S. Department of Agriculture (1915). Certain statements in this bulletin would now be altered by the author because of greatly changed conditions, but the publication still contains considerable information of value. Much detailed statistical information may be obtained from *Municipal Markets in Cities Having a Population of Over 30,000* (Bureau of the Census, 1919).

A municipal market of this kind is economically sound, for it provides a practical and necessary service not satisfactorily offered by private initiative. To be sure, wholesale and commission dealers in some cities, particularly in Philadelphia, handle a large volume of fruit and truck products from local growers, but even so, most commission firms care to accept only the business of the larger and better growers who produce few products in quantities, and grade and pack them well. The more assorted loads of the smaller grower still need the public farmers' market as an outlet.

The public farmers' market, when given half a chance, will thrive in most cities of 50,000 population and up; while much smaller cities often successfully operate them. This proves fairly well that they fill a definite need in the present system of perishable-food distribution. In Detroit, for instance, the public farmers' markets are surrounded by the stores of wholesale and commission merchants, so that the local producer has his choice of outlet. Nevertheless, practically all of the truckloads of produce brought in by the growers are sold on the farmers' markets. This indicates that the growers get better financial returns by selling in this manner, and in general are more satisfied with it. A good public farmers' market is also a most effective agency in stimulating the nearby production of fruit and truck crops and poultry products.

Should farmers' markets be retail only?

In establishing a new farmers' market the question generally arises as to whether it should be wholesale or retail in character, or both. Because of the many factors involved, no inflexible rule can be laid down. However, strictly retail, or direct-to-consumer, markets are not recommended except when (1) the city or the surrounding truck-crop production, or both, are small, so that offerings on the market are not sufficient to supply both the retail dealers and consumers, and (2) when the city already has a good wholesale public farmers' market, but wants one or more additional markets in other neighborhoods to function two or three days a week, particularly during the summer months, or (3) when most of the growers who would use the market are not large commercial truck growers, but farmers with small surpluses of garden, orchard, and poultry products to sell, and are willing to spend the time necessary to retail small quantities direct to the consumer. Even under these circumstances, it will be found that the market will usually develop faster and attract more growers if wholesale selling in the early morning hours is permitted.

The most satisfactory type of public farmers' market in cities of upwards of 50,000 population, located in a good, or even a fair, truck-producing area, is the one where wholesale selling to grocers, hucksters, and other retailers is encouraged in the early morning hours, to be followed later by direct consumer buying. In this way the market caters to the whole community, as the ninety or more percent of families who cannot, or do not, desire to go to a public market and shop are served quickly with fresh home-grown products with but one intermediate handling. This feature is relatively more important than providing facilities for direct sale to a few families. A city should aim to keep the channel between producer and consumer as straight, and the intermediate dealers as few as possible; and a market of this type fulfills this purpose. Furthermore, it suits the needs of the growers best, thus encouraging a maximum number to come in and use it. As farm labor and other costs increase, it is the more necessary that producers waste as little time as possible away from the farm in marketing their products. Therefore most of them prefer to sell the bulk of their load at wholesale, taking a little less per package, rather than spend more time retailing it in small quantities direct to the consumer, even at a higher price. In fact, the truck growers who bring in the larger loads of the best produce would find it almost impossible physically to retail all of it, and one seldom finds such growers on a strictly retail market. Practically all growers, however, are willing to retail a part of their offerings, finding the consumer trade valuable as a supplement to their wholesale business.

A farmers' market which lets selling take its normal course and serves retail dealers and consumers alike will usually find far less opposition, particularly at the time of its establishment, from retail business interests of a city. Strictly direct-to-consumer public farmers' markets are often bitterly opposed by the established retailers, and in many cities this opposition has prevented any development of farmers' market facilities.

The best location for a wholesale and retail public farmers' market is in, or immediately adjacent to, the wholesale produce district that is nearest the shopping and business center of the city. In the largest cities more than one such market is often required to serve the community adequately. If so, they should be quite widely separated and in natural centers of wholesale produce distribution. Moderate priced property for future, as well as immediate, needs is desirable.

To make the trading rapid and to conserve time of both pro-

410 PRACTICE OF MUNICIPAL ADMINISTRATION

CHAP. XXIII

Operation

ducers and buyers, the hours of business should be held to a minimum. A definite opening hour, before which sales are forbidden, is very advisable and is usually set around 5 A. M. in the summer months, and 6:30 A. M. in the winter. The market should be closed by noon on all days except Saturday, when an afternoon and evening session is sometimes desirable. If the trade will not support a daily market, it should be restricted to Tuesdays, Thursdays, and Saturdays, or possibly to two days a week, Saturday always being one. Usually it is found best to restrict the selling on the market to bona fide producers selling their own produce. If any dealers are allowed to sell, they should at least be separated from the producers and plainly designated as such. As many stalls as possible should be rented to producers on an annual or seasonal basis and reserved for the renter at least to the opening hour of the market. The appearance of a producer regularly in a certain stall helps both him and his customers. Daily fees, of course are necessary for the producer who comes only occasionally. After the market is once established as a going business, stall rentals should at least be sufficient to meet maintenance and operating charges. Since the market is a distinct service asset to the city as well as to the nearby producers, it is often considered fair for the city to finance the site and buildings, and let the rentals from farmers cover the remaining costs.[1]

Transfer of privileges

The holding of more than one or two stalls by one person inevitably leads to the sub-leasing of stall privileges for a consideration. A person renting a stall from the city should not be allowed to sell this privilege with its good will to another, but the stall, when given up, should revert to the city, to be given to the next person on the waiting list. To permit stalls to be transferred for a consideration covering intangible assets loads up the stall purchaser with an expense that makes for higher prices. The principal justification for public markets occupied by producers or dealers, or both, lies in the low prices to be gained as a result of small investment, low operating costs, and large volume of trade.[2]

Discipline

Market rules should be framed so that stall renters have no

[1] For further discussion of farmers' markets, see McFall Kerby, *Open Types of Public Markets* (U. S. Dept. of Agriculture Bulletin No. 1002, 1921). *Service and Regulatory Announcements—Markets*, No. 69 of the same Department, gives suggestions for a farmers' market ordinance.

[2] Parts of this discussion on management features are taken by Mr. G. V. Branch, from his "Public Markets," *Government of Cincinnati and Hamilton County.*

reason to feel that they have property rights in the stall. To regulate a market successfully, the city must maintain absolute control and be able to dispossess a tenant when he violates either market or health regulations, or conducts his business in a way detrimental to the best interests of the market. Where stall renters gain the impression that the stall is their property to use as they see fit, and to sell to another when they wish, one always finds a poorly conducted market, run in the interests of the stall owners instead of the public.

The retail curb market is found in many small municipalities and some larger ones, and may be successful in cities of over 10,000 population. Here, on some suitable street, local farmers and gardeners, and hucksters, are given places where they may station themselves at certain specified times and display their produce. This type of market has no buildings, so may be moved easily if the site first selected proves unsatisfactory. The farmer or huckster should pay a small fee for stand privilege, and should be permitted to keep this stand for a definite period without danger of being ousted by some other dealer. However, permanent curb markets are undesirable from the point of view of both sanitation and traffic congestion. No practical cover for perishable food products can be provided for protection from sun and rain, and produce is constantly exposed to the blowing dirt of the street.

Such markets should be placed inside of the property line and under sheds as soon, at least, as the experimental stage is passed, thereby coming in the category of farmers' markets previously discussed. This removal from the streets is most important, now that traffic congestion on city highways is becoming so acute. If such removal is not practicable, every effort should be made to minimize traffic interference by the elimination of corner stands, the removal of as many standing vehicles of stall holders as possible, the angle or parallel parking of the remaining ones, and the abolition of parking on the opposite side of the street.

Rules should forbid the sale of food products not usually washed, peeled, or cooked before being eaten; except that butter, cheese, candy, dates, and figs may be merchandised when unexposed and offered in original containers. In the case of curb markets, it has not proved practicable to require stall renters to remove their rubbish and garbage when the market period is over. If compelled to care for refuse, many vendors will dump it into the first convenient alley, where it is more costly to clean up than

412 PRACTICE OF MUNICIPAL ADMINISTRATION

CHAP. XXIII

Sanitary conditions

when left on the market place. It is also difficult to enforce a rule requiring that all decayed vegetable matter and trimmings be kept in a separate receptacle and not thrown on the pavement, but with fairly drastic supervision this can be done. It is only reasonable to demand that tenants keep their garbage and rubbish in separate containers, and clean up their stalls reasonably well when ready to leave. If arrangements are made with the garbage and street cleaning departments of the city to give immediate service when the market is over, the refuse in containers, as well as loose matter, can be picked up and removed before it is scattered about. This special service should be charged back to the stall holders in increased stall rentals, and the market department should recompense the departments responsible for refuse removal for the extra expense incurred. If stall holders refuse to respect reasonable sanitary regulations, as a last resort they should be compelled to sort, trim, unwrap, and otherwise prepare all their products for sale at their homes or place of business before bringing them to the market, even though such a procedure would be quite a hardship. Even with most careful attention, a curb market is bound to be somewhat unsightly in appearance. Open or curb markets are usually paved with brick or asphalt, the spaces sold being marked off by lines painted on the pavement.

Market administration

Public markets are often placed for general administration under the department of health, the department of public works, or the police department. Sometimes they are controlled by a market board or commission, or by a separate bureau of markets, directly responsible to the chief executive of the city. To be administered by one of the larger departments of the city government generally means that the markets will receive scant study and attention. Whether independent, or a unit in another department, a bureau of markets, in charge of a competent and experienced director, will be found advisable in larger cities. Where only one market exists, the market master of that market generally handles the administrative, clerical, and regulatory work. In such cases, the progress of the market, and the service which it renders, depends to a great extent on this man's ability, aggressiveness, and experience in marketing work.

One of the most valuable innovations in public marketing is the preparation and distribution of publicity material covering market prices and conditions. Adequate market reports following

MARKETS 413

each day's market, distributed to producers and buyers as a separately printed sheet or through the market pages of the daily press, tend to stabilize prices and encourage more producers to bring in their produce. Special stories in the news columns of the papers keep consumers advised as to when to buy at advantage, particularly for canning, pickling, and storing. Even where there is no bureau of markets to handle this service in a large way, an individual market master can do much through the press if he will exert himself in that direction.

Frequently, cities maintain public scales located in a central place, often in connection with the public farmers' market, for the weighing of farm produce and other commodities. Such scales are open at convenient hours and in charge of a weigh-master, who for a small fee, furnishes a certified copy of the weights. They are generally administered by the office of weights and measures or the market bureau.

Akin to the problem of facilitating the sale of food products at reasonable prices is that of insuring the full weight and measure of produce bought. Therefore, the regulation of weights and measures is an important activity of every city, and particularly of those larger communities whose citizens are entirely dependent upon middlemen for all food supplies.[1] Such regulation is usually lodged with the police authorities, although the wisdom of this course is sometimes questionable. The successful administration of this activity can be had only by an official who is something more than a law-enforcing officer. In addition to the quality of integrity, he must be equipped with more than ordinary intelligence, a knowledge of marketing, and ability to secure the coöperation of dealers. In many places the official in charge of public markets is best fitted to have charge of this work, which is so closely allied to his other duties. In any event the staff must be sufficiently large to cover the duties in more than a perfunctory way.

The regulation of weights and measures must be supported by adequate state law and local regulations. In some localities there is thorough-going coöperation between state and city in the administration of such regulations, the state having charge of the

---

[1] For an amplification of this subject, see an article on the "Supervision of Weights and Measures," by George K. Burgess, Director of the Bureau of Standards, U. S. Department of Commerce, in the *Municipal Index*, 1925 (American City), 38; and C. A. Crosser in the *Toledo City Journal*, VIII, Nos. 33, 34, 35.

414 PRACTICE OF MUNICIPAL ADMINISTRATION

Dual activities involved

rural areas and smaller communities that are not in a position to supply regular inspections, the cities caring for the task within their own borders. Many cities, however, have not waited for state action, but have established independent facilities for this work. Where state laws are inadequate, local ordinances must, of course, be resorted to to supply the deficiency.

Mr. Burgess suggests that the work of regulation falls into two divisions, the first having to do with the correctness of utensils for weighing and measuring, such as scales, weights, and measures; and the second, with the manner in which such equipment is used.[1] The ordinances governing the regulation of weights and measures must make provision for the regular mechanical inspection and testing of all devices used, usually annually or semi-annually; for the suitable marking of all equipment which is found accurate and proper for use; and for the rejection or condemnation of inaccurate, fraudulent, and worn-out equipment.[2] The second activity can be provided for only by such legal authority as will permit investigation of actual articles delivered by the examination of purchases made by private individuals and by purchases made by responsible officers, although not all cities provide funds for this purpose. While certain results are obtainable by prose-

[1] Burgess, *op. cit.*
[2] The following data on the subject are taken from C. A. Crosser, *op. cit.*:

Cities	Number of Persons for each Inspector	Percentages of Scales Condemned to Total Inspected	Scales Inspected Per 1,000 Inhabitants	Daily Inspections Per Inspector	Prosecutions Per 100,000 Population
All cities	73,474	8	25	6	—
Richmond	21,415	17	23	2	.0
Philadelphia	23,829	5	28	3	9.5
Worcester	25,708	3	31	3	3.3
Washington	27,183	—	—	—	26.3
Rochester	42,250	3	35	5	1.0
Jersey City	42,586	8	15	3	30.2
Boston	49,870	7	34	6	18.7
Buffalo	50,667	3	32	6	2.7
Milwaukee	57,143	—	—	—	3.0
Seattle	63,062	12	22	5	16.8
San Francisco	63,334	4	32	7	3.5
Omaha	63,867	12	18	4	7.3
St. Louis	64,408	1	48	11	12.0
Pittsburgh	65,371	12	38	9	21.2
Baltimore	73,382	2	26	7	.4
Kansas City	81,102	—	—	—	.6
Detroit	99,367	15	11	4	21.2
Toledo	121,532	7	14	7	.0
Cleveland	132,807	—	—	—	5.5
Cincinnati	200,604	13	18	13	.0

cuting persons who give fraudulent weight, the principal results come through knowledge that such regulations are in effect, through the constant investigation of complaints of shortages and by educating merchants and the purchasing public in the requirements of existing law and the proper use of weighing and measuring equipment.[1]

[1] The Bureau of Standards of the Department of Commerce is in a position to offer valuable advice and suggestions, not alone upon the mechanical side of weighing and measuring, but with respect to model laws and ordinances regulating weighing and measuring devices. In this connection, there is an annual conference, held under the auspices of this bureau, of individuals interested in the subject, and the printed proceedings are of value to the administrative officers directly concerned in the subject.

CHAPTER XXIV

ENGINEERING [1]

Public structures

Public properties cover a wide range of physical improvements and include public buildings, sewers, streets, alleys, bridges, docks, public utilities such as water plants, street railways, etc., and many miscellaneous engineering structures. In connection with all of them, certain operations are fundamental—the design, which may be undertaken by architects or engineers; the actual construction, which may be done in a variety of ways, but always under professional supervision and inspection; and current operation and maintenance.

Organization for designing

Public structures may be designed by securing competition among architects and engineers, by contract with consultants, by the establishment of a definite organization for designing as a part of the government, or, as is more usual, by a combination of these methods. The plan of competitive design is frequently used for a public building, a group of public buildings, or a bridge that is intended to be something more than a traffic way. In such cases the architectural beauty of the structure, the harmony of design with use, and the monumental features are fully as important as the structural integrity, and cost is not the first determining factor. Such competitions should be restricted to competent architects and engineers, and the choice of the best design should be entrusted to officials or others who are thoroughly equipped to pass judgment on both æsthetic and practical qualities. The city planning authorities should be qualified to lend aid in the selection of the best design and should be consulted. Usually, an unbiased and valuable opinion can be secured by polling the competitors themselves as to their second choice of design.

Competitive design

As an alternative, it is often desirable to employ a consultant

---

[1] See John P. Davies, *Engineering Office Systems and Methods* (McGraw-Hill, 1915); S. Whinery, *Specifications for Street Roadway Pavements with Instructions to Inspectors on Street Paving Work* (McGraw-Hill, 1913). For current reference, see *Proceeding of the American Society for Municipal Improvements* (annual); *Specifications of the American Society for Testing Materials;* the *Engineering News-Record* (weekly); *Public Works* (monthly); and the *American City* (monthly)

ENGINEERING

for the design of public buildings or any public work requiring specialized architectural or engineering skill of a high order. These services may be secured even though a city maintains a designing staff for ordinary structures. This procedure has, however, sometimes led to advertising for competitive bids for such special work, a practice to be earnestly deprecated. Experienced and competent architects and engineers are usually worth their established rates of compensation, else they would not have achieved their preëminence. The only persons who are interested in furnishing consulting services at reduced prices are the inexperienced who are endeavoring to establish themselves in business, or others who by reason of incapacity are unable to command standard fees. The practice of competitive bidding for consulting services is pernicious and should be discouraged in every way. None but reputable professional men of the widest possible experience should be considered as consultants for the design of public works and for the supervision of their construction.

In municipalities of any considerable size, an engineering corps is a part of the city organization. Occasionally there is also an architectural bureau, but more frequently architectural services are secured through the selection of designs submitted to a competition, or by the employment of consulting services. The engineer corps is usually recruited by civil service procedure, which should insure the employment of capable men in all of the branches of engineering work. Except in the determination of highly complicated and technical structures, as for instance a sewage treatment works or a monumental bridge, this engineering division prepares designs, specifications, and contracts for all public works.

During the progress of the construction of any public structure, it is essential that the engineer or architect or their representatives be present continuously to insure the work being prosecuted in strict accordance with the contract, the plans, and the specifications. As this inspection is an engineering function, it should be placed subordinate to the chief engineer or city engineer, and sufficient money should be appropriated to secure engineering talent. Much responsibility rests on the inspector. Not only should he be equipped to pass upon the work at hand, but he should have the ability to report progress for cost estimating. The daily reports should form the basis for an accounting system maintained by the municipality, whereby a determination of unit and job costs can be made. Such compilations are of incalculable value

418 PRACTICE OF MUNICIPAL ADMINISTRATION

CHAP. XXIV

in estimating and letting future contracts. It is unfortunate, but true, that incompetent or dishonest inspection has been the cause of failure of many well designed structures. And although absolute failure may not result from such shortcomings in inspection, the municipality has paid for and is entitled to receive the quantity and quality called for by the specifications and the contract.

Payment for engineering services

Ordinarily, general engineering services that cannot be easily allocated to a particular job are paid by appropriations from the current funds of the city. Such appropriations will cover general office expenses, the salary of the city engineer and general assistants, and the salaries of employees on construction work financed by direct taxation. It is customary to charge the salaries and expenses of engineers working on specific construction projects to the capital funds made available for such work. This procedure is entirely correct, since engineering services are as necessary to proper construction as are the physical materials that go into it. Such charges may be made directly to the separate funds, or, if they are not immediately available, may be made to a rotary fund [1] and later allocated to the proper funds.

Methods of letting contracts

Contracts are generally let to the lowest bidder, the total of whose unit costs multiplied by the estimated quantities is lowest. There are also special contracts of various types, and the so-called "force account" or "day labor" method of construction. The "low bid" is the usual form of contract for public work. By this method it is anticipated that the contract will naturally fall to the contractor with the best organization and equipment, who can undertake construction for less money and complete it faster than a contractor not so situated. With free competition, this assumption is usually correct. With an over-abundance of contract work available, or collusion among contractors, the efficacy of the low bid method is lessened. The advertising on the competitive contract plan usually reads "lowest responsible bidder" which involves not only organization and equipment, but experience and financial ability. Most invitations for bids are so worded that any or all bids may be rejected in event the bidding is for any reason unsatisfactory.

Competitive low bids

Trade group bidding

In certain types of construction, particularly of buildings, contracts are not always let to the lowest bidder as determined by the aggregate of item bids. Frequently bids will be solicited by

---

[1] A rotary fund is a fund created to temporarily finance certain costs, the fund being later reimbursed for such charges.

ENGINEERING 419

trade groups, as for example, excavating, foundations, masonry, heating, etc., and the contract awarded to the lowest bidder in each group. This procedure stimulates competition by bringing many smaller contractors into the bidding. However, it has decided disadvantages. The city really takes the place of the general contractor in sub-letting a number of small contracts, and must be prepared to give the execution of these contracts careful supervision. No single individual can be held responsible for the progress of the work, nor can penalties for delay and poor workmanship be easily collected.

<small>CHAP. XXIV</small>

The estimates of cost prepared by the city and that accompany the plans and specifications of proposed construction work are for informative purposes and enable the authorities to determine whether a project may be carried through under existing financial arrangements, and are also useful in checking the reasonableness of bids. The same care must be observed in the preparation of the cost estimates as is used in getting out the plans and specifications. The specifications should be accurately and comprehensively drawn, in order to reduce to a minimum the number of contingencies that must be allowed for, and that will increase the bids. Also, if the plans and specifications are general rather than specific in character, a low bidder may load up his estimates with "extras" which may make a low bid contract most expensive.

<small>Estimates and specifications</small>

Under ordinary procedure, a contract is prepared and approved by the legal department. It covers the subjects of definitions, scope of work, time requirements, drawings and specifications, facilities for inspection, supervision by contractor, penalties, protection from claims and losses, labor and legal requirements, additional work, payment, alterations of contract, and release on final payment. The approved document is attached to the plans and specifications and advertised in prescribed channels, sealed proposals being accepted on or before a specified date.[1]

<small>The contract</small>

It is generally stipulated that each bidder shall submit with his proposal a certified check as a guarantee of good faith that the contract will be accepted if awarded to him. This check is usually to an amount of five to ten percent of the total bid.

<small>Bid deposit</small>

As soon as the award is made, bid deposit checks are returned to unsuccessful bidders, and the successful one provides a bond

[1] A model form of contract is being prepared by the Joint Committee on Standard Municipal Contract Form of the American Society for Municipal Improvements and the Associated General Contractors.

in the amount of the contract to guarantee the fulfillment of the contract. In many municipalities the issuance of fidelity bonds is interwoven with politics, the agents are presumed to have influence with the administration, and independent contractors who resist entering into "gentlemen's agreements" with other contractors are punished by having their applications for bonds refused. The cost of bonds is naturally added to the cost of construction work, and the better contractors complain that financially weak companies obtain bonds as easily as strong ones, and that the bonding companies do not consider financial standing in determining premiums. An optional form of contract has been suggested in which in lieu of a fidelity bond, the contractor would permit the city to retain a part of payments of monthly estimates until a fidelity reserve of say ten percent of the contract price had been created. This reserve would be paid to the contractor upon the satisfactory completion of the work.[1]

On larger work, it is sometimes stipulated in the contract that before the actual work starts the successful bidder shall submit to the engineer a detailed plan of procedure. This is particularly desirable on jobs where traffic has to be maintained, or where considerable shoring and under-pinning is necessary. The contractor proceeds with the work only after such plan of procedure is approved by the authorities. It is understood, of course, that the plan may be deviated from in case unforeseen obstacles or contingencies are encountered.

While there has been considerable improvement in the relations between cities and contractors, there still remain a number of methods of manipulating the award of contracts and of fraud after the award is made. Although common honesty and common sense are more general in public business than a decade or two ago, the possibilities of trickery on the part of contractors and the possible susceptibility of honest but inexperienced officials are sufficiently serious to warrant the recitation of some of the ways by which the taxpayers of a city may be imposed upon.

The official interpretation of the term "lowest responsible bidder" is sometimes used to eliminate competition. A contractor with little experience and insufficient capital, who has defaulted on previous contracts, cannot be called a responsible bidder, and may

---

[1] See "The Lowest Bidder and the Surety Bond," *American City*, XXXIV, 353-355 (April, 1926).

ENGINEERING

justly be eliminated, although a low bidder. On the other hand, more than one bidder who was responsible in every respect has had his bid thrown out of competition on trumped up charges of irresponsibility. Happily, such instances are becoming fewer.

In cases of urgency, work may properly be undertaken without competition. An example would be the replacement of a bridge washed out by a freshet, or construction work involving the protection of the public health against sudden menace. In such cases informal bids may be taken and the award made honestly. But it is also possible for the emergency to be stretched and the short-cut procedure followed where no real necessity exists.

In nearly every city, contracts involving small outlay may be let, under specific provisions of the charter, without competition. If a large piece of construction involving a small amount of grading, a little stone work, some brick work, and other items, is split sufficiently fine, a contractor who has sufficient influence may get the entire job piecemeal. By permitting such a subterfuge to reduce or eliminate competition, city officials may be well within the law, but far from its intent.

Another crude method of favoritism is to give a favored contractor the plans and specifications before the advertising is done, and to allow so short a time thereafter for submission of bids that no one else can possibly prepare and submit a detailed bid on the work. Similarly, patented materials controlled by one contractor may be specified.

"Unbalanced" bidding constitutes another device for cheating the public. Proposals are asked for the detailed parts of a single construction job. The contractor will bid high on some parts and low on the others. The average of his bids when figured may be lower than that of his competitor. When the work is actually done, it may be found that an extraordinary number of high-priced units were necessary and the cost increased accordingly. This situation can occur only through faulty estimates, intentional or otherwise, on the part of the city engineer.

There is another type of unbalanced bidding requiring no collusion and resulting in no actual fraud or ultimate additional cost to the city, yet which is contrary to good policy. This type of bid involves a high unit bid on items of a contract which are to be completed first, and a correspondingly lower unit bid on items to be completed late in the contract period. This insures payments to

CHAP. XXIV

Emergency

Split contracts

Direct favoritism

Unbalanced bidding

the contractor of all or a substantial part of his estimated profits early in the work, and makes it possible to withdraw his working capital for other uses.

Collusion

Again, a group of contractors whose operations include practically all of the public work of a city may decide that there is work enough for all and that by collusion in bidding maximum profits can be secured. Under a gentlemen's agreement it is decided which contractor is to submit the low bid on each job, and each gets work at a profit that is entirely satisfactory to everyone but the citizen-taxpayer. A variation in this plan is found in agreements among contractors by which all submit a legitimate bid, but the one receiving the contract must pay a percentage of the total bid or of the net profits to the other members of the agreement.

Extras

The matter of "extras" has been mentioned. With proper care in the preparation of specifications, extras should be few. With a loosely drawn set of specifications, a shrewd contractor may take a contract at a price at which he would ordinarily lose money, and thereupon cover such loss, and make an outrageous profit besides, by submitting a bill for extra work necessary and not included in the specifications.

Ignoring specifications

The more usual way for a contractor to add to his profits is to ignore the specifications. At least this has been the rule throughout the United States. It is not at all unusual for contractors to supply city inspectors with intoxicating liquor and keep them unfit to make inspections for days at a time. The small investment necessary to bring about such conditions is insignificant compared to the economies practised during the absence or incapacity of the inspector. A gradual appreciation of the importance of inspection is dawning on officialdom, and the engineers of the country particularly are demanding that inspection shall be controlled by engineers and made an engineering function, rather than intrusted to incompetent, untrustworthy, and ignorant persons.

Over-stringent specifications

It should be noted that cities often unintentionally facilitate the ignoring of specifications, to the detriment of competition. When specifications are prepared it is only natural for the city engineer to insert rigorous provisions for the protection of the city. Occasionally these provisions may be entirely unnecessary and practically unenforceable. Local contractors will be aware of a city's practice with respect to the non-enforcement of such provisions and will modify their bids accordingly. The out-of-town contractor, who might otherwise be tempted to bring competition into a city, may be deterred by the apparent rigidity of the specifications, or may submit a bid unusually high because of provisions that he supposes will be enforced.

Over-inspection is a favorite disciplinary device of city officials who have combined with a ring of local contractors to prevent honest competition. Out-of-town contractors and local contractors not a party to gentlemen's agreements can be effectively curbed by an officious inspector. However specific specifications may be, their interpretation in the last analysis is the responsibility of city officials. If the engineer and inspectors are so inclined, they may condemn quantities of materials that are on the job and even compel stretches of work to be torn up on some flimsy charge. With this sort of hazing an unwelcome contractor is often fortunate to avoid bankruptcy and always glad to get out of the field with the mere loss of anticipated profits. No contractor in his right senses will go into a city where he knows officialdom is hostile to him.

Practically all cities require a guarantee of maintenance on pavements laid by contract, as a protection against unscrupulous contractors and venal inspection. This guarantee may be in the nature of a bond given by the contractor, or the city may retain a cash percentage of the contract cost of each improvement for a number of years to insure that construction has not been slighted. The period of the guarantee may extend from six months to ten years, but in a majority of cities it runs for five years. In some instances this guarantee stipulates a unit price for repairs in event they are necessitated by other reasons than failure of material or workmanship. The general opinion of engineers is strongly against this practice of maintenance guarantees. Any such guarantee naturally increases the contract price of the public work, and yet by no means accomplishes the results intended. In case of defective material and workmanship, a contractor may have sufficient influence in the city hall so that the fulfillment of the guarantee is not demanded; or court action becomes necessary to enforce the obligation; or the sureties fail. A city should use rigid inspection and careful engineering in the design and construction of all work, relieving the contractor of further responsibility upon its completion. Proceeding on these principles, it will be substantially cheaper for the city to do its own maintenance than to rely upon other means.

424 PRACTICE OF MUNICIPAL ADMINISTRATION

CHAP. XXIV

Force account or day labor work

To avoid the inherent difficulties of the competitive contract plan, and particularly to insure genuine competition, some cities have undertaken to build certain of their public structures either by entering into direct competition with contractors and submitting unit cost bids, or more often, by day labor working directly under municipal supervision. A great deal of poor construction at excessive cost has been done under the day labor plan; and, on the other hand, much good work has been done at material savings to the taxpayers. The supervisors and the workmen should have no incentive to use poor materials or to do the work in a slipshod manner. Neither have they any incentive to unusual exertion.

Arguments for and against

It may be said that a city, in undertaking its own construction work, with or without competition, does not have to figure a profit and should be able to save at least this amount. To be sure, a profit does not have to be made; but in figuring costs for comparison with contractors' estimates proper provision should be made for interest, depreciation, and sundry overhead expenses directly chargeable to the work. Also no plan by which a municipality engages to do its own work will take care of a loss in event one is incurred. If the city cannot do the work within its estimates it will do it outside the estimates, and the taxpayer will pay the bill. If a contractor cannot do the work within his bid he or his bondsman must stand the loss.

When to be undertaken

In making a choice between competitive contracts and construction by day labor, there are few arguments for the latter. However, on occasions a city may find it advantageous actually to compete with private contractors, submitting bids in the same way and at the same time. Conditions are too variable to permit of any general conclusions as to what such occasions are. Perhaps it is sufficient to say that if a city is getting satisfactory bids on its public work without undue profits being made by local contractors, and there is no indication of connivance to defraud the city by excessive bids, the city would best continue to have its work done by the contract method. If, on the other hand, there is evidence of gentlemen's agreements which are resulting in excessive prices for public work, and outside contractors cannot be induced to come into the city and compete for business, then the city would better step in and do a portion of its work itself. Under these circumstances, ample provision must be made for machinery and other equipment, with a rotary fund adequate to meet all costs until the charges can be allocated to the proper appropriations or bond funds.

CHAP. XXIV

In event a city undertakes to do a portion of its own construction work, it should submit bids in regular form in competition with the bids submitted by contractors, and if a competent private contractor is willing to undertake a job for less than the city estimate he should be permitted to do so. Also, a city should not overload its facilities so that it cannot bid on all jobs. The real value of the city entering a bid to do its own work is in the competition that it inspires. If early in the construction season the city forces assume tasks that will keep them busy throughout the year, the competitive element is lost. It is far better for the city to be in a position to bid on every job, keeping the private contractors in continual suspense; or at least for the city to submit bids on all work, even if occasionally such bids are designedly high.

Work should be competitive

In fairness both to contractors and to the public, accurate detailed cost records should be maintained, including a proper percentage for overhead, and the unit costs of each completed job should be known to officials and the public. If city work constantly exceeds the estimates, then the city would better retire from the field unless there are incidental advantages that outweigh these particular losses.

Need for cost records

Inspection of public work should be equally rigid with that done on work undertaken by private contract. Simply because a job is supervised by public officials and undertaken by public employees is no reason why carelessness will not enter in and efforts be made to keep the cost within the estimate, even at the sacrifice of sound construction. The inspection of public works should be divorced from the department undertaking the construction, and this force should be compelled to adhere rigidly to the specifications laid down. Unfortunately, it is a common occurrence to find that work done by private contractors is more thoroughly inspected and is of a better quality than that done by the city itself.

Inspection of public work

Special contracts—cost plus a percentage or cost plus a fixed sum—are used for the execution of work for which there is particular urgency, or on work where unknown factors and contingencies are likely to exist. Such contracts should be let only to contractors whose integrity is impeccable and whose ability is unquestioned. Under such schemes the contractor is under no pressure to economize on time or material, unless a **maximum cost**

Special contracts

426   PRACTICE OF MUNICIPAL ADMINISTRATION

<small>CHAP. XXIV</small>

is stipulated, and the task of ascertaining what the cost actually is often involves a great amount of adjudication. The experience of the United States government with such contracts during the World War is still sufficiently remembered to act as a deterrent, and it would be an urgent need indeed that would justify the execution of such contracts at this time.

<small>Payments on contracts</small>

Payments on contracts are usually made on a monthly basis. It is the duty of the city engineer to keep accurate information of the progress of the work and to prepare monthly a detailed estimate of the work done to date. The bases for such an estimate are the progress reports made by the inspectors and actual measurements taken in the field by the engineering corps. Such estimates are the basis for monthly payment, ten to fifteen percent of the total amount due being withheld to safeguard the city against error and faulty work and to insure continued application of the contractor to the work. Each monthly estimate should be a total of all work completed to date, not merely the sum of monthly progress figures; otherwise an error made for any individual month would carry through the entire construction period. On completion of the contract, a final estimate is calculated and the contractor is paid in full, except that ten or fifteen percent of the amount is again withheld for a short period, pending official acceptance of the work, and to meet any possible damage claims in which the city is made joint defendant with the contractor. The contractor should be required to file an affidavit setting forth that all bills for labor and materials used in the work have been paid.

<small>Operation and maintenance</small>

The operation and maintenance of public structures fall naturally to the departments for which the construction was undertaken. An important exception to this rule is the group of public buildings and miscellaneous structures. The care of special buildings may be delegated to the principal departments of government that they house, but in a city with a considerable number of public buildings this procedure is both expensive and inconvenient. It is more desirable to establish a department of buildings and grounds that will undertake to operate and keep in repair all buildings that do not pertain to departments having regular maintenance divisions. Such a division of buildings and grounds can be organized for doing the odds and ends of landscaping, repairing, painting, etc., necessary to such structures, and can properly supervise the cleaning, elevator, and heating services. These operating activities involve problems of employment, discipline, unit costs, and maintenance of adequate records that are more fully discussed in connection with the subject of education, since the department responsible for that activity makes use of many buildings.¹

In connection with the maintenance of public buildings, some word should be said concerning insurance against fire losses. Practice with respect to insurance varies so considerably in different cities, that no accepted procedure can be stated. Some municipalities insure all public buildings; others set aside each year a small percentage of the total value of all buildings, which sums, with accrued interest, constitutes a replacement fund in event of loss; and still others make no provision for insurance of any kind in the belief that the large taxing and bonding powers of the community constitute in themselves a form of self-insurance. In other words, any loss would be relatively so small that it could be met without undue burden upon the taxpayers. In any large community this last procedure is probably sound.²

CHAP.
XXIV

Fire insurance

¹ See Chap. XVI.
² See William T. Melchior, *Insuring Public School Property* (Teachers College, Columbia Univ., 1925). St. Louis, Kansas City, Los Angeles, and Portland, Ore., insure in regular companies; New York City, Chicago, Boston, San Francisco, Washington, D. C., and Detroit make no provision for insurance; Philadelphia, Newark, Rochester and Baltimore maintain funds for self-insurance. See C. A. Crosser, "Can City Carry Own Insurance?" *Toledo City Journal*, VIII, 47 (November 24, 1923).

CHAPTER XXV

PAVEMENTS [1]

Development of pavements

The importance of highways to commerce and to military operations has been recognized from very ancient times, and one who views the remains of roads built by the Cæsars is tempted to conclude that there has been little progress in this branch of engineering in almost two thousand years. Indeed, street and highway design and construction, as specialized branches of engineering science, were so inconspicuous prior to 1900 as to be negligible. This was particularly true in the United States, where railroad construction and industrial development monopolized the attention of engineers. With the present century came the development of the internal combustion engine and its application to vehicular movement. Following this, there have been astounding changes in the habits of the western world, due to new facilities of transportation.

Early city pavements

Cities had, of course, long been paving streets, the original consideration being a pavement sufficient to keep traffic out of the mud. As population increased and traffic became heavier and denser, other considerations entered. For heavy hauling, a firm foothold and a durable surface were essential. For residential streets, it was desirable to have a smooth surface and one easily cleaned. In the smaller cities, expense made it necessary to use the cheapest materials that would secure some of these requisite qualities, regardless of other considerations. Knowledge of maintenance costs as an aid in determining the type of pavement was considered unnecessary; or the figures were misleading. Many

---

[1] See F. S. Besson, *City Pavements* (McGraw-Hill, 1923); T. R. Agg, *The Construction of Roads and Pavements* (McGraw-Hill, 3d ed., 1924); I. O. Baker, *Treatise on Roads and Pavements* (Wiley, 3d ed., 1918); Arthur H. Blanchard, *Elements of Highway Engineering* (Wiley, 1915); Clifford Richardson, *The Modern Asphalt Pavement* (Wiley, 1914); and Henry W. Durham, *Street Paving and Maintenance in European Cities* (City of New York, 1915); and the numerous road publications of the Bureau of Public Roads, U. S. Department of Agriculture. Current reference should be made to the *Proceedings of the American Society for Municipal Improvements* (annual); the *Engineering News-Record* (weekly); *Public Works* (monthly); *Public Roads* (monthly); *Roads and Streets* (monthly); and *The American City* (monthly).

PAVEMENTS

pavements were patented, and vicious selling methods were applied to unscrupulous legislative bodies and to city officials. As a result, all manner of peculiar and unsatisfactory pavements were built.

CHAP. XXV

During the time when horses were used as beasts of burden in industry and business, and for pleasure purposes, the ideal pavement was one having the qualities of permanence, smoothness, quiet, ease of cleaning, and freedom from abrasion. For securing permanence, bases of earth and of concrete were used, and when concrete was laid it was made first of natural cement and later of portland cement. Various surface materials were tried out—the earth road provided with a crown and gutters, and frequently sprinkled and resurfaced; gravel and macadam roads; two and three course pavements with a concrete base and surfaces of granite block, cedar block, brick, creosoted wood block, and sheet asphalt; and many others. As traffic became congested, the noise of horse-drawn, steel-tired vehicles became more and more bothersome. For a time it was thought that creosoted wood block gave the answer to the question of noise, and at the same time possessed all other necessary qualities. This form of pavement, however, is expensive, and later developments, including changes in the type of traffic, have proved its inadequacy. With the use of the automobile and motor truck the character and volume of traffic, both urban and interurban, have been so radically modified that the entire science of street paving has changed in layout, design, selection of materials, and methods of construction.

Qualities sought

Changing factors

The street problems of a municipality include all construction between the street lines—street paving, curbs and gutters, and sidewalks. In the days before traffic had increased to anywhere near its present volume, it was a general rule to allow two-fifths of the width between street lines for sidewalk and parkways and three-fifths of the width for the roadway. Such proportioning was then quite adequate. But with present traffic and parking needs, it is often necessary to set the curb back to the sidewalk edge, and sometimes to move the street line and sidewalks. This means that the planning of street widths is essential to proper street construction, and such planning is largely dependent upon zoning. By zoning, the uses to which any given area will be put may be predetermined, and the development forecast with some accuracy. The width of streets and the character of the traffic to be borne by them may be predicted and proper provision made in the most economical way. If zoning is not to be had, the best

City planning and street paving

endeavor should still be made to provide for through traffic streets of proper width, to prevent dead-end streets, and otherwise to make most useful the work of the paving engineer.[1]

Who should decide the type of pavement?

The actual determination of type of pavement requires the closest coöperation between the city planning authorities, the city engineer, and the legislative body. The width of the paved area must be correlated with the street plan of the entire city. Depth of pavement foundation and type of pavement surface is an engineering problem to be solved through complete studies of soil, climatic conditions, and particularly traffic needs. Further, both the width and type of pavement may be influenced by the financial conditions of a city, and must therefore be approved by the city council. The best practice requires that the engineering and social problems involved in street paving be jointly determined by the engineers and the city planners and that the joint recommendations be presented to the city council for approval. If the council overrides the wisdom of its technical advisors and modifies these recommendations, it does so as the representative of the citizens and taxpayers.

Organization for street paving

Street paving is commonly an activity of a department of public works, and more specifically of a construction engineer working in conjunction with a city engineer. In smaller cities, however, a city engineer may be directly responsible for this activity—in which event, the work should be in two divisions, one having to do with construction, and the other with maintenance.

Classification of streets

In the work of city planning, considerable attention has been given to the classification of streets in accordance with their use and surroundings, and such detailed classification is entirely proper as an aid in determining street widths, areas to be paved, location of shade trees, arrangement of unpaved street areas, and other elements that enter into the usefulness and beautification of thoroughfares. A detailed classification, however, is of small interest to the engineer concerned with paving, since construction must be determined by actual traffic needs. The engineer will roughly classify streets as: (1) industrial, *i.e.*, those in which a large amount of heavy trucking is done; (2) ordinary business and higher type residential; (3) less important residential; (4) unpaved thoroughfares; and (5) alleys. Every city should plan to decrease the number of types of pavement used on these groups of streets. Pavements require maintenance, and this maintenance

[1] For a more extended discussion of this subject, see Chap. XII.

is less expensive with a few types than with many. It is recommended that the ordinary city standardize on granite block or brick for heavy trucking streets and steep grades; sheet asphalt on heavily traveled downtown streets, and on high class residential streets and boulevards; concrete on outlying residential streets and alleys; and cinderization or graveling on unpaved thoroughfares.

The decision as to type of pavement laid should be based on a careful consideration of local markets as affecting the original cost, probable maintenance costs, suitability of the material for the particular traffic or district served, and the amount of money available for the particular paving. This last item is important. For example, in the construction of a home, one may be convinced that a fireproof brick structure will be the most economical and satisfying, but the family budget may allow nothing more expensive than a frame structure. So in street construction, it may be known that sheet asphalt, brick, or creosoted wood block would be more economical and more satisfying to the pride of a community, yet something less expensive may have been laid in order to avoid an intolerable tax burden.

When undeveloped territory is acquired by a city, the establishment of both street lines and street grades should be subject to a forward-looking policy. Too often the easiest way has been the one followed. Instead of building to a predetermined grade, the first builder in a new district may build his sidewalk in conformity to the street line but at a grade that is most convenient considering the topography of the site. The sidewalk grade determines the elevation of the gutter, which in turn determines the elevation of the crown of the pavement at that point. The general effect of an entire street may thus be fixed by an unconsidered location of one sidewalk. Such haphazard construction should be impossible. It is the duty of the city engineer to bring into being as a completed entity a general street plan adequate to meet the traffic conditions. Suitable lines and grades should be established by the engineer and should be properly recorded; and public and private construction work should be made to conform.

Pavement construction involves three elements—the sub-grade, the base, and the wearing surface.

The subgrade is the natural earth below the pavement base. It may be the natural soil reached by excavation, or it may have to be constructed by making a fill of natural earth. Newly opened city streets, which usually remain as dirt roads for several years,

CHAP. XXV

will, if properly drained, produce a fairly compacted subgrade for a permanent pavement. This is particularly true if they are given a temporary surface of gravel or cinders. The subgrade is prepared in the same manner for any type of construction, *i.e.*, smoothed and rolled to a surface parallel to the proposed finished surface, although this process may cause a retention of moisture inimical to the integrity of the structure.

Drainage

The character of the soil will determine how extensive the drainage system must be. The object of the drains is to remove the moisture from the subgrade. Moisture not only lessens the sustaining power of the soil but has a direct influence on the performance of the concrete base. A gravelly or sandy soil will ordinarily give adequate drainage, while clays and loams make more elaborate provision necessary, including side and under drains. A drainage ditch at the side of a roadway will do essentially all the work of a longitudinal side tile drain. Under certain conditions, it is necessary to place tile drains under the center of the roadway, in which case transverse drains are necessary to remove the water to the side ditch or drain. The open ditch has the disadvantage of requiring constant attention and remains a perpetual traffic hazard. As the drainage capacity of the subgrade soil, its porosity, and its capillarity vary constantly with various sections of any street or highway, these qualities should be considered in the design of the pavement, with changes of the design as often as conditions require. The object should be to build a roadway of constant strength rather than one of constant thickness.

Gravel and cinder roads

So far as modern permanent pavements are concerned, it would be logical to discuss at this point the construction of permanent foundations. However, many cities find it expedient to make use of temporary construction, particularly on outlying streets and alleys. Such streets may not be immediately required as traffic ways, but it may be desirable to so improve them that building materials can be moved over them and other essential traffic facilitated. To accomplish this, the road may be graded and the crown spread with gravel and cinders, or even ashes, to several inches in depth. These materials will be compacted by traffic, and if maintained in constant repair will serve a useful purpose. In small communities properly laid gravel streets have a distinct place. These surfaces will not withstand any quantity of automobile and truck traffic, and in large cities they must be considered as temporary improvements.

PAVEMENTS

Bituminous surface treatment may be used on such roads, or in fact on almost any highway, and consists of applying superficial coats of bituminous materials, with or without being mixed with crushed stone and sand. The application of liquid bitumen of various sorts to remove dust generally results in a compact and smooth surface, but for a time is a great nuisance to traffic. The application of a thin veneer of a bituminous material is not a permanent treatment, but may be expedient on occasions. On streets so improved, the surface should be free from moisture and dust and the bitumen applied either by hand or from tanks with gravity distributors, similar to sprinkling carts. Occasionally the application is made under pressure, the material being forcibly sprayed upon the roadway. In any case, this bituminous coat is usually covered with coarse sand, fine gravel, or stone screenings.[1]

Macadam pavement has been popular for many years because of its relative cheapness, its suitability to most types of horse-drawn vehicles, and its ease of repair. Macadam consists of layers of crushed rock placed on a prepared subsoil, the rock graduated in size from large pieces at the bottom to small particles at the top. The whole is compacted by rolling. Since the surface particles are bound together by moisture, this pavement is ordinarily called water bound macadam to distinguish it from bituminous macadam. Modern automobile traffic rapidly destroys this type of pavement, and it has been discarded by most cities. Telford pavement is somewhat similar, except that the lower layer of rock is placed on end, forming a more rigid foundation.

A street having a wearing course of macadam, the interstices of which are filled with bituminous material, is called bituminous macadam. The bond is supplied by the asphaltic cement or tar product penetrating to a thickness of about two and one-half inches. Coarse aggregates are first spread and rolled to the approximate thickness of the finished surface and treated with hot bituminous cement applied under pressure. Following the application of the cement, intermediate aggregates are applied in a thin layer to fill the voids and barely cover the treatment. The surface is again thoroughly compacted and another application of cement made. After this application, fine aggregates are spread and rolled until thoroughly bonded to the road.

The usual wear on bituminous macadam removes only the top

[1] See J. T. Bullen, "Surface Treatment of Gravel Roads with Asphaltic Oils," *American City*, XXXIV, 157-161 (February, 1926).

surface. The maintenance of such a road consists, then, of reconstructing this seal coat, and a treatment of light sand or screenings and oil ordinarily will suffice. Oil, however, should be used only in small quantities, as it will cause deterioration of the cement below. The surface mat should never be allowed to wear out completely, and whenever the coarse aggregates are exposed a new surface should be constructed. Breaks or ruts may be caused by weakness of the base or subgrade conditions, and if so, the cause should be corrected before repairs are made.

The "cold patch" method of repair may often be applied economically and with satisfactory results. It is a convenient process, as heating equipment is unnecessary and a quantity of patching material may be mixed and used for several weeks after preparation. There are various materials on the market, bituminous in character, that may be used cold. Crushed stone is mixed with sand in the ratio of three to one, and the binder material is added, the mixture being made up almost anywhere.

The base of a modern pavement is the heavy foundation laid on the subgrade for the purpose of giving support to the surface or wearing layer of the pavement. In modern pavements this base is almost universally of portland cement concrete, although recently a few pavements have been built with an asphaltic foundation known as a "black base." Black base is actually bituminous concrete. Its use is still in the experimental stage, but it is said to have the advantages of flexibility, not being subject to the same minor disintegrations as portland cement concrete, and it may be used immediately after laying. On the other hand, it is reported not to withstand the strains of heavy traffic.

In repaving it is sometimes advantageous to use the old roadway in whole or in part as the base for a new surface. A surface of sheet asphalt, and particularly asphaltic concrete, can often be placed on old macadam roads with satisfactory results when financing a new pavement is out of the question. Old brick, granite, or other pavements are occasionally left in place and a surface of asphalt applied. This process is not recommended unless the base is sound, which is seldom in older pavements, or a base of substantial thickness can be added. A pavement is no better than its base, and if that is defective any amount of resurfacing will not produce a permanently smooth and durable roadway.

The thickness of the concrete base is determined by the nature of the subgrade and the amount of traffic for which the roadway

PAVEMENTS 435

is designed, the average thickness being from six to nine inches. With assumptions as to the strength of concrete when the cement is mixed with sand and gravel or other aggregates in certain proportions, the engineer will specify the "mix" of the concrete for a particular pavement. In the early years of construction with concrete these specifications called for a "lean mix," *i.e.*, containing little cement in proportion to the aggregates, and this leanness was accentuated by contractors slighting the quantities of cement or unduly increasing the quantities of aggregates. The resulting concrete was far below present-day standards. Further, no one knew precisely the effect of water on the strength of concrete, and it became the practice to mix the concrete very wet so that it would flow into place, thereby saving labor. It is now known that this additional water affects the quality adversely. With the acquisition of more technical knowledge concerning the proportioning, mixing, and placing of concrete, and of the results of deviation from established standards upon its ultimate strength, former practices have entirely changed.

CHAP. XXV

The use of concrete is very general, for there are few localities in which suitable sand, gravel, or rock is not found. These materials should be clean, the sand coarse and sharp, and the gravel or rock fairly uniform in size. The quality varies in different pits, and where much variation in size and character are found the gravel should be screened. Otherwise variations in strength of the concrete are sure to follow. While limestone is generously distributed over the country, not all limestones are satisfactory for concrete. Special investigation should be made of each quarry to determine the quality of the stone before it is used.[1]

Aggregates

It has been learned that the specification of a definite mix of concrete and aggregates in no way indicates the strength of the resulting concrete, but that this strength varies with the volume of water added and the thoroughness of mixing. As an excess of water makes the concrete more fluid, standards of consistency have been established, the tests for which are known as "slump" tests. These tests are made in a mold in the form of a truncated cone twelve inches high, the base of which is eight inches, and the top four inches, in diameter. For certain work, it is specified that after filling with concrete and tamping with a specified bar for a certain period, the concrete shall slump, or settle, a maximum of a

Water-cement ratio

[1] For detailed discussion of the proportioning of concrete materials, see the bulletins published by the Structural Materials Research Laboratory of Lewis Institute, Chicago.

436 PRACTICE OF MUNICIPAL ADMINISTRATION

certain number of inches. The proportioning of the amount of water to the cement is called the water-cement ratio. As long as a proper ratio is preserved, it serves as a natural check on the quantity of aggregates, since too large additions would cause the mixture to be too stiff to work easily.

Ratio of cement to aggregates

The ratio of cement to aggregates, and the ratio of sand to the coarse aggregates, must be determined by the strength of the concrete desired. Several methods of proportioning have been devised. It is generally accepted in accordance with the "method of voids" that "the densest and strongest concrete that can be made with any proportion of cement and any combination of aggregates is that in which the cement parts fill the voids of the sand and the resulting mortar fills the voids in the coarse aggregate." Another proposal deals with the proportioning of materials in accordance with the surface areas of the aggregates.

Inspection

It is obvious, therefore, that in establishing specifications for concrete the engineer must know definitely what kind of concrete is desired and how to get it from available materials. And it should also be clear that, to assure the engineer that specifications are being complied with, there must be continuous inspection of a high character. In early days inspection of pavement construction and other public works was a part of the political mechanism of the municipality. An inspector might have been trained in any occupation, however remote from engineering, but his qualifications for inspection were always political. Not only were such inspectors incompetent to inspect, but they often made no pretense of being on the job; and when deviations from specifications were noted they were not reported. Even in cities generally well governed, incompetency and politics combined to prevent public inspection from being what it should be. At the present time every indication points to the necessity of higher grade inspection, and there is a gradual realization of this necessity on the part of the public and its representatives. Insuring that concrete is of specified thickness, although important, is the roughest and least important of the essentials to thorough inspection. Slump tests, fineness tests, and crushing tests are only a few of the technical measurements that must be applied continuously.

Concrete handling and mixing equipment

The handling, mixing, and placing of concrete has stimulated the manufacture of equipment that enables contractors to do enormous quantities of work at costs much below those of hand-labor methods. Mixing machines were developed of both the con-

PAVEMENTS 437

tinuous and "batch" mixing types. The batch mixer is now in universal use, the equipment being designed to handle the aggregates and cement in exact proportions. The ingredients of the batch are dumped into the mixer, which is adjusted to admit the required amount of water and to mix the prescribed minimum of time, usually one minute. For paving work a boom, along which a bucket carries the whole batch of concrete, is an integral part of the mixer. This boom and bucket deposits the material at any desired point in the roadway. Machines for finishing concrete road work follow the mixer and by means of vibrating parts compact the concrete. A belt follows this tamper and is dragged transversely back and forth across the pavement, smoothing the surface. This may be followed by hand-operated floats that put on the final surface.

Experiment and observation clearly indicate that moisture and temperature have a decided effect on the integrity of concrete. Under conditions of continued wetness and high temperatures, concrete increases materially in volume; when dry and cold, it contracts. Therefore the design of concrete structures must provide means of taking care of these changes, which is accomplished by transverse expansion joints.

Before the process of applying the pavement surface to the concrete base may proceed, ample time must be allowed for the concrete to become thoroughly set. This usually takes place in about three weeks.

The wearing surface of pavements, as has been indicated, has been tried in numerous materials—the principal ones being untreated cedar blocks, creosoted wood block, vitrified brick, and various asphaltic surfaces. Local conditions may be an important factor in the choice of surface material, but, other things being equal, the surface that rides most smoothly, is economical to maintain, and is safe when wet is given preference. The present tendency is toward surfaces of asphaltic concrete, and particularly sheet asphalt, which has been used satisfactorily in both the finest residential districts and in business areas. Many cities confine their new work and rebuilding to this type of pavement, which consists of a binder and a surface course.

The binder course is made of broken stone and sand mixed uniformly with asphaltic cement and laid on the concrete base to a uniform thickness of one and one-half inches or more. The stone and sand are heated, and the hot aggregates are combined in a

438 PRACTICE OF MUNICIPAL ADMINISTRATION

CHAP. XXV

The surface course

mixer into which the asphalt is sprayed under pressure. Mixing is continued sufficiently long to produce a homogeneous mass. This material is delivered on the street at high temperatures, and is raked and leveled, and then rolled with a heavy roller. The surface course of about one and one-half inches consists of sand and a mineral filler of limestone dust, slate dust, or portland cement uniformly mixed with asphalt cement at a high temperature. The surface material is delivered on the street while hot and is placed on the binder course, preferably while the latter is warm. The surface is first raked and then rolled slowly until free from waves and no further compression results. A light surface of limestone dust or portland cement is swept over the asphalt before the final rolling.

Maintenance of sheet asphalt

Any irregularity that may develop in the surface of asphalt should be repaired promptly, and if caused by defective subgrade, drainage, or base, that defect should be remedied first. The unsatisfactory surface is cut out and cleaned, a smear of asphalt cement is applied to insure a satisfactory bond between the old and new material, and new material is applied as in new construction. When the pavement is badly broken and renewal is necessary the surface material may be satisfactorily removed by burning with a surface heater.

Asphaltic concrete

A concrete in which asphaltic cement is used instead of portland cement has been much used as a surface and has given satisfactory results. This asphaltic concrete is made in two ways—by using coarse graded aggregates in one type and fine graded aggregates in the other. These surfaces are laid on a prepared base to a thickness of about two inches. The asphaltic cement must be of essentially the same quality as is used in sheet asphalt, and the methods of mixing are comparable. On the first course of the heavier aggregates a surface treatment of hot cement is laid to which intermediate aggregates are applied, and the whole is rolled to a smooth even surface. The same temperatures are necessary as in the preparation of sheet asphalt, and comparable methods are employed throughout. In the fine graded type of asphaltic concrete the greater part of the aggregates are less than one-fourth inch in diameter, and the sand and mineral filler are the same as is used in sheet asphalt. In fact, the surface is a modified sheet asphalt pavement. "Topeka" pavements are of the fine graded type, the specifications varying slightly from those

PAVEMENTS   439

indicated. A number of patented pavements are constructed on the same general principles. <small>CHAP. XXV</small>

The sources of asphalt are diverse. Native asphalt appears almost pure in "lakes," hence the term lake asphalt. Rock asphalt appears as a limestone or sandstone, impregnated with asphalt. Oil asphalt is a residual product resulting from the refining of certain petroleums. The bitumens are distilled from coal in the process of gas-making and form a group that is much used. The principal competition among asphalts is between the lake and oil varieties. Lake asphalt has been much used, but is rapidly being supplanted by the oil product. Oil asphalt is less expensive, and experience has demonstrated that it is equally good for paving purposes. Paving specifications should be so drafted as to compel the two products to compete on equal terms. <small>Sources of asphalt and bitumen</small>

Standards as to both physical and chemical qualities have been established and should govern the use of bituminous material in the construction of pavements. These qualities are measured by numerous tests, including the penetration test, the float test, the viscosity test, test for water, test for loss on heating, distillation test, flash test, test for soluble bitumen, and test for specific gravity.[1] <small>Tests</small>

Those cities having large areas of asphalt paving have found that the construction and operation of a municipal asphalt plant is a profitable investment. Such plants may be used for resurfacing and repairing streets, and in emergencies may lay new asphalt paving, thus furnishing competition to contractors. Larger cities throughout the country have very generally made this investment, using both portable and stationary plants. <small>Municipal asphalt plants</small>

Asphalt block has been used for paving to some extent and with considerable success. The blocks are usually made of rock screenings with from six to eight percent of asphaltic cement. The block presents a wearing surface of about five by twelve inches, and is from two to three inches in thickness. These blocks are laid on portland cement foundations in a one-half inch bed of rich cement mortar. <small>Asphalt block</small>

For heavier traffic, and for horse drawn traffic particularly, pavements of brick and granite have given satisfaction, not on account of superior riding qualities, but because of the security of foothold and durability. Such pavements are noisy and more <small>Brick and granite</small>

---

[1] The details of the various tests may be had from a testing laboratory or in any of the standard treatises on paving materials and methods.

440   PRACTICE OF MUNICIPAL ADMINISTRATION

CHAP. XXV

difficult to keep clean than asphalt. Formerly, a considerable sand cushion was used between the concrete base and the brick or granite surface, but it has become a more recent practice to lay the blocks in a bed of cement mortar, as with asphalt blocks. A cement mortar filler in the interstices between the blocks makes a very rigid and enduring pavement but presents trouble in making cuts in the surface. On the latter account, a bituminous filler is more satisfactory.

Wood block

Blocks of southern yellow pine, Douglas fir, tamarack, Norway pine, and hemlock treated with creosote made a bid for popularity as a paving surface early in the century. When they were properly treated and laid, the surface presented all of the qualities of a perfect pavement for horse-drawn traffic. As the demand for blocks increased, defective treatment, and carelessness or ignorance of best practices in laying, increased maintenance expenses. The original expense of this pavement, and its slippery qualities in wet weather under automobile traffic, have brought a change in sentiment, and it is now not often used. The methods of laying wood block are similar to those used in the other block pavements.

Concrete pavements

The pavement that has come to be almost the universal hard-surface highway in rural areas, and the use of which is growing rapidly for certain urban districts, is of concrete. The wide distribution of materials suitable for aggregates and the facility with which it can be applied have made concrete advantageous as a wearing surface under certain conditions. It may be laid in one or two courses, and with or without reinforcement. In two-course pavements the practice is to make the base, or lower course, of a somewhat leaner mixture and of coarser aggregates than the top course, although this is not recommended. One-course concrete pavement is in most common use.

Mechanical equipment

To a large extent, efficiency in concrete construction is now a matter of mechanical equipment. Mechanical mixers were the first advance over the old hand methods; proportioning of all materials except water at a central plant from which they are conveyed to the mixer in cars or trucks has superseded the hand process; and the perfecting of finishing machines has improved the road surface and reduced costs.

Improvement in design

At the same time, much has been learned about the action of concrete under varying climatic changes and this knowledge is being utilized in the design. Proper design is fundamental, and

PAVEMENTS

this includes a rich mixture of concrete, for whether a reinforcement of steel bars or steel netting is used or not, a good pavement cannot be laid without using sufficient cement. And equally important with design is the matter of inspection. This includes the rigid proportioning, proper timing of the mix, proper ratio of water to cement, slump tests, breaking tests, and the assurance that the specified thickness is in place.

The first concrete roads were poured in continuous slabs. These almost invariably cracked and made maintenance necessary. It was soon realized that expansion joints were necessary, and these were provided at distances varying from thirty to one hundred feet or more. Even with the expansion joints, it was noticed that the cracking continued, in characteristic ways for various widths of road. This has been partially obviated by the introduction of longitudinal joints, one in the center for a twenty foot roadway, two for a thirty foot roadway, etc., the maximum width of a concrete slab being about ten feet. Joints for expansion purposes are made of a fibre impregnated with asphaltic cement, about one-half inch thick and placed transversely the full width of the roadway, and cut to fit the cross section of the road. These fiber joints are supplanting the metal strips once used, as the latter leave a rigid rib across the roadway after a slight wearing of the cement. Longitudinal joints are often provided by casting one-half of a roadway with a longitudinal groove. When the other side of the pavement is poured the concrete fills this groove. But a bond is not made between the two sides; a hinge effect is produced, allowing for considerable movement perpendicularly without rupture. When the whole width of the roadway is poured in one operation the joint is made by introducing a corrugated steel sheet along the section at which the joint is desired. This is held in place by metal pins through holes in the corrugations, and the top edge is below the finished surface. Sometimes this joint is not discernible until after the pavement is in use for awhile.[1]

Care should be taken in setting forms at the sides of pavement. These forms, of wood or preferably steel, should be kept in alignment and to grade, and firmly held in place with wooden or iron pegs. When a finishing machine is used, it runs on the side forms, and in such cases the necessity of having the forms clean, in proper

---

[1] See H. Eltinge Breed, "Behavior of Concrete Pavements under Service Conditions," *American City*, XXXIV, 149-153 (February, 1926).

442 PRACTICE OF MUNICIPAL ADMINISTRATION

Streets suitable for concrete paving

alignment, at proper grade, and solidly pegged in place must be emphasized. However, the same precautions are desirable in hand finishing.

The universal use of one-course cement pavements is not recommended at the present time. For the highest class streets, sheet asphalt holds a strong position as most satisfactory in all respects. The relative cheapness of concrete makes it a desirable alternative when economy is an important factor. Notwithstanding some of the less desirable features of concrete streets, largely æsthetic, they have been, and are being, built in many exclusive sections, and as far as can be learned have given entire satisfaction. On dead-end streets concrete is particularly desirable.[1]

Resurfacing concrete pavement

In many cases one-course concrete streets are laid with eight-inch curbs. This extra height of curb is provided with the idea that at some future time, when the surface of the concrete is worn, a surface of sheet asphalt may be applied without making the curb grotesquely low or requiring its change.

Patented pavements

Many cities have been inveigled into laying patented pavements, more through the artifices of competent salesmen than by reason of any unusual merit of the product. "There are no secrets, and nothing of mystery in designing and constructing good modern pavements. There are a number of pavements recognized by paving engineers as being standard types. No individuals have control of the materials entering into them; nor has a royalty to be paid for their use. None of the so-called patented pavements have qualities superior to standard pavements that are not patented, and (the administration of any city) is to be criticized for incurring the additional expense incident to using patented pavements."[2]

Paving between street railway tracks

Whether or not the electric railway is ultimately supplanted by the motor-bus, there will be much work in maintaining and rebuilding street railway lines before the transition is fully made. Due to the vertical planes of weakness between the tracks and the pavement, to variation in the wearing qualities of railway tracks and pavements, and to the differences in street railway and street traffic, the paving between the tracks is invariably a problem. With ordinary track construction, the pavement base inevitably fails at the track joints, admitting water, and eventually destroying the adjacent pavement. As track maintenance must be con-

---

[1] Because of the absence of traffic. Same authorities hold that asphalt paving must have abundant wear to retain its mechanical properties.

[2] Ezra C. Shoecraft, "City Engineering," *Government of Cincinnati and Hamilton County*, 294.

tinuous, a satisfactory solution of the paving in cities where the track is used jointly for railroad and vehicular traffic cannot be found until radical departures are made in track laying and building.

<small>CHAP. XXV</small>

The most important prerequisite of permanent track pavement is a substantial base that will prevent vertical motion at any part of either track or pavement. In Cleveland, Detroit, Bridgeport, and St. Joseph, investigations have resulted in the partial or complete adoption of this rigid type of construction. Steel ties are used, so deformed that the rail is slightly canted toward the center of the track, making the top of the rail parallel to the cone of the wheel-load. The steel tie and rail are entirely imbedded in concrete. Rail joints are welded with a plate on each side to support the rail head at the joint. The concrete slab, resting on the soil, supports the tie. The concrete above the lower slab is of the "Hassam" type, sometimes called "compressed," and is brought to the head of the rail. This upper slab is constructed by placing the aggregates of stone before mixing the mortar, these aggregates being thoroughly compacted by rolling with a heavy roller. The grout is then poured under pressure to fill the voids. While there has been slight raveling of the surface in some instances, this form of pavement is singularly free from either transverse or longitudinal cracks. The pavement is expensive in first cost, but the maintenance requirements are small, and the type has proved most satisfactory for the purposes for which it is intended.[1]

<small>Rigid track construction</small>

Within the last few years, and particularly since the net earnings of street railways have been reduced by increasing operating costs and competition from other forms of transportation, there has been considerable agitation of relieving street railways of the cost of paving within car tracks. It is urged that this paving is of no particular benefit to the street railway, but is an integral part of the paving of the entire street and is used constantly by other than street car traffic. On the other hand, it cannot be denied that the presence of car tracks increases both the initial cost and the maintenance of paving. Certain types of street railway construction cause the pavement adjacent to the rails to disintegrate rapidly and occasionally large stretches of pavement on either side of the track are destroyed. Because of the social need

<small>Cost of track pavement</small>

[1] For a discussion of the distribution of the cost of pavements between street railway tracks, see Chap. XXX.

of street railway transportation, it may be desirable for a municipality to grant a subsidy to a street railway company which may take the form of relief from the initial cost of paving between the tracks, or both paving and maintenance. If so, such subsidy should be granted with the full knowledge of its nature.[1]

Corporation cuts

In the modern city as it is ordinarily administered there are objections to pavements with surfaces that are not easily and quickly repaired. The "corporation cut" or opening in the pavement necessitated by the installation of public utility connections, or for the repair of such connections, sooner or later honeycombs the pavement and disturbs the subsoil to a considerable depth below the base. As the back-fill settles, the concrete base in the cut may not have a proper bond with the original concrete and, being over a settling ditch, settles with it. The result is a rough spot in the pavement, which is a source of possible danger, and of certain trouble. Further, even if the trench work and base are satisfactorily replaced, there is always an unsightly patch in brick, concrete, and other hard surface streets. With bituminous surfaces, the patch is obliterated, and there is the added advantage of allowing the free passage of traffic within a short time after the patch is completed.

Most cities attempt to control the extent of corporation cuts. Public utilities are usually notified in advance of the pavement of streets and requested to make any contemplated change in present installations or to place new installations. Occasionally a newly paved street will be opened its entire length to put in mains or conduits, but such instances are unusual. The troubles with corporation cuts arise from the installation of house connections. Cities have endeavored to compel the laying of these connections before paving, but the effort has not been successful, since it is difficult to foresee the exact size of connection required and an outlay of idle capital must be made. A more favored device is to penalize such cuts by compelling the payment of several times the actual cost of the work, graduated in accordance with time elapsed since the pavement was constructed. This system is not particularly effective. The owner of a vacant lot prefers to risk passing on the charges to the actual builder of a home rather than bother making an installation that may not be used for several years. To

---

[1] For detailed discussion of arguments against the relief of street railways from paving costs, see J. W. Howard, "Paying for Car Track Paving," *Municipal and County Engineering*, LXX, 104 (February, 1926).

PAVEMENTS

insure proper backfilling and street repair, cuts in pavements are usually made by the city itself, the utility being charged with the cost. Less often, the work is done by the utility under city inspection.[1]

In event that the community is unable to maintain its own engineering staff, the importance of employing reputable engineers cannot be too strongly emphasized. A reputable engineer will provide rigid inspection without which no municipality can be assured of getting the construction it is paying for. In concrete paving, possibly more than in other types, the necessity of securing contractors who are experienced and well equipped is also of vital moment. The lowest bidder, too frequently, is a tyro and is attempting to build up a business, without organization or equipment, at the expense of the municipality.

Curbs and gutters are usually constructed as parts of the street paving and included in the contract for it. The curb may be of granite or sandstone, set vertically in concrete at the curb line. In case the curb is of stone, the gutter may be of the same material as is used for the street pavement, but it is often varied, particularly if the street is on a grade where the scouring action of water must be considered. When concrete is used, the curb and gutter may be combined, or the curb may be constructed of concrete in the same general form as a curb stone. In the combined curb and gutter, a width of about twenty-four inches at the base is considered standard practice, with a thickness of nine inches in the horizontal gutter section with a curb six inches thick and six inches high. The face of the curb is given a batten of one inch, and the angle between curb and gutter is rounded to facilitate cleaning. This form of curb is probably most desirable from the standpoint of motor car drivers, as the abrasion on tires when driving to the curb is negligible. The grade of the curb determines the grade of the street and has a definite relation to the grade of the sidewalk.

In opening subdivisions, it is usual to build sidewalks in order to afford pedestrians easy access to the properties and as an added incentive to purchase. Such walks are often built at grades suitable to the local terrain and the convenience of the subdivider; the quality is generally far below the standards maintained by the city, construction being adopted with a view only to preserving its integrity long enough to sell the property. In the outskirts of

[1] See Chap. V with respect to revenues from corporation cuts.

large cities it is not uncommon to see sidewalks cracked longitudinally for the length of a block, with grass and weeds growing through the cracks. It is scarcely necessary to state that such construction constitutes an economic waste that should not be tolerated. The same criticism holds for many streets built for sales promotion purposes.

Sidewalks may be built of earth, gravel, cinders, plank, stone, brick, and concrete—both asphaltic and cement. But cement walks are now used almost universally in American municipalities. As with concrete highways, there are certain fundamentals to be observed, and they are the same as in street construction. Drainage and a firm, substantial base must be provided. Drainage is had by excavating the loam below the base, the depth varying with conditions, and providing a subgrade of cinders or gravel. This subgrade should be leveled and thoroughly compacted. The sidewalk itself may be one course or two courses, as with pavements, and should have a minimum thickness of four to five inches. The same general care should be taken in proportioning the cement with aggregates, in the addition of water, the mixing, provisions for joints, etc., as is taken in the construction of pavements. Naturally, the same careful inspection to secure compliance with specifications should be made.

Street maintenance is ordinarily under the direct charge of a maintenance engineer, who should designate and generally supervise the areas to be repaired. Depending upon size, a city is ordinarily divided into a number of maintenance districts, each in charge of a district foreman subordinate to the engineer. Each district should be equipped with the proper yard, machinery, and supplies for making repairs with a minimum of haulage and other effort. Ordinarily, these maintenance crews will make temporary repairs in winter in order to prevent disintegration of the pavement.[1]

---

[1] For the subject of financing street paving, see Chap. VI; also, Laurence I. Hewes, *Highway Bonds* (U. S. Dept. of Agriculture, Bulletin No. 136, March, 1917).

CHAPTER XXVI

WASTES [1]

The average householder has little conception of the amount of refuse material produced by a single family living under urban conditions—waste water from bathroom and kitchen, food refuse, ashes, tin cans, bottles, paper, leaves, grass, hedge trimmings, and rubbish of every description all of which must be collected and disposed of by the municipal authorities. Add to this domestic refuse the enormous quantity of wastes incidental to manufacturing, industry, and other businesses; the dust and dirt on the streets, and the greater part of all rain and snow that falls within a densely populated city with paved streets, and one has a measure of the problem confronting the public administrator.

{The problem of waste disposal}

The complete and prompt collection and disposal of refuse such as sewage, garbage, and street dirt is essential to public health; the collection and disposal of ashes and rubbish is a great public convenience, and contributes to the orderliness of a city. In the interests of public health, sewerage, street cleaning, and in practically all instances garbage collection, are undertaken by the city government; and only in rare cases is ash and rubbish collection left to private initiative.

On the basis of their nature, and also the different methods and equipment employed both in collection and disposal, these wastes fall into two distinct groups: (1) sewage, which consists almost entirely of water with only a fraction of a percent of solid matter, and (2) solid refuse. Solid refuse, in turn, may be divided into two classes because of the different methods employed in its collection; (1) street wastes, consisting of street dirt and snow,

{Classification of wastes}

---

[1] The outstanding reference on the subject is Rudolph Hering and Samuel Greeley, *Collection and Disposal of Municipal Refuse* (McGraw-Hill, 1921), although discussion of street cleaning methods is omitted. See also, William Parr Capes and Jeanne D. Carpenter, *Municipal Housecleaning* (Dutton, 1918); and *Proceedings of the International Association of Street Sanitation Officials* (annual). For generally helpful discussions, although applying to particular cities, see Bureau of Municipal Research of Philadelphia, *Municipal Street Cleaning in Philadelphia* (1924); Rochester Bureau of Municipal Research, *Report on the Problem of Street Cleaning* (1918); *Report on the Problem of Refuse Collection* (1919); and Richard T. Fox, *Reports on the Chicago Bureau of Streets* (1913). For current references see *The American City* (monthly).

448 PRACTICE OF MUNICIPAL ADMINISTRATION

CHAP.
XXVI

and (2) household wastes of three sorts, *i.e.*, garbage, rubbish, and ashes. The problems of sewage collection and disposal, *i.e.*, "sewerage," are so distinct from those involved in the collection and disposal of other refuse, that this subject has been discussed separately.[1] The present chapter deals with the solid-waste group, which by usage has come to be known as "municipal wastes."

Variable conditions affecting waste removal

Few public activities are undertaken under more variable conditions than that of waste removal. Garbage that must be collected at frequent intervals during the extreme heat of summer may be solid ice during parts of the winter, and the normal quantity will be materially augmented in certain seasons of the year by the refuse of green vegetables; ashes come only in the winter season, the quantity varying with the severity of the weather; snow falls with extreme irregularity, and its removal may be facilitated by a thaw or made more difficult by extreme cold. And in the United States the problems tend to become difficult of solution because of the extremely rapid growth of cities, involving a new, fluctuating, and therefore more or less irresponsible population, yet one prone to demand every modern convenience. The activities of street cleaning and waste collection require unceasing effort toward administrative improvement, in order that the high standard of services now demanded may be obtained.

In the discussion that follows the methods and problems of street cleaning are kept separate from those of other waste collection and disposal because of their different character. In some cities these activities are handled by distinct departments, although most communities follow the preferable practice of utilizing two distinct organizatons within the same department.

Definition of street cleaning

The satisfactory cleaning of streets and alleys, paved and unpaved, requires the removal and subsequent disposal, of any deposits which may be detrimental to health, which are unsightly,

Sources and character of street dirt

and which may interfere with the use of the highways. Street sweepings have a diversified character, but may be placed in three general classes: (1) dust and fine deposits; (2) larger and heavier materials such as papers, sticks, straw, etc., and (3) snow and ice. There are many sources of street dirt, and seasonal and climatic variations have considerable effect upon the nature of street sweepings. The more common sources are excrement of animals, soot and dust from the air, materials from passing vehicles, débris from buildings and adjacent property, refuse thrown on the streets

[1] See Chap. XXVII.

WASTES

by pedestrians, dirt dragged by wheels from unpaved to paved streets, and material from wear of pavements. Other sources are of special nature, as refuse from the construction of buildings, dead leaves, etc.

The quantity of street sweepings determines the methods of removal and disposal, and quantities vary with the location of the street, the congestion and nature of population, the proximity of unpaved streets, the age of the pavement, and the time of year. In larger cities, the weight of street sweepings will range from 150 to 300 pounds per person per year, equivalent to an average of about one-third of a cubic yard. The seasonal variation in quantities of street sweepings will modify methods, as well as the amount of equipment and personnel, and add to the difficulties of conducting the activity. The seasonal changes may cause an extreme variation of five to one in quantities, but a range of three to one is more normal. The heaviest work in cleaning occurs during the summer months, as far as sweepings are concerned. However, heavy removals of snow and ice must be reckoned with in December, January, and February.

The type of pavement and its condition decidedly affects the efficiency of cleaning operations, and therefore the methods used and the size of the force employed. It is much easier to clean a new asphalt street than a stone block or water-bound macadam pavement. The greater the number of crevices and irregularities in the surface of the street the more difficult becomes the cleaning operation, and an old pavement in need of repairs requires most careful treatment. The relative ease of cleaning various types of pavement has been estimated by street cleaning authorities on the following scale, the maximum ease being represented by 100:

New sheet asphalt	100
New bituminous concrete	90
New wood block	90
New bituminous macadam	80
Brick, grout filler	80
Concrete, average condition	70
Stone block	60
Water bound macadam	40–20
Earth and gravel	10

The relative yearly cost of cleaning various types of pavement in Rochester, on the basis of 1,000 square yards, and the ratio of that cost to the cost of cleaning asphalt pavement, is as follows:[1]

[1] See Rochester Bureau of Municipal Research, *op. cit.*

Medina, business	$22.98	per	1000	sq.	yds.	153%
Brick, residential	15.54	"	"	"	"	104%
Asphalt	14.96	"	"	"	"	100%
Wood block	13.42	"	"	"	"	96%

Effect of character and extent of traffic

A study of traffic should be made to aid in the determination of the cleaning methods since the character and extent of traffic has an important bearing on the type of machinery chosen, and the volume of traffic influences the time of cleaning. It is not expedient, for instance, to flush downtown business streets during rush hours, or even at any time during the business day because the result would be congestion and confusion. Night is the proper time for flushing business sections, while handsweeping proves the most suitable method of cleaning throughout the day. The volume and character of traffic, whether automobile or horse-drawn, also affects the quantity of sweepings.

Effect of social and industrial conditions

The location of streets will influence the extent, if not the actual method, of the cleaning operation chosen. Residential, business, and factory areas present different problems. The nature and quantity of the dirt is distinct, traffic conditions are different, and the character and condition of pavements varies with the district. The nationality and social standing of the people residing along the street generally are reflected in its appearance. Foreigners have a tendency to litter the streets with paper and rubbish, a habit which is less noticeable among the more Americanized groups. In certain New York tenement districts, all garbage and refuse is wrapped in newspapers and hurled to the street, the bundle being known as a "pidgon." In consequence, the pavements in such localities must be hand broomed several times a day and flushed frequently.

Frequency of cleaning

The frequency of street cleaning must be based first upon available funds and sanitary needs. Other influencing factors are the density of horse-drawn vehicles, the width of the street, the character of the surrounding district and its population, the nearness of unpaved streets and alleys, the location of the public buildings, parks, and playgrounds, and the condition of the pavement. In localities where there are no playgrounds or parks, children are forced to use the streets for play, and under such circumstances particular effort ought to be made to maintain a high standard of cleanliness. Frequency also depends upon the method employed. The desirable number of cleanings cannot be stated arbitrarily, but must be determined by a field study, each street constituting a separate problem.

Among the cleaning methods in common use are machine brooming, squeegeeing, machine and hand flushing, and hand sweeping. Under certain circumstances each of these methods has advantages over the others.

Machine brooming means sweeping with a rotating broom mechanically operated. The machine may be either horse-drawn or motor-driven, the revolving broom of stiff bristles, being placed at an angle with the direction of travel, and with a sprinkling device located in front of the broom. Most of the machines deposit the dirt on one side as they proceed, this deposit being designated as "the stroke." Other machines of later model have a pick-up or a vacuum attachment, so that the entire operation of cleaning and removal is performed by the one machine. Machine sweeping should always be preceded by sprinkling, using just sufficient water to lay the dust and soften street dirt, that it may be picked up easily. The cleaning unit required ordinarily consists of a sprinkling machine, two machine brooms, and a pick-up wagon. If the brooming machine combines the operations of sprinkling, brooming, and pick-up, the equipment is correspondingly reduced. Such apparatus is capable of sweeping 175,000 to 180,000 square yards of pavement a day.

When a pick-up gang follows the broom, it should follow immediately; at the worst, not more than a few hours should elapse between the brooming of a street and the gathering of the material which has been left in the gutters. Otherwise as soon as the material becomes dry it is scattered over the street by wind or traffic, and much of the work which has been done is lost. Sometimes, however, the stroke of a machine, or what is left of it, is allowed to lie in the gutters eighteen to twenty-four hours, or longer, after the machine has passed.

Squeegee machines are for use on large areas of smooth pavement which are already comparatively clean. The squeegee is built on nearly the same principle as the machine broom, the chief difference being that a cylinder with spiral rubber flaps is substituted for the broom. Such a machine is generally operated by teams and should be preceded by a sprinkling machine which completely softens the dirt. In order to clean efficiently, several machines should be used, depending upon the street width. An excellent use for the squeegee has been found in districts where automobiles are commonly parked during the day and where the streets are paved with wood block. In such districts it is practically impossible to remove the grease and dirt stuck to the pavement by means of a flusher machine, although flushing assists in loosening this material. Under such conditions, the only mechanical equipment which appears to be adapted to the work is the squeegee. This equipment can be used also along the gutters as an auxiliary to flushing.

Machine and hand flushing

Speaking generally, flushing is the cleaning method which produces best results. However, it must be supplemented by other methods and is not adaptable to all conditions. Successful machine flushing requires careful consideration of several important factors. A flusher, when horse-drawn, becomes inefficient as it empties, due to decrease in pressure, which defect can be remedied only by the installation of a separate motor for maintaining the pressure. If the flusher is motor-driven, pressure may be regulated by the driving motor, but it is advisable and really proves most efficient to install a separate pressure motor, because of irregularity in driving speed. As regards the nozzles, at least two should be operated at the same time with a discharge pressure of about forty pounds per square inch. Pressure gauges are necessary, in order that the driver may check this item. The speed of a flusher varies from eight to ten miles per hour. They are operated in gangs, the number depending upon the street width. Two flushers are satisfactory on a forty foot street. About 100,000 square yards of pavement can be cleaned in a day. Hose or hand flushing is economical for flushing comparatively small areas, and is used in both large and small cities. The method is most efficient in some respects but requires a tremendous amount of water. However, many cities have little faith in hand flushing, since its effectiveness depends entirely upon the capabilities of the men handling the hose.

Flushing methods of either type cannot always be used; for the sewerage system must have sufficient capacity and rapidity of current to remove street dirt poured into it, and even under these circumstances coarser refuse should be removed by other methods; a large amount of inexpensive water must be available; and local conditions with respect to traffic, pavements, and character of refuse must be suitable.

Hand sweeping

Hand sweeping must always be used to supplement machine sweeping and flushing. Two principles should govern the use of the method—all material should be removed at the nearest possible point to its place of origin, and it should be removed as soon as possible after it is deposited. Under obsolete methods a patrolman was assigned to a definite area and required to make a certain number of trips a day over it. The proper method is to assign the man to a certain area and have him first remove the most conspicuous deposits of the preceding night. This having been done over the entire area, the patrolman should then collect the less offensive refuse.

The factors determining the efficiency of hand sweeping are the efficiency of the labor employed, the quantity of dirt deposited, the amount and kind of traffic (the sweeper should sweep against traffic as a safety precaution), the kind and condition of pavement, and the different classes of occupancy such as industrial, business, residential, and tenement. The areas that can be kept clean by a hand sweeper range from 2,000 to 25,000 square yards and are varied by type of district and kind of pavement. The equipment of a hand sweeper usually consists of an easily transported handwagon which has a removable container, a push-broom with scraper attached, a short handled broom of the household type, and a handscraper or lightweight steel scoop.

Unpaved streets require treatment entirely different from paved highways. If such streets are properly drained, they can be kept in good condition by periodic grading and surfacing, a hand sweeper occasionally picking up larger deposits such as sticks and paper. In the summer it is also desirable to lay the dust, which can be done by the use of oil, water, or salts. Oil has been found efficient as far as dust settlement is concerned, but when first applied is apt to prove disagreeable to both householders and traffic. Recently, calcium chloride has been much used, with good results, and it may prove to be the best method of dealing with the dust question.

Street sweepings, like other wastes, require disposal. Many cities place sweepings on the city dumps, others have had some slight success in selling them to farmers for fertilizer, and still others have attempted to use them as filling material. However, street refuse has little value as fertilizer and on account of odor and instability is also undesirable for filling, even when mixed with ashes. In any event, sweepings should be dumped in remote regions so as not to become a public nuisance. The vehicles used in conveying the street waste to places of disposal are ordinarily

454 PRACTICE OF MUNICIPAL ADMINISTRATION

Cost data

Organization for street cleaning

Geographical and functional organization

horse-drawn and central disposal or loading stations are desirable in order to reduce the length of haul by this slow-moving equipment. From these central stations the accumulation may be transported to the disposal point by steam or electric railroad, or by motor truck, at substantial reduction in costs.

In general, the cost data obtainable with respect to street cleaning activities are unsatisfactory. Fluctuating prices, varying standards of cleanliness, and different local conditions make comparisons difficult and inaccurate. Also, methods of keeping costs lack standardization and uniformity.

Two principal types of organization may be applied to the work of street cleaning, and they may be designated as functional and geographical.[1] Under the geographical organization, the supervision of all the various activities is under one individual responsible for a particular area; under the functional organization, each activity is separately supervised, two or more individuals covering the same area, each superintending a particular activity. Or the organization may be both geographical and functional, *i.e.*, functional within several large administrative areas, or functional with respect to certain activities and geographical for others.[2] Under both types coördination of the work must ultimately be supervised by a responsible superintendent.

There are merits in each type of organization. In the functional type, each activity is placed in charge of a capable supervisor who can be held responsible for the proper exercise of his authority, including coördination with the other activities. In the geographical type, responsibility within a given area is absolutely fixed and complete coördination is assumed, although the technique of supervision may not be as perfect. Without attempting further analysis and comparison, it may be stated that the activities of street cleaning are not so technically diverse that one supervisor within an area cannot administer all of them. As a general proposition, therefore, the geographical type of organization is prac-

---

[1] The organization and methods discussed in this chapter are summarized from *Report on the Reorganization of the Garbage and Street-Cleaning Division of Detroit* (1924) and numerous other reports on the collection and disposal of municipal wastes by the Detroit Bureau of Governmental Research.

[2] American railway systems are organized largely on a functional basis with a single supervisor responsible for each principal activity, such as engineering, maintenance of way, maintenance of rolling stock, etc., for the entire system. Occasionally an unusually large system may be divided first into several geographical areas, as the Pennsylvania Railroad Company has divided its lines east of Pittsburgh and west of Pittsburgh. However, even then certain administrative activities cover the entire system.

ticable and has the distinct advantage of fixing definite responsibility for cleanliness in a particular district. CHAP. XXVI

At the head of the street cleaning department should be a chief superintendent, with engineering training, aided by a planning and educational division, and by an inspection corps. In street cleaning perhaps the most important duty of the superior officers is planning the work in advance, such planning to be facilitated by complete statistics of previous work, maps, and other data regarding the geographical divisions of the city. An inspection force is necessary because as the area and quantity of the work to be supervised increases, it becomes more and more difficult for the superintendent to get over the ground often or thoroughly enough to secure the information necessary for the proper administration of the work. The best plan is to have as many inspectors as there are districts. By the occasional transfer of these inspectors from one district to another, comparison of methods and results is made easily possible and a general improvement and standardization of methods can be obtained. Educational work is also necessary because if the coöperation of the public can be secured the task of cleaning the streets becomes less difficult. Less litter will find its way into the streets, and the work will be correspondingly reduced.

Superintendence and planning

Inspection

Educational work

The advantages of the organization outlined are the elimination of divided responsibility over a single area; a clear definition of the responsibility of the various officers; a concentration of supervision; and relief of the chief from details of routine work, with the result that better service is secured for the money spent and an organization is available that may be expanded without material change to meet new requirements.

The removal of snow from city streets presents an important problem in many northern cities, especially in those communities having considerable vehicular traffic. In such municipalities snow must be removed from the business district and on main thoroughfares. The areas to be cleaned, the plan of organization, and the methods to be employed should be determined in advance of the winter season. The areas decided upon must be districted and each district placed in charge of some definite individual, with an assignment of equipment and personnel. Best results will be secured by using the local street cleaning organization as a skeleton, filling in with casual labor as necessary. For such labor, provision must be made for mittens, hot coffee when temperatures are low, and

Snow removal

payment at the end of each day's work. The contract method of removal should be avoided, but when it is necessary to use contract teams and trucks, such equipment should be provided for well ahead of emergency requirement.

Principles governing snow removal

Two principles should govern the work of snow removal— first, the snow should be gotten out of the way in the shortest possible time compatible with reasonable cost; and second, traffic should be interfered with to the least possible extent. To these ends, the work of removal should begin immediately after the commencement of snowfall and the operation should be continuous until the required district is cleared of snow. Coöperation of the weather bureau should be secured to obtain forecasts of heavy snowfall.

Methods of collection

The methods used in removal must be determined by local circumstances. Ordinarily the snow will be plowed into windrows with road scrapers, and removed by wagon or truck. Such vehicles are usually loaded by hand, although cities are now using mechanical loaders. Hand piling may be used, particularly on streets with parked automobiles, but is relatively expensive. Machine brooming may be used if the snow is not too wet and deep. Where sewer manholes are available at convenient intervals, snow may be scraped directly into them without piling. Flushing is occasionally used, but only during rising temperatures for removing slush.

Disposal

When snow must be carted away, the principal requirement in the interest of both economy and speed of removal are nearby places of disposal. These facilities may be a public dump, or any low place with adequate drainage, or preferably a body of water, easily accessible and into which the snow may be dumped without reshoveling. Disposal in sewers is ideal when conditions permit. Manholes properly constructed for dumping must be placed at convenient intervals, and the size, gradient, and flow of the sewer must be sufficient to carry off the material dumped, without clogging. When physical conditions permit, new sewers constructed in the downtown section of a city, should be designed to allow their use for snow removal purposes.

Waste collection and disposal

The collection and disposal of domestic and industrial refuse is a matter of municipal housekeeping which is being considered more and more as an engineering problem. With the increase in urban population and the corresponding increase of wastes, rudimentary methods have become inadequate to meet the requirements of both convenience and health. The public is quick to criticize an administration that leaves the alleys choked with ashes, rubbish, and decaying household wastes, to become unsightly and annoying breeding places for rats and flies. Aside from æsthetic considerations, public health requires that garbage and refuse be removed rapidly and disposed of in such a manner as not to become a nuisance.

CHAP. XXVI

Aside from street sweepings and snow, already discussed, municipal wastes consist of garbage, ashes, and rubbish. Garbage consists of rejected animal and vegetable matter from the kitchen and market. Ashes are limited in general to household ashes, those from industrial establishments not being included. Rubbish includes bulky materials that cannot be classified under any other term, such as cans, metal, paper, old boxes, furniture, bottles, grass, leaves, hedge trimmings, and similar materials. Small dead animals are generally treated as garbage; large dead animals require special consideration.

Definition of waste

The determination of the average quantity of each class of waste matter is important in deciding upon the proper and suitable methods of collection and disposal, and these quantities will vary throughout the year, and from year to year. In an ordinary city having a population of 25,000 or more, the average amount of garbage is about one-half pound per person per day, with an upward tendency. The average number of pounds of garbage per person in large cities will range from 150 to 250 pounds a year. Average production of ashes and rubbish in an urban community is in the neighborhood of four-tenths of a cubic yard per person per year. The seasonal variation in the quantities of waste requires careful consideration on the part of the administrator. Based upon percentage of the average, the monthly variation for garbage will range from about sixty-eight percent in February to 146 percent in August, with July, August, and September as the months of heaviest production because of the bulky and green vegetables that are in season. Therefore, more frequent collections during the summer months are necessary. In winter the quantity of ashes is usually double that of the summer. The rubbish ratio is about the reverse.[1]

Quantity of waste

Seasonal variation

For disposal purposes, the composition of garbage must also be known. Garbage produced by urban populations contains about seventy percent water, three percent grease, twenty percent other

[1] See Hering and Greeley, *op. cit.*, and other authorities for detailed tables.

458   PRACTICE OF MUNICIPAL ADMINISTRATION

animal and vegetable matter, and seven percent general rubbish. These relative percentages vary according to both season and locality. Grease content is an important item, and the high production of grease present in the garbage of American cities is responsible for the development of the garbage reduction processes in use in this country.

Systems of waste collection

There are two principal systems of collection—the separate and the combined. In deciding which system is to be adopted by a community, the method of disposal and the general attitude of the people must be given consideration. This latter element is most important, since the approval of the public is absolutely essential to reasonable ease of administration. The separate system means that garbage, ashes, and rubbish are each collected separately; and it is used when the garbage is disposed of by reduction, by incineration, or is fed to hogs. The ashes are used for filling low places and the rubbish is sorted and the bulk of it either dumped or burned. Under the combined system, the garbage, ashes, and rubbish are usually mixed and collected together. This system is used when all waste is disposed of by dumping or by certain types of incineration. Or there may be a separate collection of ashes and the combined collection of rubbish and garbage. This system has been adopted when the garbage and rubbish are disposed of by incineration and the ashes are used for fill. The general practice in the United States is to collect the garbage separately, and either to combine or separate the collection of ashes and rubbish.

Plans of collection

Several plans of collection have been used in this country. Under the licensed collector system, certain individuals are licensed by the city to collect and dispose of wastes, arrangements being made by the collector with each householder to pay for the service. Or collection may be by contract with the municipality. Provision is made that the city pay a fixed amount annually for services, or that a certain schedule be paid by the householder, or that the contractor pay a certain sum to the city for the privilege of collecting, charging the householder for the service. In other words, the contractor may be paid wholly by the city, by special assessment, or directly by the householder. This contract system has been employed to a large extent.

The most desirable method is municipal collection, under which the city collects and disposes of the wastes, making a charge for the service only when collecting industrial rubbish. On the whole, the service can be performed more cheaply and efficiently by the city and is a task which most cities should assume. Direct and indirect costs considered, municipal service is far cheaper and more satisfactory. Municipal operation elevates the service from the level of a money-making scheme, the householder is relieved of the burden of dealing with a contractor, and more care is apt to be taken to protect streets and alleys from dumpings, and to insure that collections are made. No matter what system is adopted, an independent inspection force should be maintained by the city and all ordinances and rules enforced.

Inspection of collection service

Treatment of the garbage by the householder is of some importance. The general requirement under the separate system is that the garbage be placed in a standard container, which is usually a galvanized steel can of such size as to be easily handled by the collector. The garbage should be thoroughly drained before being placed in the can and every can ought to be cleaned frequently. Some cities having the incineration method of disposal require that the garbage be wrapped in paper before being placed in the can. In winter this wrapping prevents freezing of garbage to the can, and it always facilitates burning. As a rule, however, such a requirement is difficult to enforce. The standard container for ashes and rubbish is the bushel basket. Under the combined system, ashes, rubbish, and garbage are placed in barrels or bins. Since the most desirable and most used system in the United States is separate collection of garbage, the consideration of equipment and disposal will be from that viewpoint, assuming municipal collection.

Details of collection methods

Garbage is collected either in tank wagons having a detachable or dump tank, or in can rack wagons. The tank wagon must be metallic, fitted with covers, easily cleaned, and of such a height as to be convenient for one man to empty a can into it, thus minimizing the strains common to the occupation. Covers are necessary to prevent the spread of bad odors, and a tarpaulin is most convenient and effective for this purpose. A tarpaulin is costly, wears out quickly, and grows dirty easily, but it does not rattle and permits expansion of the load during periods when the amount of garbage is at a maximum. Steel and wooden covers are generally built in sections, but wear loose and are noisy and heavy. Such covers are invariably left off when seasonal variation requires the overloading of wagons to maintain schedules, and the spilling of garbage creates a decided nuisance. The capacity of tank wagons

Equipment for garbage collection

varies from one to four cubic yards, two or three cubic yards being a desirable content.

With the tank wagon system, the collector carries the can from the yard, empties its contents into the wagon, and returns it to the yard. Sometimes a large bucket is carried into which several cans are emptied before transferring to the wagon. In some cities, without alleys, householders are required to place their cans in front of the house at the curb. Although this method saves time in collection, it is unsightly and disagreeable.

Under the so-called can system of collection, each wagon is fitted with a rack so as to carry a certain number of cans, and the collector leaves an empty can for each full can he removes. The city must buy the cans and furnish two for each householder. The advantages of such a system are that the emptying process at the curb and the accompanying smells are avoided; the character of the service is less obvious; covers are not opened during transportation; and cans are washed regularly. The disadvantage is largely one of expense, since a limited number of cans can be placed on each wagon, the city must buy cans, and modern washing arrangements must be installed. In small cities the can system has given excellent results, but for larger municipalities the tank wagon system seems to be more desirable and less expensive.

Horse-drawn vs. motor-driven vehicles

The relative merits of horse-drawn and motor-driven vehicles for collection have furnished much material for discussion. The data available indicate that for short hauls and frequent stops the horse-drawn vehicle is cheaper, but for long hauls and few stops the motor truck has the advantage. A horse can be worked only one-half the time and travels slowly, approximating an average speed of three miles an hour. One man is sufficient for each wagon of average size, the number of horses depending upon the weight of the load. The motor truck can be used twenty-four hours a day and covers more ground, but usually requires one man in addition to the driver, and operates inefficiently when stops are frequent. Speaking generally, motor vehicles are not effective for primary collection. A combination of horse-drawn and motor-driven vehicles gives the best results in most cases, horse-drawn trailers being coupled in trains and moved by tractor at a transfer station.

Time of collection

The time of collection in most American cities is during the day. Some cities, notably New York, have attempted night collections in all districts, but night work was so distasteful to the collectors that they deliberately created unnecessary noise and forced the abandonment of the scheme. As a general rule, collections are made in residential districts during the daytime, and only in the business sections at night.

CHAP. XXVI

The number of garbage collections a week in the same district is determined by the amount of garbage. Collections vary in the different localities from once a week in the winter to two or three a week, and once a day in the business section, in the summer. This frequency is generally accepted as standard.[1]

Frequency of collection

No one type of wagon has been universally adopted for the collection of ashes and rubbish. The wagon capacity depends upon the length of haul and the topography of the city, a good average capacity being three to five cubic yards. However, when ashes are collected separately from rubbish, it is possible to use an eight or ten yard wagon, or larger, for the latter, a fact that many city authorities fail to appreciate.

Collection of ashes and rubbish

The number of men employed on each wagon depends upon the method of collection adopted. One plan employs one or two men in addition to a driver. Under the gang plan, however, a number of men precede a wagon down a street, placing receptacles at the curb for the driver to empty. A similar gang follows the wagon, returning the receptacles to the yard.

Collections of ashes and rubbish are more frequent in winter than in summer, some authorities maintaining that a minimum of two collections per month should be undertaken in the former season. The use of motor trucks in connection with ash and rubbish collection is governed by the same factors discussed with reference to the collection of garbage.

So many different factors affect the cost of collection that it is difficult to draw any general conclusions from figures available. Local conditions, as usual, play an important part. The system of collection in operation, whether separate or combined, must also be considered. Further, the methods of figuring costs are not standardized, with the result that there is a great variation in reported expenditures. Costs of collection vary from two to eight dollars a ton, with a tendency toward the higher figures. Two factors determine the cost of collection—the cost of loading and the cost of hauling. The cost of loading depends upon the method adopted—whether receptacles are removed from the curb

Cost of rubbish collection

---

[1] Professor William C. Hoad, of the University of Michigan, believes that the minimum number of collections should be twice a week in winter, and three times a week in summer.

or the premises, whether picked up by a collector and helper or by the gang system, whether collections are separate or combined, the frequency of collections, the density of population, and the cost of labor. The cost of hauling depends upon the capacity of the wagon, the rate of travel, and the length of haul. All of these elements should be noted in the establishment of a cost system in connection with this activity.

Disposal of waste matters

Ordinarily, disposal of garbage is accomplished by one of the following means: dumping into large bodies of water; filling low ground; digging into the ground; feeding to animals; incineration; and reduction.

Dumping in water

Hauling by barge to sea or into lakes, or even dumping over the banks of streams, have been methods of waste disposal employed by New York City, on the one hand, and by the smallest hamlets on the other. None of these methods has proved satisfactory. Wind, currents, tides, and high water almost invariably bring such wastes back as a nuisance or a sanitary menace to neighbors downstream, and this practice is now generally prohibited by health authorities.

Filling low ground

Filling in low ground, or the "sanitary fill" method of disposing of garbage, may be classed as a pioneer process. Swampy lands or gulleys are filled with a mixture of ashes, garbage, and rubbish, in layers, the garbage being treated with lime or other deodorant, the final oxidation of all decomposable matter being anticipated. This method has been used with some success in Chicago and may serve as an emergency measure.

Digging into the ground

Digging into the ground is a similar makeshift method. The garbage is mixed with the top soil and plowed under. After lying unused for two or three years, a field may again be used for the same purpose.

Feeding to animals

The disposal of garbage by feeding to animals is considered one of the three proper and scientific methods of disposal. Seventy-five to one hundred hogs will consume a ton of garbage a day. The fear that disease may be spread by such feeding appears to be unfounded, since garbage-fed hogs are as healthy as other hogs, and much of the prevailing criticism is really directed against poor management rather than against any inherent defects in the method itself. Loss of hogs due to disease can be reduced to a minimum through immunization. Garbage to be fed to hogs should be kept in separate containers and collected frequently, being considered as a useable food material. Cooking of garbage before feeding is not advisable, the result being a poor, soupy material, difficult to feed, not liked by the hogs, and not calculated to make them thrive. All feeding should be done on floors of limited areas that can be cleaned after every feeding. The trough method of feeding requires an excessive amount of labor and is not desirable. At the end of each day, the refuse remaining on the feeding platform should be shoveled away and used as fertilizer. In northern latitudes, to prevent freezing, provision must be made for feeding under cover.[1]

During the past fifteen years, as a method of disposal, garbage reduction has been much used, discussed, and abused; and in some cases reduction plants have been shut down and scrapped as total losses. Garbage reduction means the treatment of garbage as collected by cooking, and the extraction of the grease for commercial purposes. Ordinarily, garbage contains about three percent grease, or sixty pounds per ton. As an additional source of revenue from the process, the residue (after the grease has been extracted and the metal and broken crockery removed), known as tankage, has value as a fertilizer or fertilizer base. The value of the grease, used in making cheaper grades of soap reached as high as fourteen cents per pound during the World War. Since then, it has gone as low as two cents or less per pound, so that the profits from grease have been problematical. The tankage is a source of profit in parts of the country where farmers and gardeners are educated to the value of strengthening their soil regularly. In other parts, the market is very unreliable, at times being negligible.

The reduction method must be employed on a large scale, preferably in cities of over 100,000 population. Skilled supervision and operation and frequent replacements of equipment are necessary, and those who anticipate operation without these fundamentals will often be disappointed in the performance of the plants. The odors inevitable in the reduction process necessitate the location of plants in the country, which increases hauling

---

[1] The city of Worcester, Mass., has been successful with this method of disposal. A report made by a special commission of that city, investigating the different methods of disposal, states "that the disposal by feeding is the most economical method; that the greatest intrinsic value of the garbage, the feeding value, is made use of; that the garbage of Worcester cannot only be disposed of without cost but that the revenue from the sale of hogs has almost been sufficient to pay for the collection." This report is rather too optimistic, but much can be said for the method when used under suitable circumstances.
The flesh of garbage-fed hogs is reported to be as sound as when corn is fed.

charges. Efforts have been made to abate the odors by chlorinating the gases in the base of the smokestack, and with some success; but no plant has been rendered odorless. The reduction process resuires the separate collection of garbage from other wastes, and a maximum of ten percent of tin cans, bottles and other extraneous matter is generally prescribed in contracts between private reduction companies and municipalities.

There are two processes of reduction—the cooking process and the dry process. In the cooking process the garbage is placed in tanks and cooked for several hours under high steam pressure. The garbage is then pressed, and from the resulting liquid the grease is eventually skimmed. The remaining liquid is evaporated, mixed with the solid tankage remaining after the pressing process, and after drying is disposed of as low grade fertilizer.

The dry process is based upon the use of a solvent. A tank is filled with raw garbage and a solvent, which is a distillate of petroleum, is added. Steam is admitted into a jacket surrounding the tank and the solvent and water are volatilized. More solvent is then pumped into the tank, which circulates continually through the stirred garbage and dissolves the grease. The solvent is drawn off, distilled, and the grease obtained. The dry garbage remaining is tankage and is used as fertilizer. With this process the tankage is said to be more valuable as a fertilizer and the odors are practically eliminated. The cost of operation is greater, and there are some differences of opinion as to the advantages and disadvantages of the two methods.

In larger cities, where garbage disposal is a major factor in sanitation, there has been a marked tendency toward incineration. This is a reaction against the uncertainty of a profit by reduction methods, the long hauls ordinarily necessary to reach reduction plants, and the usual nuisance in the locality of such plants. The decision between a method that includes doubtful profits and some nuisance and one that is absolutely sanitary without nuisance and making no pretense to profit, is one that must be made by every growing community sooner or later.

Disposal of garbage by incineration has proved successful in many cities, and is particularly applicable to smaller communities. Incinerators are of two types—low and high temperature. Low temperature incinerators, frequently termed crematories, are usually cheap of construction, lacking in durability, and inefficient of operation. The crematory requires a relatively large amount of fuel, ground space, and labor. In the crematory the temperature at the inlet of the stack is as low as 800 and 900 degrees Fahrenheit, resulting in incomplete combustion, and more or less nuisance from odors. The destructor requires relatively less fuel, less ground area, and less labor. The destructor, or high temperature incinerator, has a combustion chamber through which all gases must pass before entering the stack. This chamber permits complete combustion of all gases, the temperature never falling below 1,200 degrees Fahrenheit, and also acts as a dust collector.

In incineration garbage may be burned by itself, using such fuel as is necessary to bring the garbage into condition for combustion, or by utilizing rubbish as fuel. For best results it has been found that separate collections of wastes are desirable, although experiments have been tried in which all rubbish, including ashes, have been put through the incinerators with garbage. The results have been generally unsatisfactory, however, owing to the necessarily low temperatures following the introduction of so much inert matter. Incineration has not provided a solution for the tin cans and metal problem that is so vital in all processes connected with the disposal of municipal wastes. The heat of the incinerators, despite claims that have been made, does not fuse the metals, and they appear in the ashes, making as much of a problem as ever.

If ashes are collected separately from rubbish, they should be used for filling low ground. Much apparently useless land has been reclaimed in many cities in this manner without objectionable features. If mixed with rubbish, the use of ashes for filling purposes is not so desirable. Rubbish should be sorted and then burned in an incinerator or disposed of on outlying city dumps; or its use in a garbage incinerator is very desirable. Dumps for rubbish have not been looked upon with favor in recent years, as they are dirty, unsightly, create bad odors, and are an additional fire hazard.

Several municipalities, including Washington and Buffalo, are experimenting with the salvaging of rubbish, more as a means of reducing the amount of material hauled to the dumps than as a source of revenue. Rubbish is collected at a central transfer station, dumped into bins from which it is spread, on a belt conveyor, and sorted for metal, cans, bottles, rubber, rags, paper, and wood. A ready market is found for baled cans, certain types of bottles, scrap metal, and rags. Baled paper of the kinds found in rubbish is not so easily disposed of, and Buffalo is utilizing it for the manufacture of paper board. There is little or no market for broken glass, or for rubber. A large quantity of combustible rubbish can be burned in a cheap incinerator on the spot, without any offense whatsoever, or may be used to generate steam. The balance, about one-half of the original bulk and weight, is hauled to the dumps. The installation expense of salvaging equipment is very small, and the revenues have proved more than sufficient to pay the cost of sorting, leaving the saving in haulage as a net profit.

Costs of disposal

Any cost data on the several practical methods of disposal—feeding, incineration, and reduction, must be relative. The actual costs will be modified by local circumstances, and because of loose bookkeeping methods are difficult to obtain. For cities of moderate size, and including all cities of less than 100,000 population, incineration at high temperatures is the most feasible plan of combined garbage and rubbish disposal. The initial cost of the plant will average $1,000 a ton daily capacity and the total operating cost, including depreciation, will be in the neighborhood of $2.25 a ton. No revenue can be counted upon.

A reduction plant will cost about $2,000 a ton daily capacity, and the operating cost per ton will be somewhat higher than with incineration, say $2.50 to $2.75 a ton. The revenue from the sale of products may total $4.00 per ton of garbage reduced, depending on the price of grease and tankage. However, in actual practice it is most likely that the operating costs will be higher, and the revenues smaller than any estimates made beforehand. Extravagant claims are sometimes made on behalf of hog feeding as a means of disposal. The initial cost is high, probably around $4,000 per ton daily capacity. The cost of operation is not much, if any less, than other methods, and the revenues are about the same, so far as revenues can be calculated, considering the fluctuating price of pork. The profits to be made from garbage reduction alone are largely imaginary. During the World War, the high price of grease enabled both private and municipal plants to receive substantial returns. Under ordinary circumstances, the returns cannot be expected to meet entirely the costs involved.[1]

[1] Until 1923, Detroit delivered its garbage to a private reduction company which disposed of the waste without charge to the city. A cancellation of the contract was forced by threatened bankruptcy. The new contract provides for payment by the city of $2.25 a ton, with a reduction of 10 cents a ton for every quarter-cent increase in the price of grease above 6½ cents a pound. Columbus, during 1922, collected and reduced 26,735 tons of garbage in its municipal plant. The cost of reduction was $146,252, an average cost per

WASTES 467

These figures cover the cost of disposal only and not that of collection. In estimating the entire cost of garbage removal in a city, the cost of collection plus the cost of disposal must be considered. Any profits made from disposal products should be considered. But, as a matter of fact, the collection and disposal of garbage has never been run at a profit, and the chances are it never will be. The best that can be hoped is to reduce costs to a minimum.

When it comes to the question of organization, local conditions must be considered in conjunction with the methods of collection and disposal. A fairly satisfactory organization for collection is to divide the city into districts, with a transfer station located in each district. The length of haul should be such that a horse-drawn vehicle can make several trips a day without spending too much time in travel. Collection of garbage for the short or average haul should be by horse to the transfer station. From each transfer station the accumulation of garbage should be hauled by motor truck or tractor to a central loading station. In choosing the location of the transfer station, care must be taken that it is so situated as to prevent double hauling. Some stations have been located in such a manner that a wagon has collected garbage and hauled it some five or six miles to the station and then a truck or tractor has received these loads at the transfer station and hauled them back over the very same route to the central loading station, or place of disposal. Such double hauling cannot be entirely avoided in all cases, but should be reduced to a minimum. The general rule to follow is the use of the horse for short hauls and the motor or tractor for long hauls. In the outlying districts, collection by motor truck is economical.[1]

The number of trips made each day by collectors depends upon

---

ton of $5.47. From grease and tankage there was a revenue of $98,144, or $3.67 per ton. These figures include no interest or depreciation charges, and not all of the overhead expense connected with the operation of the reduction plant. Indianapolis, during 1923, reduced 22,098 tons of garbage under contract with a private plant. The operating revenue of the plant was $80,976.50 and the operating expense, not including depreciation and interest, was $74,940.24, leaving a so-called profit of $6,036.26 for reduction only.

[1] For example, Indianapolis during the last eight months of 1923 collected 18,321 tons of garbage at a cost of $54,559.78, or $2.977 a ton, not including interest and depreciation. Indianapolis presents no difficulties in topography, and these costs are based on a modern method of collection and transportation, *i.e.*, horses and side-dump trailers for collection, and making the long haul by assembling trailers in trains drawn by tractors and trucks. Columbus, Ohio, during 1922, collected 26,735 tons of garbage at a cost of $88,895.61, or $3.325 a ton.

the length of haul, the quantity of garbage to be collected, and the district in which collection is made. A maximum of two trips a day appears to have become a standard in many cities, it making no difference whether the time taken for these trips is four hours or eight hours. The collector figures that he is through for the day at the end of the second trip, but he always receives pay for a full eight-hour day. This habit should be discouraged, and it brings up the question of productive time. A man hired to collect garbage should spend his entire time in collecting and not half of it in riding on a wagon. It should be possible to have men placed in a district whose sole duty is collection and have wagons driven to and from the stations by hired drivers. No city has yet worked out such a plan, but it is likely that it will be developed in the near future. Much more attention should also be paid to routing the collection forces so as to compel a reasonable day's work.

CHAPTER XXVII

SEWERAGE [1]

From an early stage of civilization, sewer systems have been employed to remove sanitary wastes from homes, public baths, and industrial establishments. For a long time, however, the use of sewers was limited, and sewage was disposed of by conducting it to adjacent low land or to a body of water where the dilution was so great as to reduce the danger of contamination. In the main, early sewerage systems dealt largely with storm water, which was led off by means of shallow open drains in the center of the streets. The relation of sewage disposal to public health was not generally recognized, and in some instances the inhabitants of cities took their water supply from contaminated sources. As the number and size of cities increased, such instances were multiplied, with most serious results. Modern sewerage science has developed principally in the last half century, coincident with a knowledge of sewage as a carrier of disease, particularly of typhoid fever, with the general use of baths and indoor toilet facilities, with the large industrial use of water, and with the paving of streets which has facilitated the run off of rain and melting snow.

<small>Historical development of sewerage</small>

The sewage of a city may be thought of roughly as the used water supply of a community, containing the wastes of the human body, and certain domestic and industrial wastes, plus the run off

<small>Definition of sewage</small>

---

[1] See Leonard Metcalf and Harrison P. Eddy, *American Sewerage Practice* (McGraw-Hill, 3 vols., 1916), and *Sewerage and Sewage Disposal* (McGraw-Hill, 1922). A number of recent books treat particularly of sewage disposal, including H. E. Babbitt, *Sewerage and Sewage Treatment* (Wiley, 1925); and L. P. Kinnicutt, C. E. A. Winslow, and R. W. Pratt, *Sewage Disposal* (Wiley, 1919). A brief non-technical discussion, but promoting a patented type of disposal, is W. L. D'Olier, *The Sanitation of Cities* (The Sanitary Corporation, New York, 1921). A chapter on sewage disposal with an enumeration of the methods employed in individual cities will be found in W.P. Capes and Jeanne D. Carpenter, *Municipal Housekeeping* (Dutton, 1918). A number of valuable reports have been issued on particular cities, and a more general study will be found in H. H. Wagenhals, E. J. Theriault, and H. B. Hommon, *Sewage Treatment in the United States, a Report on the Study of Fifteen Representative Plants* (U. S. Public Health Bulletin No. 132, July, 1923). For current reference, see Proceedings of the *American Society for Municipal Improvements* (annual); *Public Works* (monthly); *Engineering News-Record* (weekly); and *The American City* (monthly).

470   PRACTICE OF MUNICIPAL ADMINISTRATION

CHAP. XXVII

of storms and such ground waters as may filter into the system. The quantity of sewage varies from 100 gallons to upwards of 200 gallons per person per day. Roughly, the ratio of solid matter to liquids is one part in one thousand, about one-third of the solids being in suspension and two-thirds in solution. About one-half of the solid matter is organic, the other half being inorganic.

Separate and combined sewerage systems

Two systems of sewage collection are in use, the separate and the combined. In the separate system domestic sewage is collected in small sewers and disposed of as the situation may require. Surface water and industrial wastes are collected by larger sewers and generally run into a river or other body of water. In the combined system all sewage is carried through a single set of sewers. Both systems are in use, although the combined system is more general. No categorical rules can be laid down as to when one or the other of the plans should be adopted, and the matter should be determined by the sanitary engineer, taking into consideration topography, amount and seasonal variation of rainfall, and other factors, including means of disposal. This last factor is highly important. If all sewage must be subject to expensive treatment before disposal, the addition of immense quantities of surface water to sanitary wastes means an unreasonable increase in cost. Under some conditions this may be largely avoided by passing unusual flows of storm water around the disposal plant.

Design of sewer systems

Whatever system of sewerage is used, it is imperative that it be designed by competent engineers who will give due consideration to the numerous and important factors that must enter in—population, topography, drainage areas, rainfall, trade wastes, ultimate disposal, and other influences of an important and technical character. The system must be designed to carry off the maximum quantity of sewage that may exist at any one time and be capable of expansion to meet expected growth of population. Certain of these factors can be calculated with reasonable accuracy; others are a matter of hypothesis. However, a scientific design based on available facts, incomplete as they may be, is better than any "rule of thumb" proposals for meeting immediate needs. Millions of dollars lie buried in useless or partly useless sewers in the streets of American cities because no real wisdom was shown in their planning.

When a city is large enough to employ its own specialized engineering force, a competent engineer of sewer design is absolutely necessary. In cities where the steady employment of such a person is out of the question, a contract with a reputable engineer is satisfactory and economical. The practice of asking engineers for competitive bids for engineering services in connection with the design of sewers and disposal works has been mentioned in earlier chapters, and it cannot be too strongly denounced. Inexperienced engineers, expecting to be paid in experience, probably work for less than reputable firms will demand, but the taxpayers should not be required to stand the costs of such a system.[1]

The inspection of sewer construction, as well as of other public work, is quite as important as the engineering design. Inspection is an engineering function, and its purpose is to assure strict compliance with the plans and specifications of all materials and workmanship entering into the structure. In the average city, inspectorial positions are too often considered an adjunct to the political machinery and as legitimate spoils of victory at the polls, to the detriment of sound construction work. However, there is also a growing realization that faulty inspection permits faulty construction that may be ultimately a total loss.

It is the duty of the inspector to see that sewers are constructed to line and grade; to pass on the quality of sand, gravel, cement, brick, tile, and other materials used; to see that the mixtures of concrete and mortar are as specified, and that they are mixed sufficiently long and thoroughly; that the ratio of water to cement is proper; that the concrete is properly placed and rammed; and that when the specifications call for a three-ring sewer, three rings, and not two rings, are laid.

While the employment of engineers as inspectors by a city may be out of the question for financial reasons, it is a fact that on many jobs the use of such trained men would be real economy. In selecting inspectors, whether they are engineers or not, care should be taken that the applicant knows something about the work he is to inspect, that he will be on the job when work is under way, that he is honest, and that he has the courage and skill to get good work from the contractor, or failing that to report faulty work with the utmost fidelity.

The choice of materials for a sewerage system is a matter for economic consideration and will be determined largely by local conditions. For sewers of twenty-four inches or less in diameter,

[1] The design and construction of sewer systems is sometimes more economical when a number of neighboring cities can be treated as a unit. For a discussion of the subject of metropolitan districts, see Thomas H. Reed, *op. cit.*, Chap. XVIII.

vitrified clay pipe is almost universally used, though of late years concrete pipe of small diameter has been made and is giving satisfaction, unless the sewage is strongly acid. Vitrified clay pipe can be had in sizes up to forty-two inches in diameter, as can all the necessary pieces, such as crosses, tees, "Y's," slants, etc. As a result, the process of laying this pipe is simple and rapid. The larger sizes of vitrified pipe usually require concrete backing to give them sufficient strength to resist earth pressure. For sewers of larger size, hard burned brick has always been the most popular construction material, because of its cheapness and its resistance to scouring action and to acids. The size of the sewer and the character of the soil in which it is laid will determine the number of "rings," of courses of brick, required. Segmental blocks made of vitrified clay or of concrete are sometimes used in sewers of between thirty inches and nine feet in diameter, or even larger.

Concrete, however, is becoming a more popular and economical material for sewer construction, as more is learned concerning its properties and the technique of proportioning and placing it. Objections may be raised because of the action of acids. The probability of such action becoming so destructive on a large sewer that the structural integrity is threatened is small, though it may affect the friction in a sewer of any size. In the smaller sizes of concrete pipe the action of acid may affect the strength of the pipe, and for this reason great care must be taken that the concrete variety is not used where there is any likelihood of an acid sewage. The almost universal distribution of aggregates suitable for good concrete, and the standardization of portland cement, together with the development of mixing and conveying machinery and the standardization of steel, makes the use of concrete for sewers of the larger sizes a very attractive plan.[1]

For open trenches, the trenching machine is largely replacing the pick and shovel method of former days, although for unusual depths the older methods continue to be used.

When the size of the sewer requires a trench wider than about three feet, steam shovels, drag line buckets, and other digging equipment, together with industrial railways and trains, are used for moving the excavated spoil. In the case of trenches of exceptional width, say of twenty feet or more, care must be taken

---

[1] The Connors Creek sewer in Detroit, the largest in the world, is of three reinforced concrete barrels, each approximately seventeen feet by fifteen feet in cross section.

SEWERAGE

that the excavated earth is not piled so high as to cause caving of the sides. With large sewers in business or residenital streets, it is often advantageous to utilize tunnelling. This is done by sinking a shaft in the street to the proper grade, and in the line of the tunnel, and installing hoisting and conveying apparatus. From the bottom of the shaft, excavation is carried on in both directions, the excavated earth being conveyed up the shaft and dumped into waiting trucks for transportation to the dump. As excavation and construction progress, industrial track is laid in the tunnel for moving all waste earth and construction material. Tunnel work is generally arranged so that the brick or concrete work of one shift of workers will approximately equal the excavation done by the other shift. This reduces the necessity for the elaborate and permanent timbering which will be necessary if the tunnel is left open for any considerable time. In some soils, work must be done under air pressure to keep out water and sand. In rock, blasting is of course necessary.

The cross section of the sewer may be varied in many ways, the form being governed by local conditions. The circular sewer is most common, since it encloses a given area with a minimum perimeter, affording the highest velocities when flowing half full or more. The oval and the horseshoe section are much used whenever the dry weather flow is small as compared to the storm flow. Other sections, not so much used are the "U" shape, semi-circular, and rectangular. These sections are required on flat grades in which the bottom of the sewer must have a large cross section to secure sufficient rapidity of flow.

In laying out a sewerage system, the engineers determine as part of the design the lines and gradients at which the work is to be constructed. It is of great importance, therefore, that the field work of setting line and grade stakes be most carefully done, and that in the construction the work be brought accurately to the marks established. Irregularities in construction cause decreased capacity and add to the expense of maintenance. Uniformity of grade is desirable. If a city lies in hilly or broken districts, it may be advantageous to separate drainage districts by large intercepting sewers, thus making it possible to establish relatively uniform grades over each district. The velocity of sewage should be sufficient to keep a sewer flushed when flowing half full, or at a rate of about two feet per second, and the grade that will provide such velocity varies inversely with the diameter

Joints

Manholes

Catch basins

of the sewer. These grades are usually expressed in feet and decimals per 100 feet of sewer. If the velocity provided is insufficient, the sewer must be cleaned and flushed periodically.

When vitrified clay pipe is used, it is necessary, in addition to seeing that only sound pipe is laid, and accurately to line, to have a rigid inspection of the joints. The sewer must be tight to prevent the pollution of ground waters by leakage of sewage, to prevent ground waters from infiltrating into the sewer, and to prevent roots from entering the sewer and eventually blocking it. For this purpose cement joints are commonly used, and care must be taken to wipe the cement flush and smooth with the inside of the pipe. With a rigid point of this type the mortar may crack in case of settling, and for this reason more flexible packing is sometimes employed, particularly a mixture of sulphur and sand. Asphalt and tar joints are satisfactory, except in sewers carrying hot water; and there are a number of patented compositions having the general characteristics of asphalt without its low melting point.

A manhole is a vertical cylinder or conical shaped shaft of brick or concrete built from the sewer to the surface, and provided with a cast iron frame and cover. It is designed to admit a man into the sewer for the purpose of inspection or cleaning. Ordinarily there is no change in the grade of the sewer at the manhole. However, if the sewer has a steep gradient and it is desirable to reduce the velocity of the sewage a vertical offset will be installed, *i.e.*, the sewer outlet from the manhole will be lower than the inlet. This type is called a drop manhole. In small sewers, if the grade is changed, it should always break at the manhole. Manhole castings consist of a circular iron base and a cover. The base rests on the top of the masonry; the lid or cover, usually perforated for ventilation, fits inside a flange flush with the street surface.

A catch basin is a vertical shaft, placed in the gutter or just back of it, for the purpose of permitting surface water to get to the sewer through an inlet without carrying all of the street dirt into the sewer with it. This is accomplished by carrying the catch basin several feet below the inlet of the sewer. Water flowing in from the street falls to the bottom of the basin, loses its velocity, and drops the sand, mud, and other matter to the bottom. This gradually accumulates, necessitating the cleaning of the basin. The removal of this foreign matter reduces the likelihood of its

SEWERAGE

clogging the sewer and consequently removes a source of much expense. Since flushing is the most effective method of cleaning streets, and is becoming more popular, catch basins are to be regarded as essential accessories to sewerage systems. Care must be exercised, however, that the catch basin is not utilized by the street cleaning gangs as a receptacle for street sweepings and litter that do not belong there.

In a flat country where the question of grades is a vital one, it is often necessary to pump sewage to a higher level in order to get it to an outfall or treatment works or to get it over obstructions. Until the development of the centrifugal pump, the plunger pump was used extensively for this purpose. Centrifugal pumps for sewage should have sufficiently large clearances to give free passage to rags, paper, and other solid matter. The sewage ejector is much used when only a small lift is necessary. In this machine the sewage flows into the pot or shell through an inlet. When the pot is filled, a flat valve opens, admitting air under pressure, which drives the sewage out through the discharge pipes. Check valves prevent back flow from the discharge lines when the pot is being filled, and also prevent back flow into the inlet when it is discharging.

Explosions in sewers may be due to sewer gas, artificial or natural gas, inflammable waste, gasoline, and similar volatile materials. Leaky gas mains, from which gas filters through the ground and into the sewers, have been the source of many serious explosions. Sewer gas itself will ordinarily pass off, if the manholes are properly ventilated. Since the use of the automobile has reached its present proportions, the discharge of waste gasoline and oil from garages has become a real menace, and it is customary in all cities to have ordinances forbidding the discharge of such wastes into sewers. The gases explode when a flame is introduced, and lighted paper should be dropped into any sewer before investigation is attempted with an open lamp. Sparks from electric railway tracks and sparks from stray currents in the many underground conduits carrying electric cables are the direct cause of many explosions.

In order that sewers may be at all times in condition to maintain the flow for which they were designed, frequent inspections are necessary. Wherever any accumulation of gravel, sand, domestic sewage, or other wastes is found, it should be immediately removed and the cause of the accumulation corrected. Rough

476   PRACTICE OF MUNICIPAL ADMINISTRATION

CHAP. XXVII

cement at joints is a common source of trouble, although tree roots growing through minute crevices in joints are the most frequent causes of such stoppages. During the dry weather flow, inspection should be particularly thorough, since in such periods stoppage may occur most easily by a deposition of insoluble matter. When the heavy flow of the rainy period sets in such stoppages may result in incalculable damage to property. Repair gangs should be available at all times, in addition to the regular inspection and cleaning gangs. Catch basin cleaning may be a function of the sewer cleaning and repair division or of the street cleaning division. The latter seems most logical, for the reason that the removal of street dirt is a function of that division. This activity is most important, particularly before the seasons of heavy thunder storms in autumn and thaws in the late winter.

Sewage disposal

The natural and easiest way of getting rid of the wastes consigned to sewers is to conduct them to the nearest large body of water and discharge them into it. The danger to health that comes from the domestic use of water so contaminated with sewage has been mentioned. Untreated sewage contains unnumbered germs of many varieties. Some of these are entirely harmless, but others are pathogenic, *i.e.*, causing disease. Among these pathogenic germs is the typhoid bacillus, and a community that utilizes for domestic purposes a water supply contaminated by domestic sewage will be subject to typhoid fever in endemic form. A rough test for the purity of domestic water is the presence of colon bacilli, which are easily identified. These germs are not in themselves harmful, but they indicate the presence of other germs of human source that may be dangerous.

The relation of sewage disposal to water supply

The relationship between sewage disposal and water supply is evident. Frequently the water supply of a city is contaminated by sources beyond the immediate control of the local administrator. More often such contamination comes from local pollution. In such instances the administrator can solve the problem by either water or sewage purification, or both. It is scientifically possible to purify water of any degree of contamination, just as it is scientifically possible to do the same with sewage. It is economical and practical to do neither. Water polluted to a certain extent may be purified in large quantities at reasonable cost by processes that are now available. Similarly, the bacterial content of sewage may be materially reduced. So the administrator utilizing contaminated water for domestic purposes may at first remove such

SEWERAGE 477

contamination by a simple process. If the contamination increases, more complicated and expensive methods will have to be employed. Finally the limit of economic practicability is reached, and it becomes necessary to lessen to some degree the amount of pollution. This may be done at first by a simple treatment of the sewage, such as the removal of the coarser suspended and floating material, followed later by complicated and expensive methods. Or both processes may be undertaken at the same time.

CHAP. XXVII

No definite standards have been set up as to the maximum pollution of water that may be safely permitted before the source of pollution should be modified. The International Joint Commission, which investigated the boundary waters between the United States and Canada, reported that when water used for domestic purposes carried an average yearly count of more than 500 colon bacilli per 100 cubic centimeters, or was seriously contaminated to any extent for more than one-half of the time, it was dangerous as a source of supply even when filtered. However, this is no absolute standard. Cities along the Ohio river have been successfully purifying water containing as many as 16,000 colon bacilli per 100 cubic centimeters. One authority has stated recently that with coagulation, single stage sedimentation, filtration, and chlorination, raw water containing 8,000 B. coli per 100 cubic centimeters may be used. Where sedimentation in two separate stages is employed, the efficiency of purification is increased so that raw water with a B. coli index in excess of 10,000 for 100 cubic centimeters is not unsafe. If only chlorination is undertaken the permissible limit should be 1,000 to 1,200 B. coli per 100 cubic centimeters.[1] The entire problem is one of medicine, engineering, and finance, and each community should approach the question of a pure water supply advised by the most competent specialists that can be secured.

Standards of pollution

In the chapter dealing with water there is some consideration of practical methods of purification.[2] Therefore discussion here is restricted to the means available for purifying sewage. While a number of special processes are utilized for this purpose, many of them are based on the general principle of providing sufficient oxygen for the biological activities to proceed uninterruptedly. The bacteria of soil and water, if given plenty of oxygen, will

Principles of purification

---

[1] From J. K. Hoskins, "Relation between Stream Pollution and Extent of Sewage Treatment Required," *American City*, XXXIV, 254 (March, 1926).
[2] Chap. XXVIII.

478 PRACTICE OF MUNICIPAL ADMINISTRATION

CHAP. XXVII

completely oxidize putrescible organic matter into simple inorganic compounds that are not putrescible. Other systems reduce the amount of oxygen in order to facilitate anærobic action.

Determination of method

The determination of the proper treatment of sewage for any community is a problem by itself and one of great technical complexity. It is not a problem with which a layman can make much progress; none but experienced and competent sanitary engineers should be employed to handle problems of such vital importance to the health of the community.[1]

Dilution

Dilution is the natural, easy, and cheap method of sewage purification, provided the volume of water utilized is sufficient, although the existence of bathing beaches or oyster beds may make some treatment necessary despite practically unlimited dilution. In any event, before any sewers are laid, a thorough study of the locality should be made in order that a treatment plant can be easily installed if needed.

Land treatment

Since the earliest use of sewers, it has been a practice to conduct sewage to areas of land where purification resulted by filtration through loamy and sandy soil. This progress removes practically all suspended solids, but not those in solution. In other instances, the sewage has been conducted over agricultural areas for the purpose of enriching the soil. The success of each plan depends upon intermittent inundation and opportunity for air to get into the soil and aid in the processes of oxidation.[2]

Screens

The simplest method of removing the coarser solids in suspension is by screening. Screens are used to protect sewer machinery from injury, to remove unsightly matter from streams or from tanks in which sewage is treated, to reduce the amount of sludge settling to the bottom of sluggish streams, and to remove a part of the fine suspended matter in addition to coarser materials. This diversity of use has led to a multiplicity of types of screens that may be installed, grouped roughly as racks, grates, and screens, each with many variations. Such screens may be coarse or fine, though the distinction between coarse and fine screens is not clear. In general an opening in the screen of one-fourth inch seems to be the maximum for a fine screen.

Bar screens, set in the sewer channel, are usually interposed

---

[1] Those who are interested in the historical and technical development of sewage treatment works are referred to Metcalf and Eddy, *American Sewerage Practice*, III.

[2] This latter plan has been used successfully in Berlin, Germany, for nearly half a century.

ahead of pumps or treatment plants and remove only the coarser matter that may clog the channel or stop the pumps. These are most frequently made of inclined bars, with a spacing varying from one-half inch up to four inches or more. Such screens are cleaned by the simple process of raking occasionally by hand.

Other screens may be made of wire mesh or perforated plates and operated as belts, cylinders, or discs. Belt screens are used extensively in England, to a less extent in Germany, and very little in America. Of the cylindrical screens used in America, the Weand Segregator, the "Dorrco," and the Tark are the outstanding types. The Reinsch-Wurl disc screen is much used in Germany, and to a considerable extent in the United States. The disc may vary from eight to thirty feet in diameter; it is inclined about fifteen degrees from the horizontal, and on it is a truncated cone on whose axis the disc revolves. Both disc and cone are made up of perforated plates. The lowest point of the disc is set at the invert. *i.e.*, bottom of the sewer, and about one-third of the disc is above the sewage. The revolutions of the disc bring the screened matter above the water line where revolving brushes scrape the screenings into receptacles. It is essential that all fine screens be in duplicate at least, to allow for proper cleaning and maintenance without stopping the processes. Where sedimentation processes follow, engineers are not agreed on the necessity for fine screens of these latter types.

Grit chambers are essential when there is a considerable amount of inorganic matter in the sewage, usually sand and gravel. The presence of such matter retards the biological action; hence it is usual to enlarge the channel of the sewer where it enters the treatment works to reduce the velocity of the sewage, and to depress the bottom of such enlargement to provide a receptable for the settled detritus. There should be at least two such chambers at every treatment works, to provide uninterrupted service and to give opportunity for cleaning. Being almost entirely inorganic, the material removed from the grit chamber may be placed on any spoil bank. Occasionally skimmers are provided for the removal of oil and grease.

For the more complete removal of the suspended solids in sewage, sedimentation tanks have been used for many years, and in a number of types. For the protection of bathing beaches and shellfish beds from bacterial contamination, and for an easier and cheaper disinfection, a purer effluent than is possible by screening

480 PRACTICE OF MUNICIPAL ADMINISTRATION

<small>CHAP. XXVII</small>

may be obtained by sedimentation. The efficacy of any type of tank will vary with the character of the sewage, as determined by the industrial waste and the storm water in it. Tanks may be designed for intermittent action, termed "fill and drain" operation, and also for continuous operation. The size and shape of tanks varies, and they are built both circular and rectangular, and for both vertical and horizontal flow.

<small>Plain sedimentation</small>

Vertical sedimentation tanks were first used in Germany, and those introduced into America at the Columbian Exposition of 1893 were modelled after the tanks at Dortmund. The operation of plain sedimentation rests upon a sufficient checking of the rate of flow of sewage, so that suspended solid matter will settle quickly, and wherever such tanks are operated provision must be made for uninterrupted operation and for the prompt removal of the residue called sludge.

<small>Sedimentation and digestion</small>

Where further and more complete action than the mere removal of the larger part of the suspended solids is necessary, tanks for the decomposition or digestion of the organic matter are constructed. The general plan is the same as that of the plain sedimentation tank, but provision is made to hold the sludge until biological action has completely changed its character. The first of these processes utilizes the septic tank. In this tank, which is covered and has traps at the inlet and outlet, the work is performed by anærobic action, micro-organisms working in the dark without air, the solids being precipitated and many of them liquefied. Gases of decomposition lift the sludge, sometimes to such an extent that it forms a scum. The patents on this process were vigorously defended and few installations of magnitude have been made in this country. Septic tanks produce offensive odors and the effluent is subject to undesirable changes often requiring additional treatment before it is safe to discharge it into waterways, conditions also furnishing grounds for dislike.

<small>Septic tanks</small>

<small>Travis tank</small>

The Travis tank was developed in England and consists of a horizontal tank divided into three longitudinal chambers by partitions extending inward from near the sides at the bottom, and almost meeting at the top. Narrow openings at the bottom allow the passage of sludge from the outside compartments to the inner one along the floor, which slopes toward the center of the tank. It is the theory of the Travis tank that sedimentation will take place in the outer chambers, the sludge flowing into the center and there decomposing. The sewage in general is therefore

SEWERAGE 481

kept away from the decomposition and flows off without those ingredients that make it offensive. Sewage requires about three hours detention in these tanks and is given a secondary treatment in contact beds.

CHAP. XXVII

In 1905 a Travis tank was begun by the Emscher Drainage Board of Germany, but completion was prevented by the death of the engineer in charge. His successor, Imhoff, realized that the sewage should be got to the tank much fresher than was possible with the Travis system, and hence he designed a tank that bears his name and is known also as the Emscher tank. The Imhoff tank is designed so that the gases and scum generated in digestion do not come in contact with the sewage passing through. This tank consists essentially of two V-shaped tanks, one above the other. The bottom of the top tank, which is the sedimentation tank, is provided with slots through which the settling may slide to the lower or digestion chamber, but through which no gas may rise. Sludge remains in the digestion chamber for periods varying from a few weeks to several months, depending on local conditions. When removed, the sludge is innocuous and the cost of its removal is very much less than in other tanks. This tank was the first two-story tank of note and gained immediate popularity in America.

Imhoff tank

The aëration of sewage to promote the oxidation of organic matter has been made the subject of experimentation since 1882, but not until 1910 did the aëration of sewage in tanks receive any attention in this country. Previously, the aëration had been done in filters. Since 1910 experimentation along this line has developed a new process of treatment called the activated sludge method. The objects of aëration are to supply to the sewage an ample amount of oxygen for the aërobic action of bacteria, and to agitate the contents of the tank sufficiently to insure continuous and intimate contact of the activated sludge particles with all the sewage. For these purposes air is pumped into the tanks, varying from one-half a cubic foot to one and three-quarters cubic feet per gallon of sewage. Sometimes the introduction of the air produces sufficient agitation; sometimes mechanical agitators are used. Aëration is necessary only until the sludge is "ripened." The suspended and colloidal matter collects in small masses and comes in contact with all parts of the liquid. These little masses, or "flocculi," contain great numbers of bacteria which live on the matter absorbed by and attracted to the sludge particles. By

Activated sludge

the bacterial action the organic matter is oxidized and the nitrogen converted into nitrates—which results in "activated" sludge. This thoroughly ripened sludge is used in part to inoculate fresh sewage coming in; and after more sludge than is needed for such purposes is produced it is removed, dewatered, and disposed of.

Contact beds

The fact that the tank treatments leave some finely suspended and colloidal matter in the effluent has led to the development of further methods of treatment. The most logical of these is the use of contact or bacteria beds. These beds are water-tight open tanks, filled with broken stone, cinders, coke, or other inert matter from one-half inch to one and one-half inches in diameter. The sewage is allowed to flow into the contact beds until they are full, and remains there from one-fourth of a day to one day, the rate of operation depending on the strength of the sewage and the condition of the beds. At the end of the period the effluent is run off and the bed is allowed to remain unused for a time. The sewage bacteria located in the organic matter in the stones or other material increase rapidly and convert the organic matter in the sewage into more stable organic matter. The settling solids and colloids are deposited in the contact bed material and retained there. This material has to be removed, cleaned, and replaced at intervals of about five years. The oxidizing power of the contact bed is based on ample quantities of oxygen, absorbed for the most part during the rest periods. About one-half the cubic content of the tank is available for storing sewage, and this space is gradually reduced by accumulations.

Trickling filters

Efforts to improve this process resulted in the "trickling filter," which is similar to the contact bed. This filter is from five to ten feet deep, using one and one-half inch stone. The sewage is applied as uniformly as possible to the surface of the rock through sprinklers or other means, but instead of standing quietly in the bed, the sewage trickles through the filter. The sprinkler is allowed to operate for about five-minute periods, with ten-minute rest periods intervening. The bed absorbs oxygen continuously by this method of application. The effluent passes through drains at the bottom and may be given a secondary sedimentation before its final discharge. These filters are generally self-cleansing, which is an added advantage. The action during oxidation is essentially the same as in the contact beds. A phenomenon of this type of treatment is the periodic storage and discharge of the solids created

SEWERAGE 483

by the process. This discharge generally takes place during the first warm days of spring. CHAP. XXVII

Plain sedimentation for from six to twelve hours will usually remove from one-third to one-half of the suspended solids in sewage. By adding chemical precipitants a great deal of the finer suspended matter and the colloids may be removed. This treatment will produce a clear, colorless effluent containing but little suspended matter but much putrescible material. The results of sedimentation with chemical treatment are, therefore, not comparable to those of good filtration methods. The cost of the treatment is high, and the tendency is always to use less chemical than is necessary. This method does seem to have a real place in the treatment of industrial wastes. The chemicals most frequently used are lime, alum, copperas, ferric sulphate, and aluminoferric. Chemical precipitation

Sometimes when it is necessary to secure deodorization or a high degree of purification of sewage, the effluent is treated electrolytically, or more often chemically, after the solids have been removed by one of the previously mentioned processes. Or, if absolute freedom from bacteria is not necessary, chemical methods are effective and relatively inexpensive as a means of securing a reasonable degree of purification. Sulphuric acid is extremely effective as a germicidal agent, but its use except in emergencies is prohibited by its cost. Copper sulphate has also been tried for this purpose but found less efficient and more expensive than chloride of lime. The various combinations of chlorine, *i.e.*, chlorine gas, liquid chlorine, calcium hypochlorite, and sodium hypochlorite, have found very satisfactory application. Calcium hypochlorite, or "bleach," or chloride of lime, was first on the market and has been widely used. Liquid chlorine is very much more convenient to use and on that account is finding favor generally.[1] In cities in which considerable quantities of spent acids are discharged in connection with industrial wastes, the bacteria count of sewage is relatively small, and when streams into which sewage is received drain over areas having limestone and iron deposits the bacterial content may be affected. Sterilization

A serious problem following all of the sedimentation processes of sewage purification is the disposal of sludge. The sludge produced by an Imhoff tank will be from 300 to 750 gallons per Sludge

[1] See p. 495.

CHAP. XXVII

Sludge disposal

million gallons of sewage treated; by chemical precipitation, about 5,000 gallons; and from the activated sludge treatment from 3,000 to 6,000 gallons. Under all conditions there is some putrescible matter in sludge, and the water content ranges from seventy to ninety-nine percent. The common method of drying sludge is to run it on sand beds and allow the moisture to seep away and evaporate. From these beds the sludge may be removed by hand or by excavating equipment and destroyed or used as a low-grade fertilizer. Dewatering by pressing requires extensive equipment and is an expensive operation. Activated sludge contains more water than ordinary sludge, and this water is held tenaciously. Various types of machinery have been developed for dewatering sludge of this type, and sometimes sulphuric acid or alum is added to aid in the process. While the activated sludge has higher fertilizer value than the sludge of other settling tanks, the problem of marketing has not be solved. However, it is not fair to make the marketability of sludge the criterion by which the success or failure of the activated sludge method is determined. The test of any method is its efficiency in purifying sewage to a predetermined standard.

CHAPTER XXVIII

WATER [1]

Water is a first essential to the maintenance of all life, and the conduct of human affairs has been largely influenced by its presence or absence. The existence of springs, lakes, and streams has determined trade routes, the location of communities, and the prosperity of nations. The earliest congregations of peoples were doubtless in the vicinity of water supplies adequate to their needs, and so situated as to be easily protected from foes. As communities increased in size, they sometimes outgrew their water supplies, and natural sources were supplemented by artificial means—by the digging of wells and the building of aqueducts and storage basins. The ruined aqueducts of Athens and Rome testify to the early importance of water to civilized communities, and to the well-being of these ancient nations. The Arabian civilization of Spain also had well engineered aqueducts built during the seventh, eighth, and ninth centuries. Medieval cities in Europe, however, were content to utilize the polluted streams along which they were built. In those cradle ages of the northern races, however, nearly every art of community living retrograded rather than progressed.

The early importance of water

The scientific progress of the nineteenth century that so vitally modified industrial processes, making great cities necessary and possible, also facilitated the securing and distributing of water as a necessity of urban growth.[2] Inventions made it possible to secure

Modern development

---

[1] American Water Works Association, *Water Works Practice* (Williams and Wilkins, 1925), and F. E. Turneaure and H. L. Russell, *Public Water Supplies* (3d. ed., Wiley, 1924), treat in detail the subjects covered in this chapter. See also Edward Wegmann, *Conveyance and Distribution of Water* (Van Nostrand, 1918). Data as to water works practice in American cities will be found in the *1925 Municipal Index*, 378-409. For current reference, consult the *Journal of the American Water Works Association* (monthly); *Journal of the New England Water Works Association* (annual); *Public Works* (monthly); *Engineering News-Record* (weekly); the monthly water works and hydraulic issues of *Engineering and Contracting; Water Works Engineering* (semi-monthly); and *The American City* (monthly).

[2] Professor William C. Hoad, of the University of Michigan, makes the point that many cities, particularly those in the arid Western portions of the United States, are limited in growth because of an absence of adequate water supply.

486 PRACTICE OF MUNICIPAL ADMINISTRATION

CHAP. XXVIII

water cheaply and in abundance: the steam engine provided means for pumping; various mechanical devices and chemical agents aided in purification; and iron pipe provided an economical means of distribution.

The uses of public water

The water requirements of a modern city are determined on the basis of the average amount consumed daily by each inhabitant, taking the term "consumed" to mean water delivered to the distributing system. This amount will ordinarily be between 100 and 200 gallons per person, the size and character of the city being factors of importance in determining it, for the reason that in larger municipalities the number of users corresponds closely to the population, while in small communities some of the population will depend upon private supplies. Of even greater importance is the industrial and commercial use of water in large cities. The estimates of consumption include the entire amount delivered to the mains, not taking wastage or leakage into consideration, and is determined in several ways. The water supplied by pumps may be calculated by multiplying the number of strokes in a given time by the displacement of the plungers, with allowance for pump slippage.[1] Pump slippage will seldom amount to less than two or three percent, and in pumps in bad repair, may amount to as much as forty percent. Lately there has been a rapid increase in the use of venturi meters and pitometers for measuring the discharge from pumping stations and in gravity supply lines.

The consumption of public water may be divided into four general classes—domestic, commercial-industrial, and public—and loss and waste, this last being usually referred to as "unaccounted water."

Domestic use

The amount of water used for domestic purposes can be determined only when all services are metered. Highest class residences will use sixty gallons of water, or much more, per person per day; in the poorest dwellings the amount used may fall as low as ten gallons per person.[2] If the supply is unmetered, the consumption will average more, due to gross wastage by a few persons.

Industrial and commercial use

Industrial and commercial concerns, including office buildings, hotels, and railroads, are the largest actual consumers of water.

---

[1] Water not being forced into the mains because of wear on the plungers or failure of the supply to fill the cylinder.

[2] Turneaure and Russell, *op. cit.*, 17. For per capita consumption of water in cities of the United States, as well as other water works data, see *1925 Municipal Index*.

This industrial and commercial use varies widely in different cities, depending on the number of industries, the nature of their processes, and the availability of private water supplies.

Public use

The city government itself uses water primarily for fire protection, for street and sewer flushing, for parks, schools, and public buildings, and for incidental needs, as well as for semi-public purposes, such as churches and charities. Little water is used for ornamental purposes. It is not easy to estimate the quantities supplied to meet public and semi-public requirements as such water is seldom measured, and is ordinarily furnished free of charge. Fire departments do not use large amounts of water. Some estimates place their consumption as high as two percent, but probably the actual use is only a small fraction of this figure.

Loss and waste

It has been estimated that in some instances one-half of the water pumped in cities is wasted, due to bad plumbing, flow to prevent freezing, leaky mains, and carelessness on the part of users, although some authorities believe that excessive estimates of waste are often due to miscalculations of pumpage. Leaks in mains which are not easily detected make some of this loss unavoidable, but the great bulk of it results from mains being in poor repair or through wilful carelessness on the part of consumers. Some citizens have the idea that water is plentiful and cheap, and that therefore no bounds need be placed on its use. Water may be relatively plentiful and cheap, but the conclusion as to use does not necessarily follow. Many large cities find it increasingly necessary to go long distances to secure an adequate supply, and spend large sums in purifying the water obtained. This expense of purification must be undertaken although only a small proportion of the amount pumped is used for domestic consumption, because a duplication of supply is impractical. As a result, the waste of water means increased pumping costs, and also increased investment in equipment for supply, pumping, and distribution.

What is water?

To the average person, particularly the city dweller, water is a pure sparkling substance, agreeable in taste and adaptable in temperature, to be had by turning a tap in the kitchen or bathroom. If one is scientifically minded he further recalls that its principal components are hydrogen and oxygen. One is not so apt to remember that the sparkling product of the tap was not many days before the rain flowing down the street gutter, or a part of some neighboring lake or river—the habitat of fish and of animal and vegetable life and the depository of sewage and refuse. For all

488 PRACTICE OF MUNICIPAL ADMINISTRATION

CHAP. XXVIII

practical purposes water is something more than oxygen and hydrogen. Running over wooded slopes to the river it may have absorbed the color and taste of dead leaves and other vegetation; from the gravel and soil through which it percolated it may have taken up the color and taste of iron and manganese; and it will usually absorb calcium and magnesium, in the form of bicarbonates and sulphates, thus acquiring characteristics called "hardness." Also, it will pick up small particles of clay and sand, thus becoming turbid. But, what is of far greater importance, it may carry uncounted bacteria, some of them harmless, others pathogenic, *i.e.*, capable of producing disease when taken into the human system. To many public administrators water is not the pure sparkling gift of nature to man; it is a muddy, bacteria-laden liquid, tasting of mineral and vegetable matter, and containing substances that render it unsuitable for many purposes.

The sources of supply

The water supply of cities is from either surface or ground sources, in the latter case being surface water that has percolated through soil and rock strata to an underground stream. This water is frequently purified of bacteria by this process, but usually acquires considerable mineral matter held in solution. Such mineral content does not make the water unfit for drinking purposes unless present in excessive quantities, or of repulsive taste, as for example iron and sulphur, but may render it undesirable for cooking, laundry, and certain industrial uses. Ground water is obtained from wells, some of them of great depth and of an artesian nature; others, shallow in character, and often sunk in the dry beds of streams. Ground water sources are only occasionally sufficient to meet the needs of large communities.

Ground water

Surface water

Surface water is usually derived from lakes and rivers, and occasionally from the impounded flow of watersheds. Such water contains less mineral matter in solution than ground water, but is far more turbid, and usually more contaminated, due to human habitations upon the watersheds from which the supply is drawn and to the disposal of sewage by dilution. This pollution makes it necessary to utilize elaborate and expensive methods of treatment before such water can be used with safety for domestic purposes.

Lakes

Some communities find an abundant water supply near at home, while others are compelled to transport it from a distance. Cities bordering upon the Great Lakes, as for example Milwaukee, Chicago, Detroit, Cleveland, and Buffalo, secure an abundant water

WATER 489

supply from that source even though these lakes also receive the sewage of the same cities, so that in spite of immense dilution, extensive use of purification plants, both for sewage and water, is made highly desirable. Cities located on large rivers, such as New Orleans, St. Louis, Cincinnati, and Washington, take their supply from these streams, using elaborate purification plants. Many cities draw from small lakes and streams that are relatively uncontaminated. Others situated at a distance from sources of supply collect and store the water from small watersheds during the seasons of heavy rainfall. New York City has probably the largest works of this kind in America in the well known Groton and Catskill systems,[1] and Baltimore, Boston, Los Angeles, Portland (Ore.), and Seattle are among the cities that obtain their supply in this manner.

Cities are required to give considerable care to such catchment districts, which must be small enough to permit of sanitary control. Some cities acquire ownership of such properties, removing the inhabitants and reforesting the area, but this plan is not always practicable, nor is it necessary. In fact, a principal objection to the use of lakes as a source of supply is that it often precludes the use of the shores for residential and outing purposes. As a result, some of the catchment areas are rather heavily inhabited, and good water can be secured if a city will enact rigid sanitary regulations for such inhabitants and assume the expense of seeing that such regulations are enforced. For example, Portland, Ore., permits the use of its reservoirs for recreation purposes. The impounding of water in itself provides a means of purification, since disease germs will die from natural processes in water after a varying period of time. However, there is danger that polluted water will be drawn from such reservoirs before such processes can operate, and it is customary to make use of some additional purification process to supplement that of nature.

An impounding reservoir is constructed by damming the outlet of the catchment area, or a system of reservoirs may be formed on one or more watersheds. The location, construction, and determination of capacity, of catchment areas, reservoirs, and aqueducts are highly technical features, and should be handled by sanitary engineers who have made a particular study of the subject.

[1] Sydney, Australia, is said to have the largest impounding reservoirs in the world.

490   PRACTICE OF MUNICIPAL ADMINISTRATION

CHAP. XXVIII

Continuous attention must be given reservoirs, the accumulated muck removed, and algæ and other vegetable growths controlled. Otherwise, the physical characteristics of the water will be affected.

Desirable qualities of water

To be entirely satisfactory for domestic purposes, water should be colorless; free from turbidity and undesirable odor and taste; of a refreshing temperature; not excessively hard; and, most important of all, pure.

Color

Ground waters are usually free from color when drawn from the earth, but may change color when exposed to light. When surface waters originate on watersheds covered with dense vegetation, they often carry dissolved organic matter in solution resulting in discoloration. Ordinarily, this characteristic is offensive, but does not affect the health of consumers.

Turbidity

Surface waters are also likely to be somewhat turbid, *i.e.*, cloudy or muddy, owing to the presence of suspended clay or sand, a factor influenced by the geological nature of the watershed and the rapidity of flow. During warm seasons of the year this suspended inorganic material will be supplemented by the presence of microscopic vegetable growths, especially algæ. These are a cause of both odor and taste.[1]

Odor and taste

Unpleasant odors and tastes may result when water is impregnated with minerals such as salts of sodium, magnesium, iron, sulphur, etc., or because of the growth of certain algæ. Water designed for domestic use should be relatively free from these characteristics and owe its palatableness primarily to the presence of carbon dioxide and oxygen.

Temperature

The temperature of the water is of some importance, but is more frequently dependent on the temperature of the ground through which the pipes pass than the temperature of the water at the point of supply.

Requirements of water purification

In general, there are four elements of impurity which it may be desirable or necessary to remove from a domestic water supply [2] —turbidity, color, mineral salts (causing "hardness") and bacteria.[3] The suspended matter in surface waters may not be detrimental to health, but it is desirable to remove it, since a turbid or colored water does not comport with modern standards of cleanliness. In particular, it is desirable to eliminate any large amount of dissolved inorganic material which may be troublesome. Ordi-

---

[1] See *Water Works Practice*, 168–169.

[2] Some impurity is desirable, as chemically pure water is unpalatable.

[3] See previous citations, and Milton Stein, *Water Purification Plants and Their Operation* (3d ed., Wiley, 1926).

WATER

CHAP. XXVIII

narily there are dissolved mineral salts in all water, which may or may not make it unpalatable for drinking purposes, but if present in large quantities will be objectionable to industrial users. For these reasons the public water supply should be free, or nearly so, of inorganic salts which give it objectionable taste or the quality of hardness. Finally, water often contains bacteria, or organic pollution, which must be removed to protect the health of the community. This relation of pure water to public health has only recently been fully recognized. When water is contaminated by domestic sewage, there is continual danger of typhoid fever. The presence of such contamination, however, is not ordinarily determined by the presence of typhoid bacilli, but by colon bacilli, which are much easier to identify. These latter are not pathogenic, but indicate human pollution and hence the possible presence of bacilli of a virulent type.[1]

Plain sedimentation

The particles of clay and sand that are a principal cause of turbidity have a specific gravity of approximately 2.65 and are largely held in solution by the force of the water current. Plain sedimentation involves the stoppage or reduction of this current,

[1] The effect of water purification upon the typhoid morbidity and mortality rate in a city obtaining its supply from a polluted source is well evidenced by these data from Cincinnati:

Year	Number of Cases	Number of Deaths	Death rate per 100,000
1902	1,038	206	61.9
1903	710	144	42.7
1904	1,646	270	80.2
1905	746	155	41.1
1906	1,922	239	71.5
1907	1,252	157	45.4*
1908	235	64	18.2
1909	218	46	13.3
1910	202	21	8.8†
1911	238	43	11.4
1912	187	28	7.3
1913	266	24	6.1
1914	148	23	5.9
1915	141	29	7.3‡
1916	98	12	3.0
1917	89	16	4.0
1918	184	19	4.8
1919	56	11	2.8
1920	56	12	2.9
1921	67	14	3.4
1922	58	13	3.2
1923	62	12	3.0

* Completion of filtration plant.
† Vault elimination begins.
‡ Universal pasteurization of milk.

thus allowing clay, sand, and inorganic matter held in suspension to settle. Under such circumstances, particles as small as silt will settle out in approximately half an hour. Particles finer than silt cannot be removed in this manner because of the excessive length of time required. In practical operation, the amount of time that water should be held in storage for settling purposes must be determined by actual tests, the period ranging anywhere from twenty-four hours to three days, during which seventy-five to eighty-five percent of the suspended matter will be removed. This process of storage also eliminates bacteria to some extent and may modify color.

<small>Sedimentation with coagulation</small>

For water containing clay in a colloidal condition which approximates solution, it is necessary to resort to some method of agglomeration or coagulation by which the collected particles, owing to their size, will settle more rapidly. This process involves the use of chemicals which will form a precipitate of a gelatinous character when placed in water, and about which the particles of clay and silt settle. Because of the effect of colloidal particles upon color, any process of coagulation modifies this characteristic. For reasons of economy, coagulants are not used until the coarser materials in solution have been precipitated.

<small>Kinds of coagulants</small>

The most common coagulant is sulphate of alumina, *i.e.*, alum, added to water in minute quantities. Alum consists of alumin, sulphur, oxygen, and water of crystallization. When it is introduced into a water containing carbonates or bicarbonates of calcium and magnesium, a chemical reaction results which decomposes the bicarbonates and forms sulphates of calcium or magnesium, aluminum hydroxide, and carbon dioxide. All of these elements are tasteless and harmless. The aluminum hydroxide is gelatinous and constitutes the coagulant. These gelatinous flocculi sink, taking with them the finely suspended matter and bacteria.

Sulphate of iron has recently come into favor as a coagulant, the process being not dissimilar from that followed in the use of alum. Lime, in the form of milk of lime, is used for softening water, and to some extent it acts as a germicide and a coagulant.

By the use of coagulants it is possible to remove a high percentage of suspended matter from water in a few hours, the exact time of the process depending upon the nature of the sediment and the amount of coagulant used. No matter how long the sedimentation process may be continued, there is usually danger of some con-

WATER

tamination remaining, and water polluted with sewage is seldom used without additional means of purification.

Settling basins

Basins in which the sedimentation processes are conducted are operated by either the continuous flow or the intermittent method. Basins of the continuous flow type, in which the water is continuously entering and leaving the reservoir at a slow rate of speed, are generally conceded to be advantageous and are almost universally used. Economy in construction costs results, because one basin may be used in place of the several necessary under the intermittent, or fill and flow, system.

Softening water

Hardness of water is caused by the solution of various salts, particularly bicarbonates and sulphates of magnesium and calcium. The presence of the bicarbonates results in temporary hardness, which can be removed by boiling. Sulphates cause a type of hardness that must be modified by chemical processes which are relatively expensive. Various chemicals are used for this purpose, but principally lime and sodium carbonate, the chemical compound in solution decomposing, and its elements uniting with those of an added compound to form insoluble salts that precipitate. The process uses lime applied in the form of lime water or milk of lime. Carbonates are held in solution largely because of carbon dioxide dissolved in the water. When lime is added, carbonates of calcium and magnesium are formed, which are precipitated. This precipitation is accomplished by passing the water into settling basins, and in some instances the water is further clarified by rapid filtration. Some bacterial purification results from the softening processes, due to the action of the lime.

By use of lime

Many small private water plants, including those of industrial firms, use zeolite, both natural and synthetic, under various trade names as a softening process. Zeolite is a mineral compound of alumina, silica, and sodium. Water is passed through a granular filter of this material, the calcium and magnesium being extracted, and replaced with sodium. The filter can be regenerated by reversing the process, using a solution of common salt.[1]

Zeolite

Iron salts will be found in water which has come in contact with iron compounds, affecting both color and taste, causing a discoloring of laundry, and make it unsuitable for industrial purposes. An iron content of one-half part per million will be found

Removal of iron

---

[1] See "Water Softening by Lime and Soda," *Water Works Practice*, Chap. X.

objectionable, and some authorities place the maximum content as three-tenths of a part per million. Manganese is usually found with iron and has substantially the same result on the utility of water. Incident to the presence of iron compounds are the so-called "iron bacteria" crenothrix, which thrive in the darkness of water pipes. These bacteria aggravate the difficulties found with water containing iron, cause deposits in the water pipes which may seriously disturb the distribution system, and create bad odors and unpleasant tastes.

A number of processes are used for the removal of iron and manganese, the most common being aëration.[1] The presence of oxygen causes an oxidization of the ferrous carbonate forming an insoluble precipitate which may be removed if necessary by filtration. The amount of oxidization required varies considerably. The raising of water by air-lift pumps may be sufficient, or it may be necessary to construct elaborate aëration works.

Salt

Common salt, which occasionally finds its way into water supplies from brine wells, cannot be removed by any practical method.

Treatment for bacteria and organic pollution

In addition to the effect of plain sedimentation and of sedimentation with coagulants on water, aëration, disinfection, and filtration are the ordinary means employed for the removal of bacteria and organic pollution.[2]

Aëration

Aëration implies the introduction of oxygen into water already deficient in that element and is particularly applicable to ground waters and waters drawn from stagnant surface supplies.[3] The process is not employed as a primary means of reducing bacterial content (although it may have some effect upon this pollution), but is used principally as a means of removing unpleasant tastes and odors. The gases which give the waters these characteristics are removed and oxygen is substituted in their place. The process is not effective on all causes of disagreeable odors and tastes and is said to be entirely ineffective as a means of removing the pollution caused by coal or wood distillates.

The methods employed for aëration naturally depend upon the amount of oxygen that must be introduced in the water. Exposure in a settling basin or passage over weirs may be sufficient. The most common practices, however, are the introduction of oxygen under pressure into the water or by its passage through

---

[1] See "Removal of Iron and Manganese," *Water Works Practice*, Chap. IX.
[2] For a discussion of the limits of water pollution and the resulting burden on purification methods, see p. 477.
[3] See "Aëration," *Water Works Practice*, 189–194.

WATER 495

spraying devices. This latter is in most common use, although it is expensive because of the resulting loss of pressure when water must be pumped. In northern climates the use of sprays is impractical on account of freezing.

Disinfection

Early in the present century it was discovered that the dosing of water with chlorinated lime, known as bleaching powder or chloride of lime, resulted in a high bacterial removal when used in water reasonably free from turbidity. Recently, liquid chlorine has been substituted as being less expensive, more effective in results, and more easily handled. The chlorination process is relatively inexpensive, and easy of application, but is used principally in connection with other means of purification because its effects are not sufficiently thorough on water of a high bacterial count. The exact sterilization process of chlorine is not known, but either it is the result of chemical processes freeing oxygen or the chlorine has a toxic effect on itself. Probably the latter theory is the correct one. Chlorine can be used most effectively as a purification agent in relatively quiet water, but has been used with some success on bathing beaches.[1]

Ozone

Ozone, *i.e.*, atmosphere that has been subject to high voltage electric discharges, is used in a small way as a water disinfectant. The process is much more expensive than chlorination and is not employed in the United States, although it has been adopted in a few European plants. Ozone is an efficient disinfectant, killing pathogenic germs with certainty, where the gas comes into direct contact with the bacteria. However, difficulty has been experienced in developing satisfactory mixing devices.[2]

Other methods of sterilization

Ultra-violet rays, produced by the so-called quartz lamp, are an efficient means of sterilization, but are little used on a commercial scale because of the cost and the attention required. The water should be free from turbidity and color and must be passed in proximity to the lamps, usually arranged in batteries. This equipment is quite effective, particularly with small amounts of

---

[1] In July, 1925, the Belle Isle bathing beach at Detroit was found to be grossly polluted and due to the swiftness of the current—the water passing by the portion of the beach used by the bathers in less than two minutes—ordinary means of sterilization were found inadequate. Chlorination was accomplished by placing four liquid chlorine tanks up stream about fifty yards from the bathers and connecting them in series with common three-quarter inch garden hose of a total length of 300 feet. The hose was fitted with four millimeter glass pet cocks placed at three-foot intervals and anchored at the bottom of the river. A day's operation of this outfit costs approximately $8.00 and insures safety from typhoid fever.

[2] See *Water Works Practice*, 265-267.

496   PRACTICE OF MUNICIPAL ADMINISTRATION

CHAP. XXVIII

water, such as supplies for swimming tanks, hotels, boats, and the like.

Copper sulphate is used in minute quantities to destroy objectionable growths of algæ in reservoirs. Sufficient amounts to serve as a general germicide cannot be applied because of its deleterious effects on the human system.

Filtration

Filtration was first undertaken, not as a means of removing bacteria, but for the elimination of turbidity. In 1829 a plant was constructed in London, and the idea spread rapidly in Europe. Filtration as a means of substantially complete purification was not understood until much later, and only in the last fifty years has its value for removing bacteria been recognized in America. Both the slow and rapid type of filters are used as circumstances dictate. The latter operates at a rate of from 2,000,000 to 6,000,000 gallons per acre of filter per day, or from twenty to sixty times as fast as the former when used in conjunction with coagulation.[1]

Slow sand filters are efficient and economical as a means of purifying water of low turbidity and reasonable bacterial content. Filters of this type are much used abroad and have a place in the treatment of certain types of water under certain circumstances, particularly when purification can be effected in a single process. Slow sand filtration does not always eliminate unpleasant tastes, odors or discoloration, and cannot be used when the pollution is such as to clog the filter rapidly. The exact process by which the purification takes place is not thoroughly understood. The efficiency of the filter gradually improves with age, and a filter that has been cleaned is more effective than a new one. This is probably due to the coating of a gelatinous nature which forms over the surface of the sand, which acts to some extent as a strainer, and also destroys bacteria by chemical or electrical action.[2]

Slow sand filters usually have an area of from one-half acre to one and one-half acres. They consist of concrete reservoirs partially filled with filtering material and underlaid by drains leading to a collecting well. The water is filtered through broken stones, gravel, and sand laid in successive layers, each decreasing in size until the final top layer of several feet of sand is reached. This layer of sand is the most important part of the filter and

[1] *Water Works Practice*, 208.
[2] For the details of slow and rapid sand filtration, see Turneaure and Russell, *Public Water Supplies*, Chaps. XXI and XXII, and *Water Works Practice* Chap. VIII.

WATER

must not be allowed to become too thin. Periodic cleaning to prevent a reduction of the capacity of the filter is usually accomplished by the removal of a thin layer of sand.

The rapid or mechanical filter, much used in the United States when water purification cannot be secured by less expensive methods, is designed to accomplish rapidly the same results as can be secured through slow sand filtration. The operation of a rapid filtration system is similar to the slow sand filter in that the filtration process is accomplished by passing the water through a bed of sand overlying coarser material. However, in rapid filtration the filtration areas are smaller, some form of coagulation must be used in conjunction with filtration in order to remove the coarser suspended matter, the water is under pressure, and provision must be made for washing the filter beds. This cleaning is accomplished by reversing the flow of water, usually for a few minutes every twenty-four hours, occasionally oftener depending upon the amount of suspended matter in the water filtered. Rapid filtration is sometimes used in conjunction with slow filtration when a double treatment appears desirable.

Somewhat akin to the removal of bacteria from water for the purpose of preserving health is the addition of iodine as a means of preventing goitre. It has been known for many centuries that there was a curative, or at least a preventative, relationship between iodine and goitre, and recently it has been reasonably well demonstrated that simple goitre is caused by an absence of iodine in the thyroid gland, due principally to the absence of this chemical in food and drink. As a result, goitre is comparatively common in certain sections of the United States, particularly in states bordering on the Great Lakes and in certain mountain regions. Apparently the situation can be corrected by adding minute quantities of iodine to food such as table salt, or to water consumed for drinking purposes. As a result, a number of cities [1] have experimented with dosing their water supply for a few weeks each year. The experimentation has not continued sufficiently long to demonstrate results, but is looked upon with considerable favor by water works authorities.[2]

Whatever the source of water supply, it is essential that reservoirs provide for the storage of water to meet such emergencies

---

[1] Among them are Rochester, Sault Ste. Marie, Cleveland, and Cincinnati.
[2] See "Treatment of Water with Iodide for the Prevention of Simple Goitre," *Water Works Practice*, Chap. XII.

498   PRACTICE OF MUNICIPAL ADMINISTRATION

CHAP. XXVIII

as conflagrations and breaks in equipment, and to balance the load on filters during hours of high consumption.[1] The construction of such reservoirs follows much the same principles as are used in building impounding reservoirs except that it is desirable to have them covered. Unless water is covered there may be an increase in the growth of algae, and there is always danger of human tampering and contamination.

Standpipes and water towers

Reservoirs of a minimum capacity are frequently constructed as standpipes or water towers, particularly in cities located on comparatively level ground and without available reservoir sites. These standpipes are used to equalize the operation of the pumps, by furnishing water during peak periods of consumption, and to provide an extra supply of water for fire protection. Where such reservoirs can be constructed so that the entire contents will exert pressure they are built in the form of standpipes; otherwise the water tower is the most economical form.

Pumping

A gravity water supply eliminates, in whole or in part, the attention and costs incidental to machinery actuated by steam or other power, and hence the most expensive operating charge in a water works system. Unlike reservoirs and conduits, pumps are subject to considerable depreciation and their operation requires constant and intelligent attention. Pumping machinery must be designed in accordance with the requirements of economical and efficient operation in each particular situation. In meeting these requirements the engineer is concerned principally with power and pumps, correlating one to the other in a manner that will best meet specific needs. The pumps selected are usually one of the numerous displacement types, although the use of centrifugal pumps is increasing rapidly. These are ordinarily actuated by steam, although occasionally by internal combustion engines or electric power, and sometimes by water power.[2]

Distribution system

Materials

The pipe used for distributing water under pressure is commonly constructed of cast iron or steel, but occasionally of wrought iron, wood, vitrified clay, cement, or lead. Water pipe, if used in large quantities, should have the qualities of strength, durability, and low initial cost. Because cast iron has all of these essentials and in addition may be easily cast into various shapes, it is the most widely used material. Wrought iron and steel are

[1] See "Relation Between Filtered Water Storage and Filter Capacity," *Water Works Practice*, Chap. XIV.
[2] See D. W. Mead in Turneaure and Russell, *op. cit.*, 630; and "Pumping Station Practice," *Water Works Practice*, Chap. XV.

WATER 499

also much used, since pipes of these materials are free from sudden breaks; and the fact that steel is much lighter than iron is an item of consideration when transportation over long distances is required. However, the life of steel pipe is limited as compared with that of cast iron, which is ordinarily rated at one hundred years, and instances are available in which it has lasted much longer. Wooden pipes made of single logs were much used in early systems; they are durable and are not impractical with low pressures, but are not now used except in some communities where wood is to be had in abundance and the cost of transporting cast iron pipe is large. Pipes of wood staves are sometimes used in diameters of considerable size. Vitrified clay pipes are used occasionally, but not with high pressures on account of leakage due to both porosity and breakage. The use of reinforced concrete pipe is increasing rapidly, withstanding pressures as high as ordinarily found in cities. Lead pipes are now limited to service connections with waters that are not too soft.[1]

CHAP. XXVIII

The design of the distribution system is a highly technical matter to be determined essentially in accordance with established engineering principles. The system must first supply ordinary domestic and industrial requirements. These needs, and the size of pipe and pressure necessary to meet them, can be calculated with considerable accuracy. Secondly, it is necessary to meet the requirements of fire protection. These are to a certain extent fixed by the National Board of Fire Underwriters who will recommend that the system, both simultaneously and at certain points, be able to supply so many fire streams of 250 gallons each per minute. The problem is therefore one of correlating amount of water, size of pipes, and pressure. The ordinary main in a residential street is six or eight inches in diameter, with larger mains crossing at regular intervals in the form of a gridiron. All mains should feed in two directions so as to minimize the effect of breaks, and should have valves every 500 feet. The position of hydrants depends upon pressure and the number of fire streams that may be necessary, the average distance apart in the cities of the United States being between 500 and 600 feet.[2]

The distribution system

It is not necessary to maintain equal water pressures over an entire city, particularly if some sections are devoted to business

Pressures

[1] See G. S. Williams and Allen Hazen, "Hydraulic Tables," (Wiley, 1920); and *Water Works Practice,* Chap. XIII.
[2] For a discussion of this very technical subject of the distribution system, see Turneaure and Russell, *op. cit.,* Chap. XXVIII.

CHAP. XXVIII

and industry. Larger municipalities therefore install both low and high pressure services. In residential districts a minimum pressure of thirty pounds per square inch at the street level is sufficient to cause water to flow freely in the upper stories of buildings, while fifty pounds is desirable in business districts. These pressures are occasionally raised at time of fires, although this is contrary to best water works practice.

Leakage

As has been mentioned, it is estimated that from one-third to one-half of the water supplied by a pumping plant may serve no useful purpose, being wasted through leaky fixtures in the household or through leaky mains. This leakage is to some extent a concomitant of high pressure. The result is an unnecessary expense for pumping and increased capital costs for the plant. In a clay soil broken mains ordinarily will be revealed by water coming to the surface; in porous soil no such indication will be had. Water main leaks should be discovered by periodic pitometer surveys, the pitometer being an instrument for measuring the pressure in mains, thus indicating any marked decrease owing to leaks. The water phone is a simpler device used for locating the exact point of a leak. Main leaks are often due to electrolysis caused by pipes serving as the conductor of return currents of electric railways. No practical method of preventing deterioration from this cause has been perfected, although proper street railway construction is helpful. Leaking house fixtures cannot be located so easily. House to house inspection can be employed, and at night running faucets can be detected by applying a water phone to the curb cock. Such leaks when detected are difficult to correct, and the only substantial answer to household leaks is the installation of meters.[1]

High pressure

High pressure systems carrying a maximum pressure of 300 pounds per square inch and requiring the use of separate mains of special size and strength are constructed essentially for fire fighting purposes. This pressure is not maintained constantly, but the mains are kept full of water, and the required pressure can be secured within a minute. This water may, of course, be taken from a polluted source. High pressure systems are ordinarily operated by the fire department, rather than in connection with the supplying of domestic water.[2]

[1] See "Water Consumption," *Water Works Practice,* Chap. XIX.
[2] See Chap. XIV.

The most common and satisfactory type of hydrant is the post hydrant which is installed back of the street curb and extends two or three feet above the surface of the ground. In highly congested areas flush hydrants are installed level with the sidewalk or street. In installing hydrants it is very desirable that the nozzles be of the same standard thread as those employed by adjacent cities. On more than one occasion fire apparatus that has been borrowed from a neighboring community for a serious conflagration has been found impossible to connect with the hydrants because the hose did not fit the threads of the hydrants. In the operation of hydrants care should be taken that they are drained or pumped out after use, particularly in freezing weather. The freezing of a hydrant not only damages the mechanism, but prevents its use. Hydrants are particularly susceptible to freezing because they are on a "dead end" of the main.

Meters are not universally installed in cities because of the expense of both installation and maintenance, although their complete use is desirable, and rapidly increasing. The meters should be supplied by the department of water supply and installed without charge, but with charges for repairs when made necessary by neglect of the householder. In this way the city can standardize on a few types of meters, carry a minimum of repair parts, and secure metered service at a minimum of cost. Unless meters are actually owned by the city, repairs are necessarily difficult and costly.

Meters are of two general classes—the positive displacement and the inferential types. The former (usually designated as "disk" meters) operate by measuring a definite amount of water either through the displacement of a piston, or by the motion of a disk affected by the water flow; in the latter type the amount of water is determined by the number of revolutions of a screw. The positive displacement meter is in general use, although either type is accurate, registering an error of only a few percent when properly installed and maintained. A satisfactory meter should register accurately relatively small flows of water, and have a low initial and maintenance cost.

There is decided variation among cities in the frequency of reading meters and the billing for water consumed. About one-third of the municipalities read and bill monthly, arguing that the water department obtains financial results more quickly by this method. Many cities read meters and deliver bills quarterly, thereby saving the department considerable expense and the consumers the inconvenience of paying bills frequently.[1] A few cities require only a semi-annual settlement, except for large consumers. Experience indicates that meters passing large quantities of water should be read monthly.[2]

<small>Meter reading and billing</small>

For the purpose of meter reading a city is ordinarily laid off in districts, the meter reader being responsible for a number of districts. In large cities meters are being read and bills prepared continuously, the reading and billing organizations dealing with one district after another. In addition to a permanent and controlled record of services in the water department office, a duplicate card record of meters arranged by district and street is had, and it serves for meter reading purposes. Each day a number of these records are taken from the office, the meter read, and the amount of water consumed entered upon them. If the householder is not at home, the reader will ordinarily call back once, on the next day. If the meter cannot then be read, an estimate of consumption will be entered by the water office. In some localities the meter reader prepares and leaves the bill at the same time that the meter is read. This procedure, however, is unusual, and ordinarily the meter readings are returned to the office for billing. The billing can be done mechanically at a great saving of time and expense, and with added assurance of accuracy. In some jurisdictions, the total meter readings of a district are placed under accounting control before the billing is undertaken. This step is a precaution against dishonest practices and errors on the part of billing clerks. Collections are ordinarily undertaken by the department.

<small>Water rates</small>

With the general introduction of a water supply piped into homes, a flat charge was made to each customer regardless of the amount of water used. This crude plan was so manifestly unfair that efforts were made to gauge the possible consumption of each consumer and apply charges accordingly. Numerous criteria were developed and are still in use in many cities, among them the size of the pipe leading to the property, the number of rooms in the house, the number of water taps, the rental value of the

---

[1] George H. Fenkell and Henry Steffens, Jr., ''Water Supply,'' *The Government of Cincinnati and Hamilton County.*

[2] For data on installation of meters in many American cities, see Harry Barth, ''Water Meter Problems,'' *American City,* XXXIV, 491-496 (May, 1926).

WATER 503

property plus a fixture rate, the front feet of property served plus a fixture rate, etc. Such measures of water consumption are simple of application and eliminate much expense in connection with billing. However, with the increased cost of water production it has become necessary to develop some methods of preventing useless waste, thereby reducing the capital investment as well as the cost of distribution on the part of water departments. In consequence, many cities have undertaken to meter all or part of their individual services, and the practice is increasing. The meter rates applied may be uniform per unit of consumption regardless of the quantity of water used, or more properly may be in accordance with a decreasing sliding scale.[1] This latter plan is decidedly preferable, since the task of supplying water in large quantities is obviously less. Otherwise, the result can only be a penalization of industry that may work ultimate detriment to the economic welfare of the community.

There has been a great deal of discussion as to how much a city should collect for water service. Certainly the rates should be sufficient to cover operating expenses, which include depreciation, and interest on the bonded debt.[2] In addition, it is desirable to have a surplus which can be used for extensions and improvements. However, such extensions may be properly financed largely or totally by bonds.[3]

Determination of rates

American cities have adopted no uniform policy for meeting the cost of water pipe extensions. It is usual for the costs of large mains to be borne by the department, and these mains are laid when considered necessary and funds are available. Lateral mains are frequently laid upon the petitions of property owners, some proportion of the cost being advanced by them, which may or may not be returned when the connections are sufficient to place the service on a self-supporting basis. Other cities install laterals by special assessment, a plan which compels the private financing of much of this work and correspondingly relieves the department of capital costs. However, under such a system the department is prevented from making needed replacements and extensions to pipes of smaller sizes. In consequence, the growth of industry or

Extensions

[1] See *Water Works Practice*, 460 *et seq.* Also Allen Hazen, *Meter Rates for Water Works* (Wiley, 1918); and George H. Fenkell, *Metered Water Rates for Detroit* (Department of Water Supply, 1923).
[2] See Chapter XXXI in which are discussed the relations of depreciation charges and those for debt retirements.
[3] See *Uniform Classification of Accounts for Water Utilities* (National Association of Railway and Utilities Commissioners, 1922).

population may not be stimulated; and when conditions require an expansion of water facilities, the plan will be found impractical.[1]

Various methods are adopted by cities for the actual laying of water extensions. Smaller cities and some larger ones, notably Pittsburgh, design the extension work and furnish the water pipe but have the actual construction done by contract. Other cities undertake to lay the larger mains in the older sections by city forces, and provide for the laying of pipes in new residential districts by contract. Still other communities, as for example Detroit, which for many years has been rapidly extending its water system, do all engineering and construction work by city forces. Force account work cannot be undertaken satisfactorily unless a sufficient quantity of extensions and replacements is being made to keep designers and construction gangs actively engaged throughout the working season. Contract work is most advantageous in cities requiring only occasional jobs.[2]

Distribution records

In connection with the distribution system there should be available large scale sectional maps showing mains, valves, and hydrants and complete drawings of the supply works and pumping stations should be on file. The sectional maps should show the location and size of mains, connections, valves, and fire hydrants as well as the direction and the number of turns required to close the valves. These maps are usually photographed to reasonable size and bound into books for ready reference, the original maps being securely preserved. These records not only facilitate the operation and maintenance work of the department, but prevent unnecessary delay and resulting drainage when breaks occur in the mains.[3]

Organization of a water department

A water board, consisting of three to five members, has been the prevailing form of supervisory organization in American cities, the actual administration being left to a technical superintendent. The members of the board are occasionally elected by popular vote, but in usual practice are appointed by the chief executive. There is, however, a tendency to discard the board organization and place the management under the control of a single commissioner.[4]

[1] George H. Fenkell and Henry Steffens, Jr., *op. cit.*
[2] *Ibid.*
[3] *Ibid.*
[4] For a fuller discussion of this subject see p. 10. Munro, *op. cit.*, 158, quotes Professor George C. Whipple to the effect that the "water board with its water superintendent usually got better results than the more modern water commissioner system."

In some instances the water service is a bureau in a more comprehensive department of public works.

The actual operating head of a water department faces an unusual number of administrative problems. Not only does the work include the engineering questions of design, construction, maintenance, and repairs of the system, but these technical features must be applied to the diverse phases of supply, purification, pumping, and distribution. These duties require a staff of well trained mechanical and sanitary engineers.

The superintendent himself should have expert technical training, including some knowledge of all of these branches of engineering. The work entrusted to him demands a high degree of intelligence, and ability and training should be the sole basis of selection. The political appointee has no place in the water service. Not only may the city suffer financial losses through his blunders, but—what is of greater importance—it may suffer disease because of his incapacity.

Public ownership is taken almost for granted in the field of water supply. All of the considerations that may be advanced in favor of the municipal ownership of street railways, lighting plants, and gas plants, are pertinent as applied to water works, but in addition there are decided social reasons for public ownership.[1] The health of the community is so intimately related to the purity of its water, and the large use of water is so desirable for social reasons, that it does not seem wise to leave this service to a private corporation. Further, the public interests may be seriously affected by the water rates established and by the policy adopted with respect to extensions. Industry and manufacturing may be encouraged or repressed by the attitude taken. The majority of public water services are now publicly owned in the United States, and it is reasonable to expect that the number will be extended.

[1] See Chap. XXXI.

CHAPTER XXIX

LIGHTING [1]

Public lighting, by which is meant primarily the lighting of streets and public places, is one of the oldest, and yet one of the newest, of municipal activities. It is old in its origin; new in its conception of thoroughfares well lighted with modern appliances. Lighting art has kept reasonable pace with the demands made upon it by automobile traffic, amusements, and other innovations that have vastly increased the night use of streets. Street lighting suitable to these new requirements has been made possible by the discovery and improvement of equipment for producing light, by the more scientific use of equipment already available, and by increased public expenditures for lighting purposes.

Development of public lighting

The earliest street lighting of which we know was that practised by the Romans about 200 A. D. Their method was to suspend oil vessels containing a lighted wick at public squares. Even this was given up during the Middle Ages, when the citizen who ventured on the streets at night was expected to provide his own lighting if he wanted any. In 1415, citizens of London were required by ordinance to hang out lanterns, and about 1524 the Parisians were ordered to display a tallow candle in every window along certain streets. Tallow candles and oil lanterns were the only means of illumination in London and Berlin until shortly after 1800, when gas came into wide use throughout the civilized world wherever lighting was practised to any extent.[2]

---

[1] The principal sources of information on public lighting are articles in technical periodicals, such as *The Transactions of the Illuminating Engineering Society*, *The General Electric Review*, *The Electrical World*, and *The American City*. The articles are fragmentary, each dealing with some special phase of the question. Francis E. Cady and Henry B. Dates, ed., *Illuminating Engineering* (Wiley, 1925), deals briefly with the many elements involved. Valuable pamphlet material is issued by the General Electric Company and other corporations dealing in street lighting equipment. In 1919, the San Francisco Bureau of Governmental Research published an informing survey of street lighting in that city. The Bureau of Standards of the U. S. Department of Commerce has in preparation a study of street lighting that will be available in 1926.

[2] In 1812 the editor of the *Cologne Gazette* protested the introduction of street lighting in Cologne, as being in contravention of Divine Will.

LIGHTING

A new era in street lighting was ushered in when, in 1879, Cleveland, Ohio, first constructed and used electric arc lamps.[1] This style of lamp consisted of carbon sticks which emitted a brilliant light when brought together in an electric circuit. Later the carbon was enclosed in a glass globe and the lights were known as enclosed arcs. The next development was the magnetite arc, introduced twenty-five years later, and differing from the original arc only in the composition of the material forming the electrodes, but producing a much better light. The carbon incandescent lamp was available for commercial use at about the same time as the original arc light, but proved unsatisfactory for street lighting.[2] The invention of the tungsten filament, placed in general use in 1908, and the gas-filled tungsten lamp in 1914, made the incandescent lamp equal in every respect to the arc light for certain purposes.

_{CHAP. XXIX}

The use of electricity

Public lighting, as the term is understood in municipal administration, includes the illumination not only of city streets, but also of parks and public buildings. For the safety and convenience of pedestrian and horse-drawn traffic, adequate street lighting is important, and the common use of the automobile has made it almost imperative. It is estimated from observations made in thirty principal cities in 1920 that over seventeen percent of night traffic accidents are directly attributable to insufficiently lighted streets, and that in poorly lighted cities this proportion may increase to fifty percent. These preventable accidents in a single year involved more than 550 fatalities and cost approximately $54,000,000. At the same time, the total expenditure for street lighting in the United States was estimated at less than $50,000,000 a year.[3] It is true that a lighted automobile can be seen easily as it approaches, but the dark figure of a person against an equally dark background can scarcely be discerned. Eventually, cities may be held responsible for accidents due to inadequate lighting. Not only safety, but convenience is promoted by illumination, and the aim and purpose of public lighting officials is a thoroughfare so lighted that obstacles, and all irregularities on the surface of the street or sidewalk can be seen.

Scope of public lighting

[1] Consult Henry Schroeder, *History of Electric Light* (Pub. No. 2717, Smithsonian Institute, 1923); also W. R. Mott, "Arc Lights," *Illuminating Engineering*, 66-68.
[2] See I. H. VanHorn, "Electric Incandescent Lamps," *Illuminating Engineering*, 89-130.
[3] E. A. Anderson and O. F. Haas, "Illumination and Traffic Accidents," *Transactions of the Illuminating Engineering Society*, XVI (1921).

508 PRACTICE OF MUNICIPAL ADMINISTRATION

Street lighting is also of great aid in police protection. It has been remarked that every street lamp is a silent policeman, since a lawbreaker will hesitate to commit an offense in a place where his act and his escape may be observed. An analysis of the increase of crime in Cleveland showed a decrease of eight percent in the business section after a lighting system of high intensity had been installed, and an increase of fifty-seven percent in poorly lighted sections.[1] These data, however, are indicative rather than conclusive.

But the need of ample street lighting does not rest on accident and crime prevention alone. Well-lighted streets stimulate civic pride, improve the sanitary conditions of streets, serve public convenience, and in business sections are a distinct commercial asset.

Parks Parks need lighting, although of a type quite different from that of the heavily traveled streets. The lighting of particularly dark places, and lights of low intensity along driveways are all that is necessary, except in small, formal parks in the downtown sections. Generally the light from business houses and electric signs in the vicinity will illuminate such small parks, but it is not advisable to trust to this source, as there are hours at night when these lights are turned off.

Public buildings The lighting of public buildings involves problems of an entirely different character from those arising out of the lighting of streets and open public places. The science of interior lighting is sufficiently technical and important to have brought into existence the profession of illuminating engineering. While the public administrator is responsible for the operation and maintenance of the lighting facilities of public buildings, the initial installation of such facilities should be referred to competent technicians.[2]

How streets are lighted

Gas So far, this discussion would indicate that only electricity is used for public lighting. American cities use both electricity and gas to light their streets, but the latter is being discontinued rapidly owing to its inadequacy under some conditions, the inclination of the public to adopt modern facilities, and the exhaustion of the natural gas supply. As a rule, when gas lamps are used in cities, they are situated in the older sections and on comparatively quiet streets. Electric lamps are used on main thoroughfares, in business

---

[1] Ward Harrison, "Statistics on Street Lighting and Crime," *ibid.*
[2] See M. Luckiecsch, "Lighting of Public Buildings," *Illuminating Engineering*, 356-391.

LIGHTING

districts, and in newer residential sections. Electricity is supplanting gas so rapidly as a means of public lighting that the technical application of the latter need not be discussed in this book.

CHAP. XXIX

There are practically two types of electric street lights, the luminous arc and the incandescent lamp. The arc light was the first electric light manufactured, and was steadily improved until it became a good means of street illumination. It is commonly used in a single unit, or a double one where high intensities are required. At one time, tower clusters of arc lights were elevated to a height of 100 feet. This type of lighting was evolved when only the open arc lamp was on the market. This lamp was inherently very efficient, but the distribution of the light was poor, the maximum of the light being given at an angle of between forty-five and fifty degrees from vertical. By mounting the lamps at a higher level the distribution of light was much improved. With the improved initial distribution of light in the enclosed carbon arc and the magnetite arc, it was not necessary to mount lamps at great height, and the practice was discontinued. The arc lamp is essentially a large unit with an output of 3,000 to 8,700 lumens.[1] Within the lighting range of the arc lamp, its efficiency is high, although the equipment necessary for arc light service is more elaborate and expensive than that required for incandescent lamps.

Electricity

Arc lights

The incandescent electric light has come rapidly into favor and is now the principal type used for street lighting, its light being modified by the use of reflectors, refractors, and globes. The incandescent lamp, including the high efficiency gas-filled lamp, did not really compete with the arc lamp until it was possible by means of refractors to direct the light rays, lost in the upper zones, to the street surface. The incandescent lamp with these accessories has now supplanted the luminous arc for many purposes, not because the latter produces insufficient light, but because the incandescent light has greater flexibility, being available for a use of from 450 to 25,000 lumens, or from 40 to 2,500 candle-power. There is a noticeable trend towards the use of larger lamp sizes. It is agreed that 100 candle power lamps are the minimum size economical for street lighting, and lamps of 250

Incandescent lights

---

[1] The lumen is a unit used to designate the total amount of light radiated. One standard candle radiates 12.57 lumens.

candle power are preferable in designing new installations. With small lamps, too large a proportion of the annual cost is consumed in fixed charges on installation—this is as much as three-fourths in some instances—and too little goes for actual illumination.

The selection of one type of electric light in preference to the other is largely a question of economy, to be determined by actual cost analysis, although there is a tendency for the arc light to disappear from use.

Ornamental and non-ornamental lighting

The early idea of street lighting was the suspension of a non-ornamental lamp, usually an arc light, but sometimes in smaller cities an incandescent light, at all important street intersections.[1] Or such lamps would be projected some distance into the street by the use of simply constructed arms. In all cases the current was supplied by overhead wiring. Ornamental lighting, by which is meant the placing of arc, but more often incandescent lamps, on ornamental standards with underground wires in conduits or armored cables, was first used only in the business sections desiring intensive lighting for part or all of the night. Non-ornamental lighting is, of course, cheaper to install, and under present expenditures for public lighting must continue the principal type used by cities. However, ornamental lighting is so far superior to the non-ornamental type in attractiveness that its eventual adoption, particularly in the newer sections of a city, is inevitable. Washington and Milwaukee have attempted this ideal.

Spacing of lights

Lights are placed at intervals on both sides or in the middle of the street to be illuminated, the length of the interval depending upon the brilliancy of the light needed, the elevation of the lamps, and the obstacles that may obstruct the light. The original idea of a lamp at each intersection has given way to the installation of intermediate lamps in longer blocks. If streets are to be made as convenient and safe by night as by day, lamps should be spaced at about eight times the mounting height, and the maximum spacing should not exceed ten or twelve times the height.[2] This would mean a light every 200 feet, which would require more lights than most cities think they can afford. Some cities, however, are installing intermediate units when the distance between lights exceeds twenty times the mounting height, the intermediate

[1] See Ward Harrison, "Street Lighting," *Illuminating Engineering*, 416-427.

[2] *Scientific Street Lighting* (Booklet 250, Holophone Glass Company, New York, 1923), 4.

unit sometimes being of smaller capacity. On wide streets the lamps should be placed opposite each other. The staggered arrangement is advantageous in giving uniform illumination, but has not so attractive an appearance.

Experiment indicates that 100 candle power lamps with non-ornamental fixtures, and with refractors should be mounted eighteen feet, measured from the street surface to the height of the light center; and that lamps of 400, 600, and 1,000 candle power should be mounted from twenty to twenty-five feet. Except in business sections, a higher mounting than twenty-five feet is not advisable, as the lights usually will be obscured by the branches of trees. There is, however, a decided tendency toward high mounting because of the elimination of glare and economy of installation, and fifteen feet is now regarded by some engineers as an absolute minimum.

The height of mounting has a direct effect upon glare, which is the blinding effect of the lamps. As compared with a thirteen and one-half foot mounting, the glare is only one-half as intense at eighteen and one-half feet, and only one-quarter as intense at twenty-seven feet.[1]

Intensity of lighting is related closely to uniformity of distribution. Not only must there be enough light, but it must be distributed so as to illuminate with reasonable uniformity the entire space to be lighted. This uniformity of illumination is expressed by the ratio of maximum to minimum intensity, excluding in this comparison all other lights than street lights and all shadows of trees and buildings. While even distribution is desirable. *i.e.*, all parts of the street lighted equally well, the cost of the lighting equipment necessary to secure it is so great as to offset the advantages. The economic limit is a ratio of three to one, which means that the best illuminated spot receives only three times the light of the poorest illuminated portion, and the ratio should never exceed fifteen to one. Satisfactory uniformity is represented by a ratio of four to one, while reasonable uniformity is represented by a ratio of less than four to one but better than twelve to one.[2]

As has been mentioned, the incandescent lamp could not be used for street lighting until devices were perfected that would

[1] *Scientific Street Lighting, op. cit.*, 13.
[2] R. E. Greiner, *Street Lighting with Mazda Lamps* (Bulletin L. D. 144, Edison Lamp Works of General Electric Company, January, 1923), 9.

512 PRACTICE OF MUNICIPAL ADMINISTRATION

CHAP.
XXIX

throw the light downward. Fifty percent of the light from a Mazda lamp suitable for street lighting purposes is emitted above a horizontal plane through the center of the lamp.[1] Light emitted upward is wasted (except as building façades are illuminated), and the light emitted downward produces a relatively bright space directly under the lamp, and for a space equal to about twice the mounting height. An ordinary glass globe does not affect this light distribution, nor does an ordinary reflector, although the latter will intercept the upward light rays and turn them downward. This difficulty has been met by the introduction of refractors. The refractor is a glass globe containing prisms designed to bend downward the rays of light emitted upward, and to bend upward the excess of rays emitted downward, thus extending the radius of effective illumination. Asymmetric refractors are a further aid to lighting, as they refract the rays from side to side, permitting a greater intensity of illumination on the street surfaces than on sidewalks and toward residences.[2] The prisms of refractors are built into the globe so as to leave both the inside and outside surfaces practically smooth and thus facilitate cleaning. It may be added that not all authorities favor the use of refractors with incandescent lamps.[3]

Summary of requirements

The problem of the administrator with respect to lighting is to determine the amount of light necessary on the street surface, and the lighting mechanism, spacing, and mounting that will produce that amount of light.

Classification of streets for lighting

The determination of needed amount of light depends upon the character of the streets to be illuminated, and it is practicable to classify city streets according to their various needs for illumination.[4] A large city has streets of all types, ranging from those which must be brilliantly lighted to those which require only occasional illumination. If a satisfactory classification be made, the error of developing one part of the city at the expense of another is eliminated. In any such classification, there will, how-

[1] *Scientific Street Lighting, op. cit.,* 7.
[2] See Frank Benford, ''Iso Candles and the Asymmetric Lighting Unit,'' *General Electric Review* (April, 1925); and T. W. Rolph, ''Asymmetric Street Lighting,'' *American City*, XXXIV, 484-487 (May, 1926).
[3] The engineers of the General Electric Company have developed what is reported to be a new type of street lighting for Lynn, Mass., using this principle. The system covers streets of all characters and is said to make the use of automobile head lamps unnecessary. Ten times the former illumination is received at twice the cost.
[4] See R. E. Greiner, *op. cit.*

LIGHTING

ever, be borderline streets, which will be difficult of allocation. Such streets must be dealt with according to their own particular needs.

<small>CHAP. XXIX</small>

First, there are main business streets in the retail, hotel, and theater districts. These streets should be the best lighted of the city, the size of the community determining the type and amount of illumination used. The location of retail stores, theaters, cafés, and other focal points of night-life will guide the trend of vehicular and pedestrian traffic and the lighting should be sufficient to provide safety and convenience to the public.

<small>Business streets</small>

It is true that proprietors of shops, theaters, and other enterprises along such streets are quick to realize the drawing power of bright lights. These privately owned lights give a flood of illumination and enhance the beauty of the streets, but cannot be depended upon entirely, as there are hours of the night when part of these private lights and signs are off. Such business streets require thirty to sixty-hundredths foot candles of light measured at the street or sidewalk surfaces, which is the equivalent of as much as sixteen times full moonlight.[1] The proper illumination can be provided by the use of luminous arc lamps, set high in the air, and spaced at wide intervals. If high powered incandescent lamps of less intensity be used, they should be mounted on standards placed at closer intervals. But it must be remembered that closer spacing increases the number of lampposts and fixtures, and therefore the investment and the cost of maintenance. To increase illumination, it is preferable to use higher candle power lamps. The glare can be reduced by a higher mounting, and by means of refractors the light flux may be directed where it is needed.

Secondary business streets, or in very large cities, crosstown arteries or thoroughfares require the same type of street lighting as the main business streets. They need not be as highly illuminated, but the same spacing and character of equipment should be used, so that with business development higher power illuminants may be used.

<small>Secondary business streets</small>

Boulevards and residential thoroughfares should have ornamental lighting, some uniform design being used for the entire city, the type to be determined largely by surroundings and topography. For example, Los Angeles has designed its lamp standards

<small>Boulevards</small>

[1] For the method of measuring light intensity see p. 516.

along the lines of the Spanish Renaissance. If a street be broad, lights should be placed to illuminate the entire street surface and yet not cause a glare.

Wholesale and manufacturing districts

Wholesale and manufacturing districts, although busy sections of the city during the day, are usually deserted at night. These parts of a city contain a vast amount of valuable property and if not sufficiently lighted the shadows afford an excellent opportunity for miscreants to work. It is customary to place a high powered light at the intersections of streets which will light the street sufficiently to protect the pedestrian and aid the policeman who passes through the section by night. City authorities sometimes allow the daytime importance of these streets to influence the character of the illumination, providing greater lighting than is necessary.

Residential streets

Strictly residential streets carry little vehicular and pedestrian traffic after night, consequently the lighting should be the minimum sufficient to afford police protection and safety. The illumination should enable pedestrians to discern objects at a distance and should be equivalent to at least moonlight standard, without consideration of the illumination from residences, which is negligible. The wide thoroughfare can be lighted best by luminous arcs; on the other hand, incandescent lamps are more suitable to narrow streets.[1]

Rural highways

The lighting of highways through sparsely settled sections subject to heavy vehicular traffic but with few pedestrians becomes a municipal function only when such territory is within the confines of the city. The subject is receiving considerable attention from county authorities. When traffic warrants, such thoroughfares may be illuminated by single incandescent lamps strung overhead, 250 to 400 feet apart, or upon the simplest standards, with reflectors to throw the light upon the road.

Standards of lighting

Authorities on street illumination do not agree with respect to the lighting requirements of the several types of streets. The combined ideas of a number of authorities in the subject are incorporated in the following compilation, which may serve as a guide to the municipal administrator.[2]

---

[1] See "Symposium on Residence Street Lighting," *Transactions of the Illuminating Engineering Society*, (December, 1925).

[2] From the "Report of Committee on Street Lighting," *Proceedings of the American Society for Municipal Improvements* (1922). For other standards of street illumination, see "The Year's Progress," *Transactions of the Illuminating Engineering Society* (October, 1924).

LIGHTING

100,000 Population or Larger

Street Class	Lamp C. P. Per Post	Mounting Height	Desirable Lamp Spacing Feet	Arrangement of Lamps	Lamp C. P. Per Foot Length of Street
Principal business	1000–5000	14–25	80–150	Parallel	20–100
Secondary business	1000–2500	14–18	80–125	Parallel	10–50
Principal thoroughfares	600–1500	20–25	125–250	Parallel or Staggered	3–10
Secondary thoroughfares wholesale, and mfg. district	400–1000	20–25	125–250	Staggered	2–5
Boulevards and parks	250–1000	14–20	125–250	Parallel or One Side	1–5
Residential	250– 600	14–20	125–250	Staggered	1–4
Alleys business section	250– 600	16–20	125–250	One Side	2–5
Outlying streets and alleys	100– 250	16–20	200–400	One Side	¼–1

20,000 to 100,000 Population

Business	1000–2500	14–18	80–125	Parallel	10–50
Thoroughfares	400–1000	20–25	125–250	Staggered	2–5
Boulevards and parks	250–1000	14–20	125–250	Parallel or One Side	1–5
Residential	250– 600	14–20	125–250	Staggered	1–3
Outlying streets and alleys	100– 250	15–20	200–400	One Side	¼–1

5,000 to 20,000 Population

Business	600–1500	14–18	80–125	Parallel	5–30
Thoroughfares	400–1000	20–25	125–250	Staggered or One Side	2–5
Boulevards and parks	250– 600	14–20	125–250	Parallel or One Side	1–3
Residential	250– 400	14–20	125–250	Staggered or One Side	1–3
Outlying streets and alleys	100– 250	16–20	200–400	One Side	¼–1

5,000 Population or Smaller

Business	250– 600	12–16	80–125	Parallel or Staggered	2–10
Thoroughfares	250– 600	16–20	125–250	Staggered or One Side	1–3
Residential	250	14–20	125–250	Staggered or One Side	1–2
Alleys	100	16–20	200–400	One Side	¼–½
Highways	250– 400	25–35	300–600	One Side	¼–1

516 PRACTICE OF MUNICIPAL ADMINISTRATION

A committee representing both city officials and the lighting experts of private electric utilities makes the following recommendation with respect to minimum standards of street lighting:[1]

	Minimum Lumens Per Lineal Foot	Maximum Spacing Along Center of Street
Business section—Population over 100,000	200	125
Business section—Population 50,000 to 100,000	120	125
Business section—Population 20,000 to 50,000	80	125
Business section—Population up to 20,000	60	125
Main thoroughfare in fully developed residence district	35	150
Fully developed residence district	15	250
Outlying residence districts	10	250

In this table the standard street is taken as being forty feet from curb to curb. For streets of greater width, the values of minimum lumens per linear foot should be increased in the same ratio as the width of the street. Where secondary business districts adjoin main business districts, the equipment should be of similar design, but with an illumination of approximately one-half the lumens per linear foot.

The lighting intensities required to make streets by night essentially as safe and convenient as by day have been expressed in somewhat different terms as follows:[2]

Classification of Streets	Intensity of Illumination in Foot-Candles	Approximate Equivalency To Full Moonlight
Non-Traffic streets	.04-.05	1⅓ times
Arterial streets outside of retail business districts, carrying considerable automobile traffic and little pedestrian traffic	.12-.15	4 times
Arterial streets outside of retail business districts, carrying very great automobile traffic and little pedestrian traffic	.20-.25	7 times
Promenade streets	.50-.60	16 times

Measurement of lighting intensity

Intensity of street lighting is measured in foot-candles or fractions thereof, as at the surface of the street or sidewalk. "A foot-candle is the light shed by one unit of candle power on a surface set at right angles to the direction of the light at a distance of one linear foot. A unit of candle power is the light produced (at the candle) by one laboratory candle burning at the rate of 120 grains per hour."[3]

[1] *Report of Joint Committee on Street Lighting* (New York State Conference of Mayors and other City Officials and The Empire State Gas and Electric Association, 1924).

[2] *Scientific Street Lighting, op. cit.* 6.   [3] Munro, *op. cit.* 360.

LIGHTING 517

To appreciate the intensity of lighting expressed in foot-candles, it is well to remember that moonlight standard is about one-twenty-fifth of a foot-candle. An average illumination of one foot-candle for street illumination is intensive lighting. A well-lighted office is lighted to an average of five foot-candles, and only exceptional offices are lighted to as much as from eight to twelve foot-candles.

CHAP. XXIX

The instrument by which light intensity is measured is a photometer.[1] In making street illumination tests with this instrument certain factors that may cause erroneous conclusions must be considered before final decisions are made. A portable photometer is scarcely as reliable as a laboratory instrument, and inherent errors may be further aggravated by errors in readings made by persons inexperienced in photometry; too few lamps may be tested and undue weight may be given to the performance of a single lamp; and where a refractor or parabolic type of unit is installed, the lamp tested may not be in the proper position. Also, due allowance must be made for reflection from buildings, shadows from trees, and the condition of the road surface. Whenever possible, important decisions should be based upon data secured under the exact conditions of laboratory tests. Frequently such laboratory tests are impossible, and tests must be made in the field to determine the effects of cleaning of globes, shade, and other elements modifying actual use.[2]

Maintenance is a very important item in any street lighting system. Street lighting that is potentially adequate may be much less than that if insufficient care is given to the replacing of worn out and burned-out lamps, and to the cleaning of globes and accessories. Any system should be periodically patroled for "outages," *i.e.*, lamps that are out when they should be lighted, in addition to such supervision as will be given by the police, and all burned-out lamps should be replaced within twenty-four hours. Globes containing incandescent lights should be cleaned six times a year or oftener. Lamps that have exceeded their rated burning hours should be replaced. During the life of a lamp, the filament material vaporizes and is deposited on the bulb, causing it to darken so as to cut off some of the light emitted. There is also an increased resistance in the filament on electric circuits of constant voltage, reducing the amount of electricity consumed and the amount of light produced. On circuits arranged in series, the

Maintenance of lamps

[1] See F. E. Cady, "Photometry," *Illuminating Engineering.*
[2] *Ibid.*

518   PRACTICE OF MUNICIPAL ADMINISTRATION

CHAP.
XXIX

amount of light given off by the filament is actually increased, and more than offsets the darkening of the bulb for a time, but does not continue to do so.[1] The size of lamps, type of glassware, and height and spacing of standards are designed to give a certain distribution and intensity of light when maintained at best average efficiency. When this efficiency deteriorates, the lighting results may be decreased as much as one-half.[2]

Lighting schedules

Street lighting circuits are generally operated by a schedule prepared a year in advance, showing the exact time the lamps are to be lighted and shut off. At present, practically all street lights in important cities are operated on an all-night schedule, the lights going on thirty minutes after sunset and off thirty minutes before sunrise. Under such a schedule, each light is operated about 4,000 hours a year. Various other schedules have been worked out, but now they are mostly of historic interest, except in the small communities. Under the Freund system, all lights are operated until midnight, each light burning about 3,000 hours a year. The standard-moonlight system utilizes moonlight to a great extent, and reduces the burning time of each lamp to 2,000 hours a year. It is often the practice to operate ornamental street lights until midnight, after which time all or a part are turned off. Street lighting contracts are generally made at a low rate, and the electric companies do not meter the service, but bill on the basis of the hours burned by each lamp, according to the schedule on which they are operated. This is a simple and fairly accurate method, the only adjustment being for the outages as reported to the electric company by the police department, or other responsible persons.

Organization for public lighting

The type of municipal organization for public lighting must be determined by the nature and extent of the duties imposed upon it. These duties vary greatly in different cities, the size of the community and its lighting requirements being determining factors

[1] See Henry Schroeder and H. E. Butler, *Modern and Obsolete Street Lighting Systems* (Bulletin L. D. 152, Edison Lamp Works, General Electric Company, June, 1924).

[2] In 1923, the St. Louis Bureau of Municipal Research made a study of the effect of maintenance on park lighting. Photometric measurements indicated that the average light from a properly maintained 100 candle power lamp, twenty-two feet from the pole, was .054 foot-candle, while the measurement for a lamp with improper maintenance was .027 foot-candle. A calculation of costs indicated that a properly maintained lamp of the type involved would cost $10.54 a year, but give double the light of an improperly maintained one costing $7.53 a year. The effect of proper maintenance in decreasing the unit cost of used light is evident.

of only relative importance. The authorities responsible for public lighting in one municipality may be required only to purchase lighting from some private utility, in accordance with the terms of a contract running for a period of years. Under these conditions, the activities of the city are largely inspectorial, *i.e.*, to insure compliance with the contract, check up outages and see that additional equipment is installed as ordered. These duties may be assigned to a single individual, who in a small city will usually be a subordinate official in one of the principal departments.

Another city may elect to furnish and maintain its own lighting equipment, purchasing only the electric power necessary to operate it from a privately owned utility. Under these circumstances, the duties of the lighting authorities are more extensive, and include the installation and maintenance of lighting equipment and transmission lines. Duties of this extent warrant the establishment of a separate lighting organization, possibly within a major department, but under the jurisdiction of a person technically trained and competent to organize and operate the distinct forces necessary for lighting installation and lamp maintenance.

Again, a city may own and operate its own electric power plant, as well as its lighting equipment. If such a plant is operated solely for public lighting purposes, it seems sufficient to have its management entrusted to a superintendent responsible directly to the chief executive of the city. If the plant is also generating power for sale to private consumers, there may be merit in having a citizen board of control, appointed by the chief executive, with a professional superintendent actually in charge. It is important that the determination of rates and service be not left to the judgment of a single individual.

The comparative expense of public lighting is usually calculated on the annual cost per capita, per lamp, per unit of candle power, or per mile of street illuminated. Cost varies widely in different cities, depending not only upon the amount of illumination, but also upon the cost of labor, power, and other items. For this reason comparative figures must be accepted as indicative rather than conclusive. To determine whether a city is spending too much or too little for public illumination requires an investigation on the spot by an illuminating engineer.[1]

Authorities on public lighting state that, at a minimum, public

[1] For detailed lamp costs see *Report on Street Lighting Costs in the Larger Cities of the United States,* prepared by F. W. Ballard & Co. (Cleveland, 1925).

520   PRACTICE OF MUNICIPAL ADMINISTRATION

CHAP.
XXIX

lighting should cost a city approximately one dollar per capita per year.[1] Many believe, however, that this figure was satisfactory only in the days of horse-drawn vehicles, and that it still prevails merely because cities have not revised their lighting standards to meet the new traffic hazards or present conceptions of proper street illumination. For example, it is reported that the amount of electricity measured in kilowatt hours used for street lighting in New York State, outside of New York City, was not increased to any extent between 1914 and 1924.

A more satisfactory standard for public lighting consonant with modern requirements is placed at $1.50 to $2.50 per person per year. This expenditure has been translated into the following approximate schedule of annual costs per foot length of street:[2] business district with high intensity, $1.00 to $4.00; thoroughfares and boulevards, $0.30 to $1.29; residential streets, $0.20 to $0.80.[3] It is obvious, too, that the annual budget for public lighting must show a considerable amount for extensions and replacements.

Cost of gas and electricity

Although gas lighting is rapidly becoming obsolete, something should be said concerning its cost. In cities contiguous to natural gas or oil wells, gas lights are less expensive than electricity per unit of light delivered. The actual investment necessary to gas lighting is comparatively small and the principal element of cost

[1] The Bureau of Standards of the U. S. Department of Commerce has compiled costs and other illumination data during 1925 for 730 American cities based on the 1920 census. In the following table these cities are arranged in 10 groups according to population, of which the average population only is given:

Group	Average Population	Miles Illuminated	Pop. per Mile of St.	Lumens per Mile	Lumens per Capita	Annual Cost per Mile	Cost per Capita
1	376,000	622	656	57,600	86	$558	$0.85
2	236,500	398	633	62,800	91	604	.93
3	169,500	332	560	38,800	58	427	.74
4	122,000	172	760	53,200	69	708	.86
5	87,500	194	510	41,300	82	487	.93
6	60,900	136	540	40,700	80	474	.94
7	44,400	87	658	47,500	78	554	.94
8	34,400	77	544	43,700	79	471	.91
9	24,100	64	479	36,200	74	414	.90
10	13,750	41	410	30,000	74	408	1.02

[2] "Report of Committee on Street Lighting," *Proceedings of the American Society for Municipal Improvements*, 1922.

[3] The San Francisco Bureau of Governmental Research compiled the cost of lighting in 59 cities of over 100,000 population for 1919. The per capita expenditure ranged from 43 cents in Tacoma to $1.50 in Rochester. For a discussion of per capita costs, see *Engineering News-Record*, XCI, 850 (November 22, 1923).

is labor. No satisfactory mechanical device has been perfected for lighting and extinguishing these lamps, so that men must still be employed for the purpose.[1]

Electric lighting presents a somewhat different cost problem. Labor costs are not so important, but overhead expense in the form of interest and depreciation is large. However, the expense of the large capital investment necessary to electric lighting is reduced materially if the investment can be kept continually productive. If a utility supplies electricity principally for lighting purposes, its highest or peak production will be during the few hours from dusk to midnight. During the balance of the day, output must be curtailed sharply and much equipment be idle. Under satisfactory conditions, utilities endeavor to maintain a comparatively even distribution by the sale of industrial power during the daylight hours, special inducements being offered such consumers in the form of reduced rates. Economical public lighting cannot be divorced from the industrial and domestic consumption of electric power.

Since the majority of American cities do not own and operate their own electric light plants, it is necessary that contracts be entered into with private producers for the electric energy required; or, if lighting equipment is not furnished by the city, for the supply and operation of the different type lamps in use at a given price per unit. In either case the city must pay for meeting its requirements at the "after supper" peak load of the utility. It is most advantageous for a city to own its equipment and purchase only the current, because contracts for electric energy alone are not particularly difficult to make. If, however, a city accepts complete lighting service from a private corporation, it is essential that the standards of service be specified in considerable detail. The type and power of the lamps, the amount of light to be emitted from each lamp, the placing of lamps, the cleaning of lamps, allowance for outages, and some provision for taking advantage of improvements in the art of lighting, all should be covered in the specifications. A most important factor is the establishment of good will between the parties to a contract that at best must be more or less flexible in its terms, to the end that the spirit as well as the letter of its provisions may be observed.

The pressure for municipal ownership of all the facilities necessary to public lighting is not so urgent as in the case of

[1] Cincinnati uses a solenoid control for this purpose.

522 PRACTICE OF MUNICIPAL ADMINISTRATION

CHAP.
XXIX

Municipal
vs. private
ownership
in street
lighting

certain other utilities. In larger cities, and particularly those of an industrial character, the power requirements for public lighting purposes form only a small percentage of the total power generated. For example, in Detroit, in 1925, the peak load of the Detroit Edison Company is 330,000 kilowatts per hour, while the peak consumption of the municipality for street lighting is between 7,000 and 8,000 kilowatts per hour. The maximum possible production of the Detroit Edison Company is 540,000 kilowatts per hour. Under these circumstances, it is obvious that the municipality would have little reason for engaging in the generation of electric energy for public lighting purposes only. A private corporation capable of producing seventy times the power consumed by the municipality is in a position to meet the city's requirements at a much lower cost than that at which the city can manufacture a small quantity of power for its own use. In the particular instance of Detroit, however, the city finds it necessary to provide power for both public lighting and the publicly owned street railway. The combined requirements are so large that probably the muncipality can produce the necessary power as cheaply as a private corporation. Also a private corporation might be unwilling to give the city so large a proportion of its output, considering that the contract might be discontinued upon expiration. It may be concluded that larger cities using power for only street lighting and public buildings can buy service from a private corporation cheaper than that service can be secured under municipal ownership.

This is not always true for small communities, and particularly those that have few or no industries and are not served by the suburban service of some great electric utility. In these communities the largest requirement for electricity is for street lighting purposes. Here, municipal power production is practicable, particularly when the city is in a position to furnish power to private consumers. If the city plant adequately meets the street lighting requirements, there will be little incentive for a private corporation to go into the electrical business. Obviously, in the long run, a city must meet all requirements or none of them.[1]

[1] For arguments against public ownership in this field, see James Mavor, *Niagara in Politics* (Dutton, 1925); and *Political Ownership and the Electric Light and Power Industry* (National Electric Light Association, 1925).

CHAPTER XXX

CONTROL OF UTILITIES [1]

A public utility is ordinarily a corporation that renders necessary or important services to a large number of persons, utilizing special rights granted by the public. Water and gas mains, heating pipes, conduits, poles, and rails must be laid in public streets, and on occasions private property that cannot be secured through negotiations with the owners must be taken by eminent domain, although the exercise of this latter right is limited to certain utilities and for specific purposes. The more important special privilege of using public property by a utility originates in the specific grant of a franchise or indeterminate permit given by an authority competent to make such grants. Usually this authority is the legislative body of a city, although state legislatures also have on occasions granted special rights. In some cities an affirmative vote of the people is necessary to confirm any privileges granted by other authority.

A franchise is a contract granting a utility the right to put poles, mains, conduits, rails, etc., in the city streets to the practical exclusion of all others, to render service to the public requiring it, and to make certain charges for that service. On the other hand, the utility undertakes to furnish the service specified, to make its charges in accordance with the rates stipulated in the franchise or as determined by the authorities regulating utilities, and sometimes to pay the municipality certain sums for the privileges extended it. Franchises and indeterminate permits

Public utilities have the important economic characteristic of being natural monopolies. Ordinary business provides opportunity for competition which usually establishes reasonable prices Utilities are natural monopolies

---

[1] There are many worthwhile publications on the subject of public utility regulation. Some of the most recent are L. R. Nash, *The Economics of Public Utilities* (McGraw-Hill, 1925); John Bauer, *Effective Regulation of Public Utilities* (Macmillan, 1925); William M. Wherry, Jr., *Public Utilities and the Law* (Writer's Pub. Co., 1924); William G. Raymond, *The Public and Its Utilities* (Wiley, 1925); Henry C. Spurr, *Guiding Principles of Public Utility Regulation* (2 vols., Public Utility Reports, Inc., 1925); and Morris L. Cooke, ed., *Public Utility Regulation* (Ronald, 1924). See also the state laws and the reports of the Public Utility Commission of the state in which interested. For current reference, consult *Public Utility Reports* (fortnightly).

and satisfactory service. This freedom of trade does not exist when buying a necessity furnished by a public utility. The service rendered at the established price must be accepted or done without. By natural economic law, two utilities furnishing the same service cannot well operate in the same territory. To be sure, it is physically possible for two sets of mains or poles or conduits to be placed in the same street, and for competing street railway lines to serve the same area, but such duplications are not economically possible, and in most instances in which they have been tried they have failed. Not infrequently, public officers have endeavored to circumvent the monopolistic character of an existing franchise by granting a new franchise for the same service, particularly in the case of telephones and electric service. For a time the competing utilities struggle along side by side, rendering unsatisfactory service, causing great annoyance, and frequently a duplication of expense to citizens required to patronize both services. In the end, there is a consolidation of the two companies, to the relief of every one concerned.

The causes underlying the monopolistic character of public utilities, and the impracticability of successful competition, will be apparent on careful thought, although officials and citizens, on many occasions, have neglected to do such thinking. If a public utility must provide facilities sufficient to give service to all citizens, and then has only one-half of those citizens as customers, it follows that the interest and depreciation charged to the consumer will be doubled. In a similar manner, the expense of superintendence and other overhead costs must be prorated over the fewer units of product or service sold. Furthermore, the low manufacturing costs that generally go with large output cannot be secured. The combined results are higher charges to the consumer, or reduced profits to the utility, each of which can be obviated only by consolidation and reversion to monopoly.

Public utilities are alike in so far as they enjoy special privileges and are monopolistic in character. They are unlike in that certain of them are revenue producing and others are not. The organization and operation of all revenue producing utilities is substantially the same, whether privately or publicly owned. In this group are found the agencies furnishing water, gas, heat, electricity, transportation and communication. In each instance a sufficient charge must be made for the service rendered to pay the ordinary costs of operation and a return upon the capital invested. In the other group are those facilities that have been so long socialized that they are not thought of as utilities at all, *e.g.*, streets, sidewalks, sewers, bridges, and parks. These are publicly owned and made non-revenue producing because of their universal use and their absolute importance in the daily life of the people. How far this socialization will proceed is problematical. Occasionally it is suggested that street railways should be municipally owned and operated without charge to the riders, and a few cities provide a minimum amount of free water to each consumer. There appears to be no positive rule for determining what services shall be free. It would be difficult to charge for certain facilities, such as streets and sidewalks. Yet the use of sanitary sewers is scarcely more universal than the use of water, and an annual charge could easily be made for each sewer connection. The only prediction to be made safely is that the socialization of public facilities will increase rather than lessen.

It is unthinkable that citizens would knowingly and voluntarily place themselves in a position where they must purchase a commodity essential to community life from a single corporation, pay whatever price is asked, and accept whatever service is rendered. There might be occasions when a utility under such circumstances would give good service at a reasonable price, but such philanthropy is not to be expected from a corporation owned by many and changing stockholders and operated by professional managers chosen for their ability to produce dividends. The almost universal conduct of uncontrolled monopolies has been anything but philanthropic, and their operations have been characterized by the slogan of "the public be damned." Only such service has been given as would show immediate profit; extensions of service have been denied when such profit was not apparent; arbitrary and irritating rules have been enforced; and rates have been fixed at "all the traffic would bear." "All the traffic will bear" means a rate that will bring sufficient consumption to insure a maximum profit. A lower rate might bring about a larger consumption, and a higher rate a smaller consumption, each, however, with less profit than the rate established.

These conditions have been gradually understood by the public, and in a halting way, and in spite of obstacles, control has been sought through three methods, *i.e.*, the stipulation of specific conditions in franchises, regulation by especially authorized authorities, and public ownership and operation.

526 PRACTICE OF MUNICIPAL ADMINISTRATION

CHAP. XXX

The possibilities of control through franchises

It is generally conceded that the effort to regulate public utilities by the contractual provisions of ordinary franchises has not been a decided success, and has injected a baneful influence into municipal policies.[1] Early franchises were granted under political and social conditions that do not generally obtain now. These contracts were for excessively long terms, sometimes in perpetuity; little control was had of rates and service; and corruption was rampant in their granting.[2] The legislatures and the courts[3] have to some extent mitigated the harshness of existing provisions but these controls have proved insufficient to meet the needs of practical regulation. The impracticability of controlling utilities by contractual means, even where the best of intentions prevail on the part of the city authorities, or on the part of both parties for that matter, can be appreciated. Consider the persons in whose hands

Experts vs. laymen

the negotiations are placed. On the side of the utility is the most able engineering and legal talent that money will buy, formulating terms in private conferences of experts, executives, and directors. On the side of the city is the short-term public officer, by no means a specialist in utility control. The public's terms cannot be decided upon in secret, but must be mulled over by the city council, and furnish headlines for the local press. A franchise is a lengthy technical document, replete with opportunities for clauses of innocent and unimportant appearance that may loom large after the papers have been signed and sealed.[4]

---

[1] Consult Delos F. Wilcox, *Municipal Franchises*, 2 vols. (*Engineering News*, 1911) and *Analysis of the Electric Railway Problem* (Macmillan, 1921).

[2] For a picture of disgraceful municipal politics at the end of the last century by one of the then styled "muckrakers" read Lincoln Steffens, *The Shame of the Cities* (McClure-Phillips, 1904). Professor W. B. Munro summarizes the situation, *op. cit.*, 403-404.

[3] "In practice there have been two general ways of accomplishing this latter result. The courts have repeatedly held that reservations in the constitution or laws of the state at the time of the granting of a franchise, providing for the future revocation or modification of franchises, would by implication become a part of the terms of every franchise granted during the existence of such reservations, thus subjecting it to subsequent revocation or modification by its own terms. Again, the courts have held that there are certain fundamental powers of sovereignty, notably the police power, which cannot be compromised or granted away by a franchise, and consequently that no reasonable police regulation can be construed as an impairment of the obligation of a contract." Chester M. Maxey, *An Outline of Municipal Government* (Doubleday, Page, 1924) 236-237.

[4] For example, the city of Dayton at one time contracted with a corporation for the "disposal of *all* garbage." The city could not require every establishment to give its garbage to the collectors, and the company collected many thousands of dollars in damages. Nevertheless, a new group of officials, unfamiliar with conditions, was quite willing that the same clause should be incorporated in a renewal of the contract.

How long an otherwise acceptable franchise should run has never been determined to the satisfaction of both utilities and the public. The company naturally insists upon a long term as an ostensible aid in financing, and the city on a relatively shorter period. Perhaps a solution will be found in the indeterminate permit or franchise which have been substituted in various jurisdictions for perpetual and term franchises. It is usually provided that the city shall take over the utility property at an agreed arbitrated value when an indeterminate franchise is canceled.[1] Usually no consideration is given to the disposal of property upon the expiration of ordinary franchises, the utility knowing that with its facilities in the streets and with service being rendered, it is reasonably sure of a satisfactory renewal.

It is the detailed provisions concerning service and rates that give rise to the greatest difficulties in contractual control. Schedules of charges and standards of service may be agreed upon as reasonable, but once incorporated in the contract they must stand for its entire life. With this in mind, contemplate the changes in costs and service that the mechanical progress of the last few years has made possible—improvements in the methods of producing gas and electricity; in the construction of telephones, street cars, and electric lamps; and in the methods of reducing labor costs. Rates and service reasonable and modern a decade ago may be unreasonable and obsolete today. When conditions work in favor of the utility, they are always taken advantage of; when they work against it, the utility is in a position to negotiate amendment of the franchise under threat of curtailing service.

Curiously enough, in the recent rise of prices of labor and materials, fixed franchise rates have been a detriment to utilities. With a rapid increase in the ratio of operating costs to gross in-

---

[1] Massachusetts and the District of Columbia were the leaders in the development of the bare indeterminate permit under which the franchise granting authority has the power to revoke the franchise at any time without compensation. In the District of Columbia this may be done by act of Congress. In Massachusetts this power of revocation relates chiefly to street railways. Wisconsin adopted the indeterminate permit as a part of its public utilities law in 1907 and coupled with the permit a system of practically exclusive state control and a guarantee of monopoly, except where competition is found by the state commission to be necessary. This Wisconsin system has been followed quite closely in Indiana, and indeterminate permit legislation in one form or another has been enacted in several other states. Sometimes it is incorporated in the city charter as, for example, in the new charters of Kansas City and Los Angeles. See Delos F. Wilcox, *The Indeterminate Permit and Its Relation to Home Rule and Municipal Ownership* (Public Ownership League, Bulletin 34, 1926).

528   PRACTICE OF MUNICIPAL ADMINISTRATION

CHAP. XXX

come, many utilities have been forced into receivership or to secure increased rates. Such increases were sometimes secured by negotiation, but often the public service commission, acting under legislative authority, has set aside the conditions contained in public utility franchises pertaining to rates and service, so far as necessary to give the utilities relief. These actions are taken under the theory that the state, being the source of municipal power, has the right to surrender on behalf of the public any advantages which the municipality may have secured through contract. Of course, a state commission cannot change the conditions of a franchise contract to the detriment of the public utilities without their consent, if these conditions were lawful at the time the contracts were entered into. On the other hand, a commission appears entirely free to change the conditions of the contract to the detriment of the municipality without the latter's consent, except where some home rule provision of the state constitution intervenes.[1]

Contracts are not self-executing

Utilities are operated by professional managers, employed for their training and abilities, and continuing in office as long as they render satisfactory service. It is the business of these men to see that the city performs its part of the franchise obligation. The city's interests are represented by laymen, holding office for brief duration, and who have many problems more pressing than those involved in a franchise granted by their predecessors.[2] Sometimes franchises provide boards of arbitration to which many questions of service are to be referred. More often they do not, and the cities interested are unprotected through default of action.[3]

The abuses of unregulated franchises

The abuses of restricted service and unreasonable rates arising from attempts to control utilities by contractual stipulations have already been mentioned; but amplification of these points is desirable. The rates permitted by franchise are not always employed by the utilities, because such rates may not bring consumption to the most profitable point. Utilizing a fixed rate for service, or even

"Watered stock"

[1] During this period the Detroit United Railways arbitrarily placed in effect a five-cent fare on certain lines where a three-cent fare was required by franchise, and later announced a six-cent fare on all lines, although the legal maximum rate was five cents. The city protested but paid.
[2] Another example may be taken from Dayton, Ohio. The city, under suspicious circumstances, leased valuable business property to a utility for a long term of years, with the proviso that the rent should be adjusted every ten years by an arbitrator. For many years no revision was made, because it was not the specific business of any official to institute the necessary procedure.
[3] Occasionally fidelity bonds are posted to compel specific performance of franchise obligations.

a voluntary rate sufficiently generous to provide large earnings, the task of the utility is to arrange its finances so that excessive profits will not be too apparent to the public. This arrangement was simple in other days when the control of security issues was unsupervised by state authorities. For example, many companies that now operate are a consolidation of a number of smaller corporations. In making such consolidations it was relatively easy to capitalize the new company, not upon a basis of actual investment in plant, but on a basis of the earnings at prevailing charges. Frequently, subsidiary corporations were bought at excessively high prices, either in cash or stock of the new corporation. Sometimes the franchises of the underlying corporations were actually secured by the officials of the consolidated company and the construction done by construction corporations in which they were interested. In this fashion, there was a profit to be received in construction and a profit to be received from the sale of the company, all of which "water" was finally transmuted into valuable securities.

CHAP. XXX

A more modern device for concealing excessive earnings is to "plow in" the surplus above reasonable dividends, *i.e.*, to reinvest it in extensions of plant.[1] In this fashion the equity of the stockholders is constantly increased and the foundation laid for future stock issues representing actual increased values. This stricture would by no means be agreed to by all utility authorities. Many maintain that the tests of a fair rate are reasonableness of charges as compared to those in effect in other cities, high character of service rendered, and freedom from extravagance in both investment and operation. Assuming that these conditions are satisfactory, they would hold that surplus may properly be invested in extensions. Similarly, depreciation reserves may be so excessive as to constitute an illegitimate burden, requiring unreasonable earnings to meet their requirements.

"Plowing in" earnings and depreciation reserves

Another unsatisfactory condition arising under franchises is the payment by some utilities of excessive salaries to officials, which is in reality a dividend to the management at the expense of both the stockholders and the public. A similar abuse arises through the promiscuous payment of retainers to numerous attorneys. In some few instances there has been flagrant "stock job-

Excessive salaries

"Stock jobbing"

---

[1] The Detroit United Railways used to advertise publicly that it paid only eight percent dividends, surplus earnings being put back into the Company in the form of extensions and new equipment.

bing" by utility officials. They have been able to suppress earnings, or to stimulate difficulties with the public authorities, thereby depressing stock values. Then the true earnings were made known, or the difficulties cleared away by a conciliatory attitude, with a rise in prices, and consequent profit to the "insiders."

Exercise of political influence

It is important to recognize the baneful influence that public utilities have had on American municipal politics. The selfish control exercised by utilities in Chicago, Philadelphia, New York, St. Louis, and other large communities is an evidence of the benefits to be received by these monopolies through controlling city councils and administrative officials. With friends in the city hall, no drastic action contrary to utility interests was to be anticipated. Also, additional franchises and extensions to present franchises were to be had at a minimum of expense and on the most satisfactory terms. Happily, this situation is passing away, and cities are gradually regaining control of their streets and securing needed services at reasonable rates.

"Footballs of politics"

The utilities are not to be blamed entirely for their selfish interest in politics. Politicians have been ever ready to take a selfish interest in utilities. Controversies have continued for years for the reason that their settlement would have closed an easy road to political preferment. When an unpopular utility is involved, the easiest way to get public office and to keep it, is for the candidate to condemn the corporation, propose impossible settlements, and finally do nothing.

Out-of-town ownership

The relations of utilities and the public are further affected by out-of-town ownership. While some utilities have been financed by local money, more often "foreign capital" has been brought in, or "foreign control" secured after the original financing. Today there exist numerous great holding corporations which own or control strings of gas, electric, and street railway companies, spread over large areas.[1] A city is sometimes less reasonable with such companies than with those whose stock is owned by its own citizens, and it cannot be expected that out-of-town stockholders and managers will have large incentive to cultivate friendly relationships.

Payment for franchises

When cities began to realize that utilities receiving franchises were reaping inordinate profits at the rates designated in the

[1] Examples of these holding corporations are the American Electric Power Company, American Gas and Electric Co., American Light and Traction Company, Cities Service Company, Middle West Utilities Company, North American Company, Stone and Webster, American Bell Telephone Company, etc.

contracts, efforts were made to reduce the returns by special taxation. Practically all of the more recent franchises provide that the corporation shall pay some portion of their income into the city treasury. This contribution may be a small percentage of the gross or net income, or it may be a charge based on rough units of service. Frequently additional provision is made to pay for services rendered by the city, such as original paving, street repair, and snow removal between street-car tracks. There is no doubt about the propriety of charges for actual services rendered. When a utility has a rate fixed in its franchise, the collection of a special tax may be an absolute gain to the public. When a utility operates under a rate ostensibly based on the cost of service, there is a question as to the advisability of such special taxes, since they may be added to the other costs of operation and reflected in higher rates charged the consumer.

Service at cost

As an alternative to the fixing of rates and service by contract, the service-at-cost franchise has been developed. This plan is not new, but was given impetus by the Cleveland settlement of 1910, ending a conflict between the city and the street railway company over the question of a three-cent fare, and is commonly known as the Tayler plan, after Judge Robert W. Tayler. The Cleveland franchise provides for a rate of fare that will return the company six percent on an agreed valuation, although a maximum rate of fare is also fixed. Provision is made, too, for the charges that will be allowed for operation, maintenance, renewals, depreciation, etc., and the physical operations and accounting of the company are under the detailed supervision of a street railway commissioner employed by the municipality. Changes in the rate of fare are facilitated by the creation of an equalization fund which is set aside to care for variations in earnings. When this fund reaches a maximum of $700,000 the fares are reduced, and when it falls to a minimum of $300,000 they are correspondingly increased.

The Tayler plan

The advantages of this plan are apparent, perhaps more apparent than real. Service is ostensibly rendered at cost, which is all any citizen can ask, and the city can specify the amount and character of service it requires. In consequence, the plan has many friends. However, some disadvantages have been noted. A main difficulty is that of establishing the value upon which the rate of return is to be allowed. Outstanding capital stock cannot be accepted as an evidence of value, because there is seldom any

Advantages

Disadvantages

relation between the two. Determining value by appraisal involves problems that are more fully discussed at a later point, as does determination of a fair rate of return.[1] Nor can a fair rate of return be assured by merely increasing fares. Unfortunately, economic law establishes the highest charge that can be made, almost as effectively as if it were written into the franchise contract. There is always some point beyond which price cannot go without consumption and profits being unduly curtailed. With respect to actual operation, it will be observed that the utility is under no obligation to accept losses originating in faulty management or industrial depression. This is an advantage enjoyed by no private industry. In consequence there is no incentive to economy in operation. Waste, inefficiency, and downright pilfering must be compensated for by the public. This obstacle can can be only partially overcome by minute supervision of affairs on the part of the city. The result is likely to be little or no control, or a control in such detail as to handicap the effective operation of the utility.

The Boston sliding scale

The plan for regulating the price of gas in Boston and environs, established in 1906, is a somewhat similar service-at-cost scheme, except that an incentive is offered for economy in operation. The plan employs the principle of the so-called sliding scale. A standard price for gas and rate of dividends to stockholders were established by an act of the Massachusetts legislature, the rate being such as to secure a fair return to the stockholders upon their investment. For every reduction in the price of gas, the company is allowed a corresponding increase in dividends. The standard price is set at ninety cents per thousand cubic feet, and the rate of dividend at seven percent on the established value. Provision is made for an increase of one percent in the dividend rate for every reduction of five cents in the price of gas. The act of the legislature also provides that a reserve fund for emergency purposes shall be set aside each year up to one percent of the capital, until it becomes equal to five percent. Excess earnings from the sale of gas are to be paid to towns in which gas is sold at a rate determined per mile of main in use there. After the first ten years of operation, a board of gas and electric light commissioners has power to raise or lower the standard rate to facilitate meeting of greater or lesser burdens, whether due to changes in prices of materials, or to improved methods of manufacture, or

[1] See p. 537 *et seq.*

CONTROL OF UTILITIES 533

to other conditions affecting the general cost or manufacture of gas.

With the expiration of existing franchises, or to secure extensions of service for which no franchise will be given, cities often enter into "day to day" agreements for service. Such agreements are nothing more than indeterminate franchises revocable at the will of the city. They usually provide for the current adjustment of rates by some agreed method, and for the disposition of the property in event the permit is canceled.[1] These agreements are most useful only when some purchase clause can be legally appended, under which conditions the utility is in a position to borrow money for original installations or extensions.

The fixing of rates and service by local or state boards of regulation becomes necessary when no contractual rates and service are established in a franchise, when operation is to be started under a franchise providing for such regulation, when existing franchises expire, when franchises are voluntarily given up by a utility, or when the terms of a franchise are canceled. Under any of these conditions a valuation must be determined and a rate established that will pay a reasonable return upon that value. Utilities are no different from private persons, in that their property may not be taken "without due process of law."[2]

Regulation may be secured either through the enforcement of legislative enactments by the courts or through the enforcement of these enactments and administrative regulations by a special regulatory authority designated for the purpose. The first method is now seldom used, as legislative bodies are seldom competent to prescribe or courts to enquire into the technical details of public utility operation and regulation.[3] Control through special regulatory authorities is largely a function of the state. The present regulatory commissions are a gradual outgrowth of earlier railway commissions, their powers and jurisdictions having been extended to embrace supervisory control over motor transportation, water, gas, electric, telephone, and street railway companies. It is natural that public utility regulation should lie largely with the state, although some weighty arguments are advanced in behalf of local

[1] Detroit secured large extensions to city street railway service through day-to-day agreements with the Detroit United Railways, additional franchises being refused. The rate of fare continued to be that charged on other lines, and it was provided that extensions so constructed could be taken over by the city at cost of construction, less depreciation as determined by a board of arbitration.
[2] See earlier references.   [3] Maxey, *op. cit.*, 242.

534 PRACTICE OF MUNICIPAL ADMINISTRATION

CHAP. XXX

regulation, particularly in larger cities. Probably the future will see a distribution of regulatory functions between the state and the city, with the necessary administrative coöperation.[1]

Some arguments for state regulation

As an argument for state rather than city regulation it is urged that a state authority is in the best position to secure sufficient data for intelligent regulation of public utility companies having an intercorporate character. The jurisdiction of a local commission may be too limited always to permit the application of its rules to an entire corporation. Also, a utility corporation with holdings in several municipalities may reasonably deny information to a local commission concerning operations not within its jurisdiction, and may reasonably object to the enforcement of different regulations in each municipality in which it operates. Aside from the securing of information, state regulation may be desirable to protect this interurban service from discriminating regulation on the part of the dominating city; for only a state authority is capable of deciding justly as between the diverse interests of neighboring cities. State regulation is also necessary if there are to be uniform methods of accounting and control of capitalization.

State jurisdiction is wide

Unfairness among cities prevented

Uniform regulations secured

Expert advice available

The determination of matters having to do with regulation is technical in its nature and requires expert consideration of a high order. Such expert advice is not obtainable by small cities, and not always by larger ones. The state authorities, however, with the wealth of the state to command, can employ experts who can give the same skilled service to all communities alike. Lastly, a state authority is in a position to protect the investor in utility concerns. Operations can be controlled in the interest of the stockholders, and unethical practices on the part of the management and the sale of worthless stock and bonds prevented. The so-called "blue-sky" laws that have been enacted by many states make it compulsory for individuals, firms, and corporations to file with the proper state officers a detailed financial statement, copies of their constitution and by-laws, and any other information required, and to secure a permit before they can sell any stocks, bonds, or other securities. They thus illustrate the thoroughness with which a state may operate in instances where a municipality would be practically helpless.

Protection of investors

Some arguments for local regulation

While local regulation is in some of its phases admittedly impracticable, there are still some arguments to be advanced for it. The local regulating authority will be composed of individuals

[1] See Morris L. Cooke, *op. cit.*, Chap. XI.

who know, or should know, local conditions. This knowledge of the methods and business habits of the utility operating in a city, and of the prejudices and opinion of citizens, should be of very great value. These detailed local conditions can never be presented competently to the state authority in any utility hearing, even by municipalities that maintain their own staffs for the investigation of utilities and the collection of data supplementary to that secured through the investigations of state agents.

Speaking generally, the utilities favor state regulation and the larger cities desire to avoid it. With the growth of the home rule idea, and the reluctance of larger cities to surrender any authority to the state, a solution may be found in the establishment of state regulation supplemented by special regulatory coöperative boards for metropolitan areas, with a jurisdiction sufficient to cover the territorial ramifications of the utilities centering in the predominating city. Such metropolitan authorities would meet many of the objections raised against purely local regulation, and would have many advantages pertaining to such local regulation.[1]

The regulatory control exercised by public authority, whether state or local, should permit of sufficient income to provide for the efficient operation of the plant, for adequate maintenance and depreciation, and for a reasonable return upon the investment. In addition, the public should be protected from inefficient and extravagant operation, and the stockholders from transactions inimical to their interests.

An enumeration of these standards suggests some of the difficulties that militate against public utility control by this method to the entire satisfaction of all concerned. As in most administrative matters, successful operation depends upon personnel. If the regulatory authority consisted always of men of highest integrity and ability, trained in public utility affairs, keen to detect specious arguments presented for consideration, and adamant to influence, whether political, social, or economic, the regulation of public utilities would be effectively undertaken, and more drastic action on the part of the public with respect to utilities would be rendered

---

[1] For a time two public service commissions existed in New York, that for the First District having to do with New York City. This local commission was abolished in 1921, its duties being transferred to a single commission for the entire state. A transit commission was established to control street railways and busses.

See Harold F. Kumm, "The Legal Relations of City and State with Reference to Public Utility Regulation," *Minnesota Law Review* (December, 1921, and January, 1922).

unnecessary. Regulation ordinarily rests with several individuals constituting a board appointed by the governor, or in the event of local regulation, by the mayor; although sometimes they are elected, and in a few instances they are subject to recall. The tenure of office is from two to ten years. Compensation, while substantial, is ordinarily not sufficient to command the services of the most competent persons.

It does not require much imagination to appreciate the absurdity of electing officers for duties of this character. With rare exceptions, men do not become candidates for offices of limited remuneration unless their abilities command even less compensation than that which the office pays, or the office can be used as a stepping stone to greater political preferment or to lucrative employment by the utilities themselves. And a judicial or quasi-judicial office should never be used for this latter purpose. Members of regulatory commissions should always be appointed. Even this method of selection is not always, however, a guarantee of proper qualifications. Governors occasionally appoint henchmen of the utilities, since these corporations have a way of helping in politics; or use these positions to liquidate political obligations, appointing personnel primarily because the appointees strengthen the control of the political party in some section of the state. It is to be expected that such appointees will give more weight to the political than to the economic considerations brought to their attention, and formulate decisions having in them larger elements of popular approval than abstract justice. Constituted as they sometimes are, public utility commissions have been considerably more impartial than they might have been expected to be.

The influence of the public on decisions

On the other hand, the regulatory authorities are primarily agents of the public and not of the utility, and are sometimes amenable to the influence of extended newspaper campaigns, petitions by commercial, civic, and labor organizations, and the exhortations of their friends who represent the public. And the public is not always reasonable in its demands. It has little or no understanding of the technicalities of public utility operation, and little patience with rate-making that does not give a minimum charge to the maximum number of people, regardless of whether justice is done. These specious issues are often created and supported by newspapers and politicians who would curry public favor at the expense of others.

Labor, too, usually has its own point of view to urge before

CONTROL OF UTILITIES 537

the commission, and its opinions may not coincide with those of either the public or the utility. Labor is usually opposed to the introduction of devices that will reduce the amount of labor employed, and always in favor of reducing the number of hours of employment regardless of disproportionate costs that may be involved. The influence of labor, organized as well as unorganized, is always large with local officials, and not infrequently with state authorities.

In still other respects the utility is at an advantage before the regulatory authority. Usually, the utilities have been more ably represented in the legislative body that enacted the regulatory law than has the public. Though now espoused by the public service corporations as a preferable alternative to public ownership, public regulation has not had the genuine support of such corporations, and the regulatory laws enacted will be the least stringent that can be secured. From this favorable starting point, the utilities appear before the commission in the person of the most able legal and technical representatives that can be secured. A city sometimes has able counsel; the utility always has. Further, the representatives of the utilities appear with all available data to support their contentions; the representatives of the city appear with such facts as have been pried out of reluctant informants, with half truths instead of whole truths, and with superficial enlightenment instead of ready familiarity with the intricacies of public utility ownership and operations.

But, assuming fair legislation fairly applied, there will remain technical problems of magnitude before a rate can be established that will give a reasonable return upon a fair valuation.[1] What is a fair value? What is a reasonable return? What rate or rates shall be applied to produce that return?

Determining a fair value as a "rate base" involves translating the tangible and intangible assets of the corporation into terms of dollars so equitably that it cannot be maintained successfully that any property has been taken without compensation. The capital stock and bonds outstanding of a utility are not a satisfactory evidence of fair value. In private corporations, not subject to serious public control, there is little connection between securities and value; in a public utility some connection may exist, but not

[1] Some utility operators will deny the right of the public to establish a "rate base," insisting that the reasonableness of rates is determined by comparison with the rates in other cities. They would permit dividend rates to be regulated, any surplus earnings to be reinvested in plant.

538   PRACTICE OF MUNICIPAL ADMINISTRATION

CHAP.
XXX

necessarily so. Enough has been said already in connection with the subject of franchises to indicate the methods of inflation employed by fortunately a decreasing number of utilities. On the other hand, the actual assets of many utilities exceed outstanding securities. Securities are a concomitant of assets, not assets a concomitant of securities. To rule otherwise, results in injustice either to the public or to the utility.

Franchise values

Should a city acquire a utility that is operating under a franchise, that franchise has a value that must be purchased, unless otherwise specified in the grant itself, or unless the grant is in the nature of an indeterminate permit. The public has sold or given away the right to collect certain charges for service, and it must pay for that right when it reacquires it. Adequate regulation of rates, however, implies the lack of any right in the company to establish a rate under a franchise. If such a right exists, there are no grounds for rate regulation, unless the rate is too low. If the company has no right to fix rates, or has voluntarily surrendered such a right, there are no grounds for considering the value of the franchise in rate regulation. To value a franchise in rate regulation is to reason in a circle. The value of a franchise is the capitalization of the potential earnings possible under its terms, regardless of the physical equipment essential to those earnings. To capitalize such an intangible asset is to authorize the company to go ahead and collect a rate it is legally authorized to collect already, which is nonsense. This does not mean that franchises do not have values under certain conditions, but only that values are not determined by potential earnings. A corporation, subject to regulation, may own franchises for which it paid actual cash, or its equivalent, to a city. When such payments are actual, and were made in good faith, they represent cash actually invested in the property, and become part of the value of the corporation.

"Going value"

When an individual or a corporation starts in business, there is a construction period during which there are no returns. Money cannot be invested one day and be found represented the next by a fully constructed and paying street railway or gas plant. After the holders of stocks and bonds have paid in their cash, a long period may elapse before construction is completed and operations undertaken. In the meantime, interest must be paid on bonds; and the stock must go without dividends. The absence of earnings during the construction period are as much a cost of constructing the utility as is the cost of rails and generators, and should be so included as a part of "going value." It has been urged in some quarters that losses in operation after construction should be capitalized as "going value," but this position is seldom sustained before commissions or the courts.

CHAP. XXX

Ordinarily, a private business is not established by merely manufacturing or purchasing a stock of goods and opening the doors for business. Customers must be had, and they are secured only by diligent effort. Once secured, these customers become an established clientele, which, with proper management, can be expected to continue. They constitute the good will of the private business and really determine its earnings. Frequently this good will is a much more valuable asset than the goods on the shelves or in the warerooms.

Good will

Can a public utility have good will of this character, such as must be considered as an asset of the corporation in determining fair value? It cannot. By definition, a public utility is a monopoly. Citizens must buy its product whether they like it or not, and no matter what its name may be; its clientele comes through no unusual act of its own, but by natural economic law. To create a value out of this compulsory patronage is to capitalize the monopolistic character of the utility as is done when the potential earnings of a franchise are capitalized.

There are other items of intangible value to be considered, such as the capitalization of unusual losses, expenses incident to securing franchises, unusual legal expenses, etc., but they are incidental as compared with the items of franchise value and good will, the correct treatment of which is essential to proper rate making. The conclusions as given with respect to these two items are those followed by substantially all regulatory authorities.[1]

Other intangible values

With the question of intangibles decided, the regulatory authority is confronted with the task of determining the fair value of the physical assets belonging to the utility.[2] Physical assets can

Determination of physical value

[1] Prof. Henry E. Riggs of the University of Michigan, a well known utility specialist, comments: "I think you have rather over-emphasized this element of intangibles. In general very little is getting into modern valuations on this ground."
[2] The most important treatise on the subject of valuation is possibly the "Final Report of the Special Committee of the American Society of Civil Engineers to Formulate Principles and Methods of Valuation for Railroads and Other Public Utilities," *Transactions of the Am. Soc. Civil Engs.*, LXXXI, 1311-1620. See also earlier citations, and H. H. Hartman, *Fair Value* (Houghton Mifflin, 1920); C. E. Grunksy, *Valuation, Depreciation and the*

be inventoried. Agents of the commission can enumerate lands, buildings, ties, rails, generators, cars, and other items used in utility service. The accuracy of such enumeration is in the realm of facts and can be agreed upon by all parties to a controversy. Agents can also estimate the extent to which such properties are depreciated at the time the enumeration is made, such depreciation to be deducted to determine present value. Inventorying and estimating can, of course, be over done. Excessive detail means excessive cost, and may add nothing to the real facts of the case. "Valuation is not an exact science, it is somebody's estimate, and the greater the volume of detail, the greater the likelihood of error."[1] The less detailed inventories and estimates frequently check accurately with those of a more detailed character.

But with the inventory of physical properties at hand, what values shall be assigned to each item—its original cost, its cost of reproduction at present prices, or its cost at some average figure taken over a period of years? Public utility experts, public utility commissions, and the courts have adopted no uniform practice, necessary as uniform standards are to the success of utility regulation. It must be remembered that practically every utility now in operation in any important city had its origin at a time when the price scale was considerably lower than now exists, and additions have been made at constantly increasing costs. Sometimes large profits have been "plowed in" by reinvestment in additional assets,[2] or are concealed as depreciation reserves.[3] When a private citizen owns a piece of property that has increased in value, either on account of a rise in cost of construction or for other reasons, he is sometimes permitted by the law of supply and demand to receive a return upon the new value. On this theory, a public utility should be allowed to earn on its cost were the plant replaced at present prices. But a public utility is not a private individual. Utilities have been subject to some sort of regulation almost since their beginnings. They have enjoyed certain rights

Rate Base (Wiley, 1916); H. Barker, *Public Utility Rates* (McGraw, 1917); H. V. Hayes, *Public Utilities, Their Fair Present Value and Return* (Van Nostrand, 1915); W. G. Raymond, *What Is Fair?* (Wiley, 1918). For an economic discussion, see John R. Commons, *Legal Foundations of Capitalism* (Macmillan, 1924).

[1] Professor Henry E. Riggs. See also the discussion of Justice Brandeis in the Missouri telephone case, footnote p. 541.

[2] See discussion of "plowed in" earnings, p. 529.

[3] Excessive depreciation reserves are severely criticized by some utility specialists. Without doubt the treatment of depreciation requires utmost care both in purchasing and regulating utilities.

CONTROL OF UTILITIES 541

which do not appertain to private industry. Once rendering service, they are ordinarily permitted to continue service at a rate sufficient to give them a fair return. Under these circumstances, it is at least a debatable question whether an appreciated value that comes through no efforts of their own should be allowed to redound to their benefit.

Some experts, particularly those with a leaning toward municipal interests, have maintained that the earnings of utilities should be based on the absolute cost of the plant to the company, less depreciation.[1] The United States Supreme Court holds that these earnings must be a fair return upon the reasonable value of the property at the time it is being used by the public. Regulatory authorities have not agreed as to the method of appraisal to be used, but there is a leaning among the commissions toward utilizing the actual cost of the property. Many appraisals are substantially a compromise between the two methods.[2]

The matter of plowed-in surpluses for the present is largely academic. "Possession is nine points in law," and usually the public has so many more possible points to maintain in rate cases that it is content to let bygones be bygones and not contest the right to assets not represented by initial investment.

One of the questions that will be discussed hotly in every important rate case is depreciation, and the amount that values shall be reduced because of it. It would seem that no one could very well deny that "things made by the hands of man deteriorate with age and use";[3] yet such denial has been entered, to all intents and purposes, in many valuation cases, and no subject having to do with valuations is so confused by intellectual dishonesty and downright stupidity.

Depreciation may be defined as the reduction in the value of a

CHAP. XXX

Depreciation

Definition of depreciation

---

[1] This accounts for the wide range of values that are set when a rate case is considered. For example, in the recent Denver Tramway Case, the minimum value of the railway less depreciation was placed at about $7,200,000. The court allowed a value of $23,514,769. In the Kansas City Railway case the values ranged from $7,800,000 to $50,000,000, and the property subsequently sold at auction for $8,000,000. It is difficult to reconcile such disparity until one understands the differences in fundamental theory governing the appraisals.

[2] For an illuminating discussion on the fixing of value, see the opinion of Justice Brandeis in the State of Missouri *ex rel.* Southwestern Bell Telephone Co. *vs.* Public Service Commission of Missouri (May 21, 1923). Also Edwin C. Goddard, "Fair Value of Public Utilities," *Michigan Law Review*, XXII (May and June, 1924).

[3] Delos F. Wilcox, *Depreciation in Public Utilities* (National Municipal League, 1925). This monograph is a valuable discussion of the question of depreciation on the "elapsed life" theory.

542   PRACTICE OF MUNICIPAL ADMINISTRATION

CHAP. XXX

property due to wear and tear, age, physical decay, inadequacy, obsolescence, or supersession, *not made good by maintenance*. The wearing out of a plant is an element in the cost of operation just as much as is the cost of fuel or labor, although the payment of the cost may be deferred for a long period, perhaps many years. If this cost is not met in some manner it means that eventually the plant will be worn out, nothing will have been set aside to replace it, and the outstanding stocks and bonds will be represented by no values; it means that the current operating statements will understate the total cost of operation, and that the periodic balance sheets will evidence assets that do not exist.

Reduction in value because of depreciation

It is common practice to deduct depreciation in any determination of utility values for purposes of acquisition or rate making. This usage has not been conceded by the utilities without a struggle; they have contended that the setting aside of a depreciation fund has not been required by law, and that to penalize them for acts not contrary to their rights "would seem of doubtful morality to say the least."[1] This point of view has not been sustained by the courts, and the Supreme Court of the United States has held that a utility must exact sufficient returns to keep its investment unimpaired, and if it fails to do so the fault is its own.[2] It would appear that if the presence of current depreciation could be accepted, the presence of accrued depreciation would follow as a corollary. And if a correct charge for current depreciation is established, it should follow that the accumulation of these charges over a period of years, and not offset by maintenance, would represent the accrued depreciation.[3] But this corollary is not conceded by many utility experts, and it is the principal cause of the wide variations in the values that may be presented for the same utility.

Two methods of calculating depreciation

The difference in the two theories of depreciation turns on the phrase "not made good by maintenance," and experts adopt either the elapsed life or the impairment of investment theory.

The elapsed life method

The elapsed life method of calculation assumes that every item used in public utility operation has a calculable period of life, at the end of which time it must be replaced. This period of life

---

[1] James E. Allison, Chief Engineer of the St. Louis Public Service Commission, quoted *in extenso* by Wilcox, *op. cit.*, 36. Occasionally depreciation is neglected in order to maintain dividends.
[2] Knoxville *vs.* Knoxville Water Company, 212 U. S. 1.
[3] Dr. Milo R. Maltbie has referred to current and accrued depreciation as "Siamese twins," the one not existing without the other.

CONTROL OF UTILITIES 543

can be estimated with some degree of accuracy, the rates of depreciation varying only slightly from time to time with the actual life of units. In the same manner, but with some less accuracy, provision may be made for obsolescence,[1] the depreciation that occurs because an asset ceases to be useful, although it may be still in good physical condition. It is maintained that this deterioration goes on accumulating even though the property is maintained in good condition and gives highly satisfactory service; that rails, cars, and generators may be kept in repair and do good work, yet in spite of the attention given them must be replaced at the end of some period to be calculated with reasonable accuracy. Therefore, in calculating the ravages of depreciation, experts of this school will divide the calculable period of life of each unit into the period it has been in use, and conclude that the resulting fraction of useful life is past. Of course, the calculable period of life depends to an extent upon the character of current maintenance given, and allowance must or at least should be made accordingly.

CHAP. XXX

Experts of the impairment of investment school hold that the elapsed life plan is highly theoretical and should have no place in utility valuation.[2] It is argued that the amount of depreciation depends upon the character of use, the extent of use, and the amount and quality of maintenance, as well as obsolescence, and the general age of the property. Both the elapsed life and the impairment of investment group are in entire accord on this statement. The disagreement arises in the method of its application. The elapsed life adherents urge that, considering all these qualifying conditions, reasonably correct life tables can and must be made. The impairment of investment group holds that every utility is being maintained constantly in a certain physical condition through replacements from maintenance, and that this degree

The impairment of investment method

---

[1] "Changes in the arts, due to the versatility of the human mind in the face of need, municipal requirements maturing as the political and civic exigencies of the community mature, the overmastering influence of economic revolutions, the shifting tides of population and industry,—all these lie concealed behind the drawn curtains of the future, and with them are hidden the ways and times of obsolescence." Wilcox, *op. cit.*, 7.

[2] "... the use of the so-called life tables is the most extreme form of hypothesis, and no weight has been given to any estimates based on assumed life. *Report of the Arbitrators in the Proceedings to Determine the Value of the "Day to Day" Lines Purchased by the City of Detroit from the Detroit United Railways, 1921.* "You want to know if you can accurately foretell the lives (of units of property)? ... I think you could do that about as well as you would guess how fast different birds can fly." S. Z. Mitchell, President, Electric Bond and Share Co.

544   PRACTICE OF MUNICIPAL ADMINISTRATION

of physical condition can be determined best by careful observation of the property and equipment taken as a unit capable of producing service.

If the life tables are correct and the observations are correct—and possibly both are guesses—the methods should produce the same conclusions with respect to the amount of depreciation from a "new" condition. The disparity arises because of the inclination of the observation group to correlate closely operating condition and physical condition, and to maintain that the degree of operating condition should represent the approximate degree of physical condition. Under this plan a utility having a 100 percent operating condition would have a physical condition of say about 85 percent of new, 15 percent representing the degree of depreciation.[1] The opposing interests urge that a utility might have a 100 percent operating condition and a physical condition gravitating downward to fifty percent.

The elapsed-life school urge that the issues at stake between these two methods are large. They estimate that the difference in the amount of accrued depreciation for all of the utilities in the country as calculated on the two plans is twenty-five percent of cost new. There are probably fifteen billion dollars invested in utilities; hence the amount of depreciation involved is between three and four billion dollars, and the amount of possible return to be allowed is between two hundred and three hundred million dollars.[2] On the other hand, the opponents state that if a utility were renewed as new it would be no better, no safer, no more valuable than now, and that ten or twenty years hence it will be in the same condition as now.

A layman might summarize the discussion in this fashion: One group holds that utilities are so large and contain so many different operating units, that all losses due to wear and obsolescence can and should be made up from current maintenance, and that the public is not concerned with the small resulting variation between condition new and an excellent operating condition; the other group maintains that depreciation can never be met adequately from current maintenance, that the difference can be

[1] Professor Henry E. Riggs states: "The impairment of investment theory says that actual loss of capacity for service, or failure to keep up a proper standard for service is depreciation, measurable by the full amount of money that the management would be economically justified in spending to restore a proper condition,—not a hypothetical 'new' condition, but to maximum service condition."

[2] Wilcox, *op. cit.*, 40.

CONTROL OF UTILITIES 545

calculated on age-life tables, and that the variation of condition new from excellent operating condition is large and important.[1] Perhaps the type and size of utility has something to do with the discussion, and wear and obsolescence can easily be made good from maintenance in one instance and not in another.[2] And perhaps all maintenance should be made from depreciation reserves, the unexpended balance representing accrued depreciation.

Under either theory it is admitted that when a new property is placed in operation, and is properly maintained, it gradually depreciates in value to a certain stabilized point dictated by operating necessity, at which point it is continued through current maintenance. The property can never be maintained at its original value. Therefore, if depreciation reserves are accumulated they are used for three purposes—first, to make good the loss in investment between cost new and the point of stabilization; second, to care for current loss after the point of stabilization is reached, and which may be merged properly with maintenance; and third, to care for unusual items of current maintenance, *i.e.*, to stabilize operating expense. This last is only a phase of the second purpose, and neither one has anything to do with accrued depreciation.[3]

The use that should be made of depreciation reserves is dictated by the purposes for which they are accumulated. After the point of stabilization is reached by a property, depreciation becomes an element of maintenance, and the depreciation fund may be expended for such purpose. Funds for accrued depreciation may

[1] See Wilcox, *op. cit.*, and Henry E. Riggs, *Depreciation of Public Utility Properties* (McGraw-Hill, 1922).

[2] "A continental railroad system with its power plants cut into hundreds or thousands of units, having absolutely no major unit, can approximate the condition which Judge Ransom holds out as ideal—namely, the charging to each year's expenses of such substitutions or betterments as will maintain the value and operating efficiency of the plant. An electric power company may find itself (and most of them have already found themselves) in circumstances where items up to ten or fifteen percent of total plant value ought to be retired in a single year. A gas company is betwixt-and-between in such matters, and the telephone companies are clearly at the opposite end of the list from the railroads, and telephone methods are no more suitable for an electric light and power company than are the methods of the railroads, for the converse reason"—Alex Dow, *Some Ethical Aspects of Replacement Reserves* (Association of Edison Illuminating Companies, 1925), 55. This pamphlet contains a reply to Mr. Dow's position by Mr. William Ransom, rate counsel for the New York Edison Co., etc., and constitutes an interesting and valuable discussion of the subject.

[3] Professor E. Riggs states: "On small properties it (depreciation reserve) is quite essential as it is the only way in which recurring replacements can be spread uniformly. On large companies it is not only unnecessary, but I think of very questionable public policy."

be returned to the investors in the form of special dividends representing amounts of capital no longer invested in the plant, or may be invested in extensions and betterments, sufficient to preserve the original investments. Because of the expanding requirements of most utilities, the latter method is the more prevalent. In some private industries, particularly mining, the former method is used, such dividends representing depletion of capital.

The measure of depreciation

Depreciation is measured by the difference between the original cost of a unit of property and its scrap or salvage value, the accumulated depreciation fund being sufficient to return to the investor the original investment. This is the usual position of utility experts, and is based on the theory that a utility is worth what it actually cost, and not what it would cost to reproduce it at current prices.[1] If the new unit costs more than the replaced one, the increase is treated as an addition to capital invested. Certain authorities, however, leaning towards the theory that the cost of reproduction should be the fair value of a utility, hold that sufficient depreciation reserves should be accumulated to replace the depreciated unit at its current cost.[2]

Straight line vs. sinking fund accumulations

Depreciation charges are generally accumulated on either the straight-line or sinking fund plan. The straight-line plan involves dividing the original cost of a unit by its life expectancy, and setting aside the resulting fraction of the total each year. The use of this method, which is customary, is predicated upon the current investment of accrued depreciation reserves in new assets or in their return to the investor. The sinking fund plan contemplates setting aside in a sinking fund an amount each year which, with accumulated earnings, will equal the cost of the depreciated unit at the end of its calculated life. By this method the utility retains as an asset of the company all accrued depreciation in the form of sinking fund securities. The current earnings of the corporation must be sufficient to pay a reasonable return to the investor on both physical and sinking fund assets during this period of accumulation. The sinking fund method is complicated and has no particular merit over the straight-line plan.

[1] "It is not the theory of a renewal reserve that it should provide the full cost of a physical replacement, when that cost is greater than the original cost less salvage value of the unit replaced. If the new unit costs more than the old one, the difference is not a replacement of capital but an addition to capital, even though the new physical unit may not be intrinsically any more valuable than the old one was." Wilcox, *op. cit.*, 30.

[2] *Depreciation Requirement of the San Francisco Municipal Railway* (San Francisco Bureau of Governmental Research, 1925).

CONTROL OF UTILITIES 547

Assuming that the amount of depreciation and the other questions incidental to fair value have been agreed upon in a rate-making case, the problem of reasonable return still remains. With the fair value definitely decided, what constitutes a reasonable return upon money invested in a public utility? The yearly cost of money ranges anywhere from three percent when bought by the United States government with tax exempt bonds to twenty-four percent or more, when bought with a chattel mortgage as security. Somewhere within this range is a fair rate for utility investments, the exact rate being determined by the current cost of money, security of investment, probability of continuing return, and possibilities of speculative reward. Regulatory authorities must provide a rate of return that will attract capital in competition with other investments. A utility cannot meet expanding service requirements unless it can secure new investments, and it is foolhardy to fix a rate that will not command that investment. A utility is a natural monopoly and has a degree of security that does not adhere to competitive private industry. But that security is not absolute. Whole utilities have suddenly become obsolete, as did the cable system of street railways, as interurban electric railways are doing, and as electric street railways may do. The security of the return is in about the same degree as the security of the investment. Since the beginning of the period of regulated rates the possibilities of speculative enhancement of values have been small.

In the last analysis, the rate of return on invested capital must be determined by the courts. These resulting decisions have covered a wide range of years, but have specified a relatively narrow range of returns. A reasonable return is understood to be between six percent and eight percent dependent upon local conditions and the need of the utility for additional capital. Probably seven percent could be considered as average.

It is one thing to determine fair value and reasonable rate of return, and quite another to specify the proper rates to produce that return. Aside from specifying certain general principles in rate making, the regulatory authorities ordinarily leave the working out of detailed rates to the utilities themselves, subject to final approval by the commission. These detailed rates involve some fine concepts of abstract justice, since the rule of all the traffic will bear has been discarded. Present-day practice in rate making is to apportion the income from operations over the different

548 PRACTICE OF MUNICIPAL ADMINISTRATION

CHAP. XXX

classes of consumers on an equitable basis. Such apportionment involves the fixing of flexible rates which will charge each class of consumer approximately what it costs to serve them. Such scheduling of charges is difficult in some utilities, and is not always used in those to which it can be applied.

Readiness to serve

Every customer of a utility, no matter how small his consumption of service may be, necessitates a certain fixed expense on the part of the utility for the costs of capital invested in facilities, the reading of the water, gas, or electric meters, and accounting and other record keeping. The utility incurs these expenses in order to be ready to serve the consumer who has indicated a desire for service. It is only fair that the customer should pay enough to cover this cost, whether or not he avails himself of the service. This readiness to serve is covered by a minimum periodic charge for each meter installed. Occasionally all service is charged at regular rates in addition to the minimum charge, but it is more usual to allow this minimum to apply against consumption.

Overhead expense

It is axiomatic in industry that the more units of output, the less the cost per unit. Not only is large-scale production more economical because of the lower direct costs of manufacturing, but the fixed charges and expenses of management are distributed over a larger output. This conclusion holds true of water, gas, and electric production, but not of telephone services, because the installation of each new telephone increases the possible service to the customer and correspondingly increases the cost of service, in excess of any resulting unit decrease in overhead expense. Large-scale production is made possible by large-scale consumption, and it is only reasonable that these large consumers should profit proportionately, and no more, by the reduction in cost that they make possible. Unfortunately, these large consumers are relatively few, and their voice in rate-fixing is not always as influential as are the voices of the large number of small consumers.[1] Sometimes the rates on large consumption are fixed so high as to induce the production of the service by the private consumer.

Peak load and rates

In dealing with the subject of public lighting some consideration has already been given to the peak load of utilities and the additional equipment made necessary by that load.[2] Every utility must provide facilities to supply the maximum demand for its

---

[1] See Charles M. Fassett, "Electric Rates and Rate Making," *The American City*, XXV (August and September, 1921).

[2] Chap. XXIX.

CONTROL OF UTILITIES 549

service, even though that demand may prevail for only a few hours each day. This peak load is so marked in the electric power industry that it is practical to differentiate between ordinary users and those who consume power at other times. These off-time consumers, particularly industries, may materially reduce the cost per unit of production, and special rates are usually given in consequence. Daytime domestic consumption of electricity is also stimulated through the use of domestic labor-savings devices. In a few cities, separate rates are given for such use, and separate meters provided. However, this distinction has not proven practicable. Such special rates must be further adjusted to provide for intermittent users of service. In these cases the utility must increase its facilities for a stand-by service, *i.e.*, be ready to provide service when required, and this readiness must be charged for.

<small>CHAP. XXX</small>

<small>Stand-by service</small>

Ideal billing to the consumer for the service should be based on monthly meter readings and present the following data: the new reading, the last old reading, the subtraction, the rate, the discount for prompt payment and the amount due. The utility and the consumer are benefited by bills that can be read and understood by both. Service should be discontinued promptly upon failure to pay undisputed charges. With municipally owned utilities, the charge can be made a lien against the property served exactly as are delinquent taxes and special assessments. With privately owned utilities, an initial deposit is frequently required of those who are not owners of real estate.

<small>Billing and collection</small>

A further important problem of utility regulation has to do with labor. Wages always constitute a large proportion of production costs, and are especially large in street railway service. The policy of the utility toward its employees concerns the consumer in two respects; first, the rate of compensation and the hours worked directly modify the rates that must be paid for service; second, a strike of employees interrupts service that is essential to the general welfare. Therefore, shall the labor problems of a utility be left to the solution of the company and its employees, or shall the regulatory authority attempt to prescribe the hours and pay of labor, and attempt to prevent strikes? The former course has been adopted generally, inconsistent with adequate regulation as it may appear. Many persons hold, and the feeling is growing, that just as a utility stands in an unusual relationship to the public, so that it will have its charges prescribed and will not be allowed to discontinue service, so persons

<small>Labor problems</small>

550 PRACTICE OF MUNICIPAL ADMINISTRATION

The industrial court

who choose to be employed by a utility must consent to have their compensation regulated and must not be allowed to endanger the public by striking. It is almost unnecessary to say that this position is vigorously opposed by labor, although it seems consistent with common sense and public necessity.[1]

The only definite recognition that the conflicting elements in the operation of public utilities have a public character, and involving an attempt to determine their relationship by judicial action, is found in the legislation establishing the Kansas Court of Industrial Relations.[2] This legislation provided for an industrial board to hear all disputes between capital and labor, and specified that a strike or lockout might not be ordered until the grounds for such a conflict had been heard by the court and a decree entered. After such decree, laborers might cease work as individuals, but an actual strike was made illegal. The act applied to disputes in private industry as well as public utilities, and was not sustained in the courts. Had the test been restricted to utilities, perhaps another conclusion would have resulted.

The proposal has sufficient merit to warrant a statement of the issue involved. This issue was propounded in a debate between Henry J. Allen, then governor of Kansas, and father of the plan, and the late Samuel Gompers, then president of the American Federation of Labor, as follows: "When a dispute between capital and labor brings on a strike affecting the production or distribution of the necessities of life, thus threatening the public peace and impairing public health, has the public any right in such a controversy, or is it a private war between capital and labor?"

Ordinarily when capital and labor quarrel, the public suffers and pays the costs involved, while it has no part in bringing on the fight or in deciding the struggle. Under these circumstances, it is maintained that the public may assert a right to share in the settlement, for reasons already stated. The extreme defenders of trade unionism counter that the prevention of the right to strike is a form of industrial slavery; and that in the long run, the interests of the public and of labor are identical. Accordingly, the

[1] For a clear discussion of the right to strike, see Delos F. Wilcox, *Analysis of the Electric Railway Problem* (Grand Rapids, 1921), 341-563.

[2] This legislation will be found in Laws of 1920, Chap. 29. The important features of the act were found unconstitutional in Wolff *vs.* Court of Industrial Relations, *1925 Supreme Court Advance Opinions* (May, 1925), 499.

public should bear with a good grace the inconveniences and suffering incident to the struggles of labor and capital.[1]

The Plumb plan is a different method of settlement that is concerned directly with the interests of the general public as well as with those of labor, and aims to harmonize the conflicting elements of capital, labor, and consumer.[2]

The plan is so named for the late Glenn E. Plumb, who proposed the plan while special attorney for the railroad brotherhoods. The plan proposes to increase the compensation and reduce the hours of labor, and at the same time to give labor a share in the control of industry and in the responsibility for maintaining production. It recognizes that there are definite limits upon the gains to labor that are to be had from reducing hours and raising money wages, and that additional gains must come from increased efficiency. The Plumb plan was proposed for railroad operation, but may be applied with equal force to the operation of any public utility. Under it capital, labor, and consumer would each have a voice in service, rates, and profits through membership on the board of directors of an industry or business. If efficiency of operation results in an unusually large return, it will be shared, not by capital alone as in unregulated industry, or by the consumer, as in a service-at-cost scheme, but by all three parties or elements concerned. Theoretical arguments are made both for and against this proposal, but to date the scheme has not been tried in America. As yet, therefore, these arguments have no conclusive weight; and the student can only look for some experiment to reveal the degree of practicability of the plan.[3]

---

[1] In addition to a large amount of periodical literature on the subject, reference should be made to Henry J. Allen, *The Party of the Third Part* (Harper, 1921).

[2] See Carl D. Thompson, *Public Ownership* (Crowell, 1925).

[3] A clear editorial on the Industrial Court and the Plumb Plan will be found in *The New Republic*, June 1, 1921, under the title of "The Kansas Challenge to Unionism."

CHAPTER XXXI

MUNICIPAL OWNERSHIP [1]

Municipal ownership an alternative to regulation

The advocates of municipal ownership insist that public regulation of utilities has been an abject failure, and that the only alternative is municipal ownership and operation. In support of this contention can unquestionably be cited numerous instances in which regulation has been unsuccessful on account of the incompetency of the regulatory authorities to deal with the complex problems of utility control. On the other hand, many instances can be cited in which public regulation has been both intelligent and honest, and has had results satisfactory to all interests concerned.

Is regulation a failure?

Regulation is a relatively new endeavor on the part of the public, and the principles upon which it rests are being slowly evolved. Illogical conclusions cannot long prevail, and it may be anticipated that sound principles will be developed and accepted, guiding the regulatory authorities in the determination of fair value and fair return, and facilitating a degree of technical control as yet unrealized. Public regulation is not yet an instrument for completely solving the many questions involved in the operation of public utilities, but it cannot properly be discarded, on that ground, in its present experimental stage. The arguments for municipal ownership and management must rest on surer ground.

Social policies underlying public ownership

Present-day obstacles to successful municipal operation of utilities are so great that its adoption as a general policy must originate in needs that cannot be met by the most successful regulation. Education, sewerage, and water supply—activities once conducted through private initiative—are now municipally owned and operated. This socialization has resulted, not because these services are more difficult to regulate than gas plants and street

---

[1] The student of public utility administration will be interested particularly in W. G. Raymond, *The Public and Its Utilities* (Wiley, 1925). This book covers in detail many of the subjects discussed in this chapter. See also L. R. Nash, *The Economics of Public Utilities* (McGraw-Hill, 1925); the *Journal of Land and Public Utility Economics* (quarterly); and the numerous citations throughout the chapter. For current questions of public utility operation, consult the trade journals in the various fields.

railways, but because public welfare calls for a universality of service not to be secured under private ownership. Practically every one in a city makes use of schools, and especially sewers and water supply, and it is highly desirable that they shall do so, even if such use must be secured by legal compulsion. Children are required to attend school; houses must be connected with sewers, and the use of wells and similar sources of domestic water supply is forbidden. Should social conditions become so changed—and who can say what modifications will take place?—that common welfare should require that every one make use of gas, telephones, and street railways, and that the city forbid other means of heating, communication, and transportation, then it may be anticipated that municipal ownership and operation will prevail in these fields, regardless of the advantages of public control and of the disadvantages of public ownership.

The words ownership and operation are coupled in speaking of the municipalization of utilities because genuine municipal ownership implies both ownership and operation. It has been suggested by some persons that all the benefits and none of the evils of public ownership could be secured by permitting the private operation of publicly owned utilities, just as it is sometimes suggested that the United States government should own the railways and leave their operation in private hands. This is really begging the question of utility control. The problems of municipalization arise mainly out of operation, not out of mere ownership. Cincinnati owns the Cincinnati Southern Railroad, and Philadelphia owns its gas plant; and both are leased to private corporations for operating purposes. But none of the problems of service, rates, and labor are solved by this mere circumstance. If benefits are to come from municipalization, they are to be benefits derived from municipal operation. Boston does not own the Boston Elevated Railway Company, and Detroit has guaranteed many millions of dollars of bonds privately issued by its street railway. But in both of these cases there is municipal operation, and practically all of the advantages and disadvantages of complete municipal ownership are present.

Municipal ownership has never had the vogue in American cities that it has had in Europe, and its extent varies greatly with different utilities.[1] The utility most frequently city owned

[1] See Chester C. Maxey, *An Outline of Municipal Government* (Doubleday, Page, 1924), 252-255; and W. B. Munro, *Municipal Government and Administration* (Macmillan, 1923), 419-421. For a more detailed discussion, see Carl D. Thompson, *Public Ownership* (Crowell, 1925).

554   PRACTICE OF MUNICIPAL ADMINISTRATION

CHAP.
XXXI

and operated is water supply. Electric lighting plants are by no means universally owned by the public, but are often so in smaller cities. In larger cities, municipally owned lighting plants are used exclusively for public lighting, but in the smaller communities they often sell power to private consumers.[1] The necessity for smaller cities and villages to enter the field of electric power production has been discussed in the chapter on public lighting. The movement has been facilitated by the public ownership of water works, of which electric current in some respects can be made a by-product. Recently the development of large scale production and distribution of electric energy from metropolitan centers has caused many public plants to discontinue. Only occasionally are gas plants [2] and street railways owned by the public.[3]

Practically no steps have been taken to municipalize telephone systems.[4] There is no urgent need in this direction, and an isolated publicly owned telephone system would be out of keeping with the national character of the utility. A municipality would scarcely be in a position to undertake the research work that has brought such marked improvements in telephone facilities, or to bargain with the parent corporation for the use of patented equipment. In fact, the payments made by local companies for leased and patented instruments, as well as the intercity long distance service, interfere with successful regulation by local and state authorities, and may eventually necessitate national control of the industry. A few unimportant heating plants are publicly owned.[5]

The arguments for and against the public ownership of util-

---

[1] More than 2,000 cities and villages in the United States own and operate lighting plants. For a list, see Carl D. Thompson, *Municipal Electric Light and Power Plants* (Public Ownership League of America, Chicago, 1922).

[2] There are municipally owned gas plants in Omaha, Richmond, Va., Duluth, Holyoke, Mass., and about forty smaller American cities. Philadelphia owns its gas plant but does not operate it. Hamilton, Ohio, owns its distribution system.

[3] Three important cities own their street railway systems, *i.e.*, Detroit, San Francisco, and Seattle. Municipal systems are also found in Ashtabula, O.; St. Petersburg, Fla.; Pekin, Ill.; Lincoln, Ill.; Fort Collins, Co., and several smaller communities. The New York subways are in part owned by the city, but leased to operating companies. The Boston street railways, except the subways, are privately owned, but are operated by the city. See *Public Ownership and Operation of Electric Railways* (Bulletin 56, American Electric Railway Association, December, 1925).

[4] Municipal systems are reported in Brookings, S. D.; Barnsville, Minn., and Galtry, Okla.

[5] Reported in Sabetha, Kan.; Newton, Mass.; Bloomington, Ind.; Brookings, S. D., and Cleveland, O.

ities have been presented at such length and in so many different mediums, and are so generally understood by even the casual student of public affairs, that it is unnecessary to restate them extensively.[1] As has been mentioned, the fundamental argument for municipal ownership is based upon public convenience and welfare. By owning and operating a utility the public can examine its problems from the point of view of its own interests, ignoring at least the idea of profits, and facing the utility problem as it affects the morals, health, and convenience of the public. For example, street car lines can be extended with a view to relieving downtown congestion, even though such extensions are operated at the expense of other branches of the same utility; water can be furnished to sparsely settled communities at the expense of the denser populations; and so on. Such treatment of the question is no doubt legitimate, just as public education in poor districts is supported increasingly by wealthier sections, because the public welfare is more important than abstract justice in taxation. Additional social arguments come from the inclination of cities to treat their employees more fairly than is customary with private corporations, and the growing antipathy against strikes on the part of municipal employees. This subject is discussed more fully in another place.[2]

On the economic side, it is urged that the much vaunted efficiency of American business men in private industry has been highly overrated, and that the average municipal activity is conducted with as great economy and effectiveness as is the average private business; that expert supervision can be secured by a city for less money than under private ownership, with a resulting saving in managerial salaries; and that the capital required by cities can be borrowed at a much lower rate of interest than by private persons. These combined economies, if realized, would be sufficient to make a decided reduction in the cost of services rendered.

Aside from the alleged and probably actual efficiency of private

[1] For a clear interesting statement of these arguments, see Munro, *op. cit.*, 421-441. Some of the most highly recommended works on the subject are Leonard Darwin, *Municipal Trade* (Dutton, 1907); Bernard Shaw, *Common Sense of Municipal Trading* (Lane, 1911); C. L. King, *The Regulation of Municipal Utilities* (Appleton, 1912); W. S. Murray, *Government Owned and Controlled Compared with Privately Owned and Regulated Electric Utilities* (National Electric Light Assoc., 1922); *Report of the Federal Electric Railways Commission* (Department of Commerce, 1920); and the numerous publications of the Public Ownership League, 1439 Unity Building, Chicago.

[2] See pp. 550 and 563.

business, and the daring of private capital that will venture into developments that public capital cannot enter, the principal arguments for private ownership with public control center around the assumed incompetency of public business.[1] To be sure, American city governments have increased their effectiveness to an amazing extent in the past decade. But as yet they can scarcely be selected as models of business efficiency. Ineffective operation of municipally owned utilities arises primarily from the appointment of incompetent persons to public positions, frequent changes in personnel, slipshod financial methods, and establishment of discriminating rates for service.

The political rather than business character of American city governments, and the use of public positions as rewards for political activity, regardless of the qualifications that the appointees may have, have become notorious. Privately owned utilities are not simon-pure in their employment policies, and may find ample room in their organizations for the relatives and friends of officers and prominent stockholders. Yet their first purpose remains profit-making operation and not the reward of favorites. Civil service has eliminated to some extent the selection of incompetents for minor positions in public service, but the technique of satisfactory appointment by merit is still undeveloped, and civil service selections are still manipulated for political ends.

The "labor turnover" in public employment is well known and furnishes one pertinent reason for the lack of effectiveness in public work. Some subordinates may be retained in service too long for public good, but because of the larger rewards in private service there is a constant incentive for the best men to leave. In the higher ranks the rewards are relatively small for the training and ability required, and the protection of the merit system is seldom provided.[2] It requires years of service to understand thoroughly the detailed operations of an important activity of a city government, and no private corporation would tolerate ousting

[1] Mr. Henry Steffens, Jr., Controller of the City of Detroit during the period of acquisition and initial operations of the municipal street railways, and who supervised the city's cases in the rate hearings on electricity, gas, and telephones, believes that, under regulation of rates based upon valuation, the utilities have no greater incentive to efficient operation than under public ownership.

[2] For example, in the decade 1916-25 the city of Detroit had five commissioners of public works, five commissioners of police, and five controllers, the average period of service being about two years. The managers of the city's utilities have had a more permanent tenure.

MUNICIPAL OWNERSHIP

an efficient management every two or three years, either for political reasons or because of inadequate compensation.

Financial legerdemain, or at least incomplete and inaccurate reporting, characterizes practically every municipally owned utility in the country. Proper allowances are seldom made for taxes, depreciation, services rendered to other departments in the form of electric current or water supplied, services rendered the utility for street widenings and other construction work made necessary by utility operations, or accounting, purchasing, and legal work done by other branches of the government.

Somewhat akin to financial juggling is the fixing of inadequate rates so that deficits in operation must be made up directly or indirectly from taxation, and the fixing of unscientific rates because of political expediency. Political influence can reach the management of a private utility only by indirect pressure brought to bear through the regulatory authorities, but it finds a direct affect when applied on the officers of a city. It is not unusual for municipal utility rates to be dictated by the demands of the voting public rather than by abstract justice, or even the less apparent best interests of the city.[1]

Dr. Delos F. Wilcox has formulated the practical prerequisites deemed necessary to the successful operation of utilities by a municipality. These are:[2] (1) the absolute exclusion of politics from the operation of municipal utilities; (2) continuity of intelligent and faithful service; (3) complete and carefully analyzed financial statements showing the true cost of construction and operation and the true revenues earned by the plant; and (4) a scientific schedule of charges calculated to produce sufficient revenues, and at the same time to distribute the burden of the cost of service among the consumers without unjust discrimination.

Much has been written concerning the success or failure of public ownership, and much that has been written is of no worth. Men, otherwise of honor and honesty, have put no restraint on their

---

[1] For example, the Cincinnati municipal water plant has one of the lowest minimum rates for water in the country—$1.20 quarterly for 1,000 cubic feet of water used through a five-eighths inch service, as compared with $4.00 in Philadelphia. Ordinarily this rate would decrease with increased consumption, but in Cincinnati political expediency has caused it to be otherwise. A factory using 1,200,000 cubic feet of water quarterly through a three-inch service would pay $1440 as compared with $523.50 in Philadelphia.

[2] *Financial and Administrative Preparation for Municipal Ownership*, an address before the National Public Ownership Conference, Chicago, 1917.

558 PRACTICE OF MUNICIPAL ADMINISTRATION

CHAP.
XXXI

enthusiasms and prejudices in extolling the advantages of municipal ownership or in decrying its disadvantages. The proponents have at least been inspired by an unselfish faith in what they believe to be a great cause; the opponents too often have been motivated by selfish interest. Neither has told the whole truth, nor is competent to tell it, since the truth is not available to tell.[1] The results of both private and public ownership have been cunningly concealed in a maze of intricate and false accounting. The facts, both at home and abroad, are so bound up in complex balance sheets and operating records, and in adjustments that must be made for comparative purposes, that the student is left about as much in the dark at the end of his studies as he was at the beginning.

A basis for conclusions

The administrator who is considering the desirability of public ownership in his own community must rest his case on certain more or less a priori conclusions. First, public ownership may be necessary in one city and not in another, in spite of its apparent success or failure as such results are usually judged. Public necessity may require public ownership regardless of other considerations. Franchises may have expired, and the public may have refused to renew them; no reasonable operating agreement with the utility may be obtainable; the utility may be unable to raise funds for imperative increases in equipment and service; or other circumstances may force public action, the wisdom of which would be otherwise debatable. Second, public ownership may be a success in one city and not in another, and may be a success with respect to one utility and not with another in the same city. Certain city governments operate with a high degree of efficiency, while others do not; although there are available no definite criteria of effectiveness by which absolute judgments can be made. However, a city administration sodden with politics and corruption obviously cannot be trusted with the acquisition and management of a utility, when a reasonably clean city administration can be. Third, certain legal restrictions will hamper the acquisition and operation of utilities in one city and not in another, and such restrictions are much more prevalent in America than abroad. Fourth, public opinion may not be ready for certain ventures in public ownership, although it is reconciled to others. The public

[1] Though out of date, the outstanding study of the results of municipal ownership has been the report on *Municipal and Private Operation of Public Utilities*, prepared and published by the National Civic Federation (3 vols., 1907). Other references have been previously cited.

may insist that one utility shall be well managed, while showing indifference to other activities; or, it may consider one utility well managed, and be highly critical of another. A large body of public opinion not convinced of the necessity or desirability of public ownership will mean difficulties for the administrator, regardless of results produced.¹ Fifth, irrespective of results, the proponents of public ownership will make statements difficult to substantiate, and the opponents will criticize and villify with little regard to facts.² However, if responsible for the operation of a publicly owned utility, the administrator will be more interested in certain specific problems that confront him than in theoretical or implied allegations with respect to success or failure.

Public ownership of utilities would have advanced farther in the United States were it not for legal obstacles that repeatedly thwart the public will. Cities operate under authority delegated by the state, and their powers are enumerated precisely. Members of a state legislature from rural communities, unfamiliar with the problems that beset urban life, are reluctant to permit the municipalities to go adventuring into "socialistic" experiments. When authority to acquire and operate utilities is granted, it is frequently so hedged about with restrictions as to be practically inoperative.

One of the most serious of these restrictions relates to the incurring of public debt. The most wide-sweeping powers with respect to municipal enterprises are useless when a city cannot bond itself sufficiently to permit the exercise of them. And the use of complete authority with respect to both acquisition and the incurrence of debt may be estopped by the laws of a state a thousand miles away. Bonds authorized must be sold, and the usual market for bonds in sufficiently large quantities to purchase a public utility is found in the eastern states. These states so rigidly control the legal investments of their public and semi-public institutions as to constitute an effective bar to the rapid or extensive municipal ownership in cities in other parts of the country.³

¹ In Detroit the operations of the municipally owned water plant are seldom criticized by the public, while the operations of the municipally owned street railways are under constant fire.
² A further example of this condition may be taken from the Detroit Street Railways. The writer by no means approves of all the accounting methods employed and reports made by the city in connection with this activity, but the statements so secured are far nearer the truth than the unsupported allegations of deficits and operating losses spread broadcast over the country.
³ The banking laws of New York State, a principal market for city bonds, provides that savings banks may not buy the bonds of a city whose net debt

560   PRACTICE OF MUNICIPAL ADMINISTRATION

CHAP. XXXI

Difficulties of acquiring franchises

A further restriction is found in the safeguards thrown about private property by the constitution of the United States, as well as by the constitutions of the states. A franchise is property; once granted by a city, it cannot be reacquired except by the payment of its value, in addition to what must be paid for the physical property. Fortunately, many franchises granted years ago are now expiring, in whole or in part, and the physical properties can be acquired for what they are worth.

Methods of financing public ownership

Having covered the hurdle of acquisition, the administration is faced with the task of financing the purchase. The ordinary method is the issuance of public utility bonds, which are really general city bonds secured to the investor by the faith and credit of the city. If bonds in sufficient amount can be issued legally they have the same marketability as other city bonds. Care must be taken, however, that the total city debt is not so great as to make the bonds of the city illegal investments for savings banks and other financial institutions in the states in which the issues are to be marketed. This restriction is of little moment to smaller cities with a limited debt and a local market for city securities. But it is an effective bar to the complete municipalization of utilities by larger cities with large debts, and whose bonds have a limited local market.

Public utility bonds

Guarantee of private bonds

The financial arrangements made with the utility purchased may have an influence on the methods of financing. The bond holders of the company may agree to the guaranteeing of these bonds by the city as an alternative to having them called in and paid, the amount of bonds guaranteed being applied on the purchase price.[1] This procedure is, of course, merely a substitute for the issuance of city securities, but is advantageous under certain circumstances. Or it may be possible to buy a utility on a purchase contract with only a small initial payment, the utility itself being the security for the contract. Such a contract is not computed as a part of the city debt, since the faith and credit of the city are not involved, and it eliminates the necessity of utilizing the city's bonding authority.[2]

Purchase contract

exceeds seven percent of its assessed valuation. In calculating net debt, water works bonds are not included, but no other public utility issues are so favored.

[1] This course was followed by Bay City, Mich., in the acquisition of a water system.

[2] The urban portion of the Detroit United Railways was purchased by the city of Detroit for $19,850,000. Only $2,770,000 was paid in cash, the balance of $17,080,000 being in the form of a purchase contract, $500,000

MUNICIPAL OWNERSHIP 561

Somewhat similar to the purchase contract plan is the scheme of issuing mortgage bonds. Such bonds are issued by, but place no obligation upon, a city, being secured by a lien upon the property and earnings of the utility for which they are issued. Such bonds may be issued to any amount, the only restriction being the very practical one of marketability. Accompanying such an issue of bonds must be a mortgage and a conditional franchise stating the terms upon which the bondholders may operate the utility in the event of foreclosure. The use of such bonds has been limited.¹ The interest rate must be relatively high, since the security of principal is no better than if the utility were owned privately. Probably the question of a suitable conditional franchise will also be a stumbling block to their use.

CHAP. XXXI

Mortgage bonds

The extensive use of special assessments has been proposed as a means of financing public utility construction, particularly in connection with street railways and rapid transit. The reasons for the assessment of benefits in rapid transit construction are apparent. The building of rapid transit lines into undeveloped territory creates enormous values that benefit only the real estate owner, except as the city may receive back a small portion in property taxes on increased assessments. The public, whose use of this real estate creates the new values, pays not only for the transportation system that makes that use possible, but for the increased values as well. If a transportation system is to make a limited number of real estate owners wealthy, it seems only fair that a substantial portion of the cost of that system should be paid by them. The law under which the New York City subways are constructed permits the assessment of benefits, but no use has been made of this authority.²

Special assessments

The most ambitious proposals for financing transportation in

being payable semi-annually for ten years, and a sinking fund of $7,580,000 being created to make the final payment.
¹ Provision is made for the issuance of mortgage bonds in connection with the financing of both the Detroit street railways, and the proposed rapid transit system, but none have been issued. Los Angeles has authorized the issue of such bonds in connection with municipal housing projects.
² The detailed proposals of the Detroit Rapid Transit Commission will be found in *Proposed Financial Plan for a Rapid Transit System for the City of Detroit*, published by the Rapid Transit Commission, November 27, 1923, the proposals being legalized by Act 224 of the Public Acts of Michigan for 1925, and Chapter XXIV of the City Charter. The New York City authorization will be found in the *Rapid Transit Act of 1891 as Amended*. The financial benefits accruing from rapid transit construction in New York are discussed in *Building of Rapid Transit Lines in New York City by Assessment Upon Property Benefited*, prepared by the City Club of New York, in 1908.

562 PRACTICE OF MUNICIPAL ADMINISTRATION

CHAP. XXXI

part by the assessment of benefits are found in the rapid transit plans of Detroit. Legislation has been secured permitting the rapid transit authorities to build a rapid transit system, seventeen percent of the cost to be paid by the city at large, fifty-one percent by the benefited property owners, and thirty-two percent by the riders. .The assessment of accruing benefits is based on both the street frontage and the actual values affected.

Responsibility for public operation

In acquiring and operating a utility, the public and the administrator must be guided by two general principles. First, the principal purpose of public ownership and operation is to obtain certain social benefits that cannot be secured otherwise. Public service, rather than private profit, must become the controlling motive. Hence, the operating authorities must have constantly before them the opportunities for public welfare, and their actions must be guided accordingly. Second, so far as is consistent with the first principle, the utility must be operated as if privately owned, *i.e.*, independently of political control with respect to the selection of personnel, the establishment of rates, and general conduct of the business.[1] How can operation with these interrelated motives be best secured? It is generally conceded that the greatest efficiency of operation in any public activity can be brought about by the centralization of responsibility. Such centralization implies a single operating head appointed by and directly subordinate to the chief executive of the municipality. In city government there is a marked tendency in the direction of such organization even with respect to publicly owned utilities. For example, the water plants of only three of the ten largest cities of the United States are operated by boards rather than by single commissioners.[2] In addition to effective organization, the single commissioner means an intimate contact with the political head of the city and a ready response to public demands for modification in service and charges.

But it is exactly this ready response to public demand that makes the single-headed control of a utility dangerous. It is well enough to appreciate public wishes, but such wishes are not always reasonable and consistent with efficient operation. In such instances a too ready response is undesirable and can best be prevented by a buffer body between the political and the operating

[1] The charter of Detroit provides: "The Board, subject to the approval of the mayor, shall have supervision, management, control of the entire public street railway system of Detroit, both in its construction and maintenance and operation, as fully and completely as if said board represented private owners."
[2] These three exceptions are Detroit, Baltimore, and Los Angeles.

head. Such a buffer can be secured by intrusting operations to a board of reasonable size, appointed by the executive for fixed terms, and removable only for cause. Such a board, if made up of the highest type of citizen, serving without financial compensation, is the best security against political manipulation of a utility. Absence of compensation is essential. Even the smallest financial reward proves an almost irresistible incentive to the appointment of political henchmen of inferior ability. Such a board will be, or can be made, conversant with the wishes of the public; but, removed from pressure, it can sit as a deliberative body, operating the utility through a subordinate professional officer in such a manner as to serve best all interests concerned. Such organization is not recommended for the ordinary activities of local government, nor for cities in which political influences do not prevail.[1]

One of the stock arguments urged against public ownership is the undue influence that may be had by labor under such conditions. A city is a relatively large employer, whose employees have an exceptional unity because of the nature of their work, the method of their appointment, and their security of tenure. While not ordinarily unionized, except in the skilled trades, municipal employees usually belong to one of several associations, such as those of firemen, policemen, or school teachers, or to a general association open to all employees. These associations make demands respecting compensation and other conditions of work directly to the legislative body of the city. But their greatest effectiveness comes through activity in political campaigns. When one considers the votes of relatives and friends that can be marshalled by a single individual, the voting influence of a great group of city employees can be appreciated. The acquisition of each utility aggravates an already serious situation. Municipal ownership will be a matter of indifference to the public if the rapacity of organized employees with respect to wages is substituted for that of a private corporation for profits, and exorbitant rates and curtailed service result.

However, the public employment of large bodies of men and women is not an unmitigated evil. The employees of private corporations frequently are unionized; the employees of cities seldom are, and city charters often forbid the recognition of unions. In consequence, the employees of private utilities are in a better posi-

[1] The subject of administrative boards is discussed at greater length in Chap. I.

564   PRACTICE OF MUNICIPAL ADMINISTRATION

CHAP. XXXI

tion to enforce demands by strikes, with resulting hardship to citizens, than are public employees. Further, a strike of the workmen of a privately owned utility is to the public largely a private quarrel in which their sympathies are frequently against an already unpopular employer. On the other hand, strikes of public employees are highly unpopular, and any sane group of public servants will exhaust every other effort, and submit to many grievances, before resorting to a cessation of labor to attain a desired objective. Strikes of firemen and policemen have been beaten in every instance,[1] and there is a growing sentiment that organized cessation of labor on the part of public employees will not be tolerated.

The diverse interests of labor and capital, whether capital appears in the form of a few security holders or of a great public, can scarcely be reconciled by a few simple principles that a public administrator can make effective. There is no reason to believe, however, that such reconciliation will not be made eventually. In the meantime, the administrator can minimize his difficulties by providing for selection and security of tenure under the merit system, pensions and other rewards for long and satisfactory service, the arbitration of disputes, and some voice of labor in management, particularly with respect to discipline.

Accounting and reporting

It is not sufficient that a publicly owned utility be operated effectively; the public must know that it is so operated. It is not so much a question of what things are, as of what folks think they are, and a clear conscience on the part of the administrator is no substitute for honest confidence on the part of the public. The public will not always be interested, and will not always understand, but the few leaders that guide public opinion will. No administrator can afford to neglect honest reporting, on the ground that the public is not interested, or to adopt dishonest reporting, on the ground that the public is too stupid to discover the chicanery. Either policy spells ultimate defeat.[2]

Properly maintained accounts of financial transactions and operating results mean: first, that earnings will be credited properly and expenses charged properly, so that the net cost of operating

---

[1] Such strikes failed in Boston and Cincinnati.
[2] These criticisms of accounting and reporting for municipally owned utilities must not be interpreted as an approval of all private utility accounting. Often the first requisite of such accounting is to show an earning and thus protect the investor. See William Z. Ripley, ''Stop, Look, Listen!'' *Atlantic*, CXXXVIII, 380-400 (September, 1926).

may be obtained readily, and changes in future operating income be estimated accordingly; second, that the comparative costs of units of service will be available as a guide to future economies and to the extension of activities; and third, that the actual values invested in the utility may be known and preserved from inefficient and dishonest management.

<small>CHAP. XXXI</small>

The maintenance of such accounts should result in three important statements—first, the balance sheet, showing on one side the fixed assets of the business, such as buildings and property, and the floating assets such as cash, materials on hand, and evidences of credit, and on the other side the capital liabilities, such as stocks, bonds, and floating liabilities, such as notes and accounts payable, together with the reserves for losses, contingencies, depreciation, and amortization; second, the operating statement, showing the costs and revenues of the business for the period; and third, the surplus statement showing the disposal of revenues over and above operating expenses. The operating statement, when compared with the statistics of operation, will indicate the unit costs of operation for the period involved. The mere existence of these accounts does not, however, insure the honesty or intelligence of their maintenance. Particularly are the accounts of municipal utilities under suspicion with respect to the items of taxes, interdepartmental charges, and depreciation and amortization.

<small>Suspicion of municipal accounts</small>

Were the same public paying taxes and consuming a utility product, and the taxpayers utilizing the utility service in substantial proportion to the amount of taxes paid, then the taxes on a utility could be remitted with justice to all concerned. But these conditions never exist. The public that uses street cars or consumes water and gas is by no means the public that pay taxes; the largest taxpayers may use none of these services. Under these circumstances, the remission of taxes to a publicly owned utility amounts to the granting of a subsidy at the expense of the taxpayers, and an unwarranted advantage extends to municipal ownership and operation. In the name of common honesty, publicly-owned utilities should pay taxes to the city on a fair valuation, exactly as if privately owned. Similarly, the city should pay the utility for services rendered to other departments. The municipal water works should not be expected to furnish water for street flushing, fire service, and public and semi-public buildings without payment. The charges for taxes and interdepartmental services may counterbalance one another, but no one knows that they do,

<small>Taxes</small>

<small>Interdepartmental charges</small>

566 PRACTICE OF MUNICIPAL ADMINISTRATION

CHAP. XXXI

Depreciation and amortization

and in the meantime ignoring them brings municipal accounting into the disrepute it so often merits.

In the same category are charges for depreciation, a subject discussed in the preceding chapter. Depreciation is a cost of operation, and operating statements and balance sheets should so consider it. It is not sufficient for a publicly owned utility to pay certain amortization charges and maintain that such amortization offsets depreciation. There is no connection between depreciation and amortization. One is a charge to operation, the other a charge to surplus; one is measured by the physical decay of the plant, the other by the arbitrary terms of outstanding securities.[1]

It is recognized that municipal utilities are usually required by law to retire, out of earnings, the bonds outstanding against them. In a privately-owned utility such bonds ordinarily would be refunded upon falling due. It would be unreasonable and unjust to the consumers to expect a municipal utility to maintain its capital investment intact through depreciation reserves, and at the same time liquidate an equal amount of outstanding liabilities through amortization reserves. But the double charges are reconcilable. As has been stated, depreciation reserves may be used for investment in new assets or to retire outstanding liabilities. The effect on the surplus reflected in the balance sheet is exactly the same. A publicly-owned utility faced with debt retirement should transfer from its depreciation reserves to its amortization reserves any amounts required for this latter purpose not provided from surplus. If this process leaves the depreciation reserves inadequate to maintain the plant properly, that deficiency may be made good legitimately from additional bond issues. In any event, the utility is no worse off than if no depreciation reserves were established, and its accounting has been maintained in an honest and intelligent fashion.

Industries clothed with a public interest

It has been stated that special rights have been granted to utilities because their operations are clothed with a public interest. There are, however, other industries that furnish supplies or services so essential to the welfare of citizens that the public has more than an ordinary interest in the prices charged and the character of service rendered, even though no special use is made of public property and no special rights are required in conduct-

[1] This position with respect to depreciation will not be concurred in by many public utility experts. It is maintained by some that depreciation should be met by current maintenance and that reserves for such should not be established except in small plants. See p. 545.

MUNICIPAL OWNERSHIP

ing their business. In great cities, the furnishing of coal, ice, milk, bread, and housing is assuming something of a public character, and efforts are being made by the public to control prices and service, either by legal regulations or by municipal competition, or both. For example, cities have ordinances governing the weight of loaves of bread, the weighing of coal and ice upon delivery, and the purity of milk and ice. With respect to housing, state laws or ordinances have been enacted in some instances regulating the amount of rent that may be charged. During the coal shortage at the time of the World War, several cities went into the distribution of coal from municipality owned and operated coal yards.[1]

CHAP. XXXI

At least two cities [2] have endeavored to take over the distribution of milk, and the question of milk supply has given many cities concern. There may be some justification for making this industry a public undertaking on the grounds that the pure milk supply necessary to public health cannot be obtained otherwise. However, the quality of milk, as to both purity and fat content, is fairly well regulated in most cities. The more obvious defect in milk distribution is the costly duplication of service in connection with a food product absolutely required for public well-being. The late home-comer or early riser cannot but be impressed with the intermittent parade of different milk carts that pass down every residential street at dawn, and this overlapping of service is reflected in the cost of every bottle left on the doorstep. But the distribution of dairy products is no simple industry, and does not begin and end with the pasteurization, bottling, and delivery of domestic milk. The successful conduct of a modern dairy involves the ownership and operation of farms and herds, delicate negotiations and formal contracts with other milk producers, the transportation of milk over long distances, and the manufacture and sale of ice cream, butter, and cheese. In fact, the bottling and distribution of milk to householders may be said to be a by-product of more profitable, if somewhat less important, activities of the dairy industry.

Milk distribution

[1] For a statement of municipal experience with temporary coal yards, see Carl D. Thompson, *op. cit.*

[2] In 1920 Jamestown, N. Y., voted $150,000 to construct a municipal milk plant and distribution system. The project was ultimately prevented on legal grounds. In 1919 the City Commission of Kalamazoo approved a project to municipalize the bottling and distribution of milk in that city, but almost immediately rescinded its action. Opposition came from the milk distributors and citizens opposed to municipal ownership.

568   PRACTICE OF MUNICIPAL ADMINISTRATION

CHAP. XXXI

Abattoirs

Public control of meats has come to the fore in recent years. The United States Department of Agriculture maintains a stringent inspection of all meats entering into interstate commerce, and such government inspected meat constitutes the greater portion of the supply of every large city. There remain, however, many small local slaughtering houses—so many that local inspection is difficult. It has been urged that cities should prevent such indiscriminate slaughtering by owning a municipal abattoir where the preparation of meats for market could be carried on by individuals upon the payment of a small fee.[1]

Ice plants

Efforts of cities to operate municipal ice plants have not been very successful, owing to the legal difficulties of establishment.

Port facilities

Larger cities of the United States having access to navigable water have gone extensively into the developing of public wharves, warehouses, and terminal facilities in an effort to stimulate trade, and with the development of the St. Lawrence waterway it is anticipated that a number of lake cities will undertake similar projects. These enterprises are ordinarily managed by special authorities, and are substantially self-supporting.[2] Several American cities own and operate ferry systems.[3]

Ferries

Housing

A great deal has been written in connection with the housing situation, and cities have been urged to undertake housing projects. As yet, no serious efforts have been made in this field.[4]

Burial places

It is not unusual for towns and villages to buy and maintain cemeteries. Doubtless this function grew out of the absolute necessity of a burial place in every community, and the impracticability of providing these facilities by private initiative in smaller cities and villages.[5] It has been suggested also that cities should engage in funeral management as a means of reducing costs.[6]

[1] Municipal abattoirs are reported in Montgomery, Nashville, Dubuque, Los Angeles, Grand Forks, N. D., and Paris, Texas.
[2] Such facilities are reported on a significant scale in Seattle, New Orleans, New York, Baltimore, Los Angeles, Boston, San Francisco, Chicago, and Oakland. The investment of the public in the New Orleans development is nearly $50,000,000, and the projects in other cities have cost many millions.
[3] San Francisco, New York, and Portsmouth, Va.
[4] Both the city and county of Milwaukee own stock in the Garden Homes Company which is building and disposing of houses at low prices and easy terms. The new charter of Los Angeles authorizes a similar activity. New York State is preparing to give aid to housing projects.
[5] It is estimated that there are 2,000,000 deaths annually in the United States, and more than 89,000 cemeteries, or an average of 30 for each county.
[6] Quincy L. Dowd, *Funeral Management and Costs* (Univ. of Chicago Press, 1921). A bibliography on municipal cemeteries will be found in Gordon R. Merrick, *City Cemetery Administration* (Bulletin No. 58, League of Kansas Municipalities, June 1, 1926).

While recognizing the importance of these industries that are not public utilities, yet have a public interest, probably the safest present course for cities to pursue is to avoid efforts at municipal ownership and operation. The time may come when such steps will be necessary and expedient, but it is not here now. The full effects of municipal regulation have not yet been secured. Somewhat the same pressure for consolidation is at work with these industries as with public utilities, and with the same results of improved service and lowered cost. As this consolidation proceeds and these industries assume the character of monopolies, it may be expected that means will be found for their better regulation.

INDEX

Abattoirs, municipal ownership of, 568.
Absent voting, 27.
Accident insurance, 318.
Accidents, traffic, and street lighting, 507; investigation of, 358; loss from, 341.
Accounting, 136-141.
Accounts, classification of, 143; unpaid, 100.
Activated sludge, see sewage treatment.
Adams, Thomas, "Modern City Planning," 186, 189, 190.
Adler, Herman M., "Psychiatry and Medical Relations," 360.
Administration, fundamentals of, 5.
Administrators, characteristics of, 11; permanent, 7; selection of, 11.
Adult education, see education.
Aëration of water, 494.
Agg, T. R., *Construction of Roads and Pavements*, 428.
Agriculture, Dept. of, see United States Dept. of Agriculture.
Allen, Henry J., *Party of the Third Part*, 551.
Allen, William H., on operation audits, 14; *Universal Training for Citizenship and Public Service*, 11.
Allison, James E., on depreciation, 542.
Almshouses, 313.
American Association for Community Organization, 312.
American City, 76, 186, 224, 270, 271, 294, 341, 416, 428, 447, 469, 485, 506; "Lowest Bidder and the Surety Bond," 420; "To Park or not to Park," 350.
American City Bureau, *Know and Help Your Schools*, 270, 271.
American Child Health Association, *Health Survey of 86 Cities*, 243; *Transactions* of, 257.
American Electric Railway Association, *Public Ownership and Operation of Electric Railways*, 554.
American Engineering Standards Committee, *special code for*, 212.

American Hospital Association, *Proceedings* of, 263.
American Institute of Architects, *Journal* of, 186.
American Institute of Criminal Law and Criminology, *Modern Criminal Science Series*, 379; *Journal of Criminal Law and Criminology*, 360, 379.
American Institute of Park Executives, *Concessions and Privileges in Public Parks*, 305.
American Journal of Public Health, 243.
American Judicature Society, *Bulletins 4-A and 4-B*, 367; *Journal* of, 360, 379.
American Medical Association, see National Education Association.
American Prison Association, definition of crime, 379; *Proceedings* of, 379.
American Public Health Association, *Appraisal form for City Health Work*, 265; *Half Century of Public Health*, 245; *Model Health Code* by, 251; *Proceedings* of, 243; *Report on Committee of Municipal Health Department Practice*, 243.
American School Board Journal, 266.
American School of Correspondence, *Cyclopedia of Fire Prevention*, 224.
American Society of Civil Engineers, "Final Report of the Special Committee to Formulate Principles and Methods of Valuation for Railroads and Other Public Utilities," 539.
American Society of Mechanical Engineers, boiler code of, 212.
American Society for Municipal Improvements, 520; *Proceedings* of, 416, 428, 469, 514; *Standard Contract Form*, 419.
American Society for Testing Materials, *Specifications* of, 416.
American Water Works Association, *Water Works Practice*, 485; *Journal* of, 485.
Amundsen, George, "Public Health Education," 265.

571

572 INDEX

Anderson, E. A., and Haas, O. F., "Illumination and Traffic Accidents," 507.
Anderson, William, *American City Government*, 4, 77.
Annals of the American Academy, *Automobile, Its Province and Problems*, 341; *Competency and Economy in Public Expenditures*, 53; *Legal Aid Work*, 185, 316, 371; *Municipal Markets*, 399; *Public Budgets*, 53, 55.
Annuity bonds, see bonds.
Appointments, provisional, 41; temporary, 40.
Appreciation, 144; of structures, 90.
Appropriation, balances, 143; ordinance, 70.
Appropriations, allotment, 60; continuing, 58; control of, 140; lump sum, 68; segregated, 69.
Arc lights, 509.
Arcading, 348.
Arrests, 363.
Arson, 228.
Art, 189, 196, 300.
Ashes, collection of, 461.
Asphalt, block, 439; plants, 439; sources of, 439; testing of, 439; see also pavements.
Assessing, manuals, 92; organization, 79; system, 79-80.
Assessments, description of property for, 81; equalization of, 92; methods of determining, 83; preparation of, 80; review of, 92; rules of, 84.
Assessments, special, see special assessments.
Assessors, selection of, 79.
Assets, forms of, 145.
Associated General Contractors, *Standard Municipal Contract Form*, 419.
Atkinson, R. C., *Effects of Tax Limitations upon Local Finance in Ohio, 1911-1922*, 93; on tax limitation, 93; "Tax and Debt Limit Laws," 93, 120.
Attendance, enforcing school, 285.
Attorney, see legal advisor, legal aid.
Audits, operation, 14, 74; state control of, 149.
Auto patrol, 328.
Automobile, see motor equipment.
Automotive Industries, 167.
Automatic alarm and sprinklers, 239.
Auxiliary fire squads, 235.

Ayres, Leonard P., *Laggards in Our Schools*, 284.
Ayres, Leonard P., see also Gulick, Luther H., jt. auth.

Babbitt, H. E., *Sewerage and Sewage Treatment*, 469.
Babcock, Frederick M., *Appraisal of Real Estate*, 84, 87, 88.
Bail, 364.
Baker, I. O., *Treatise on Roads and Pavements*, 428.
Balance sheet, 142.
Baldwin, Roger, and Flexner, Bernard, *Juvenile Courts and Probation*, 375.
Ballard, F. W., & Co., *Report on Street Lighting Costs in the Larger Cities of the United States*, 519.
Ballots, 24.
Baltimore, pre-billing of taxes in, 128.
Barker, H., *Public Utility Rates*, 540.
Barnett, J. D., "Compulsory Voting in Oregon," 28.
Barrow, A. Mable, "Public Defender, a Bibliography," 371.
Barth, Harry, *Water Meter Problems*, 502.
Bassett, Edward M., "Zoning," 199, 200.
Bates, Frank G., "State Control of Local Finance in Indiana," 93.
Bates, Sanford, *Individualization of Punishment*, 382.
Bath houses, 300.
Bathing beaches, 300.
Bauer, John, *Effective Regulation of Public Utilities*, 523.
Bay City, Mich., mortgage bonds in, 105; purchase of water plant by, 560.
Beard, Charles A., *Municipal Government of Tokyo*, 14.
Benford, Frank, "Iso Candles and the Asymmetric Lighting Unit," 512.
Bernard, Alfred D., *Some Principles and Problems of Real Estate Valuation*, 84, 85, 89, 90.
Besson, F. S., *City Pavements*, 428.
Bettman, Alfred, and Burns, Howard F., "Prosecution," 60.
Beyer, W. C., "Hire of Firemen and Policemen," 333.
Bidding, methods of, 418; unbalanced, 421.
Billboards, regulation of, 203, 218, 219.
Bingham, Robert F., see McMichael, Stanley, jt. auth.
Bituminous surfaces, 433.

INDEX

Black base, 434.
Blanchard, Arthur H., *Elements of Highway Engineering*, 428.
Block and lot description, 81.
Blucher, Walter, on city planning, 186.
Boards, administrative, 10.
Bode, Boyd, *Fundamentals of Education*, 266.
Boilers, regulation of, 218.
Bolton, R. P., *Building for Profit*, 89.
Bond budgets, see budgets, bond.
Bond bureau, 369.
Bonding, abuses in, 369.
Bonds, 107-115; fidelity, 420; mortgage, 561; public utility, 560; surety, 420.
Bondsmen, professional, 368.
Boston, budget procedure in, 69; planning metropolitan area in, 188; pre-billing of taxes in, 128; sliding scale, 532; subways in, 195.
Bostwick, A. E., *American Public Library*, 282.
Boulevards, 304; lighting of, 513.
Bowen, W. P., and Mitchell, E. D., *Practice of Organized Play*, 294; *Theory of Organized Play*, 294.
Bradway, J. S., see Smith, R. H., jt. auth.
Branch, G. V., "Markets," 412, 413; *Retail Public Markets*, 407.
Breckinridge, Sophonisba P., *Family Welfare Work in a Metropolitan Community*, 317.
Breed, H. Eltinge, "Behavior of Concrete Pavements under Service Conditions," 441.
Brick, see pavements.
Brown, Dorothy K., *Federal Aid to the States*, 269.
Brown, Fraser, *Municipal Bonds*, 105.
Buck, A. E., *Municipal Budgets and Budget Making*, 53, 60; *Municipal Finance*, 76; on special assessments, 61.
Buck, A. E., see also, Cleveland, F. A., jt. auth.
Budget, classification of, 62; control, 71; definition of, 53; statement, 66.
Budget procedure, defects of, 54; failure of, 72; publicity of, 68.
Budgets, bond, 59; sinking fund, 59; trust fund, 59.
Builders, licensing of, 216.
Building codes, 205.
Building construction, examination of plans, 213; inspection of, 214.
Building control, see safety engineering.

Building inspection, see inspection of buildings.
Building Officials Conference, *Proceedings* of, 204.
Buildings, classification of, 209; lighting of, 508; location of, 196; regulation of area of, 199; regulation of height of, 198; special, 212.
Bullen, J. T., "Surface Treatment of Gravel Roads," 433.
Buncel, Bessie, "Working Paper Procedure," 257.
Bureau of Municipal Research of Philadelphia, on bond issues, 113; on codification of ordinances, 178; *Municipal Street Cleaning in Philadelphia*, 447.
Bureaus of municipal research, 13.
Burgess, George K., "Supervision of Weights and Measures," 43.
Burial places, see cemeteries.
Burkhardt, Margaret R., see Winslow, C. E. A., jt. auth.
Burnham, W. H., *Normal Mind*, 283.
Burns, Howard F., see Bettman, Alfred, jt. auth.
Burton, Frank, "Construction of the Building Code," 207; on preparation of building codes, 207; "Some Legal Aspects of Building Codes and Their Enforcement," 208.
Business manager of schools, see schools, business manager of.
Business taxes, 95.

Cabot, Richard C., *Social Work*, 317.
Cady, F. E., "Photometry," 517.
Cady, F. E., and Dates, Henry B., *Illuminating Engineering*, 506.
Cahalane, C. F., *Police Practice and Procedure*, 320; *Policeman*, 320.
Caldwell, O. W., and Courtis, S. A., *Then and Now in Education*, 283.
Cambridge Health Education Conference, 287.
Camps, summer, 299; tourists, 304.
Candle power, definition of, 516.
Cannon, Lucius H., *Smoke Abatement*, 218.
Capes, William Parr, and Carpenter, Jeanne D., *Municipal Housecleaning*, 447, 469.
Catch basins, see sewers.
Catchment areas, see water.
Cemeteries, municipal ownership of, 568.
Census, see United States Bureau of the Census.
Census, school, see schools, census.

INDEX

Chamber of Commerce of the United States, *Auto Tourist Camps*, 305.
Chamberlain, Lawrence, *Principles of Bond Investment*, 105.
Chapman, Frank E., *Hospital Organization and Operation*, 263.
Chapman, J. Crosby, and Counts, George S., *Principles of Education*, 266.
Charity, 310.
Chicago Bureau of Public Efficiency, *Report on Excess Condemnation*, 202.
Chicago, consolidation inspection in, 223; pay-as-you-go plan in, 118; terminal markets in, 402.
Chicago Teachers' Federation, *Report on Detroit Platoon System*, 277.
Children's Bureau, see United States Children's Bureau.
Children's homes, 314.
Chlorination purification of water, 495.
Cincinnati, purchasing in, 155, 159; water purification in, 491; water rates in, 557.
Cities, council, 6; growth, causes of, 3.
City Club of New York, *Building of Rapid Transit Lines in New York*, 561.
City manager plan, 6.
City planning, 186.
Civic centers, 196.
Civil service, 30.
Clark, Mary A., "Venereal Disease Control," 255.
Cleveland, election officials in, 20.
Cleveland, F. A., "Evolution of the Budget Idea in the United States," 55.
Cleveland, F. A., and Buck, A. E., *Budget and Responsible Government*, 53.
Cleveland Foundation, *Criminal Justice in Cleveland*, 320, 360, 379; *Cleveland School Survey*, 266; *Recreation Survey Report*, 294.
Cleveland Hospital Council, *Cleveland Health and Hospital Survey*, 243.
Clinics, psychopathic, 372.
Coal yards, municipal ownership of, 567.
Cole, W. M., *Cost Accounting for Institutions*, 263.
Colleges, municipal, 279.
Collins, Charles W., *National Budget System*, 53.
Cologne, street lighting in, 506.
Commerce, Dept. of, see United States Dept. of Commerce.

Commons, John R., *Legal Foundations of Capitalism*, 540.
Communicable diseases, 251.
Community centers, 296.
Compulsory voting, 28.
Concerts, 301.
Concessions, park, see parks.
Concrete, see pavements.
Condemnation proceedings, 201.
Confidential exchange, 316.
Conn, H. W., and Harold J., *Bacteriology*, 244.
Contact beds, see sewage treatment.
Contagious diseases, see hospitals, contagious disease.
Continuation schools, see schools, continuation.
Contracts, fraud in, 420; methods of letting, 418; payments on, 426; split, 421.
Convertible bonds, see bonds.
Cooke, Morris L., *Public Utility Regulation*, 523.
Corcoran, Harry J., "Selection, Care and Operation of Fire Fighting Equipment," 230.
Corner influence, 85, 87.
Corporation counsel, see legal advisor.
Corporation cuts, 444.
Correction, see punishment.
Cost records, on public work, 425.
Counts, George S., see Chapman, J. Crosby, jt. auth.
Coupon bonds, see bonds.
Court docket, 377; records, 376.
Courtis, S. A., definition of education, 266; *Standard Tests*, 282; *Why Children Succeed*, 282.
Courtis, S. A., see also, Caldwell, O. W., jt. auth.
Courts, 365-376; felony, 362; juvenile, 375; misdemeanant, 362; municipal, 376; night, 375; regulation of utilities by, 533; traffic, 374; unified, 366; women's, 377.
Crane, R. T., *Loose Leaf Digest of City Manager Charters*, 138.
Crathorne, A. R., see Rietz, H. L., jt. auth.
Crime and street lighting, 508.
Crime, definition of, 379; in England, 380.
Crobaugh, Clyde J., "Centralizing Fiscal Tendencies in State and Local Relations," 95.
Croker, E. F., *Fire Prevention*, 224.
Crosby, E. W., Fiske, H. A., and Forster, H. W., *Handbook of Fire Protection*, 224, 227, 239.

INDEX

Crosser, C. A., "Can City Carry Own Insurance?" 427; on election districts, 18-19; "Housing the Voter," 20; "How Your Police Department Functions," 320; on regulation of weights and measures, 413, 414; "Report on Toledo Fire Department," 235, 237; "Some Election Facts and Tendencies," 16.

Cubberly, E. P., *Public School Administration*, 266, 275, 276, 282, 285; on special instruction, 284; *Supplementary Report on the Organization and Administration of School District No. 1 in the City and County of Denver*, 268, 269, 271, 273.

Cubberly, E. P., and Elliott, E. C., *State and County School Administration*, 269.

Culpin, Ewart, *Garden City Movement Up to Date*, 197.

Culture and education, 268.

Curbs, 445.

Curtis, H. S., *Practical Conduct of Play*, 294.

Cushman, R. E., *Excess Condemnation*, 202.

Dana, J. C., *Library Primer*, 282.

Darwin, Leonard, *Municipal Ownership*, 555.

Dates, Henry B., see Cady, Francis E., jt. auth.

Davies, John P., *Engineering Office Systems and Methods*, 416.

Davis, Michael M., and Warner, Andrew R., *Dispensaries*, 258.

Day labor work, 424.

Day to day agreements, 533.

Dayton, centralized purchasing in, 154; defects in accounting methods, 136; garbage collection contract in, 526; general nursing in, 258; sinking funds in, 112.

Dean, A. S., *Analytic System for the Measurement of Relative Fire Hazards*, 241.

Dean's schedule, 241.

Debt, extent, 119; floating, 99; limitations on, 120; redemption of, 110.

Debt, see also bonds.

Democracy and education, 267.

Depreciation, 144, 541, 566; measure of, 546; methods of calculation, 542; on motor equipment, 175; on structures, 90; reserves, 540, 545.

Detectives, 333.

Determinism, see punishment.

Detroit Board of Assessors, *Manual of Assessments*, 80.

Detroit Board of Education, *Effectiveness of Half-Time Sessions*, 286.

Detroit Bureau of Governmental Research, Inc., *Architectural Services in Eight Cities*, 288; *Consolidation of Inspection*, 223; *Growth of a City*, 4; *Lot and Block Method of Describing Property for Taxation Purposes*, 82; *Memorandum on Retirement Funds*, 48; *Memorandum to the Detroit Civil Service Commission re Rating of Examination Papers*, 37, 40; *Method of Securing Architectural Services and Planning of School Buildings*, 288; *New House of Correction*, 391; *Organization and Administration of the Business Department of the Detroit Board of Education*, 274; *Organization and Administration of the Engineering and Janitorial Service of the Detroit Board of Education*, 289; *Public Employment in Detroit*, 46; *Report on the Administration of Civil Service in Detroit*, 35, 40; *Report on the Maintenance of School Property*, 290; *Report on the Organization and Administration of Centralized Purchasing*, 291; *Report on the Organization and Administration of the Detroit Recreation Commission*, 295; *Reorganization of the Garbage and Street Cleaning Division of Detroit*, 454; *Studies of the Detroit Recorder's Court*, 367; *Study of 250,000 Arrests*, 360; *Ten-Year Financial Program for Detroit*, 59.

Detroit City Plan Commission, *A Building Zone Plan for Detroit*, 198; *Zoning and Its Application to Detroit*, 198.

Detroit Dept. of Street Railways, Budget System, 69.

Detroit Federation of Labor, "Platoon School," 277.

Detroit Rapid Transit Commission, *Proposed Financial Plan for a Rapid Transit System for the City of Detroit*, 561; *Proposed Superhighway Plan for Greater Detroit*, 192.

Detroit Street Railway Arbitrators, *Proceedings to Determine the Value of the Day to Day Lines*, **543.**

Detroit, changes in personnel in, 556; Connors Creek sewer in, 472; early elections in, 16; garbage disposal in, 466; mortgage bonds in, 105; pre-billing of taxes in, 128; purification of bathing beaches in, 495; special assessments in, 122; street railway accounting methods, 559; turnover of prisoners in House of Correction, 396; water plant in, 559.

Detroit United Railways, 528, 529, 533, 560.

Devine, Edward T., *Misery and Its Causes*, 309.

De Voss, J. C., see Monroe, W. S.

Dewey, John, *School and Society*, 266.

Dillon, John F., *Commentaries on the Law of Municipal Corporations*, 177, 364.

Dinsmore, John C., *Purchasing Principles and Practice*, 153.

Disease, germ theory of, 244.

D'Olier, W. L., *The Sanitation of Cities*, 469.

Donaldson, W. T., "Compulsory Voting and Absent Voting," 28.

Dow, Alex, *Some Ethical Aspects of Replacement Reserves*, 545.

Dowd, Quincy L., *Funeral Management and Costs*, 568.

Drivers, regulation of, 356.

Dublin, Louis I., *Some Problems of Life Extension*, 246; "Vital Statistics," 251.

Durham, Henry W., *Street Paving and Maintenance in European Cities*, 428.

Eddy, Harrison P., see Metcalf, Leonard, jt. auth.

Education, 266-292; adult, 281; collegiate, 279; platoon plan of, 277; recreation in, 287; six-three-three plan, 278; traditional plan of, 276; vocational, 279.

Eggleston, D. C., *Municipal Accounting*, 126, 135.

Ehrmann, H. B., see Smith, R. H., jt. auth.

Elapsed life method of calculating depreciation, 542.

Elections, 16.

Electric lighting, see lighting.

Electric Railway Journal, 341.

Electrical World, 506.

Eligible lists, 40.

Elliott, E. C., see Cubberly, E. P., jt. auth.

Ellis, Ellen D., "City Manager as a Leader of Policy," 7.

Empire State Gas and Electric Association, 516.

Employees, associations of, 51; classifications of, 34-35; political activities by, 52; recruiting of, 34.

Employment agencies, 316.

Engineering, consulting services in, 417; organization for, 416; payment for, 418.

Engineering and Contracting, 485.

Engineering News-Record, 355, 416, 428, 469, 485.

Equipment, 146; disposal of, 165.

Evans, Harry C., *American Poor Farm and Its Inmates*, 313.

Examinations, civil service, 35-37.

Excess condemnation, 202.

Extras, on contracts, 422.

Fair value, see value.

Fales, W. Thurber, "Expenditures of Health Departments," 264.

Fales, W. Thurber, see also Hiscock, Ira B., jt. auth.

Farm produce distribution, see markets.

Fassett, Charles M., "Electric Rates and Rate Making," 548.

Faust, Martin L., *Custody of State Funds*, 126.

Fees, 95, 96, 97, 103.

Felonies, definition of, 361; prosecution of, 371.

Fenkell, George H., and Steffens, Henry, Jr., "Water Supply," 502, 504.

Ferries, municipal ownership of, 568.

Fidelity bonds and franchises, 528; deposits, 158; bonds, see bonds.

Filters, water, 496.

Filtration, water purification by, 496.

Financial Statistics of Cities, see U. S. Bureau of the Census.

Fines, 383.

Fire Engineering, 224.

Fire protection, 227-240.

Firemen, 236-238.

Firemen's Herald, 224.

Fiscal year, 150.

Fiske, H. A., see Crosby, E. W., jt. auth.

Fitzpatrick, E. A., *Budget Making in a Democracy*, 53; "Inter-relationships of Hospitals and Communities," 263.

Flexner, Bernard, see Baldwin, Roger, jt. auth.

Flushing, machine and hand, 452.

INDEX 577

Folks, Homer, *Care of Destitute, Neglected and Delinquent Children,* 314.
Food, inspection of, 259.
"Footballs of politics," 530.
Forbes, Russell, "Centralized Purchasing in Governments of the United States and Canada," 153; on centralized control of motor equipment, 169; on use of automobiles, 167.
Force account work, 424.
Ford, James, *Social Problems and Social Policy,* 309.
Forster, H. W., see Crosby, E. W., jt. auth.
Fosdick, Raymond B., *American Police Systems,* 320, 325; *European Police Systems,* 320; "Police Administration," 320.
Foulke, William D., *Fighting the Spoilmen,* 31.
Fox, Richard T., *Report on the Chicago Bureau of Streets,* 447.
Franchises, 523, 526, 527, 528, 530, 538.
Freeman, Allen W., "The Health Board and the Health Officer," 248.
Freeman, Allen W., and Fales, W. Thurber, "Control of Communicable Diseases," 253.
Fuld, Leonard F., *Police Administration,* 320.
Funds, deposit of, 131.

Garage, central, 170.
Garbage collection, 459; disposal, 462, 463, 466.
Garden cities, 197.
Gardens, home and school, 299.
Gardner, Mary S., *Public Health Nursing,* 258.
Gary plan, see education.
Gas lighting, see lighting.
Gas plants, municipal ownership of, 554.
Gasoline tax, 171.
General Electric Co., 506.
Gibbon, I. G., "Municipal Government in the United States," 7.
Gillin, John L., *Criminology and Penology,* 379.
Gladstone, William E., on budgets, 55.
Glover, J. W., *Tables of Applied Mathematics in Finance Insurance Statistics,* 111.
Glover, J. W., see also Hewes, Lawrence I.

Goddard, Edwin C., "Fair Value of Public Utilities," 541.
"Going Value," 538.
Goldrich, Leon W., *Manual for Cottage Mothers and Supervisors,* 314.
Goldman, M. C., *Public Defender,* 371.
Good will, 539.
Gorgas, Marie D., and Hendrick, Percy J., *William Crawford Gorgas,* 244.
Gosnell, H. F., see Merriam, C. E., jt. auth.
Governmental research, see bureaus of municipal research.
Governmental Research Conference, *Character and Functioning of Municipal Civil Service Commissions in the United States,* 30, 32, 33, 42.
Grades, standardization of, 45-46.
Grand juries, 364.
Granite, see pavements.
Graper, Elmer O., *American Police Administration,* 320.
Greeley, Samuel, see Hering, Rudolph, jt. auth.
Greiner, R. E., *Street Lighting with Mazda Lamps,* 511, 512.
Grunsky, C. E., *Valuation, Depreciation and the Rate Base,* 539.
Guarantees, maintenance, see maintenance guarantees.
Gulick, Luther H., on new sources of revenue, 101.
Gulick, Luther H., and Ayres, Leonard P., *Medical Inspection of Schools,* 287.
Gutters, 445.

Haas, O. F., see Anderson, E. A., jt. auth.
Harley, Herbert, "Model Municipal Court," 367.
Harris, C. L., see Jordan, J. P., jt. auth.
Harris, H. J., see Winslow, C. E., jt. auth.
Harris, Joseph P., *Registration for Voting in the United States,* 22.
Harris, Louis J., *Clinical Types of Occupational Diseases,* 258; *Industrial Hygiene,* 258; *Occupational Causes of Ill Health,* 258; *Opportunities which Industrial Hygiene Offers to the General Practitioner,* 258.
Harrison, Aleck P., "Organization of a City Health Department," 246.

Harrison, Ward, "Statistics on Street Lighting and Crime," 508; "Street Lighting," 510.
Hart, Hastings H., *Plans and Illustrations of Prisons and Reformatories*, 391.
Hartman, H. H., *Fair Value*, 539.
Hatton, A. R., on budgets, 55.
Hauer, Roy, and Scragg, George H., *Bus Operating Practice*, 167.
Hayes, H. V., *Public Utilities*, 540.
Hazen, Allen, *Meter Rates for Water Works*, 503.
Hazen, Allen, see also Williams, G. S., jt. auth.
Health education, 264.
Health insurance, 318.
Health officers, 249.
Health Survey of 86 Cities, 248, 249, 251, 253, 255, 256, 257, 258, 259, 260, 265.
Health work, 245-265; in schools, 286.
Healy, William, *Individual Delinquent*, 382.
Heating plants, municipal ownership of, 554.
Henderson, C. R., *Cause and Cure of Crime*, 379; *Correction and Prevention*, 379.
Hendrick, Percy J., see Gorgas, Marie D., jt. auth.
Herwig, Rudolph, and Greeley, Samuel, *Collection and Disposal of Municipal Wastes*, 447.
Hewes, Lawrence I., and Glover, James W., *Highway Bonds*, 110, 446.
High pressure water system, 236, 500.
Highways, by-pass, 346; crosstown, 346; super, in Detroit, 195.
Hiscock, Ira B., "Food and Drug Inspection," 259; "Infant Hygiene," 256; "Milk Inspection," 259; "Sanitary Inspection and Sanitation," 260, 261.
Hiscock, Ira B., and Fales, W. T., "School Health Supervision," 257.
Hiscock, Ira B., and Hiscock, Margaret S., "Public Health Laboratories," 260.
Hiscock, Margaret S., see Hiscock, Ira B., jt. auth.
Hoffmaster, P. J., "Tourist Camp Site," 305.
Holding companies, examples of, 530.
Holophone Glass Co., *Scientific Street Lighting*, 510, 511, 512, 516.
Hommon, H. B., see Wagenhals, H. H., jt. auth.

Hood, William C., on waste collection, 461; on water supply, 485.
Hoover, Herbert, on building codes, 207; on organization of government, 10.
Horwood, Murray T., *Public Health Survey*, 243.
Hose wagons, 232.
Hoskins, J. K., "Stream Pollution and Extent of Sewage Treatment Required," 477.
Hospitals, 261-263; beds in, 262; charity, 315; communicable disease, 251, 262.
House of Representatives, see U. S. House of Representatives.
Housing, betterment of, 186; control of, 260; municipal ownership of, 568.
Howard, Ebenezer, *Garden Cities of Tomorrow*, 197.
Howard, J. W., "Paying for Car Track Paving," 444.
Hubbard, H. V., and Kimball, Theodora, *Introduction to the Study of Landscape Design*, 305.
Hunt, G., *Writings of James Madison*, 268.
Hurd, Richard M., *Principles of City Land Values*, 84.
Hydrants, water, 501.
Hysell, Helen, *Science of Purchasing*, 153.

Ice plants, municipal ownership of, 568.
Identification of criminals, 334.
Illuminating Engineering Society, *Transactions* of, 506, 514.
Imhoff tanks, see sewage treatment.
Improvements, methods of financing, 106.
Incandescent lighting, 509.
Incarceration, 385.
Incendiarism, see arson.
Incineration, 464.
Income and expense statement, 142.
Income, control of, 139.
Indebtedness, see debt.
Indeterminate permits. see permits.
Indianapolis, garbage disposal in, 467.
Indictments, 364.
Industrial compensation, 318; courts, 550; training, 267.
Industries, revenues from, 98.
Inspection, of buildings, 206, 216; consolidation of, 222; of construction, 417; of public work, 423; of purchases, 156.

INDEX

Insurance, fire, 240, 427; health, 318; rates, 241-242; unemployment, 318.
Intelligence tests, 38.
Inter-departmental charges, 565; services, 74.
Interest, see funds.
International Association of Dairy and Milk Inspectors, *Proceedings of*, 259.
International Association of Street Sanitation Officials, *Proceedings of*, 447.
International Health Education Conference, *Report* of, 287.
Interest payments, reductions in, 102.
Iodine, treatment of water with, 497.

Jacobs, Philip P., *Tuberculosis Worker*, 254.
Jails, prisoners in, 368.
Jails, see also prisons.
"Jay-walkers," 345.
Jensen, Carl C., "Our Convict Slaves," 396.
Job costs, 146.
Johnson, Alexander, *Almshouse*, 313.
Jordan, J. P., and Harris, G. L., *Cost Accounting*, 147.
Journal of Accountancy, 135; of *Land and Public Utility Economics*, 552.
Judicial procedure, 362.
Junior college, see education, collegiate.

Kales, A. M., "Legal Education," 360.
Kansas City Public Service Institute, on costs of registration, 23.
Kansas Court of Industrial Relations, 550.
Kelly, F. J., see Monroe, W. S., jt. auth.
Kelso, Robert W., *History of Public Poor Relief in Massachusetts*, 309, 310.
Kenlon, John, *Fires and Fire Fighters*, 226.
Kerby, McFall, *Open Types of Public Markets*, 410.
Kershaw, John B. C., *Fuel Economy and Smoke Prevention*, 218.
Kimball, Theodora, *Manual of Information on City Planning and Zoning*, 186.
Kimball, Theodora, see also Hubbard, H. V., jt. auth.
King, Clyde L., *Lower Living Costs in Cities*, 399; *Regulation of Municipal Utilities*, 555.

Kinnicult, L. P., Winslow, C.E.A., and Pratt, R. W., *Sewage Disposal*, 469.
Kipling, Rudyard, *Rewards and Fairies*, 244.
Krumwiege, Charles, see Parks, W. H., jt. auth.
Kumm, Harold F., "Legal Relations of City and State with Reference to Public Utility Regulations," 535.

Labor, Department of, see United States Dept. of Labor.
Laboratory, health, 260.
Ladder trucks, 231.
Land, valuation of, 82.
Land value maps, 82.
Law enforcement, break down of, 362.
Lawyers, shyster, 370.
Lee, Joseph, *Play in Education*, 294.
Legal action against cities, 180.
Legal advisor, 179.
Legal aid, 184, 315.
Leonhauser, V. L., 136.
Lewis, Burdette C., *Penal and Correctional Treatment*, 379.
Lewis, E. E., *Personnel Problems of the Teaching Staff*, 274.
Lewis Institute, Structural Materials Research Laboratory, 435.
Lewis, Nelson P., *Planning of the Modern City*, 186.
Lewis, Sinclair, *Arrowsmith*, 249.
Liabilities, control of, 139.
Libraries, 281.
Library Journal, 282.
Licenses, 95, 103, 336.
Lighting, street, 507-522.
Link, Chas. H., *Employment Psychology*, 38.
Loans, 99.
Local regulation of utilities, 534.
Lodging houses, 314.
London, replanning of, 186; Traffic Branch of the Board of Trade, 350.
Los Angeles, mortgage bonds in, 105, 561; pedestrian control in, 353.
Lowrie, S. Gale, *The Budget*, 53.
Luckiecsch, M., "Lighting of Public Buildings," 508.
Lumen, definition of, 509.
Lutz, Harley L., *Public Finance*, 77.
Lyle, W. T., *Park and Park Engineering*, 305.
Lynn, Mass., street lighting in, 512.

Macadam, see pavements.
McBain, Howard L., *American City Progress and the Law*, 218, 219.

McClellan and Juntersfeld, *1925 Transportation Survey of the City of Washington, D. C.*, 341.
McClintock, Miller, *Street Traffic Control*, 341, 343, 345.
McFarland, Horace, "Proposal to Control Billboards," 219.
Machine brooming, 451.
Mackall, K. W., "Operation and Control of Traffic Signal System," 354.
McLure, J. R., *Ventilation of School Buildings*, 290.
McMichael, Stanley and Bingham, Robert F., *City Growth and Values*, 84.
McNutt, J. Scott, *Manual for Health Officers*, 243, 245, 247, 249.
McQuillen, Eugene, *Treatise on the Law of Municipal Corporations*, 95, 122, 177, 364.
Maintenance guarantees, 423.
Maltbie, Milo R., on depreciation, 542.
Mandel, Arch, "Getting and Keeping Good Policemen," 330; Police, 320.
Manholes, see sewers.
Markets, 399-413; curb, 406, 411; retail, 405, 408, 410; retail farmers, 408; wholesale farmers, 404; wholesale terminal, 403.
Markets, see also, United States Bureau of Markets.
Marsh, Edward C., *Civil Service*, 30, 31.
Martin, Edward M., "Aptitude Test for Policemen," 330; "Experiment in New Methods of Selecting Policemen," 330.
Maryland budget law, 57.
Massachusetts bond law, 106.
Massachusetts Bureau of Statistics, *Report of a Special Investigation Relative to Sinking Funds and Serial Loans*, 111.
Massachusetts, civil service in, 31.
Massachusetts Constitutional Convention, Bulletins, 92; on, "Absent Voting," 27; "Compulsory Voting," 28; "Eminent Domain and Excess Condemnation," 202; Methods of Borrowing, "Sinking Funds vs. Serial Bonds," 110.
Mavor, James, *Niagara in Politics*, 522.
Maxey, Chester C., *Outline of Municipal Government*, 526, 533, 553.
Mayers, Lewis, *Federal Service*, 31, 33.
Mead, D. W., "Pumping Station Practice," 498.

Meat, inspection of, 259, 568.
Medical service, charity, 315.
Melchior, William T., *Insuring Public Property*, 291, 427.
Mellon Institute, *Some Engineering Phases of Pittsburgh's Smoke Problem*, 218.
Merit system, see civil service.
Meriam, Lewis, *Principles Governing the Retirement of Public Employees*, 48.
Merriam, Charles E., "Compulsory Voting in Czechoslovakia," 28; *Municipal Revenues in Chicago*, 101.
Merriam, C. E., and Gosnell, H. F., *Non-Voting*, 28.
Merrick, Gordon R., *City Cemetery Administration*, 568.
Metsalf, Leonard, and Eddy, Harrison P., *American Sewerage Practice*, 469, 478; *Sewerage and Sewage Disposal*, 469.
Meters, water, 501.
Metropolitan Life Insurance Co., *Traffic Problem*, 341.
Metz, Herman A., *Manual of Accounting and Business Procedure of the City of New York*, 13, 135, 136.
Michigan, sinking funds in, 111, 112.
Michigan State Teachers Association, *Uniform Financial Procedure for the Public Schools of Michigan*, 292.
Milk distribution, municipal ownership of, 567; supervision of, 258.
Miller, Cyrus C., "Municipal Terminal Markets," 403.
Milwaukee Citizens' Bureau, *Milwaukee's Tax Problem*, 101.
Milwaukee School Board, *Reports of the Special Committee named to Investigate Platoon Schools*, 277.
Minneapolis, *A Million a Year; A Five Year School Building Program*, 59.
Minnesota Tax Commission, *Assessor's Manual*, 80.
Misdemeanants, character of, 393; supervision of, 393.
Misdemeanors, definition of, 361.
Mitchell, E. D., see Bowen, W. P., jt. auth.
Mitchell, John P., 7.
Mitchell, S. Z., on depreciation, 543.
Modern Hospital, 263.
Moehlman, Arthur B., *Child Accounting*, 285; *Public Education in Detroit*, 266; *Public School Finance*, 271, 275.

INDEX 581

Moley, Raymond, *Missouri Crime Survey*, 360.
Monroe, W. S., De Voss, J. C., and Kelly, F. J., *Educational Tests and Measurements*, 282.
Morey, Lloyd, *Introduction to Governmental Accounting*, 135; *Manual of Municipal Accounting*, 135.
Morley, John, *Life of Gladstone*, 55.
Mortgage bonds, see bonds.
Moses, Robert, *Civil Service in Great Britain*, 31.
Moss, F. A., see Telford, Fred, jt. auth.
Mothers' pensions, 319.
Motor buses, 194.
Motor dispatch, 172.
Motor equipment, 167-176; use of by building inspectors, 222.
Motor Transport, 167.
Motor Trucks, 167.
Mott, W. R., "Arc Lights," 407.
Mounted patrol, 328.
Municipal functions, 8.
Municipal Index, 1925, 305, 485, 486; "Codification of Municipal Ordinances," 183.
Municipal ownership, 552-566.
Munro, W. B., *Government of American Cities*, 14; *Municipal Government and Administration*, II, 181, 245, 266, 268, 270, 272, 280, 344, 380, 504, 516, 526, 553, 555.
Murray, W. S., *Government Owned and Controlled Compared with Privately Owned and Regulated Electric Utilities*, 555.

Nash, Jay B., "Organizing a City's Play and Recreation Assets," 298.
Nash, L. R., *Economics of Public Utilities*, 523, 552.
National Assembly of Civil Service Commissions, *Proceedings* of, 30.
National Association of Controllers and Accounting Officers, *Proceedings* of, 135.
National Association of Public School Business Officials, *Proceedings* of, 274.
National Association of Purchasing Agents, *Proceedings* of, 153.
National Association of Railway and Utilities Commissioners, *Uniform Classification of Accounts for Water Utilities*, 503.
National Board of Fire Underwriters, *Building Codes*, 207; *Estimate of Fire Losses*, 224; *Retirement of Firemen*, 237; *Standard Schedule of Grading Cities and Towns of the United States*, 240.
National Catholic Welfare Conference, *Health Thru the School Day*, 257.
National Civic Federation, *Municipal and Private Operation of Public Utilities*, 558.
National Civil Service Reform League, 45.
National Conference of Social Work, *Proceedings* of, 309.
National Conference on City Planning, *Proceedings* of, 186.
National Conference on Street and Highway Safety, *Publications* of, 341; resolutions on speed, 352.
National Education Association, *Health Education*, 257.
National Education Association, *Journal* of, 266; *Research Bulletin* of, 266.
National Electric Light Association, *Political Ownership and the Electric Light and Power Industry*, 522.
National Federation of Federal Employees, 51.
National Fire Protection Association, *Electrical Code* of, 212.
National Highway Traffic Association, *Publications* of, 341.
National Industrial Conference Board, *Report* of, 30; *Tax Burdens and Exemptions*, 102.
National Municipal League, "Model Election System," 16, 17, 22; *Personnel Problem in the Public Service*, 30, 33; *Public Markets in the United States*, 399; *Report of the Committee on Civil Service*, 30, 31.
National Municipal Review, 23, 53, 76.
National Safety Conference, *Publications* of, 341.
National Tax Association, "Plan of a Model System of State and Local Taxation," 78; *Proceedings* of, 76; "Report of the Committee on Methods of Selecting Assessors," 79.
National Team and Motor Truck Owners Conference, *National Standard Truck Cost System*, 175.
National Tuberculosis Association, *Final Summary Report of Framingham Experiments*, 253; *Transactions* of, 254.
Newark Chamber of Commerce, *Traffic, Transit and Transportation*, 341.

582　　　　　　　　　　INDEX

New England Water Works Association, *Journal* of, 485.
New Jersey bond law, 106; civil service in, 31; reformation in, 395; tax foreclosures in, 130.
New Jersey State League of Municipalities, *New Sources of Revenue for New Jersey Municipalities*, 101.
New Republic, 342, 381, 551; *A Symposium: The Child, the Clinic, and the Court*, 375.
New sources of revenue, 101.
New York Bureau of Municipal Research, 54; *Handbook of Municipal Accounting*, 126, 135; *Next Steps in the Development of a Budget Procedure for the City of Greater New York*, 53, 68, 70; *Survey of San Francisco*, 320, 339.
New York City bond law, 106; election of officials in, 20; *Final Report of the Committee on Taxation of the City of New York*, 101; health department budget, 54; *Municipal Wholesale Terminal Markets and Their Relation to the Food Problem*, 403; Pay-as-you-go plan in, 118; *Report of the Commission on New Sources of Revenue*, 107; *Report of the Mayor's Market Commission*, 399; standardization of supplies in, 164; subways in, 195; terminal markets in, 403.
New York State Bureau of Information, *Municipal Public Markets*, 399.
New York State, civil service in, 32; Conference of Mayors and other City Officials, 516; *Rapid Transit Act of 1891 as Amended*, 561; *Report of Commission on Ventilation*, 290; *Report of the Joint Legislative Committee on Taxation and Retrenchment*, 101; tax exemptions in, 102; tax foreclosures in, 130.
New York State Probation Commission, *Manual for Probation Officers*, 385; *Methods of Supervising Persons on Probation*, 385.
Nolan, John, *City Planning*, 186, 203.
Norfolk, Va., central garage in, 170.
Norton, W. J., on charity, 309.
Nott, Charles C., Jr., ''Coddling Criminals,'' 381.
Nuisances, control of, 260.
Nursing, public health, 258.

Oakey, Francis, *Principles of Government Accounting and Reporting*, 58, 76, 77, 95, 135, 142.

Oakey, Imogen B., *A Sketch of the History of Civil Service Reform in England, India, and the United States*, 31.
Obsolescence, 89.
Occupation taxes, 95.
Occupational diseases, control of, 257.
Odum, H. W., and Willard, D. W., *Systems of Public Welfare*, 309, 314.
Offenders, disposition of, 382; habitual, 390; segregation of, 386.
Offenses, civil, 380; criminal, 380; nature of, 360.
Ohio bond law, 106.
Ohio, civil service in, 32.
Ohio Institute, on results of health work, 246.
Old age pensions, 318.
Oliver, John R., ''Criminology and Common Sense,'' 382, 389.
Omwake, Katherine T., ''Value of Photographs and Handwriting in Estimating Intelligence,'' 38.
Operating reports, 151.
Ordinances, codification of, 183; violations of, 181.
Organization, city, 6-10.
Ostrander, Jessie M., ''One Hundred and Fifty Policemen,'' 39, 330.
Outdoor relief, 313.
Owings, Chloe, *Women Police*, 336.
Ozone, water purification by, 495.

Pardons, 386.
Paris, replanning of, 186.
Parking, of automobiles, 350.
Parks, 195, 305; lighting of, 508.
Parks and Recreation, 294, 303, 306.
Parks, W. H., Williams, Anna W., and Krumwiege, Charles, *Pathogenic Micro-Organisms*, 244.
Parmelee, M. F., *Poverty and Social Progress*, 309.
Parole, 387, 388; misdemeanant, 388.
Pavements, 347, 428-445.
Pay-as-you-go, 117-119.
Payrolls, checking, 37; control of, 147; padding, 148; payment of, 133; preparation of, 132.
Pedestrians, 353.
Pendleton Act, 31.
Pennsylvania, budget procedure in, 61; regulation of billboards in, 219.
Pennsylvania Railroad Company, organization of, 454.
Pensions, see mothers' pensions, old age pensions, retirement pension.
Peoria, Ill., bounty bonds in, 111.
Pepys, Samuel, *Diary*, 243.

INDEX

Permits, indeterminate, 523, 527.
Personalty, assessment of, 91.
Pest houses, 262.
Philadelphia, collection of delinquent taxes, 130; election of officials in, 20; terminal markets in, 403; see also, Bureau of Municipal Research of Philadelphia.
Phillips, T. Glenn, "City Planning," 190; *City Tree Planting*, 192; on parks, 303; on playgrounds, 298.
Phillips, T. Glenn, and Huttenlock, George, "Parks," 299, 303.
Pittenger, B. F., *Introduction to Public School Finance*, 293.
Planning, city, 187-190.
Platoon plan, see education.
Playground and Recreation Association of America, *Bulletins* of, 294; *Community Music*, 296; *Home Play*, 296; *Layout and Equipment of Playgrounds*, 296; *Normal Course in Play*, 294; *Proceedings* of, 294; *Rural and Small Community*, 296.
Playgrounds, 195, 296, 298.
Play leaders, qualifications of, 307.
"Plowed-in" surplus, 529.
Plumb plan, 551.
Plummer, H. E., "Efficiency in a Building Department," 221.
Police, 321-336.
Police Journal, 320.
Police Magazine, 320.
Policewomen, 336.
Pollock, James K., Jr., "Absent Voting," 27.
Pollock, Walter W., "An Equitable Standard for Land Valuation," 84.
Poor houses, 313.
Population, congestion of, 344.
Port facilities, municipal ownership of, 568.
Poverty, causes of, 311.
Pratt, R. W., see Kinnicult, L. P., jt. auth.
Prendergast, William A., *Report Submitting Plan of Proposed System for the Central Purchase and Distribution of Supplies for the City of New York*, 153.
Price agreements, 160.
Prison Association of New York, *Publications* of, 379.
Prison farms, 396.
Prisons, 389-397.
Prisons and Prison Building, 391.
Prisoners, 390-396.
Probation, 371, 384.
Probationary periods, of employees, 41.

Procter, Arthur W., *Principles of Public Personnel Administration*, 30, 32, 34, 36, 38, 42, 44, 46.
Promotions, of employees, 42.
Property, acquisition of, 200; control of, 140; dedication of, 200; regulation of use of, 199.
Psychopathic clinics, see clinics, psychopathic.
Public defender, 370.
Public Health Service, *Report of the Committee on Municipal Health Department Practice*, 243.
Public interest, industries clothed with, 566.
Public Libraries, 282.
Public litigation, 180.
Public Ownership League, *Publications* of, 555.
Public Personnel Studies, 30.
Public Roads, 342.
Public utilities, see utilities.
Public Utility Reports, 523.
Public Works, 201, 416, 428, 469, 485.
Public works, maintenance of, 426; operation of, 426; see also detailed operations in.
Pump slippage, 486.
"Pumpers," 231.
Punishment, theories of, 379-382.
Pupils, promotion of, 284.
Purcell, F. X. A., *Purchasing for Large Cities*, 160.
Purchase contracts, 560.
Purchase orders, 160.
Purchasing, procedure of, 156-165.
Purdy, Lawson, on assessing rules, 84; *Assessment of Real Estate*, 84.

Quarantine, see communicable diseases.
Queen, Stuart A., *Social Work in the Light of History*, 310.

Rainwater, Clarence, *Play Movement in the United States*, 294.
Ransom, William, on depreciation, 545.
Rapid transit, 194.
Rate base, 537.
Rates, fixing for utilities, 547.
Ravenel, Mazyck C., see American Public Health Association.
Raymond, William G., *The Public and Its Utilities*, 523, 552; *What Is Fair?* 540.
Readiness-to-serve charge, 548.
Real estate, public, 103.
Rear lot condemnation, 202.

Receipts, departmental, 61.
Recreation, 287-308.
Reduction, garbage, see garbage reduction.
Reed, Thomas H., "Compulsory Voting in Belgium," 28; *Municipal Government in the United States*, 4, 181, 188, 471.
Reeder, R. R., *How Two Hundred Children Live and Learn*, 314.
Refractors, 511.
Registration, for voting, 23.
Refuse, see wastes.
Reinsch-Wurl screens, see screens.
Releases, court, 369.
Relief agencies, subsidies for, 318.
Relief, poor, 313.
Reports, operation, 74.
Rescue squads, 232.
Research in government, need for, 12-13.
Research, social, 316.
Reservoirs, water, 489, 497.
Retirement pensions, 48-50.
Revenue, see New sources of revenue.
Revenues, assessment and collection of, 78; classification of, 60; definition of, 76; miscellaneous, 97; sources of, 77; utility, 103.
Richardson, Clifford, *Modern Asphalt Pavement*, 428.
Richmond, Mary E., *Social Diagnosis*, 317; *What Is Social Case Work?* 317.
Rietz, H. L., Crathorne, A. R., and Rietz, J. C., *Mathematics of Finance*, 111.
Rietz, J. C., see Rietz, H. L., jt. auth.
Riggs, H. E., on depreciation, 544, 545; *Depreciation of Public Utility Properties*, 545; on valuation of intangibles, 539; on valuations, 540.
Rightor, C. E., on city debt, 105; "How Detroit's Financial Program Was Prepared," 59.
Ringlemann chart, 217.
Ripley, William Z., "Stop, Look, Listen!" 564.
Riter, Frank H., "Permanent Registration for Elections Unsuitable for Large Cities," 23.
Roads, see United States Bureau of Public Roads.
Roads and Streets, 428.
Robinson, Charles, *City Planning*, 186.
Robinson, Louis, N., *Penology in the United States*, 379, 391.
Rocca, Helen M., *Registration Laws*, 22.

Rochester Bureau of Municipal Research, *Report on the Administration of the Bureau of Buildings*, 204; *Report on the Assessment of Real Property in the City of Rochester*, 84; *Report on the Building Department*, 215; *Report on the Problem of Refuse Collection*, 447; *Report on the Problem of Street Cleaning*, 447.
Rosewater, Victor, *Special Assessments*, 122.
Routh, J. W., "Thoughts on the Manager Plan," 7.
Rubbish collection, 461; see also, wastes.
"Running cards," 233.
Rural highways, lighting of, 514.
Russell, H. L., see Turneaure, F. E., jt. auth.
Russell Sage Foundation, *Regional Plan of New York and Its Environs*, 341.

Sachs, Emanie N., "Being Human," 7.
Safety engineering, 204.
St. Louis Bureau of Municipal Research, on maintenance of street lights, 518.
St. Paul Bureau of Municipal Research, on pay of firemen, 240.
Salaries, schedules of, 66; standardization of, 45.
Saleilles, Raymond, *The Individualization of Punishment*, 382.
Salvage, 235.
Salvage of wastes, see wastes, salvage of.
San Francisco Bureau of Governmental Research, on cost of street lighting, 520; *Depreciation Requirements of the San Francisco Municipal Railway*, 546; *Some Phases of the Miscellaneous Revenue Situation in San Francisco*, 101; *Survey of Street Lighting in San Francisco*, 506.
Scales, public, 413.
Schools, 273-290; see also education; all year, 280; business management of, 273; census, 285; continuation, 278; half time sessions in, 286; health work in, 256; high, 279; standardization of design of, 288.
Schroeder, Henry, *History of Electric Light*, 507.
Schroeder, Henry, and Butler, H. E., *Modern and Obsolete Street Lighting Systems*, 518.

INDEX

Screens, belt, 479; Dorrco, 479; Reinsch-Wurl, 479; Tark, 479; Weand segregator, 479.
Securities, lost, 117.
Sentences, indeterminate, 386; suspended, 383.
Septic tanks, see sewage.
Serial bonds, see bonds.
Serums, use of, 252.
Service at cost, 531.
Service records, 43, 148.
Setbacks, 202.
Settling basins, 493.
Sewage, definition of, 409; treatment of, 476-483.
Sewers, 471-475.
Sewerage, development of, 469; separate and combined systems of, 470.
Shaw, Bernard, *Common Sense in Municipal Trading*, 555.
Sheffield, Ada E., *The Social Case History*, 317.
Sheriffs, Police, and Peace Officers Review, 320.
Shoecraft, Ezra C., "City Engineering," 442.
Sidewalks, 445.
Sinking funds, 110-113.
Six-three-three plan, see education.
Slippy, J. C., *How Pittsburgh Solved Its Official Transportation Problem by the Adoption of Public Taxicab Service*, 172.
Sludge, 483; disposal, 484.
Smith, Bruce, *State Police*, 320.
Smith, R. H., *Justice and the Poor*, 360, 376.
Smith, R. H., and Bradway, J. S., *Growth of Legal Aid Work in the United States*.
Smith, R. H., and Ehrmann, H. B., "Judicial Administration," 360.
Smoke prevention, 217.
Smoke Prevention Association, *Manual of Smoke and Boiler Ordinances and Requirements in the Interest of Smoke Regulation*, 218.
Snow, removal of, 455.
South Carolina bond law, 106; budget procedure, 60.
Spain, Charles L., *Platoon School*, 277, 282; "Platoon School in Detroit," 277.
Special assessments, 121; for utility financing, 561.
Specifications, on public works, 419; standardization of, 155, 158, 162, 163.
Spero, S. D., *Labor Movement in a Government Industry*, 52.

Sports, competitive, 301.
Sprague, E. Z., *The Accountancy of Investment*, 111.
Spurr, Henry C., *Guiding Principles of Public Utility Regulations*, 523.
Squeegee machines, 451.
Stand-by service, charge for, 549.
Standards, see United States Bureau of Standards.
Standpipes, water, 498.
State medicine, 264.
State regulation of utilities, 533.
Steffens, Henry, Jr., "Business Procedure of the Board of Education," 290; on regulation of utilities, 556; see also Fenkell, George H., jt. auth.
Steffens, Lincoln, *Shame of the Cities*, 526.
Stein, Milton, *Water Purification Plants and Their Operation*, 490.
"Stock jobbing," 529.
Stoner, J. Ben, *Systems of Equalizing, Assessing and Collecting Taxes*, 84.
Stop streets, see streets, through.
Stores records, 164.
Stourm, Rene, *The Budget*, 53.
Strayer, George D., and others, *Problems in Educational Administration*, 266.
Street cars and traffic, 347.
Street railway tracks, construction of, 443; paving between, 442.
Street railways, 194; municipal ownership of, 554.
Streets, classification of, 430; classification of for lighting, 512; cleaning of, 448; congestion in, 344; gravel and cinder, 432; lighting of, 508; see also lighting; lines and grades of, 431; naming of, 192; numbering of, 219; offset, 349; one-way, 356; ornamentation of, 192; paving of, see paving; planning of, 191; signs on, 193; through, 353; unpaved, cleaning of, 453; width of, 348.
Strong-mayor plan, 7
Structures, assessing, 89.
Studensky, Paul, *Pension Problem and the Philosophy of Contributions*, 48.
Stutzman, J. O., *Curing the Criminal*, 382.
"Suburbanites," 231.
Sullivan, J. W., *Markets for the People*, 399.
Supplies, control of, 164.
Surety bonds, see bonds.

Survey, 309.
Sutherland, Edwin H., *Criminology*, 379.
Swan, Herbert S., and Tuttle, George W., "Land Subdivision and the City Plan," 191, 201, 349.
Sweeping, hand, 452.
Sydney, Australia, reservoirs in, 489.

Tannenbaum, Frank, on prisons, 397.
Tax loans, see loans.
Tax maps, 82.
Taxation, classification of property for, 91; exemption from, 78; limiting exemptions from, 102.
Taxes, accounting control of, 92; collection of, 127, 129; limitation of, 92; special, 95.
Taxicabs, control of, 357.
Taxicab service, 172.
Taylor plan, 531.
Taylor, E. S., see Young, H. E., jt. auth.
Taylor, R. E., *Municipal Budget Making*, 53.
Teachers, 275.
Technical Advisory Corporation, *City Plan of Cincinnati*, 341.
Telephones, municipal ownership of, 554.
Telford, Fred, and Moss, F. A., "Suggested Tests for Patrolmen," 330.
Term bonds, see bonds.
Tests, performance, 14.
Theis, Sophie V., *How Foster Children Turn Out*, 314.
Theriault, E. J., see Wagenhals, H. H., jt. auth.
Thom, Charles, and Hunter, Albert C., *Hygienic Fundamentals of Food Handling*, 260.
Thomas, Arthur A., *Principles of Government Purchasing*, 153, 155, 158, 160, 163, 164.
Thompson, Carl D., *Municipal Electric Light and Power Plants*, 554; *Public Ownership*, 551, 553, 556.
Thompson, Russell, on voting by mail, 27.
Thorne, W. V. S., "A Central Purchasing Agency for the City of New York," 160; *Hospital Accounting and Statistics*, 263.
Thurstone, L. L., "Intelligence of Policemen," 39, 330.
Tokyo, replanning of, 186.
Toledo City Journal, 4, 18.
Toledo, Ohio, *Report for 1918 of the Division of Health*, 207.

Town Planning Institute of Canada, *Journal* of, 186.
Traffic regulation, 335-357.
Train, Arthur, *Confessions of Artemas Quibble*, 370.
Transfer of employees, 42, 43.
Transportation, mass, 194.
Travis tank, see sewage treatment.
Treasurer, 126; records of, 134.
Trials, 365; misdemeanant, 363.
Trickling filters, see sewage treatment.
Triple combinations, 231.
Truancy, school, 285.
Trust fund budgets, see budgets, trust fund.
Trust funds, 101.
Tuberculosis, control of, 253.
Turneaure, F. E., and Russell, H. L., *Public Water Supplies*, 485, 486, 496.
Turner, E. H., *Repayment of Local and Other Loans*, 111.
Tuttle, George W., see Swan, Herbert, jt. auth.
Twyford, H. B., *Purchasing and Storing*, 153.

Umbrascope, 225.
Unit costs, 74, 146.
Unit depth rules, 85.
United States Bureau of the Census, *Financial Statistics of Cities*, 76, 77, 105; *Municipal Markets in Cities*, 399, 407; *Statistics of Fire Departments*, 240.
United States Bureau of Education, *Annual Report of Conference on Health Education and the Preparation of Teachers*, 257; support for, 209.
United States Bureau of Markets, *Markets*, 410.
United States Bureau of Public Roads, *Publications* of, 428.
United States Bureau of Standards, on street lighting costs, 520; study of street lighting, 506; on weights and measures, 415.
United States Dept. of Agriculture, score cards for milk supervision, 258.
United States Dept. of Commerce, *Minimum Live Loads Allowable*, 207; *Recommended Minimum Requirements for Masonry Wall Construction*, 207; *Recommended Minimum Requirements for Plumbing in Dwellings and Similar Buildings*, 207; *Report of the Federal Electric

INDEX

Railways Commission, 535; *Vehicular Traffic Congestion and Retail Business*, 350.
United States Dept. of Labor, *Growth of Legal Aid Work in the United States*, 185, 316, 376; Publications of, 257.
United States House of Representatives, *National Budget System*, 53.
Upson, Lent D., "Budget Making for Small Cities," 70; *Government of Cincinnati and Hamilton County*, 14; see also separate reports; "Half Time Budget Methods," 72; "Increasing Activities and Increasing Costs," 4; *Sources of Municipal Revenues in Illinois*, 101.
Utilities, public, 523-547; revenues, collection of, 98.
Utility bonds, see bonds.
Utility regulation, standards of, 535; state vs. local, 533.

Vaccines, use of, 252.
Value, fair, 537.
Van Waters, Miriam, *Youth in Conflict*, 375.
Venereal disease, control of, 254.
Veteran preference, 40.
Violation bureaus, 358.
Virginia, budget procedure in, 61.
Vital statistics, 250.
Vollmer, August, on vice, 334.
Voting, absent, 27; compulsory, 28, 29; by machines, 26, 27; by mail, 27; methods of, 25.

Wagenhals, H. H., Theriault, E. J., and Hommon, H. B., *Sewage Treatment in the United States*, 469.
Waite, Herbert H., *Disease Prevention*, 245.
Waite, John B., "Protection from the Police," 363.
Walton, John M., *Manual of Accounting, Reporting and Business Procedure of the City and County of Philadelphia*, 135.
Warner, Amos G., *American Charities*, 309, 311.
Warner, Andrew R., see Davis, Michael M.
Warrants, 362.
Wastes, 447-465.
Water meters, 501, 502.
Water purification, 489-495.
Water rates, 502, 503.
Water supply, 485-500.

Water system, municipal ownership of, 505.
Water towers, 232, 498.
"Watered stock," 528.
Waterworks development, 195.
Waterworks engineering, 485.
Water Works Practice, 490, 493, 494, 495, 496, 497, 499, 500, 503.
Wayne County (Mich.) Board of Auditors, *Regulations and Requirements for Laying out, Planning and Subdividing Land*, 201.
Weeks, A. L., "School Building Construction," 288.
Wegmann, Edward, *Conveyance and Distribution of Water*, 485.
Weights and measures, 336, 413.
Welfare departments, 319.
Wheeler, J. L., *The Library and the Community*, 282.
Wherry, William M., Jr., *Public Utilities and the Law*, 523.
Whinery, S., *Specifications for Street Roadway Pavements with Instructions to Inspectors on Street Paving Work*, 416.
Whipple, George C., on water organization, 504.
White, Leonard D., *Introduction to the Study of Public Administration*, 3.
White, Percival, *Motor Transportation*, 167.
Wilcox, Delos F., *Analysis of the Electric Railway Problem*, 526, 550; *Depreciation in Public Utilities*, 541, 543, 544, 545, 546; *Financial and Administrative Preparation for Municipal Ownership*, 557; *Indeterminate Permit and Its Relation to Home Rule and Municipal Ownership*, 527; *Municipal Franchises*, 526.
Willard, D. W., see Odum, H. W., jt. auth.
Williams, Anna W., see Parks, W. H., jt. auth.
Williams, C. C., on building codes, 208.
Williams, Frank B., "The Law of the City Plan," 187; *Law of City Planning and Zoning*, 186, 187, 200, 202.
Williams, G. S., and Hazen, Allen, *Hydraulic Tables*, 499.
Willoughby, W. W., *Movement for Budgetary Reform in the States*, 53; *Problem of the National Budget*, 53.
Wiltsie, Charles H., on collection of delinquent taxes, 130.

Wines, Frederick H., *Punishment and Reformation*, 379, 391.
Winslow, C. E. A., *Fresh Air and Ventilation*, 290.
Winslow, C. E. A., and Baker, Gertrude S., "Tuberculosis," 253.
Winslow, C. E. A., and Burkhardt, Margaret R., "Public Health Nursing," 258.
Winslow, C. E. A., and Harris, H. I., "An Ideal Health Department for a City of 100,000 Population," 243, 249.
Winslow, C. E. A., see Kinnicult, L. P., jt. auth.
Wisehart, M. K., "Newspaper and Criminal Justice," 360.
Wolpert, N. N., "Observations on the Naming and Marking of Streets," 192, 194.
Wood, Thomas D., and Powell, Hugh G., *Health Through Prevention and Control of Diseases*, 287.
Woodruff, C. R., *New Municipal Program*, 367.

Woods, Arthur, *Crime Prevention*, 320; *Policemen and Public*, 320.
Worcester, Mass., garbage disposal in, 463.
Working papers, 256, 257.
Work-study-play plan, see education.
Wright, Joseph, *Selected Readings in Municipal Problems*, 181.

Young, H. E., and Taylor, E. S., on rotary traffic, 355.

Zangerle, John A., on corner influence, 87; on assessment methods, 84; *Principles of Real Estate Appraising*, 84, 87, 88, 89, 90; *Unit Value Land Maps*, 84.
Zeolite, 493.
Zoercher, Philip, "Central Supervision of Local Expenditures," 93.
Zoning, 197, 200, 346; by general law, 198; by private restrictions, 197.
Zukerman, T. David, *Voting Machine*, 26.